Lecture Notes in Computer Science

Vol. 245: H.F. de Groote, Lectures on the Complexity of Bilinear Problems. V, 135 pages. 1987.

Vol. 246: Graph-Theoretic Concepts in Computer Science. Proceedings, 1986. Edited by G. Tinhofer and G. Schmidt. VII, 307 pages. 1987.

Vol. 247: STACS 87. Proceedings, 1987. Edited by F.J. Brandenburg, G. Vidal-Naquet and M. Wirsing. X, 484 pages. 1987.

Vol. 248: Networking in Open Systems. Proceedings, 1986. Edited by G. Müller and R.P. Blanc. VI, 441 pages. 1987.

Vol. 249: TAPSOFT '87. Volume 1. Proceedings, 1987. Edited by H. Ehrig, R. Kowalski, G. Levi and U. Montanari. XIV, 289 pages. 1987.

Vol. 250: TAPSOFT '87. Volume 2. Proceedings, 1987. Edited by H. Ehrig, R. Kowalski, G. Levi and U. Montanari. XIV, 336 pages. 1987.

Vol. 251: V. Akman, Unobstructed Shortest Paths in Polyhedral Environments. VII, 103 pages. 1987.

Vol. 252: VDM '87. VDM – A Formal Method at Work. Proceedings, 1987. Edited by D. Bjørner, C.B. Jones, M. Mac an Airchinnigh and E.J. Neuhold. IX, 422 pages. 1987.

Vol. 253: J.D. Becker, I. Eisele (Eds.), WOPPLOT 86. Parallel Processing: Logic, Organization, and Technology. Proceedings, 1986. V, 226 pages. 1987.

Vol. 254: Petri Nets: Central Models and Their Properties. Advances in Petri Nets 1986, Part I. Proceedings, 1986. Edited by W. Brauer, W. Reisig and G. Rozenberg. X, 480 pages. 1987.

Vol. 255: Petri Nets: Applications and Relationships to Other Models of Concurrency. Advances in Petri Nets 1986, Part II. Proceedings, 1986. Edited by W. Brauer, W. Reisig and G. Rozenberg. X, 516 pages. 1987.

Vol. 256: Rewriting Techniques and Applications. Proceedings, 1987. Edited by P. Lescanne. VI, 285 pages. 1987.

Vol. 257: Database Machine Performance: Modeling Methodologies and Evaluation Strategies. Edited by F. Cesarini and S. Salza. X, 250 pages. 1987.

Vol. 258: PARLE, Parallel Architectures and Languages Europe. Volume I. Proceedings, 1987. Edited by J.W. de Bakker, A.J. Nijman and P.C. Treleaven. XII, 480 pages. 1987.

Vol. 259: PARLE, Parallel Architectures and Languages Europe. Volume II. Proceedings, 1987. Edited by J.W. de Bakker, A.J. Nijman and P.C. Treleaven. XII, 464 pages. 1987.

Vol. 260: D.C. Luckham, F.W. von Henke, B. Krieg-Brückner, O. Owe, ANNA, A Language for Annotating Ada Programs. V, 143 pages. 1987.

Vol. 261: J. Ch. Freytag, Translating Relational Queries into Iterative Programs. XI, 131 pages. 1987.

Vol. 262: A. Burns, A.M. Lister, A.J. Wellings, A Review of Ada Tasking. VIII, 141 pages. 1987.

Vol. 263: A.M. Odlyzko (Ed.), Advances in Cryptology – CRYPTO '86. Proceedings. XI, 489 pages. 1987.

Vol. 264: E. Wada (Ed.), Logic Programming '86. Proceedings, 1986. VI, 179 pages. 1987.

Vol. 265: K.P. Jantke (Ed.), Analogical and Inductive Inference. Proceedings, 1986. VI, 227 pages. 1987.

Vol. 266: G. Rozenberg (Ed.), Advances in Petri Nets 1987. VI, 451 pages. 1987.

Vol. 267: Th. Ottmann (Ed.), Automata, Languages and Programming. Proceedings, 1987. X, 565 pages. 1987.

Vol. 268: P.M. Pardalos, J.B. Rosen, Constrained Global Optimization: Algorithms and Applications. VII, 143 pages. 1987.

Vol. 269: A. Albrecht, H. Jung, K. Mehlhorn (Eds.), Parallel Algorithms and Architectures. Proceedings, 1987. Approx. 205 pages. 1987.

Vol. 270: E. Börger (Ed.), Computation Theory and Logic. IX, 442 pages. 1987.

Vol. 271: D. Snyers, A. Thayse, From Logic Design to Logic Programming. IV, 125 pages. 1987.

Vol. 272: P. Treleaven, M. Vanneschi (Eds.), Future Parallel Computers. Proceedings, 1986. V, 492 pages. 1987.

Vol. 273: J.S. Royer, A Connotational Theory of Program Structure. V, 186 pages. 1987.

Vol. 274: G. Kahn (Ed.), Functional Programming Languages and Computer Architecture. Proceedings. VI, 470 pages. 1987.

Vol. 275: A.N. Habermann, U. Montanari (Eds.), System Development and Ada. Proceedings, 1986. V, 305 pages. 1987.

Vol. 276: J. Bézivin, J.-M. Hullot, P. Cointe, H. Lieberman (Eds.), ECOOP '87. European Conference on Object-Oriented Programming. Proceedings. VI, 273 pages. 1987.

Vol. 277: B. Benninghofen, S. Kemmerich, M.M. Richter, Systems of Reductions. X, 265 pages. 1987.

Vol. 278: L. Budach, R.G. Bukharajev, O.B. Lupanov (Eds.), Fundamentals of Computation Theory. Proceedings, 1987. XIV, 505 pages. 1987.

Vol. 279: J.H. Fasel, R.M. Keller (Eds.), Graph Reduction. Proceedings, 1986. XVI, 450 pages. 1987.

Vol. 280: M. Venturini Zilli (Ed.), Mathematical Models for the Semantics of Parallelism. Proceedings, 1986. V, 231 pages. 1987.

Vol. 281: A. Kelemenová, J. Kelemen (Eds.), Trends, Techniques, and Problems in Theoretical Computer Science. Proceedings, 1986. VI, 213 pages. 1987.

Vol. 282: P. Gorny, M.J. Tauber (Eds.), Visualization in Programming. Proceedings, 1986. VII, 210 pages. 1987.

Vol. 283: D.H. Pitt, A. Poigné, D.E. Rydeheard (Eds.), Category Theory and Computer Science. Proceedings, 1987. V, 300 pages. 1987.

Vol. 284: A. Kündig, R.E. Bührer, J. Dähler (Eds.), Embedded Systems. Proceedings, 1986. V, 207 pages. 1987.

Vol. 285: C. Delgado Kloos, Semantics of Digital Circuits. IX, 124 pages. 1987.

Vol. 286: B. Bouchon, R.R. Yager (Eds.), Uncertainty in Knowledge Based Systems. Proceedings, 1986. VII, 405 pages. 1987.

Vol. 287: K.V. Nori (Ed.), Foundations of Software Technology and Theoretical Computer Science. Proceedings, 1987. IX, 540 pages. 1987.

Vol. 288: A. Blikle, MetaSoft Primer. XIII, 140 pages. 1987.

Vol. 289: H.K. Nichols, D. Simpson (Eds.), ESEC '87. 1st European Software Engineering Conference. Proceedings, 1987. XII, 404 pages. 1987.

Vol. 290: T.X. Bui, Co-oP A Group Decision Support System for Cooperative Multiple Criteria Group Decision Making. XIII, 250 pages. 1987.

Vol. 291: H. Ehrig, M. Nagl, G. Rozenberg, A. Rosenfeld (Eds.), Graph-Grammars and Their Application to Computer Science. VIII, 609 pages. 1987.

Vol. 292: The Munich Project CIP. Volume II: The Program Transformation System CIP-S. By the CIP System Group. VIII, 522 pages. 1987.

Vol. 293: C. Pomerance (Ed.), Advances in Cryptology – CRYPTO '87. Proceedings. X, 463 pages. 1988.

Vol. 294: R. Cori, M. Wirsing (Eds.), STACS 88. Proceedings, 1988. IX, 404 pages. 1988.

Vol. 295: R. Dierstein, D. Müller-Wichards, H.-M. Wacker (Eds.), Parallel Computing in Science and Engineering. Proceedings, 1987. V, 185 pages. 1988.

Lecture Notes in Computer Science

Edited by G. Goos and J. Hartmanis

326

M. Gyssens J. Paredaens
D. Van Gucht (Eds.)

ICDT '88

2nd International Conference on Database Theory
Bruges, Belgium, August 31 – September 2, 1988
Proceedings

Springer-Verlag
Berlin Heidelberg New York London Paris Tokyo

Editors

Marc Gyssens
Jan Paredaens
Department of Mathematics and Computer Science
University of Antwerp
Universiteitsplein 1, B-2610 Antwerp/Wilrijk, Belgium

Dirk Van Gucht
Computer Science Department, Indiana University
Bloomington, Indiana 47405-4101, USA

CR Subject Classification (1987): D.3.3, E.2, F.1.3, F.4.1, H.2, I.2.4

ISBN 3-540-50171-1 Springer-Verlag Berlin Heidelberg New York
ISBN 0-387-50171-1 Springer-Verlag New York Berlin Heidelberg

Printed in Germany

Printing and binding: Druckhaus Beltz, Hemsbach/Bergstr.
2145/3140-543210

Preface

The International Conference on Database Theory (ICDT) is organized every two years under the auspices of the European Association for Theoretical Computer Science (EATCS). It intends to provide a European forum for the international research community working on theoretical issues related to database systems. The first ICDT conference was organized in September 1986 in Rome. The proceedings of this meeting were published in LNCS 243.

The University of Antwerp, Belgium, has organized the second ICDT conference from August 31 to September 2, 1988, in Bruges, the world-famous charming city, not far from the North Sea, often nicknamed "Venice of the North" for its medieval atmosphere and the numerous small canals crossing the city.

The main topics of ICDT '88 were

Dynamic Aspects of Databases
Logic and Deductive Databases
Complexity and Optimization
Object Oriented Databases
Data Models and Query Languages
Miscellaneous Topics

From a total of 87 submitted papers from 18 countries, 23 have been selected for presentation.

There were also three invited talks:

Nancy Lynch: "A Theory of Atomic Transactions"
Serge Abiteboul: "Updates, a New Frontier"
Catriel Beeri: "Data Models and Languages for Databases".

The Program Committee consisted of twelve members:

F. Bancilhon (France)	J. Biskup (Germany)
W. de Jonge (The Netherlands)	M. Gyssens (Belgium)
R. Hull (California,USA)	G. Jaeschke (Germany)
P. Kanellakis (Rhode Island,USA)	P. Larson (Canada)
M. Özsoyoğlu (Ohio,USA)	J. Paredaens - Chairman (Belgium)
D. Sacca (Italy)	D. Van Gucht (Indiana,USA)

They were assisted by 45 referees:

J. Allwein	H. Aly	P. Apers
J. Blakeley	H. Bruggemann	P. Celis
N. Coburn	B. Convent	P. Dadam
A. Deshpande	V. Deshpande	F. Dignum
E. Chan	P. van Emde Boas	S. Ginsburg
D. Guozhu	Y. Hsiu-hsen	S. Jianwen
U. Kelter	M. Kersten	S. Kitchel
E. Lambrichts	U. Lipeck	M. Kersten
K. Kwast	N. Martin	V. Martin
Z. Nong	D. van Oosten	G. Özsoyoğlu

P. Pistor	U. Rasch	L. Sankar
P. Schmitt	W. Schonfeld	A. Siebers
M. Smid	N. Sudkamp	D. Tahon
L. Tanca	V. Vianu	G. Weddell
H. Weigand	W. Wernecke	R. Wieringa

We gratefully acknowledge the support of the sponsors of ICDT '88:

Agfa-Gevaert
Apple Computer N.V.
Bell Telephone Mfg. Company
Generale Bank
IBM Belgium
Indiana University
Infotex Sydes sales organisation
Ministerie van de Vlaamse Gemeenschap
Nationaal Fonds voor Wetenschappelijk Onderzoek
Olivetti Belgische nv
Sabena Belgian World Airlines
Universitaire Instelling Antwerpen.

Finally we wish to thank all the others who helped us with the organization of ICDT '88, especially Lydia Janssens, Francine Schoeters, Marc Gemis and Jan Van den Bussche.

Antwerp, June 15, 1988

Marc Gyssens
Jan Paredaens
Dirk Van Gucht

Contents

Invited Lectures

Logic and Deductive Databases

Complexity and Optimization

Object Oriented Databases

Data Models and Query Languages

Dynamic Aspects of Databases

Miscellaneous Topics

UPDATES, A NEW FRONTIER

Serge Abiteboul
I.N.R.I.A., 78153 Le Chesnay, France
(abitebou@inria.inria.fr)

Abstract: We consider the main features of updates in databases. Recent results on updates are briefly described and used to raise various questions. It is argued that well-accepted query properties like safety and determinism should not be strictly enforced in the context of updates. The issue of declarative versus procedural update languages is also addressed. Finally, update-based database specifications are considered and compared to more traditional approaches.

1 Introduction

Since Codd's original proposal in the beginning of the seventies [16], the relational model has been the basis of a wide variety of theoretical research [41,50,64]. This research has focused primarily on (i) how can information be effectively extracted from the database? and (ii) what are the static properties of data? This was due both to the origin of the relational model in traditional logic and to the nature of early database applications, which were mostly business oriented. Although important in practice, the database evolution in time has somehow been less central for the researchers of the field.

Two powerful query languages, a calculus and an algebra, have long served as a yardstick for measuring expressive power of relational query languages. In contrast, no such yardstick exists for update languages, which have traditionally provided just the most basic update capabilities: tuple insertion, deletion and modification. The common justification for this weakness is that query constructs can be used in conjunction with updates if more power is needed. Indeed, one could use for update language any query language together with the capability to assign the result of a query to a base relation. While queries and updates certainly share important characteristics, we argue in the paper that updates differ from queries in several basic respects and that they deserve separate study.

The problems raised by queries and updates differ widely in special contexts such as databases with incomplete information, deductive databases and user views. The fundamental reason is the inherent non-monotonicity of updates. The nice first-order setting underlying both "classical" and "deductive" database theories is of little use. In the present paper, we try to exhibit the principles underlying update languages. Roughly speaking, we argue that:

$$\textit{updates} \neq \textit{relational calculus} + \textit{assignment}$$

and address the question: what is an update language?

We emphasize issues differentiating updates from queries. These include:

1. the need for non-determinism in updates,

2. safety and the modification of the database active domain by updates,

3. declarative versus procedural update languages, and

4. specification of database behavior using updates.

To illustrate our presentation, we often use the families of update languages DL and TL introduced in [8,9] and the language DLL of [55].

To conclude this introduction, we briefly discuss incomplete information, deductive databases and user views, from an update perspective, to highlight the fundamental difference between updates and queries.

Incomplete databases

An incomplete database involves the representation of many possible worlds. Querying databases with incomplete information is now fairly well understood, from the point of view of both semantics [39,34,61] and complexity [66,3,38]. On the other hand, little is known on how to update incomplete databases. A proof-theoretic approach is proposed in [31,29]. The database is viewed as a first-order theory and an update as a post condition. To handle updates, they introduce and study sets of theories called "flocks". The proof theoretic approach is too much "syntax" driven: the database may react differently to two distinct but logically equivalent formulas. Furthermore, the computation of the resulting state is intractable. A model-theoretic approach is followed in [2,73]. Roughly speaking, some representation of a set of models is chosen and updates map representable sets of models to representable ones. In the model theoretic approach, the choice of updates and their semantics is somewhat arbitrary. In [22], modal logic is used to specify update semantics in presence of incomplete information. Despite of these various investigations, it can be considered that the update problem for incomplete databases has not yet been solved. An overview of the area can be found in [74].

User views

The problem of querying views coincides with the general query problem and is therefore well understood. On the other hand, updating views seems to lead to insurmountable problems in the general case. Intuitively, when specifying an update on a view, the user does not provide enough information for the system to perform a "real" update on the database. The problem has been extensively investigated, for instance in [27,15,30,23,42,49]. In particular, an elegant framework is provided in [15]: a view complement is provided and the update is realized (if possible) by translating the update into an update on the database which leaves unchanged the view complement. In [23], complexity issues are considered and it is shown that the problem cannot be solved in its full generality. A purely operational approach is followed in [17]. More recently, a sophisticated update language was used in [55] to specify the semantics of view updates using explicit translation given in a logic-based language.

Deductive databases

Deductive databases are based on a proof-theoretic approach. In this field, most of the effort has focused on the semantics and evaluation strategies for queries. The update problem is related to issues in non-monotonic reasoning addressed for instance in [26,43] in an A.I. framework. In the deductive database context, the problem has recently been considered. For instance, in [4], the problem of the impact of simple updates on the database extension is considered. The problem of integrating updates in a logic program is not yet understood. Existing solutions such as *assert* and *retract* in Prolog are not generally considered satisfactory in logic programming, and are even less so in the context of databases. First, *assert* and *retract* are non declarative constructs. Furthermore, their semantics is unclear and varies from one Prolog implementation to another. A discussion on the nonlogical aspects of *asserts* can be found in a section of [72] under the title: "the evils of assert". Similar issues are addressed in [58] where the problem of introducing the notion of transaction in a Prolog environment is considered. Update semantics in a rule-based context is also considered in [55,57]. Obviously, much is left to be done in that direction.

The paper is organized as follows. In Section 2, the notions of updates and queries are compared, and formal definitions of updates and update completeness presented. The family TL of procedural languages is presented in the next section to illustrate those concepts. Declarative update languages are considered in Section 4. Specification of behaviour using updates is considered in Section 5. Conclusions are given in a last section.

2 Updates

We adapt the formal notion of computable query of Chandra and Harel [20] to the context of updates. We also discuss two key issues for updates: non-determinism and the modification of the active domain. But first, we present some preliminaries.

2.1 Preliminaries

We assume the existence of two infinite sets of symbols: The set **att** of *attributes* and the set **dom** of *constants*. A *relational schema* is a finite set of attributes, and a *database schema*, a finite set of relational schemas. A *tuple* over a relational schema R is a mapping from R to **dom**. A *relation* over R is a finite set of tuples. An *instance of* a database schema $\mathcal{R}$ is a pair (Σ, I) where Σ is a finite subset of **dom**, and I a mapping from $\mathcal{R}$ to corresponding relations with values in Σ. The set Σ is called the *active domain*. We sometimes omit Σ and talk about database I. It is then understood that the active domain coincides with the set of constants occurring in I. The set of instances over $\mathcal{R}$ is denoted inst($\mathcal{R}$).

The following query languages are popular in databases. *Relational calculus* [16] is a function-free first-order logic. *Datalog* is a language based on function-free Horn clauses. *Fixpoint calculus* is a function-free first-order logic augmented with a fixpoint construct [20].

2.2 Simple updates

We first take the view that the difference between updates and queries concerns primarily the interpretation of the results, rather than the computation involved. Therefore, we do not emphasize (for the time being) distinctions between queries and updates.

In defining computable updates, we basically start from Chandra and Harel's computable queries. Thus an update is a partial recursive mapping. We also follow the usual requirement that instances over a fixed schema be mapped to instances over another fixed schema. As in [20], we require that constants be essentially viewed as uninterpreted, although we do allow for a *finite* number of constants to be interpreted. Intuitively, those constants are privileged constants such as constants in a newly inserted tuple, or constants occurring in a selection condition. This is captured by the following fundamental property [20,37]. (Related concepts have been presented in [12,60,5].)

Definition 2.1 Let $\mathcal{R}$ and $\mathcal{S}$ be database schemas and C a finite set of constants in **dom**. A mapping τ from inst($\mathcal{R}$) to inst($\mathcal{S}$) is *C-generic* if τ commutes with every permutation of **dom** leaving C invariant, i.e., for each bijection ρ over **dom** which is the identify on C,

$$\rho(\tau(\Sigma, I)) = \tau(\rho(\Sigma, I)).$$

Note that mappings considered in databases are in general C-generic. Relational calculus queries (using $=$, $\neq$ only) and Datalog queries are C-generic. Insertions, deletions and modifications are also C-generic. Natural join is ϕ-generic, $select_{A=5,B=6}$ and $insert(5,6,5)$ are $\{5,6\}$-generic.

Coming back to the definition, when queries only are considered, the set C is not of any importance. For selections with constants, we can always assume that these constants are already stored in the database. Indeed, Chandra and Harel use ϕ-genericity (genericity for short). On the other hand, if we want to study the evolution of the database in time, we have to consider possibly infinite sequences of instances

$$(\Sigma_1, I_1), \ldots, (\Sigma_n, I_n), \ldots$$

with finite but non identical active domains. It is thus necessary to be able to modify the active domain in some controlled way. The set C above serves that purpose.

We are now ready to define the notions of deterministic [1] updates and update completeness [9].

[1] Yes indeed, there will be non-deterministic ones.

Definition 2.2 A *deterministic update* is a mapping from inst($\mathcal{R}$) to inst($\mathcal{S}$) (for some $\mathcal{R}$, $\mathcal{S}$) which is partial recursive and C-generic for some finite set C. A language is *deterministic update complete* iff all state transformations expressible in the language are deterministic updates and if all deterministic updates are expressible in the language.

We will present later several deterministic update complete languages. First, however, we discuss non-determinism.

2.3 Non-Determinism

In this section, we argue that non-determinism is really intimately connected to updates.

The information that we have on the real world may be incomplete. This is the starting point of the work on incomplete databases. It is also natural to consider that our information on state transitions may be incomplete. For instance, consider the piece of information

EMPLOYEE(John,toy) ∨ EMPLOYEE(John,book).

There are at least two ways of interpreting the "arrival" of this information.

First, the formula is understood as some incomplete information on the real world, i.e. as the sentence: *John is in the toy or book department.* Then John should be in the answer to the query: *Who are the employees in the toy or book department*; and if the system is sophisticated enough, queries such as *Can John be in the toy department?* should be answered positively. This interpretation forces us to deal with incomplete databases representing sets of possible worlds. Queries can be answered by inspection of the answer of the queries on all possible worlds. In this first interpretation, the formula is viewed as an incompletely specified update on the database.

There is a second interpretation that may be more appropriate in certain circumstances. Intuitively, the formula is understood as: *Hire John in the toy of book department!* The system chooses non deterministically one possible world, that is John is hired in exactly one of the two departments and the answer to the query *Is John in the CS department?* will depend on the choice. In that case, the database remains complete. Queries can therefore be answered using a classical relational system and the computational problems raised by incomplete information are not encountered.

This second interpretation and the non-determinism implied by it are the topic of this section. We now present three other examples of updates where inherent non-determinism is essential.

Example 2.1 To follow tradition, consider *the* deductive database example, i.e., the ancestor example. It uses the rule

$$R(x,y) \leftarrow R(x,z),\ R(z,y)$$

to derive new facts. Now consider the inverse which maps a transitively closed relation to some "minimal" relation of which it is the closure. This can be computed using the *Transaction Language* (TL) of [8] by the following non-deterministic program. (The semantics of TL will be explained later but should be obvious in the example.)

while $R(x,z)$, $R(z,y)$, $R(x,y)$
  do $delete_R(x,y)$ *done.*

Note that they may be several outcomes for the same input relation R. However, if the graph is acyclic, there is a unique result. □

Example 2.2 Consider a unary relation S and the update: *insert 0 in S, if S has an even number of tuples.* This is computed by the following program which uses a temporary relation T:

$while\ S(x),\ \neg\ T(x)$
$\quad do\ insert_T(x)\ done;$
$while\ T(x),\ T(y),\ x \neq y$
$\quad do\ delete_T(x);\ delete_T(y)\ done;$
$if\ empty(T)\ then\ insert_S(0).$

Note that this program has a deterministic effect although the computation is inherently non-deterministic. Indeed, to obtain the same effect with a deterministic language, the language would need the capability to count up to the size of S which is not needed with a non-deterministic language. □

The last example is taken from [55]. It uses the language DLL. Again, the semantics should be understandable from the context.

Example 2.3 To enroll students in a course with two sections, the following update procedure can be used:

<*enroll*(*name*)> ← <+*sec1*(*name*)>(*size*(*sec*1,N) & N<30)
<*enroll*(*name*)> ← <+*sec2*(*name*)>(*size*(*sec*2,N) & N<20)

If *enroll*(John) is called, John is enrolled in Section 1 or 2 (non-deterministically) based on the availability of the section. We will come back to DLL later. □

We now formally introduce the notions of (non-deterministic) update and update completeness.

Definition 2.3 A (non-deterministic) *update* is a recursively enumerable, C-generic[2] subset of inst($\mathcal{R}$) × inst($\mathcal{S}$) (for some $\mathcal{R}$, $\mathcal{S}$ and some finite set C). A language is *update complete* iff all (non-deterministic) state transformations expressible in that language are updates and if all updates are expressible in that language.

We will discuss various proposals which use non-deterministic updates. In particular, the procedural language TL [8] is non-deterministic, so are the declarative languages DL, RDL1 [52] and DLL.

Another proposal [57] presents a non-deterministic semantics, and then focuses on programs which have deterministic effects (Church-Rosser property). A basic issue is that it is not decidable whether a program in [57] has a deterministic effect. This is also the case for languages mentioned above. Another consequence of their expressive power is that program termination cannot be guaranteed for those languages.

Termination and determinism are two fundamental properties for programs. In the next section, we consider another property of major importance, namely safety.

2.4 Safety

In this section, we discuss the modification of the active domain of the database and the resulting power.

It is generally assumed that the result of a query should depend only of the values present in the database. Such a restriction is not realistic for updates. As mentioned above, one wishes to be able to modify the active domain of the database during a transaction. We use the term "invented" for those values that "appear" in the active domain in some miraculous ways. In fact, these values are in general supplied as procedure parameters. To illustrate this fact, consider the database consisting of two relations R(NUM,NAME,ADD) and S(NUM,DEP). Suppose that users only see the projection on NAME, ADD and DEP of the natural join of R and S. Values in column NUM can be viewed as "internal" identifiers for persons in the database. The following update procedure can be used to introduce a new person in the database: (The syntax is again that of TL.)

[2] The notion of C-genericity is extended to relations in the obvious way.

procedure insertion(name,add,dep) =
  with new z do $insert_R$*(z,name,add);* $insert_S$*(z,dep) done.*

As we shall see, the introduction of invented values is a very powerful mechanism. Indeed, if the database schema is fixed and only values from the input can be used, there is only a finite number of possible database states that can be reached during the computation. It is therefore hopeless to achieve the computational power of computable queries/updates. Indeed, Chandra and Harel relax the fixed schema requirement in their proposal (temporary predicates are not typed and can be arbitrarily "wide" in the course of a computation) to obtain completeness. Using invented values, a counter can be simulated in a fixed arity predicate. For instance, a counter can be represented by the number of tuples in a unary relation R with the following *increment* and *decrement* TL procedures:

procedure increment =
  with new x *do* $insert_R$(x);
procedure decrement =
  if R(x) *then* $delete_R$(x).

As we shall see, the presence of a mechanism for inventing new values will lead to complete languages.

With this notion of invented value, we can now reconsider the concept of genericity. Consider a unary relation R. The (non-deterministic) update consisting of inserting an arbitrary value in R corresponds to the relation

$$\tau = \{< I, I \cup \{a\} > \mid I \text{ in } inst(R),\ a \text{ in } \mathbf{dom}\ \}.$$

It is easy to see that τ is generic. It is therefore possible to modify the active domain non-deterministically in a generic manner. The reader can check that it is impossible to do so deterministically. This motivates the use of C-genericity which allows the interpretation of a finite number of values, and thus the modification of the active domain even in a deterministic setting.

To conclude this discussion on invented values, it should be noted that languages in object-oriented databases [13] usually provide mechanisms to create new objects. The creation of new objects (like value invention) provides additional computational power independently from the other powerful mechanisms usually found in object-oriented database languages.

3 The TL family

In this section, we briefly present a family of procedural update languages, namely TL [8]. The TL languages are based on *insert* and *delete* operations, *composition* (denoted by ";"), a *while* loop to perform iterations, and a construct called *with new* to introduce new domain values. We informally present the languages and completeness results.

Syntax: We first present the common syntax for all languages in the family.

We assume the existence of an infinite set **var** of symbols called *variables*. These variables will range over **dom**.

Let $\mathcal{R}$ be a database schema. A *condition* on $\mathcal{R}$ is a conjunction of atomic formulas of the form $R(r)$, $\neg R(r)$, $x = y$, $x \neq y$, where R is in $\mathcal{R}$, r is a tuple (possibly containing variables), and x, y are constants or variables. For each condition without variables, the fact that a database satisfies that condition is defined in the straightforward manner.

Informally, parameterized transactions are transactions with *free* variables (not bound to any condition), which are used in a manner analogous to procedure parameters. A ***p-transaction*** (for ***parametrized*** transaction) over a database schema $\mathcal{R}$ is an expression obtained as follows:

1. for R in $\mathcal{R}$, and for each tuple r over R, $i_R(r)$ and $d_R(r)$ are p-transactions (insertion and deletion);

2. if t and t' are p-transactions over $\mathcal{R}$, then $t; t'$ is a p-transaction over $\mathcal{R}$;

3. if t is a p-transaction and Q a condition over $\mathcal{R}$, then *while* Q *do* t *done* is a p-transaction over $\mathcal{R}$; and

4. if t is a p-transaction over $\mathcal{R}$ and z a variable, then *with new* z *do* t *done* is a p-transaction over $\mathcal{R}$.

The scope of a variable and the notion of free variable in a parameterized transaction are defined in the obvious way.

To illustrate the language, consider the following program which computes in S the transitive closure of R:

while $R(x,y) \wedge \neg\, S(x,y)$
 do $i_S\,(x,y)$ *done*;
while $R(x,y) \wedge S(y,z) \wedge \neg\, S(x,z)$
 do $i_S\,(x,z)$ *done.*

Semantics: In order to define the semantics of transactions, we need the auxiliary concept of valuation of p-transactions and conditions. Let t be a p-transaction. Let X be the set of free variables in t. A ***valuation*** v of t is a mapping from X into **dom**. A valuation v of t transforms t into vt obtained by replacing in t each occurrence of a free variable x by $v(x)$.

Finally, a TL program defines a relation between databases over the input schema and databases over the output schema. Insert and delete statements allow the insertion and deletion of tuples. The *while* statement permits an iteration as follows: in a statement *while* Q *do* t *done*, a valuation v such that vQ is true in the current state is non-deterministically chosen, and vt is performed. This is iterated until there is no such valuation. A statement *with new* z *do* t is interpreted as follows. If (Σ, I) is the state of the database, a value not in Σ is arbitrarily chosen and t is performed with z replaced by this value; and the new value is added to the domain.

Formally, the update semantics is described as follows. A database state is a set of possible worlds. The semantics of a program is a binary relation between database states (i.e., is an update as defined above). This is in the spirit of Kripke semantics for Modal Logic [48].

The language thereby obtained is called TL. The language obtained by prohibiting the *with new* construct is called safe TL. It is proved in [10] that:

Theorem 3.1 TL is update complete. Safe TL defines the non-deterministic updates which can be computed using polynomial space.

One can restrict syntactically the invented values to be used only in temporary relations. This allows to characterize updates where non-determinism is finite in the sense that for a given instance and a given update, there is finitely many possible outcomes.

We next turn to determinism. Note that non-determinism may result from: (a) the presence of invented values in the result and (b) the choice of a valuation in the *while*.

We call detTL the language obtained by forbidding the insertion of invented values in an output relation. (This can be guaranteed syntactically.) The semantics of the *while* is modified in the following way. For a statement *while* Q *do* t *done*, all the valuations that make Q true are applied "in parallel". The result of one step is the ***union*** of the results for all valuations. This is again iterated until no valuation can be found.

Some subtlety of the semantics should be pointed. Considering all alternatives in parallel is obviously a clean way of removing the non-determinism, however the combination of results from all branches somewhat privileges inserts versus deletes: a tuple is inserted as the consequence of an insertion in *one* of the alternatives; whereas it must be deleted in *all* of them to be effectively deleted.

Without going into more details, we have [10]:

Theorem 3.2 detTL is deterministic update complete. Safe detTL contains the fixpoint queries and is strictly included in PSPACE.

It should be noted that if an ordering of **dom** is provided, safe detTL has exactly the power of PSPACE.

4 Declarative languages

In this section, we consider the introduction of updates in declarative languages. As we shall see, this is intimately connected to the introduction of control.

Update and queries are not correctly integrated by the current database technology (e.g., C+SQL) which tries to mix a declarative query language with a procedural application language. A solution is to move to all-procedural for queries and updates. This is the solution of the object-oriented community and probably the most feasible in the immediate future. However, following the tradition of relational calculus, recent database languages are often declarative (e.g., Datalog). It is therefore important to understand how to merge update features in a declarative language.

In this section, we consider various ways of introducing updates in declarative languages. This is achieved by introducing some control features thereby departing from a purely declarative semantics. Paraphrasing an overused sentence,

$$update = logic + control.$$

Not surprisingly, the introduction of control will lead to an increase of power. We distinguish two ways of introducing control.· We do not view them in any respect as final solutions to the problem. They only indicate possible directions of research. The first one is related to a bottom-up evaluation of the rules and will consist in having imperative statements in heads of rules. The control will be obtained by considering a semantics related to the inflationary semantics of [36]. The second one is tied to a top-down evaluation of rules with imperative statements in the body. The control will correspond to the control strategy of the resolution.

As mentioned above, the introduction of updates in declarative languages is primarily an issue of control. In the last PODS, there have been several proposals [IN,KP,NK,AV4] to provide semantics for Datalog with negation in the body of rules (Datalog$^\neg$) which seem to converge towards a a merge of declarative and procedural features. It should be noted that the detTL language presented above (without *delete*) can be seen as participating to this trend. We first briefly review two proposals for introducing control in Datalog$^\neg$ programs. They will provide some basis for comparison with the update languages presented below.

4.1 Control and negation

In this section, we briefly present two proposals for introducing some limited control in Datalog with negation.

Stratified Datalog$^\neg$ [21,1,67,56] has been proposed as a solution to extend Datalog with negation in the body of the rules. A Datalog$^\neg$ rule is a function-free Horn clause with possibly negative literals in the body. A program may have more than one minimal model because of negations. If it is "stratified", a natural way of choosing one minimal model is provided. This particular model can be computed using a sequence of fixpoints, one for each stratum. The intuition is that *when* a negative literal is used to derive new facts, then the extension of the corresponding predicate will not be modified any more. It is important to note the "*when* ...". The semantics assumes some sequentiality between the applications of the rules. This establishes some implicit control strategy. The strategy is implicit since the user specifies a *set* of rules and the system is responsible for choosing an order of evaluation. However, the user must be aware of the sequencing to understand the program semantics.

Imielinski and Naqvi [40] propose an explicit specification of control based on a *rule algebra*. They start with with Datalog$^\neg$ rules, and build algebraic expressions using $\cup$, sequential composition and '*' (saturation). For instance, let r, s and t be rules. The expression

$$r\ (\ s \cup t\ )^*$$

requires to apply r once, then $s \cup t$ (i.e., apply s and t and take the union) until saturation. Similar constructs are found in update languages.

4.2 Updates in body

In this section, we briefly present the DL family of languages [9]. This is also an extension of Datalog with some implicit control like in stratified Datalog$^\neg$. The language is viewed primarily as an update language and literals in heads are interpreted as insertions. We then consider the language RDL1 which follows a similar philosophy but also allows deletions in heads.

We first present the DL languages. A DL rule is a Datalog rule where negations are allowed in the body and with (possibly) multiple literals in the head. In [9], a non-deterministic and a deterministic semantics are given to such programs. We now describe them.

We first consider the non-deterministic semantics. Instantiations of rules in the program are applied non-deterministically until a fixpoint is reached. Variables occurring in the head of a rule and not in the body are interpreted as values *outside* of the active domain and thus serve for introducing invented values.

For instance, consider the following rule where Q is a base relation, and $\tilde{Q}$, $\hat{Q}$ are derived:

$$\tilde{Q}(x,y,z), \hat{Q}(x,y) \leftarrow Q(x,y),\ \neg\ \hat{Q}(x,y).$$

Intuitively, Q is copied in $\hat{Q}$ and in $\tilde{Q}$. Furthermore, each tuple in $\tilde{Q}$ is given some identifier which is stored in the third column. In some sense, variables occurring in the body are viewed as universally quantified, those occurring only in the head as existentially quantified; and the invented values can be interpreted as skolems in the manner of [38].

A safe version of the language can be considered by forcing all variables in heads to be "positively bound", i.e., to also occur in a positive literal of the body. Now we have:

Theorem 4.1 DL is non-deterministic update complete. Safe DL is included in the set of non-deterministic updates which can be computed using polynomial space (and equals NPTIME on ordered domains).

The precise characterization of the power of safe DL is still open.

The difference between TL and DL is the limited control mechanism of DL compared to the explicit control provided in TL. Note that the power of safe DL is less than the power of the corresponding procedural language (safe TL). This illustrates the fact that, in general,

loss of control results in loss of power.

However, in presence of invented values, TL and DL have the same power. This is due to the power of invented values that can be used to simulate sophisticated control.

A deterministic semantics can be given to obtain the language detDL. Indeed, to make DL deterministic, we follow the same pattern as for the TL language. All facts that can be derived by one application of some rule are added simultaneously. This is again iterated up to saturation. We may also require safety and obtain safe detDL. In safe detDL, multiple heads are not needed, so we can use the Datalog$^\neg$ syntax.

The language safe detDL has been independently proposed by Kolaitis and Papadimitriou [47] under the name inflationary Datalog$^\neg$. Their terminology is based on the fact that the semantics corresponds to the inflationary fixpoint semantics of [36]. It is shown in [46] that the language thereby obtained is strictly more powerful than stratified Datalog$^\neg$. Furthermore, it is shown in [10] that it has the power of the fixpoint queries. One surprising consequence is that the set of updates computable in safe detDL is closed under complement. For example, the program below computes in U the complement of the transitive closure of a base relation P in inflationary Datalog$^\neg$. (One may argue whether this is a natural way of expressing the complement of transitive closure.)

$R(x,y) \leftarrow P(x,y);$
$R(x,y) \leftarrow R(x,z),\ R(z,y);$
$S(x,y) \leftarrow R(x,y);$
$T(x,y) \leftarrow R(x,y), R(x',z'), R(z',y'), \neg R(x',y');$
$U(x,y) \leftarrow \neg\ R(x,y),\ S(x',y'),\ \neg\ T(x',y').$

Intuitively, S is a copy of R with a delay of one iteration. T also constructs a copy of R (with a delay of one) until R is saturated. The tuples that are obtained in R at the last stage are not copied in T. Then S and T differ, which triggers the computation of the complement of R by the last rule.

The power of deterministic DL languages is characterized in the following result [10]:

Theorem 4.2 detDL is deterministic update complete. Safe detDL computes exactly the fixpoint queries.

As in the previous result, we obtain the maximum power in the unsafe case. This comes from the power of invented values. It should be noted that the simulation of control is much more intricate in the deterministic case.

Let us compare the power of Datalog, stratified Datalog$^\neg$ and safe detDL:

$$\text{Datalog} \subset \text{stratified Datalog}^\neg \subset \text{inflationary Datalog}^\neg = \text{safe detDL}.$$

We can view this as introducing increasing degrees of control starting from a purely declarative language. Datalog is easy to learn, but its expressive power is quite limited. For instance, Datalog cannot express all relational calculus. The DL family provides more power, but consider the example above. If what the programmer wants to do is (i) compute the transitive closure, and (ii) take the complement, there must be more natural ways to express it than this safe detDL program! In these examples, the power of the language is enhenced by introducing more procedurality. It is still unclear whether this is a basic flaw of the declarative approach, or this is just that our view of it is still too limited. I would tend to believe that if control is needed, it is bad strategy to "hide" it, and the language should provide explicit control. Obviously, the question is what form of control.

The update languages described above can be interpreted as containing imperative insert statements in heads of rules. The same philosophy can be followed to provide deletions. The rule

$$\neg\ R(x) \leftarrow S(x)$$

can be interpreted by: if $S(x)$ then delete x from R. This semantics is intimately connected to a bottom-up interpretation of rule programs: if the body holds, perform the update. The "updates in heads" semantics is the approach followed in the language RDL1 [52]. The following example is given there. Note that updates are explicit in heads, the '+' indicating an insertion and '–' a deletion. Arbitrary first order formulas are allowed in bodies. The semantics is in the spirit of the *safe* DL semantics.

Example 4.1 A tuple $G(x, y, r)$ indicates that a resistance r is present between vertices x and y. Two serial edges are replaced by a unique one as follows:

$$
\begin{aligned}
&-G(x,y,r);\ -G(y,z,r');\ +G(x,z,r+r') \\
&\quad \leftarrow G(x,y,r),\ G(y,z,r), \\
&\qquad \forall\, w,s\ (G(w,y,s) \Rightarrow w = x\ ), \\
&\qquad \forall\, w,s\ (\ G(y,w,s) \Rightarrow w = z\ ).\ \square
\end{aligned}
$$

It should be noted that the language RDL1 is also non-deterministic. Due to the presence of deletions, termination of RDL1 programs cannot be guaranteed.

It is interesting to note that in a follow-up paper [53], de Maindreville and Simon propose to add some explicit control to the rules, supporting our earlier remark that control should not be hidden if control is necessary. They advocate a clean separation between the logic part (rules with updates in heads) and the control part, and propose to use for control: union, sequential composition and some iteration until saturation. Indeed, the control that they propose resembles the control of the rule algebra of [40].

4.3 Updates in bodies

The problem of updates has also been considered by the logic programming community. Interpreters for standard Prolog suggest the introduction of updates in the body of rules. Indeed, traditionally *assert* and *retract* served that purpose. In [72], Warren criticizes the notoriously non-declarative semantics of these operators and proposes instead a modal operator "assume". The idea of viewing an update as a modality is elaborated in [28,55,40]. The language proposed in [57] goes even further in that direction by introducing more control in the updates that are considered. Indeed, they introduce control features resembling those of the rule algebra of [40]. To highlight the essence of the approach, we concentrate on the simple and elegant language DLL of [55].

The formal semantics proposed by [55] is based on Kripke's semantics for dynamic logic. Like for TL and DL, the semantics is based on (non-deterministic) updates, i.e., relations between sets of states. Indeed, there are deep connections between the languages DL and DLL. A key difference is the body versus head occurrence of updates which are related, respectively to forward and backward chaining perspectives.

We describe DLL through an example [55].

Example 4.2 In a database, the relation *ES* stores the salary of each employee, and the relation *ED* the department of each employee. A tuple *AS*(*dep*,*avg*) indicates that the average salary of department *dep* is *avg*. Consider first the following Prolog program:

:- *assert*(*ES*(John,200K)), *assert*(*ED*(John,toy)), *AS*(toy,*avg*), *avg* < 50K.

Intuitively, it is intended to hire John in the toy department with a salary of 200K if the average salary of the department stays below 50K. However, because of Prolog semantics, if the average salary after hiring John is more than 50K, John has nevertheless been hired. (The reader might try to write the "correct" Prolog program.)

Now consider the following DLL update procedure:
<*hire* (*emp*,*sal*,*dep*)> ←

<+*ES*(*emp*,*sal*)> (<+*ED*(*emp*,*dep*)> (*AS*(*dep*,*avg*) & *avg* < 50K))

A call *hire*(John,200K,toy) hires John in the toy department only if after hiring him, the average salary of the department stays below 50K. The "+" symbols indicates an insertion. The parenthesis after the insertions in *ES* and *ED* indicates that after the two tuples have been inserted the condition must hold. Otherwise, the update is not realized (i.e., the system backtracks). Tuple insertions and deletions in DLL can be viewed as modal operators. A key difference with Prolog *assert* is that the database updates are "undone" while backtracking. □

Note that control is introduced in DLL, but that this control is essentially non-deterministic like in DL. The elegance of the language lies in the careful mix between what can be seen as "static" predicates (the query part) and "dynamic" predicates (the update part). This allows the binding of values in updates to results of queries and vice versa, and can be used in a variety of ways such as the expression of pre and post conditions.

To conclude this section, let us note that DLL allows recursion in update procedures. This gives the power of simulating a *while* in TL or the fixpoint semantics of DL. Invention of values is not considered in DLL. Because of deletion of tuples, DLL cannot guarantee termination. However, we conjecture that DLL with inserts only has exactly the power of safe DL.

5 Updates as Constraints

The introduction of static semantics in relational databases is the topic of dependency theory. (See [32] for a survey.) Dynamic semantics of applications can be described declaratively using dynamic integrity constraints as in the work of Vianu [68,69,70,71]. In other proposals [18,19], some forms of modal logic are used to describe valid state transitions. Since the focus of the paper is on updates, we now concentrate on capturing semantics using updates. More precisely, we describe recent work on "transactional schemas" [7,11].

In the context of the relational model, valid database states have traditionally been described using static integrity constraints. More recently, it has been argued that valid database states should not be defined in a static framework alone, but should be viewed as the results of applying particular valid operations to the database [14,18,19,24,45,51,54,62]. The specification of the legal database states by transactions rather than constraints leads to the notion of a *transactional schema*. Informally, a transactional schema provides a finite set of "procedures". The valid transitions correspond to calls to those procedures, and the valid states are all instances which can be constructed starting from the empty instance, by repeated calls to the procedures of the schema.

An analogy can be found between on one hand queries and static constraints, and on the other, updates and dynamic constraints. Yannakakis and Papadimitriou have shown that queries can be used to specify static integrity constraints [75]. They proposed the notion of algebraic dependencies based on inclusion between certain queries and proved the equivalence between algebraic dependencies and a natural class of dependencies. In an analogous way, it is shown in [11] that updates can serve to specify natural classes of integrity constraints both static and dynamic.

Let us first consider an example:

Example 5.1 Consider a database consisting of two relations, TA(NAME, COURSE), and PHD(NAME, ADDRESS). It is assumed that each PHD student has exactly one address, each TA teaches one course, and each TA is also a PHD student. This is formalized by the following dependencies:

$$\text{NAME} \rightarrow \text{COURSE},$$
$$\text{NAME} \rightarrow \text{ADDRESS, and}$$
$$\text{TA(NAME)} \subset \text{PHD(NAME)}.$$

Suppose that the legal operations are defined by the procedures:

$hiring(x, y, z) =$
  $delete_{TA}(\text{NAME}{=}x)$; $insert_{TA}(x, y)$;
  $delete_{PhD}(\text{NAME}{=}x)$; $insert_{PhD}(x, z)$;
$firing(x) = delete_{TA}(\text{NAME}{=}x)$.

Consider the transactional schema

$$< R, \{hiring, firing\} >.$$

The valid states generated by this transactional schema are exactly those satisfying the dependencies. □

Various choices of update/transaction languages lead to different specifying capabilities. In the previous example, line programs with only inserts and deletes can generate an interesting family of instances. The class of families of instances generated with very simple update languages can be surprisingly rich. For instance, consider the language of line programs consisting of inserts, deletes and modifications using simple selection conditions [6]. It generates a class of instances which is comparable to the set of recursively enumerable sets [7]. This indicates the potential power of operational specifications of database semantics and highlights a fundamental limitation of the classical approach based on static constraints (where only recursive sets of instances can be specified).

As a consequence, even for very restricted update languages, many basic questions such as *Can a particular instance be constructed?* are not decidable, i.e., it may be impossible to statically check the integrity of the database at a given time, unless some history has been recorded.

Obviously, applications will be more adapted to the transactional approach and others to the classical constraint-based approach. Not surprisingly, the two approaches are in general incomparable. However, large classes of dependencies (functional, and acyclic inclusion dependencies) do have equivalent transactional schemas even for the simple language of line programs [7]. Other dependencies, such as join dependencies, require more powerful update languages [9].

It is also interesting to relate usual static constraints and properties of dynamic specifications. One property is of particular interest: *determinism.* Intuitively, a set of valid state transitions is deterministic if it can be specified using deterministic procedures. Clearly, determinism is a natural restriction to impose on state transitions. It is shown in [11] that the sets of valid states described by large classes of dependencies are deterministic, i.e. can be generated by a transactional schema using deterministic procedures. However, functional dependencies together with inclusion dependencies and embedded join dependencies are generally *not* deterministic, i.e. they would require non-deterministic procedures in corresponding transactional schemas.

The results which we briefly mentioned above are just a first step in understanding the connection between static and dynamic specifications of a database. Many questions of interest remain open. For instance, a complete characterization of static constraints defining deterministic database families is desirable. Other properties of dynamic specifications, such as complexity, should also be investigated.

6 Conclusion

Some results on updates have been exhibited and many questions raised. It has been argued that determinism and safety, although standard properties of queries, are too restrictive for updates. In that spirit, extensions of the notion of computable query have been proposed and complete languages presented. Also, update-based specification has been considered via the notion of transactional schema.

A major open problem facing database theory, is to introduce update capabilities in declarative languages. This involves introducing control in an elegant way into "toy" declarative languages such as Datalog.

We have considered DL languages where an inflationary semantics provides some control mechanism. We have also mentioned other attempts at introducing updates in bodies or heads of logic programs. A number of questions have to be answered:

1. how much can be achieved in a purely declarative manner?

2. should the control be completely implicit or should it be explicit? How much procedurality should the user be aware of?

3. in a rule-based context, should the control be specified "inside" a logic program, or should it be supplied by the user "beside" the program?

4. where does the notion of transaction gets into the picture?

Even before answering such questions, philosophical issues, from which we tried to stay away in the present paper, will have to be answered such as *what is declarative and what is not.* (Being able to specify the semantics in terms of dynamic logic is clearly *not* a sufficient criteria.)

While all the above questions are subject to debate and are likely to remain open for the near future, some consensus may be developed on the following aspects of update languages:

1. the updates of interest are "updates" in the sense of Section 3, i.e., C-generic mappings between fixed schemas interpreting at most a finite number of values. (For instance, the result should not depend on the ordering of facts in the database.)

2. update semantics should be defined in some formal ways. (Dynamic logic is a possible candidate.)

3. control should not be hidden in programs, e.g., the semantics should not depend on the order of rules or the order of subgoals in a rule.

4. non-determinism and unsafety are acceptable in some cases. Not being able to guarantee update termination may be a necessary price to pay for computational power(?).

While the results described in this paper apply to the relational model, most practical attempts at capturing behavior in databases were made using other models usually object-based. We believe that results obtained for the relational model form the necessary groundwork for understanding the problem of behavior in the context of more complex models. However, notions such as object and object identity have a substantial impact on the update problem.

More work is clearly needed to help understand database behaviors. Such work should lead to the development of better database design tools integrating behavioural and structural aspects, better means for checking the soundness of a specification, and more efficient ways of ensuring database integrity.

Acknowledgements: Many results presented here were obtained with Victor Vianu. The user thanks Francois Bancilhon, Paris Kanellakis, Michel Scholl, Eric Simon and Victor Vianu for very carefully reading a first draft of the paper and making many suggestions to improve it.

References

[1] Apt, K., H. Blair, A. Walker, Toward a theory of declarative knowledge, Foundations of Deductive Databases and Logic Programming, (J. Minker ed.) (1988).

[2] Abiteboul S., Grahne, G., Update Semantics for Incomplete Databases, Proceedings of the 11th VLDB, Stockholm, 1985.

[3] Abiteboul, S., P. Kanellakis, G. Grahne, On the Representation and Querying of Sets of Possible Worlds, Proc. of the ACM SIGMOD Conference on the Management of Data, (1987)

[4] Apt, K., J.M. Pujin, Maintenance of Stratified Databases viewed as a belief revision system, Proc. ACM SIGACT-SIGMOD-SIGART Symp. on Principles of Database Systems (1988)

[5] Aho, A.V., J.D. Ullman, Universality of Data Retrieval Languages, Proc. 6th ACM Symp. on Principles of Prog. Languages, San Antonio, Texas (1979)

[6] Abiteboul, S., V. Vianu, Equivalence and optimization of relational transactions. Journal of the ACM, 35,1 (1988).

[7] Abiteboul, S., V. Vianu, Transactions and constraints. Fourth ACM SIGACT-SIGMOD Symp. on Principles of Database Systems, (1985).

[8] Abiteboul, S., V. Vianu, A transaction language complete for database update and specification. Proc. ACM SIGACT-SIGMOD-SIGART Symp. on Principles of Database Systems (1987).

[9] Abiteboul, S., V. Vianu, Procedural and declarative database update languages. Proc. ACM SIGACT-SIGMOD-SIGART Symp. on Principles of Database Systems (1988).

[10] Abiteboul, S., V. Vianu, Transaction languages for database update and specification. I.N.R.I.A. Technical Report No.715 (1987). Invited to special issue of J. of Computer and Systems Science, scheduled to appear in 1988.

[11] Abiteboul, S., V. Vianu, The connection of static constraints with determinism and boundedness of dynamic specifications. Proc. 3rd Int'l. Conf. on Data and Knowledge Bases (1988).

[12] Bancilhon, F., On the Completeness of Query Languages, Proc. 7th Symp. on Mathematical Foundations of Computer Science, Zakopane, Poland (1978)

[13] Bancilhon, F., Object-Oriented Database Systems, Proc. ACM SIGACT-SIGMOD-SIGART Symp. on Principles of Database Systems (1988).

[14] Brodie, M.L., On modelling behavioral semantics of data, VLDB (1981).

[15] Bancilhon, F., N. Spyratos, Update semantics of relational views, ACM TODS (1981).

[16] Codd, E.F., a relational model of data for large shared data banks, CACM (1970).

[17] Carlson, C.R., A.K. Arora, UPM: a formal tool for expressing database update semantics, in Entity-Relationship Approach to Software Engineering, Elsevier Science Publish., (1983).

[18] Castillo, I.M.V., M.A. Casanova, A.L. Furtado, A temporal framework for database specifications. Proc. 8th Int. Conf. on Very Large Databases (1982), 280-291.

[19] Casanova, M.A., A.L. Furtado, A family of temporal languages for the description of transition constraints.

[20] Chandra, A., D.Harel, Computable queries for relational databases. J. of Computer and Systems Science, (1980).

[21] Chandra, A., D.Harel, Horn Clause queries and generalization, J. of Logic Programming, (1985).

[22] Cholvy, L., Update semantics under Domain Closure assumption, Proc., of Intern. Conf. on Database Theory, (1986).

[23] Cosmadakis, S.S., C.H. Papadimitriou, Update of relational views, JACM (1984)

[24] Cerri, S., G. Pelagetti, G. Bracchi, Structured methodology for designing static and dynamic aspects of database applications. Information Systems, Vol. 6, No. 1, pp. 31-45.

[25] Clifford, J., D.S. Warren, Formal semantics for time in databases. ACM Transactions on Database Systems, Vol. 8, No. 2, June 1983, 214-254.

[26] Doyle, J., A Truth Maintenance System, Artificial Intelligence, pp 231-272, (1979)

[27] Dayal, U., P.A. Bernstein, On the correct translation of update operations on relational views, ACM TODS (1982).

[28] Farinas, L., A. Herzig, Reasoning about Database Updates, Workshop on Foundations of Logic Programming and Deductive Databases, J. Minker, ed. (1986).

[29] Fagin, R., G. Kuper, J.D. Ullman, M.Y. Vardi, Updating Logical Databases, Advances in Computing Research, vol 3, JAI Press (1986)

[30] Furtado, A.L., K.C. Sevcik, Permitting Updates through views of Databases, Information Systems (1979).

[31] Fagin, R., J.D. Ullman, M.Y. Vardi, On the semantics of updates in databases, Proc. ACM SIGACT-SIGART-SIGMOD Symp. on Principles of Database Systems, (1983).

[32] Fagin R., M. Vardi, The Theory of Data Dependencies: A Survey, Mathematics of Information, (M. Anshel and W. Gewirtz, eds.), Symp. in Applied Math. 34 (1986).

[33] Gallaire, H., Impacts of logic on databases, Proc. 7th Int. Conf. on Very Large Data Bases (1981), pp. 248-259.

[34] Gallaire, H. J, Minker, J.M. Nicolas, Logic and Databases: a Deductive Approach, ACM Computing Surveys

[35] Golshani, F., T.S.E. Mailbaum, M.R. Sadler, A model system of algebras for database specification and query/update language support, Proc. Ninth Int. Conf. on Very Large Data Bases (1983), pp. 331-339.

[36] Gurevich, Y., S. Shelah, Fixed-point extensions of first-order logics, FOCS (1985).

[37] Hull, R. Relative information Capacity of Simple Relational Database Schemata. USC Technical Report 1984, To appear in SIAM J. of Computing.

[38] Imielinski, T., Incomplete Deductive Databases, submitted to publication (1987).

[39] Imielinski, T., W. Lipski, Incomplete Information in Relational Databases, Journal of Assoc. Comp. Mach., 31,4 (1984)

[40] Imielinski, T., S. Naqvi, Explicit control of Logic Programs through Rule Algebra, Proc. ACM SIGACT-SIGART-SIGMOD Symp. on Principles of Database Systems, (1988).

[41] Kanellakis, P.C., Elements of Relational Database Theory, to appear as a chapter in Handbook of Theoretical Computer Science, North-Holland.

[42] Keller, A., Algorithms for translating view updates to database updates for views involving selections, projections and joins, Proc. ACM SIGACT-SIGART-SIGMOD Symp. on Principles of Database Systems, (1985).

[43] de Kleer, J., An Assumption-Based Truth Maintenance System, Artificial Intelligence, pp. 127-162 (1986)

[44] Klopprogge, M.R., P.C. Lockemann, Modelling information preserving databases: consequences of the concept of time, Proc. Ninth Int. .Conf. on Verg Large Data Bases (1983), pp. 399-416.

[45] King, R., D. McLeod, The event database specification model, Proc. Second International Conf. on Databases: Improving Usability and Responsiveness, Israel (1982)

[46] Kolaitis, P., The expressive power of stratified logic programs, manuscript (1987).

[47] Kolaitis, P., C. Papadimitriou, Why not negation by fixpoint? Proc. ACM SIGACT-SIGART-SIGMOD Symp. on Principles of Database Systems, (1988).

[48] Kripke, S., Semantical considerations on Modal Logic, Acta Philosophica Fennica, Helsinki (1963)

[49] Keller, A., J.D. Ullman, On complementary and independent mappings, Proc. ACM SIGMOD (1984).

[50] Maier, D., The Theory of Relational Databases, Computer Science Press (1983).

[51] Mylopoulos, J., P.A. Bernstein, H.K.T. Wong, A language facility for designing interactive 'database–intensive applications, ACM Trans. on Database Systems (June 1980).

[52] de Maindreville, C., E. Simon, a production rule based approach to deductive databases, Proc. Conf. on Data Engineering (1988).

[53] de Maindreville, C., E. Simon, Modelling a Production Rule Language for Deductive Databases, Proc. Conf. on Very Large Data Bases (1988).

[54] Maier, D., J.Stein, A.Otis, A.Purdy, Development of an Object-Oriented DBMS, ACM SIGPLAN Not. 21 (11), (1986).

[55] Manchanda S., D.S. Warren, A logic-based language foe database updates, Foundations of Logic Programming and Deductive Databases, ed. J. Minker (1987).

[56] Naqvi, S., a logic for negation in database systems, Proc. Workshop on Logic Databases (1986).

[57] Naqvi, S., R. Krishnamurthy, Database Updates in Logic Programming, Proc. ACM SIGACT-SIGART-SIGMOD Symp. on Principles of Database Systems, (1988).

[58] Naish, L., J.A. Thom, K. Ramamohanaro, Concurrent database updates in Prolog, U. de Melbourne, Australia.

[59] Nicolas, J.M., Yazdanian, Integrity checking in deductive data bases, Logic and Databases H. Gallaire and J. Minker, (Eds.), Plenum Press (1978).

[60] Paredaens, J., On the Expressive Power of the Relational Algebra, Inform. Processing Letters (1978)

[61] Reiter, R., Towards a logical reconstruction of relational database theory, in On Conceptual Modelling, Springer-Verlag pp. 191-233 (1984)

[62] Rolland, C., Event driven synchronization in REMORA. Third Scandinavian Symp. on Information Modelling, Tampere, Finland, 1984.

[63] Snodgrass, R., The temporal query language t quel, Proc. Third ACM SIGACT-SIGMOD Symp. on Principles of Database Systems (1984), pp. 204-212.

[64] Ullman, J.D., Principles of Database and Knowledge Base Systems, Computer Science Press (1988).

[65] Ulrich, Schiel, An abstract introduction to the temporal-hierarchical data model, Proc. Ninth Int. Conf. on Very Large Data Bases (1983), pp. 322-330.

[66] Vardi, M., Querying Logical Databases, Proc. Fourth ACM SIGACT-SIGMOD Symp. on Principles of Database Systems (1985)

[67] van Gelder, A., Negation as failure using tight derivations for general logic programs, Proc. IEEE symposium on Logic Programming (1986).

[68] Vianu, V., Dynamic constraints and database evolution. Proc. Second ACM SIGACT-SIGMOD Symp. on Principles of Database Systems (1983), 389-399.

[69] Vianu, V., Dynamic functional dependencies and database aging. Journal of the ACM, 34,1 (1987).

[70] Vianu, V., Database survivability under dynamic constraints. Acta Informatica, 25, (1988).

[71] Vianu, V., Object projection views in the dynamic relational model. ACM Transactions on Database Systems, 13, 1, (1988). (1984).

[72] Warren, D.,S., Database Updates in pure Prolog, Proc. of Inter. Conf. on 5th Generation Computer Systems (1984).

[73] Winslett, M., A model theoretic approach to updating logical databases, Proc. ACM SIGACT-SIGART-SIGMOD Symp. on Principles of Database Systems, (1986).

[74] Winslett, M., A framework for the comparison of update semantics, Proc. ACM SIGACT-SIGART-SIGMOD Symp. on Principles of Database Systems, (1987).

[75] Yannakakis, M., C. Papadimitriou, Algebraic Dependencies, J. CSS 25, 2 (1982).

DATA MODELS AND LANGUAGES FOR DATABASES †

Catriel Beeri

Department of Computer Science
The Hebrew University, Jerusalem, Israel

ABSTRACT

The seventies have been the decade of the relational model. In the eighties, there is a renewed interest and activity in the database area. Most of it is concerned with so called "advanced systems for new types of applications". In this activity, much emphasis is placed on the development of new data models and languages. The data models include complex objects, which are in essence hierarchical structures, and various flavors of object oriented models. Data manipulation languages include extensions of the classical algebra and calculus based languages to some of the new models, logic programming style languages, and versions of object oriented languages. The paper discusses extensions of the relational model that allow users to specify and manipulate structurally complex objects and their languages. The emphasis is on formal models and languages. In particular, we describe a formal model for objects with identity, and declarative languages for the model.

1. INTRODUCTION

The seventies, for the database area, were the decade of the relational model. This model emphasizes simple structuring mechanisms, and declarative languages. The languages currently in use for the relational model are restricted versions of the relational algebra and calculus (augmented with special constructs, such as aggregate functions). Query evaluation and optimization for these languages are well understood, and commercial implementations abound.

In the eighties, the database community has discovered that the relational model and its aforementioned languages, although quite satisfactory for the commercial and administrative application domains, are inadequate for other data intensive domains. These include, in particular, knowledge based and engineering applications [LP, U2]. The desire to be able to support "knowledge manipulation" or "intelligent behavior" led to a concentrated effort to develop Horn-clause-like query languages and optimization methods for recursive queries (e.g., [BaR, BeR, CH2, Sa, U2]. Efforts to develop database systems that are better suited for engineering applications have been generating a plethora of new systems, models and languages, that are described by terms such as *extensible*, *complex objects*, and *object-oriented*. Numerous efforts to implement such systems are currently under way [Ver, CM, CaD, Dad, PSSWD, SR].

† This research was partially supported by USA-Israel Binational Science Foundation, grant #85/00082

There is currently no agreement on the meaning of *object oriented* in the database context. The characteristics of object oriented systems have been described in several recent surveys [SB, We]; for a discussion in the database context, see [Ban, Di]. Characteristics usually attributed to "object-oriented" include the following: *Complex structures*, using a variety of data constructors, allow for the description of complex entities. The most basic are hierarchic structures. The use of *object identities* allows objects to share subobjects, thus making possible the construction of general networks. *Class hierarchies* provide a facility for more precise descriptions of the relationships between entities to be made known to the system. These three characteristics relate to the structural approach to objects. *Methods, messages*, and *information hiding*, relate to the behavioral approach. The significance of the different features for database systems is still under debate [Di, KLW, RS]. The systems that are now under development contains many of the features above, as well as many others. Many of the proposed languages are navigational, rather than declarative, and systems descriptions often mix implementation and high level details. This can be attributed, at least partially, to the fact that there is no general formal model for object-oriented databases.

In this paper we discuss recent efforts to extend the relational model and its languages so as to capture some of the features implied by the concept of object-oriented. We deal only with the structural aspect; we are not aware of similar work on the behavioral aspects. The main idea that we try to pass to the reader is that there exist a precise formal model in which the structural aspects of objects, including hierarchic and network structures, identity and classes, are adequately represented, and that declarative languages, that generalize those of the relational model, exist for this model. The paper is a survey. However, some of the work we describe is quite recent, and some of it is not adequately described in widely available literature. We hope that this survey will draw the attention of the database community to ideas and results that we consider to be important and that deserve further attention. To make the paper readable, and yet be able to present a complete picture, we have made an effort to avoid complex notation. The details of the formalisms can be found in the references.

The plan of the paper is as follows: Section 2 is a short reminder of the relational model and the declarative languages that are associated with it. A model for hierarchically structured objects, called here *complex objects* or *nested relations*, and its languages are described in Section 3. Results about the expressive power of the languages are presented. The notion of object identity is introduced in Section 4. We describe there some of the pitfalls and problems that have been encountered in efforts to develop a formal model, then we describe a model that avoids the problems. We also discuss query languages, and we conclude with a short discussion of updates. Section 5 presents conclusions.

2. LANGUAGES FOR THE RELATIONAL MODEL.

The following are often cited as the advantages of the relational model: Simplicity of the user view of data; a precise, formal model, with close connection to formal logic, allowing the use of concepts and tools from proof theory and model theory; a declarative language, based on the first order calculus; the equivalence of the relational calculus and relational algebra. While we cannot hope to preserve simplicity as we move to more complex models, we can hope to preserve the other advantages. The last two, in particular, are important to our discussion of other models. A declarative language means that no special evaluation strategy is implied by the formulation of a query. Hence an implementor has the freedom of choosing the most efficient strategy that can be found for each query. The algebra consists of a small number of constructs, each embodying a certain style of looping. We can, therefore, invest our efforts in optimizing these constructs, relying on a good understanding of their properties and relationships [Ma1, U1]. The equivalence of calculus and algebra, "the algebraization of calculus", is often viewed as a cornerstone of query optimization. However, this view is somewhat simplistic; the rest of this section briefly explains why.

Current relational systems support languages that are equivalent to a restricted version of the relational algebra (or calculus). The queries are those that can be expressed by the *project, select, join, union* operations (PSJU queries). For this algebra, optimization using rules such as "push selections inside," is effective in translating a declarative query into an access plan that uses to advantage existing access paths. The full power of the algebra can be realized by applying the difference operation to the results of such queries; optimization, however, deals only with PSJU queries. There are very few papers that try to extend optimization to difference or to universal quantifiers, see [Day1, Day2]. Thus, algebraization by itself is no guarantee that queries in a language can be efficiently optimized. The knowledge we have about the operations and their properties is crucial.

Recent research on recursive queries deal with a language commonly called Datalog, that extends the class of PSJU queries. A Datalog program is a collection of rules, each of the form *head :– body*, where *body* is a conjunction of literals, and head is a single literal. The predicates appearing in a body can be database relation names, or new names denoting *derived* relations; the predicate in the head must be derived. There are good reasons for considering this language. Datalog programs are easy to understand, and have a simple declarative meaning. As a matter of fact, Datalog is a pure version of Prolog, which is widely used for the implementation of knowledge based systems. Thus, one expects that systems based on Datalog will be accepted by users. (Whether such systems will provide good support for knowledge based systems still remains to be seen; probably some extensions to the language are needed.) The semantics of Datalog can be defined in several ways. The *proof theoretic* semantics views a Datalog program as a conjunction of formulas, and its meaning is the set of formulas that are implied by it. The *model theoretic* semantics considers the meaning of the program to be the smallest model for it. The *fixpoint* semantics defines the meaning of a program as the least fixpoint of an associated monotone operator. When one is interested only in ground atomic facts, the three approaches are equivalent, which shows that for this language, the semantics is a robust and natural concept, and is closely related to formal concepts and tools. The language is completely declarative; no evaluation order is implied by the program. The proof theoretic and least fixpoint approaches induce the top-down and bottom-up evaluation strategies. These can be refined in many ways, so there is a fertile ground for the development of optimizations. In particular, bottom-up evaluation is suitable to database style, set-at-a-time processing. Although no "algebraization" of the language is known, various optimization strategies have been developed [BaR, Sa]. In particular, the concept of "pushing selections" have been extended to Datalog, although it does not rely on algebraic rules any more [BeR].

Assume that negation is added to Datalog, but it may be used only in the bodies of rules. Consider the program $p(a) :- \neg q(a)$; $q(a) :- \neg p(a)$. It has several minimal, incomparable, models; the operator associated with the program is not monotone; the set of ground atomic facts implied by the program is empty. Further, it seems there is no natural, intuitive way to associate semantics with the program. *Stratification* is a condition that disallows cycles involving negation in a program [ABW, N]. For example, if the second rule above is replaced by $s(a) :- \neg p(a)$, then we have a stratified program. We can now compute the extension for q, which in this case is empty (no rule has q in its head); fixing it, we obtain $\{p(a)\}$ as the extension for p, using the first rule only; then we obtain an empty extension for s using the second rule. This is the currently accepted semantics of such a program. The connection to proof theory is lost, however - the program does not imply $p(a)$. The language is commonly called *stratified Datalog*.

There is a general feeling that in stratified Datalog we still have a reasonable notion of declarative semantics, and since it involves a bottom up computation, we can hope to extend optimization methods developed for Datalog to stratified Datalog. Note, however, that the language is strictly more powerful than the full first order calculus: it can express any first order query, since negation can be used; it can also express the transitive closure query, which is not first order [AU]. Optimization strategies for stratified Datalog should in particular work also for the first order calculus. A general framework for optimizing stratified Datalog programs is not yet known.

Many additional languages, utilizing a rich repertoire of programming constructs, have been identified and their expressive power has been studied extensively; see [Ch] for a recent survey. We mention here some of them: *FO* is the language of first order calculus; It is in turn contained in *FP* - the language of fixpoint queries, which is contained in *SO* - the language of *second order* calculus, i.e., the calculus with relational variables. ("contain" here means more expressive). While many of these languages are declarative, they are currently considered candidates for implementation (except possibly for *FO* and stratified Datalog); they can express queries that are too complex. Perhaps the key point is the following: there are indeed queries that cannot be expressed in *FO*, or in Datalog, or in stratified Datalog. It may be of theoretical interest to consider efficient implementations for more expressive languages, or look for a "algebraizations". However, we currently seem to have almost no idea on how to do that. Furthermore, it is not clear that an increase in the expressive power of the query language is what is needed for better database systems. Actually, those who are now implementing new systems are looking in altogether different directions.

3. COMPLEX OBJECTS

The first extensions of the relational model that have been studied deal with hierarchically structured objects, referred to as nested relations or complex objects. Although various languages for complex objects have been considered, comparative studies have been undertaken only recently [ABe, RKS]. We present here some recent results concerning the expressive power of those languages. Our presentation of the languages is brief; details can be found in [ABe, ABVG, KR, RKS, SS].

3.1 The Model

Codd required relations to be in First Normal Form (1NF), thus avoiding the need to have in the languages facilities for composing or decomposing attribute values [C]. The shortcomings of 1NF for data representation were first observed in [Mak]. Note that the absence of set-valued attributes causes problems even for languages like SQL. Indeed, aggregate functions in such languages have set arguments, which are not first class citizens of the model. The query *select SUM(*) from S*, computes the number of tuples in *S*; however, the argument * in SQL usually stands for an arbitrary tuple, rather than for the set of all tuples, so its role is ambiguous. Numerous models that partially or completely remove the 1NF restriction, with associated languages, have been proposed [BK, Kl, FT, JS, OOM] ; see [ABVG, KR] for recent surveys and additional references. The proposed models can roughly be classified either as *nested relations*, or as general *complex objects*. In a nested relation, an attribute value may be either atomic or a relation. The constructors that are used in the model are the *set* and the *tuple* constructors, and they must alternate. A complex object is obtained from atomic values by using these constructors, but there is no restriction on the order in which they are used. Thus, we may have a tuple in which one of the components is a tuple, and we may have a set of atoms, or a set of sets, and so on.

Complex object types are defined as follows. First, *domains names*, denoting atomic domains, are types. (We assume a finite set of domain names.) If T, $T_1, \ldots, T_n$ are types, and A, $A_1, \ldots, A_n$ are distinct attributes then $[A_1{:}T_1, \ldots, A_n{:}T_n]$ is a *tuple* type, and $\{A{:}T\}$ is a *set* type. Given an assignment of a set of values to each domain name, we can apply the same constructors to obtain *complex objects*. Thus, for each type, there is a set of objects of that type, that can be constructed from elements of these domains. Types and objects are classified as *atomic* or *complex*, and further, by their principal constructor, as *tuples* or *sets*.

Nested relations (also called $\neg$1NF, or NFNF, or NF ^{2} relations) are particular cases of complex objects in which the set and tuple constructors alternate. That is, if, $T_1, \ldots, T_n$ are atomic or nested types, then $T = \{A{:}[A_1{:}T_1, \ldots, A_n{:}T_n]\}$ is a *nested type*. A complex object of type T is called a *nested relation*. Many of the proposals for nested relations further assume that in each tuple there is at least one atomic component, and that the atomic components in a relation contain a key for the relation. Such nested relations are called *V*-relations in [ABi], and *PNF* relations in [RKS]

A *database type* (or *schema*) is a tuple of set types $\boldsymbol{DB} = [R_1{:}T_1, \ldots, R_n{:}T_n]$. A *database instance* is a structure consisting of the domains assigned to the domain names, and of objects $R_1, \ldots, R_n$ of types $t_1, \ldots, T_n$, respectively. Each R_i is called a *database relation*. A *query* is a function from the instances of $\boldsymbol{DB}$ to a set type T. For nested relations, T must be a nested type.

3.2 The Calculus

The calculus for the model is a typed first-order language. *Terms* include *constants and variables*, each associated with a type. (Thus, the domain names are used in the language, in type expressions.) Also, if t is a term of tuple type, and A is a component name of that type, then $t.A$ is a term. The set of predicates includes the predicate names $\boldsymbol{R}_1, \ldots, \boldsymbol{R}_n$, and for all types S, $T=\{S\}$ the predicates: $\in_{S,T}$ (membership predicate), and $=_{SS}$ (equality predicate). Predicates applied to terms (of the appropriate types) yield *atomic* formulas. In particular, $\boldsymbol{R}(t)$), (meaning $t \in \boldsymbol{R}$), $t \in s.A$, and $t \in s$ are formulas, as are similar formulas constructed with the equality predicate. Finally, the connectives $\wedge, \vee, \neg$ and the quantifiers $\forall$, $\exists$ are used to construct non-atomic formulas.

An *interpretation* assigns domains to the domain names names, and objects $R_1, \ldots, R_n$ to $\boldsymbol{R}_1, \ldots, \boldsymbol{R}_n$ (of appropriate types). That is, it is a database instance. Given an interpretation, a domain of values is determined for each type that uses only the domain names of the given scheme. Thus, an interpretation assigns a meaning to the quantifiers, and truth values for formulas can be defined in the standard way. A *(c-)query* is an expression $q \equiv <A:t \mid \phi>$, for some formula $\phi(t)$, such that t is its only free variable. Let the type of t be T. The c-query q *defines* a query, i.e., a mapping from instances of $\boldsymbol{DB}$ to instances of $\{A:T\}$, as follows:

$$q(DB) = \{ v \text{ of type } A:T \mid \phi(v) \text{ is true in } DB \}$$

Obviously, the calculus can serve also for the nested relation model. The result of a query must be a nested relation - a set of tuples. Every set in the formula is a component of a tuple. Therefore, only tuple variables need to be used. See [RKS].

Example 1: Let the schema be S:$\{B:[C, D:\{E\}]\}$. The queries are:

(1) The powerset of the relation S.

$$t \mid \forall u\, (u \in t \rightarrow S(u))$$

(2) The collection of subsets of the second component of tuples of S, which do not contain 2, 4, or 5.

$$t \mid \exists s\, (\, S(s) \wedge \forall w\, (\, w \in t \rightarrow (w \in s.D \wedge w \notin \{2,4,5\})\,)\,)$$

(3) The relation S, with the value of the C component added to the set value of the D component, and the C component eliminated. The result is of type $\{D:\{E\}\}$. Let $\boldsymbol{R}$ be a predicate name of type $[C, D]$. The following formula *represents* the desired function on elements of type $[C, D]$.

$\forall w(w \in t \leftrightarrow w \in \boldsymbol{R}.D \;\vee\; w = \boldsymbol{R}.C\,)$, or simply,

$t = \boldsymbol{R}.D \cup \{\boldsymbol{R}.C\}$.

(Note that this representation differs from that used for queries.) The query is now easily obtained:

$t \mid \exists s\, (\, S(s) \wedge t = s.D \cup \{s.C\}\,)$. □

It is well known that the calculus is "closed" under query composition [CH1]. The third example illustrates a general mechanism, called *apply-to-all* in [Ba], for performing restructuring - applying a function to each element of a set. Such a mechanism is particularly useful in the context of complex objects, since it can be used recursively.

Recall that the domain names are used only in the definitions of the types. Nevertheless, the truth value of a formula may depend not only on the relations assigned to the R_i's, but also on the domains assigned to the D_j's, since the domains determine the ranges for the variables. A query is *domain independent* if it has the same value on any two structures that differ only in their domains [Fa]. the *domain independent calculus* is the calculus, restricted to domain independent formulas.

3.3 The Algebra

The algebra contains the classical operations: *union, intersection difference, cross product, select, project*, extended to accept arbitrary objects of set type as arguments. A nontrivial, new, operation is the *powerset*, which creates the set of all subsets of a set. As we deal with complex objects, the algebra is used not only to define the contents of the result, but also its shape - its type. It is used for restructuring. For nested relations, two well known operations are *nest*, that has an effect resembling that of "group-by", and *unnest*. (They are not suitable for general complex objects.) These two, with *select, project* and *cross* provide for a rich set of restructuring transformations.

There is still a need to be able to operate on sub-objects. Using *nest, unnest* operations, one can "flatten" a relation, operate on it, than "unflatten" the result. This leads to a non-recursive algebra. One problem here is that the two operations are not always inverses. (They are inverses for *PNF* relations.) An alternative approach is to allow algebraic operations to be used recursively on sub-objects [Ja, SS]. The most general approach presented so far, is probably that of [ABe], who include in the algebra the "apply-to-all" functional form, which they call a *replace*. The general format is $replace<G>(\mathbf{R})$, where G is a *replace specification*. The specification represents the function to be applied to each element of the set R that is substituted for $\mathbf{R}$. Specifications are algebraic expressions constructed from predicate names, constants and attribute names, using tuple and set constructors, a conditional constructor, and application of operations. In particular, a specification may itself contain a replace subexpression, so the definition is recursive. It turns out that *project, select,* and many other restructuring operations are special cases of *replace*.

Example 1 (continued) : Recall the schema $S{:}\{\ B{:}[C,\ D{:}\{E\}\ \}$. The algebraic expression for the queries are:

(1) $powerset(\mathbf{R})$.

(2) $set{-}collapse\ (\ replace<powerset(D-\{2,4,5\})>(S)\ )$.

(*set-collapse* replaces a set of sets by its union.)

(3) $replace<D\cup\{C\}>(S)$ □

Whereas arbitrary formulas of the calculus are not guaranteed to be domain independent, The algebra is a domain independent language. We can now state the first equivalence result.

Theorem [ABe] : The algebra and the domain independent calculus are equivalent. □

The proof follows the classical proof presented in [U1]. In the reduction from the calculus to the algebra, the first step is to construct for each variable in a formula an algebraic expression (i.e., query) that represents the domain of values this variable can take on in a database instance. Once such *domain expressions* are given, the construction proceeds by induction on the structure of the formula, and rather weak algebraic operations are used. Now assume, say, that the type of a variable t is "set of atoms". We can construct an algebraic expression for the set of atoms that appear in the database by applying projections to the database relations, then union. The domain of t is the powerset of the set described by that expression. Hence the need for the powerset in the algebra.

3.3 Safety and Strict Safety

It is known, even for the classical relational calculus, that domain independence is undecidable [DiP, Va1]. Traditionally, one uses syntactic restrictions that guarantee domain independence. Following [U1], formulas that are syntactically restricted, by a condition that guarantees domain independence, are called *safe*. The accepted approach to making a formula safe is to attach to each variable a *range formula* that restricts the values that can be assigned to it to those that are obtained from the database relations. Safety is defined in [ABe] for complex objects, and in [RKS] for nested relations. The idea is that in any formula there should be a partial ordering of the variables such that the range formula for a variable restricts its values to those obtained from constants of the formula, from the database relations, or from values of variables that precede it in the ordering. This guarantees that the atomic elements in a value assigned to any variable during the evaluation of a formula are only those that appear in the database or in constants in the formula. A range formula for a variable t may state that t is a tuple in some $\boldsymbol{R}_i$, or that t is a tuple of s, or that t is obtained by collecting into a tuple components of $s_1, \ldots, s_k$, and so on. In each case, the variables used in the range formula for t (e.g., $s, s_1, \ldots, s_k$) must precede t in the ordering. Note that to be able to generate powersets, to make the safe calculus as expressive as the domain independent calculus, it is necessary to include

(*) $\exists s\ (\ \phi(s) \wedge t \subseteq s)\ ),$

where s precedes t in the ordering, as a valid range restriction. As for the relational model, we have:

Theorem [ABe]: The algebra, the safe calculus, and the domain independent calculus, are equivalent. □

The proof is by reduction from the algebra to the safe calculus, and vice versa. The only change in the reduction from safe calculus to the algebra is in the first step, in the construction of the algebraic domain expressions. Instead of taking the relations apart, then reconstructing the domains for the types of the variables, we can now construct the domain expressions directly from the range formulas.

The powerset is an expensive operation. Can one do without it? A stronger version of safety, called *strict safety* in [ABe] is obtained by dropping (*) from the collection of range formulas.

Theorem [ABe]: The algebra without the *powerset* and the strictly safe calculus are equivalent. □

A similar approach has been adopted in [RKS]. They define safety for the calculus by range formulas that do not allow the formation of powersets, and they do not include the powerset in the algebra. Their algebra is different from that used in [ABe, SS]. The problem they face is that most operations do no preserve the*PNF* property. Thus they change the definitions of the operations to make them *PNF* preserving

3.4 Recursive Languages

Among the Horn-clause based languages recently introduced, many allow sets as components of tuples, and they use set predicates ($\in$, in particular) and operations in the rules. In LDL [TZ], a *grouping* operation, similar to the "group-by" of SQL, is introduced. In a rule

$$p(X, <Y>) :- \text{body}(X, Y, Z)$$

a tuple of p contains an X-value, and the set of *all* Y-values such that, for some Z-value, the body is satisfied. The set predicates $\cup$ and $\in$ are also used, and negation is allowed. Although a data model is not formally described, it is obviously a complex object model.

As noted in [BNRST], the use of *grouping* (which contains an implicit universal quantifier) causes problems in defining semantics of programs, similar to those caused by negation. Stratification with respect to both negation and grouping is offered as a solution. (As shown there, additional restrictions, such as allowing only typed predicates, may be needed.) Other language constructs that have been proposed include *data functions*, used in [AG], and explicit *universal quantification over set variables* (ranging over finite sets) in [Ku2]. However, it turns out that, in the presence of negation, the different set predicates and operations have the same power. In [ABe] it is shown that with membership and negation it is possible to simulate union, and also grouping. Similar results are proved in [Ku3]. Also, in [BNRST] it is shown that grouping can simulate negation. Thus, it seems that we have a collection of operations on sets such that languages having some or all of them are equivalent.

Assume a recursive language that uses membership, negation and union, with semantics based on stratification.

Theorem [ABe]: A query is expressible as a layered recursive query, if and only if it is expressible in the safe calculus (or the powerset algebra). □

3.5 Discussion

As we have stated, the algebra, the domain independent calculus, the safe calculus, and the recursive, stratified-Datalog-like, language, are equivalent. In particular, although the transitive closure cannot be expressed in the relational calculus, it can be expressed in the complex object calculus. Given a binary relation, we project it on the two attributes and take the union, to obtain the set of all elements in it. We take the cross product of this set with itself, obtaining a binary relation that contains the transitive closure. Next, we generate all the subsets of this relation, using the powerset construction; using variables that range over the elements of that powerset we describe the properties of the transitive closure, namely that it is the minimal set that contains the given relation and is transitively closed. The equivalence of the calculus and the recursive language is proved in [ABe] by generalizing this idea.

What is the complexity of this class of queries? Although a precise characterization is not known, there are some clear indications. We may consider queries on a relational database, with a relation as a result, that use intermediate complex types. As shown in [HS], the class of queries that is obtained contains *SO* - the second order calculus. Also note that to generate the powerset of a relation takes exponential time. A user may generate powersets nested to arbitrary depths. Obviously. unrestricted use (probably any use) of powerset is too expensive. In contrast, if we consider the strictly safe calculus, and the equivalent algebra (without powerset), they have a much more restricted expressive power and the queries they define belong to a more "reasonable" complexity class. Another indication that the powerset is not a useful operation is the construction of the transitive closure described above. It is certainly not the natural way to define the transitive closure, and it implies a very expensive method for computing it. It is way beyond the capabilities of current optimizers to transform such a definition into a bottom-up direct computation. Again, algebraization does not guarantee that queries can be optimized.

Our study of complex object languages can be couched in terms of *safety*. The unrestricted calculus can express queries that are ambiguous, from the users' viewpoint, since their results depend on the domains, which are not visible to the users. Also, results may be infinite (for infinite domains). Safety implements the concept of domain independence, solving this problem. The solution is satisfactory for the relational model, but not for the complex object model, since it still allows the generation of all subsets of the domain, hence the expression of second order queries. Our feeling is that strict safety, or a similar idea, is the right concept here, as it limits queries to elements that are constructed in a simple way from the database objects.

4. OBJECTS WITH IDENTITY

4.1 The Model

The complex object model, like the relational model, is *value based* [U3], that is, entities and relationships are represented by values. In a value based model, object sharing may only be accomplished by the introduction of artificial identifiers. Dealing with these identifiers and with the attendant normalization issues is the users' responsibility. When objects have a permanent identity, separate from the values associated with them, it is possible for objects to share subobjects. An early example is the DBTG network model. Surprisingly few works treat such models and their declarative languages formally [Ja, Ku1, KV1, KV2, Ma2, Ry]. Our presentation outlines some of the difficulties, and a solution. We follow, in general, the ideas in [Ku, KV1, Ma2, Ry], although we diverge from these works in many details. We note that the main idea has been known and used by logicians; see [En].

Informally, an object oriented database is a collection of objects of various types. Some of the types correspond to *atomic* domains; the elements of these domains are *printable*, i.e., can be shown on a screen or printed. Objects of other types are not printable. Objects of tuple types have attribute values associated with them. These may be of any type, not necessarily atomic. An object of set type is associated with a (finite) set of objects. (However, a tuple object is not a tuple. Rather, it is associated with a value that is a tuple. Similarly, a set object is not a set, but its value is a set.) Relationships may be represented in several ways. A one-many relationship may be represented as an attribute whose value is a set object. An n-ary many-many relationship can be represented as an n-ary tuple object. An object may belong to any number of sets, and be a component of any number of tuples. Our goal is to describe a formal model in which declarative languages, in particular a calculus, may be used.

The first issue is how to specify the types for the objects. The notation for type definitions that we discussed (very briefly) in Section 3 can be viewed as equations, where in an equation, the type on the left side is defined by the type expression on the right side. To obtain a general notation, we allow a type name to be used in more than one equation, and we allow recursion. The atomic types may not appear on the left; they are given, not definable. We assume that each type is defined once only, and is either a tuple or a set type. A tuple type is defined by an equation of the form $T = [A_1{:}T_1, \ldots, A_n{:}T_n]$. A set type is defined by an equation of the form $T = \{A:S\}$. If we want to allow one-to-many attributes (as in [Ry]), we use in the tuple constructor the name of the appropriate set type, which of course needs to be defined in another equation. An (n-ary) relationship is an object of tuple type. Its type is defined by an equation with the type name on the left, and the tuple of types of the components of the relationship on the right. Such a set of type definitions is called an *object scheme.*

Example 2: Consider the following university database. The atomic domains are Name, B_Date. The object types are Student, Course, Professor. We assume that the relationship between students and courses is many-many. Each professor has a set of courses that he/she teaches. The type equations are (attribute names are omitted in most cases):

$Student = [Name,\ B\_Date]$

$S\_C = [Student,\ Course]$

$Course = [Name]$

$Set\_of\_C = \{C\}$

$Professor = [Name,\ B{-}Date,\ Courses{:}Set\_of\_C]$ □

Note that in a definition such as $S\_C = [Student,\ Course]$, the name S_C denotes a type, hence it refers to a set of $[Student,\ Course]$ pairs.

An *object calculus* may now be easily defined. The terms are constants and variables. As in Section 3 and in [Ja], we may assume that each constant and variable is associated with a type. Alternatively, we may use untyped variables, but require that each variable v appears in a range formula of the form $T(v)$, where T is a type. The approaches are equivalent. We use in the examples below the second approach.

Components of a tuple type are selected using dot notation, as e.g., in the term *x.Name*. The predicate symbols are $\in_{S,T}$ and $=_{S,S}$, and $T(v)$, where T is a type name. Using them we obtain the atomic formulas. The set of formulas is closed under the connectives and quantifiers.

Now, let us consider structures. Given type definitions, and an assignment of domains to the atomic domain names, what are the sets of possible values for the types? Jacobs defines those sets to be the least fixpoint solution of the recursive type equations [Ja]. For the hierarchic case, one obtains precisely our definition of Section 3. For the general case, the approach is not satisfactory. First, although the scheme may contain cycles, the data does not contain cycles - data items are *well-founded*. For example, consider the following type equation.

Person = [*Name*, *Person*]

We may use such an equation to define the type of persons, where each person is a pair of a name and a spouse. Thus, the data we are interested in is a collection of pairs, where each element in a pair points to the other element of the pair. However, such pairs are not part of the domain as described in [Ja].

There are other problems with Jacob's approach. Even when the atomic domains are finite, the collection of values for a given type may be infinite, even when using Jacob's definition. This is the case for the type *Person* defined above. Thus, as noted in [Va2], one may not be able to compute the truth value of a formula, given an assignment of values to its free variables, and some queries are not computable. Further, Jacobs proved that the logic is second order. In this case, as domains are infinite, it makes the computations not just more expensive (as in the relational case), but infinitely so.

The solution is the following. Given a set of type definitions, we associate with it a *many-sorted* first order logic. Each type is identified with a *sort* (for which we may use the same name). In particular, each atomic domain is also a sort. For a tuple type $T = [A_1{:}T_1, \ldots, A_n{:}T_n]$, the association between T and $A_i{:}T_i$ is represented by a binary predicate T_A_i. The dot notation, as in *x.Name*, where x is of type *Student*, is then simply a short notation for "the unique y such that $Student\_Name(x, y)$ holds". Attributes that are single valued may be represented as functions; the dot notation then represents function application. (An alternative approach is to associate a single n-ary predicate with the tuple type. These approaches are equivalent as far as we are concerned.) Each predicate is typed, that is, a type is associated with each position, and similarly for functions. If we choose to represent single valued attributes as predicates then the single-valued property is represented by a formula. (This is not a problem - the type definitions usually do not restrict the instances to those that are of interest, so we need formulas as part of the scheme anyway.) Finally, consider set types. If T is a type, and S is the type $\{T\}$, then a sort is associated with S, like with any other type. The relationship between an object of type S and its elements of type T is just like any other relationship. It is represented by a predicate, say, $mems_{S,T}$.

Example 2 (cont'd): The sorts and predicates for the example are as follows (types of predicate positions are omitted where they are obvious. Names are abbreviated for convenience.):

Types: *Name*, *B_Date*, *Student*, *Course*, *Set_of_Course*, *Professor*,

Predicates: $S\_Name(-,-)$, $S\_B\_Date(-,-)$, $S\_C(-,-)$, $C\_Name(-,-)$, $mem_{\{C\},C}(Set\_of\_C,\ C)$,

$P\_Name(-,-)$, $P\_B\_Date(-,-)$, $P\_Cs(Professor, Set\_of\_C)$ □

The description above defines a correspondence between the object calculus and the many sorted first order calculus. A restriction that is induced from the many sorted logic is that variables in the object calculus may only be of the types defined in the scheme, just as variables of the many sorted language can only be of one of the sorts. Given this restriction, each formula in the object calculus can be translated to a formula in the many sorted calculus, and vice versa. Although we do not guarantee that the translations are inverses, they preserve equivalence of formulas.

The next step is to consider the concept of structure for the many sorted logic, and induce from it a definition for structure for the object model. Recall that a structure for the many sorted logic consists of a domain for each sort, and an assignment of a relation to each predicate and a function to each function symbol. From that we obtain a definition of an *object structure.* It consists of an assignment of a collection of objects to each type defined in the scheme, and in addition, of an association of a value with each object. The value of an atomic object is itself, the value of a non-atomic object is a tuple or a set, as described informally above. The only divergence from Jacob's definition is, therefore, that the domains of the types are arbitrary and independent, rather than determined by the atomic domains and the type definitions. (Note that no domains are associated with types not defined in the scheme; this is not a problem, as variables can only be of the types of the scheme.) The concept of identity is represented in a very simple way - each object is its own identity. (The concept of *l*-value used by [KV1] can be viewed as a lower level representation, just as object identity is internally represented in a system by some identifier. The value of an object is the *r*-value of [Ku1, KV1]). A structure is finite iff each of the domains is finite.

It can easily be seen that there is now a one to one correspondence between object structures and many sorted structures (which preserves the finiteness property). We can now define truth values for formulas of the object calculus in an object structure. The correspondence between formulas of the two languages preserves truth values. It follows that the object calculus, with the new definition of semantics (via the new definition of object structure) is first order, and in a finite structure, queries are computable.

Why is the calculus now first order, although quantification over set typed variables is allowed? The reason is that the range of a quantified variable of type $\{T\}$ is not the collection of all (finite) sets one can construct on the domain of T, but rather a given, independent, collection. (In contrast, in the complex object model, each type has an associated domain that is constructed from the atomic domains, and they range over the domains that are so constructed, using the constructors. We may use arbitrary types for the variables but then we have a second order language.) The approach may, at first, seem to be profoundly different from the way structures are treated in Mathematical Logic.However, as mentioned above, the logicians have discovered the usefulness of this approach to "correct" problems associated with second order logic. Our object structures are special cases of the *general structures* of [En]. The approach is certainly natural from the database viewpoint. Consider the concept of safety. Its stated purpose is to free users from the need to consider the domains of a structure, and regard queries as relating to the database relations only. Since users are not aware of the domains, we want to avoid queries whose results depend on the domains; such queries are ambiguous, and probably not what the user meant anyway. They may also have infinite results. Now, the definition of semantics for the object model that we have presented (i.e., the association of the language with object structures), has safety built in - quantifiers do not range over the set of all elements that *potentially* could be of the given types, but are restricted to those that are given in the structure. In addition to the reasons mentioned above for imposing safety, we have here a situation that unsafe queries are not computable, hence we have an even stronger motivation to concentrate on safe queries. The model is constructed so that safety is, in a sense, an intrinsic property.

4.2 Databases and Queries

We have not yet defined what a database is. We may define the database to be the given structure, as is done in [Ku1, KV1, Ma2, Ry]. Each type name is considered to be a relation name, denoting the collection of all elements of the type in the structure. The definition diverges from the accepted notion of a database: Not every type deserves to be a relation. E.g., we have no reason to regard *Set_of_C* as a relation. That can be solved easily: add to the scheme a list of the types that are the database relations. This is the approach we adopt. (Alternatively, we may add a list of constants, of the appropriate types, and treat those as the database relations.) Note that in a structure there may exist elements of various types that do not appear in any of the relations. To make the results of queries independent of the choice of domains for the types, we should add range restrictions, as was done for the previous models. That is, we should impose safety restrictions in addition to those that are built in.

Example 2 (cont'd): We have seven types, of which two are atomic, and five are non-atomic. The database contains four relations namely, *Student, Course, Professor, S_C*. The fifth, *Set_of_C*, is not considered a relation. □

A point that deserves attention is that we are not forced to make everything an object. We can use predicates to represent relationships that we do not want to consider as objects. That is, we may include in the scheme names and definitions of predicates. The list of database relations will, in general, contain both types, denoting sets of objects, and predicates names, denoting "normal" relations. This is crucial for the definition of declarative query languages. One of the most important properties of the relational model is that results of queries are relations, hence query expressions can be composed. If the model recognizes only (collections of) objects, then the result of a query must be an object, or a set of objects, of a type that usually is not one of the types in the scheme. That means that query expressions define *new* objects. This is the approach taken in [Ku1, KV1]. However, as shown in [Ku1], the definition of new objects by formulas is problematic. We still do not know how to do it in the general case. (This subject is discussed again below.) In contrast, if predicates are first rate citizens of the model, the result of a query may be a relation, composition is well defined, and there is no need to invent new objects. This is the approach we adopt.

An *o-query* is a formula of the object calculus, with free variables; the target list contains precisely the free variables. (As in the relational tuple calculus, we may take shortcuts: if we are interested in the A component of a variable v, we may write in the target list $v.A$, and leave v as a free variable in the formula, whereas the formal definition requires that v be existentially quantified, and a new free variable, whose value is equated to $v.A$, is introduced.) The answer of a query on a given database is the set of tuples of values for the free variables that satisfy the formula. These tuples are not new objects, they are simply tuples of objects from the database. Recall that all variables in a formula are required to be of the types of the scheme. A query, then, defines a new, nameless, predicate. Note that the tuples of this predicate contain objects. Thus, we still have "pointers" to the objects in the database that appear in the result. We can use them later for updates. See [Ja, Ry] for examples that use the results of queries for subsequent updates. This is an important property, not shared by value based systems.

The definition of a query as defining a "flat" relation may be too restrictive. We may want to define more elaborate structures. For that we may use the ideas of Section 3. Given an object scheme ***DB***, let us consider, for a query, an auxiliary set of types that are defined in terms of the types in ***DB***, such that the new types define a hierarchic structure with respect to the given scheme. That is, the new types define a forest, whose leaves are all types of ***DB***. Then, given a finite object structure for ***DB***, we obtain a finite domain for each of the new types, using the construction of Section 3 (which is identical to the bottom-up construction of [Ja]). We may now use variables of these new types in the language, and in particular, obtain structured results. Note, however, that the new types and variables are treated in a value-based manner. The values are not new objects, but simply complex objects in the sense of Section 3, that is, hierarchically structured relations, composed of values that are objects in the database.

A technical remark: Kuper and Vardi have in their language two versions of equality, denoted $=_l$, $=_r$. The first denotes equality of objects; in our language $=$ is used for that. The second denotes equality of the values of the objects. There is no predicate in our language for that. However, for atomic objects, it is the regular equality; for tuple objects, it is a conjunction of equalities for the components; for set objects, it can be expressed by a formula that states that the two objects contain the same members. Thus $=_r$ can be considered as an abbreviation in our language. It is, nevertheless, a very useful abbreviation.

A final remark: A user should be aware that the result of a query contains objects that are not printable. The language contains the facilities to select only printable values for the result.

Example 2 (cont'd): We consider queries on the university database.

(1) Print the names of all courses taken by the student named 'jones'.

$$x.Name \mid \exists y(\,Student(y) \wedge Course(x) \wedge y.Name = \text{'}jones\text{'} \wedge S\_C(y,\, x)\,)$$

(2) Print names of pairs of courses with a common student taking them, and a common professor teaching them.

$$x,\, y \mid \exists s \exists p(\,Student(s) \wedge Professor(p) \wedge Course(x) \wedge Course(y)$$

$$\wedge S\_C(s, x) \wedge S\_C(s, y) \wedge x \in p.Courses \wedge y \in p.Courses\ )$$

(3) Suppose we want to remove Jones from all the courses he is taking, since he is temporarily suspending his studies. Then we can retrieve the set of courses he takes, as in (1) above, but with x instead of $x.Name$ in the target list. If we put the result of the query into a relation R, then we may perform the deletion by

$$delete\ x \mid S\_C(x) \wedge x.Course \in R$$

This may not be the most straightforward way to perform the deletion in this case, but it illustrates how objects that are retrieved can be used later in updates. □

As for other languages, there is no problem to define a Datalog version of the calculus. The rules define new predicates, but not new types. The defined predicates may be used in the bodies of the rules.

Example 3: Let the types be *Person, Parent,* where the latter is a tuple type, relating a person to one of its parents. Then we may define an ancestor predicate as follows:

$$anc(x, y) :- Parent(z),\ z.1 = x \wedge z.2 = y.$$

$$anc(x, y) :- Parent(z),\ z.1 = x \wedge z.2 = u \wedge anc(u, y).$$ □

Note that if we view $=_r$ as an abbreviation, than its expansion for set objects cannot appear in the body of a rule, since it contains a universal quantifier. It can be seen, however, that if we take $=_r$ as a built-in predicate of the language, the semantics of rules and programs is still well defined. As a matter of fact, $=_r$ for set types can be defined by a stratified program.

Similarly, it is possible to adopt the algebra of [ABe], or other algebras proposed for complex objects, to apply to the object model. We have to be careful, to define the result of each of the operations to be a set (of objects, or of tuples of objects), rather than a new object. We conjecture that the algebra, the calculus and a stratified version of the recursive language are equivalent.

4.3 Classes and ψ-Terms

Class hierarchies are a well known feature of object-oriented systems. They can be incorporated into the model as follows. Each class is one of the types in the scheme. Each type is essentially a unary predicate. A statement "*Student ISA person*" is expressed by the calculus formula $\forall x(Person(x) \leftarrow Student(x))$. Similarly, other constraints on the hierarchy, such as "*Person* is a disjoint union of *Student* and *Employee*" can be expressed as first order sentences. All these sentences are included as part of the scheme.

How can such scheme information be used in our model? It may be used, for example, by a compiler when it checks that a query is well formed. Assume that the scheme contains the types *Person, Student,* and one of the attributes declared for *Person* is *Name.* If the scheme includes the statement *Student ISA person,* then a query that contains $Student(x) \wedge x.Name = \text{'}jones\text{'}$ is legal, since

Name is defined for x. Note that this is the only meaningful notion of *inheritance* in our model, namely the scheme-level information that a subclass has the predicates and functions of the superclass. On the instance level, there is no inheritance. If an object o is a student, it is also a person. It does not inherit a name from anything else; it has a name. Also, issues such as should we store all information on students in one file, or should we store the *Person* part in a different file, are implementation issues. They can not be described in the model.

Ait-Kaci has introduced the notation of ψ-*terms*, to describe complex types [A-K]. His notation extends naturally to instances, and is particularly suited for the object model, since it allows easy access to components of an object. The notation replaces the dot notation. Instead of $x.Name$ = *'jones'* we write x (*Name* ==> *'jones'*). The notation is convenient especially when we have several conditions on an object. Thus, we may write

$$
\begin{aligned}
x\,(&Name \Longrightarrow y\,(First \Longrightarrow \text{'steve'},\ Last \Longrightarrow \text{'jones'})\\
&\quad B\_Date\,(Day \Longrightarrow 12\\
&\qquad\quad Month \Longrightarrow 05\\
&\qquad\quad Year \Longrightarrow 45)\\
&\quad Father\,(Name \Longrightarrow (First \Longrightarrow \text{'john'})\,)\ )
\end{aligned}
$$

instead of the conjunction

$$x.Name = y \ \wedge\ y.First = \text{'steve'} \cdots .$$

Note that every such term is a short notation for a conjunction. Using such terms is a matter of convenience only.

Originally, ψ-terms were introduced in [A-K] as type descriptions. Assume, for example that we have a set of type names, with an ISA hierarchy, or a lattice structure. If *Student ISA Person* is in the scheme, and if every student has an advisor attribute, then *Student* (*Advisor* ==> *Full*−*professor*) denotes a subtype of all students whose advisor is a full professor. The (potentially infinite) collection of types that can be defined in this way inherits the structural properties of the original set of types; if the scheme defines a a lattice, then the induced set of types is a lattice, and so on. Such type expressions may be used, for example, as integrity constraints in the scheme. We may also use such type expressions in queries, to describe succinctly, for example, that a given object is of type student, and further, that its advisor is a full professor. That is, we may allow subexpressions of the form A==> *type* in a term denoting an object, meaning that the A-value for the object is of the specified type. All these terms can be translated into the object calculus. Note that given such terms, the notation $T(x)$ may no longer be convenient. The notation proposed by Maier, T:x, where T is a type specifier, may be more suitable.

To conclude the discussion of ψ-terms, we recall an observation of [A-K] that Prolog programmers often use function symbols to denote types, as e.g., in *person*(*'jones'*, 1945). His system of type notations was meant to formalize and extend this usage. However, although he has worked out the theory of the types, the semantics of his theory cannot be defined in the framework of Prolog (or Datalog). In the value based Herbrand universe that underlies the semantics of Prolog, the type names correspond to function symbols; the terms *Student*(*'jones'*, 1945) and *Person*(*'jones'*, 1945) are different and the only relationship is the common values. There is no meaning to the claim *student ISA Person*. The correct semantics is found in the object model, where the type names are interpreted as predicates. Now, *Student ISA Person* has a translation into a formula, and is a meaningful constraint on the databases of a given scheme.

4.4 Updates - the New Frontier

We have defined the results of queries so that no new objects are generated. Kuper and Vardi, however, assume that queries do generate new objects. Their motivation, as explained in [Ku1], is that since the model deals with objects, the results need to be objects, so queries can be composed. As shown above, the composition problem can be solved without introducing the need to generate new objects. There is, nevertheless, motivation for considering object generation, namely the need (or desire) to have a powerful, declarative, language for updates. We sketch here briefly some ideas relating to updates.

Maier proposes the following notation for updates: $t <== f$ [Ma2]. In this expression, f is a query, and t is a term, or a conjunction of terms. When all the variables in t appear in f, the meaning is that for every instantiation that makes f true, we change the database such that t becomes true. We may thus change connections between objects, insert objects into classes, and so on. By allowing negation in t we may perform deletion.

Example 2 (cont'd): We show how to perform the deletion of (3) above.

$$\neg S\_C(z) \mid \exists y(\mathit{Student}(y) \wedge y.\mathit{Name} = \text{'jones'} \wedge z.\mathit{Student} = y)) \quad \Box$$

While changes to existing objects and their relationships may be specified using this notation, the issue of adding objects is not so easily solved. The most general way of specifying collections of new objects is to extend the given scheme by a *query scheme*, and use a formula with variables ranging on the variables of both schemes [Ku1]. However, this approach is fraught with problems. First, we do not have domains for the new types given to us, so we have no ranges defined for the variables with these types. Even if we restrict attention to acyclic extensions, we cannot easily use the approach that was proposed above for queries, namely to construct the domains for the new types bottom up. Although such a construction gives us a precise idea of the values of the objects in of these types, remember that different objects may have the same values. Given a formula, there may exist numerous extensions of the database in which it is satisfied. Which one should we choose? The most natural choice is the least extension. However, it is undecidable in general if a query has a unique minimal result, even when the database is fixed [Ku1].

The approach of [Ku1, KV1] is: (1) Extend the scheme by one type at a time, and do not allow cyclic extensions. To extend a scheme by several new types, add them one at a time. (2) In the formula for a single type extension, the free variable is of the new type, but all other variables are of the types in the database scheme. The result of the query is defined in the following way. First, compute the values defined by the query. Then "attach" a new object to each such value. They prove that the result is unique, up to isomorphism, and is minimal in a well defined sense.

We conclude the section with a proposal to combine Maier's and Kuper and Vardi's approaches. Define a *rule* to be an expression of the form *head* :– *body*, where *body* is a conjunction of atomic formula, and *head* is also a conjunction. We need more than one atom in the head since we may want, for example, to create a new object, and connect it to several existing objects. It is customary to regard such a rule as a (universally) quantified formula, and its effect on a structure is to change it, so that the rule, as a formula, becomes true. If all the variables in the head appear in the body, then this is Maier's approach, as explained above. Assume that the head contains variables that do not appear in the body. Then these are considered as *existentially* quantified variables, and the operational semantics of the rule is that *if* the rule is not satisfied in the given database, then a new object is created and given a value so that the rule is satisfied. The fact that a new object is not created if an existing object is crucial. We want to use the rules in a recursive program. If a rule always adds objects, the program will never stop.

Another crucial decision is how to quantify the rule. Assume that we have a rule $head(x, y, z)$:– $body(x, y, w)$. The customary quantification in Prolog is universal quantification for all variables. This is inappropriate here since there is no meaning to a universal quantification on z. An existential quantifier is more appropriate. We propose the quantification $\forall xy \exists z \, \forall w(\, rule\,)$. In that, we disagree with [Ma2], in which the existential quantifier is at the end of the quantifier list. The motivation is that since only x and y appear in the head, the new object should be a function of their values only. As an example, assume we change the ancestor program so it generates objects for ancestors tuples. If the new object representing an ancestor of x and y depends also on the intermediary z, we will obtain many such objects for a given pair x, y. If the data is cyclic, we obtain an infinite number of them.

A program is now defined as a collection of rules, possibly with recursion. We conjecture that a minimal model semantics for such programs can be defined. Intuitively, each rule is essentially an existential query in the sense of [KV1]. Thus, the effect of a rule is well defined. What remains to be done is the extension on the result to include recursion, i.e., an an unbounded number of rule applications.

5. CONCLUSIONS

We have presented in this paper extensions of the relational model that capture the structural aspects of object-oriented systems. We have also presented calculus based and algebraic languages for these extensions. Thus, the main properties of the relational model, except possibly for simplicity, have been generalized.

Our results indicate that the unrestricted calculus may be too powerful in the general setting of object-oriented models. The same remark applies to the recursive languages that have been recently proposed. More research is needed to classify the complexity of these and other languages in object models. It is, in particular, necessary to consider restrictions on the languages that will guarantee acceptable complexity. We note that a restriction such as "use only existential quantification, and no negation", although used in the relational model, may not be acceptable. While universal quantification over a, relation may be considered too expensive, this need not be the case for quantification over a set that is a component of a tuple. Anyway, another look at optimization for queries involving universal quantifiers may be profitable. One direction that looks promising is the use of "higher level" constructs in calculus based languages. Such constructs include *set formation* of the form $\{t \mid \phi(t)\}$ [Kl, RKS], and *subset*, used in POSTGRES [RS]. Note that both can be used to simplify the queries in Example 1.

More generally, the challenge is to extend other subjects that were treated in the relational model to the more general models. Of particular interest are query optimization, view updates, and constraint checking. In particular, the object models we have presented allow the natural representation of queries that deal with sets, and this should help in formalizing the theory. Last, but not least, we have shown that in a model in which objects have identity, declarative updates become possible. Understanding the issue of declarative is a formidable but extremely interesting challenge.

REFERENCES

[ABe] Abiteboul, S., and C. Beeri, "On the power of languages for complex objects," Research Report, INRIA and Hebrew University (April 1988).

[ABi] Abiteboul, S., and Bidoit, N., "Non first normal form relations: an algebra allowing data restructuring", *J. Comp. System Sci.* (1986),

[ABVG] Abiteboul S., C. Beeri, D. Van Gucht, and M. Gyssens, "An introduction to the completeness of languages for complex objects and nested relations," manuscript, (May 1988).

[AG] Abiteboul, S., and S. Grumbach, "A logical approach to the manipulation of Complex Objects," *Proc. EDBT* (March 1988), Springer Verlag Lecture Notes in Computer Science 303.

[A-K] Ait-Kaci, H., "An algebraic semantics approach to the effective resolution of type equations," *TCS* 45 (1986), pp. 293-351.

[AU] Aho, A.V., J.D. Ullman, "Universality of data retrieval languages," *Proc. POPL* (1979).

[ABW] Apt, K., H. Blair, and A. Walker, "Toward a Theory of Declarative Knowledge," In *Foundations of deductive databases and logic programming,* J. Minker (ed.), Morgan Kaufmann publishers (1988)

[Ba] Backus, J., "Can programming be liberated from the von Neuman style? A functional style of programming and its algebra of programs," 1977 Turing Award Lecture, *CACM* 21:8 (Aug. 1978).

[Ban] Bancilhon, F., "Object-oriented database systems," *Proc. 7th PODS* (March 1988), pp. 152-162.

[BaR] Bancilhon, F., and R. Ramakrishnan, "An amateur's introduction to recursive query processing strategies," *Proc. ACM-SIGMOD Conf.* (1986), Also in *Foundations of Deductive Databases and Logic Programming* (J. Minker, ed.) Morgan Kaufmann (1988).

[BK] Bancilhon, F., and S. Khoshafian, "A calculus for complex objects, *Proc. 4th PODS* (March 1985).

[BNRST] Beeri, C.,S. Naqvi, R. Ramakrishnan, O. Shmueli, and S.Tsur, "Sets and Negation in a Logic Database Language," *Proc. 6th PODS* (March 1987), pp. 21-37.

[BeR] Beeri, C. and R. Ramakrishnan, "On the power of magic," *Proc. 6th PODS* (March 1987).

[C] Codd, E.F., "A relational model for large shared data banks," *CACM* 13:6 (1970), pp. 377-387.

[CaD] Carey, M, D. DeWitt, D. Frank, G. Graefe, J. Richardson, E. Shekita, and M. Muralikrishna, "The architecture of the EXODUS extensible DBMS," *Proc. of the Int'l Workshop on Object Oriented Database Systems* Pacific Grove, Ca (1986).

[Ch] Chandra, A. K., "Theory of database queries," *Proc. 7th PODS* (march 1988), pp. 1-9.

[CH1] Chandra, A. K., and D. Harel, "Structure and complexity of relational queries," *J. Comp. System Sci* 25:1 (Aug. 82), pp. 99-128.

[CH2] Chandra, A. K., and D. Harel, "Horn clause queries and generalizations," *J. Logic Programming* 1:1 (1985), pp. 1-15.

[CM] Copeland, G. and D. Maier, "Making Smalltalk a database system," *Proc. ACM-SIGMOD Conf.* (1984), pp. 316-325.

[Dad] Dadam, P. et al, "A DBMS prototype to support extended NF ^{2}-relations: An integrated view on flat tables and hierarchies," *Proc. ACM-SIGMOD Conf.* (1986), pp. 376-387.

[Day1] Dayal, U., "Processing queries with quantifiers: A horticultural approach," *Proc. 2nd PODS* (1986).

[Day2] Dayal, U., "Of nests and trees: A unified approach to processing queries that contain nested subqueries, aggregates and quantifiers," *Proc. 13th VLDB*, Brighton, England (Sept 1987), pp. 197-208.

[Di] Dittrich, K. R., "Object-oriented database systems: The notion and the issues," *Proc. Int'l Workshop on Object-Oriented Database Systems*, Pacific Grove, Ca (Sept 1986), pp. 2-6.

[DiP] Di Paola, R.A.,"The recursive unsolvability of the decision problem for the class of definite formulas," *JACM* (April 1969).

[En] Enderton, H. B., *A mathematical introduction to logic*, Ch.4.4, Academic Press (1972).

[Fa] Fagin, R., "Horn clauses and database dependencies," *JACM* 29:4 (Oct. 1982).

[FT] Fischer, P., and S. Thomas, "Operators for non-first-normal-form relations," *Proc. 7th COMPSAC*, Chicago,(Nov. 1983).

[HS] Hull, R. and J. Su, " On the expressive power of database queries with intermediate types," *Proc. 7th PODS* (March 1988).

[Ja] Jacobs, B., "On database logic," *JACM* 29:2 (April 1982).

[JS] Jaeschke, B., and H.-J. Schek, "Remarks on the algebra of non first normal form relations," *Proc. 1st PODS* (March 1982).

[Ka] Kanellakis, P., personal communication (1987).

[Kl] Klug, A., "Equivalence of relational algebra and calculus query languages having aggregate functions," *JACM* 29:3 (July 1982).

[KLW] Kemper, A., P. C. Lockemann, and M. Wallrath, "An object-oriented database system for engineering applications," *Proc. ACM-SIGMOD Conf.* (1987), pp. 292-310.

[KR] Korth, H. F., and M. A Roth, "Query languages for nested relational databases," TR-87-45, University of Texas at Austin (Dec. 1987).

[Ku1] Kuper, G. M., "The logical data model: A new approach to database logic," Ph.D thesis, Stanford University (Sept. 1985).

[Ku2] Kuper, G.M.,"Logic Programming with Sets," *Proc. 6th PODS* (1987)

[Ku3] Kuper, G. M., "On the expressive power of Logic programming languages with sets," *Proc. 7th PODS* (March 1988), pp. 10-14.

[KV1] Kuper, G.M., M.Y. Vardi, "A new approach to database logic," *Proc. 3rd PODS* (1984)

[KV2] Kuper, G.M., M.Y. Vardi, "On the expressive power of the logical data model," *Proc. ACM SIGMOD Int'l Conf.* (1985).

[LP] Lorie, R., and W. Plouffe, "Complex objects and their use in design transactions," *Proc. ACM-SIGMOD Conf., Engineering Design Applications*, (May 1983), pp. 115-122.

[Ma1] Maier, D., "Why database languages are a bad idea," *Proc. Workshop on Database Programming Languages*, Roscoff, France (Sept. 1987), pp. 334-344.

[Ma2] Maier, D., "A logic for objects," manuscript, Oregon Graduate Center (Nov. 1987).

[Mak] Makinouchi, A., "A consideration on normal form of not-necessarily normalized relations in the relational model," *Proc. 3rd VLDB* (Oct. 1977).

[N] Naqvi, S.A., "A Logic for Negation in Database Systems," *Proc. Foundations of Deductive Databases and Logic Programming* (1986)

[OOM] Ozsoyoglu, G, Z.M. Ozsoyoglu, and V. Matos, "Extending relational algebra and relational calculus with set-valued attributes and aggregate functions," *TODS* 12:4 (Dec. 1987).

[PSSWD] Paul, H.-B., H.-J. Schek, M. Scholl, G. Weilkum, and U. Deppisch, "Architecture and implementation of the Darmstadt database Kernel System," *Proc. ACM SIGMOD Conf.* (1987).

[RKB] Roth, M.A., Korth, H.F., and D. Batory, "SQL/NF - A query language for ¬1NF relational databases," *Information systems* 12:1 (19870, pp. 99-114.

[RKS] Roth, M.A., H.F. Korth, and A. Silberschatz , "Extended algebra and calculus for ¬NF relational databases," manuscript, TR-84-36, Department of Computer Science, University of Texas at Austin, 1984, revised, 1985, to appear, *TODS*.

[RS] Rowe, L., and M. Stonebraker, "The POSTGRESS data model," *Proc. 13th VLDB*, Brighton, England (1987), pp. 83-96.

[Ry] Rybinski, h., "On first order languages," *TODS*12:3 (June 1987), pp. 325-349.

[Sa] Sagiv, Y.,"Optimizing Datalog programs," *Proc. 6th PODS* (March 1987), pp. 349-362, also in *Foundations of deductive databases and Logic Programming* (J. Minker, ed.), Morgan Kaufmann (1988).

[SB] Stefik, M., and D. G. Bobrow, "Object-oriented programming: Themes and variations," *the AI Magazine* (1986), pp. 40-62.

[SS] Schek H.-J, and M. Scholl, "An algebra for the relational model with relation-valued attributes," *Information Systems.* 11:2 (1986).

[SR] Stonebraker, M., and L. Rowe, "The design of POSTGRESS," *Proc. ACM SIGMOD Conf.* (1986).

[TZ] Tsur, S. and Zaniolo, C., "LDL: A logic-based data-language," *Proc. 12th VLDB*, Kyoto, Japan (1986).

[U1] Ullman, J.D., *Principles of Database systems*, Computer Science Press, 2nd ed. (1982).

[U2] Ullman, J. D., "Implementation of logical query languages for databases," *ACM TODS* 10:3 (1985), pp. 289-321.

[U3] Ullman, J. D., "Database theory - past and future," *6th PODS* (1987), pp. 1-10.

[Va1] Vardi, M. Y., "The decision problem for database dependencies," *Inf. Proc. Letters* (Oct. 1981).

[Va2] Vardi, M. Y., "Review of [Ja]," *Zentralblatt fur Mathematic,* 497.68061 (1983).

[Ver] Verso, J., "VERSO: A database machine based on non 1NF relations," rapport de Recherche INRIA 523 (1986).

[We] Wegner, P., "The object-oriented classification paradigm," in *Research Directions in Object-Oriented Programming* (B. Shriver, P. Wegner, eds.), The MIT Press (1987), pp. 479-560.

A Theory of Atomic Transactions

Nancy Lynch, M.I.T.
Michael Merritt, AT&T Bell Labs
William Weihl, M.I.T.
Alan Fekete, M.I.T.

Abstract:

This paper describes some results of a recent project to develop a theory for reasoning about atomic transactions. This theory allows careful statement of the correctness conditions to be satisfied by transaction-processing algorithms, as well as clear and concise description of such algorithms. It also serves as a framework for rigorous correctness proofs.

1 Introduction

The notion of "atomic transaction", originally introduced for databases, is now used in programming systems for general (data-oriented) distributed computing such as Argus [Liskov] and Camelot [SS]. Roughly speaking, a transaction is a sequence of accesses to data objects; it should execute "as if" it ran with no interruption by other transactions. Moreover, a transaction can complete either successfully or unsuccessfully, by "committing" or "aborting". If it commits, any alterations it makes to the database should be lasting; if it aborts, it should be "as if" it never altered the database at all. The execution of a set of transactions should be "serializable", that is, equivalent to an execution in which no transactions run concurrently and in which all accesses of committed transactions, but no accesses of aborted transactions, are performed. Another condition often considered is "external consistency", which asserts that the order of transactions in the equivalent serial execution should be compatible with the order in which transaction invocations and responses occur.

In order for transactions to be useful for general distributed programming, the notion needs to be extended to include nesting. Thus, in addition to accesses, a transaction can also contain subtransactions. The transaction nesting structure can be described by a forest, with the top-level transactions at the roots and the accesses to data at the leaves. The semantics of nested transactions generalize those of ordinary transactions as follows. Each set of sibling transactions or subtransactions is supposed to execute serializably. As for top-level transactions, subtransactions can commit or abort. Each set of sibling transactions runs as if all the transactions that committed ran in serial order, and all the transactions that aborted did not run at all. An external consistency property is also required for each set of siblings.

Nested transactions provide a very flexible programming mechanism. They allow the programmer to describe more concurrency than would be allowed by single-level transactions, by having transactions request the creation of concurrent subtransactions. They also allow localized handling of transaction failures. When a subtransaction commits or aborts, the commit or abort is reported to its parent transaction. The parent can then decide on its next action based on the reported results. For example, if a subtransaction aborts, its parent can use the reported abort to trigger another subtransaction, one that implements some alternative action. A good mechanism for handling failures is especially important in distributed systems, where failures are common because of the unreliability of communication.

---

[1]The work of the first author (and through her, the work of the fourth author) was supported in part be the office of Naval Research under Contract N00014-85-K-0168, by the National Science Foundation under Grant CCR-8611442, and by the Defense Advanced Research Projects Agency (DARPA) under Contract N00014-83-K-0125. The work of the third author was supported in part by the National Science Foundation under Grant CCR-8716884, and by the Defense Advanced Research Projects Agency (DARPA) under Contract N00014-83-K-0125.

The idea of nested transactions seems to have originated in the "spheres of control" work of [Davies]. Reed [Reed] developed the current notion of nesting and designed a timestamp-based implementation. Moss [Moss] later designed a locking implementation that serves as the basis of the implementation of the Argus programming language.

There are two reasons why a formal model is needed for reasoning about atomic transactions. First, the implementors of languages that contain transactions need a model in order to reason about the correctness of their implementations. Some of the algorithms that have been proposed for implementing transactions are complicated, and informal arguments about their correctness are unsatisfying. In fact, it is not even obvious how to state the precise correctness conditions to be satisfied by the implementations; a model is needed for describing the semantics of transactions carefully and formally. Second, if programming languages containing transactions become popular, users of these languages will need a model to help them reason about the behavior of their programs.

There has been considerable prior work on a theory for atomic transactions, described, for example, in [BHG]. This "classical" theory is primarily applicable to single-level transactions, rather than nested transactions. It treats both concurrency control and recovery algorithms, although the treatments of the two kinds of algorithms are not completely integrated. The theory assumes a system organization in which accesses are passed from the transactions to a "scheduler", which determines the order in which they are to be performed by the database. The database handles recovery from transaction abort and media failure, so that each access to one data object is performed in the state resulting from all previous non-aborted accesses to that object. The notion of "serializability" in this theory corresponds to "looking like a serial execution, from the point of view of the database". Proofs for some algorithms are presented, primarily based on one main combinatorial theorem, the "Serializability Theorem". This important theorem states that serializability is equivalent to the absence of cycles in a certain graph representing dependencies among transactions.

There are some limitations of this prior work. First, the notion of correctness is quite restrictive, stated as it is in terms of the object boundary in a particular system organization. The object interface that is described is suitable for single-version locking and timestamp algorithms (in the absence of transaction aborts), but it is much less appropriate for other kinds of algorithms. Multi-version algorithms and replicated data algorithms, for example, maintain object information in a form that is very different from the (single-copy latest-value) form used for the simple algorithms, and the appropriate object interface is also very different. The correctness conditions presented for the simple algorithms in [BHG] thus do not apply without change to these other kinds of algorithms. It seems more appropriate, and useful in not unduly restricting possible implementations, to state correctness conditions at the user interface to the system, rather than the object boundary.

Second, the transactions are not modelled explicitly in the earlier work, but rather implicitly, in terms of axioms about their executions. It is sometimes interesting to reason about the control within a transaction, e.g., to describe how the same transaction would behave when it is placed in different systems. Such reasoning is facilitated by an explicit model which clarifies which actions occur under the transaction's control, and which are due to activity of the environment. Furthermore, it will turn out that the "user interface" mentioned above can be modelled by the boundary between the transactions and the rest of the system; in order to state correctness conditions at this boundary, it is useful to have an explicit model for the transactions.

Third, the prior model does not seem to extend well to treat nested transactions. This seems to be primarily because not everything that needs to be described is modelled explicitly. For example, a subtransaction may have been created only because an earlier attempt aborted, so we must model the abort explicitly to capture this dependence.

Our model remedies the deficiencies described above for the earlier model. This improvement does not come for free: our model contains more detail than the earlier model, and may therefore seem more complicated. It seems to us, however, that this extra detail is necessary. In fact, we believe that the extra detail is useful for understanding not just nested transactions, but also ordinary single-level transactions.

We have already used our theory to present and prove correctness of many transaction-processing algorithms, including locking and timestamp-based algorithms for concurrency control, algorithms for managing replicated data and algorithms for managing "orphan" transactions. This work has been presented in research papers [LM, FLMW1, FLMW2, HLMW, GL, AFLMW, Perl], and we are currently writing a book [LMWF] to unify all the work. There is still much that remains to be done, in particular in modelling the very interesting and complex algorithms that have been developed to implement transactions in the presence of crashes that destroy volatile memory.

In this paper, we present some of the basic results of our theory and attempt to compare them to the corresponding results of the classical theory. In particular, we describe the correctness conditions that we use for transaction systems - notions similar to "serializability" but stated in terms of the transaction boundary. We then present our "Serializability Theorem", a general theorem containing a sufficient condition for proving serializability. Although this theorem is more complicated to state than the classical Serializability Theorem, it is similar in spirit: it shows that the existence of a single ordering of transactions that is consistent with the processing of accesses at each object is sufficient to prove serializability. We use our Serializability Theorem elsewhere to prove correctness for locking [FLMW2] and timestamp algorithms [AFLMW], but in this paper, we only present the theorem itself in detail and mention some of its consequences.

The rest of the paper is organized as follows. Section 2 contains an outline of the I/O automaton model, the basic model for concurrent systems that is used for presenting all of our transaction work. Section 3 contains a description of "serial systems", extremely constrained transaction-processing systems that are defined solely for the purpose of stating correctness conditions for more liberal systems. Section 4 contains a description of "simple systems", very unconstrained transaction-processing systems that represent the common features of most transaction-processing systems. Section 5 contains our Serializability Theorem, stated in terms of simple systems. Section 6 contains a discussion of some applications of the Serializability Theorem and Section 7 contains some final remarks.

2 The I/O Automaton Model

In order to reason carefully about complex concurrent systems such as those that implement atomic transactions, it is important to have a simple and clearly-defined formal model for concurrent computation. The model we use for our work is the recently-developed *input/output automaton* model [LT]. Since its introduction, the model has been used for describing and reasoning about several different types of concurrent systems, including network resource allocation algorithms, communication algorithms, concurrent database systems, shared atomic objects, and dataflow architectures. This section contains an introduction to a simple special case of the model that is sufficient for use in this paper.[2]

2.1 Overview of the Model

I/O automata provide an appropriate model for discrete event systems consisting of concurrently-operating components.[3] The components of a discrete event system can be regarded as discrete event systems themselves. Such a system may be "reactive" in the sense that it interacts with its environment in an ongoing manner (rather than, say, simply accepting an input, computing a function of that input and halting).

Each system component is modelled as an "I/O automaton", which is a mathematical object somewhat like a traditional finite-state automaton. However, an I/O automaton need not be finite-state, but can

---

[2]In this paper, we only consider properties of finite executions, and do not consider "liveness" or "fairness" properties.

[3]By a "discrete event system" we mean an entity that undergoes sudden changes that may be named and observed, and through which the system interacts with its environment.

have an infinite state set. The actions of an I/O automaton are classified as either "input", "output" or "internal". This classification is a reflection of a distinction in the system being modelled, between events (such as the receipt of a message) that are caused by the environment, events (such as sending a message) that the component can perform when it chooses and that affect the environment, and events (such as changing the value of a local variable) that a component can perform when it chooses, but that are undetectable by the environment except through their effects on later events. In the model, an automaton generates output and internal actions autonomously, and transmits output actions instantaneously to its environment. In contrast, the automaton's input is generated by the environment and transmitted instantaneously to the automaton. Our distinction between input and other actions is based on who determines when the action is performed: an automaton can establish restrictions on when it will perform an output or internal action, but it is unable to block the performance of an input action.

The fact that our automata are unable to block inputs distinguishes our model from others, such as Hoare's Communication Sequential Processes ("CSP") [Hoare], or Milner's Calculus of Communicating Systems ("CCS") [Milner]. In these models, communication between two components only occurs when both components are willing to communicate. Thus, for example, a sender of a message is blocked until the corresponding receiver is ready to receive the message. In CSP-like models, input blocking is used for two purposes: as a way of eliminating undesirable inputs, and as a way of blocking the activity of the environment. Our model does not have any way of blocking the environment, but does have other ways of coping with unwanted inputs. For example, suppose that we wish to constrain the behavior of an automaton only in case the environment observes certain restrictions on the production of inputs. Instead of requiring the automaton to block the bad inputs, we permit these inputs to occur; however, we may permit the automaton to exhibit arbitrary behavior in case they do. Alternatively, we may require the automaton to detect bad inputs and respond to them with error messages. Thus, we have simple ways of describing input restrictions, without including input-blocking in the model.

I/O automata may be nondeterministic, and indeed the nondeterminism is an important part of the model's descriptive power. Describing algorithms as nondeterministically as possible tends to make results about the algorithms quite general, since many results about nondeterministic algorithms apply *a fortiori* to all algorithms obtained by restricting the nondeterministic choices. Moreover, the use of nondeterminism helps to avoid cluttering algorithm descriptions and proofs with inessential details. Finally, the uncertainties introduced by asynchrony make nondeterminism an intrinsic property of real concurrent systems, and so an important property to capture in a formal model of such systems.

Often, a single discrete event system can also be viewed as a combination of several component systems interacting with one another. To reflect this in our model, we define an operation called "composition", by which several I/O automata can be combined to yield a single I/O automaton. Our composition operator connects each output action of the component automata with the identically named input actions of any number (usually one) of the other component automata. In the resulting system, an output action is generated autonomously by one component and is thought of as being instantaneously transmitted to all components having the same action as an input. All such components are passive recipients of the input, and take steps simultaneously with the output step.

When a system is modelled by an I/O automaton, each possible run of the system is modelled by an "execution", an alternating sequence of states and actions. The possible activity of the system is captured by the set of all possible executions that can be generated by the automaton. However, not all the information contained in an execution is important to a user of the system, or to an environment in which the system is placed. We believe that what is important about the activity of a system is the externally visible events, and not the states or internal events. Thus, we focus on the automaton's "behaviors" — the subsequences of its executions consisting of external (i.e., input and output) actions. We regard a system as suitable for a purpose if any possible sequence of externally-visible events has appropriate characteristics. Thus, in the model, we formulate correctness conditions for an I/O automaton in terms of properties of the automaton's behaviors.[4]

One convenient way to specify properties of an I/O automaton's behaviors is in terms of another I/O automaton. That is, we can define a particular "specification automaton" B and say that any automaton A is "correct" if it "implements" B, in the sense that each finite behavior of A is also a finite behavior of B. Often, B will be a simple system that is impractical as a real solution because it is too inefficient or uses global information, while A will be a more efficient or distributed algorithm.

The model permits description of the same system at different levels of abstraction. Abstraction mappings can be defined, which describe the relationship between automata that include implementation detail to more abstract automata that suppress some of the detail. Such mappings can be used as aids in correctness proofs for algorithms: if automaton B is an image of automaton A under an appropriate abstraction mapping, then it can be shown that A implements B.

The model allows very careful and readable descriptions of particular concurrent algorithms. We have developed a simple language for describing automata, based on "precondition" and "effect" specifications for actions. This notation has proved sufficient for describing all algorithms we have attempted so far. However, the model does not constrain the user to describe all automata in this manner; for example, the model is general enough to serve also as a formal basis for languages that include more elaborate constructs for sequential flow of control.

The model also allows clear and precise statement of the correctness conditions that an automaton must satisfy in order that the system modelled by the automaton be said to solve a problem; such conditions can be stated independently of any particular proposed solution. As described above, such properties are often conveniently formulated in terms of implemention of a given automaton, but any other method of specifying properties of external behaviors could be used instead. Finally, once both an algorithm and the correctness condition it is supposed to satisfy have been described in the model, it is then possible to use the model as a basis for a rigorous proof that the algorithm satisfies the given conditions.

2.2 Action Signatures

The formal subject matter of this paper is concerned with finite and infinite sequences describing the executions of automata. Usually, we will be discussing sequences of elements from a universal set of *actions*. Since the same action may occur several times in a sequence, it is convenient to distinguish the different occurrences. Thus, we refer to a particular occurrence of an action in a sequence as an *event*.

The actions of each automaton are classified as either "input", "output", or "internal". In the system being modelled, the distinctions are that input actions are not under the system's control, output actions are under the system's control and are externally observable, and internal actions are under the system's control but are not externally observable. In order to describe this classification formally, each automaton comes equipped with an "action signature".

An *action signature* S is an ordered triple consisting of three pairwise-disjoint sets of actions. We write *in(S)*, *out(S)* and *int(S)* for the three components of S, and refer to the actions in the three sets as the *input actions*, *output actions* and *internal actions* of S, respectively. We let *ext(S)* = in(S) ∪ out(S) and refer to the actions in ext(S) as the *external actions* of S. Also, we let *local(S)* = int(S) ∪ out(S), and refer to the actions in local(S) as the *locally-controlled actions* of S. Finally, we let acts(S) = in(S) ∪ out(S) ∪ int(S), and refer to the actions in acts(S) as the *actions* of S. An *external action signature* is an action signature consisting entirely of external actions, that is, having no internal actions. If S is an action signature, then the *external action signature* of S is the action signature *extsig(S)* = (in(S),out(S),∅), i.e., the action signature that is obtained from S by removing the internal actions.

[4]This viewpoint differs from that taken in much of the algorithm specification work in the research literature, in which properties of the states are taken to be of primary concern.

2.3 Input/Output Automata

An *input/output automaton* A (also called an *I/O automaton* or simply an *automaton*) consists of four components:

- an action signature *sig(A)*,
- a set *states(A)* of *states*,
- a nonempty set *start(A)* $\subseteq$ states(A) of *start states*, and
- a transition relation *steps(A)* $\subseteq$ states(A) $\times$ acts(sig(A)) $\times$ states(A), with the property that for every state s' and input action π there is a transition (s',π,s) in steps(A).[5]

Note that the set of states need not be finite. We refer to an element (s',π,s) of steps(A) as a *step* of A. The step (s',π,s) is called an *input step* of A if π is an input action, and *output steps*, *internal steps*, *external steps* and *locally-controlled steps* are defined analogously. If (s',π,s) is a step of A, then π is said to be *enabled* in s'. Since every input action is enabled in every state, automata are said to be *input-enabled*. The input-enabling property means that an automaton is not able to block input actions.

If A is an automaton, we sometimes write *acts(A)* as shorthand for acts(sig(A)), and likewise for in(A), out(A), etc. An automaton A is said to be *closed* if all its actions are locally-controlled, i.e., if in(A) = $\emptyset$.

An *execution fragment* of A is a finite sequence $s_0\pi_1s_1\pi_2...\pi_ns_n$ or infinite sequence $s_0\pi_1s_1\pi_2...\pi_ns_n...$ of alternating states and actions of A such that (s_i,π_{i+1},s_{i+1}) is a step of A for every i. An execution fragment beginning with a start state is called an *execution*. We denote the set of executions of A by *execs(A)*, and the set of finite executions of A by *finexecs(A)*. A state is said to be *reachable* in A if it is the final state of a finite execution of A.

The *schedule* of an execution fragment α of A is the subsequence of α consisting of actions, and is denoted by *sched*(α). We say that β is a *schedule* of A if β is the schedule of an execution of A. We denote the set of schedules of A by *scheds(A)* and the set of finite schedules of A by *finscheds(A)*. We say that a finite schedule β of A *can leave* A *in* state s if there is some finite execution α of A with final state s and with sched(α) = β. The *behavior* of a sequence β of actions in acts(A), denoted by *beh*(β), is the subsequence of β consisting of actions in ext(A). The *behavior* of an execution fragment α of A, denoted by *beh*(α), is defined to be beh(sched(α)). We say that β is a *behavior* of A if β is the behavior of an execution of A. We denote the set of behaviors of A by *behs(A)* and the set of finite behaviors of A by *finbehs(A)*.

An *extended step* of an automaton A is a triple of the form (s',β,s), where s' and s are in states(A), β is a finite sequence of actions in acts(A), and there is an execution fragment of A having s' as its first state, s as its last state and β as its schedule. (This execution fragment might consist of only a single state, in the case that β is the empty sequence.)

If β is any sequence of actions and Φ is a set of actions, we write $\beta|\Phi$ for the subsequence of β consisting of actions in Φ. If A is an automaton, we write $\beta|A$ for $\beta|$acts(A). We call this the *projection* of β on A. It can be thought of as the portion of β observable by A.

2.4 Composition

I/O automata may be combined by means of a composition operator, as defined in this section. As a preliminary step, we first define composition of action signatures. Let I be an index set that is at most countable. A collection $\{S_i\}_{i\in I}$ of action signatures is said to be *strongly compatible*[6] if for all i, j $\in$ I,

---

[5] I/O automata, as defined in [LT], also include a fifth component, an equivalence relation *part(A)* on local(sig(A)). This component is used for describing fair executions, and is not needed for the results described in this paper.

[6] A weaker notion called "compatibility" is defined in [LT], consisting of the first two of the three given properties only. In this paper, only the stronger notion will be required.

we have

1. $out(S_i) \cap out(S_j) = \emptyset$,
2. $int(S_i) \cap acts(S_j) = \emptyset$, and
3. no action is in $acts(S_i)$ for infinitely many i.

Thus, no action is an output of more than one signature in the collection, and internal actions of any signature do not appear in any other signature in the collection. Moreover, we do not permit actions involving infinitely many component signatures.

The *composition* $S = \Pi_{i \in I} S_i$ of a collection of strongly compatible action signatures $\{S_i\}_{i \in I}$ is defined to be the action signature with

- $in(S) = \cup_{i \in I} in(S_i) - \cup_{i \in I} out(S_i)$,
- $out(S) = \cup_{i \in I} out(S_i)$, and
- $int(S) = \cup_{i \in I} int(S_i)$.

Thus, output actions are those that are outputs of any of the component signatures, and similarly for internal actions. Input actions are any actions that are inputs to any of the component signatures, but outputs of no component signature.

Now we define composition of automata. A collection $\{A_i\}_{i \in I}$ of automata is said to be *strongly compatible* if their action signatures are strongly compatible. The *composition* $A = \Pi_{i \in I} A_i$ of a strongly compatible collection of automata $\{A_i\}_{i \in I}$ has the following components:[7]

- $sig(A) = \Pi_{i \in I}\, sig(A_i)$,
- $states(A) = \Pi_{i \in I}\, states(A_i)$,
- $start(A) = \Pi_{i \in I}\, start(A_i)$, and
- steps(A) is the set of triples (s',π,s) such that for all $i \in I$, (a) if $\pi \in acts(A_i)$ then $(s'[i],\pi,s[i]) \in steps(A_i)$, and (b) if $\pi \notin acts(A_i)$ then $s'[i] = s[i]$.[8]

Since the automata A_i are input-enabled, so is their composition, and hence their composition is an automaton. Each step of the composition automaton consists of all the automata that have a particular action in their action signature performing that action concurrently, while the automata that do not have that action in their signature do nothing. We will often refer to an automaton formed by composition as a "system" of automata. Using the obvious isomorphisms, composition of automata is associative and commutative when defined.

If $\alpha = s_0\pi_1 s_1 \ldots$ is an execution of A, let $\alpha|A_i$, the *projection* of α on A_i, be the sequence obtained by deleting $\pi_j s_j$ when π_j is not an action of A_i, and replacing the remaining s_j by $s_j[i]$. Recall that we have previously defined a projection operator for action sequences. The two projection operators are related in the obvious way: $sched(\alpha|A_i) = sched(\alpha)|A_i$, and similarly $beh(\alpha|A_i) = beh(\alpha)|A_i$.

We close this subsection with some basic results relating executions, schedules and behaviors of a system of automata to those of the automata being composed. The first result says that the projections of executions of a system onto the components are executions of the components, and similarly for schedules, etc.

Proposition 1: Let $\{A_i\}_{i \in I}$ be a strongly compatible collection of automata, and let $A = \Pi_{i \in I} A_i$. If $\alpha \in execs(A)$ then $\alpha|A_i \in execs(A_i)$ for all $i \in I$. Moreover, the same result holds for finexecs, scheds, finscheds, behs and finbehs in place of execs.

---

[7]Note that the second and third components listed are just ordinary Cartesian products, while the first component uses a previous definition.

[8]We use the notation s[i] to denote the ith component of the state vector s.

Certain converses of the preceding proposition are also true. In particular, we can prove that schedules of component automata can be "patched together" to form a schedule of the composition, and similarly for behaviors. In order to prove these results, we first state two preliminary lemmas, one involving schedules and one involving behaviors, that say that executions of component automata can be patched together to form an execution of the composition.

Lemma 2: Let $\{A_i\}_{i\in I}$ be a strongly compatible collection of automata, and let $A = \Pi_{i\in I}A_i$. Let α_i be an execution of A_i, for all $i \in I$. Suppose β is a sequence of actions in acts(A) such that $\beta|A_i$ = sched(α_i) for every i. Then there is an execution α of A such that β = sched(α) and $\alpha_i = \alpha|A_i$ for all i.

Lemma 3: Let $\{A_i\}_{i\in I}$ be a strongly compatible collection of automata, and let $A = \Pi_{i\in I}A_i$. Let α_i be an execution of A_i, for all $i \in I$. Suppose β is a sequence of actions in ext(A) such that $\beta|A_i$ = beh(α_i) for every i. Then there is an execution α of A such that β = beh(α) and $\alpha_i = \alpha|A_i$ for all i.

Now the results about patching together schedules and patching together behaviors follow easily.

Proposition 4: Let $\{A_i\}_{i\in I}$ be a strongly compatible collection of automata, and let $A = \Pi_{i\in I}A_i$.

1. Let β be a sequence of actions in acts(A). If $\beta|A_i \in$ scheds(A_i) for all $i \in I$, then $\beta \in$ scheds(A).
2. Let β be a finite sequence of actions in acts(A). If $\beta|A_i \in$ finscheds(A_i) for all $i \in I$, then $\beta \in$ finscheds(A).
3. Let β be a sequence of actions in ext(A). If $\beta|A_i \in$ behs(A_i) for all $i \in I$, then $\beta \in$ behs(A).
4. Let β be a finite sequence of actions in ext(A). If $\beta|A_i \in$ finbehs(A_i) for all $i \in I$, then $\beta \in$ finbehs(A).

Proof: By Lemmas 2 and 3.

Proposition 4 provides a method for showing that certain sequences are behaviors of a composition A: first show that its projections are behaviors of the components of A and then appeal to Proposition 4.

2.5 Correspondences Between Automata

In this subsection, we define the notion of "implementation" which is useful in stating correctness conditions to be satisfied by automata. Let A and B be automata with the same external action signature, i.e., with extsig(A) = extsig(B). Then A is said to *implement* B if finbehs(A) $\subseteq$ finbehs(B). One reason for the usefulness of the notion of implementation as a correctness condition is the following fact: if A implements B, then replacing B by A in any system yields a new system in which all finite behaviors are behaviors of the original system. In fact, as the following proposition shows, we can take any collection of components of a system and replace each by an implementation, and the resulting system will implement the original one.

Proposition 5: Suppose that $\{A_i\}_{i\in I}$ is a strongly compatible collection of automata, and let $A = \Pi_{i\in I}A_i$. Also suppose that $\{B_i\}_{i\in I}$ is a strongly compatible collection of automata, and let $B = \Pi_{i\in I}B_i$. If for each index i in I, A_i implements B_i, then A implements B.

In order to show that one automaton implements another, it is often useful to demonstrate a correspondence between states of the two automata. Such a correspondence can often be expressed in the form of a kind of abstraction mapping that we call a "possibilities mapping", defined as follows. Suppose A and B are automata with the same external action signature, and suppose f is a mapping from states(A) to the power set of states(B). That is, if s is a state of A, f(s) is a set of states of B. The mapping f is said to be a *possibilities mapping* from A to B if the following conditions hold:

1. For every start state s_0 of A, there is a start state t_0 of B such that $t_0 \in f(s_0)$.

2. Let s' be a reachable state of A, t' ∈ f(s') a reachable state of B, and (s',π,s) a step of A. Then there is an extended step, (t',γ,t), of B (possibly having an empty schedule) such that the following conditions are satisfied:

   a. $\gamma|\text{ext}(B) = \pi|\text{ext}(A)$, and

   b. $t \in f(s)$.

Proposition 6: Suppose that A and B are automata with the same external action signature and there is a possibilities mapping, f, from A to B. Then A implements B.

2.6 Preserving Properties

Although an automaton in our model is unable to block input actions, it is often convenient to restrict attention to those behaviors in which the environment provides inputs in a "sensible" way, that is, where the interaction between the automaton and its environment obeys certain "well-formedness" restrictions. A useful way of discussing such restrictions is in terms of the notion that an automaton "preserves" a property of behaviors: as long as the environment does not violate the property, neither does the automaton. Such a notion is primarily interesting for properties that are "prefix-closed" and "limit-closed": formally, a set of sequences P is *prefix-closed* provided that whenever $\beta \in P$ and γ is a prefix of β, it is also the case that $\gamma \in P$. A set of sequences P is *limit-closed* provided that any sequence all of whose finite prefixes are in P is also in P.

Let Φ be a set of actions and P be a nonempty, prefix-closed, limit-closed set of sequences of actions in Φ (i.e., a nonempty, prefix-closed, limit-closed "property" of such sequences). Let A be an automaton with $\Phi \subseteq \text{ext}(A)$. We say that A *preserves* P if $\beta\pi \in \text{finbehs}(A)$, $\pi \in \text{out}(A)$ and $\beta|\Phi \in P$ together imply that $\beta\pi|\Phi \in P$. Thus, if an automaton preserves a property P, the automaton is not the first to violate P: as long as the environment only provides inputs such that the cumulative behavior satisfies P, the automaton will only perform outputs such that the cumulative behavior satisfies P. Note that the fact that an automaton A preserves a property P does not imply that all of A's behaviors, when restricted to Φ, satisfy P; it is possible for a behavior of A to fail to satisfy P, if an input causes a violation of P. However, the following proposition gives a way to deduce that all of a system's behaviors satisfy P. The lemma says that, under certain conditions, if all components of a system preserve P, then all the behaviors of the composition satisfy P.

Proposition 7: Let $\{A_i\}_{i \in I}$ be a strongly compatible collection of automata, and suppose that A, the composition, is a closed system. Let $\Phi \subseteq \text{ext}(A)$, and let P be a nonempty, prefix-closed, limit-closed set of sequences of actions in Φ. Suppose that for each $i \in I$, one of the following is true.

1. $\Phi \subseteq \text{ext}(A_i)$ and A_i preserves P, or

2. $\Phi \cap \text{ext}(A_i) = \emptyset$.

If $\beta \in \text{behs}(A)$, then $\beta|\Phi \in P$.

3 Serial Systems and Correctness

In this section, we develop the formal machinery needed to define correctness for transaction-processing systems. Correctness is expressed in terms of a particular kind of system called a "serial system". We define serial systems here, using I/O automata.

3.1 Overview

Transaction-processing systems consist of user-provided transaction code, plus transaction-processing algorithms designed to coordinate the activities of different transactions. The transactions are written by application programmers in a suitable programming language. In some transaction-processing systems such as the Argus system, transactions have a nested structure, so that transactions can invoke subtransactions and receive responses from the subtransactions describing the results of their processing. In addition to invoking subtransactions, transactions can also invoke operations on data objects.

In a transaction-processing system, the transaction-processing algorithms interact with the transactions, making decisions about when to schedule the creation of subtransactions and the performance of operations on objects. In order to carry out such scheduling, the transaction-processing algorithms may manipulate locks on objects, multiple copies of objects, and other convenient data structures. One popular organization divides the transaction processing into a "scheduler algorithm" and a "database" of objects. In this organization, the scheduler has the power to decide when operations are to be performed on the objects in the database, but not to perform more complex manipulations on objects (such as maintaining multiple copies). Although this organization is popular, it does not encompass all the useful system designs.

In our work, each component of a transaction-processing system is modelled as an I/O automaton. In particular, each transaction is an automaton, and all the transaction-processing algorithms together comprise another automaton.

It is not obvious at first how one ought to model the nested structure of transactions within the I/O automaton model. One might consider defining special kinds of automata that have a nested structure, for example. However, it appears that the cleanest way to model this structure is to describe each subtransaction in the transaction nesting structure as a separate automaton. If a parent transaction T wishes to invoke a child transaction T', T issues an output action that "requests that T' be created". The transaction-processing algorithms receive this request, and at some later time might decide to issue an action that is an input to the child T' and corresponds to the "creation" of T'. Thus, the different transactions in the nesting structure comprise a forest of automata, communicating with each other indirectly through the transaction-processing automaton. The highest-level user-defined transactions, i.e., those that are not subtransactions of any other user-defined transactions, are the roots in this forest.

It is actually more convenient to model the transaction nesting structure as a tree than a forest. Thus, we add an extra "root" automaton as a sort of "dummy transaction", located at the top of the transaction nesting structure. The highest-level user-defined transactions are considered to be children of this new root. The root can be thought of as modelling the outside world, from which invocations of top-level transactions originate and to which reports about the results of such transactions are sent. We often find that the formal reasoning we want to do about this dummy root transaction is very similar to our reasoning about ordinary transactions; thus, regarding the root as a transaction leads to economy in our formal arguments.

The primary goal of this section is to define correctness conditions to be satisfied by transaction-processing systems. As we discussed in the introduction, it seems most natural and general to define correctness conditions in terms of the actions occurring at the boundary between the transactions (including the root transaction) and the transaction-processing automaton. For it is immaterial how the transaction-processing algorithms work, as long as the outside world and the transactions see "correct" behavior. We define correct behavior for a transaction-processing system in terms of the behavior of a particular and very constrained "serial" transaction-processing system, which processes all transactions serially.

Serial systems consist of transaction automata and "serial object automata" composed with a "serial scheduler automaton". Transaction automata have already been discussed above. Serial object automata serve as specifications for permissible object behavior. They describe the responses the objects should make to arbitrary sequences of operation invocations, assuming that later invocations wait for responses to previous invocations. Serial objects are very much like the ordinary abstract data objects that are used in sequential programming languages.

The serial scheduler handles the communication among the transactions and serial objects, and thereby controls the order in which the transactions take steps. It ensures that no two sibling transactions are active concurrently — that is, it runs each set of sibling transactions serially. The serial scheduler is also responsible for deciding if a transaction commits or aborts. The serial scheduler can permit a transaction to abort only if its parent has requested its creation, but it has not actually been created. Thus, in a serial system, all sets of sibling transactions are run serially, and in such a way that no aborted transaction ever performs any steps.

A serial system would not be an interesting transaction-processing system to implement. It allows no concurrency among sibling transactions, and has only a very limited ability to cope with transaction failures. However, we are not proposing serial systems as interesting implementations; rather, we use them exclusively as specifications for correct behavior of other, more interesting systems. In our work, we describe many systems that do allow concurrency and recovery from transaction failures. (That is, they undo the effects of aborted transactions that have performed significant activity.) We prove that these systems are correct in the sense that certain transactions, and in particular T_0, cannot distinguish them from corresponding serial systems. It appears to the transactions as if all siblings are run serially, and aborted transactions are never created, even though in reality, the systems allow concurrency and recovery from transaction failures.

In the remainder of this section, we develop the necessary machinery for defining serial systems and correctness. First, we define a type structure used to name transactions and objects. Then we describe the general structure of a serial system — the components it includes, the actions the components perform, and the way the components are interconnected. We define several concepts involving the actions of a serial system. We then go on to define the components of a serial system in detail, and state some basic properties of serial systems. Finally, we use serial systems to state correctness conditions for transaction-processing systems.

3.2 System Types

We begin by defining a type structure that will be used to name the transactions and objects in a serial system.

A *system type* consists of the following:

- a set $\mathcal{T}$ of *transaction names*,
- a distinguished transaction name $T_0 \in \mathcal{T}$,
- a subset *accesses* of $\mathcal{T}$ not containing T_0,
- a mapping *parent*: $\mathcal{T} - \{T_0\} \rightarrow \mathcal{T}$, which configures the set of transaction names into a tree, with T_0 as the root and the accesses as the leaves,
- a set $\mathcal{X}$ of *object names*,
- a mapping *object*: accesses $\rightarrow \mathcal{X}$, and
- a set $\mathcal{V}$ of *return values*.

In referring to the transaction tree, we use standard tree terminology, such as "leaf node", "internal node", "child", "ancestor", and "descendant". As a special case, we consider any node to be its own ancestor and its own descendant, i.e. the "ancestor" and "descendant" relations are reflexive. We also use the notion of a "least common ancestor" of two nodes.

The transaction tree describes the nesting structure for transaction names, with T_0 as the name of the dummy "root transaction". Each child node in this tree represents the name of a subtransaction of the transaction named by its parent. The children of T_0 represent names of the top-level user-defined transactions. The accesses represent names for the lowest-level transactions in the transaction nesting structure; we will use these lowest-level transactions to model operations on data objects. Thus, the only transactions that access data directly are the leaves of the transaction tree. The internal nodes model transactions whose function is to create and manage subtransactions, but not to access data directly.

The tree structure should be thought of as a predefined naming scheme for all possible transactions that might ever be invoked. In any particular execution, however, only some of these transactions will actually take steps. We imagine that the tree structure is known in advance by all components of a system. The tree will, in general, be an infinite structure with infinite branching.

Classical concurrency control theory considers transactions having a simple nesting structure. As modelled in our framework, that nesting structure has three levels; the top level consists of the root T_0, modelling the outside world, the next level consists of all the user-defined transactions, and the lowest level consists of the accesses to data objects.

The set $\mathcal{X}$ is the set of names for the objects used in the system. Each access transaction name denotes an access to some particular object, as designated by the "object" mapping. If $X \in \mathcal{X}$, the set of accesses T for which object(T) = X is called *accesses(X)*.

The set $\mathcal{V}$ of return values is the set of possible values that might be returned by successfully-completed transactions to their parents. If T is an access transaction name, and v is a return value, we say that the pair (T,v) is an *operation* of the given system type. Thus, an operation designates a particular access to an object and a particular value returned by the access.

3.3 General Structure of Serial Systems

A serial system for a given system type is a closed system consisting of a "transaction automaton" A(T) for each non-access transaction name T, a "serial object automaton" S(X) for each object name X, and a single "serial scheduler automaton". Later in this chapter, we will give a precise definition for the serial scheduler automaton, and will give conditions to be satisfied by the transaction and object automata. Here, we just describe the signatures of the various automata, in order to explain how the automata are interconnected.

The following diagram depicts the structure of a serial system.

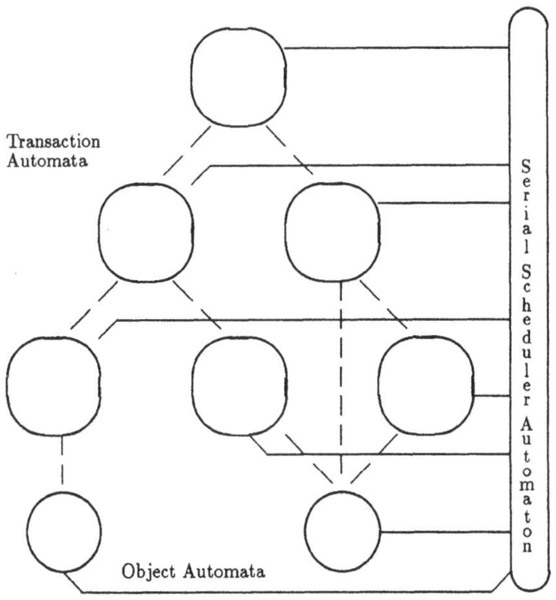

Figure 1: Serial System Structure

The transaction nesting structure is indicated by dotted lines, and the direct connections between automata (via shared actions) are indicated by solid lines. Thus, the transaction automata interact directly with the serial scheduler, but not directly with each other or with the object automata. The object automata also interact directly with the serial scheduler.

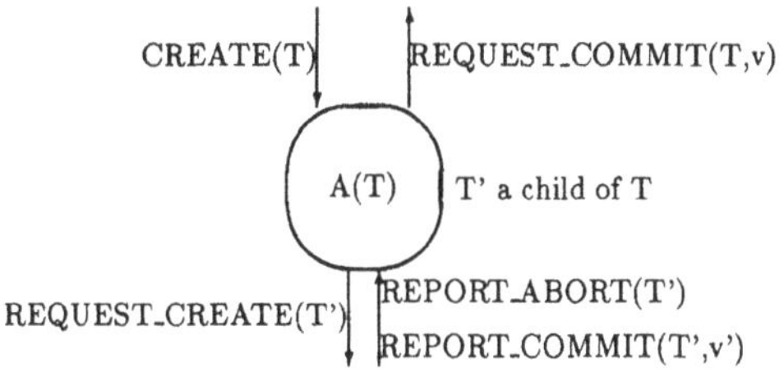

Figure 2: Transaction Automaton

Figure 2 shows the interface of a transaction automaton in more detail. Transaction T has an input CREATE(T) action, which is generated by the serial scheduler in order to initiate T's processing. We do not include arguments to a transaction in our model; rather we suppose that there is a different transaction for each possible set of arguments, and so any input to the transaction is encoded in the name of the transaction. T has REQUEST_CREATE(T') actions for each child T' of T in the transaction nesting structure; these are requests for creation of child transactions, and are communicated directly to the serial scheduler. At some later time, the scheduler might respond to a REQUEST_CREATE(T') action by issuing a CREATE(T') action, an input to transaction T'. T also has REPORT_COMMIT(T',v) and REPORT_ABORT(T') input actions, by which the serial scheduler informs T about the fate (commit or abort) of its previously-requested child T'. In the case of a commit, the report includes a return value v that provides information about the activity of T'; in the case of an abort, no information is returned. Finally, T has a REQUEST_COMMIT(T,v) output action, by which it announces to the scheduler that it has completed its activity successfully, with a particular result as described by return value v.

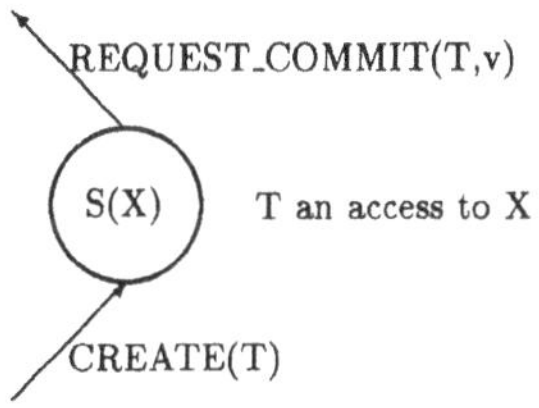

Figure 3: Object Automaton

Figure 3 shows the object interface. Object X has input CREATE(T) actions for each T in accesses(X). These actions should be thought of as invocations of operations on object X. Object X also has output actions of the form REQUEST_COMMIT(T,v), representing responses to the invocations. The value v in a REQUEST_COMMIT(T,v) action is a return value returned by the object as part of its response. We have chosen to use the "create" and "request_commit" notation for the object actions, rather than the more familiar "invoke" and "respond" terminology, in the interests of uniformity: there are many places in our formal arguments where access transactions can be treated uniformly with non-access transactions, and so it is useful to have a common notation for them.

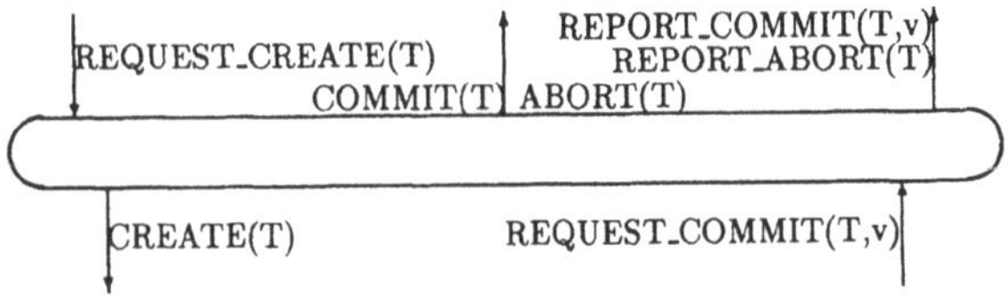

Figure 4: Serial Scheduler Automaton

Figure 4 shows the serial scheduler interface. The serial scheduler receives the previously-mentioned REQUEST_CREATE and REQUEST_COMMIT actions as inputs from the other system components. It produces CREATE actions as outputs, thereby awakening transaction automata or invoking operations on objects. It also produces COMMIT(T) and ABORT(T) actions for arbitrary transactions $T \neq T_0$, representing decisions about whether the designated transaction commits or aborts. For technical convenience, we classify the COMMIT and ABORT actions as output actions of the serial scheduler, even though they are not inputs to any other system component. Finally, the serial scheduler has REPORT_COMMIT and REPORT_ABORT actions as outputs, by which it communicates the fates of transactions to their parents.

As is always the case for a composition of I/O automata, the components of a serial system are determined statically. Even though we refer to the action of "creating" a child transaction, the model treats the child transaction as if it had been there all along. The CREATE action is treated formally as an input action to the child transaction; the child transaction will be constrained not to perform any output actions until such a CREATE action occurs. A consequence of this method of modelling dynamic creation of transactions is that the system must include automata for all possible transactions that might ever be created, in any execution. In most interesting cases, this means that the system will include infinitely many transaction automata.

3.4 Serial Actions

The *serial actions* for a given system type are defined to be the external actions of a serial system of that type. These are just the actions listed in the preceding section: CREATE(T) and REQUEST_COMMIT(T,v), where T is any transaction name and v is a return value, and REQUEST_CREATE(T), COMMIT(T), ABORT(T), REPORT_COMMIT(T,v), and REPORT_ABORT(T) where $T \neq T_0$ is a transaction name and v is a return value.

In this subsection, we define some basic concepts involving serial actions, for use later in the paper. All these definitions are based on the set of serial actions only, and not on the specific automata in the serial system. For this reason, we present the definitions here, before going on (in the next subsection) to give more information about the system components.

3.4.1 Basic Definitions

The COMMIT(T) and ABORT(T) actions are called *completion* actions for T, while the REPORT_COMMIT(T,v) and REPORT_ABORT(T) actions are called *report* actions for T.

We define the "transaction" of an action that appears in the interface of a transaction or object automaton — that is, of any non-completion action. Let T be any transaction name. If π is one of the serial actions CREATE(T), REQUEST_COMMIT(T,v), or REQUEST_CREATE(T'), REPORT_COMMIT(T',v') or REPORT_ABORT(T'), where T' is a child of T, then we define *transaction*(π) to be T. If π is a completion action, then transaction(π) is undefined. We will sometimes want to associate a transaction with completion actions as well as other serial actions; since a completion action for T can be thought of as occurring "in between" T and parent(T), we will sometimes want to associate T and sometimes parent(T) with the action. Thus, we extend the "transaction(π)"

definition in two different ways. If π is any serial action, then we define *hightransaction(π)* to be transaction(π) if π is not a completion action, and to be parent(T), if π is a completion action for T. Also, if π is any serial action, we define *lowtransaction(π)* to be transaction(π) if π is not a completion action, and to be T, if π is a completion action for T. In particular, hightransaction(π) = lowtransaction(π) = transaction(π) for all serial actions other than completion actions.

We also require notation for the object associated with any serial action whose transaction is an access. If π is a serial action of the form CREATE(T) or REQUEST_COMMIT(T,v), where T is an access to X, then we define *object(π)* to be X.

We extend the notation in the preceding paragraphs to events as well as actions. For example, if π is an event, then we write *transaction(π)* to denote the transaction of the action of which π is an occurrence.

Recall that an *operation* is a pair (T,v), consisting of a transaction name and a return value. We can associate operations with a sequence of serial actions, as follows. If β is a sequence of serial actions, we say that the operation (T,v) *occurs* in β if there is a REQUEST_COMMIT(T,v) event in β. Conversely, we can associate serial actions with a sequence of operations. For any operation (T,v), let *perform(T,v)* denote the two-action sequence CREATE(T) REQUEST_COMMIT(T,v), the expansion of (T,v) into its two parts. This definition is extended to sequences of operations in the natural way: if ξ is a sequence of operations of the form ξ'(T,v), then perform(ξ) = perform(ξ') perform(T,v). Thus, the "perform" function expands a sequence of operations into a corresponding alternating sequence of CREATE and REQUEST_COMMIT actions.

Now we require terminology to describe the status of a transaction during execution. Let β be a sequence of serial actions. A transaction name T is said to be *active* in β provided that β contains a CREATE(T) event but no REQUEST_COMMIT event for T. Similarly, T is said to be *live* in β provided that β contains a CREATE(T) event but no completion event for T. Also, T is said to be an *orphan* in β if there is an ABORT(U) action in β for some ancestor U of T.

We have already used projection operators to restrict action sequences to particular sets of actions, and to actions of particular automata. We now introduce another projection operator, this time to sets of transaction names. Namely, if β is a sequence of serial actions and $\mathcal{U}$ is a set of transaction names, then $\beta|\mathcal{U}$ is defined to be the sequence $\beta|\{\pi\text{: transaction}(\pi) \in \mathcal{U}\}$. If T is a transaction name, we sometimes write $\beta|T$ as shorthand for $\beta|\{T\}$. Similarly, if β is a sequence of serial actions and X is an object name, we sometimes write $\beta|X$ to denote $\beta|\{\pi\text{: object}(\pi) = X\}$.

Sometimes we will want to use definitions from this subsection for sequences of actions chosen from some other set besides the set of serial actions — usually, a set containing the set of serial actions. We extend the appropriate definitions of this subsection to such sequences by applying them to the subsequences consisting of serial actions. Thus, if β is a sequence of actions chosen from a set Φ of actions, define *serial(β)* to be the subsequence of β consisting of serial actions. Then we say that operation (T,v) *occurs* in β exactly if it occurs in serial(β). A transaction T is said to be *active* in β provided that it is active in serial(β), and similarly for the "live" and "orphan" definitions. Also, $\beta|\mathcal{U}$ is defined to be serial(β)$|\mathcal{U}$, and similarly for projection on an object.

3.4.2 Well-Formedness

In the definition of a serial system in the following subsection, we will place very few constraints on the transaction automata and serial object automata. However, we will want to assume that certain simple properties are guaranteed; for example, a transaction should not take steps until it has been created, and an object should not respond to an operation that has not been invoked. Such requirements are captured by "well-formedness conditions", certain properties of sequences of external actions of the transaction and object components. We define those conditions here.

First we define "transaction well-formedness". Let T be any transaction name. A sequence β of serial actions π with transaction(π) = T is defined to be *transaction well-formed* for T provided the following conditions hold.

1. The first event in β, if any, is a CREATE(T) event, and there are no other CREATE events.
2. There is at most one REQUEST_CREATE(T') event in β for each child T' of T.
3. Any report event for a child T' of T is preceded by REQUEST_CREATE(T') in β.
4. There is at most one report event in β for each child T' of T.
5. If a REQUEST_COMMIT event for T occurs in β, then it is preceded by a report event for each child T' of T for which there is a REQUEST_CREATE(T') in β.
6. If a REQUEST_COMMIT event for T occurs in β, then it is the last event in β.

In particular, if T is an access transaction name, then the only sequences that are transaction well-formed for T are the prefixes of the two-event sequence CREATE(T) REQUEST_COMMIT(T,v). For any T, it is easy to see that the set of transaction well-formed sequences for T is nonempty, prefix-closed and limit-closed.

Now we define "serial object well-formedness". Let X be any object name. A sequence of serial actions π with object(π) = X is defined to be *serial object well-formed* for X if it is a prefix of a sequence of the form CREATE(T_1) REQUEST_COMMIT(T_1,v_1) CREATE(T_2) REQUEST_COMMIT(T_2,v_2) ..., where $T_i \neq T_j$ when $i \neq j$. The following connection between serial object well-formedness and transaction well-formedness is immediate.

Lemma 8: Let β be a sequence of serial actions π with object(π) = X. If β is serial object well-formed for X and T is an access to X, then $\beta|T$ is transaction well-formed for T.

3.5 Serial Systems

We are now ready to define "serial systems". Serial systems are composed of transaction automata, serial object automata, and a single serial scheduler automaton. There is one transaction automaton A(T) for each non-access transaction name T, and one serial object automaton S(X) for each object name X. We describe the three kinds of components in turn.

3.5.1 Transaction Automata

A *transaction automaton* A(T) for a non-access transaction name T of a given system type is an I/O automaton with the following external action signature.

Input:
  CREATE(T)
  REPORT_COMMIT(T',v), for T' a child of T, and v a return value
  REPORT_ABORT(T'), for T' a child of T
Output:
  REQUEST_CREATE(T'), for T' a child of T
  REQUEST_COMMIT(T,v), for v a return value

In addition, A(T) may have an arbitrary set of internal actions. We require A(T) to preserve transaction well-formedness for T, as defined in the previous section. As discussed earlier, this does not mean that all behaviors of A(T) are transaction well-formed, but it does mean that as long as the environment of A(T) does not violate transaction well-formedness, A(T) will not do so. Except for that requirement, transaction automata can be chosen arbitrarily. Note that if β is a sequence of actions, then $\beta|T = \beta|\text{ext}(A(T))$.

Transaction automata are intended to be general enough to model the transactions defined in any reasonable programming language. Of course, there is still work required in showing how to define appropriate transaction automata for the transactions in any particular language. This correspondence depends on the special features of each language, and we do not describe techniques for establishing such a correspondence in this paper.

3.5.2 Serial Object Automata

A *serial object automaton* S(X) for an object name X of a given system type is an I/O automaton with the following external action signature.

Input:
  CREATE(T), for T an access to X
Output:
  REQUEST_COMMIT(T,v), for T an access to X

In addition, S(X) may have an arbitrary set of internal actions. We require S(X) to preserve serial object well-formedness for X, as defined in the previous section. As with transaction automata, serial object automata can be chosen arbitrarily as long as they preserve serial object well-formedness.

3.5.3 Serial Scheduler

There is a single serial scheduler automaton for each system type. It runs transactions according to a depth-first traversal of the transaction tree, running sets of sibling transactions serially. The serial scheduler can choose nondeterministically to abort any transaction after its parent has requested its creation, as long as the transaction has not actually been created. In the context of this scheduler, the "semantics" of an ABORT(T) action are that transaction T was never created. The scheduler does not permit any two sibling transactions to be live at the same time, and does not abort any transaction while any of its siblings is active. We now give a formal definition of the serial scheduler automaton.

The action signature of the serial scheduler is as follows.

Input:
  REQUEST_CREATE(T), $T \neq T_0$
  REQUEST_COMMIT(T,v)
Output:
  CREATE(T)
  COMMIT(T), $T \neq T_0$
  ABORT(T), $T \neq T_0$
  REPORT_COMMIT(T,v), $T \neq T_0$
  REPORT_ABORT(T), $T \neq T_0$

Each state s of the serial scheduler consists of six sets, denoted via record notation: s.create_requested, s.created, s.commit_requested, s.committed, s.aborted and s.reported. The set s.commit_requested is a set of operations. The others are sets of transactions. There is exactly one start state, in which the set create_requested is $\{T_0\}$, and the other sets are empty. We use the notation s.completed to denote s.committed $\cup$ s.aborted. Thus, s.completed is not an actual variable in the state, but rather a "derived variable" whose value is determined as a function of the actual state variables.

The transition relation of the serial scheduler consists of exactly those triples (s',π,s) satisfying the preconditions and yielding the effects described below, where π is the indicated action. By convention, we include in the effects only those conditions on the state s that may change with the action. If a component of s is not mentioned in the effects, it is implicit that the set is the same in s' and s.

REQUEST_CREATE(T), $T \neq T_0$
Effect:
  s.create_requested = s'.create_requested $\cup$ {T}

REQUEST_COMMIT(T,v)
Effect:
  s.commit_requested = s'.commit_requested $\cup$ {(T,v)}

CREATE(T)
Precondition:
  T $\in$ s'.create_requested - s'.created
  T $\notin$ s'.aborted

siblings(T) $\cap$ s'.created $\subseteq$ s'.completed
Effect:
s.created = s'.created $\cup$ {T}

COMMIT(T), $T \neq T_0$
Precondition:
(T,v) $\in$ s'.commit_requested for some v
T $\notin$ s'.completed
Effect:
s.committed = s'.committed $\cup$ {T}

ABORT(T), $T \neq T_0$
Precondition:
T $\in$ s'.create_requested - s'.completed
T $\notin$ s'.created
siblings(T) $\cap$ s'.created $\subseteq$ s'.completed
Effect:
s.aborted = s'.aborted $\cup$ {T}

REPORT_COMMIT(T,v), $T \neq T_0$
Precondition:
T $\in$ s'.committed
(T,v) $\in$ s'.commit_requested
T $\notin$ s'.reported
Effect:
s.reported = s'.reported $\cup$ {T}

REPORT_ABORT(T), $T \neq T_0$
Precondition:
T $\in$ s'.aborted
T $\notin$ s'.reported
Effect:
s.reported = s'.reported $\cup$ {T}

Thus, the input actions, REQUEST_CREATE and REQUEST_COMMIT, simply result in the request being recorded. A CREATE action can occur only if a corresponding REQUEST_CREATE has occurred and the CREATE has not already occurred. Moreover, it cannot occur if the transaction was previously aborted. The third precondition on the CREATE action says that the serial scheduler does not create a transaction until each of its previously created sibling transactions has completed (i.e., committed or aborted). That is, siblings are run sequentially. A COMMIT action can occur only if it has previously been requested and no completion action has yet occurred for the indicated transaction. An ABORT action can occur only if a corresponding REQUEST_CREATE has occurred and no completion action has yet occurred for the indicated transaction. Moreover, it cannot occur if the transaction was previously created. The third precondition on the ABORT action says that the scheduler does not abort a transaction while there is activity going on on behalf of any of its siblings. That is, aborted transactions are dealt with sequentially with respect to their siblings. The result of a transaction can be reported to its parent at any time after the commit or abort has occurred.

The following lemma describes simple relationships between the state of the serial scheduler and its computational history.

Lemma 9: Let β be a finite schedule of the serial scheduler, and let s be a state such that β can leave the serial scheduler in state s. Then the following conditions are true.

1. T $\in$ s.create_requested exactly if $T = T_0$ or β contains a REQUEST_CREATE(T) event.
2. T $\in$ s.created exactly if β contains a CREATE(T) event.

3. $(T,v) \in$ s.commit_requested exactly if β contains a REQUEST_COMMIT(T,v) event.

4. $T \in$ s.committed exactly if β contains a COMMIT(T) event.

5. $T \in$ s.aborted exactly if β contains an ABORT(T) event.

6. $T \in$ s.reported exactly if β contains a report event for T.

7. s.committed $\cap$ s.aborted $= \emptyset$.

8. s.reported $\subseteq$ s.committed $\cup$ s.aborted.

The following lemma gives simple facts about the actions appearing in an arbitrary schedule of the serial scheduler.

Lemma 10: Let β be a schedule of the serial scheduler. Then all of the following hold:

1. If a CREATE(T) event appears in β, then a REQUEST-CREATE(T) event precedes it in β.
2. At most one CREATE(T) event appears in β for each transaction T.
3. If a COMMIT(T) event appears in β then a REQUEST-COMMIT(T,v) event precedes it in β for some return value v.
4. If an ABORT(T) event appears in β then a REQUEST-CREATE(T) event precedes it in β.
5. If a CREATE(T) or ABORT(T) event appears in β and is preceded by a CREATE(T') event for a sibling T' of T, then it is also preceded by a completion event for T'.
6. At most one completion event appears in β for each transaction.
7. At most one report event appears in β for each transaction.
8. If a REPORT-COMMIT(T,v) event appears in β, then a COMMIT(T) event and a REQUEST_COMMIT(T,v) event precede it in β.
9. If a REPORT-ABORT(T) event appears in β, then an ABORT(T) event precedes it in β.

Proof: By Lemma 9 and the serial scheduler preconditions.

The final lemma of this subsection says that the serial scheduler preserves the well-formedness properties described earlier.

Lemma 11:

1. Let T be any transaction name. Then the serial scheduler preserves transaction well-formedness for T.
2. Let X be any object name. Then the serial scheduler preserves serial object well-formedness for X.

Proof: By the definitions and the characterization given in Lemma 10.

3.5.4 Serial Systems, Executions, Schedules and Behaviors

A *serial system* of a given system type is the composition of a strongly compatible set of automata indexed by the union of the set of non-access transaction names, the set of object names and the singleton set {SS} (for "serial scheduler"). Associated with each non-access transaction name T is a transaction automaton A(T) for T. Associated with each object name X is a serial object automaton S(X) for X. Finally, associated with the name SS is the serial scheduler automaton for the given system type. When the particular serial system is understood from context, we will sometimes use the terms *serial executions*, *serial schedules* and *serial behaviors* for the system's executions, schedules and behaviors, respectively.

A fundamental property of serial behaviors is that they are well-formed for each transaction and object name.

Proposition 12: If β is a serial behavior, then the following conditions hold.

1. For every transaction name T, $\beta|T$ is transaction well-formed for T.
2. For every object name X, $\beta|X$ is serial object well-formed for X.

Proof: For non-access transaction names T, or arbitrary object names X, the result is immediate by Lemma 7, the definitions of transaction and object automata, and Lemma 11. Suppose that T is an access to X. Since $\beta|X$ is serial object well-formed for X, Lemma 8 implies that $\beta|T$ is transaction well-formed for T.

Another fundamental property of serial behaviors is that the live transactions always form a chain of ancestors, as indicated below.

Proposition 13: Let β be a serial behavior.

1. If T is live in β and T' is an ancestor of T, then T' is live in β.
2. If T and T' are transaction names such that both T and T' are live in β, then either T is an ancestor of T' or T' is an ancestor of T.

In the remainder of the paper, we fix an arbitrary system type and serial system, with A(T) as the non-access transaction automaton for each transaction name T, and S(X) as the serial object automaton for each object name X.

3.6 Correctness Conditions

Now that we have defined serial systems, we can use them to state correctness conditions for other transaction-processing systems. It is reasonable to use serial systems in this way because of the particular constraints the serial scheduler imposes on the orders in which transactions and objects can perform steps. We contend that the given constraints correspond precisely to the way nested transaction systems ought to appear to behave; in particular, these constraints yield a natural generalization of the notion of serial execution in classical transaction systems. We arrive at a number of correctness conditions by considering *for which system components* this appearance must be maintained: for the external environment T_0, for all transactions, or for all non-orphan transactions.

To express these correctness conditions we define the notion of "serial correctness" of a sequence of actions for a particular transaction name. We say that a sequence β of actions is *serially correct* for transaction name T provided that there is some serial behavior γ such that $\beta|T = \gamma|T$. (Recall that if T is a non-access, we have $\beta|T = \beta|ext(A(T))$ and $\gamma|T = \gamma|ext(A(T))$. If T is a non-access transaction, serial correctness for T is a condition that guarantees to implementors of T that their code will encounter only situations that can arise in serial executions.

The principal notion of correctness that we will use in this paper is the serial correctness of all finite behaviors for the root transaction name T_0. This says that the "outside world" cannot distinguish between the given system and the serial system.

Many of the algorithms we study satisfy stronger correctness conditions. A fairly strong and possibly interesting correctness condition is the serial correctness of all finite behaviors for all transactions names. Thus, neither the outside world nor any of the individual user transactions can distinguish between the given system and the serial system. Note that the definition of serial correctness for all transactions does not require that all the transactions see behavior that is part of the same execution of the serial system; rather, each could see behavior arising in a different execution.

We will also consider intermediate conditions such as serial correctness for all non-orphan transaction names. This condition implies serial correctness for T_0 because the serial scheduler does not have the action ABORT(T_0) in its signature, so T_0 cannot be an orphan. Most of the popular algorithms for concurrency control and recovery guarantee serial correctness for all non-orphan transaction names. Our Serializability Theorem gives sufficient conditions for showing that a behavior of a transaction-processing system is serially correct for an arbitrary non-orphan transaction name, and can be used to prove this property for many of these algorithms. The usual algorithms do not guarantee serial correctness for orphans, however; in order to guarantee this as well, the use of a special "orphan management" algorithm is generally required. Such algorithms are described and their correctness proved in [HLMW].

We close this subsection with a proposition that shows that serial correctness with respect to a transaction name T, a notion defined in terms of behaviors of T, implies a relationship between executions of T in the two systems.

Proposition 14: Let $\{B_i\}_{i\in I}$ be a strongly compatible set of automata and let $B = \Pi_{i\in I}B_i$. Suppose that non-access transaction name T is in the index set I and suppose that B_T and A(T) are the same automaton. Let α be a finite execution of B, and suppose that beh(α) is serially correct for T. Then there is a serial execution α' such that $\alpha|B_T = \alpha'|A(T)$.

Proof: Proposition 1 implies that $\alpha|B_T$ is an execution of B_T, and then Lemma 3 can be used to patch together the desired execution.

4 Simple Systems

It is desirable to state our Serializability Theorem in such a way that it can be used for proving correctness of many different kinds of transaction-processing systems, with radically different architectures. We therefore define a "simple system", which embodies the common features of most transaction-processing systems, independent of their concurrency control and recovery algorithms, and even of their division into modules to handle different aspects of transaction-processing. A "simple system" consists of the transaction automata together with a special automaton called the "simple database". Our theorem is stated in terms of simple systems.

Many complicated transaction-processing algorithms can be understood as implementations of the simple system. For example, a system containing separate objects that manage locks and a "controller" that passes information among transactions and objects can be represented in this way, and so our theorem can be used to prove its correctness. The same strategy works for a system containing objects that manage timestamped versions and a controller that issues timestamps to transactions.

4.1 Simple Database

There is a single simple database for each system type. The action signature of the simple database is that of the composition of the serial scheduler with the serial objects:

Input:
  REQUEST_CREATE(T), $T \neq T_0$
  REQUEST_COMMIT(T,v), T a non-access
Output:
  CREATE(T)
  COMMIT(T), $T \neq T_0$
  ABORT(T), $T \neq T_0$
  REPORT_COMMIT(T,v), $T \neq T_0$
  REPORT_ABORT(T), $T \neq T_0$
  REQUEST_COMMIT(T,v), T an access

States of the simple database are the same as for the serial scheduler, and the initial states are also the same. The transition relation is as follows.

REQUEST_CREATE(T), $T \neq T_0$
Effect:
  s.create_requested = s'.create_requested $\cup$ {T}

REQUEST_COMMIT(T,v), T a non-access
Effect:
  s.commit_requested = s'.commit_requested $\cup$ {(T,v)}

CREATE(T)
Precondition:
$T \in$ s'.create_requested - s'.created
Effect:
s.created = s'.created $\cup$ {T}

COMMIT(T), $T \neq T_0$
Precondition:
(T,v) $\in$ s'.commit_requested for some v
$T \notin$ s'.completed
Effect:
s.committed = s'.committed $\cup$ {T}

ABORT(T), $T \neq T_0$
Precondition:
$T \in$ s'.create_requested - s'.completed
Effect:
s.aborted = s'.aborted $\cup$ {T}

REPORT_COMMIT(T,v), $T \neq T_0$
Precondition:
$T \in$ s'.committed
(T,v) $\in$ s'.commit_requested
$T \notin$ s'.reported
Effect:
s.reported = s'.reported $\cup$ {T}

REPORT_ABORT(T), $T \neq T_0$
Precondition:
$T \in$ s'.aborted
$T \notin$ s'.reported
Effect:
s.reported = s'.reported $\cup$ {T}

REQUEST_COMMIT(T,v), T an access
Precondition:
$T \in$ s'.created
for all v', (T,v') $\notin$ s'.commit_requested
Effect:
s.commit_requested = s'.commit_requested $\cup$ {(T,v)}

The next two lemmas are analogous to those previously given for the serial scheduler.

Lemma 15: Let β be a finite schedule of the simple database, and let s be a state such that β can leave the simple database in state s. Then the following conditions are true.

1. T is in s.create_requested exactly if $T = T_0$ or β contains a REQUEST_CREATE(T) event.
2. T is in s.created exactly if β contains a CREATE(T) event.
3. (T,v) is in s.commit_requested exactly if β contains a REQUEST_COMMIT(T,v) event.
4. T is in s.committed exactly if β contains a COMMIT(T) event.
5. T is in s.aborted exactly if β contains an ABORT(T) event.
6. T is in s.reported exactly if β contains a report event for T.
7. s.committed $\cap$ s.aborted = $\emptyset$.
8. s.reported $\subseteq$ s.committed $\cup$ s.aborted.

Lemma 16: Let β be a schedule of the simple database. Then all of the following hold:

1. If a CREATE(T) event appears in β, then a REQUEST-CREATE(T) event precedes it in β.
2. At most one CREATE(T) event appears in β for each transaction T.
3. If a COMMIT(T) event appears in β, then a REQUEST-COMMIT(T,v) event precedes it in β for some return value v.
4. If an ABORT(T) event appears in β, then a REQUEST-CREATE(T) event precedes it in β.
5. At most one completion event appears in β for each transaction.
6. At most one report event appears in β for each transaction.
7. If a REPORT-COMMIT(T,v) event appears in β, then a COMMIT(T) event and a REQUEST_COMMIT(T,v) event precede it in β.
8. If a REPORT-ABORT(T) event appears in β, then an ABORT(T) event precedes it in β.
9. If T is an access and a REQUEST_COMMIT(T,v) event occurs in β, then a CREATE(T) event precedes it in β.
10. If T is an access, then at most one REQUEST_COMMIT event for T occurs in β.

Proof: By Lemma 15 and the simple database preconditions.

Thus, the simple database embodies those constraints that we would expect any reasonable transaction-processing system to satisfy. The simple database does not allow CREATEs, ABORTs, or COMMITs without an appropriate preceding request, does not allow any transaction to have two creation or completion events, and does not report completion events that never happened. Also, it does not produce responses to accesses that were not invoked, nor does it produce multiple responses to accesses. On the other hand, the simple database allows almost any ordering of transactions, allows concurrent execution of sibling transactions, and allows arbitrary responses to accesses. We do not claim that the simple database produces only serially correct behaviors; rather, we use the simple database to model features common to more sophisticated systems that do ensure correctness.

Lemma 17: Let T be any transaction name. Then the simple database preserves transaction well-formedness for T.

Proof: By the definitions and the characterization given in Lemma 16.

4.2 Simple Systems, Executions, Schedules and Behaviors

A *simple system* is the composition of a compatible set of automata indexed by the union of the set of non-access transaction names and the singleton set {SD} (for "simple database"). Associated with each non-access transaction name T is a transaction automaton A(T) for T, and associated with the name SD is the simple database automaton for the given system type. When the particular simple system is understood from context, we will often use the terms *simple executions, simple schedules* and *simple behaviors* for the system's executions, schedules and behaviors, respectively.

Lemma 18: If β is a simple behavior and T is a transaction name, then $\beta|T$ is transaction well-formed for T.

Proof: By Lemma 17 and the definition of transaction automata.

The Serializability Theorem is formulated in terms of simple behaviors; it provides a sufficient condition for a simple behavior to be serially correct for a particular transaction name T.

5 The Serializability Theorem

In this section, we present our Serializability Theorem, which embodies a fairly general method for proving that a concurrency control algorithm guarantees serial correctness. This theorem expresses the following intuition: a behavior of a system is serially correct provided that there is a way to order the transactions so that when the operations at each object are arranged in the corresponding order, the result is a behavior of the corresponding serial object. The correctness of many different concurrency control algorithms can be proved using this theorem.

This theorem is the closest analog we have for the classical Serializability Theorem of [BHG]. Both that theorem and ours hypothesize that there is some ordering on transactions consistent with the behavior at each object. In both cases, this hypothesis is used to show serial correctness. Our result is somewhat more complicated, however, because it deals with nesting and aborts. In the next two subsections, we give some additional definitions that are needed to accomodate these complications.

5.1 Visibility

One difference between our result and the classical Serializability Theorem is that the conclusion of our result is serial correctness for an arbitrary transaction T, whereas the classical result essentially considers only serial correctness for T_0. Thus, it should not be surprising that the hypothesis of our result does not deal with all the operations at each object, but only with those that are in some sense "visible" to the particular transaction T. In this subsection, we define a notion of "visibility" of one transaction to another. This notion is a technical one, but one that is natural and convenient in the formal statements of results and in their proofs. Visibility is defined so that, in the usual transaction-processing systems, only a transaction T' that is visible to another transaction T can affect the behavior of T.

A transaction T' can affect another transaction T in several ways. First, if T' is an ancestor of T, then T' can affect T by passing information down the transaction tree via invocations. Second, a transaction T' that is not an ancestor of T can affect T through COMMIT actions for T' and all ancestors of T' up to the level of the least common ancestor with T; information can be propagated from T' up to the least common ancestor via COMMIT actions, and from there down to T via invocations. Third, a transaction T' that is not an ancestor of T can affect T by accessing an object that is later accessed by T; in most of the usual transaction-processing algorithms, this is only allowed to occur if there are intervening COMMIT actions for all ancestors of T' up to the level of the least common ancestor with T.

Thus, we define "visibility" as follows. Let β be any sequence of serial actions. If T and T' are transaction names, we say that T' is *visible* to T in β if there is a COMMIT(U) action in β for every U in ancestors(T') - ancestors(T). Thus, every ancestor of T' up to (but not necessarily including) the least common ancestor of T and T' has committed in β.

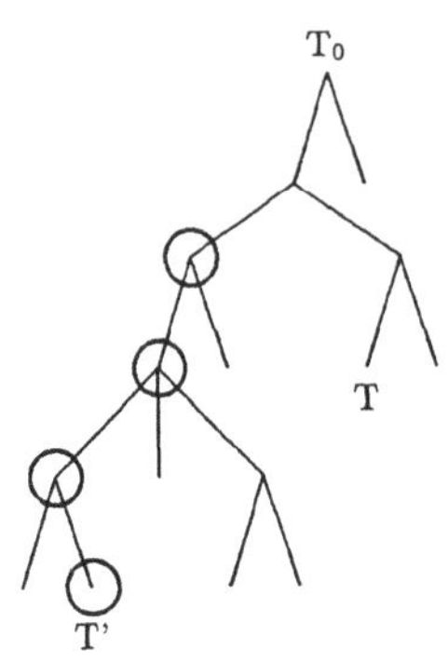

Figure 5: Visibility

Figure 5 depicts two transactions, T and T' neither an ancestor of the other. If the transactions represented by all of the circled nodes have committed in some sequence of serial actions, then the definition implies that T' is visible to T.

The following lemma describes elementary properties of "visibility".

Lemma 19: Let β be a sequence of actions, and let T, T' and T'' be transaction names.

1. If T' is an ancestor of T, then T' is visible to T in β.
2. T' is visible to T in β if and only if T' is visible to lca(T,T') in β.
3. If T'' is visible to T' in β and T' is visible to T in β, then T'' is visible to T in β.
4. If T' is live in β and T' is visible to T in β, then T is a descendant of T'.
5. If T' is an orphan in β and T' is visible to T in β, then T is an orphan in β.

We use the notion of "visibility" to pick, out of a sequence of actions, a subsequence consisting of the actions corresponding to transactions that are visible to a given transaction T. More precisely, if β is any sequence of actions and T is a transaction name, then *visible(*β*,T)* denotes the subsequence of β consisting of serial actions π with hightransaction(π) visible to T in β. Note that every action occurring in visible(β,T) is a serial action, even if β itself contains other actions. The following obvious lemma says that the "visible" operator on sequences picks out either all or none of the actions having a particular transaction.

Lemma 20: Let β be a sequence of actions, and let T and T' be transaction names. Then visible(β,T)|T' is equal to β|T' if T' is visible to T in β, and is equal to the empty sequence otherwise.

5.2 Event and Transaction Orders

The hypothesis of the theorem refers to rearranging the operations at each object according to a given order on transactions. The definitions required to describe the appropriate kind of ordering to use for this purpose are provided in this subsection.

5.2.1 Affects Order

We first define a partial order "affects(β)" on the events of a sequence β of serial actions. This will be used to describe basic dependencies between events in a simple behavior; any appropriate ordering will be required to be consistent with these dependencies. We define the affects relation by first defining a subrelation that we call the "directly-affects" relation and then taking the transitive closure. For a sequence β of serial actions, and events ϕ and π in β, we say that ϕ *directly affects* π in β (and that $(\phi,\pi) \in$ directly-affects(β)) if at least one of the following is true.

- transaction(ϕ) = transaction(π) and ϕ precedes π in β,[9]
- ϕ = REQUEST_CREATE(T) and π = CREATE(T)
- ϕ = REQUEST_COMMIT(T,v) and π = COMMIT(T)
- ϕ = REQUEST_CREATE(T) and π = ABORT(T)
- ϕ = COMMIT(T) and π = REPORT_COMMIT(T,v)
- ϕ = ABORT(T) and π = REPORT_ABORT(T)

If β is a simple behavior, and $(\phi,\pi) \in$ directly-affects(β), then it is easy to see that ϕ precedes π in β. For a sequence β of serial events, define the relation affects(β) to be the transitive closure of the relation directly-affects(β). If the pair (ϕ,π) is in the relation affects(β), we also say that ϕ *affects* π in β. The following is immediate.

---

[9]This includes accesses as well as non-accesses.

Lemma 21: Let β be a simple behavior. Then affects(β) is an irreflexive partial order on the events in β.[10]

The conditions listed in the definition of "directly-affects" should seem like a reasonable collection of dependencies among the events in a simple behavior. Here we try to give some technical justification for these conditions. In the proof of the theorem, we will attempt to extract serial behaviors from a given simple behavior. The transaction orderings used to help in this construction will be constrained to be consistent with "affects"; this will mean that the sequences we construct will be closed under "affects" and that the orders of events in these sequences are consistent with "affects". Thus, if β is a simple behavior and $(\phi,\pi) \in$ directly-affects(β), all the serial behaviors we construct that contain π will also contain ϕ, and ϕ will precede π in each such behavior.

The first case of the "directly-affects" definition is used because we are not assuming special knowledge of transaction behavior; if we included π and not ϕ in our candidate serial behavior, we would have no way of proving that the result included correct behaviors of the transaction automata. The remaining cases naturally parallel the preconditions of the serial scheduler; in each case, the preconditions of π as an action of the serial scheduler include a test for a previous occurrence of ϕ, so a sequence of actions with π not preceded by ϕ could not possibly be a serial behavior.

As before, we extend the "affects" definition to sequences β of arbitrary actions by saying that ϕ affects π in β exactly if ϕ affects π in serial(β).

5.2.2 Sibling Orders

The type of transaction ordering needed for our theorem is more complicated than that used in the classical theory, because of the nesting involved here. Instead of just arbitrary total orderings on transactions, we will use orderings that only relate siblings in the transaction nesting tree. We call such an ordering a "sibling order". Interesting examples of sibling orders are the order of completion of transactions or an order determined by assigned timestamps.

Let *SIB* be the (irreflexive) sibling relation among transaction names, for a particular system type; thus, $(T,T') \in SIB$ if and only if $T \neq T'$ and parent(T) = parent(T'). If $R \subseteq SIB$ is an irreflexive partial order then we call R a *sibling order*. Sibling orders are the analog for nested transaction systems of serialization orders in single-level transaction systems. Note that sibling orders are not necessarily total, in general; totality is not always appropriate for our results.

A sibling order R can be extended in two natural ways. First, R_{trans} is the extension of R to descendants of siblings, i.e., the binary relation on transaction names containing (T,T') exactly when there exist transaction names U and U' such that T and T' are descendants of U and U' respectively, and $(U,U') \in R$. This order echoes the manner in which the serial scheduler runs transactions when it runs siblings with no concurrency, in the order specified by R. Second, if β is any sequence of actions, then $R_{event}(\beta)$ is the extension of R to serial events in β, i.e., the binary relation on events in β containing (ϕ,π) exactly when ϕ and π are distinct serial events in β with lowtransactions T and T' respectively, where $(T,T') \in R_{trans}$. It is easy to see that R_{trans} is an irreflexive partial order, and for any sequence β of actions, $R_{event}(\beta)$ is an irreflexive partial order.

The concept of a "suitable sibling order" describes two basic conditions that will be required of the sibling orders to be used in our theorem. The first condition is a technical one asserting that R orders sufficiently many siblings, while the second condition asserts that R does not contradict the dependencies described by the affects relation. Let β be a sequence of actions and T a transaction name. A sibling order R is *suitable* for β and T if the following conditions are met.

1. R orders all pairs of siblings T' and T'' that are lowtransactions of actions in visible(β,T).

---

[10]An *irreflexive partial order* is a binary relation that is irreflexive, antisymmetric and transitive.

2. $R_{event}(\beta)$ and affects(β) are consistent partial orders on the events in visible(β,T).[11]

5.3 The Serializability Theorem

We now present the main result. It says that a simple behavior β is serially correct for a non-orphan transaction name T provided that there is a suitable sibling order R for which a certain "view condition" holds for each object name X. The view condition says that the portion of β occurring at X that is visible to T, reordered according to R, is a behavior of the serial object S(X). In order to make all of this precise, suppose β is a finite simple behavior, T a transaction name, R a sibling order that is suitable for β and T, and X an object name. Let ξ be the sequence consisting of those operations occurring in β whose transaction components are accesses to X and that are visible to T in β, ordered according to R_{trans} on the transaction components. (The first condition in the definition of suitability implies that this ordering is uniquely determined.) Define *view(β,T,R,X)* to be perform(ξ).

Thus, view(β,T,R,X) represents the portion of the behavior β occurring at X that is visible to T, reordered according to R. Stated in other words, this definition extracts from β exactly the REQUEST_COMMIT actions for accesses to X that are visible to T; it then reorders those REQUEST_COMMIT actions according to R, and then inserts an appropriate CREATE action just prior to each REQUEST_COMMIT action. The theorem uses a hypothesis that each view(β,T,R,X) is a behavior of the serial object S(X) to conclude that β is serially correct for T.

Theorem 22: (Serializability Theorem) Let β be a finite simple behavior, T a transaction name such that T is not an orphan in β, and R a sibling order suitable for β and T. Suppose that for each object name X, view(β,T,R,X) $\in$ finbehs(S(X)). Then β is serially correct for T.

Proof: Given β, T and R, the needed serial behavior is constructed explicitly. The construction is done in several steps. First, visible(β,T), the portion of β visible to T, is extracted from β. This sequence is then reordered according to R and affects(β). (There may be many ways of doing this.) The reordered sequence is then truncated at an appropriate place, just after the last action involving T or any of its descendants. The resulting sequence γ is shown to be a serial behavior by showing separately that its projections are behaviors of the transaction automata, of the serial object automata, and of the serial scheduler, and then applying Proposition 4.

If T' is a nonaccess transaction name, Proposition 1 implies that $\beta|T'$ is a behavior of A(T'). Proposition 20 and the fact that $R_{event}(\beta)$ is consistent with affects(β) ensure that $\gamma|T'$ is a prefix of $\beta|T'$ and so is a behavior of A(T'). Thus, the projection of γ on each of the transaction automata is a behavior of that automaton.

For each object name X, unwinding the definitions shows that $\gamma|X$ is a prefix of view(β,T,R,X). The "view condition" hypothesis of the theorem, that view(β,T,R,X) $\in$ finbehs(S(X)), implies that $\gamma|X$ is a behavior of S(X). Thus, the projection of γ on each of the serial object automata is a behavior of that automaton.

Finally, an explicit argument by induction on the length of γ shows that γ is a behavior of the serial scheduler automaton. Consistency with affects(β) is used to show that certain events are included in γ; this implies that the serial scheduler preconditions involving occurrence of certain events are satisfied. The properties of the "visible" operator are used to show that certain events, e.g., those involving live transactions neither ancestors nor descendants of T, are not included in γ; this implies that the serial scheduler preconditions involving nonoccurrence of certain actions are satisfied.

The theorem has a straightforward corollary that outlines a strategy for showing that a particular system satisfies the correctness condition in which we are mainly interested, i.e., that all its finite behaviors are serially correct for T_0.

---

[11]Two binary relations R and S are *consistent* if their union can be extended to an irreflexive partial order (or in other words, if their union has no cycles).

Corollary 23: Let $\{B_i\}_{i \in I}$ be a strongly compatible set of automata and let $B = \Pi_{i \in I} B_i$. Suppose that the name T_0 is in the index set I, and that the automaton $A(T_0)$ is associated with T_0 in B. Suppose that for every finite behavior β of B, the following conditions hold.

1. serial(β) is a simple behavior.
2. There exists a sibling order R suitable for serial(β) and T_0, such that for each object name X, view(serial(β),T_0,R,X) $\in$ finbehs(S(X)).

Then every finite behavior of B is serially correct for T_0.

6 Applications of the Serializability Theorem

We use this theorem elsewhere in our work to reason about the correctness of a wide variety of algorithms for implementing atomic transactions. In particular, we carry out correctness proofs for several algorithms that use locking and others that use timestamps.

The locking algorithm of Moss [Moss] is designed for data objects that are accessible only by read and write operations. We have developed a similar algorithm, in [FLMW2], that accomodates arbitrary data types. These algorithms involve simultaneous locking at different levels of the transaction nesting tree. A transaction is only permitted to access a data object if it has a suitable lock on that object. Sometime after a transaction commits, its locks are passed up to its parent and associated modifications to the data are made available to the parent and its other descendants. On the other hand, when a transaction aborts, its locks are released and its modifications to the data are discarded. The decision about whether to permit an access transaction to obtain a lock is based on whether any locks for "conflicting" operations are held by transactions that are not ancestors of the given access.

Using Corollary 23 above, we can prove that all the finite behaviors of a system B are serially correct for T_0 if B uses these algorithms. Although the locking algorithms include more actions than the simple system, it is not hard to see that serial(β) is a simple behavior, for every finite behavior β of B. The sibling order R used in the proof is the "completion order", i.e., the order in which sibling transactions commit and abort. Proving correctness of this algorithm using the Serializability Theorem highlights the key reason why locking algorithms work: roughly speaking, the condition that view(β,T_0,R,X) $\in$ finbehs(S(X)) says that the processing at any object is "consistent" with the transaction completion order. The "consistency" mentioned here means that reordering the appropriate, "visible" portion of the processing at each object in completion order yields a correct behavior for the corresponding serial object automaton. We can also use the Serializability Theorem to prove the stronger statement that the locking algorithms mentioned above are serially correct for all non-orphan transactions.

Our correctness proofs for these algorithms have an interesting structure. Namely, we describe each algorithm as the composition of a component automaton for each object plus one global "controller" automaton that simply manages communication among the other automata. A local condition called "dynamic atomicity" is defined; this condition essentially says that the object satisfies the view condition using the completion order. The Serializability Theorem implies that if all the objects are dynamic atomic, the system guarantees serial correctness for all non-orphan transaction names. The rest of the proof involves showing that the objects that model the given locking algorithms are dynamic atomic.

This proof structure allows us to obtain much stronger results than just the correctness of the given algorithms. As long as each object is dynamic atomic, the whole system will guarantee that any finite behavior is serially correct for all non-orphan transaction names. Thus, we are free to use an arbitrary implementation for each object, independent of the choice of implementation for each other object, as long as dynamic atomicity is satisfied. For example, a simple algorithm such as Moss' can be used for most objects, while a more sophisticated algorithm permitting extra concurrency by using type-specific information can be used for objects that are "hot spots" (that is, very frequently accessed.) The idea of a local condition that guarantees serial correctness was introduced by Weihl [Weihl] for systems without transaction nesting.

The timestamp algorithm of Reed [Reed] is designed for data objects that are accessible only by read and write operations. We have developed a similar algorithm, in [AFLMW], that accomodates arbitrary data types. (This work generalizes work of Herlihy [Herlihy] giving a timestamp algorithm for single-level transactions using arbitrary data types.) These algorithms both involve assignment of ranges of timestamp values to transactions in such a way that the interval of a child transaction is included in the interval of its parent, and the intervals of siblings are disjoint. Responses to accesses are determined from previous accesses with earlier timestamps.

We again analyze these algorithms using the Serializability Theorem and its Corollary. This time, the sibling order used is the timestamp order. Now the condition that view(β,T_0,R,X) $\in$ finbehs(S(X)) says that the processing of accesses to X is "consistent" with the timestamp order, in that reordering the processing in timestamp order yields a correct behavior for the corresponding serial object automaton. The Corollary then implies that all finite behaviors are serially correct for T_0, and the Serializability Theorem implies that the timestamp algorithms are serially correct for all non-orphan transaction names. Once again, each algorithm is described as the composition of object automata and a controller. This time, a local condition called "static atomicity" is used, saying that an object satisfies the view condition using the timestamp order. As long as each object is static atomic, the whole system is serially correct for non-orphan transactions. We show that both Reed's algorithm and our version of Herlihy's algorithm ensure static atomicity. Again, we have the flexibility to implement objects independently as long as static atomicity is guaranteed.

Objects can be proved to be dynamic atomic or static atomic using standard assertional proof techniques and connections between the object's state and history. It is also possible to prove that some objects are dynamic atomic or static atomic by showing that they implement other objects of the same kind. Possibilities maps and Proposition 6 can be used to show this. This strategy is especially useful in cases where the object keeps information in a compact form, whereas the required local property is easy to prove for a less compact variant of the algorithm. We refer the interested reader to [FLMW2] and [AFLMW] for more details.

7 Conclusions

In this paper, we have presented correctness conditions for atomic transaction systems. These conditions are stated at the user interface to the system, which is the interface of primary interest. The fact that the conditions are stated at this interface makes them quite general; they can be used to state appropriate correctness conditions for a wide variety of different algorithms. We have also described one general theorem, the Serializability Theorem, which is useful for proving correctness of many interesting and apparently dissimilar algorithms.

The Serializability Theorem is not the only tool we use for our correctness proofs. There are several other techniques that we use for decomposing proofs of transaction-processing algorithms. For example, in [GL], we provide proofs for replicated data algorithms based on the quorum consensus technique of Gifford [Gifford]. We consider replication management algorithms in combination with concurrency control and recovery algorithms. Our presentation separates the concerns very cleanly: the algorithm is divided into modules that handle replication and modules that handle the concurrency control and recovery. Correctness conditions for the two separate algorithms are combined to yield correctness for the complete algorithm. In particular, all that is required of the concurrency control and recovery algorithms is that they guarantee serial correctness for non-orphan transactions (with respect to the individual copies of the data objects); thus, there is considerable flexibility in the choice of concurrency control and recovery algorithms. We remark that transaction nesting provides a particularly good way to organize this decomposition: the replication part of the algorithm is formally described in terms of new copy-management subtransactions that are called by the user-level transactions in place of the original user-level accesses to objects.

We expect that our model in general, and the Serializability Theorem in particular, will prove quite useful for reasoning about many more algorithms than those that we have already considered. We are also particularly interested in understanding how to reason about multi-level locking algorithms such as that considered in [BBG], and in understanding complicated algorithms that are used for concurrency control and recovery in an environment having volatile memory which is lost during a crash. Understanding these ideas in our model is work remaining to be done.

Finally, we remark that our Serializability Theorem still seems somewhat more complicated than the classical theorem, even taking the generalizations into account. The classical theorem was stated in simple combinatorial terms, while our theorem involves a more complicated fine-grained treatment of individual actions. We wonder if it is possible to combine the advantages of the two approaches: perhaps there is a simple combinatorial condition that takes suitable account of nesting and failures, and that implies the natural and general correctness conditions described in this paper.

8 References

[AFLMW] Aspnes, J., Fekete, A., Lynch, N., Merritt, M., and Weihl, W., "A Theory of Timestamp-Based Concurrency Control for Nested Transactions," Proceedings of 14th International Conference on Very Large Data Bases, to appear.

[BBG] Beeri, C., Bernstein, P. A., and Goodman, N., "A Model for Concurrency in Nested Transaction Systems," Technical Report, Wang Institute TR-86-03, March 1986.

[BHG] Bernstein, P., Hadzilacos, V., and Goodman, N., "Concurrency Control and Recovery in Database Systems," Addison-Wesley, 1987.

[Davies] Davies, C. T., "Recovery Semantics for a DB/DC System," Proceedings of 28th ACM National Conference, 1973, pp. 136-141.

[FLMW1] Fekete, A., Lynch, N., Merritt, M., and Weihl, W., "Nested Transactions and Read/Write Locking," Proceedings of 6th ACM Symposium on Principles of Database Systems, 1987, pp. 97-111. An expanded version is available as Technical Memo MIT/LCS/TM-324, Laboratory for Computer Science, Massachusetts Institute of Technology, Cambridge, MA., April 1987.

[FLMW2] Fekete, A., Lynch, N., Merritt, M., and Weihl, W., "Nested Transactions, Conflict-Based Locking and Dynamic Atomicity," Technical Memo MIT/LCS/TM-340, Laboratory for Computer Science, Massachusetts Institute of Technology, Cambridge, MA., September 1987. Submitted for publication.

[Gifford] Gifford, D., "Weighted Voting for Replicated Data," Proceedings of 7th ACM Symosium on Operating System Principles, 1979, pp. 150-162.

[GL] Goldman, K., and Lynch, N., "Nested Transactions and Quorum Consensus," Proceedings of 6th ACM Symposium on Principles of Distributed Computation, 1987, pp. 27-41. An expanded version is available as Technical Report MIT/LCS/TR-390, Laboratory for Computer Science, Massachusetts Institute of Technology, Cambridge, MA., May 1987.

[Herlihy] Herlihy, M., "Extending Multiversion Time-Stamping Protocols to Exploit Type Information," IEEE Transactions on Computers C-36, April 1987.

[HLMW] Herlihy, M., Lynch, N., Merritt, M., and Weihl, W., "On the Correctness of Orphan Elimination Algorithms," Proceedings of 17th IEEE Symposium on Fault-Tolerant Computing, 1987, pp. 8-13.

[Hoare] Hoare, C. A. R., "Communicating Sequential Processes," Prentice Hall International, 1985.

[Liskov] Liskov, B., "Distributed Computing in Argus," Communications of ACM, vol. 31, no. 3, March 1988, pp. 300-312.

[LM] Lynch, N., and Merritt, M., "Introduction to the Theory of Nested Transactions," Technical Report MIT/LCS/TR-367, Laboratory for Computer Science, Massachusetts Institute of Technology, Cambridge, MA., July 1986. To appear in Theoretical Compter Science.

[LMWF] Lynch, N., Merritt, M., Weihl, W., and Fekete, A., "Atomic Transactions," in preparation.

[LT] Lynch, N., and Tuttle, M., "Hierarchical Correctness Proofs for Distributed Algorithms," Proceedings of 6th ACM Symposium on Principles of Distributed Computation, 1987, pp. 137-151. An expanded version is available as Technical Report MIT/LCS/TR-387, Laboratory for Computer Science, Massachusetts Institute of Technology, Cambridge, MA., April 1987.

[Milner] Milner, R., "A Calculus of Communicating Systems," Lecture Notes in Computer Science 92, Springer Verlag, 1980.

[Moss] Moss, J. E. B., "Nested Transactions: An Approach To Reliable Distributed Computing," Ph.D. Thesis, Technical Report MIT/LCS/TR-260, Laboratory for Computer Science, Massachusetts Institute of Technology, Cambridge, MA., April 1981. Also, published by MIT Press, March 1985.

[Perl] Perl, S., "Distributed Commit Protocols for Nested Atomic Actions," M.S. Thesis, M.I.T. September 1987.

[SS] Spector, A., and Swedlow, K. (eds), "Guide to the Camelot Distributed Transaction Facility: Release 1," Carnegie Mellon University, Pittsburgh, PA., October 1987.

[Reed] Reed, D. P., "Naming and Synchronization in a Decentralized Computer System," Ph.D Thesis, Technical Report MIT/LCS/TR-205, Laboratory for Computer Science, Massachusetts Institute of Technology, Cambridge, MA., September 1978.

[Weihl] Weihl, W., "Specification and Implementation of Atomic Data Types," Ph.D. Thesis, Technical Report MIT/LCS/TR-314, Laboratory for Computer Science, Massachusetts Institute of Technology, Cambridge, MA., March 1984.

Improving Integrity Constraint Checking in Deductive Databases

P. Asirelli, P. Inverardi, A. Mustaro

Istituto di Elaborazione della Informazione - CNR
via S. Maria n. 46
I-56100 Pisa

1. INTRODUCTION

In this paper the description of a new method for integrity constraints checking in deductive databases is given and its correctness is proved. Our method extends and integrates two well known approaches in the literature, namely [Lloyd&Topor 85], [Lloyd&Topor 86], [Lloyd et al. 87] that has been proposed for stratified databases [Apt et al. 87], and [Nicolas 82] that was instead proposed for relational databases.
Like in the other approaches we assume that the database satisfies the integrity constraints before the update and, therefore, any new violation of the constraints must involve the update, so that, it will be sufficient to check the instances of those constraints which could be invalidated by the update.
Our method tries to minimize, as much as possible, the number of constraint instances to be checked, it works on stratified databases, thus including definite and hierarchical databases, and on the same kind of constraint formulas of [Lloyd et al. 87].
The method can be splitted into four steps:
First step: a certain number of sets of atoms is defined to obtain a set of atoms which could falsify the integrity constraints. These sets contain all atoms that falsifies the integrity constraint. Even if inspired by [Lloyd et al. 87] the definition of the sets is different, the number of atoms computed is less than those computed with that method and, furthermore they are more instantiated.
Second step: two set of substitutions Θ_{new} and Ψ_{new} are defined so that each substitution contained in one of these sets is the mgu of an atom which is part of an integrity constraint W and of an atom included in one of the sets computed in the first step. This second step ends with the generation of instances of the integrity constraint formula W obtained by applying the substitutions in $\Theta_{new} \cup \Psi_{new}$ to W itself.
Third step: like in [Nicolas 82] we try to simplify the obtained instances of W with the atoms pre-evalutation and with the application of the absorption rules.
Fourth step: by using the SLDNF we try to prove that each simplified instance is a logical conseguence of the completion of the database.

Comparisons with other methods
Here we briefly anticipate the differences among our method and [Lloyd et al. 87], [Nicolas 82], [Sadri&Kowalsky 87], [Decker 86] , that will be better motivated in section **5**.
Differently from [Lloyd et al. 87], we put in our sets $N^{*}v_{ins}$, $N^{*}v_{del}$, $P^{*}v_{ins}$, $P^{*}v_{del}$, only those atoms that were true before the update and that could be false after the update ($N^{*}v_{ins} \cup N^{*}v_{del}$) or the atoms that could be false before the update and that are true after the update ($P^{*}v_{ins} \cup P^{*}v_{del}$), while they insert

all the atoms that *could* be false after the update, set N, and all those that *could* be true after the update, set P.
Furthermore in [Lloyd et al. 87] the third step connected to constraints simplification is missing.
[Decker 86] builts exactly the difference between the two models, of the old database before the update and of the new database after the update. For that reason it introduces a greater number of substitutions than ours and therefore a greater number of constraint instances has to be checked. Besides, the algorithm used by Decker to compute the difference between the two models is more expensive than our's because it does not take advantage of the information that we mantain from the first step. In this case the third step is missing too.
Finally, [Sadri&Kowalsky 87] proposes a method which is based on an extension of the SLDNF resolution procedure. This method, too, assumes that the database satisfies its integrity constraints before the update. It will be shown in section **5**, that we obtain a significant improvement also with respect to this method.

2. BASIC DEFINITIONS

The following are basic definitions that we give to make the paper easier to read, but they can be found in the literature, [Lloyd 87], [Lloyd et al. 87].

Def1: A *database clause* is a first order formula such as: $A \leftarrow W$ where A is an atom and W is a conjunction of literals $L_1,\dots, L_n$, with $n \geq 0$. A is the head of the clause while W is the body. All variables in A and all free variables in W are considered universally quantified in front of the clause.

Def2: A *database* (often referred to as db) is a finite set of db clauses.

Def3: An *Integrity Constraint* formula is a closed first order formula.

Since we are dealing with general clauses, i.e. clauses whose body can contain a negative atom, the notion of integrity constraint satisfaction requires the introduction of the completion of a database, *comp(D)*. The definition of the completion we use is exactly that one defined in [Lloyd 84], that is, it contains the completed definition for each predicate and the equality theory including the domain closure axiom.

Def4: An atom A *occurs positively* in A; if an atom A occurs positively (negatively) in a formula W, then A *occurs positively* (*negatively*) in $\exists x W$ or $\forall x W$ or $W \wedge V$ or $W \vee V$ or $W \leftarrow V$. If an atom A occurs negatively (positively) in a formula W, then A *occurs negatively* (*positively*) in $\neg W$ or $V \leftarrow W$.

Def5: Let D be a db and G a goal: $\leftarrow W$, a *correct answer substitution* for comp(D) $\cup\{G\}$ is an answer substitution θ s.t. $\forall\,(W\theta)$ is a logical consequence of comp(D).

Def6: Let D be a db s.t. comp(D) is consistent, and let W be an integrity constraint formula. We say that D *satisfies* W iff W is a logical consequence of comp(D); otherwise we say that D *violates* W.

Def7: A *level mapping* of a db is a mapping from its set of predicates to the non negative integers. This mapping assigns to each predicate the value of its level.

Def8: A db is *stratified* if it has a level mapping s.t. in every clause $p(t_1,...,t_n) \leftarrow W$, the level of the predicate of every atom occuring positively in W is less or equal to the level of *p* and the level of the predicate of every atom occuring negatively in W is less than the level of *p*.

Def9: A transaction t is a finite sequence of deletions $(del_1,...,del_n)$ and of insertions $(ins_1,..., ins_m)$.

We assume that in a transaction there is no insertion and deletion of the same clause. Furthermore, since the order is not significant, we will consider all the deletions performed before the insertions.
With respect to integrity checking a transaction is considered as an atomic transformation on the data base, thus integrity checking is performed only at the end of a transaction.

Def10: Given two substitutions σ, σ', σ *subsumes* σ' iff $\sigma' \supseteq \sigma$ that is iff for each pair v_i/c_i in σ there is a pair v_j'/c_j' in σ' s.t. $v_j' = v_i$ $c_j' = c_i$. The empty substitution ε subsumes any substitutions.

Subsumption Lemma: Given a wwf F in prenex normal form and any interpretation I of F. Given two substitutions σ_i and σ_j which deal, on the one hand with variables in F which are universally quantified variables but not governed by an existentially quantified one, and on the other hand with elements in I. If σ_i subsumes σ_j then : if $F(\sigma_i)$ is true in I then so is $F(\sigma_j)$.
Proof: see [Nicolas 82]

3. DEFINITION OF COMPUTED SETS

In this section we define all the sets that are necessary in our method. Let us first introduce some notations. The sets we are going to define have generic elements whose form is the following: $E=[A,L_1,\dots,L_n]$ where A is an atom, and $L_1,\dots,L_n$ are literals; we will denote A with *head (E)* and $L_1,\dots,L_n$ with *tail (E)*.

Let Del denote the set of clauses deleted, and Ins denote the set of clauses inserted i.e.:
Del $=\{ A_i \leftarrow L_i \mid$ where $L_i = L_{i1},...,L_{in}$; $i \geq 0$, $A_i \leftarrow L_i \in D$ and it is *deleted* i.e $A_i \leftarrow L_i \notin D'\}$
Ins $=\{ A_i \leftarrow L_i \mid$ where $L_i = L_{i1},...,L_{in}$; $i \geq 0$, $A_i \leftarrow L_i \notin D$ and it is *inserted* i.e $A_i \leftarrow L_i \in D'\}$

Def11: $pos^0_{ins} := \{[A,L_1,...,L_n] \mid A \leftarrow L_1,...,L_n \in Ins \text{ and } n > 0\} \cup \{[A, \#] \mid A \leftarrow \in Ins\}$
The # symbol denotes that the coupled atom is certainly a logical consequence of Comp(D').

$$pos^{n+1}_{ins} := \{[B\sigma, A', L_1\sigma,...,L_{i-1}\sigma, L_{i+1}\sigma,..., L_n\sigma] \mid \exists E \in P^n_{ins} \text{ with}$$

-head (E) = A'

- $\exists$ a rule $B \leftarrow L_1,...,L_{i-1}, A^{\sim}, L_{i+1},...,L_n \in D$ s. t. $A' = A^{\sim}\sigma$

$$\cup \{[B\sigma, A', L_1\sigma,...,L_{i-1}\sigma, L_{i+1}\sigma,..., L_n\sigma] \mid \exists E \in N^n_{ins} \text{ with}$$

-head (E) = A'

- $\exists$ a rule $B \leftarrow L_1,..., L_{i-1}, \neg A^{\sim}, L_{i+1},...,L_n \in D$ s. t. $A' = A^{\sim}\sigma$

Def12: $neg^0_{ins} := \{ \}$

$$neg^{n+1}_{ins} := \{[B\sigma, L_1\sigma,...,L_{i-1}\sigma, L_{i+1}\sigma,..., L_n\sigma, A'] \mid \exists E \in P^n_{ins} \text{ with}$$

-head (E) = A'

-$\exists$ a rule $B \leftarrow L_1,\ldots, L_{i-1}, \neg A^{\sim}, L_{i+1},\ldots,L_n \in D$ s. t. $A' = A^{\sim}\sigma$

$\cup$ $\{[B\sigma, L_1\sigma,\ldots,L_{i-1}\sigma, L_{i+1}\sigma,\ldots, L_n\sigma, A'] \mid \exists E \in N^n_{ins}$ with

-head (E) = A'

- $\exists$ a rule $B \leftarrow L_1,\ldots, L_{i-1}, A^{\sim}, L_{i+1},\ldots,L_n \in D$ s. t. $A' = A^{\sim}\sigma$

Def13 $P^n_{ins} = pos^n_{ins} \setminus H^n_P$ where

$H^n_P = \{ E \in pos^n_{ins} \mid E$ is an instance of $E' \in pos^j_{ins}$, $j \leq n$, regardless literals order and variables renaming$\}$

$\cup \{ E \in pos^n_{ins} \mid E = [A, L_1,\ldots,L_m]$ and it exists an index $i \leq m$ s.t., $L_i = A \}$

The set P^n_{ins} is necessary to record only the elements of pos^n_{ins} that are not subsumption of other elements of all pos^i_{ins} for $1 \leq i \leq n$ and to eliminate recursive elements. In the same way it is possible to define:

Def14 $N^n_{ins} = neg^n_{ins} \setminus H^n_N$ where

$H^n_N = \{E \in neg^n_{ins} \mid E$ is an instance of $E' \in neg^j_{ins}$, $j \leq n$, regardless literals order and variables renaming$\}$

$\cup \{ E \in neg^n_{ins} \mid E = [A, L_1,\ldots,L_m]$ and it exists an index $i \leq m$ s.t., $L_i = A \}$

The construction terminates at step r when: $P_{ins}^{r} = N_{ins}^{r} = \emptyset$
Termination is ensured if no function symbol is used. More precisely problems arises in the case of function symbols used in clauses such as: $P(f(X)) \leftarrow P(X)$. In any case it is possible to deal with such cases similarly to [Lloyd et al. 87].

Now we define the two final sets P_{ins}, N_{ins}:

$P_{ins} = \cup_{j \leq r} P^j_{ins} \setminus \{E \in P^j_{ins} \mid E$ is an instance of an E' already included in $P_{ins}\}$

Since each P^j_{ins} ensure that its elements are either unique or subsumption of elements of other preceeding P^j_{ins}, P_{ins} is necessary to obtain all possible, most general, deducible elements. Analogously:

$N_{ins} = \cup_{j \leq r} N^j_{ins} \setminus \{E \in N^j_{ins} \mid E$ is an instance of an E' already included in $N_{ins}\}$

Remember that W is an integrity constraint formula we now define two new sets:

Def15 $P^*_{ins} = \{ E \mid E \in P_{ins}$ and head(E) is an instance of an atom which occurs negatively in W $\}$

Def16 $N^*_{ins} = \{ E \mid E^* \in N_{ins}$ s.t. head(E) is an instance of an atom which occurs positively in W$\}$

These set are built to obtain all partially instantiated clauses which potentially may affect the IC. Thus N^*_{ins} and P^*_{ins} contain all those clauses whose conclusion can affect the IC.
Let us give two more definitions:

Def17 $P^{*v}_{ins} = \{B \mid E=[B,\#] \in P^{*}_{ins}\} \cup \{B \mid B$ is an atom and $\exists E \in P^{*}_{ins}$ s.t.
- $E=[A,L_1,\dots,L_n]$
- $A\theta = B$ where θ is a correct answer substitution SLDNF for $D' \cup \{\leftarrow L_1,\dots,L_n\}\}$

P^{*v}_{ins} is built by taking all elements of P^{*}_{ins} and computing exactly those atoms which are certainly true in D', probably not true in D and that can falsify W.

Analogously, let us now define N^{*}_{ins}. The idea here is to include in the set, all atoms that were true in D, might be false in D', might affect W.

Def18 $N^{*v}_{ins} = \{B \mid B$ is an atom and $\exists E \in N^{*}_{ins}$ s.t.
- $E=[A,L_1,\dots,L_n]$
- $B=A\theta$ where θ is a correct answer substitution SLDNF for $D \cup \{\leftarrow L_1,\dots,L_n\}\}$

with respect to the above construction we can now assume:

- $\forall B \in P^{*v}_{ins}$	B is true in D'	- $\forall B \in N^{*v}_{ins}$	B is true in D
- $\forall B \in P^{*v}_{ins}$	B may be false in D	- $\forall B \in N^{*v}_{ins}$	B may be false in D'
- $\forall B \in P^{*v}_{ins}$	B may affect W	- $\forall B \in N^{*v}_{ins}$	B may affect W

Let us now deal with the deletions, we will show how to construct the analogous sets for deletions:

pos_{del}	P_{del}	P^{*}_{del}	P^{*v}_{del}
neg_{del}	N_{del}	N^{*}_{del}	N^{*v}_{del}

Def19: $neg_{del}^{0} := \{[A, L_1,\dots,L_n] \mid A \leftarrow L_1\dots L_n \in Del\} \cup \{[A,\$] \mid A \leftarrow \in Del\}$

The symbol $ is used instead of # since a deletion does not guarantee that the deleted fact will be no more derivable (due to redundancy)

$neg^{n+1}_{del} := \{[B\sigma, A', L_1\sigma,\dots, L_{i-1}\sigma, L_{i+1}\sigma,\dots, L_n\sigma] \mid \exists E \in P^{n}_{del}$ with
- head (E) = A'
- $\exists$ a rule $B \leftarrow L_1,\dots,L_{i-1}, \neg A^{\sim}, L_{i+1},\dots,L_n \in D$ s. t. $A' = A^{\sim}\sigma$

$\cup \{[A, A_1,\dots,A_{i-1},A_{i+1},\dots, A_n, A'] \mid \exists E \in N^{n}_{del}$ with
- head (E) = A'
- $\exists$ a rule $B \leftarrow L_1,\dots, A^{\sim},\dots,L_n \in D$ s. t. $A' = A^{\sim}\sigma$

Def20: $pos^{0}_{del} := \{\}$

$pos^{n+1}_{del} := \{[B\sigma, A', L_1\sigma,\dots, L_{i-1}\sigma, L_{i+1}\sigma,\dots, L_n\sigma] \mid \exists E \in P^{n}_{del}$ with
- head (E) = A'
- $\exists$ a rule $B \leftarrow L_1,\dots,A^{\sim},\dots,L_n \in D$ s. t. $A' = A^{\sim}\sigma$

$\cup$ $\{[B\sigma, A', L_1\sigma,..., L_{i-1}\sigma, L_{i+1}\sigma,..., L_n\sigma] \mid \exists E \in N^n{}_{del}$ with

-head (E) = A'

- $\exists$ a rule $B \leftarrow L_1,..., \neg A^{\sim},...,L_n \in D$ s. t. $A' = A^{\sim}\sigma$

Def21 $P^n{}_{del} = pos^n{}_{del} \setminus K^n{}_p$ where

$K^n{}_p = \{E \in pos^n{}_{del} \mid$ E is instance of $E' \in neg^j{}_{ins}$, $j \leq n$, regardless literals order and variables renaming$\}$

$\cup\{ E \in pos^n{}_{del} \mid E = [A, L_1,...,L_m]$ and it exists an index $i \leq m$ s.t., $L_i = A\}$

In the same way it is possible to define

Def22 $N^n{}_{del} = neg^n{}_{del} \setminus K^n{}_N$ where

$K^n{}_N = \{ E \in neg^n{}_{del} \mid$ E is an instance of $E' \in neg^j{}_{del}$, $j \leq n$, regardless literals order and variables renaming$\}$

$\cup\{ E \in neg^n{}_{del} \mid E = [A, L_1,...,L_m]$ and it exists an index $i \leq m$ s.t., $L_i = A\}$

The construction terminates at step r when: $P_{del}{}^r = N_{del}{}^r = \varnothing$

The two final sets P_{del}, N_{del} are:

$P_{del} = \cup_{j \leq r} P^j{}_{del} \setminus \{E \in P^j{}_{del} \mid$ E is an instance of an E' already included in $P_{del}\}$

$N_{del} = \cup_{j \leq r} N^j{}_{del} \setminus \{E \in N^j{}_{del} \mid$ E is an instance of an E' already included in $N_{del}\}$

Def23 $P^*{}_{del} = \{ E \mid E \in P_{del}$ s.t. head(E) is an instance of an atom that occurs negatively in W$\}$

Def24 $N^*{}_{del} = \{ E \mid E \in N_{del}$ s.t. head(E) is an instance of an atom that occurs positively in W$\}$

Again $N^*{}_{del}$ and $P^*{}_{del}$ contain all those clauses whose conclusion can affect the IC.

Def25 $P^{*v}{}_{del} = \{B \mid E=[B,\$] \in P^*{}_{del}\} \cup \{B \mid$ B is an atom and $\exists E \in P^*{}_{del}$ s.t.

- $E=[A,L_1,...,L_n]$
- $A\theta = B$where θ is a correct answer substitution SLDNF for $D' \cup \{\leftarrow L_1,...,L_n\}$ $\}$

Def26 $N^{*v}{}_{del} = \{B \mid$ B is an atom and $\exists E \in N^*{}_{del}$ s.t.

- $E=[A,L_1,...,L_n]$
- $B=A\theta$ where θ is a correct answer substitution SLDNF for $D \cup \{\leftarrow L_1,...,L_n\}$ $\}$

with respect to the above construction we can now assume:

- $\forall B \in P^{*v}{}_{del}$ B is true in D'
- $\forall B \in P^{*v}{}_{del}$ B may be false in D
- $\forall B \in P^{*v}{}_{del}$ B may affect W

- $\forall B \in N^{*v}{}_{del}$ B is true in D
- $\forall B \in N^{*v}{}_{del}$ B may be false in D'
- $\forall B \in N^{*v}{}_{del}$ B may affect W

Remember that an integrity constraint has the following form: $W = \forall x_1 \ldots \forall x_n W'$

Def27 Let $\Theta = \{\theta \mid \theta$ is the restriction to $x_1 \ldots x_n$ of θ' where $A\theta' = L$ and
- $A \in P^{*v}_{ins}$ and L occurs negatively in W, or
- $A \in N^{*v}_{ins}$ and L occurs positively in W $\}$

Let Θ_{new} be the obtained from Θ by removing subsumed substitutions.

Def28 Let $\Psi = \{\psi \mid \psi$ is the restriction to $x_1 \ldots x_n$ of ψ' where $A\psi' = L$ and
- $A \in P^{*v}_{del}$ and L occurs negatively in W, or
- $A \in N^{*v}_{del}$ and L occurs positively in W $\}$

Let Ψ_{new} be the obtained from Ψ by removing subsumed substitutions.

4. BASIC THEOREMs

In this section the correctness of the proposed method is proved. In order to do that we will use a result from [Lloyd et al. 87] which shows that the instances, with respect to a certain preinterpretation j, of the set of atoms (P, N) computed with their method, $posinst_{D,D',J}$ and $neginst_{D,D',J}$, properly contain the difference between (suitably related) models for comp(D) and comp(D').

Def29 Let POS = $\{head(E) \mid E \in P^n_{del} \cup P^n_{ins}\}$ and NEG = $\{head(E) \mid \in N^n_{del} \cup N^n_{ins}.\}$

Proposition 0 The set POS and the set NEG are, respectively, equal to the set P and the set N as defined in [Lloyd et al. 87].

Proof: Straightforward by construction.

Thus the result of the following lemma, taken from [Lloyd et al. 87] also applies for the instances computed on the sets of atoms POS and NEG. Let E denote the equality theory.

Lemma (from [Lloyd et al. 87]) Let D and D' be stratified databases such that $D' \supseteq D$, let J be a preinterpretation of D.

a) Let M' be an interpretation based on J for D' such that $M' \cup E$ is a model for comp(D'). Then there exists an interpretation M based on J such that $M \cup E$ is a model for comp(D), $posinst_{D,D',J} \supseteq M' \setminus M$ and $neginst_{D,D',J} \supseteq M \setminus M'$.

b) Let M be an interpretation based on J for D such that $M \cup E$ is a model for comp(D). Then there exists an interpretation M' based on J such that $M' \cup E$ is a model for comp(D'), $posinst_{D,D',J} \supseteq M' \setminus M$ and $neginst_{D,D',J} \supseteq M \setminus M'$.

The above result guarantees that the two sets POS and NEG correctly capture the differences between D and D'.

Let us now prove the following proposition:

Proposition 1: If A is true in Comp (D') and A is false in Comp (D) and it exists in W an $L = \neg A^{\sim}$ s.t. $A\sigma = A^{\sim}$ then it exists a substitution δ s.t. δ subsumes σ and $A\delta \in P^{*v}_{del} \cup P^{*v}_{ins}$ (i.e. A is an instance of a B s.t. $B \in P^{*v}_{del} \cup P^{*v}_{ins}$)

Sketch of the proof: From the hypothesis and from the above lemma we have that A is an instance of an atom $A' \in$ POS, i.e. $A\delta = A'$, and therefore it exists an element $E \in P^{n}_{del} \cup P^{n}_{ins}$ s.t. head(E) = A'. Since A may violate W by construction $A\delta \in P^{*v}_{ins}$ and $A\delta \in P^{*v}_{del} \cup P^{*v}_{ins}$.
Let us remember that P^{*v}_{ins} contains all facts certainly true in D' which are in pos_{ins} and that can violate W while in P^{*v}_{del} there are all facts certainly true in D' which are in pos_{del} and that can violate W.

Proposition 2: If A is true in Comp (D) and A is false in Comp (D') and it exists in W an L s.t. $A\sigma = L$, then it exists a substitution δ s.t. δ subsumes σ and $A\delta \in N^{*v}_{ins} \cup N^{*v}_{del}$ (i.e. A is an instance of a B s.t. $B \in N^{*v}_{del} \cup N^{*v}_{ins}$).

Sketch of the proof: The proof is analogous to **proposition 1**, when considering the sets NEG, N^{*v}_{del}, N^{*v}_{ins} instead of the sets POS, P^{*v}_{del}, P^{*v}_{ins}

Def30 Let $\forall W^{\wedge}\,'\varphi$ be the simplified form of $\forall W\,'\varphi$ defined in the following way:
1) substituting each atom A =True in Comp (D')with the symbol $\mathbb{T}$ and each atom A'=False in Comp (D') with the symbol $\mathbb{F}$ and 2) applying the following absortion rules:

i) $A \wedge B \in I$ iff $B \wedge A \in I$
ii) $A \vee B \in I$ iff $B \vee A \in I$
iii) $A \wedge B \wedge A \in I$ iff $A \wedge B \in I$
iv) $A \vee B \vee A \in I$ iff $A \vee B \in I$

Proposition 3 D' satisfies $\forall W^{\wedge}\,'\varphi$ iff D' satisfies $\forall W\,'\varphi$.
proof Straightforward.

Let us describe the main theorem:

Theorem 1
Let D and D' be stratified data bases, t the transaction that when applied to D produces D'. Let t be a sequence of deletions followed by a sequence of insertions. Let $W \equiv \forall x_1 \ldots \forall x_n\, W'$ an integrity constraint in Prenex Normal Form. Let D satisfy W and Θ_{new} and Ψ_{new} defined in the previous section. Then it holds that:

i) D' satisfies W iff D' satisfies $\forall W^{\wedge}\,'\varphi$ for every $\varphi \in \Theta_{new} \cup \Psi_{new}$ where $\forall W^{\wedge}\,'\varphi$ is the simplified form of $\forall W'\varphi$.
ii) If $D' \cup \{\leftarrow \forall W^{\wedge}\,'\varphi\}$ has a SLDNF refutation for every $\varphi \in \Theta_{new} \cup \Psi_{new}$ then D' satisfies W.
iii) If $D' \cup \{\leftarrow \forall W^{\wedge}\,'\varphi\}$ has a finite failure SLDNF tree for some $\varphi \in \Theta_{new} \cup \Psi_{new}$ then D' does not satisfy W.

Proof:

i) *First half* : If D' satisfies W then D' satisfies $\forall$ W'φ for every $\varphi \in \Theta_{new} \cup \Psi_{new}$. Trivial for definition of satisfiability.

Second half: For **proposition 3** we will prove that if D' satisfies $\forall$ W'φ for every $\varphi \in \Theta_{new} \cup \Psi_{new}$ then D' satisfies W. From the hypothesis, D satisfies W that is W is true in Comp (D) and we know that $\forall \varphi \in \Theta_{new} \cup \Psi_{new}$, $\forall$ W'φ is true in Comp(D') ; we must show that W is true in Comp (D').
Let us suppose that this is not true, that is W is not true Comp (D') thus Comp (D') does not satisfy W. This means that the transaction t modified the structure of D in one of the following two cases:

1. It exists a ground atom A s.t. A is true in Comp(D') and A is false in Comp(D) and it exists in W a literal L=$\neg$B s.t. Aσ = B and $\forall$ W'σ is not true in Comp (D');
2. It exists a ground atom A s.t. A is true in Comp (D) and A is not true in Comp (D') and it exists in W a literal L = B s.t. Aσ' = B and $\forall$ W'σ' is not true in Comp (D').

1 . For hypothesis it holds **proposition 1**, that is it exists a δ such that : $A\delta \in P^{*v}_{del} \cup P^{*v}_{ins}$ this means that, by construction, it exists a substitution $\delta' \in \Theta_{new} \cup \Psi_{new}$ and δ' subsumes σ . Since $\forall \varphi \in \Theta_{new} \cup \Psi_{new}$, $\forall$ W'φ is true in Comp (D') it results $\forall$ W' δ' is true in Comp (D') and for the subsumption lemma (sect. 2.) $\forall$ W'σ is true in Comp(D') that leads to a contradiction.

2. For hypothesis it holds **proposition 2**, that is it exists a δ such that :$A\delta \in N^{*v}_{del} \cup N^{*v}_{ins}$ this means that, by construction, it exists a substitution $\delta' \in \Theta_{new} \cup \Psi_{new}$ and δ' subsumes σ' . Since $\forall \varphi \in \Theta_{new} \cup \Psi_{new}$, $\forall$ W'φ is true in Comp (D') it results $\forall$ W' δ' is true in Comp (D') and for the subsumption lemma (sect. 2.) $\forall$ W'σ' is true in Comp (D') that leads to a contradiction.

ii) Follows from i) and from the correctness of the SLDNF procedure.

iii) It is immediate too; if D' $\cup$ {$\leftarrow\forall \hat{W}'\varphi$} has a finite failure SLDNF tree for some $\varphi \in \Theta_{new} \cup \Psi_{new}$ then it holds that $\neg\forall \hat{W}'\varphi$ is a logical consequence of comp(D'). Thus for the consistency of D it follows that D ' does not satisfy W.

Two corollaries hold in case in which the transaction is either a single insertion or a single deletion.

Corollary 1. Let D a stratified data base, C a data base clause and D'=D $\cup$ {C} Let W $\equiv \forall x_1 \ldots \forall x_n$ W' an integrity constraint . Let D satisfy W and Θ_{new} be defined as in the previous section, then it holds that:

i) D' satisfies W iff D' satisfies $\forall \hat{W}'\theta$ for every $\theta \in \Theta_{new}$.
ii) If D' $\cup$ {$\leftarrow\forall \hat{W}'\theta$} has a SLDNF refutation for every $\theta \in \Theta_{new}$ then D' satisfies W.
iii) If D' $\cup${$\leftarrow\forall \hat{W}'\theta$} has a finite failure SLDNF tree for some $\theta \in \Theta_{new}$ then D' does not satisfy W.

Corollary 2. Let D a stratified data base, C a data base clause and D'=D - {C} Let $W \equiv \forall x_1 \ldots \forall x_n$ W' an integrity constraint . Let D satisfy W and Ψ_{new}. be defined as in the previous section, t then it holds:

i) D' satisfies W iff D' satisfies $\forall \hat{W'} \psi$ for every $\psi \in \Psi_{new}$.

ii) If $D' \cup \{\leftarrow \forall \hat{W'}\psi\}$ has a SLDNF refutation for every $\psi \in \Psi_{new}$ then D' satisfies W.

iii) If $D' \cup \{\leftarrow \forall \hat{W'}\psi\}$ has a finite failure SLDNF tree for some $\psi \in \Psi_{new}$ then D' does not satisfy W.

5. EXAMPLES and COMPARISONS

In this section we give some examples to compare our method to the other referred methods [Sadri&Kowalsky 87], [Lloyd et al. 87], [Decker 86]. These examples are taken from [Sadri&Kowalsky 87] . In order to compare the methods we will compare the number of resolution steps in the SLDNF trees.

Example 1

The first example considers the following DB:

1. $N(x) \leftarrow P(x)$
2. $R(x,y) \leftarrow P(x), Q(y)$
3. $Q(b)$
4. $M(a)$

$IC \equiv W \equiv N(x),R(x,y),M(y) \rightarrow$ Update : insert P(a)

In [Sadri&Kowalsky 87] it has been shown that in this case [Lloyd et al. 87] works better than [Sadri&Kowalsky 87] thus we will compare our method only with [Lloyd et al. 87].

In [Lloyd et al. 87] we have the following sets:

$pos^0 = \{P(a)\}$

$pos^1 = \{N(a), R(a,y)\}$

$P = \{P(a), N(a), R(a,y)\}$

$\Theta = \{\theta_1 = [x/a]\}$ $W\theta_1 = N(a), R(a,y), M(y) \rightarrow$ at this point it is issued the goal

$$
\begin{array}{c}
\leftarrow N(a), R(a,y), M(y) \\
| \\
P(a),R(a,y), M(y) \\
| \\
R(a,y), M(y) \\
| \\
P(a), Q(y), M(y) \\
| \\
Q(y), M(y) \\
| \\
M(b) \\
| \\
fail
\end{array}
\qquad (1)
$$

Let us show our method:

pos^0_{ins} = {[P(a),#]}

pos^1_{ins} = { [N(a), #] , [R(a,y), Q(y)]}

P_{ins} = {[P(a),#], [N(a), #] , [R(a,y), Q(y)]}

P^*_{ins} = { [N(a), #] , [R(a,y), Q(y)]}

```
← Q(y)
 |                                        (2)
succ [ y/b]
```

P^{*v}_{ins} = { N(a), R(a,b)}

$\Theta = \Theta_{new} = \{\theta_1 = [x/a]\}$

$W\theta_1$ = N(a), R(a,y), M(y) → ≡ 𝕋, R(a,y), M(y) → ≡ R(a,y), M(y) →

at this point it is issued the goal

```
← R(a,y), M(y)
       |
P(a), Q(y), M(y)                          (3)
       |
  Q(y), M(y)
       |
     M(b)
       |
     fail
```

It is easy to see that (1) is larger than (2)+(3). In particular, (3) is only a part of (1).

Example 2

Let us now show another example where our method behaves better than [Sadri&Kowalsky 87] that in turn is better than [Lloyd et al. 87] [Decker 86].

Consider the following DB:

1. R(x,y) ← P(x), Q(y)
2. S(x,y) ← R(x,y)
3. M(x) ← ¬P(x), N(x)
4. L(x,y) ← S(x,y)
3. N(a)
4. Q(b)

IC ≡ W ≡ L(x,y) → H(x,y)   Update : insert P(a)

We will consider Kowalski :

```
            P(a)
           /    \
R(a,y)← Q(y)   ¬M(a)          (1)
    |             |
  R(a,b)        succ
    |
  S(a,b)
    |
  L(a,b)
    |
  H(a,b)
    |
   fail
```

Let us see with our method:

$pos^0_{ins} = \{[P(a),\#]\} = P^0_{ins}$

$neg^0_{ins} = \{\} = N^0_{ins}$

$pos^1_{ins} = \{[R(a,y), Q(y)]\} = P^1_{ins}$

$neg^1_{ins} = \{[M(a),N(a), \neg P(a)]\} = N^1_{ins}$

$pos^2_{ins} = \{[S(a,y), R(a,y)]\} = P^2_{ins}$

$neg^2_{ins} = \{\} = N^2_{ins}$

$pos^3_{ins} = \{[L(a,y), S(a,y)]\} = P^3_{ins}$

$neg^3_{ins} = \{\} = N^3_{ins}$

$P^4_{ins} = N^4_{ins} = \{\}$ STOP

$P_{ins} = \{[P(a),\#], [R(a,y), Q(y)], [S(a,y), R(a,y)], [L(a,y), S(a,y)]\}$

$N_{ins} = \{[M(a),N(a), \neg P(a)]\}$

$P^*_{ins} = \{[L(a,y), S(a,y)]\}$ $\qquad N^*_{ins} = \{\}$

```
← S(a,y)
     |
   R(a,y)
     |
  P(a), Q(y)                  (2)
     |
    Q(y)
     |
  succ [ y/b]
```

$P^*v_{ins} = \{L(a,b)\}$

$\Theta = \Theta_{new} = \{\theta_1 = [x/a, y/b]\}$ $\qquad W\theta_1 = L(a,b) \rightarrow H(a,b) \equiv \mathbb{T} \rightarrow H(a,b) \equiv H(a,b)$

```
← H(a,b)
     |                        (3)
   fail
```

Also in this case it is easy to see that with our method we get, considering (2) +(3), a simpler tree than (1).

Example 3

Let us now show how the method works in case of updating that are deletions, in this case we will compare our method only with [Lloyd et al. 87].

1. C(a,b)
2. D(b,a)
3. E(a)
4. G(b)
5. B(b,a)
6. R(x,y) ← A(x,y)
7. A(x,y) ← B(x,y), C(x,y)
8. C(x,y) ← B(x,y), D(y,x)
9. D(x,y) ← B(x,y), E(x), G(y)
10. F(x,y) ← E(x), B(x,y)
11. C(y,x) ← D(y,x), E(x)
12. A(x,y) ← C(x,y), D(y,x)

IC ≡ W ≡ C(x,y) → A(x,y); Update : delete E(a)

In [Lloyd et al. 87] we have the following sets:

P = {E(a), D(a,y), F(a,y), C(y,a), C(a,y), A(y,a), A(a,y), R(y,a), R(a,y)}

$\Psi = \{\psi_1, \psi_2\}$; $\psi_1 = [x/a]$; $\psi_2 = [y/a]$;

$W\psi_1 = C(a,y) \rightarrow A(a,y)$

$W\psi_2 = C(x,a) \rightarrow A(x,a)$

at this point are issued the goals

```
                  ← C(a,y)
           /          |          \
succ [y/b]   B(a,y), D(y,a)   \
                  |              D(a,y) E(y)
                 fail                  |
                           B(a,y), E(a), G(y), E(y)        (1)
                              |
                             fail
```

thus we try ← A(a,b)

```
                  ← A(a,b)
                  /        \
      B(a,b), C(a,b)     C(a,b), D(b,a)            (2)
           /                   |
       fail                 D(b,a)
                               |
                             succ
```

$W\psi_1$ is satisfied

Let us prove the second instance of the constraint $W1\psi_2 = C(x,a) \rightarrow A(x,a)$:

```
              ← C(x,a)
             /         \
  B(x,a) D(a,x)       D(x,a), E(a)
        |              /        \
     D(a,b)         E(a)     B(x,a) E(x) G(a) E(a)        (3)
        |             |                |
B(a,b) E(a) G(b)    fail       E(b) G(a) E(a)
        |                              |
      fail                           fail
```

$W\psi_2$ is satisfied

Let us now use our method:

N^*_{del} = {[A(y,a), B(y,a), C(y,a)], [A(y,a), D(a,y), C(y,a)], [A(a,y), B(a,y), C(a,y)],
[A(a,y), D(y,a), C(a,y)]}

Now we construct the set N^{*v}_{del}. This set contains instances of head(N^*_{del}) that were true in Mod(D) and might be false in Mod(D'). In order to do this we issue the following goals: e.g.tail ([A(y,a), B(y,a), C(y,a)]) = B(y,a),C(y,a) thus

```
      ←B(y,a),C(y,a)                        ←D(a,y), C(y,a)
            |                                      |
         C(b,a)                          B(a,y), E(a),G(y) ,C(y,a)
         /     \                                   |
B(b,a),D(a,b)  D(b,a),E(a)                        fail
      |             |
B(a,b), E(a),G(b)  E(a)
      |             |
    fail          fail

   ←B(a,y),C(a,y)                           ←D(y,a),C(a,y)
         |                                         |
       fail                                     C(a,b)
                                                   |
                                               succ y/b
```

Thus we obtain N^{*v}_{del} = {A(a,b)}

$W \equiv C(x,y) \rightarrow A(x,y)$ $\Psi = \psi_1 = [x/a, y/b]$;

$W\psi_1 = C(a,b) \rightarrow A(a,b)$

```
           ←C(a,b)
              |                          (1')
            succ
           ←A(a,b)
           /       \                     (2')
  B(a,b), C(a,b)   C(a,b), D(b,a)
         |                |
       fail            D(b,a)
                          |
                        succ
```

$W\psi_1$ = is satisfied so does W

With respect to the previous method it is evident that we need less resolution steps at the cost of the amount of storage needed to record the N^*v_{del} set. Althought the fourth steps has not been applied, due to the particular form of the constraint, it is clear that with more general constraints formula and wider databases our method is much more convenient.

6. CONCLUSIONS

The method we have shown will be implemented to be integrated in the EDBLOG system which is a logic DBMS whose integrity checking mechanism is at present based on [Asirelli et al. 85].
Further improvements are under consideration and mainly concern an adeguate ordering of the literals in the element of the computed sets (e.g. reordering the tail from left to right, with the more instantiated first). In this work we mainly concentrated on the foundations of the method and comparisons with other methods are carried out informally on the base of examples. Anyway we believe that they can be sufficient to convince on the improvement obtained.

REFERENCES

[Apt et al. 87] Apt, K. R., Blair, H., and Walker, A., Towards a theory of Declarative Knowledge, in: J. Minker (ed.), *Foundations of Deductive Databases and Logic Programming,* Morgan Kaufman, Los Altos, 1987.
[Asirelli et al. 85] Asirelli, P., De Santis, M., Martelli, M., Integrity Constraints in Logic Data Bases, *Journal of Logic Programming*, 2 (3), 1985.
[Decker 86] Decker, H., Integrity Enforcement on Deductive Databases, *1st International Conference on Expert Database Systems,* Charleston, S.C., 1986, pp. 271-285.
[Lloyd 84] Lloyd, J. W, *Foundations of logic programming*, Symbolic Computation Series, Springer, 1984.
[Lloyd 87] Lloyd, J. W, *Foundations of logic programming*, Second Edition, Symbolic Computation Series, Springer, 1987.
[Lloyd&Topor 85] Lloyd, J. W, and Topor, R. W, A Basis for Deductive Database Systems, *J. Logic Programming*, 2 (2): 93 -109, 1985.
[Lloyd&Topor 86] Lloyd, J. W., and Topor, R. W., A Basis for Deductive Database Systems II, *J. Logic Programming* 3 (1): 55 -67, 1986.
[Lloyd et al. 87] Lloyd, J. W., Sonenberg, E.,A., Topor, R. W., Integrity Constraint Checking in Stratified Databases, *J. Logic Programming* 4 (4): 331-343, 1987.
[Nicolas 82] Nicolas, J. M., Logic for Improving Integrity Checking in relational Data Bases, *Acta Informatica* 18 (3): 227-253 (1982).
[Sadri&Kowalsky 87] Sadri, F., Kowalsky , R. A., A Theorem-Proving Approach to Database Integrity, in: J. Minker (ed.), *Foundations of Deductive Databases and Logic Programming,* Morgan Kaufman, Los Altos, 1987.

On the Composition and Decomposition of Datalog Program Mappings[1]

Guozhu Dong
Computer Science Dept, USC, LA, CA 90089-0782

Abstract The composition and decomposition of datalog program mappings are investigated for the purpose of optimization. Composability is studied using an algebraic axiom system. Also considered are (i) the decomposability of a subclass of linear recursive programs into single-rule programs; (ii) the structure of the class of prime programs; and the factorizability of bounded recursive programs into single-rule primes.

Introduction

Current research on deductive databases emphasizes the optimization of individual datalog programs (or mappings) used as queries [BaRa]. Clearly, queries or views are often computed in a compositive manner, with the top level queries computed using the compositions of the mappings defining the intermediate queries. The consideration of composition mappings offers new directions to optimizing datalog queries by using equivalence among compositive queries. (Only one of the equivalent ones needs to be evaluated for each input database.) Due to the difference at the component level, sometimes such optimization cannot be obtained without considering composition. Furthermore, two equivalent composition mappings may have different forms, thus optimization techniques not applicable in one may be applicable in the other. That is, more freedom is possible in applying existing optimization techniques on single programs. When one of the equivalent composition mappings is a program, all these composition mappings are decompositions of the program. Even in this limited case, earlier work on optimization can be improved. For example, let $P = \{R(x,y) \rightarrow R(y,x), R(x,y) \ \& \ R(y,z) \rightarrow R(x,z)\}$. Then P is optimized in Sagiv's sense [Sa]. However, P can be further optimized using decomposition. Indeed, let $P_1 = \{R(x,y) \rightarrow R(y,x)\}$ and $P_2 = \{R(x,y) \ \& \ R(y,z) \rightarrow R(x,z)\}$. Then the query P is the same as the query P_1 followed by the query P_2 [see Example 2.2]. Clearly, the latter query is more efficient since the interaction among different rules are removed.

In a sense, the composition operation generalizes "stratification" [ABW], a mechanism introduced for handling negation. Also, composition seems to capture in spirit some aspects of semantic query optimization [CFM] by combining a query and the underlying constraint.

This paper is an extended abstract of [Do1], and is organized into three sections. Section 1 reviews the preliminaries; Section 2 considers the composability of datalog mappings; and Section 3 concerns decomposition, primes and factorization.

---

[1]Supported by the National Science Foundation under grant CCR-86-18907.

1 Preliminaries

We present the formalisms of relational databases, datalog programs, mappings (or datalog queries) and the composition of datalog mappings (or compositive datalog queries).

Throughout the paper we shall assume three pairwise disjoint infinite sets of abstract elements called constants (or domain values), relation names, and variables respectively; and each relation name R has an arity. We shall usually use integers to denote constants, R (possibly with a subscript) relation names, and v, x, y, and z (possibly with a subscript) variables.

For all relation names R and constants $a_1, \cdots, a_k$ (where k is the arity of R), $R(a_1, \cdots, a_k)$ is a fact. A database is a finite set of facts.

Let *Ancestor* and R be relation names with arity 2. Then $\{R(1,2), R(2,3), Ancestor(1,3)\}$ is a database.

The definition in the literature of a Horn clause varies, depending on the purpose at hand. Usually the difference arises in whether or not the constant, equality and inequality symbols are allowed. For simplicity, the definition which allows no constant, equality and inequality symbols is adopted here.

For all relation names R and variables $v_1, \cdots, v_k$ (where k is the arity of R), $R(v_1, \cdots, v_k)$ is a formula. A Horn clause (or rule) is an expression of the form $A_1\&...\&A_m \rightarrow H$, where $m \geq 1$, A_1 $\cdots$, A_m and H are formulas, and each variable appearing in H appears in some A_i. For each rule $r = A_1\&...\&A_m \rightarrow H$, $A_1\&...\&A_m$ and H are called the body and the head, resp., of r, and denoted $B(r)$ and $H(r)$, resp. We also write $B(r)$ as $\{A_1, \cdots, A_m\}$ and r as $B(r) \rightarrow H(r)$.

Suppose *Ancestor* and R are relation names, each with arity 2. Then "$R(x,y) \rightarrow R(y,x)$" and "$Ancestor(x,y)\&Ancestor(y,z) \rightarrow Ancestor(x,z)$" are Horn clauses. However, "$R(x,y) \rightarrow R(x)$," "$\rightarrow R(x,y)$," "$R(x,x) \rightarrow R(1,1)$," and "$R(x,y) \rightarrow R(x,z)$" are not Horn clauses.

Definition. A datalog program (or simply program) is a finite set of Horn clauses.

$\{Ancestor(x,y)\&Ancestor(y,z) \rightarrow Ancestor(x,z), R(x,y) \rightarrow R(y,x)\}$ is a datalog program.

An assignment is a mapping from variables to constants. For each assignment τ and formula $R(x_1, \cdots, x_k)$, let $\tau(R(x_1, \cdots, x_k))$ denote the fact $R(\tau(x_1), \cdots, \tau(x_k))$.

For each datalog program, one can associate a mapping on all the databases of interest.

Definition. Suppose P is a datalog program.

(a) Let P^1 be the mapping defined (for each database D) by $P^1(D) = D \cup D'$, where $D' = \{\phi(H(r)) \mid \text{there exist } r \text{ in } P \text{ and assignment } \phi \text{ such that } \phi(B(r)) \subseteq D\}$.

(b) Suppose i is a positive integer such that P^i is already defined. Let $P^{i+1} = P^1 \circ P^i$.

(c) Finally, let P^ω (called a datalog mapping) be the mapping defined (for each database D) by $P^\omega(D) = \bigcup_{i=1}^{\infty} P^i(D)$.

Several points should be noted here. First, some authors [Ll] denotes the mappings P^i and P^ω as $T_P\uparrow i$ and $T_P\uparrow\omega$ respectively. Second, for each input, P^ω returns the least fixpoint containing the input

xample 1.1 Consider the datalog program $P = \{R(x,y)\ \&\ R(y,z) \rightarrow R(x,z),\ R(x,y) \rightarrow R(y,x)\}$ ıd the database $D = \{R(1,2),\ R(2,3),\ R(3,4)\}$. Then,

$$P^1(D) = D \cup \{R(1,3), R(2,4), R(2,1), R(3,2), R(4,3)\},$$

$$P^2(D) = \{R(i,j) \mid 1 \leq i,j \leq 4 \textit{ and } (i,j) \neq (4,1)\}, \text{ and}$$

$$P^\omega(D) = P^3(D) = \{R(i,j) \mid 1 \leq i,j \leq 4\}.\square$$

Let P and Q be programs. Then P logically implies Q, written $P \vdash Q$, if $D = P^\omega(D)$ implies $= Q^\omega(D)$ for all D. If $P \vdash Q$ and $Q \vdash P$, then P and Q are logically equivalent (denoted $P \equiv Q$).

For all mappings h from A into B and g from C into D, with $B \subseteq C$, the mapping $g \circ h$ (called e composition of g and h) is from A to D and defined by $g \circ h(x) = g(h(x))$ for all x in A. (Parentheses e omitted for grouping purposes since $\circ$ is associative.)

The definition of composition is quite general. However, we shall limit ourselves to datalog and lated mappings. Thus all the domains A, B, C and D are equal to the set of databases.

efinition. The class of composition mappings is defined recursively as follows: (i) Each datalog mapng is a composition mapping; and (ii) If q_1 and q_2 are composition mappings, then so is $q_1 \circ q_2$.

Composability of datalog programs

haracterizations and sufficiency conditions for composability are given. Typical conditions are idem-tency, preservation, and commutativity. Also given are invariant properties of composability.

Instead of proving the composability results for datalog programs directly, an axiom system (called a omposition system") approximating the datalog mappings is introduced and the results are established this more general framework. Using this approach, cleaner proofs are obtained. Furthermore, the eory developed can be applied to another situation studied in [Do].

1 Motivation

efinition. Suppose P_i $(1 \leq i \leq m)$ are datalog programs. If there is a datalog program P such that $= P_1^\omega \circ \cdots \circ P_m^\omega$, then $(P_1, \cdots, P_m)$ is composable and P is a composite of $(P_1, \cdots, P_m)$.

Clearly, if P is a composite of $(P_1, \cdots, P_m)$ and $Q^\omega = P^\omega$, then Q is also a composite of $(P_1, \cdots, P_m)$. ı the other hand, suppose P_i $(1 \leq i \leq m)$ and Q_j $(1 \leq j \leq n)$ are datalog programs such that $\circ \cdots \circ P_m^\omega = Q_1^\omega \circ \cdots \circ Q_n^\omega$. Then $(P_1, \cdots, P_m)$ is composable iff $(Q_1, \cdots, Q_n)$ is.

There are several reasons for considering composability. Most important of all, the results for mposability shed light on the "decomposition" of datalog programs (defined formally in Section 3), ıich in turn can be used to gain efficiency. (Indeed, Theorem 2.1, Corollarys 2.2 and 2.3, and eorems 2.2 and 2.3 can be reformulated for decomposability.) From a computational point of view, it is advantageous to know if one program is the composite of some other programs since the composition mapping, carried out in a stratified fashion, is more efficient. (Indeed, "decomposing" P into parts P_1 and P_2 may minimize the interactions among its components P_1 and P_2.)

In contrast, the "horizontal decomposition" of P^ω into $P_1^\omega + P_2^\omega$ was discussed in [LaMa]. (For mappings h and g over a domain with a union operation $\cup$, $(h+g)(x)$ is defined to be $h(x) \cup g(x)$.) Our "vertical" decomposability generalizes their "horizontal decomposability," that is, $P^\omega = P_1^\omega + P_2^\omega$ implies $P^\omega = P_1^\omega \circ P_2^\omega$ when $P = P_1 \cup P_2$.

2.2 Characterization

We start out with the definition of our axiom system.

Notation. Let $h_1, \cdots, h_n$ be mappings over a poset S. Then the mapping $(\sqcup_{i=1}^n h_i)$ is defined (for each x in S) by $(\sqcup_{i=1}^n h_i)(x)$ is the smallest y in S such that $x \subseteq y$ and $h_i(y) = y$ for each i $(1 \leq i \leq n)$, if such y exists, and is undefined otherwise.

Definition. A set $\mathcal{H}$ of total mappings over a poset S is a composition system if:

Increasing law. For each h in $\mathcal{H}$ and x in S, $x \subseteq h(x)$.

Monotonic law. If h is in $\mathcal{H}$ and x and y are in S such that $x \subseteq y$, then $h(x) \subseteq h(y)$.

Idempotent law. For each h in $\mathcal{H}$, $h \circ h = h$.

Finitely reachable law. For all $h_1, \cdots, h_n$ in $\mathcal{H}$, $\sqcup_{i=1}^n h_i$ is in $\mathcal{H}$. And for each x in S, there exists a positive integer m such that, for each integer $k \geq m$, $(\sqcup_{i=1}^n h_i)(x) = (h_1 \circ \cdots \circ h_n)^k(x)$.

Proposition 2.1 *The set of datalog mappings is a composition system.*

Similar to datalog mappings, one can define composability for composition systems (omitted).

Our characterization theorem for composability encompasses three equivalences. The first equivalence, (b) in the theorem, is idempotency. The second, (c), is "absorption on the left." From a computational point of view, (c) asserts that P_i^ω computations are redundant in the presence of $P_1^\omega \circ \cdots \circ P_m^\omega$. The third, (d), says the composite (if it exists) is $\cup_{i=1}^m P_i$ up to logical equivalence. (Theorem 5.13 of [ABW] gives a sufficiency condition using a notion of "local" for when (d) holds.)

All results in the rest of this section holds for composition systems, although they are stated for datalog programs only. That is, their proofs only require the conditions as provided by the axioms of composition systems.

Theorem 2.1 (Characterization) *For all programs $P_1, \cdots, P_m$, the following conditions are equivalent:*

(a) $(P_1, \cdots, P_m)$ *is composable;*

(b) $P_1^\omega \circ \cdots \circ P_m^\omega$ *is idempotent;*

(c) $P_i^\omega \circ P_1^\omega \circ \cdots \circ P_m^\omega = P_1^\omega \circ \cdots \circ P_m^\omega$ *for each* i, $1 \leq i \leq m$; *and*

(d) $(P_1 \cup \cdots \cup P_m)^\omega = P_1^\omega \circ \cdots \circ P_m^\omega$.

roof. Clearly, (d) implies (a). We shall prove that (a) implies (b), (b) implies (c), and (c) implies (d).

We first show that (a) implies (b). Thus suppose $(P_1, \cdots, P_m)$ is composable. Then there exists a atalog program P such that $P^\omega = P_1^\omega \circ \cdots \circ P_m^\omega$. Since P^ω is idempotent, so is $P_1^\omega \circ \cdots \circ P_m^\omega$. Hence (b) olds.

To prove that (b) implies (c), suppose that

$$P_1^\omega \circ \cdots \circ P_m^\omega \textit{ is idempotent.} \tag{1}$$

et D be an arbitrary database and i $(1 \le i \le m)$ be fixed. Then

$$\begin{aligned} P_1^\omega \circ \cdots \circ P_m^\omega(D) &\subseteq P_i^\omega \circ P_1^\omega \circ \cdots \circ P_m^\omega(D), \text{ by the increasing law} \\ &\subseteq P_1^\omega \circ \cdots \circ P_m^\omega \circ P_1^\omega \circ \cdots \circ P_m^\omega(D), \text{ by the increasing law and the monotonic law} \\ &\subseteq P_1^\omega \circ \cdots \circ P_m^\omega \circ P_1^\omega \circ \cdots \circ P_m^\omega(D), \text{ by the increasing law} \\ &= P_1^\omega \circ \cdots \circ P_m^\omega(D), \text{ by (1).} \end{aligned}$$

ence, $P_1^\omega \circ \cdots \circ P_m^\omega(D) = P_i^\omega \circ P_1^\omega \circ \cdots \circ P_m^\omega(D)$. Therefore $P_i^\omega \circ P_1^\omega \circ \cdots \circ P_m^\omega = P_1^\omega \circ \cdots \circ P_m^\omega$, and (c) proven.

To see that (c) implies (d), suppose

$$P_i^\omega \circ P_1^\omega \circ \cdots \circ P_m^\omega = P_1^\omega \circ \cdots \circ P_m^\omega \tag{2}$$

r each i, $1 \le i \le m$. Let D be an arbitrary database. By the finitely reachable law, there exists me integer n such that $(\cup_{i=1}^m P_i)^\omega(D) = (P_1^\omega \circ \cdots \circ P_m^\omega)^n(D)$. Applying (2) repeatedly, it follows that $(P_1^\omega \circ \cdots \circ P_m^\omega)^n(D) = P_1^\omega \circ \cdots \circ P_m^\omega(D)$. Thus, $(\cup_{i=1}^m P_i)^\omega(D) = P_1^\omega \circ \cdots \circ P_m^\omega(D)$, and (d) holds. □

The question arises: Is the composition of two datalog mappings a datalog mapping? The answer general is no.

xample 2.1 Let $P_1 = \{R(x,y) \rightarrow R(y,x)\}$ and $P_2 = \{R(x,y) \;\&\; R(y,z) \rightarrow R(x,z)\}$. Then $P_1^\omega \circ P_2^\omega$ $(P_1 \cup P_2)^\omega$. (Consider $D = \{R(1,2), R(2,3)\}$.) Thus, (P_1, P_2) is not composable by Theorem 2.1. □

Since (P_1, P_2) in the above example is not composable, there is no datalog program P such that $^\omega = P_1^\omega \circ P_2^\omega$. Thus, the set of composition mappings is more expressive than the datalog mappings.

We now present three corollaries to Theorem 2.1. The first says that all composites of a sequence datalog programs are logically equivalent, and the second that a sequence of datalog programs is mposable if a certain subsequence of it is. The third characterizes the composability of two datalog ograms using the notion of "preservation," a concept similar in spirit to dependency preservation [Sa].

orollary 2.1 *Let Q and P_i $(1 \le i \le m)$ be datalog programs. Then $Q \equiv \cup_{i=1}^m P_i$ if Q is a composite of $P_1, \cdots, P_m)$. Furthermore, all composites (if any) of $(P_1, \cdots, P_m)$ are logically equivalent.*

orollary 2.2 *For all programs P_i $(1 \le i \le n)$ and m integers k_j $(1 \le k_1 < \cdots < k_m \le n)$ such that $\cup_{i=1}^n P_i \equiv \cup_{j=1}^m P_{k_j}$, $(P_1, \cdots, P_n)$ is composable if $(P_{k_1}, \cdots, P_{k_m})$ is. In this case, each composite of the tter is a composite of the former.*

Using Corollary 2.2, it can be shown that composability is invariant under replacement of the par-ticipating programs by appropriate logically "stronger" programs. That is, if $(P_1, \cdots, P_n)$ is composable Q is a program and j is an integer such that $\cup_{i=1}^{n} P_i \vdash Q$ and $Q \vdash P_j$, then $(P_1, \cdots, P_{j-1}, Q, P_{j+1}, \cdots, P_n$ is also composable.

Definition. A datalog program P_1 is said to preserve another datalog program P_2, denoted $P_1 \vdash_p P_2$, i $P_2^\omega(P_1^\omega(D)) = P_1^\omega(D)$ for $P_2^\omega(D) = D$.

$P_1 \vdash_p P_2$ if $P_1 \vdash P_2$ or $P_2 \vdash P_1$. Also, $P_1 \vdash_p P_2$ if there is no common relation name which occurs i both P_1 and P_2. In the latter case, it is the "logical independence" that causes P_1 to preserve P_2.

Corollary 2.3 *For all datalog programs P_1 and P_2, (P_1, P_2) is composable iff P_1 preserves P_2.*

Example 2.2 Let P_1 and P_2 be as in Example 2.1 and $P = P_1 \cup P_2$. By using Corollary 2.3, we ca prove that (P_2, P_1) is composable by showing that $P_2 \vdash_p P_1$. □

In passing, we note that the composability results can be used to establish equivalence betwee different composition mapping representations. For example, suppose P_1, P_2 and Q are programs suc that $P_1 \vdash_p Q$ and $Q \vdash_p P_2$. By Theorem 2.1 (d) and Corollary 2.3, it is easily seen that $(P_1 \cup Q)^\omega \circ P_2^\omega =$ $P_1^\omega \circ (P_2 \cup Q)^\omega = (P_1 \cup Q)^\omega \circ (P_2 \cup Q)^\omega = P_1^\omega \circ Q^\omega \circ P_2^\omega$. Also, new equalities can be obtained from ol ones. For instance, if q is a composition mapping and P_1, P_2 and Q are programs such that $P_1 \vdash_p Q$ $P_2 \vdash_p Q$ and $q \circ P_1^\omega = q \circ P_2^\omega$, then $q \circ (P_1 \cup Q)^\omega = q \circ (P_2 \cup Q)^\omega$.

2.3 Closure properties of composability

We first establish the invariance of composability under union.

Theorem 2.2 *For all datalog programs P_i $(1 \leq i \leq n)$,*

(a) $(\cup_{i=1}^{n-1} P_i, P_n)$ is composable if (P_i, P_n) is composable for each i, $1 \leq i < n$; and

(b) $(P_1, \cup_{i=2}^{n} P_i)$ is composable if (P_1, P_i) is composable for each i, $1 < i \leq n$.

Proof. By induction, we only prove the proposition for $n = 3$. We consider (b), (a) being similar. Thu suppose (P_1, P_i) is composable for each i, $2 \leq i \leq 3$. By Theorem 2.1,

$$P_i^\omega \circ P_1^\omega \circ P_i^\omega = P_1^\omega \circ P_i^\omega \qquad (1$$

for each i, $2 \leq i \leq 3$. By the idempotent law, $P_1^\omega \circ P_1^\omega \circ (P_2 \cup P_3)^\omega = P_1^\omega \circ (P_2 \cup P_3)^\omega$. By Theorem 2.1 (c it suffices to show that $(P_2 \cup P_3)^\omega \circ P_1^\omega \circ (P_2 \cup P_3)^\omega = P_1^\omega \circ (P_2 \cup P_3)^\omega$. To this end, let D be an arbitrar database. By the finitely reachable law, there exists an integer k such that $(P_2 \cup P_3)^\omega(P_1^\omega \circ (P_2 \cup P_3)^\omega(D)) =$ $(P_2^\omega \circ P_3^\omega)^k(P_1^\omega \circ (P_2 \cup P_3)^\omega(D))$. Thus, it is enough to show that $P_i^\omega \circ P_1^\omega \circ (P_2 \cup P_3)^\omega(D) = P_1^\omega \circ (P_2 \cup P_3)^\omega(D$ for each i, $2 \leq i \leq 3$. We shall show the above equation for $i = 2$, the case for $i = 3$ following by symmetr By the finitely reachable law, there exists an integer m such that

$$(P_2 \cup P_3)^\omega(D) = (P_2^\omega \circ P_3^\omega)^m(D). \tag{2}$$

en

$$\begin{aligned} P_2^\omega \circ P_1^\omega \circ (P_2 \cup P_3)^\omega(D) &= P_2^\omega \circ P_1^\omega \circ (P_2^\omega \circ P_3^\omega)^m(D), \text{ by (2)} \\ &= P_1^\omega \circ P_2^\omega \circ P_3^\omega \circ (P_2^\omega \circ P_3^\omega)^{m-1}(D), \text{ by (1)} \\ &= P_1^\omega \circ (P_2 \cup P_3)^\omega(D), \text{ by (2)}. \end{aligned}$$

erefore $(P_2 \cup P_3)^\omega \circ P_1^\omega \circ (P_2 \cup P_3)^\omega = P_1^\omega \circ (P_2 \cup P_3)^\omega$, and thus (b) is verified. □

Using Theorem 2.2, we can establish a result on the composability of a sequence of datalog programs sed on the composability of its subsequences of length two.

eorem 2.3 *For all datalog programs P_i $(1 \le i \le n)$, $(P_1, \cdots, P_n)$ is composable if (P_i, P_j) is compos-le for each i and j, $1 \le i < j \le n$.*

4 Commutativity

efinition. Datalog programs P and Q are called <u>commutative</u> if $P^\omega \circ Q^\omega = Q^\omega \circ P^\omega$.

Clearly, datalog programs using disjoint sets of relation names are commutative. For a "nontrivial" ample of commutative programs, consider $P_1 = \{R(x,y) \ \& \ R(y,z) \rightarrow R(y,y)\}$ and $P_2 = \{R(x,y) \ \&$ $y,z) \rightarrow R(x,z)\}$.

heorem 2.4 *For all programs P_1 and P_2, (P_2, P_1) and (P_1, P_2) are composable iff P_1 and P_2 are mmutative.*

The "if" can be generalized. Indeed, suppose $(P_1, \cdots, P_m)$ and $(Q_1, \cdots, Q_n)$ are composable. Then $\circ \cdots \circ P_m^\omega = Q_1^\omega \circ \cdots \circ Q_n^\omega$ if $\cup_{i=1}^m P_i \equiv \cup_{i=1}^n Q_i$. In particular, the equation holds if $P_1^\omega \circ \cdots \circ P_m^\omega$ is a rmutation of $Q_1^\omega \circ \cdots \circ Q_n^\omega$.

Not every pair of datalog programs is commutative. (Consider $\{R(x,y) \rightarrow R(y,x)\}$ and $\{R(x,y) \ \&$ $y,z) \rightarrow R(x,z)\}$.)

orollary 2.4 *For all programs P_i $(1 \le i \le 3)$, $(P_3, P_1 \cup P_2)$ and $(P_1 \cup P_2, P_3)$ are composable if P_3 mmutes with P_1 and P_2.*

orollary 2.5 *For all programs P_i $(1 \le i \le 3)$, P_3 commutes with $P_1 \cup P_2$ if P_3 commutes with both P_1 d P_2.*

Decomposition, primes and factorization

nis section presents an investigation of three closely related topics regarding decomposition, including e decomposition of a special class of linear recursive programs into single-rule programs; the structure the class of primes; and the factorizability of programs in three special classes ("bounded recursive," ingle-body" and "local") into single-rule primes.

3.1 Decomposition of strongly linear programs

Definition. A datalog mapping P^ω is decomposable if there are programs $P_1, \cdots, P_n$ such that $P^\omega = P_1^\omega \circ \cdots \circ P_n^\omega$. In this case, we say P^ω is decomposable into $P_1^\omega \circ \cdots \circ P_n^\omega$; or $P_1^\omega \circ \cdots \circ P_n^\omega$ is a decomposition of P^ω. The decomposition is nontrivial if $P_i^\omega \neq P^\omega$ for each i $(1 \leq i \leq n)$.

As mentioned earlier, decomposition is a method useful for minimizing the unwanted interactions among the rules in a program in the evaluation process. This method is especially beneficial when the programs in the decomposition are nicer in some sense, e.g., when the programs are smaller than the original. The best one can hope for is to obtain decompositions into single-rule programs, since no interaction is present among different rules in single-rule programs. (However, interactions may exist around one rule.)

Notation. For all r_1 and r_2, write $r_1 \succ r_2$ if the relation name occurring in $H(r_2)$ occurs in $B(r_1)$.

Definition. Suppose P is a program. For all rules r_1 and r_2 in P, r_1 is said to depend on r_2 (with respect to P), denoted $r_1 \succ^P r_2$, if either $r_1 \succ r_2$, or there is a rule r in P such that $r_1 \succ^P r$ and $r \succ^P r_2$

Thus, r_1 depends on r_2 if the evaluations of r_2 may eventually "trigger" computations using r_1.

Definition. A rule r in a program P is terminal if r does not depend on itself; and nonterminal otherwise. A relation name is recursive in a program P if it occurs in the head of a nonterminal rule in P.

Definition. A program P is linear if, for each nonterminal rule r in P, there is at most one recursive relation name occurring in $B(r)$. A program P is strongly linear if it is linear and, for each nonterminal rule r in P, there is exactly one nonterminal rule r' in P such that $r \succ r'$.

Linear programs are believed to cover most real life programs, and have been studied by a number of authors [BaRa, Va].

Example 3.1 Consider the program $P = \{r_0, r_1, r_2, r_3\}$, where

$$r_0 = R_1(x,y)\&R_2(y,z,y) \to R_0(x,z),\ r_1 = R_0(x,y)\&R_3(y,z) \to R_1(x,z),$$
$$r_2 = R_0(x,y)\&R_2(y,x,y) \to R_4(y,x), \text{ and } r_3 = R_5(y,x)\&R_6(x,x,z) \to R_0(x,y).$$

Then $r_0 \succ r_1$, $r_1 \succ r_0$, $r_1 \succ r_3$, $r_3 \not\succ r_1$, $r_0 \succ^P r_3$. The rule r_3 is terminal, whereas r_0 is not. Furthermore, P is strongly linear. For $r = R_0(x,y)\&R_6(y,x,z) \to R_1(x,z)$, $P \cup \{r\}$ is not strongly linear. □

Lemma 3.1 *Suppose Q is a strongly linear program. If $r \succ^Q r'$ for all r and r' in Q, then there is an effectively constructible decomposition of Q into at most $2\#(Q)$ single-rule programs, of which exactly one is recursive.*

Lemma 3.2 *For all programs $P_1, \cdots, P_m$, if $r_i \not\succ r_j$ for all i and j $(1 \leq i < j \leq m)$ and rules r_i in P_i and r_j in P_j, then $(\cup_{i=1}^m P_i)^\omega = P_m^\omega \circ \cdots \circ P_1^\omega$.*

We are now able to present the major result.

Theorem 3.1 *Each strongly linear program P is effectively decomposable into at most $2\#(P)$ single-rule programs.*

roof. Let P be a strongly linear program. For each rule r in P, let Q_r denote the set $\{r, r' \text{ in } P \mid r \succ^P r'$ ıd $r' \succ^P r\}$. For all r and r' in P, we write $Q_r \succ Q_{r'}$ if there are r_1 in Q_r and r_1' in $Q_{r'}$ such that $\succ r_1'$. Clearly, $Q_r \succ Q_{r'}$ and $Q_{r'} \succ Q_r$ implies that $Q_r = Q_{r'}$. Let $\mathcal{P} = \{Q_r \mid r \text{ in } P\}$ and $m = \#(\mathcal{P})$. et $r_1, \cdots, r_m$ be defined as follows:

(i) r_1 is in P such that $Q_{r_1} \not\succ Q$ for any Q in $\mathcal{P}$; and

(ii) Suppose $r_1, \cdots, r_k$ are defined for an integer k $(1 \le k < m)$. Let r_{k+1} be in P such that $_{r_{k+1}} \not\succ Q$ for any Q in $\mathcal{P} - \{Q_{r_1}, \cdots Q_{r_k}\}$.

Clearly, $\cup_{i=1}^m Q_{r_i} = P$. Furthermore, $r_i' \not\succ r_j'$ for all i and j $(1 \le i < j \le m)$ and rules r_i' in Q_{r_i} and in Q_{r_j}. By Lemma 3.2, $P^\omega = Q_{r_m}^\omega \circ \cdots \circ Q_{r_1}^\omega$. For each i, if Q_{r_i} is not a single-rule program, then it is fectively decomposable into at most $2\#(Q_{r_i})$ single-rule programs by Lemma 3.1. Replace $Q_{r_i}^\omega$ by the ecomposition thus constructed. Then the final decomposition is effectively obtained, and contains at ıost $2\#(P)$ programs. □

We now give a tight bound on the number of recursive programs in the decomposition provided in ıe above proof. We call a subset Q of a program P a cluster in P if $r_1 \succ^P r_2$ for all r_1 and r_2 in Q; and is a maximal cluster if there is no proper superset of Q which is also a cluster in P. By Lemma 3.1, r each cluster there is exactly one recursive program in its decomposition. Thus, there is at most ne recursive program in the final decomposition of P for each maximal cluster. Hence, the number of ecursive programs is bounded by the number of maximal clusters in P.

xample 3.1 (continued). For the program P, the decomposition as constructed in the proof of heorem 3.1 is $Q_4^\omega \circ Q_2^\omega \circ Q^\omega \circ Q_3^\omega \circ Q_2^\omega \circ Q_1^\omega$, where $Q_1 = \{r_3\}$, $Q_2 = \{r_1\}$, $Q_3 = \{r_0\}$, $Q = R_0(x, y_1) \& R_3(y_1, y) \& R_2(y, z, y) \to R_0(x, z)\}$, and $Q_4 = \{r_2\}$. □

.2 Prime programs

Ve study when a program can (or cannot) be decomposed nontrivially. Three major results and several ıformative examples are presented.

efinition. A program P is <u>composite</u> if it has a nontrivial decomposition; and <u>prime</u> otherwise.

otation. For each rule $r = B(r) \to R(y_1, \cdots, y_n)$, one-to-one assignment τ, and fact $f = R(c_1, \cdots, c_n)$ $P^\omega(\tau(B(r))) - \tau(B(r))$ (where $P = \{r\}$), let $r_{f,\tau}$ (or simply r_f if no confusion arises) denote the rule

$$B(r) \to R(\tau^{-1}(c_1), \cdots, \tau^{-1}(c_n)).$$

Clearly $r \vdash r_f$. However, the converse does not hold in general. (Consider the rule in (c) of xample 3.2.)

efinition. A program P is called <u>symmetric</u> if P is of the form $\{r\}$, and there exists a one-to-one ssignment τ such that $r_{f,\tau} \equiv r$ for each fact f in $P^\omega(\tau(B(r))) - \tau(B(r))$.

From the definition of symmetric, it seems that one needs to test the condition for all one-to-one ssignments until a suitable witness is found. Happily, it can be verified that this is not the case.

Example 3.2 We now present two types of symmetric programs and exhibit a nonsymmetric program.

(a) For each prime number p, the "permutation" program $\{R(x_1,\cdots,x_p) \to R(x_2,\cdots,x_p,x_1)\}$ is symmetric.

(b) Suppose τ_c is a one-to-one assignment. For each program $P = \{r\}$ such that $\#(P(\tau_c(B(R)))) = \#(\tau_c(B(R))) + 1$, P is symmetric since $r_f = r$ for each f in $P(\tau_c(B(R))) - \tau_c(B(R))$. In particular, the transitive closure program $\{R(x,y)\&R(y,z) \to R(x,z)\}$ is symmetric.

(c) The program $Q = \{r\}$ is not symmetric, where

$$r = R(x_1,x_2)\&R(x_2,x_3)\&R(y_1,y_2)\&R(y_2,y_3) \to R(x_3,y_3),$$

and x_1 and y_1 may be equal (tree) or distinct (forest of paths). □

We are now ready to present our first major result.

Theorem 3.2 *Each symmetric program is prime.*

Example 3.2 (cont). The types of programs given in (a) and (b) are prime by Theorem 3.2. □

Although the converse of the above theorem remains open, it seems very likely that it is true.

Conjecture. A single-rule program is prime iff it is symmetric.

Our next result shows that there are arbitrarily large primes.

Definition. A program P is <u>nonredundant</u> if (a) $P \not\equiv (P - \{r\})$ for each r in P, and (b) for each r in P (with $\#(B(r)) \geq 2$) and F in $B(r)$, $P \not\equiv (P \cup \{r_0\} - \{r\})$, where $r_0 = (B(r) - \{F\}) \to H(r)$.

In a sense, a large nonredundant program is indeed large since no part can be eliminated.

Theorem 3.3 *Arbitrarily large primes (in terms of rules) exists. More precisely, for each integer $n \geq 2$, there is a nonredundant prime program with n rules over n binary relation names.*

Proof. Consider the case for $n = 2$, the general case being similar but more complicated. Intuitively, we shall construct a program with two rules. For each rule, its body contains all but one of the formulas over three variables, and its head is the missing formula. Formally, let R_1 and R_2 be binary relation names. For each i ($1 \leq i \leq 2$), let r_i be defined by $B(r_i) = \{R_k(x_j,x_\ell) \mid 1 \leq k \leq 2,\ 1 \leq j,\ell \leq 3\} - \{R_i(x_1,x_3)\}$ and $H(r_i) = R_i(x_1,x_3)$. Let $P = \{r_1,r_2\}$. Then P is prime. □

Surprisingly, even single-rule programs can be composite.

Example 3.3 Consider $\{R(x_1,x_2)\&R(x_2,x_3)\&R(x_3,x_3)\&R(x_3,x_4)\&R(x_4,x_5) \to R(x_1,x_5)\}$. □

More surprisingly, for each integer k, there is a single-rule program which is nontrivially decomposable into k primes. (This example makes use of the arity of a relation.)

Example 3.4 Let p_1, $\cdots$, p_k be k distinct prime numbers and $\{x_j^i \mid 1 \leq i \leq k, 1 \leq j \leq p_i\}$ a set of $\Sigma_{i=1}^k p_i$ variables. Consider $\{R(x_1^1,\cdots,x_{p_1}^1,\cdots,x_1^k,\cdots,x_{p_k}^k) \to R(x_2^1,\cdots,x_{p_1}^1,x_1^1,\cdots,x_2^k,\cdots,x_{p_k}^k,x_1^k)\}$. □

Each nonredundant nonrecursive program containing at least two rules is composite. However, the ;uation for recursive programs is very intricate. In order to present the major theorem for when a ogram is composite, some essential preliminary symbolisms are needed.

Intuitively, we need a notation which denotes the most general substitution of formulas in the body a rule by the bodies of some other rules.

We shall assume the knowledge of some auxiliary symbolisms from automatic theorem proving, cluding substitution, unifier, and most general unifier [ChLe]. For each rule r and one-to-one mapping on variables, the rule $\mu(r)$ is a new copy of r.

otation. Suppose (a) r_1 and $r_2 = H_1\&\cdots\&H_m \to H$ are rules, and (b) $j_1, \cdots, j_\ell$ are distinct integers $\leq j_1, \cdots, j_\ell, \leq m$), such that H_{j_i} and $H(r_1)$ are unifiable for each i ($1 \leq i \leq \ell$). For each i ($1 \leq i \leq \ell$), t r_1^i be a new copy of r_1 using new variables. Let σ be a mgu for $(H(r_1^1), \cdots, H(r_1^\ell))$ and $(H_{j_1}, \cdots, H_{j_\ell})$. hen $r_2[r_1, j_1, \cdots, j_\ell]$ denote the rule $\sigma(A_1)\&\cdots\&\sigma(A_m) \to \sigma(H)$, where, for each k ($1 \leq k \leq m$), $_k = H_k$ if k is not in $\{j_1, \cdots, j_\ell\}$; and $A_k = B(r_1^i)$ if $k = j_i$ for some i ($1 \leq i \leq \ell$).

Note that not all formulas unifiable with H_1 need be replaced.

From the semantics of P^1, it is easily seen that the new rule $r_2[r_1, j_1, \cdots, j_\ell]$ is independent of the ıoice of new copies of r_1 (up to logical equivalence).

xample 3.5 Consider the two rules $r_1 = R_1(x,y)\&R(y,z) \to R_1(x,z)$ and $r_2 = R(x,y)\&R_1(y,z) \to$ (x,z). Then $r_2[r_1, 2] = R(x,y)\&R_1(y,y_1)\&R(y_1,z) \to R(x,z)$. □

otation. For each program P and rule r_1 in P, let $P_{[r_1]}$ denote the program $\{r[r_1, j_1, \cdots, j_\ell] \mid r =$ $_1\&\cdots\&H_m \to H$ in P, and $H(r_1)$ unifiable with H_{j_s} for each s, $1 \leq s \leq \ell\}$.

xample 3.5 (cont). For $P = \{r_1, r_2\}$, $P_{[r_1]} = \{r_1[r_1, 1], r_2[r_1, 2]\}$. □

We are now ready to present our major theorem for when a program is composite.

heorem 3.4 *Let P be a nonredundant program consisting of at least two rules. If there exists a rule in P such that* $(P - \{r_0\}) \cup P_{[r_0]} \not\vdash r_0$, *then P is composite.*

roof. Suppose r_0 is a rule in P such that $(P - \{r_0\}) \cup P_{[r_0]} \not\vdash r_0$. Let $P_1 = (P - \{r_0\}) \cup P_{[r_0]}$ and $_2 = \{r_0\}$. Clearly, $P \vdash P_i$ for each i ($1 \leq i \leq 2$). Since $P_1 \not\vdash r_0$, $P_1 \not\vdash P$. Let D be an arbitrary database. nce $P \vdash P_i$ for each i ($1 \leq i \leq 2$), $P^\omega(D) \supseteq P_2^\omega \circ P_1^\omega(D)$. Intuitively, for the inverse containment, the roof proceeds by constructing a P^ω computation via substituting two or more rules (including at least ıe occurrence of r_0) to by a rule of the form $r[r_0, ...]$; and leaving other rules unchanged. □

xample 3.5 (cont). P is nonredundant, and $\{r_2\} \cup P_{[r_1]} \not\vdash r_1$. By Theorem 3.4, P is composite. □

It can be shown that the condition given in the above theorem is not necessary. In passing, we note ıat there are arbitrarily large composite programs.

3.3 Factorization of bounded recursive programs

We consider the factorization of bounded recursive programs into single-rule primes. The main result says that each bounded recursive program is factorizable into single-rule symmetric primes.

Definition. A factorization of a program P is a nontrivial decomposition into primes.

From a computational point of view, factorizations are among the most efficient decompositions. Several immediate problems concerning factorization arise:

- When does a program have a factorization?
- How to obtain a factorization effectively?
- When does a program have a unique factorization (in a reasonable sense)?

Using results in Section 2, we can establish a condition for when there is a factorization: A program P has a factorization if P has a nontrivial decomposition $P_1^\omega \circ \cdots \circ P_m^\omega$ and for each P_i there exists a program Q_i such that (a) $P \vdash Q_i \vdash P_i$ and $Q_i \not\vdash P$; and (b) Q_i has a factorization.

Our major concern is on the factorization of bounded recursive programs.

Definition. A program P is said to be bounded if there is a positive integer n such that $P^\omega = P^n$.

In [Io] boundedness was called "uniform boundedness" and a graph characterization was given. Several other authors [NaSa, Va, etc.] also studied the class of bounded programs regarding decision problems. In general, such programs are preferred for their efficient evaluations. The factorizability into symmetric single-rule programs indicates that bounded programs have very nice properties.

Lemma 3.3 *For each single-rule program P, one can effectively construct symmetric single-rule primes $Q_1, \cdots, Q_m$ such that (a) $P \vdash Q_i$ for each i $(1 \le i \le m)$, and (b) $P^1(D) \subseteq Q_m^\omega \circ \cdots \circ Q_1^\omega(D)$ for each database D.*

We are now able to present the major result of the section.

Theorem 3.5 *Each bounded composite program has an effectively constructible factorization into symmetric single-rule primes.*

Proof. Let $P = \{r_1, \cdots, r_m\}$ $(m \ge 1)$ be a bounded composite program. Then there exists a positive integer n such that $P^\omega = P^n$. Let $P_i = \{r_i\}$ for each i $(1 \le i \le m)$. Clearly, $P^1(D) \subseteq P_1^1 \circ \cdots \circ P_m^1(D)$. For each i $(1 \le i \le m)$, by Lemma 3.3, there exist symmetric single-rule programs $P_{i1}, \cdots, P_{ik_i}$ such that $P_i \vdash P_{ij}$ for each j and $P_i^1(D) \subseteq P_{i1}^\omega \circ \cdots \circ P_{ik_i}^\omega(D)$ for each database D. Then, $P^\omega = (P_{11}^\omega \circ \cdots \circ P_{1k_1}^\omega \circ \cdots \circ P_{m1}^\omega \circ \cdots \circ P_{mk_m}^\omega)^n$. By Lemma 3.3 and the construction of the P_i's, the above factorization is effectively obtained. □

Not every program factorizable into symmetric single-rule primes is bounded. Consider $P = \{R(x,y) \to R(y,x), R(x,y) \& R(y,z) \to R(x,z)\}$, $P_1 = \{R(x,y) \to R(y,x)\}$ and $P_2 = \{R(x,y) \& R(y,z) \to R(x,z)\}$. Then $P^\omega = P_2^\omega \circ P_1^\omega$, and P_1 and P_2 are symmetric. But P is not bounded.

We now establish three consequences of Theorem 3.5.

orollary 3.1 *Each nonrecursive program is factorizable into symmetric single-rule primes.*

efinition. A program is single-body if each r in the program has exactly one formula in its body.

orollary 3.2 *Each single-body program is factorizable into symmetric single-rule primes.*

efinition. A program P is ℓ-local (ℓ an integer) if, for each database with ℓ or more facts, $P^{\omega}(D) = P^{\omega}(D_{\ell})$, where the union is over all subdatabases of ℓ facts. P is local if it is ℓ-local for some ℓ.

orollary 3.3 *Each local program is factorizable into symmetric single-rule primes.*

A program is bounded if it is either nonrecursive, single-body, or local [Dol].

It is open whether locality is equivalent to boundedness. It can be shown that a subset of a bounded ogram can be unbounded. It is also open whether each composite program has a factorization.

We now turn to the uniqueness of factorization.

Since datalog mappings are idempotent, the uniqueness factorizations has to exclude adjacent duicate of datalog mappings. Since there are commutative prime programs, their union has many facrizations. Hence one cannot hope for a uniqueness condition involving the ordering of programs in a ctorization. Combining the above two reasons, it seem reasonable to describe uniqueness in terms of e set of participating programs.

efinition. A set S is called a factorization base for P if $P^{\omega} = P_1^{\omega} \circ \cdots \circ P_m^{\omega}$, where each P_i is in S. A ctorization base is minimal if no subset is also a factorization base.

Unfortunately, factorizations need not be unique even in terms of the set of participating programs. deed, consider the permutation program

$$P = \{R(x_1^1, \cdots, x_{p_1}^1, \cdots, x_1^k, \cdots, x_{p_k}^k) \rightarrow R(x_2^1, \cdots, x_{p_1}^1, x_1^1, \cdots, x_2^k, \cdots, x_{p_k}^k, x_1^k)\}$$

in Example 3.4, where $k = 3$, $p_1 = 2$, $p_2 = 3$ and $p_3 = 5$. Let P_1 permute the first two elements; P_2 rmute the next three while using the result of P_1; and P_3 permute the last five while using the result both P_1 and P_2. Let Q_1, Q_2 and Q_3 be constructed similarly but the order is the last five, the middle ree, and the first two. Then both $P_3^{\omega} \circ P_2^{\omega} \circ P_1^{\omega}$ and $Q_3^{\omega} \circ Q_2^{\omega} \circ Q_1^{\omega}$ are factorizations for P.

Happily, we are able to present the following result on uniqueness using conditions combining mmetric and factorization base.

roposition 3.1 *For each program P_0, there is at most one (up to logical equivalence) minimal singlele symmetric factorization base S of P_0 such that $P_0^{\omega}(\tau_c(B(r))) = P^{\omega}(\tau_c(B(r)))$ for each $P = \{r\}$ in , where τ_c is a one-to-one assignment. (The choice of τ_c is not essential.)*

Using the proposition, we now present an example.

Example 3.6 Consider the program $P_0 = \{r_1, r_2\}$, where $r_1 = R_1(x,y)\&R(y,z) \rightarrow R_1(y,x)$ and r_2 = $R_2(x,y)\&R_2(y,z)\&R(x,z) \rightarrow R_2(x,z)$. Let $P_i = \{r_i\}$ for each i $(1 \leq i \leq 2)$. Then, using an argumen similar to that given in Example 2.2, it can be shown that $P_0 = P_2^\omega \circ P_1^\omega$. It is easily verified that $\{P_1, P_2$ is a minimal single-rule symmetric factorization base of P_0. By Proposition 3.1, such factorization bas is unique. □

Conclusion

In this paper we have studied two major topics on the composition of datalog mappings. Firstly, w investigated the composability, which is useful for undersanding the general representation problem composition mappings. A number of characterizations and sufficiency conditions and several invarianc properties were given. Typical conditions are idempotency, preservation, and commutativity.

An axiom system (called a "composition system") approximating the datalog mappings was in troduced and the composability results were established in this general framework in a clean manne Furthermore, the theory developed can be applied to another situation involving a construct calle datalog module [Do].

Secondly, we considered decomposition, prime and factorization. We showed that strongly linea programs are decomposable into single-rule programs. We described the structure of primes. In par ticular, we saw that most but not all single-rule programs are prime; most multiple rule programs ar composite; and arbitrarily large primes exist. We established that bounded recursive programs ar factorizable into single-rule primes. We also investigated the uniqueness of factorizations.

Although the study is carried out for datalog programs only, a similar study (with possibly differen answers) is possible for other rule-based systems, such as expert systems, knowledge base systems, an logic programming.

Acknowledgement: The author is thankful to R. Hull, M. Kifer, S. Kurtzman, V. Vianu, and especiall S. Ginsburg for a number of useful discussions. He is also grateful to the referees for helpful comment

References

[ABW] Apt, K.R., Blair, H., and Walker, A. Towards a theory of declarative knowledge. In *Foun dations of Deductive Databases and Logic Programming*, J. Minker, Eds., Morgan Kaufman Publishers, Los Altos, 1988, 89-148.

[BaRa] Bancilhon, F., and Ramakrishnan, R. An amateur's introduction to recursive query processin strategies. In *Proceedings of the ACM SIGMOD Conference*, 1986, 16-52.

[CFM] Chakravarthy, U.S., Fishman, D.H., and Minker, J. Semantic query optimization in exper systems and database systems. In *Expert Database Systems, Proceedings of the 1st Interna tional Workshop on Expert Database Systems*, L. Kerschberg, Eds., 1984, 326.

hLe] Chang, C., and Lee, R.C. *Symbolic Logic and Mechanical Theorem Proving*, Academic Press, 1973.

o] Dong, G. On cooperative query answering using datalog program modules. Computer Science Department, USC, 1988.

ol] Dong, G. On the composition and decomposition of datalog program mappings. Computer Science Department, USC, 1988.

] Ioannidis, Y.E. A time bound on the materialization of some recursively defined views. In *Proceedings of 11th International VLDB Conference*, Stockholm, Sweden, 1985.

aMa] Lassez, J.L., and Maher, M.J. Closures and fairness in the semantics of programming logic. *Theoretical Computer Science*, 29 (1984), 167-184.

.] Lloyd, J.W. *Foundations of Logic Programming.* Springer-Verlag, 1984.

aSa] Naughton, J., and Sagiv, Y. A decidable class of bounded recursion. In *Proceedings of the 6th PODS*, 1987, 227-236.

a] Sagiv, Y. Optimizing datalog programs, In *Proceedings of the 6th PODS*, 1987, 349.

a] Vardi, M.Y. Decidability and undecidability results for boundedness of linear recursive programs. In *Proceedings of the 7th PODS*, 1988, 341-351.

On the Semantics of Rule-Based Expert Systems with Uncertainty*

Michael Kifer and Ai Li
Department of Computer Science
SUNY at Stony Brook, NY 11794, U.S.A.

ABSTRACT

We present a formal semantics for rule-based systems with uncertainty (this field has also become known as "quantitative logic programming"). Unlike previous works, our framework is general enough to accommodate most of the known schemes of reasoning with uncertainty found in the existing expert systems. We provide a rigorous treatment of the issue of evidential independence, and study its impact on the semantics. To the best of our knowledge, this issue has not been addressed before in the literature on quantitative logic programming. In expert systems evidential independence received only an ad hoc treatment, while the approaches found in the theory of evidential reasoning are feasible only in small scale systems. We discuss the problem of query optimization and, as a first step, present a quantitative semi-nave query evaluation algorithm – generalization of a method well-known in deductive databases. Treatment of negation and conflicting evidence based on, so called, support logic is given in the last part of the paper, where we extend the semantics of stratified programs to deal with uncertainty.

1. Introduction

In recent years rule-based systems became popular tools for developing a wide range of knowledge-based applications [8, 20]. By supporting the very concepts of a rule, forward/backward chaining, certainty factors, etc., these systems are of a great help to the application developer. Despite that, building expert systems remains a largely an ad hoc and a very labor-intensive activity [13, 19, 20].

Expert system shells are environments built around rule-based languages for programming knowledge based systems. These languages normally require the users to be aware of such low-level details as backtracking, cuts, and even whether rules are to be applied in forward or backward chaining. As programming languages, these systems inherit most of the disadvantages of Prolog [11], aggravating them even further by adding new features intended to cope with knowledge representation idiosyncrasies. For instance, as in Prolog, queries to expert systems are not guarantied to terminate and/or retrieve all answers, the notion of query/program optimization is virtually nonexistent, and computational efficiency is almost solely a user's responsibility. Many expert system languages allow rules to be fired both forwards and backwards, making it likely that some answers to a query will be lost. All this renders expert system development a very time-consuming and error-prone task.

Our contention is that this situation can be improved dramatically by utilizing the recent achievements in the deductive database research (e.g., [7, 15, 23, 38]). We believe that expert system programming can be made more declarative, thereby releaving the developer from the burden of specifying most of the nitty-gritty details of the control strategy. This burden should be taken over by the system which will use various query optimization techniques to achieve desirable response time.

This is not to say that the user necessarily has to relinquish all his control over program execution. Some query optimization strategies permit users to specify certain kinds of control information (e.g., ***sideways propagation graphs*** [23], or ***sideways information passing strategy*** [7]). However, it is our thesis that the purpose of control information should be improving the efficiency of a program, not changing its semantics (as it currently is the case in rule-based systems, or languages such as Prolog). Thus, it should be possible to add or delete control information at any time without affecting correctness of a program. As we remarked earlier, none of the commercial or experimental expert system shells we are aware of attempts any serious query optimization. Instead, they supply numerous ways of specifying control information, heavily relying on user's experience in the art of what became known as "knowledge engineering".

In many problem domains (medical, military, etc.) expert systems have to deal with pieces of knowledge which are uncertain or incomplete. A well known example of such system is MYCIN [8]. Not surprisingly, the aforesaid problems become only worse when users have to face uncertain data or imprecise reasoning. In this paper we concentrate on such systems, making first couple of steps towards our

* Work supported in part by the NSF grant DCR-8603676.

declared goal of rendering expert systems programming a less demanding enterprise.

First, we propose a declarative semantics for general rule-based systems which utilize certainty factors as a means of representing incomplete or imprecise knowledge. At this point we would like to stress that the theory of evidential, probabilistic, or fuzzy reasoning is *not* our concern here. That is, we do not address the issue of how different evidences for the same fact can be combined together to yield a new (possibly stronger) evidence. Surveys of this field can be found in [8: Chapters 10-13, 14: Chapter 7, 22, 27]. Instead, a model-theoretic semantics is described for a rather large class of theories of evidential reasoning, which is specified by a number of requirements to how strength of causal links is computed. In particular, all the theories considered in [27] fall under this category. Neither do we want to get into a discussion of the controversial issue of where do the certainty numbers come from. Our goal here is more modest. It consists in providing formal grounds for a class of practical problems which so far received only an ad hoc treatment.

Second, we define a fixpoint semantics for programs with uncertainty, and show that it coincides with the model-theoretic semantics. The fixpoint semantics is especially important to us, because, as in the database theory, it can become a basis for an efficient implementation. Although on the surface the proposed fixpoint semantics seems quite similar to that of Horn programs [36], a number of difficult problems arise concerning the computation of certainties of answers to the queries. We then propose ways of solving that problem.

In the rest of this section we survey the relevant work on declarative semantics of logic programs with uncertainty. Lee [24] describes a model-theoretic semantics and the resolution principle for one of the fuzzy logics, called K-standard sequence logic [12]. Essentially the same semantics is described in [30], although in the latter paper the formalism of Post algebras is used instead of models.

van Emden [37] also deals with K-standard sequence logic, providing both model-theoretic and fixpoint semantics for that special case of inferencing, which he calls *quantitative reasoning.* Shapiro [33] considers essentially the same logic, although his framework for computing certainties is more general than in [37]. He describes a model theoretic semantics and discusses some implementational issues, but does not provide the fixpoint semantics.

Subrahmanian [34] extends the work of van Emden [37] by allowing negative information to be represented explicitly. For instance, in this extended logic it is perfectly acceptable for both p and $\neg p$ to have some supporting evidences. Unfortunately, the solutions proposed in [34] is somewhat counterintuitive. For instance, if p is known with a high degree of certainty while the certainty of $\neg p$ is low, then, according to [34], this should result in a contradiction - an unlikely course of action in most problem domains (cf. MYCIN [8]). We propose a different solution based on *support logic* [4, 5].

Work has also been reported on fuzzy relational calculus [39, 40]. These studies have also concentrated on the aforesaid K-standard sequence logic. In addition, being based on first-order (fuzzy) calculus, no recursively defined predicates can be allowed in these query languages.

Example 1. Consider the following program:

1. $close(X,X){:}1$
2. $edge(X,X){:}1$
3. $line(Line,X,Y){:}\alpha \leftarrow edge(Edge,X,Y){:}\alpha$
4. $close(X,Y){:}\dfrac{alpha*beta}{1+\delta} \leftarrow close(X,Z){:}\alpha,\ close(Z,Y){:}\beta,$
5. $line(concat(E,L),X,Y){:}\alpha*\beta*\gamma^2 \leftarrow edge(E,X,Z){:}\alpha,\ line(L,Z,Y){:}\beta,\ aligned(E,Z,L){:}\gamma$
6. $edge(Line,X,Y){:}\alpha*\beta^2 \leftarrow line(Line,X,Y){:}\alpha,\ close(X,Y){:}\beta$

The fourth statement says that any two points are "close" to each other if there is an intermediate point Z which is close to both X and Y. Statements 3,5, and 6 describe some simplified version of the line detection procedure in image recognition. In addition, there is a database of facts about close points and simple lines in the image. Variables α, β, and γ denote certainties of the assertions they are attached to. In this example certainties range from 0 (unknown) to 1 (known to be true). □

Example 1 highlights one drawback of the previous approaches to quantitative reasoning. For instance, [34, 37] do not allow such relatively complex certainty functions as those used in the example. A closer look at [33] reveals that the allowed certainty functions are required to have (a single) set-valued argument. This entails that such functions should not depend on the order of elements in the set argument, i.e., that they should be commutative. On the other hand, the certainty functions in rules 5 and 6 do not have this property.

Another weakness of the aforementioned approaches is that they all use K-standard fuzzy logic. In this logic, given a pair of evidences of strengthes α and β for the same fact p, the combined evidence to p is assumed to be of strength $max(\alpha,\beta)$. This may be inappropriate in some problem domains. For instance, MYCIN [8] uses, so called, stochastic logic [12] in which the combined evidence would be $\alpha+\beta-\alpha*\beta$.

All this suggests considering more general theories of quantitative reasoning. Our approach is not restricted to any of the above logics. We only assume that evidences are combined subject to certain natural restrictions, which are general enough to accommodate several popular methods. In this general situation, new difficult issues arise, which are mostly due to the problem of independence of different evidences supporting the same fact. We show in Section 4.1 that in the special situation considered in [33, 34, 37] this problem does not arise, which makes it, in this sense, the easiest case of quantitative reasoning. However, as mentioned earlier, this case is not general enough to accommodate the most popular reasoning systems, such as MYCIN.

We describe the general semantics in Section 3, and show the impact of evidential independence on the meaning of a program. The need to verify independence of evidences makes query evaluation more involved. In Section 4 we discuss these difficulties, and generalize the well-known semi-naive query evaluation algorithm [2, 6, 18, 35] to deal with general quantitative (Horn) logic programs. The semantics and the semi-naive algorithm described in Sections 3 and 4 are decoupled from the choice of any specific notion of evidential independence, adding another degree of generality to our approach. Of course, the *cost* of query evaluation does depend on this choice, which is also discussed in Section 4.2.

It is often argued that associating a single certainty factor with each fact in the database is not enough for many applications. For instance, in MYCIN each fact has a measure of belief and a measure of disbelief. This technique is often used to cope with contradictory information commonly arising in medical, military, and other domains. A promising approach utilizing this idea is based on, so called, support logic. Resently several calculi for computing combined evidence in such logics were proposed [4, 5, 16]. However, no formal logical semantics exists for such logics, and their implementations still share most of the drawbacks of the rule-based languages mentioned earlier. This lack of semantics prevents any systematic study of optimization in support logic systems. In Section 5 we outline a declarative semantics for such systems.

2. Preliminaries

We assume some knowledge of Logic Programming at a level of the first few chapters of [26]. Certain familiarity with database terminology and query optimization (e.g., [7, 23, 35]) is also required.

Literals in our logic are constructs of the form $p:\tau$, where p is a literal in the usual predicate calculus, and τ is a term representing certainty information about p (called *certainty term* of p). When confusion is possible, we will call the usual first-order literals, the *d-literals* (for data literals). D-literals are of the form $p(x,y,...)$ or $\neg p(x,y,...)$, where p is a predicate symbol and x, y, etc. are variables or constants. We thus do not allow function symbols in such literals. Ground d-literals will be called *d-facts*.

We also assume a finite collection of interpreted *certainty functions* (usually some arithmetic functions). A k-ary such function maps $[0,1]^k$ into $[0,1]$. Certainty terms are built in a usual way out of these functions, *certainty variables* (which are different from the usual logic variables), and *certainty constants* which will be taken from the domain of real numbers in the interval [0, 1].

D-literals annotated with certainty 1 are considered as *definitely true* facts. Certainty values between 0 and 1 mean that there is some inconclusive evidence that the fact is true, while the facts with certainty 0 have no supporting evidence whatsoever. This does not imply anything about the falsehood of the fact, contrary to the assumption made, say, in [34, 37]. Dealing with negative information, and representing falsehood of facts is postponed until Section 5.

A (Horn) rule is a statement of the form

$$p:\tau \leftarrow q_1:\sigma_1, \ldots, q_n:\sigma_n, \tag{1}$$

where p, q_1, q_2, ... are positive d-literals, and τ, σ_1, σ_2, ... are certainty terms. All the variables in (1), including certainty variables, are assumed to be universally quantified outside the clause. We also assume that variables in the head of the rule (including certainty variables) also appear in the body of that rule. In practice there does not seem to be many applications for the full generality of rule (1); in this paper we will be considering only the rules of the following simpler form:

$$p(x,\ldots):f(\alpha,\beta,\ldots,\gamma) \leftarrow a(y,\ldots):\alpha,\ b(z,\ldots):\beta,\ \ldots,c(u,\ldots):\gamma, \tag{2}$$

where α, β, ..., γ are certainty variables or constants and f is a certainty function *associated with this rule.* We will be also talking about *d-versions*, or *d-instances* of rules, etc., meaning the rules (or instances thereof) with the certainty information striped off.

We assume that bodies of the rules are nonempty. Particularly, unlike in Prolog, facts are not viewed just as rules with empty bodies: they are not rules according to our definition at all. All predicate symbols are partitioned into two categories. The first category consists of the *base* predicates. These predicates can appear only in the bodies of rules, and their extensions (sets of facts) are known in advance. The second category consists of the *derived* predicates. Extensions of these predicates are initially empty, and the corresponding facts are derived by the rules. Derived predicates can appear in the heads of the rules as well as their bodies. This assumption is common in deductive databases, and is known to be equivalent to the general case (used in Logic Programming).

An *expert system* is a combination of a Horn program **P** (i.e., a collection of rules) and of a set of facts, **D**, for the base predicates of **P**. In keeping with the database tradition, we will sometimes call **P** the *intentional database* (IDB) and **D** - the *extensional database* (EDB). For simplicity we assume that each ground d-fact appears in **D** at most once, i.e., for each $p(\vec{a})$ there is at most one fact of the form $p(\vec{a}):\alpha$ in **D**. If no $p(\vec{a}):\alpha$ appears in **D** for some $p(\vec{a})$, then we assume that $p(\vec{a}):0 \in$ **D**.

As suggested by the form of the rules, certainty function associated with a rule is a measure of strength of the causality link between the rule premises and the consequent. We impose the following natural restrictions on these functions:

1. *Monotonicity*: $f(x_1, \ldots, x_n) \leq f(y_1, \ldots, y_n)$, if $x_i < y_i$ for $i = 1,\ldots,n$. Informally this means that higher certainty of premises should yield a higher certainty of the consequent.
2. *Boundedness*: $f(x_1, \ldots, x_n) \leq x_i$, for $i=1,\ldots,n$. This states that conclusion of a rule can be only as good as its premises.
3. *Continuity*: $f(\ldots)$ is continuous w.r.t. each of its arguments. This technical assumption is needed in order to ensure the agreement between the model-theoretic and the fixpoint semantics introduced later. Most of the known certainty functions satisfy this requirement.

In expert systems, strengthes of evidences obtained from different sources all supporting the same fact are combined to determine strength of the overall support for the fact[1]. In different problem domains and, perhaps, for different types of facts, combination methods may be different. Furthermore, different researchers are fond of different theories of evidential reasoning. In order to be independent from any such theory, we postulate that associated with each predicate symbol, p, there is a unique *combination function*, F_p, used to calculate strength of combined evidences for p. Combination functions accept a single multiset-valued[2] argument, which implies that the combined strength of evidences for a fact is independent from the order in which these evidences are obtained. Some researchers have argued that it should not be that way, i.e., evidences obtained prior to some other evidences may increase significance of the latter evidences [21]. Acknowledging controversy of this issue, we note, however, that the majority of the known theories of evidential reasoning (see [27]) satisfy the commutativity requirement. We thus impose the following natural restrictions on combination functions:

1. *Commutativity:* Each combination function has a single argument which is a multiset of certainty factors (i.e., multiset of values in the range [0,1]).
2. *Monotonicity*: $S \leq S'$ implies $F(S) \leq F(S')$. The order on the multisets is defined in the usual way: $S \leq S'$ if there is a 1-1 mapping τ from S into S' s.t. for every $s \in S$, $s \leq \tau(s)$. This

[1] We postpone the discussion of conflicting evidences until Section 5.

[2] In a multiset, the same element can have several occurrences.

condition ensures that stronger evidences yield stronger overall support for a fact.

3. *Associativity*: $F(S \bigcup S') = F(S \bigcup F(S'))$. Here $\bigcup$ is a union of multisets which retains duplicate occurrences of the same element. According to this requirement, the order in which evidences are combined is immaterial. In order to obtain the overall strength of support for a fact there is no need to wait until all evidences for that fact are obtained. Instead, one can evaluate the support incrementally. Strictly speaking, this requirement is not needed in order to describe the semantics of programs. However, without associativity, evidential support cannot be evaluated incrementally, burying any hope for efficient query evaluation. We will use this property in Section 4.2.

4. *No-Information Rule*: $F(S \bigcup \{0\}) = F(S)$. That is, a non-evidence cannot change the overall support.

5. *Correctness*: $F(\{\alpha\}) = \alpha$. This means that the combined support provided by a single evidence is exactly as strong as the evidence itself.

6. *Continuity*: $F(...)$ is continuous w.r.t. the order $\geq$ on multisets defined in (2). Continuity of combination functions is needed for the same reason as in the case of certainty functions.

The following useful properties of combination functions can be derived from the aforementioned ones:

7. *Support enhancement*: $F(S) \geq \alpha$ for every $\alpha \in S$. This follows directly from (2) and (5). It means that every new evidence is potentially useful, because it may increase the overall support for a fact.

8 *Unconditional support*: $F(S \bigcup \{1\}) = 1$. This property follows form (7); it postulates that if an evidences establishes a fact beyond any doubt then the fact is unconditionally true and the rest of the evidences do not matter.

Our next step will be defining interpretations and models in which we follow the outline of [37]. For our purposes it suffices to consider only Herbrand interpretations, although general interpretations can be also defined. Given an expert system $\mathbf{E} = \mathbf{P} \bigcup \mathbf{D}$, the *domain* $D_{\mathbf{E}}$ of any Herbrand interpretation $\mathbf{E}$ is a collection of all the constants mentioned in $\mathbf{E}$. A *Herbrand base* of $\mathbf{E}$ is a collection of all ground facts of the form $p(a_1, \ldots, a_n){:}\alpha$, where p is an n-ary predicate symbol in $\mathbf{P}$, a_is all belong to $D_{\mathbf{E}}$, and $\alpha \in [0,1]$ is a certainty factor of $p(a_1, \ldots, a_n)$. A *Herbrand interpretation* I of $\mathbf{E}$ is a subset of the Herbrand base of $\mathbf{E}$. Without loss of generality we also assume that for every d-fact p there is at most one fact $p{:}\alpha \in I$. If $p{:}\alpha \notin I$ for all $\alpha > 0$ then we assume that $p{:}0 \in I$.

A fact $p(a_1, \ldots, a_n){:}\alpha$ is *true* under I iff there is $p(a_1, \ldots, a_n){:}\beta \in I$ such that $\beta \geq \alpha$. We thus postulate that whenever a fact is known with a higher certainty, β, it is also known with any other certainty which is smaller than β.

A ground rule $p(\vec{a}){:}f(\alpha_1, \ldots, \alpha_k) \leftarrow q_1(\vec{e}_1){:}\alpha_1, \ldots, q_k(\vec{e}_k){:}\alpha_k$ is true in I iff whenever all the $q_i(\vec{e}_i){:}\alpha_i$s are true in I, the head of the rule, $p(\vec{a}){:}f(\alpha_1, \ldots, \alpha_k)$, is also true in I. A (nonground) rule is true in I iff all its ground instances are true. In our framework, ground rules are used as evidences to the facts in their heads. However, not every true rule can serve as an evidence. We say that the above rule *supports* $p(\vec{a}){:}f(\alpha_1, \ldots, \alpha_k)$ in I if all its literals (head and body) are true in I. We will also refer to such rules as *evidences*.

A program, $\mathbf{P}$, is true if all its rules are true, *and*, in addition, the following *combination requirement* is satisfied:

For every set of *independent* (explained later) ground instances of the rules of $\mathbf{P}$ with the same head d-literal

$$p(\vec{a}){:}f_1(\alpha_{11},\ldots,\alpha_{k_1 1}) \leftarrow q_{11}(\vec{e}_{11}){:}\alpha_{11},\ldots,q_{k_1 1}(\vec{e}_{k_1 1}){:}\alpha_{k_1 1}$$

$$\ldots \qquad \ldots \qquad \ldots$$

$$p(\vec{a}){:}f_m(\alpha_{1m},\ldots,\alpha_{k_m m}) \leftarrow q_{1m}(\vec{e}_{1m}){:}\alpha_{1m},\ldots,q_{k_m m}(\vec{e}_{k_m m}){:}\alpha_{k_m m}$$

such that each individual rule supports its head literal in I, the literal $p(\vec{a}){:}F_p(\{f_1(\alpha_{11}, \ldots, \alpha_{k_1 1}), \ldots, f_m(\alpha_{1m}, \ldots, \alpha_{k_m m})\})$ should be true in I[3]. Notice that f_i and f_j would be identical certainty functions if the i-th and the j-th rules above are instances of the same rule of $\mathbf{P}$; they may be different otherwise.

---

[3] Observe that, since base predicates cannot appear in the rule heads, $p(\vec{a})$ cannot be an EDB fact. Hence, no EDB fact need be combined with the above evidences to $p(\vec{a})$.

The last definition expresses the fact that independently obtained evidences for the same fact are combined to obtain a possibly stronger evidence. An unusual consequence of this definition is that although each individual rule of a program might be true, the program itself may not be satisfied by the interpretation, because some of the facts may not be known with sufficient certainty to satisfy the combination requirement (since $F(S) \geq \alpha$ for any combination function F and for each $\alpha \in S$).

Another important point is that the combination requirement stated above implicitly depends on the assumption about what independent evidences are. Our semantics does not rely on the specifics of any of the variety of such assumptions, which makes it very general. The only requirement is that, to be combinable, supporting evidences should be absolutely independent form each other. Thus, even partially dependent evidences are never combined. We discuss the consequences of this assumption in Section 6. Notice that evidential independence may be defined differently for different predicates, which makes our framework even more flexible. We list two of the many possible candidates for the notion of independence.

Independence-1: A pair of ground rules $p:\alpha \leftarrow q_1:\beta_1,...,q_n:\beta_n$ and $p:\gamma \leftarrow r_1:\delta_1,...,r_m:\delta_m$ *provide independent evidences* for the fact p iff $\{q_1,...,q_n\}$ and $\{r_1,...,r_m\}$ are different, being considered as sets of ground literals.

Independence-2: A pair of ground rules $p:\alpha \leftarrow q_1:\beta_1,...,q_n:\beta_n$ and $p:\gamma \leftarrow r_1:\delta_1,...,r_m:\delta_m$ provide independent evidences for p iff the sets $\{q_1,...,q_n\}$ and $\{r_1,...,r_m\}$ are incomparable w.r.t. $\subseteq$.

Independence-1 is the minimal requirement for rules to be independent; it is too weak for most purposes. Its importance is in serving as a basis for studying other, practically more interesting, independence requirements. Independence-2 is given as a simple alternative to the first notion. In the full paper we will discuss several additional important cases of evidence independence.

Rule independence is crucial for the semantics to make sense. Indeed, counting the supports provided by dependent rules may yield bizarre results. For instance, in the degenerated case one could repeat the same rule (supporting, say, p, with a positive strength α) several times, raising the overall support for p to $F_p(\alpha,\alpha,...)$. Thus, if F_p is a MYCIN function for combining beliefs ($F_p(\alpha,\beta) = \alpha+\beta-\alpha*\beta$), then the certainty of p in any model necessarily has to be 1. To see this, notice that the certainty of p after combining α with itself n times, denoted γ_n, is related to the certainty γ_{n+1} obtained after the (n+1)-th combination by the following equation: $\gamma_{n+1} = \alpha+\gamma_n-\alpha*\gamma_n$. In the limit we have that the certainty of p, γ, is related to α as follows: $\gamma = \alpha+\gamma-\alpha*\gamma$. Hence, $\gamma = 1$. This, of course, does not look like the right thing.

We say that I is a *model* of $\mathbf{E} = \mathbf{P} \bigcup \mathbf{D}$ iff $\mathbf{P}$ and each fact in $\mathbf{D}$ is true in I. We also write $\mathbf{E} \models p(\vec{q}):\alpha$ if $p(\vec{q}):\alpha$ is true in every model of $\mathbf{E}$. A *partial order* on the interpretations is defined as follows: $I \subseteq J$ iff for every $p(\vec{q}):\alpha \in I$ there is $p(\vec{q}):\beta \in J$ s.t. $\alpha \leq \beta$. Clearly, $I = J$ iff $I \subseteq J$ and $J \subseteq I$.

Intersection of a collection of interpretations, $\{I_k\}_{k \in K}$, is the interpretation $\bigcap_{k \in K} I_k = \{p:\alpha \mid \alpha = \inf_{k \in K} \alpha_k$, where $p:\alpha_k \in I_k$, for all $k \in K\}$. Similarly, the *union* of the above collection of interpretations is defined to be $\bigcup_{k \in K} I_k = \{p:\alpha \mid \alpha = \sup_{k \in K} \alpha_k$, where $p:\alpha_k \in I_k$, for all $k \in K\}$.

It can be verified that intersection of any number of models of an expert system $\mathbf{E} = \mathbf{P} \bigcup \mathbf{D}$ is also a model. Therefore, $\mathbf{E}$ has a unique least model, which is called the *intended* model of $\mathbf{E}$.

3. The Fixpoint Semantics

In this section we present a fixpoint semantics for logic programs with uncertainties. Following the outline of [36, 37] we introduce operator $T_{\mathbf{E}}$ associated with the expert system $\mathbf{E} = \mathbf{P} \bigcup \mathbf{D}$. Given an interpretation I of $\mathbf{E}$, $T_{\mathbf{E}}(I)$ is another interpretation of $\mathbf{E}$, defined as follows. Let $a(\vec{q})$ be an arbitrary d-fact. If $a(...)$ is a base predicate then $a(\vec{q}):\alpha \in T_{\mathbf{E}}(I)$ iff $a(\vec{q}):\alpha \in \mathbf{D}$. If $a(...)$ is a derived predicate and for no certainty $\alpha > 0$, $a(\vec{q}):\alpha$ is supported by a rule in $\mathbf{P}$, then $a(\vec{q}):0$ is in $T_{\mathbf{P}}(I)$. Otherwise, suppose that $a(\vec{q}):\alpha$ is supported for some $\alpha > 0$. Consider a set of *independent* ground rules of $\mathbf{P}$ defining

$a(\vec{q})$ whose bodies are true in I:

$$
\begin{aligned}
&a(\vec{q}):\beta_1 \leftarrow \textbf{body}_1 \\
&\cdots \quad \cdots \quad \cdots \\
&a(\vec{q}):\beta_k \leftarrow \textbf{body}_k .
\end{aligned}
\tag{3}
$$

Then $a(\vec{q}):\gamma$ is in $T_E(I)$, where $\gamma = \max_{\beta}\left\{ F_a(\{ \beta_1, \ldots, \beta_k \}) \right\}$, and *max* ranges over the collection of all multisets of certainty factors $\beta = \{ \beta_1, \ldots, \beta_k \}$ produced by all possible bundles of independent ground rules (3).

Notice the requirement of independence of rules in this definition. It is needed in order to account for non-independent evidences which should not be combined using combination functions. The fixpoint semantics, like the model-theoretic one depends on evidential independence, but is general enough to accommodate any suitable notion of independence, or a combination thereof.

Our definition of T_E is somewhat more involved than in [37] because with general combination functions, MYCIN's for example, it is possible that $F(S) > \max(S)$. In this case, as explained in Section 2, one has to be very careful not to combine dependent evidences. In contrast, in [33, 34, 37], $F(S) = \max(S)$, in which case evidence independence does not have any significance.

Finally, we define $T_E^0(I) = I$ and $T_E^n(I) = T_E^{n-1}(T_E(I))$ for $n > 0$. The following results are quite standard [36]:

Lemma 1. T_E is *monotonic*, i.e., $I \subseteq J$ implies $T_E(I) \subseteq T_E(J)$, and *continuous*, i.e., for any monotonically increasing sequence of interpretations $I_1 \subseteq I_2 \subseteq I_3 \subseteq \ldots$, $T_E(\bigcup_j I_j) = \bigcup_j T_E(I_j)$. []

Proposition 1. The least fixed point of T_E is equal to $\bigcup_{i=0}^{\infty} T_E^i(\emptyset)$, where $\emptyset$ is the interpretation in which every fact is assigned certainty 0.

Proof. This follows from Lemma 1 in a standard way [36]. []

It can be seen from the definitions and Proposition 1 that $M = \bigcup_{i=1}^{\infty} T_E^i(\emptyset)$ is also a model of E. Furthermore, for any other model M', $M \subseteq M'$. We thus have the following result:

Proposition 2. The least fixed point of T_E is the least (w.r.t. $\subseteq$) model of **E**. In other words, the least fixed point of T_E coincides with the intended model of **E**. []

4. Computing Intended Models

4.1. Finite Termination Property

It was demonstrated by the database research that the iterative fixpoint computation described in the previous section can effectively serve as a basis of an operational semantics. One important advantage of this procedure is that (when function symbols do not appear in the rules) it always terminates. Unfortunately, in general, this is not the case in the presence of uncertainty. Consider the following simple example.

Example 2. Let the system E be as follows: $p(a,b)$: .6, $r(a,a)$: .5

$q(X,Y):\tau \leftarrow p(X,Y):\tau$
$q(X,Y):\alpha * \beta \leftarrow r(X,Z):\alpha,\ q(Z,Y):\beta$,

where α, β, and τ are certainty variables. Let the combination function be the same as that used in MYCIN to combine measures of belief. If is recursively defined by the following rules: $F_q(\{\ \}) = 0$, and for any multiset of certainty factors S and a factor α, $F_q(\alpha \bigcup S) = \alpha + F_q(S) - \alpha * F_q(S)$.

Applying the iterative process of the previous section yields the following. The first application of T_E to $\mathbf{D} = \{ p(a,b)\text{: .6}, r(a,a)\text{: .5}\}$ creates a new fact $q(a,b)$: .6. The next application adds the fact $q(a,b)$: .3, which is then combined with $q(a,b)$: .6, yielding $q(a,b)$: .72, since $F_q(\{ .6, .3\}) = 0.6 + 0.3 - 0.6 * 0.3 = 0.72$. After the third iteration, certainty of $q(a,b)$ raises to 0.744. It is easy to see that this process continues indefinitely, each time producing a better approximation to the certainty of $q(a,b)$ in the intended model of **E**. []

On the other hand, we could compute the certainty of $q(a,b)$ in the intended model using the following argument. Let the certainty of this fact after the n-th iteration be α_n and its certainty after the $n+1$-st iteration be α_{n+1}. It is easy to see that these two numbers are related by the following equation: $\alpha_{n+1} = 0.5 * \alpha_n + 0.6 - 0.6 * 0.5 * \alpha_n$. After the simplification, we obtain $\alpha_{n+1} = 0.6 + 0.2 * \alpha_n$. In the limit we get $\alpha = 0.6 + 0.2 * \alpha$, where α is the certainty of $q(a,b)$ in the intended model. Solving this equation yields 0.75, which is the desired certainty.

The problem illustrated in Example 2 stems from the possibility of a cyclic inferencing of the same fact, each time with a slightly higher certainty. We have also shown that this iterative process can be bypassed, which allows computing certainties exactly. In the next subsection we will generalize this argument to arbitrary programs. Another interesting question is finding out when the problem of Example 2 does not arise. In the rest of this subsection we deal with this issue.

Let us say that a program **E** has *finite termination property* if after a certain step n, $T_{\mathbf{E}}^{n}(\emptyset) = T_{\mathbf{E}}^{n+1}(\emptyset)$ for every $\mathbf{E} = \mathbf{P} \bigcup \mathbf{D}$. Obviously, the problem spotted earlier may happen to a program if and only if the program does not have finite termination property. All nonrecursive programs, or those without uncertainties, obviously possess that property. A large important class of such programs was considered in [33, 34, 37]. This class can be characterized by the fact that all recursive predicates have the same combination function max(...)[4]. That is, given a number of evidences for a fact, p, the combined support provided by these evidences equals the support provided by the strongest of the evidences.

THEOREM 1. If all combination functions for the recursive predicates of **P** are *max*(...)-functions, then **P** has a finite termination property. []

4.2. A Quantitative Semi-Naive Algorithm

In this subsection we generalize the idea of the semi-naive bottom-up query evaluation [2, 6, 18] to the case of quantitative logic programming. The main difficulty here stems from the need in computing certainty factors and dealing with evidential independence.

As illustrated by Example 2, certainty factors cannot be computed just by accumulating new certainties and combining them with the old ones. The discussion following this example suggests that recurrent equations involving certainty factors might be helpful.

Accordingly, we associate an equation with each d-fact. At the very beginning, these equations are all of the form $\tau_{p(\vec{a})} = 0$ for each d-fact $p(\vec{a})$, where $\tau_{p(\vec{a})}$ is a special certainty variable associated with $p(\vec{a})$. This initial equation says that at the beginning no evidence is available for the derived facts, and therefore, their certainty is 0. As the evaluation proceeds, the equations are updated to reflect new evidences obtained during the evaluation process. In general, we end up with recursive equations (like the one obtained in Example 2), which have to be solved to find the desired certainties. We discuss ways of solving these equations later in this section.

First we present a *basic* quantitative semi-naive algorithm assuming the simplest (independence-1) notion of evidential independence. Then we show how to extend this algorithm to accommodate any other notion of independence. We assume the following conventions.

Besides the unique certainty variable $\tau_{p(\vec{a})}$ associated with each fact, $p(\vec{a})$, there is an equation $\tau_{p(\vec{a})} = expr_{p(\vec{a})}$. Here $expr_{p(\vec{a})}$ is an expression involving certainty variables associated with other facts, as well as, possibly, $\tau_{p(\vec{a})}$ itself. As explained earlier, initially $expr_{p(\vec{a})} = 0$ for all facts which are not in the EDB **D** (i.e., for the derived facts). For the EDB-facts from **D**, $expr_{p(\vec{a})}$ simply equals the certainty of $p(\vec{a})$ in **D**. As in the regular semi-naive algorithm (e.g., [2]), we keep track of the ground d-facts obtained in the current iteration (which are kept in the set *NOW*). Facts derived during the previous iteration are kept in the set *LAST*, and those obtained even prior to that are saved in the set *OLD*. The algorithm is depicted in Figure 1.

It is easy to see that because of the associativity of combination functions, at the end of the run of the algorithm of Figure 1, the equation obtained for an arbitrary fact, say $p(\vec{a})$, is equivalent to

$$\tau_{p(\vec{a})} = F_p\left(f_{R_1}(\tau_{q_{11}(\vec{b}_{11})}, \ldots, \tau_{q_{k_1 1}(\vec{b}_{k_1 1})}), \ldots, f_{R_m}(\tau_{q_{1m}(\vec{b}_{1m})}, \ldots, \tau_{q_{k_m m}(\vec{b}_{k_m m})}) \right), \tag{4}$$

where $R_1, \ldots, R_m$ are all the ground d-instances of the rules in **P** with the same head $p(\vec{a})$ used in the

[4] In fact, this class is slightly more general than the one considered in [33, 34, 37].

$OLD := \emptyset$
$LAST :=$ **D** (the EDB)
repeat
  $NOW := \emptyset$
  for each rule $R \in \mathbf{P}$ **do**
  (* Let R be $p(\vec{X}){:}f(\alpha_1, ..., \alpha_n) \leftarrow q_1(\vec{Y}_1){:}\alpha_1, ..., q_n(\vec{Y}_n){:}\alpha_n$.
    Suppose there are ground d-facts $q_1(\vec{b}_1), ..., q_n(\vec{b}_n) \in OLD \cup LAST$ such that:
    (i) $p(\vec{a}) \leftarrow q_1(\vec{b}_1), ..., q_n(\vec{b}_n)$ is a ground d-instance of R,
    (ii) at least one of the $q_i(\vec{b}_i)$s is in $LAST$ *)
   replace $\tau_{p(\vec{a})} = expr_{p(\vec{a})}$ **by** $\tau_{p(\vec{a})} = F_p(f(\tau_{q_1(\vec{b}_1)}, ..., \tau_{q_n(\vec{b}_n)}), expr_{p(\vec{a})})$
   if $p(\vec{a}) \notin OLD \cup LAST$ **then** $NOW := NOW \cup \{p(\vec{a})\}$
  end (* for each *)
  $OLD := OLD \cup LAST$
  $LAST := NOW$
until $NOW = \emptyset$

Figure 1 - The Basic Quantitative Semi-Naive Algorithm

---

algorithm; f_{R_i} are certainty functions associated with these rules, and the d-version of each R_i is $p(\vec{a}) \leftarrow q_{1i}(\vec{b}_{1i}), ..., q_{k_i i}(\vec{b}_{k_i i})$.

Equations associated with the EDB-facts are much simpler: $\tau_{r(\vec{a})} = \alpha$, where α is the certainty of $r(\vec{a})$ in **D**. This is because base predicates cannot appear in the heads of the rules of **P**, and therefore certainties of the EDB-facts do not change. In summary, we obtain a system of equations

$$\left\{ \tau_{p(\vec{a})} = \phi_{p(\vec{a})}(\cdots \tau_{q(\vec{b})} \cdots) \right\}_{p(\vec{a}) \in FACTS} \tag{5}$$

where $FACTS$ is the set of d-facts derived by the semi-naive algorithm plus the facts in **D**; $\phi_{p(\vec{a})}$ stands for the composition of functions in (4). Since all combination and certainty functions are monotonically increasing, all $\phi_{p(\vec{a})}$ are too. These functions are also upper-bounded by 1. The equations in (5) can be also viewed as a definition of an operator, $\Phi_{\mathbf{E}}$: $[0,1]^g \rightarrow [0,1]^g$, where $g = |\mathbf{D}|$ is the number of facts in the EDB. Because of the monotonicity and boundedness, this operator has the least fixed point in $[0,1]^g$, which obviously is a solution to the equational system (5).

THEOREM 2. Consider the semantics under the independence-1 assumption. Then certainty factors for all d-facts in the intended model of **E** are given by the least fixpoint solution of the operator $\Phi_{\mathbf{E}}$ corresponding to the equational system (5). []

It is now easy to generalize the basic algorithm to handle any notion of evidential independence other than independence-1. Let *IND* denote *some* such notion. Recall that in (4) each certainty term $f_R(...)$ corresponds to a unique ground rule used as an evidence for $p(\vec{a})$. Denote the collection of all such rules by S. Let $S_1, ..., S_l$ be all the maximal sets of ***independent*** (according to IND) rules from S, and let $T_1, ..., T_l$ be the corresponding sets of certainty terms. Then, in order to replace independence-1 by IND in the basic semi-naive algorithm, one only has to transform every equation (4) produced by that algorithm into the following form:

$$\tau_{p(\vec{a})} = \max_{i=1,...,l} (F_{p(\vec{a})}(T_1), ..., F_{p(\vec{a})}(T_l)) \tag{6}$$

We will then obtain a different equational system similar to (5):

$$\left\{ \tau_{p(\vec{a})} = \max_{i=1,\ldots,l} \{ \ \ldots \psi^{i}_{p(\vec{a})}(\ldots \tau_{q(\vec{b})} \ldots) \ldots \} \right\}_{p(\vec{a}) \in FACTS} \tag{7}$$

Associated with system (7) is another operator, $\Psi_{E,IND}$, mapping $[0,1]^g$ into $[0,1]^g$, which also possesses the monotonicity and boundedness properties. In particular, as the earlier system (5), it has the least fixed point solution.

THEOREM 3. Assume an arbitrary definition of evidence independence IND. Suppose also that system (7) is obtained from (5) by selecting maximal sets S_1, ..., S_l of independent rules according to IND. Then certainty factors for all d-facts in the intended model of **E** are given by the least fixpoint solution of the operator $\Psi_{E,IND}$ corresponding to the equational system (7). []

Example 8. Consider the following system: EDB $\mathbf{D} = \{ q(a,b): .3, q(a,a): .2, s(b,c): .1, r(c,c): .7 \}$. Rules

$$p(X,Y):\alpha \leftarrow s(X,Y):\alpha$$
$$p(X,Y):\alpha * \beta \leftarrow q(X,Z):\alpha,\ p(Z,Y):\beta$$
$$p(X,Y):\alpha * \beta * \gamma \leftarrow q(X,Z):\alpha,\ p(Z,V):\beta,\ r(V,Y):\gamma$$

Let us trace the execution of the algorithm of Figure 1 assuming the independence-2 notion of evidential independence. Initially OLD = NOW = $\emptyset$, and LAST = **D**. At the first iteration we derive $p(b,c)$: .1 using the first rule. We thus have $p(b,c) \in NOW$, and then $OLD := \mathbf{D}$, $LAST := \{ p(b,c) \}$.

At the next iteration rules 2 and 3 are applied yielding the fact $p(a,c) \in NOW$ twice. This leads to creation of the following equation for $p(a,c)$: $\tau_{p(a,c)} = F_p(\tau_{q(a,b)} * \tau_{p(b,c)}, \tau_{q(a,b)} * \tau_{p(b,c)} * \tau_{r(c,c)})$. Then $p(b,c)$ moves to OLD and $p(a,c)$ to LAST. Notice that the two rules that created $p(a,c)$ were *not* independent according to independence-2.

During the third iteration, rules 2 and 3 are applied once again, but with slightly different data (using $q(a,a)$ instead of $q(a,b)$). This yields the fact $p(a,c)$ two more times, updating the equation for that fact to

$$\tau_{p(a,c)} = F_p(\tau_{q(a,b)} * \tau_{p(b,c)}, \tau_{q(a,b)} * \tau_{p(b,c)} * \tau_{r(c,c)}, \tau_{q(a,a)} * \tau_{p(a,c)}, \tau_{q(a,a)} * \tau_{p(a,c)} * \tau_{r(c,c)}).$$

At this point the derivation terminates since no new ground rule can be applied. However, not all evidences for $p(a,c)$ are independent. According to independence-2, the 1-st and the 2-nd, and the 3-d and the 4-th rules do not provide independent evidences. To take this into account we transform the above equation into the form (6):

$$\begin{aligned}\tau_{p(a,c)} = \max(\ & F_p(\tau_{q(a,b)} * \tau_{p(b,c)}, \tau_{q(a,a)} * \tau_{p(a,c)}), \\ & F_p(\tau_{q(a,b)} * \tau_{p(b,c)}, \tau_{q(a,a)} * \tau_{p(a,c)} * \tau_{r(c,c)}), \\ & F_p(\tau_{q(a,b)} * \tau_{p(b,c)} * \tau_{r(c,c)}, \tau_{q(a,a)} * \tau_{p(a,c)}), \\ & F_p(\tau_{q(a,b)} * \tau_{p(b,c)} * \tau_{r(c,c)}, \tau_{q(a,a)} * \tau_{p(a,c)} * \tau_{r(c,c)})\ ).\end{aligned}$$

Values of all variables except $\tau_{p(b,c)}$ and $\tau_{p(a,c)}$ are known from the initial equations $\tau_{q(a,a)} = 0.2$, $\tau_{q(a,b)} = 0.3$, $\tau_{r(c,c)} = 0.7$, and $\tau_{s(b,c)} = 0.1$. Substituting, we obtain a set of linear equations[5], which can be easily solved, yielding certainties of all facts involved in the query evaluation. []

Unfortunately, the situation is not always that simple as the above example might suggest. First, under a more sophisticated independence requirement (than independence-1), we may have to solve the equational system (7) instead of (5). Solving such a system usually amounts to breaking up the max(...)-functions in (7) and creating a number of simpler equational subsystems of the form (5). These systems are then solved independently. The solution of (7) is the maximum of solutions to the above subsystems. The problem here is that breaking up (7) may create an exponential number of subsystems to solve. Second, the number of equations in (5) or (7) may be as large as the number of relevant facts used in the query evaluation.

Another, perhaps more serious, problem is that, in general, functions ϕ or ψ in (5) and (7) may turn out to be polynomials of an arbitrarily high degree, even though the certainty and combination functions are not more than quadratic. The danger here is that variables τ_p involved in these equations may be mutually dependent on each other. In general, such systems can be solved only approximately. One obvious method is finding the least fixpoint solution to (5) by iterating over the set of equations (5) (i.e., by iteratively applying Φ_E to the vector <0,...,0> of initial values for τ_p s), each time getting better approximations to the actual solutions. For certain types of combination and certainty functions it is

---

[5] Here we assume that F_p is the MYCIN combination function.

possible to find reliable error estimates for the iterative method, but we are unaware of any such method for the general case.

On the bright side, note that if the rules are non-recursive then the iterative method always yields exact solutions. In this case, solving equations (5) or (7) can be done by simple substitution. This does not cause much overhead, since in this case the equations in (7) are non-recursive, and computing certainty factors can be done on-the-fly at the time of rule application. There is no need in this case in splitting the equational system (7) in order to eliminate max(...), since the arguments to max(...) will be always fully evaluated. This argument can be extended to recursive rules as follows.

Let $\mathbf{E} = \mathbf{P} \bigcup \mathbf{D}$ be an expert system. Consider the set H of all d-facts actually used in the query evaluation. Construct the *fact dependence graph* $G(H, \mathbf{P})$ on H w.r.t. $\mathbf{P}$ as follows. An arc from a fact q to p is drawn if and only if there is a ground instance of a rule in $\mathbf{P}$ s.t. its head is p, one of its premises is q, and all other premises are in H.

THEOREM 4. If the fact dependence graph, $G(H, \mathbf{P})$, is acyclic then the iterative method of finding solutions to equational systems (5) and (7) always terminates. The number of iterations over the equations is the same as the number of rule applications in the semi-naive evaluation algorithm. □

Thus, if there are no cyclic facts (note: recursive predicates *are* allowed), then the quantitative semi-naive algorithm can be used without much overhead compared to the regular semi-naive algorithm. We conjecture that in real-life applications there is rarely a need in cyclic facts. Even when they are inherently necessary, we believe that they are small in number, in which case the iterative or other approximate techniques may be acceptable.

There are several possible optimizations to the algorithm presented in Figure 1 which take advantage of Theorem 4. The idea is to evaluate the equations on-the-fly at the rule application time. However, if certain fact is determined to be recursive, we switch to another mode (for that fact) and start generating recursive equations as in Figure 1. Technical details of this optimization are rather tedious and are omitted.

5. Semantics of Conflicting Evidences and Negation

In this section we extend our framework to allow negative literals to appear in rule premises as well as their consequences. The latter is particularly useful when dealing with incomplete knowledge, in which case different evidences may contradict each other. We use the term *support logic* as a generic name for a number of related approaches to coping with such situations[6]. Although this logic suffers from some philosophical problems (as is the case with many other non-standard logics), it was proven practically useful, and we know of at least one commercial implementation [3]. However, we are unaware of any formal semantics for such logics. We attempt to rectify this drawback by extending the semantics described in Sections 2 and 3. Because of the space limitation the results of this section are rather sketchy.

In support logic, each fact, p, has a *measure of belief*, MB, ($\equiv$ certainty in the terminology of Section 2) and a *measure of disbelief*, MD. The latter is the measure of belief in $\neg p$. It is convenient to deal with $1 - MD$ instead of MD, viewing this new quantity as an upper limit on the belief in p. Thus, each fact, p, is assigned an interval $[low, high]$, meaning that the strength of belief in p is somewhere in-between low and $high$. The difference $high - low$ is the *knowledge gap* about p[7]. Under this convention it may seem unnecessary to consider negative literals, since the interval assigned to $\neg p$ is $[1{-}high, 1{-}low]$, which is uniquely determined by the interval for p. However, body occurrences of $p:[l,h]$ and $\neg p:[1{-}h, 1{-}l]$ are treated differently, since certainty functions use interval $[l,h]$ as an argument in the former case, and $[1{-}h, 1{-}l]$ in the latter. Besides, it is often convenient to use negative literals explicitly, even though they could be replaced by their positive counterparts.

Literals in support logic are of the form $p:[\tau,\sigma]$ or $\neg p:[\tau,\sigma]$, where p is a d-literal, and τ, σ are certainty terms. A negative literal, $\neg p:[\tau,\sigma]$, should be perceived as $(\neg p):[\tau,\sigma]$ rather than $\neg(p:[\tau,\sigma])$, which will be clear from their semantics. Rules are as in Section 2 (see (2)), except for the following two differences:

(i) Certainty terms/variables are replaced by intervals of certainty terms/variables.

---

[6] This view is consistent with the spirit of [5].

[7] The measure of belief is sometimes called *credibility* or *necessity* measure, while the disbelief measure is referred to as *possibility* or *plausibility* measure [12, 27].

(ii) Negative literals can appear in rule bodies as well as their heads.

It will be convenient to introduce partial order on the certainty intervals, which will also help to see the succession between the definitions in the current and the previous sections. Thus, we write $[\alpha,\beta] \underline{\lessdot} [\gamma,\delta]$ iff $[\gamma,\delta] \subseteq [\alpha,\beta]$. The motivation here is that a bigger (w.r.t. $\underline{\lessdot}$) certainty interval means that stronger positive and negative evidences are available for the associated fact. We augment the domain of all certainty intervals by adding the *maximal* element, $\top$, representing all *inconsistent* intervals, i.e., intervals $[\alpha,\beta]$ s.t. $\alpha > \beta$. Thus, $[\gamma,\delta] \underline{\lessdot} \top$. Interval [0,1] is, obviously, the smallest certainty interval. It is also easily seen that certainty intervals form a complete lattice: glb (greatest lower bound) of a set of intervals is the smallest (w.r.t. $\subseteq$) interval containing each of the intervals in the set. The least upper bound, lub, of that collection is the largest interval contained in each of the intervals in the set, if it exists; it is $\top$, otherwise. This partial order can be naturally extended to literals so that for the same d-literal p, $p:[\alpha,\beta] \underline{\lessdot} p:[\gamma,\delta]$ iff $[\alpha,\beta] \underline{\lessdot} [\gamma,\delta]$. We also write $p:[\alpha,\beta] \lessdot p:[\gamma,\delta]$ if $p:[\alpha,\beta] \underline{\lessdot} p:[\gamma,\delta]$, but $p:[\alpha,\beta] \neq p:[\gamma,\delta]$.

Herbrand base of a system $\mathbf{E} = \mathbf{P} \bigcup \mathbf{D}$ is now a collection of all positive ground facts $p(\vec{a}):[\alpha,\beta]$, where $[\alpha,\beta]$ is a certainty interval (or $\top$), p is a predicate symbol from $\mathbf{P}$, and $\vec{a}$ is a vector of values from the domain $D_{\mathbf{E}}$. A fact $p:\top$ is called an *inconsistent* fact. Interpretations are, as before, subsets of the Herbrand base. Without loss of generality we assume that every d-fact, p, may appear in I in conjunction with at most one certainty interval. For convenience, we also assume that if p does not appear in I in conjunction with any interval, then $p:[0,1] \in I$, meaning that no information is available about p and $\neg p$ (i.e., the truth of p and $\neg p$ is undefined). Intervals [0,0] and [1,1] mean the usual *false* and *true*, respectively.

A ground positive fact, $p:[\alpha,\beta]$, is true in an interpretation, I, if there is $p:[\gamma,\delta] \in I$ such that $[\alpha,\beta] \underline{\lessdot} [\gamma,\delta]$. A negative fact, $\neg p:[\alpha,\beta]$, is true in I iff $p:[1-\beta, 1-\alpha]$ is true in I.

Certainty (resp. combination) functions now map sequences (resp. multisets) of intervals (including $\top$) into the set of all certainty intervals plus $\top$. Satisfaction of rules by I is established in the standard way, as in Section 2. The definition of satisfaction of programs by interpretations carries over from Section 2 without change, except that each certainty variable/constant α_{ij} should be replaced by an interval $[\underline{\alpha}_{ij}, \overline{\alpha}_{ij}]$ of certainty variables/constants.

Since certainty intervals can be viewed as a lattice of truth values, our semantics can be regarded as an extension of [31], although the latter is described in quite different terms. On the other hand, our notions of implication, model, and entailment are different from another related proposal [17] in which truth values are also organized in a lattice. Notice that an interpretation containing inconsistent literals of the form $p:\top$ may still be a model of an expert system. However, in our logic, inconsistent facts cannot cause much damage, since they may affect only the facts which are directly dependent on them. Thus, it is possible in our semantics to detect an inconsistency, and proceed with other inferences without getting into deep troubles. This is particularly useful in analyzing, say, intelligence information.

The partial order on interpretations and other definitions carry over from Section 2 without much change. Let I and J be a pair of interpretations of $\mathbf{E}$. We write $I \subseteq J$ iff for every positive fact $p:[\alpha,\beta] \in I$ there is a fact $p:[\gamma,\delta] \in J$ such that $[\alpha,\beta] \underline{\lessdot} [\gamma,\delta]$. The notions of intersection and union of interpretations carry over directly with the exception that $\underline{\lessdot}$ replaces the usual ordering on real numbers in the interval [0,1] which was used in Section 2.

It is now easy to see that the framework of Section 2 is a special case of support logic once we replace each literal $p:\alpha$ of Section 2 by a support logic literal of the form $p:[\alpha,1]$.

Because of the negative information (either in the form of negative literals, or as disbelief measures), defining model-theoretic semantics is much more involved than it was in Section 2. As in Logic Programming, non-Horn programs may have no unique least model. Instead, they usually have several minimal models, and it is not always clear which one should be preferred. We will handle this situation along the lines suggested in [1, 28], developing a theory of stratified programs in the framework of support logic.

In pursuing this line we have an additional difficulty, though. The semantics of [1] is a manifestation of the, so called, *closed world assumption* (CWA) [29], in which a fact is assumed false unless there is an evidence to the contrary. However, negation is already present in our framework in the form of disbelief factors, and we do not always want to jump to a negative conclusion whenever there is a knowledge gap about some fact. Namely, if, say, $p(a):[.4, .8]$ is known then in response to the query $p(a):[\alpha,\beta]$? we would still expect the answer $p(a):[.4, .8]$, not $p(a):[.4, .4]$, as CWA would suggest. As in Logic Programming, we take the position that the intent of jumping to a negative conclusion should be explicitly stated in the rule. We will view some negative body literals as such an explicit declaration, which is, again, consistent with the approach taken in Logic Programming and Deductive Databases [1, 10, 25].

Thus, negative information either in the form of disbelief measures of positive literals or in the form of negative head literals will be treated according to the *open world assumption* (OWA) [29] while certain specially annotated negative body literals will be treated according to CWA. Treating negative literals using CWA has the following consequence. Suppose $p:[.2, .6] \in \mathbf{E}$. Then the answer to the query $p:[\alpha,\beta]$? would be $p:[.2, .6]$, while the answer to $\neg p:[1-\beta,1-\alpha]$? is $p:[.2, .2]$, even though the literals in these two queries are logically equivalent[8]. This effect is not a shortcoming of the proposed semantics, but merely a manifestation of different meanings attached to these queries.

It was argued that not all models capture equally well the causality aspect hidden in the syntactic structure of logic rules [28]. The appropriate semantics is given by the, so called, *perfect models* [28]. In this section we extend this notion to accommodate uncertainty.

Suppose a program has a rule $\ldots \leftarrow \ldots \neg p:[\alpha,\beta] \ldots$, and the interpretation I contains a fact $\neg p:[\gamma,\delta]$. Then jumping to a negative conclusion (using CWA) corresponds to assuming that I actually contains the fact $\neg p:[\delta,\delta]$, or, equivalently, $p:[1-\delta,1-\delta]$. Hence, certainty of p in I is also changed, which may affect validity of other rules involving p. However, the idea is to view an appearance of a negative literal in a rule as a declaration of the intention to jump to a negative conclusion in *this particular rule*, without effecting other rules.

To provide a suitable model-theoretic semantics, we assume that, in the program, certain occurrences (not necessarily all) of negative body literals are specially annotated with "$^{\mathbf{o}}$" to indicate that they should be treated under CWA[9]. Then we replace (as in [9]) each occurrence of an annotated negative literal, $\neg q^{\mathbf{o}}:[\alpha,\beta]$, by a *new* positive literal $q_{\neg}:[\alpha,\beta]$. In addition, we add the rule $q_{\neg}(\vec{X}):[\gamma,\delta] \leftarrow \neg q(\vec{X}):[\gamma,\delta]$ for each symbol $q_{\neg}$ (and remove the annotation). From now on we assume that the program $\mathbf{P}$ is modified in this way. Predicates of the form $q_{\neg}$ introduced by this modification will be called *CWA-predicates*; the remaining predicates will be called OWA-predicates.

To introduce stratification into $\mathbf{P}$ we first define *predicate dependence graph.* Given $\mathbf{P}$, its predicate dependence graph, $G_{\mathbf{P}}$, has predicate symbols of $\mathbf{P}$ as its nodes. It has an unlabeled arc $<q,p>$ between a pair of nodes in the graph iff $\mathbf{P}$ has a rule $\mu\, p(\ldots) \leftarrow \ldots, \lambda\, q(\ldots), \ldots$, where μ and λ can be either "$\neg$" or a blank (i.e., no negation). A *CWA-cycle* in $G_{\mathbf{P}}$ is a directed cycle passing through at least one CWA predicate. A program is *stratified* if its predicate dependence graph has no CWA-cycles. An expert system $\mathbf{E} = \mathbf{P} \bigcup \mathbf{D}$ is stratified if its intentional part, $\mathbf{P}$, is stratified. We can define a *stratification ordering* (in fact, a partial quasi-order) on predicate symbols appearing in a stratified program: $q \leq p$ if there is a path from q to p in $G_{\mathbf{P}}$. If at least one node on the path is a CWA-node (including p or q) then we write $q < p$.

Next we extend the notion of *perfect* models [28] to our framework. First, we need to extend the $\preceq$ order defined on OWA ground literals to include the CWA-literals which were added to replace negative literals in the rule bodies. This is done by assuming that for each CWA d-literal $q_{\neg}:[\alpha,\beta] \preceq q_{\neg}:[\gamma,\delta]$ iff $\alpha \geq \gamma$ and $\beta \geq \delta$. Notice that the $\preceq$ ordering on CWA literals differs from the case of OWA literals only in that the first inequality is reversed.

We extend $\preceq$ even further by writing $p(\vec{a}):[\ldots] \prec q(\vec{b}):[\ldots]$, where p and q are predicate symbols in $\mathbf{P}$, iff $p \prec q$ in the stratification ordering. Of course, with this extension $\preceq$ is no longer a partial order, in general, but it is a partial order if $\mathbf{P}$ is stratified. We say that an interpretation I of $\mathbf{P}$ is *preferable* to J (abbr. $I << J$) iff for every ground atom $p:[\alpha,\beta]$ which is true in I but false in J, there is a ground atom $q:[\gamma,\delta]$ which is true in J but false in I such that $q:[\gamma,\delta] \prec p:[\alpha,\beta]$. A model of $\mathbf{P}$ is *perfect* if it is minimal with respect to the preference relation $<<$.

In Logic Programming, stratified programs possess many nice properties. First, each such program has a unique perfect model, which represents its intended semantics. Second, computing perfect models is relatively inexpensive because the intended model can be obtained by applying the rules subject to the partial order imposed by stratification, in which case one never has to retract any fact previously derived in the computation. Unfortunately, in the quantitative case, stratification alone does not ensure such behaviour.

---

[8] More precisely, initially we get $\neg p:[.4,.8]$ as an answer, but after closing the knowledge gap under CWA the result is $\neg p:[.8,.8]$ or, equivalently, $p:[.2,.2]$.

[9] Note: we allow some occurrences of a literal to be treated under CWA, while others under OWA.

To make things work, we assume that the certainty and combination functions satisfy all the requirements for these functions listed in Section 2, where, as before, scalar certainties are replaced by intervals of certainties, and the usual order $\leq$ on [0,1] is replaced by $\trianglelefteq$ on the intervals. Again, it is easy to see that the requirements in Section 2 represent a special case of the new requirements, once each scalar entity, α, is replaced by the interval $[\alpha,1]$.

Although simple and intuitively appealing, these assumptions are no longer that natural as they were in Section 2. For instance, it may be desirable to assume that, as the belief in $\neg p$ increases, the belief in p should decrease. The monotonicity assumption about the certainty and combination functions rules this possibility out. Particularly, one of its deplorable casualties is the famous Dempster-Shafer combination rule [32]. On the other hand, our theory is still useful in many problem domains. For instance, the above requirements are satisfied by the functions computing the belief and disbelief measures in MYCIN. Extension of our semantics to include other important combination rules is a topic for future research. From now on we assume that the above requirements are satisfied.

PROPOSITION 3. Every stratified expert system has a unique perfect model. []

We will call the unique perfect model of **P** the *intended* model. This model can be computed similarly to [1] by successively applying the fixpoint operators corresponding to different strata of the program (in the stratification ordering). We will refer to this process as the *fixpoint computation.* Notice that it may turn out during the computation that the intended model of **P** contains inconsistent facts of the form $p:[\alpha,\beta]$, where $\alpha > \beta$. However, as noted earlier, this problem is localized to the inconsistent facts themselves, and to the facts which are directly dependent on them.

Example 4. Suppose the EDB **D** is $\{ p:[0, .5] \}$, and consider the following pair of logically equivalent sets of rules: $\mathbf{P}_1 = \{ p:[1,1] \leftarrow \neg q:[1,1] \quad p:[.3, .5] \leftarrow \neg r:[.3, .5] \}$, and $\mathbf{P}_2 = \{ p:[1,1] \leftarrow \neg q^{\circ}:[1,1] \quad p:[.3, .5] \leftarrow \neg r^{\circ}:[.3, .5] \}$. Recall that $\neg q^{\circ}$ is $\neg q$ designated for treatment under CWA. In $\mathbf{P}_1$ none of the rules can be applied, and the intended model would be identical to **D**. In contrast, in $\mathbf{P}_2$ both rules are applicable (since $\neg r:[.5, .5]$ and $\neg q:[1,1]$ are derived under CWA) and we obtain $p:[.3, .5]$ and $p:[1,1]$. Because of the monotonicity of combination functions, the combined evidence would be $p:[1, .5]$ ($\equiv p: \top$) - an inconsistent fact. []

Notice that although in the above example programs $\mathbf{P}_1$ and $\mathbf{P}_2$ are logically equivalent, they are interpreted differently by the CWA. However, this is similar to the corresponding situation in Deductive Databases and Logic Programming where, say, $p \vee q$ is handled differently than $p \leftarrow \neg q$.

THEOREM 5. The fixpoint computation yields the intended model of **P**. []

Quantitative semi-naive algorithms of Section 4 can also be extended to handle support logic queries. This issue will be dealt with in the full version of the paper. We conclude this section with a classic example of "Flying Tweety", slightly modified to illustrate some of the issues discussed in this section, including conflicting evidences.

Example 5. Suppose the EDB contains a single fact $bird(tweety):[.7, .9]$, and consider the following rule:

$$flies(X):[min(\alpha,\gamma),max(\beta,\delta)] \leftarrow bird(X):[\alpha,\beta],\ \neg abnormal^{\circ}(X):[\gamma,\delta].$$

Applying the rule yields $flies(tweety):[.7, 1]$. If, in addition, there would be an evidence that Tweety is abnormal, e.g., $abnormal(tweety):[.4, .7]$, then we can only conclude $flies(tweety):[.3, .9]$, thereby decreasing our belief in Tweety's ability to fly. On the other hand, if we were told that $abnormal(tweety):[.7, 1]$ (say, because Tweety looks like a penguin), then the conclusion would be $flies(tweety):[0, .9]$, eliminating our belief in Tweety being a flying creature, while leaving some small evidence to the contrary.

Suppose now that we had another rule, $\neg flies(X):[\alpha,\beta] \leftarrow abnormal(X):[\alpha,\beta]$, and the combination function for $flies(...)$ were $F(\{ [x,v],[y,w] \}) = [x+y-x*y, v*w]$. Here $abnormal$ is treated under OWA. Assuming $abnormal(tweety):[.7, 1]$, we get $flies(tweety):[0, .3]$ from the last rule. Combining this with $flies(tweety):[0, .9]$ which was obtained earlier, we conclude $flies(tweety):[0, .27]$, strongly suggesting that Tweety cannot fly.

Of course, these conclusions are not too surprising, since our semantics is an extension of that given in [1, 25, 28]. []

6. Conclusions and Future Work

We presented a model-theoretic and fixpoint semantics for rule-based expert systems with uncertainty. Our approach to the problem is much more general than the earlier works on that issue [33, 34, 37]. We have also considered some new aspects of the problem such as evidential independence, conflicting evidences, etc. Our treatment of negation accommodates both the closed and the open world assumptions.

As a first step towards query optimization in expert systems, we presented a generalization of the well-known semi-naive evaluation algorithm widely used in deductive databases [2, 6, 18]. Although some optimization methods from deductive databases (e.g. [7, 23]) can be directly applied to the quantitative case discussed in this paper, more work needs to be done in order to be able to recognize and eliminate low-certainty facts from the query evaluation process.

Our treatment of conflicting evidences is not as general as one would like it to be. For instance, as noted in Section 5, Dempster-Shafer combination rule is precluded by our assumptions about monotonicity of certainty and combination functions. Extending this framework is also a topic for the future. Nevertheless, our logic is still useful for a wide range of applications. Another intriguing issue is the ability of that logic to tolerate inconsistent information, yet be able to make sensible inferencing. This feature is very important in certain problem domains (e.g, military, medicine).

Additional cases of evidential independence need to be studied. The two independence criteria presented in Section 2 do not always produce the desired effect. For instance, under both criteria, combination of the rule $p:\alpha \leftarrow p:\alpha$ and a fact $p: .0001$ would lead us to conclude $p:1$. This conclusion may not be the desired one in many situations. Likewise, given the following three rules: $p \leftarrow b$, $p \leftarrow a$, and $a \leftarrow p$, we may not want to view the first pair of rules as being independent (because $a \leftarrow p$). Independence criteria appropriate to that situation will be presented elsewhere.

Finally, the very concept of independence may be too restrictive. The problem is that we view rules as being either totally independent, or totally dependent on each other. In practice, however, one may want to think of a pair of rules $p \leftarrow a,b$ and $p \leftarrow a,c$ as being only *partially* dependent (because of the common premise a). This means that different evidences supplied by the two rules should not be combined to a full extent, as it would be in the case of totally independent rules. We are currently pursuing several possibilities for accommodating partial independence in the proposed framework.

7. References

1. K. R. Apt, H. Blair and A. Walker, "Towards a Theory of Declarative Knowledge", in *Foundations of Deductive Databases and Logic Programming*, J. Minker, (ed.), Morgan-Kaufmann, 1988, 89-148.
2. I. Balbin and K. Ramamohanarao, "A Generalization of the Differential Approach to Recursive Query Evaluation", *J. of Logic Programming*, **4**, (1987), 259-262.
3. J. F. Baldwin, T. P. Martin and B. W. Pilsworth, *FRIL Manual*, EQUIPU-AIR, Ltd., Bristol, UK, 1987.
4. J. F. Baldwin and M. R. M. Monk, "Evidence Theory, Fuzzy Logic and Logic Programming", ITRC Tech. Rep.# 109, University of Bristol, UK, 1987.
5. J. F. Baldwin, "Evidential Support Logic Programming", *Fuzzy Sets and Systems*, **24**, (1987), 1-26.
6. F. Bancilhon, "Naive Evaluation of Recursively Defined Relations", Tech. Rep.# DB-004-85, MCC, 1985.
7. C. Beeri and R. Ramakrishnan, "On the Power of Magic", *Proc. of the ACM SIGACT-SIGMOD Symp. on Prin. of Database Systems*, 1987, 269-283.
8. B. G. Buchanan and E. H. Shortliffe, (eds.), *Rule-Based Expert Systems*, Addison-Wesley, 1984.
9. A. K. Chandra and D. Harel, "Horn Clauses and Generalizations", *J. of Logic Programming*, 1985, 1-15.
10. K. L. Clark, "Negation as Failure", in *Logic and Databases*, H. Gallaire and J. Minker, (eds.), Plenum Press, New York, 1978, 293-324.
11. W. F. Clocksin and C. S. Mellish, *Programming in Prolog*, Springer Verlag, Berlin-Heidelberg-New York, 1981.
12. D. Dubois and H. Prade, (eds.), *Fuzzy Sets and Systems: Theory and Applications*, Academic Press, 1980.
13. E. A. Feigenbaum, "The Art of Artificial Intelligence: 1. Themes and Case Studies of Knowledge Engineering", *IJCAI-77*, 1977, 1014-1029.
14. R. Frost, *Introduction to Knowledge Base Systems*, Macmillan Publishing C., 1986.
15. G. Gardarin, "Magic Functions: A Technique to Optimize Extended Datalog Recursive Programs", *Proc. of the ACM Intl. Conf. on Very Large Data Bases*, 1987, 21-30.

16. M. L. Ginsberg, "Nonmonotonic Reasoning Using Dempster's Rule", *AAAI-84*, Austin, TX, 1984, 126-129.

17. M. L. Ginsberg, "Multivalued Logics", in *Readings in Non-Monotonic Reasoning*, M. L. Ginsgerg, (ed.), 1987, 251-255.

18. U. Guntzer and W. K. A. R. Bayer, "On Evaluation of Recursion in Deductive Database Systems by Efficient Differential Fixpoint Iteration", *3-d Int. Conf. on Data Engineering*, 1987, 120-129.

19. F. Hayes-Roth, D. Waterman and D. Lenat, (eds.), *Building Expert Systems*, Addison-Wesley, 1983.

20. F. Hayes-Roth, "Rule-Based Systems", *Comm. ACM*, **28**, 9 (Sep. 1985), 921-932.

21. D. E. Heckerman and E. J. Horovitz, "On the Expressive Power of Rule-Based Systems for Reasoning with Uncertainty", *Automated Reasoning*, 1987, 121-126.

22. L. N. Kanal and J. F. Lemmer, (eds.), *Uncertainty in Artificial Intelligence (Machine Intelligence and Pattern Recognition, vol. 4)*, North Holland, 1986.

23. M. Kifer and E. L. Lozinskii, "A Framework for an Efficient Implementation of Deductive Database Systems", *Proceedings of the 6-th Advanced Database Symposium*, Tokyo, Japan, Aug. 1986.

24. R. C. T. Lee, "Fuzzy Logic and the Resolution Principle", *J. of ACM*, 1972, 109-119.

25. V. Lifschitz, "On the Declarative Semantics of Logic Programs with Negation", in *Foundations of Deductive Databases and Logic Programming*, J. Minker, (ed.), Morgan-Kaufmann, Los Altos, CA, 1988, 177-192.

26. J. W. Lloyd, *Foundations of Logic Programming (Second Edition)*, Springer Verlag, 1987.

27. H. Prade, "A Synthetic View of Approximate Reasoning Techniques", *IJCAI*, 1983, 130-136.

28. T. C. Przymusinski, "On the Declarative Semantics of Deductive Databases and Logic Programs", in *Foundations of Deductive Databases and Logic Programming*, J. Minker, (ed.), Morgan-Kaufmann, Los Altos, CA, 1988, 193-216.

29. R. Reiter, "On Closed World Databases", in *Logic and Databases*, H. Gallaire and J. Minker, (eds.), Plenum Press, New York, 1978, 55-76.

30. D. C. Rine, "Some Relationships between Logic Programming and Multiple-Valued Logic", *Symp. on Multiple-Valued Logic*, 1986, 160-163.

31. E. Sandewall, "A Functional Approach to Non-Monotonic Logic", *IJCAI-85*, 1985, 100-106.

32. G. Shafer, *A Mathematical Theory of Evidence*, Princeton University Press, 1976.

33. E. Shapiro, "Logic Programs with Uncertainties: A Tool for Implementing Rule-Based Systems", *IJCAI-83*, 1983, 529-532.

34. V. S. Subrahmanian, "On the Semantics of Quantitative Logic Programs", *IEEE Symposium on Logic Programming*, 1987, 173-182.

35. J. D. Ullman, *Principles of Database and Knowledge-Base Systems*, Computer Science Press, Rockville, MD, 1988.

36. M. H. van Emden and R. A. Kowalski, "The Semantics of Predicate Logic as a Programming Language", *J. ACM*, **23**, 4 (Oct. 1976), 733-742.

37. M. H. van Emden, "Quantitative Deduction and its Fixpoint Theory", *The Journal of Logic Programming*, 1986, 37-53.

38. L. Vieille, "Recursive Axioms in Deductive Databases: The Query-Subquery Approach", *Proc. of the 1-st Conf. on Expert Database Systems*, Charleston, SC, 1986, 179-196.

39. M. Zamankova-Leech and A. Kandel, *Fuzzy Relational Databases - a Key to Expert Systems*, Verlag TUV Rheinland, Koln, 1984.

40. A. Zvieli, "A Fuzzy Relational Calculus", *Proc. of the 1-st Int. Conf. of Expert Database Systems*, Charlestone, SC, 1986, 225-240.

Efficient Consistency Control in Deductive Databases *

Guido Moerkotte
Stefan Karl

Fakultät für Informatik
Universität Karlsruhe
D–7500 Karlsruhe 1

Abstract

In this paper a theoretical framework for efficiently checking the consistency of deductive databases is provided and proven to be correct. Our method is based on focussing on the relevant parts of the database by reasoning forwards from the updates of a transaction, and using this knowledge about real or just possible implicit updates for simplifying the consistency constraints in question. Opposite to the algorithms by Kowalski/Sadri and Lloyd/Topor, we are neither committed to determine the exact set of implicit updates nor to determine a fairly large superset of it by only considering the head literals of deductive rule clauses. Rather, our algorithm unifies these two approaches by allowing to choose any of the above or even intermediate strategies for any step of reasoning forwards. This flexibility renders possible the integration of statistical data and knowledge about access paths into the checking process. Second, deductive rules are organized into a graph to avoid searching for applicable rules in the proof procedure. This graph resembles a connection graph, however, a new method of interpreting it avoids the introduction of new clauses and links.

1 Introduction

A database is intended to be a truthful model of a given universe of discourse. Constraints that have been observed in this given miniworld are usually modelled as consistency constraints. Hence, these constraints should not be violated by database updates and have to be checked for validity at the end of any transaction. Since constraint checking is rather expensive, one should try to avoid inspecting the entire database. Exploiting the assumption that the constraints are satisfied before the transaction starts, it seems preferable to check only those parts of the database really affected by the transaction. Therewith, one has to take into account that in deductive databases the addition (deletion) of a fact may result in implicit additions and deletions of other facts as well.

A method for avoiding redundant checking of constraints in a relational database was proposed by Nicolas ([5]). His algorithm utilizes the database update in question to instantiate the consistency constraints, i.e. to replace variables by appropriate constants, and then to evaluate this possibly smaller set of simplified constraints by querying the database. This method was extended for deductive databases by Lloyd and Topor ([4], refered to as L/T). However, they determine a superset of the set of implicit updates by only considering the head literals of rule clauses. A method of (exactly) reasoning forwards from the updates of the transaction was proposed by Kowalski, Sadri and Soper ([2], refered to as K/S) who use an extended SLDNF proof procedure to check for consistency.

*This work was partly supported by Deutsche Forschungsgemeinschaft, Sonderforschungsbereich 314 "Artificial Intelligence and Knowledge-Based Systems", Project X4.

Both approaches exhibit deficiencies when applied to certain combinations of facts, rules, and constraints. These deficiencies can be overcome by unifying the ideas of L/T and K/S to a more general approach. Our key idea is that the procedure for determining the implicit consequences of an update should not be fixed for the whole process of forward chaining. Rather, in any step (i.e. given an explicit or implicit update, what are its consequences ?) one should be free to decide whether to reason exactly, to instantiate the head literal of the applicable rule as least as possible, or to choose an intermediate strategy. This decision could be based for example on statistical data about the amount of facts, the selectivity of certain attributes, or the availability of access paths.

We are convinced that the rules of a deductive database can be stored in main memory. Therefore, to further optimize consistency checking, we propose to establish a graph for representing the rules and consistency constraints, and feasible unifications between their literals. Utilizing a connection graph was already proposed in ([2]). However, using the algorithms from [1] for processing it, results in the introduction of new clauses and links at every deduction step. To avoid this, we propose an interpreting mechanism for our graph which deals with a set of substitutions only and never introduces new clauses or links.

The rest of the paper is organized as follows. In chapter 2 we sketch the methods of L/T and K/S and give counterexamples with respect to their efficiency. Chapter 3 describes our generalized approach for more efficient integrity checking. It introduces a data structure similar to a connection graph and a new method for interpreting it. Chapter 4 revisits the examples using the method developed in 3, and chapter 5 concludes with an outlook to further extensions.

2 Evaluation of Existing Techniques

The aim of this chapter is to exhibit the pros and cons of each method (L/T and K/S) and to argue for integrating them to a generalized approach. We present three simple examples of deleting a fact in a deductive database. The first two examples stress the merits of the one and the deficiencies of the other method, the third one reveals both methods to be inadequate. Prior to this, we introduce some terminology and sketch the proposed simplification algorithms as far as necessary to understand the examples (for details see [4], [2]).

We assume a database to be a set of facts, rules in the form of Horn–clauses, and consistency constraints in general clausal form. We call a fact deleted, if it was derivable from the database, and is not derivable from the updated database, i.e. after the execution of a transaction.

The Method by Lloyd/Topor. For an explicitly deleted fact A, L/T define $atom^0 := \{A\}$, and recursively $atom^{n+1} := \{A\theta | A \leftarrow A_1, ..., A_m \in DB, B \in atom^n, \exists i \exists \theta : \theta = mgu(A_i, B)\}$. Let $atom$ be identical to $\bigcup_{i=0}^{n} atom^i$ where n is the least integer such that $atom^{n+1}$ is subsumed by $\bigcup_{i=0}^{n} atom^i$, i.e. $atom$ is the maximum set of facts eventually no longer derivable due to the deletion of A. Now, S is defined as a subset of $atom$ such that $\forall l \in atom\ \exists l' \in S\ \exists \theta : l'\theta = l$. Finally, checking an arbitrary constraint c will be substituted by testing all instantiations $c\theta$, where $\theta \in \{mgu(l_1, l_2) \mid l_1 \in S, l_2\ is\ a\ positive\ literal\ in\ c\}$.

The Method by Kowalski/Sadri. K/S give a set of six rules for defining the refutation Refute(s u) of an update u in a database state s. Since one has to refute $\neg f$, if f is the deleted fact, we need only consider the rules R1, R2, R5, and R6, which are given below in a slightly modified version.

R1: Refute(s {})

R2: Refute(s c)←
Select(l c) and
In(d s) and

Resolve(d c l r) and
Refute(s r).

R5: Refute(DT∪IT $\{\neg l\}$)←
In($\{a\} \cup b$ DT) and
On($\neg l$ b) and
Deleted(DT D a) and
Refute(DT∪IT $\{\neg a\}$).

R6: Deleted(DT D a)←
Refute(D $\{\neg a\}$) and
NOT(Refute(DT $\{\neg a\}$)).

Therewith, D is the database, DT is the updated one, and IT is the set of consistency constraints. Select(l c) selects a literal l from a clause c. Remove(c l r) removes a literal l from a clause c which results in r. Resolve(d c l r) means that resolving clauses d and c on literal l yields the resolvent r. In(d s) means d is a clause in s. On(l b) means literal l occurs in b. Finally, if the literal l is no longer valid in DT, i.e. it has been deleted by the transaction, then Refute(DT ∪ IT $\{\neg l\}$) checks for consistency.

Now, we are prepared to understand the examples. In the first one, we give a database with a consistency constraint and a transaction where no simplification by instantiation is possible. Thus, using L/T the original consistency constraint has to be checked and nothing is gained at all. We will see that K/S works quite well in this situation. The second example emphasizes the other extrem. Here K/S might be quite inefficient while L/T simplifies the given constraint to one which is easily verified. In the following, we assume x, y, z to denote variables, and a, b, c, d, e, f to denote constants.

Example 1: There are only two rules in the first data base:

$$p_1(x, y) \wedge q(y, z) \Longrightarrow r(y, y)$$
$$p_2(x, y) \wedge r(y, z) \Longrightarrow q(x, z).$$

The consistency constraint considered here is:

$$p_2(x, y) \Longrightarrow q(x, y).$$

The transaction applied is : delete $p_2(b, a)$.

Following L/T the *atom* sets are computed as follows:

$$\begin{aligned} atom^0 &= \{p_2(b, a)\} \\ atom^1 &= \{q(b, z)\} \\ atom^2 &= \{r(b, b)\} \\ atom^3 &= \{q(x, b)\} \\ atom^4 &= \{r(x, x)\} \\ atom^5 &= \{q(x, z)\} \\ atom^6 &= \{r(x, x)\} \end{aligned}$$

Here the stopping rule is applied, and we get the following set S:

$$S = \{p_2(b, a), q(x, z), r(x, x)\}$$

Thus, for our consistency constraint we do not have any substitution besides the identity.

Let us now turn to K/S and imagine that the database contains the following facts:

$p_1(a,b)$	$p_2(b,a)$	$r(a,a)$
$p_1(b,c)$	$p_2(c,b)$	
$p_1(c,d)$	$p_2(d,c)$	
$p_1(d,e)$	$p_2(e,d)$	

Then, K/S yields the following refutation straightforwardly:

$$\{\neg p_2(b,a)\}$$
R5
$$\{\neg q(b,a)\}$$
R5
$$\{\neg r(b,b)\}$$
R5
$$\{\neg q(c,b)\}$$
R2
$$\{\neg p_2(c,b)\}$$
R2
$$\square$$

Example 2: Let us assume the single rule

$$p(x,y,z) \wedge q(x,y) \Longrightarrow r(x,z)$$

and the following consistency constraint:

$$s(x,z) \Longrightarrow r(x,z)$$

The database shall contain the following facts:

q(a,b)	p(a,b,c_1)	r(a,c_1)	s(a,c_{50})
	p(a,b,c_2)	r(a,c_3)	
	p(a,b,c_3)	r(a,c_5)	
	...	...	
	p(a,b,c_{100})	r(a,c_{99})	

The transaction under consideration now deletes the fact q(a,b) which violates the consistency constraint. Using K/S we have to apply rule R5. Since not all instances of r(a,z) have been deleted, we first have to look for one (and in the case of consistency for all) instantiation(s) of z such that r(a,z) is deleted implicitly. This might be a quite exhaustive search. In our case, for example, those r(a,c_i) with i odd are still valid. The second step consists of proving for some deleted r(a,c_i) whether this yields a refutation. There is success for r(a,c_{50}) only, and a lot of time has been vasted for $i \neq 50$.

Further, using K/S we get all the well known inefficiencies of SL-Resolution. These inefficiencies are well described by Kowalski ([1]) who additionally presents a method called the connection graph procedure to overcome them. K/S only propose to investigate the integration of connection graphs into their proof procedure. Unfortunately, they do not elaborate on this idea.

Let us now apply the method of L/T to example 2. This yields $atom^0 = \{q(a,b)\}$, $atom^1 = \{r(a,z)\}$ and $atom^2 = \{\}$. Hence, the original consistency constraint is simplified to $s(a,z) \Longrightarrow$

$r(a, z)$. There exists only one possibility to satisfy s(a,z), namely s(a,c_{50}). Thus, the constraint further simplifies to r(a,c_{50}) which should be checked easily.

Consequences and Improvements. From the examples above we learn that it is not advisable to rely on just one of the consistency checking methods proposed in the literature. Determining the exact set of implicit updates may result in a large amount of unnecessary searching and different proof trees, whereas determining just a superset of the relevant updates may fail to find any simplification at all.

Even worse, however, there are situations in which neither of the two methods is really adequate. We shall prove this by slightly modifying example 1 by assuming the additional facts

$$q(a, f_{50}) \qquad r(a, f_1) \qquad \ldots \qquad r(a, f_{100})$$

in the database. Since L/T do not take into account the fact base at all when reasoning forwards, we yield the same result as in example 1, i.e. no simplification of the original constraint is found. Whereas K/S worked well in example 1, we now get a rather blown up proof tree. Its deficiency consists of treating all literals $\{\neg q(b, f_i)\}$ seperately, and thus identically repeating the last three steps of refutation a hundred times.

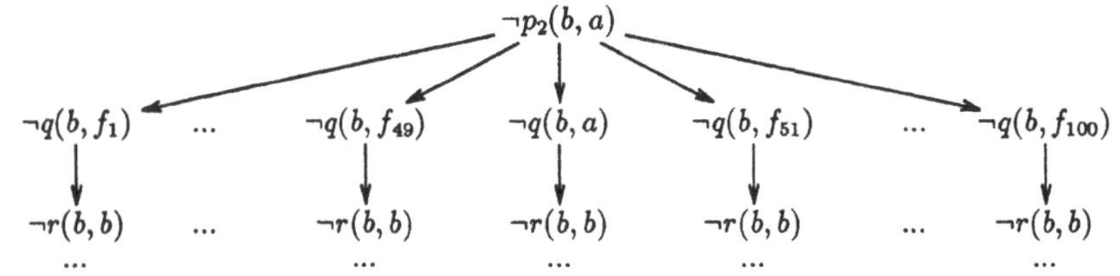

This last example motivates one of the improvements we propose. For any step of forward reasoning there should be the independent choice whether to reason exactly (K/S) or to consider a superset of the implied updates (L/T). Here, it would have been profitable to first follow L/T and then to proceed according to K/S.

An even more ambitious improvement not captured in our examples results from intermediate strategies. Assume a deductive rule having a head literal $p(x, y)$ and an update concerning the premise of the rule, but yielding an instantiation neither for x nor for y. Hence, L/T will have $p(x, y) \in atom^i$ and in K/S it might be necessary to instantiate both x and y. Taking into account statistical knowledge it could be worth-while to choose an intermediate strategy, i.e., for example, to instantiate x but to leave y uninstantiated.

The data structure and algorithms presented in the next chapter do support these proposals.

3 The Consistency Constraint Connection Graph

We now introduce the new method formally. This has the advantage that the correctness of the method can be proven. For this, we first need some basic definitions for a common notational basis. Then, we precisely capture the difference between the old and the updated database.

Throughout the rest of the paper let DB, DB_{old}, and DB_{new} be definite databases, $\mathcal{C}$ a set of constraints in clausal form, and TA a transaction. f and f_i will denote ground atoms. For a negative literal $\neg f$, $|\neg f|$ is defined as f. For a positive literal, $|\;|$ is the identity. TA is always of the form: $TA = \{del\ f_1, ..., del\ f_m, add\ f_{m+1}, ..., add\ f_n\}$, $f_i \neq f_j$ for all $i \neq j$. Define $DB(TA) = (DB \setminus \{f_1, ..., f_m\}) \cup \{f_{m+1}, ..., f_n\}$. In this chapter $DB_{new} := DB_{old}(TA)$ always holds. We further define

$$\alpha(TA) := \{\neg f_i | 1 \le i \le m, DB_{old} \vdash f_i, DB_{new} \not\vdash f_i\} \cup$$
$$\{f_j | m < j \le n, DB_{old} \not\vdash f_j, DB_{new} \vdash f_j\},$$

the set of explicit additions and deletions. Note that the definition for $\alpha(TA)$ is symmetric with respect to additions and deletions. We only use those f_i ($\neg f_i$) which are really added (deleted). This contrasts K/S who use all clauses $f_{m+1}, ..., f_n$ as top clauses.

$$\Delta A := \{f | DB_{old} \not\vdash f, DB_{new} \vdash f\} \cup \{\neg f | DB_{old} \vdash f, DB_{new} \not\vdash f\}.$$

is the set of all explicit and implicit updates caused by the transaction. $M(DB) := \{f | DB \vdash f\} \cup \{\neg f | DB \not\vdash f\}$ can be interpreted as a model of comp(DB) ([3]) or DB under the closed world assumption ([6]).

Since $M(DB_{new}) = (M(DB_{old}) \cap M(DB_{new})) \cup \Delta A$, $M(DB_{new}) \cup \mathcal{C}$ is inconsistent iff there exists a linear resolution refutation with an element in ΔA as a top clause. In general, this statement is no longer true if we substitute $\alpha(TA)$ for ΔA. One possible ad hoc idea, to avoid checking the consistency constraints as a whole after each transaction, is to compute ΔA and to use every element in ΔA as a top clause for a linear resolution proof. However, this is quite inefficient too. Nevertheless, we will keep this idea in mind and will have a closer look at ΔA.

The remainder of this chapter is organized as follows. First, we structure the set ΔA. In analogy to this structuring, we define the consistency constraint connection graph (C^3G). Then, we show that $M(DB_{new}) \cup \mathcal{C}$ consistent iff every path in this graph satisfies a certain condition. There are several alternatives for testing this path condition. In the next chapter we will see how they correspond to L/T and K/S. The advantage of our method is that at any step one can choose independently the kind of operation one wants to perform. This decision might be based on statistical knowledge and the knowledge about access paths.

Let $\mathcal{R} = \{r_i\}$ be the set of rules in DB_{old}, and hence in DB_{new}, and $r_i = \{r_{i,j}\}$. $\mathcal{C}$ is structured similarily. Let $\mathcal{C}^+/r_i^+(\mathcal{C}^-/r_i^-)$ be the set of all positive (negative) literals in $\mathcal{C}/r_i$, $\mathcal{L} := \{r_{i,j}\} \cup \{c_{i,j}\}$, $\mathcal{L}_A$ the set of all atoms contained in $\mathcal{L}$, and $\mathcal{S}$ be the set of all substitutions. We define A^i to be the set of explicit and implicit updates using i steps of forward reasoning. Then, $\Delta A = \bigcup A^k$ holds.

$$A^0 := \alpha(TA)$$

$$\begin{aligned} A^{k+1} := A^k \cup \{r_{i,j_2}\sigma\tau | \quad & r_i \in \mathcal{R}, r_{i,j_1} \in r_i^-, r_{i,j_2} \in r_i^+, g \in A^k, \sigma = mgu(|r_{i,j_1}|, g), \tau \in \mathcal{S} \\ & r_{i,j_2}\sigma\tau \text{ ground}, DB_{old} \not\vdash r_{i,j_2}\sigma\tau, DB_{new} \vdash r_{i,j_2}\sigma\tau\} \\ \cup \{\neg r_{i,j_2}\sigma\tau | \quad & r_i \in \mathcal{R}, r_{i,j_1} \in r_i^-, r_{i,j_2} \in r_i^+, g \in A^k, \sigma = mgu(r_{i,j_1}, g), \tau \in \mathcal{S} \\ & r_{i,j_2}\sigma\tau \text{ ground}, DB_{old} \vdash r_{i,j_2}\sigma\tau, DB_{new} \not\vdash r_{i,j_2}\sigma\tau\} \end{aligned}$$

In order to understand the following definition of the graph, it might be useful to take a look at fig.1 and fig.2 in chapter 4. Here, the C^3G graphs for the examples from chapter 2 are represented. The top line represents the consistency constraints. The bottom line that part of $\mathcal{L}_A$ relevant for the deleted fact. These literals are intended to be entry points into the graph, i.e. any literal in $\alpha(TA)$ can be matched against one of them. $C^3G \subseteq (\mathcal{L}_A \cup \mathcal{L}) \times \mathcal{L} \times \{R, S\}$ is defined as follows. (It might be useful to read S as Supports, and R as Resolves.)

$$\begin{aligned}
C^3G_{\mathcal{L}_A,\mathcal{C}^+} &:= \{(l, c_{i,j}, S) | l \in \mathcal{L}_A, c_{i,j} \in c_i^+, ex.\ \theta \in \mathcal{S} : l\theta = c_{i,j}\theta\} \\
C^3G_{\mathcal{L}_A,\mathcal{C}^-} &:= \{(l, c_{i,j}, R) | l \in \mathcal{L}_A, c_{i,j} \in c_i^-, ex.\ \theta \in \mathcal{S} : l\theta = |c_{i,j}|\theta\} \\
C^3G_{\mathcal{L}_A,\mathcal{R}^-} &:= \{(l, r_{i,j}, R) | l \in \mathcal{L}_A, r_{i,j} \in r_i^-, ex.\ \theta \in \mathcal{S} : l\theta = |r_{i,j}|\theta\} \\
C^3G_{\mathcal{R}^+,\mathcal{R}^-} &:= \{(r_{h,l}, r_{i,j}, R) | r_{h,l} \in r_h^+, r_{i,j} \in r_i^-, ex.\ \theta \in \mathcal{S} : r_{h,l}\theta = |r_{i,j}|\theta\} \\
C^3G_{\mathcal{R}^-,\mathcal{R}^+} &:= \{(r_{i,j}, r_{i,h}, R) | r_{i,j} \in r_i^-,\ r_{i,h} \in r_i^+\} \\
C^3G_{\mathcal{R}^+,\mathcal{C}^+} &:= \{(r_{h,l}, c_{i,j}, S) | r_{h,l} \in r_h^+, c_{i,j} \in \mathcal{C}^+, ex.\ \theta \in \mathcal{S} : r_{h,l}\theta = c_{i,j}\theta\} \\
C^3G_{\mathcal{R}^+,\mathcal{C}^-} &:= \{(r_{h,l}, c_{i,j}, R) | r_{h,l} \in r_h^+, c_{i,j} \in \mathcal{C}^-, ex.\ \theta \in \mathcal{S} : r_{h,l}\theta = |c_{i,j}|\theta\}
\end{aligned}$$

$$\begin{aligned} C^3G := & C^3G_{\mathcal{L}_A,\mathcal{C}^+} \cup C^3G_{\mathcal{L}_A,\mathcal{C}^-} \cup C^3G_{\mathcal{L}_A,\mathcal{R}^-} \cup \\ & C^3G_{\mathcal{R}^-,\mathcal{R}^+} \cup C^3G_{\mathcal{R}^+,\mathcal{R}^-} \cup C^3G_{\mathcal{R}^+,\mathcal{C}^+} \cup C^3G_{\mathcal{R}^+,\mathcal{C}^-} \end{aligned}$$

Having defined the graph, we now have to give a method of interpreting it. In the following we are interested in those paths in the graph that begin with an element in $\mathcal{L}_A$ and end with a literal in some consistency constraint. Thus, in fig.1 and fig.2 a path would have the overall direction from bottom to top. For a literal $l \in \alpha(TA)$ a path p begins with an element in $\mathcal{L}_A$ which is unifiable with l. For each pair (l,p) we will define $I(l,p)$. $I(l,p)$ will depend on certain decisions we make during our walk along the path p. This decision is mainly the one of choosing L/T or K/S, i.e. of applying an "inexact" vs. an "exact" reasoning step. This will correspond to $\Theta_h = \emptyset$ and $\Theta_h = \Theta^{\pm}$, respectively (see below). Thus $I(l,p)$ is not really one element. Instead, it corresponds to a set of elements. One $I(l,p)$ is a tupel (A,B). Only A, the set of substitutions will be relevant in detail. For B, we are only interested in the fact whether B = $\emptyset$ or not. After having computed $I(l,p)$, checking the original consistency constraint can be reduced to checking all simplified versions of it which are generated by applying one of the substitutions in A to the constraint. First, we have to define a path formally.

For every f $(\neg f) \in \alpha(TA)$ we define $p = (l_{i_0,j_0},...,l_{i_n,j_n})$ to be a path of f $(\neg f)$ iff f is unifiable with $l_{i_0,j_0} \in \mathcal{L}_A$, and $(l_{i_{h-1},j_{h-1}}, l_{i_h,j_h}, z) \in C^3G$ for all h=1,...,n. If c_i is a consistency constraint, then $(l_{i_0,j_0},...,l_{i_n,j_n})$ is defined to be a path of $f(\neg f)$, with respect to c_i, iff $(l_{i_{n-1},j_{n-1}}, l_{i_n,j_n}, R)$ $((l_{i_{n-1},j_{n-1}}, l_{i_n,j_n}, S)) \in C^3G$, and $l_{i_n,j_n} = c_{i,j}$ for some j. For a path $p = (l_{i_0,j_0},...,l_{i_n,j_n})$, and $h \leq n$, we define $p_h := (l_{i_0,j_0},...,l_{i_h,j_h})$.

In order to define I we need the following two definitions. Let $\delta(r_i)$ be a substitution which renames all variables that occur in r_i to new variables, $\delta(c_i) = \epsilon$, the empty substitution, for a consistency constraint c_i. The δ's are only of technical importance, not to get confused with the variables equal in several rules and consistency constraints. For a literal l we define

$$\Theta^+(l) := \{\theta | DB_{old} \not\vdash l\theta,\ DB_{new} \vdash l\theta\}$$
$$\Theta^-(l) := \{\theta | DB_{old} \vdash l\theta,\ DB_{new} \not\vdash l\theta\}.$$

Note the analogy between $\Theta^{\pm}$ and ΔA if $l\theta$ is ground.

Be $p := (l_{i_0,j_0},...,l_{i_n,j_n})$ a path for f $(\neg f)$, $l_{i_h,j_h} = r_{i_h,j_h}$ for $1 \leq h \leq n$, and δ a renaming substitution.
We define $I(f, l_{i_0,j_0}) := I(\neg f, l_{i_0,j_0}) := (\{mgu(f, l_{i_0,j_0}\delta)\}, \emptyset)$. If $(l_{i_{h-1},j_{h-1}}, l_{i_h,j_h}, R) \in C^3G_{\mathcal{R}^-,\mathcal{R}^+}$ then $I(\neg f, p_h) := I(\neg f, p_{h-1})$. Otherwise, I is defined as follows (I_i denotes the projection on the i-th component.):

$$\begin{aligned} I(f,p_h) \ := & (\{\sigma\sigma'\theta | \sigma' \in I_1(f,p_{h-1}),\ \delta_h = \delta(r_{i_h}),\ \sigma = mgu(r_{i_{h-1},j_{h-1}}\delta_{h-1}, r_{i_h,j_h}\delta_h), \\ & \theta \in \Theta_h \subseteq \Theta^+(r\delta_h\sigma),\ \theta = \epsilon \ if\ \Theta_h = \emptyset \ \ or\ l_{i_h,j_h} \in c_i \text{ for some } i,\ r \in r^+_{i_h}\}, \\ & I_2(f,p_{h-1}) \cup \{r\sigma | \Theta_h \neq \emptyset \wedge \Theta_h \neq \Theta^+\}) \end{aligned}$$

$$\begin{aligned} I(\neg f,p_h) := & (\{\sigma\sigma'\theta | \sigma' \in I_1(\neg f,p_{h-1}),\ \delta_h = \delta(r_{i_h}),\ \sigma = mgu(r_{i_{h-1},j_{h-1}}\delta_{h-1}, r_{i_h,j_h}\delta_h), \\ & \theta \in \Theta_h \subseteq \Theta^-(r\delta_h\sigma),\ \theta = \epsilon \ if\ \Theta_h = \emptyset \ \ or\ l_{i_h,j_h} \in c_i \text{ for some } i,\ r \in r^+_{i_h}\}, \\ & I_2(\neg f,p_{h-1}) \cup \{r\sigma | \Theta_h \neq \emptyset \wedge \Theta_h \neq \Theta_-\}) \end{aligned}$$

Please notice that the definition of I depends on the choice of the set Θ_h. Choosing $\Theta_h = \emptyset$ corresponds to L/T since only the most general unifier of $r_{i_{h-1},j_{h-1}}$ and r_{i_h,j_h} is taken into account. Thus, we have an inexact step because there is no check whether all instantiations of the head literal of r_{i_h} are really deleted. On the other hand, $\Theta_h = \Theta^{\pm}$ corresponds to K/S since due to its definition Θ^+ (Θ^-) does only contain those substitutions for the head literal of r_{i_h} that yield facts really added to (deleted from) the database by the transaction.

In the definition of I, we do not really need $\Theta_h = \Theta^{\pm}$. Indeed, we may choose Θ_h such that it subsumes $\Theta^{\pm}$, i.e. for every substitution $\theta \in \Theta^{\pm}$ there exist substitutions $\sigma \in \Theta_h$, $\tau \in \mathcal{S}$ such that $\theta = \sigma\tau$. This corresponds to what was called intermediate strategy in chapter 2. The proofs below stay the same. Hence, our method stays correct.

The following technical lemma states that for every literal $l \in \Delta A$, we have an element $s_0 \in A^0$, a path p for s_0, and the last element of p is unifiable with l, using substitutions in $I_1(s_0, p)$.

Lemma 1: $\forall k > 0\, \forall l \in A^k, k \text{ minimal } \exists r_i \in \mathcal{R}, r_{i,j_1} \in r_i^-, r_{i,j_2} \in r_i^+ \,\exists s_0 \in A^0, \exists s \in \mathcal{L}_A \,\exists\, path\ p = (s, ..., r_{i,j_2})\ \forall I(s_0, p), I_2(s_0, p) = \emptyset\ \exists \theta \in I_1(s_0, p) \exists \delta, \tau \in \mathcal{S} : r_{i,j_2}\delta\theta\tau = |l|$.

Proof: (by induction on k)

<u>$k = 1$:</u> Definition of A^1 yields:

$r_i \in \mathcal{R}, r_{i,j_1} \in r_i^-, r_{i,j_2} \in r_i^+,\ g \in A^0, \sigma, \tau \in \mathcal{S} : |r_{i,j_2}|\sigma\tau = |l|, |r_{i,j_1}|\sigma = |g|$.
Then, $p = (|r_{i,j_1}|, r_{i,j_1}, r_{i,j_2})$ is a path for g. For a renaming substitution δ' choose $\sigma' \in \mathcal{S}$ with $r_i\sigma = r_i\delta'\sigma'$. Then, $I(g, |r_{i,j_1}|) = (\{\sigma'\}, \emptyset)$. For another renaming substitution δ'' choose $\sigma'' \in \mathcal{S}$ with $r_i\sigma' = r_i\delta''\sigma''$. Then, $I(g, p) = (\{\sigma''\sigma'\}, \emptyset)$, or $I(g, p) = (\{\sigma''\sigma'\theta | \theta \in \Theta^{\pm}\}, \emptyset)$. In both cases we are done.

<u>$k + 1$:</u> Definition of A^{k+1} yields:

$r_i \in \mathcal{R}, r_{i,j_1} \in r_i^-, r_{i,j_2} \in r_i^+,\ g \in A^k, \sigma_1, \tau_1 \in \mathcal{S}$:
$|r_{i,j_1}|\sigma_1 = |g|,\ |r_{i,j_2}|\sigma_1\tau_1 = |l|$

Induction hypothese for g: $\exists r_{i'} \in \mathcal{R}, r_{i',j_1'} \in r_{i'}^-,\ r_{i',j_2'} \in r_{i'}^+, s_0 \in A^0,\ s \in \mathcal{L}_A$: $\exists p' = (s, ..., r_{i',j_2'})$ path for s_0 and $\forall I(s_0, p), I_2(s_0, p) = \emptyset\ \exists \theta' \in I_1(s_0, p), \exists \delta', \tau' \in \mathcal{S}$: $r_{i',j_2'}\delta'\theta'\tau' = |g|$

Now $p = (s, ..., r_{i',j_2'}, r_{i,j_1}, r_{i,j_2})$ is a path for s_0 since $r_{i',j_2'}$ and $|r_{i,j_1}|$ are unifiable because they have a common ground instance $|g|$. Moreover, we have $(r_{i',j_2'}\delta'\theta')\tau' = |g|,\ |r_{i,j_1}\sigma_1| = |g|$, and $(r_{i,j_2}\sigma_1)\tau_1 = |l|$. Since g, l are ground, σ_1, τ_1 instantiate the variables in r_i, and θ', τ' instantiate the variables in r_i'. Let δ be a renaming substitution such that the variables of $r_i\delta$ are distinct from all variables in r_i', θ', τ'. Define $\sigma = mgu(r_{i',j_2'}\delta', |r_{i,j_1}|\delta)$. Then, there exist σ_1', τ_1' such that $r_{i,j_2}\delta\sigma\sigma_1'\tau_1' = |l|$, and hence $r_{i,j_2}\delta\sigma\theta'\tau'\tau_1' = |l|$. Applying the definition of I completes the proof. □

The following theorem states the correctness of our approach.

Theorem: Be $c_i \in \mathcal{C}$.

$M(DB_{new}) \cup c_i$ inconsistent
    $\prec\!\succ$ $\exists l \in \alpha(TA)\ \exists$ path p for l with respect to c_i $\exists \theta \in I_1(l, p), I_2(l, p) = \emptyset$:
        $M(DB_{new}) \cup \{c_i\theta\}$ inconsistent.
    $\prec$ $\exists l \in \alpha(TA)\ \exists$ path p for l with respect to c_i $\exists \theta \in I_1(l, p),\ I_2(l, p) \neq \emptyset$:
        $M(DB_{new}) \cup \{c_i\theta\}$ inconsistent.

Proof:

$M(DB_{new}) \cup \{c_i\}$ inconsistent $\succ$ $\exists \sigma_g \in \mathcal{S}, c_i\sigma_g$ ground: $\forall j : M(DB_{new}) \cup \{c_{i,j}\sigma_g\}$ inconsistent.
$M(DB_{old}) \cup \{c_i\}$ consistent $\succ$ $M(DB_{old}) \cup \{c_i\sigma_g\}$ consistent
$\succ$ $\exists j_0 : M(DB_{old}) \cup \{c_{i,j_0}\sigma_g\}$ consistent.
This implies $\neg c_{i,j_0}\sigma_g \in \Delta A$.
The following lemma completes the proof. □

Lemma 2: $\forall l \in \Delta A, |l| = |c_{i,j}|\sigma_g$, for some i, j, σ_g, and l, $c_{i,j}$ of opposite sign, $\exists s_0 \in A_0$ $\exists p$ path for s_0 $\forall I(s_0, p)$ with $I_2(s_0, p) = \emptyset\ \exists \theta \in I_1(s_0, p) \exists \sigma_g' \in \mathcal{S}$: $|l| = |c_{i,j}|\theta\sigma_g'$.

Proof: We only show the case $l = \neg f$ ($l = f$ is shown analogously). Since l is a negative literal, $c_{i,j}$ is positiv. The lemma is proven by induction on k, where $l \in A^k$:

k = 0: p = $(c_{i,j}, c_{i,j})$ is a path for l because $(c_{i,j}, c_{i,j}, S) \in C^3G$. Define $\sigma' = mgu(|l|, c_{i,j})$. Then, $I_1(l,p) = \{\sigma'\}$, and we are done with $s_0 = l$.

k+1: For the literal l Lemma 1 yields a path $p = (l_{i_0,j_0}, ..., l_{i_n,j_n})$ for some $s_0 \in A^0$. Further there exist $\delta \in \mathcal{S}, \theta \in I_1(s_0, p)$ and $\tau \in \mathcal{S}$ with $l_{i_n,j_n}\delta\theta\tau = |l|$. Then $p' = (l_{i_0,j_0}, ..., l_{i_n,j_n}, c_{i,j})$ is a path for s_0 because l_{i_n,j_n} and $c_{i,j}$ are unifiable, and there exists $\theta' \in I_1(s_0, p')$ and $\tau' \in \mathcal{S}$ such that $c_{i,j}\theta'\tau' = |l|$. This completes the proof.

□

In the case of $I_2(l,p) \neq \emptyset$, Θ_h was choosen to be unequal to the empty set and unequal to $\Theta^{\pm}$. Consider again example 2. Since $q(a,b)$ has been deleted all instantiations of $r(a,z)$ with $z \in \{c_2, c_4, ..., c_{100}\}$ are deleted. If we only check for $\Theta_h = \{[z \leftarrow c_{22}], [z \leftarrow c_{44}], [z \leftarrow c_{88}]\}$ we do not get any refutation for $s(x,z) \Longrightarrow r(x,z)[x \leftarrow a]\theta$, $\theta \in \Theta_h$. In fact, we do not get a refutation, and hence proof of inconsistency unless $[z \leftarrow c_{50}] \in \Theta_h$. This shows that the "$\succ$" direction in the second case of our theorem cannot be derived in general, but only if Θ_h subsumes $\Theta^{\pm}$.

4 Examples revisited

In this chapter we show the application of the C^3G graph to the examples from chapter 2. Part of the C^3G graph for the first example is given in fig. 1. The following consistency check with $\Theta_h = \Theta^-$ in every step simulates the K/S refutation. We give the I-tupel for the deletion of $p_2(b,a)$. Let I^i denote the I-tupel in a distance of i nodes from the starting node ($p_2(x,y)$ in this example). The renamings δ_h used should be obvious.

$$\begin{array}{ll}
I^0 = (\{\{x_0 \leftarrow b,\ y_0 \leftarrow a\} =: \sigma_0\}, \emptyset) & \sigma_0 = \{x_0 \leftarrow b, y_0 \leftarrow a\} \\
I^1 = (\{\{x_1 \leftarrow x_0,\ y_1 \leftarrow y_0, z_1 \leftarrow a\}\sigma_0 =: \sigma_1\}, \emptyset) & \sigma_1 = \{x_1 \leftarrow b, y_1 \leftarrow a, z_1 \leftarrow a\} \\
I^2 = (\{\{y_2 \leftarrow x_1, z_2 \leftarrow z_1\}\sigma_1 =: \sigma_2\}, \emptyset) & \sigma_2 = \{y_2 \leftarrow b, z_2 \leftarrow a\} \\
I^3 = (\{\{x_3 \leftarrow c,\ y_3 \leftarrow y_2, z_3 \leftarrow y_2\}\sigma_2 =: \sigma_3\}, \emptyset) & \sigma_3 = \{x_3 \leftarrow c, y_3 \leftarrow b, z_3 \leftarrow b\} \\
I^4 = (\{\{x \leftarrow x_3,\ y \leftarrow z_3\}\sigma_3 =: \sigma_4\}, \emptyset) & \sigma_4 = \{x \leftarrow c, y \leftarrow b\}
\end{array}$$

Now $C\sigma_4$ is equal to $\{\neg p_2(c,b), q(c,b)\}$. q(c,b) may be deleted because the last step has been a $\Theta_h = \Theta^-$ step. $\{\neg p_2(c,b)\}$ is refuted by looking up the fact $p_2(c,b)$ in DB_{new}. The variant of the first example which caused problems for L/T and K/S, is processed by our method as follows. We first take an inexact step, and then proceed with exact steps only. This results in the following I^i.

$$\begin{array}{ll}
I^0 = (\{\{x_0 \leftarrow b,\ y_0 \leftarrow a\} =: \sigma_0\}, \emptyset) & \sigma_0 = \{x_0 \leftarrow b, y_0 \leftarrow a\} \\
I^1 = (\{\{x_1 \leftarrow x_0,\ y_1 \leftarrow y_0\}\sigma_0 =: \sigma_1\}, \emptyset) & \sigma_1 = \{x_1 \leftarrow b, y_1 \leftarrow a\} \\
I^2 = (\{\{y_2 \leftarrow x_1, z_2 \leftarrow z_1\}\sigma_1 =: \sigma_2\}, \emptyset) & \sigma_2 = \{y_2 \leftarrow b, z_2 \leftarrow z_1\} \\
I^3 = (\{\{x_3 \leftarrow c,\ y_3 \leftarrow y_2, z_3 \leftarrow y_2\}\sigma_2 =: \sigma_3\}, \emptyset) & \sigma_3 = \{x_3 \leftarrow c, y_3 \leftarrow b, z_3 \leftarrow b\} \\
I^4 = (\{\{x \leftarrow x_3,\ y \leftarrow z_3\}\sigma_3 =: \sigma_4\}, \emptyset) & \sigma_4 = \{x \leftarrow c, y \leftarrow b\}
\end{array}$$

I^1 and I^2 are different from the solutions we got before. However, σ_4 is still the same. Thus, we have gained the same efficiency as K/S in the unmodified example.

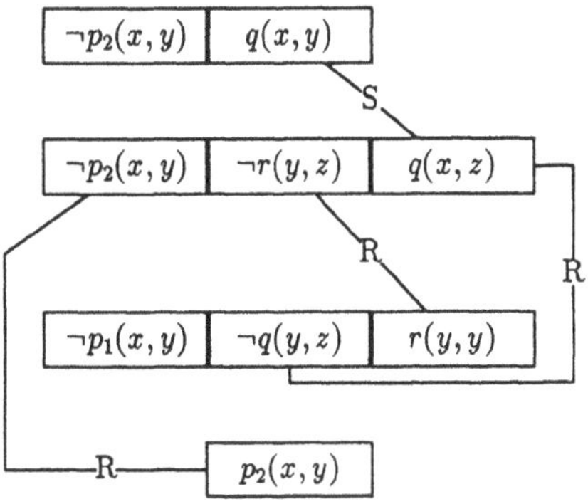

Fig. 1

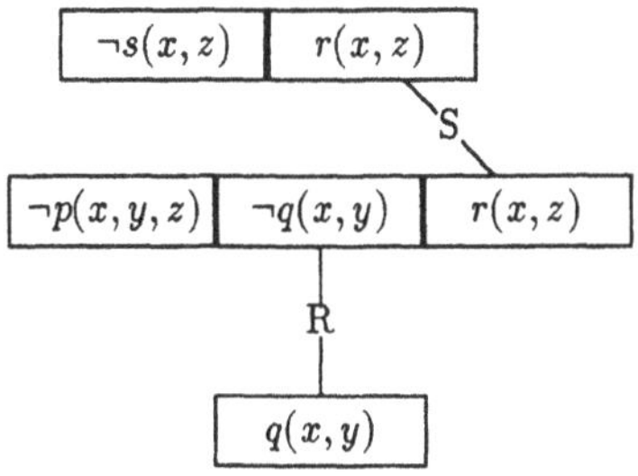

Fig. 2

Fig. 2 shows the C^3G for the second example. Simulating the L/T method with $\Theta_h = \emptyset$ in every step yields:

$$I_0 = (\{\{x_0 \leftarrow a, y_0 \leftarrow b\} =: \sigma_0\}, \emptyset) \qquad \sigma_0 = \{x_0 \leftarrow a, y_0 \leftarrow b\}$$
$$I_1 = (\{\{x \leftarrow x_0, z \leftarrow z_0\}\sigma_0 =: \sigma_1\}, \emptyset) \qquad \sigma_1 = \{x \leftarrow a, z \leftarrow z_0\}$$

Hence, the original constraint can be simplified to $C\sigma_1 = \{\neg s(a, z_0), r(a, z_0)\}$, which is easily refuted by looking up s(a,c_{50}) and disproving r(a,c_{50}).

It should be quite obvious that the advantage of the additional flexibility provided by our mechanism heavily depends on a good procedure for deciding whether to take an exact, unexact, or even intermediate step. This decision could be based on statistical knowledge about the database, such as the number of stored facts or the selectivity of predicate arguments. In the variant of the first example there is a small number (4) of explicit facts for predicate p_2 and a rather large number (100) for predicate r. Let us further assume the system has gained some statistical knowledge about the low selectivity of the first argument of r. Then, the decision for first taking an unexact step, and proceeding with exact steps only can be motivated as follows.

The deletion of $p_2(b, a)$ yields $\sigma_0 = \{x_0 \leftarrow b, y_0 \leftarrow a\}$ and the upper rule in fig. 1 is simplified to $\{\neg p_2(b, a), \neg r(a, z_1), q(b, z_1)\}$. Now, one may proceed with either $q(b, z_1)$ or all of its implicitly deleted instantiations. The latter, however, are likely to be numerous since the large number of r-facts and the low selectivity of the first argument will probably result in a large number of instantiations of $r(a, z_1)$. Hence, we choose to reason unexactly which – using the other deductive rule – yields the head literal $r(b, b)$. Since that is already ground it can easily be checked for being really deleted (exact step). Proceeding from $r(b, b)$ we again reach the upper rule which is now simplified to $\{\neg p_2(x_3, b), \neg r(b, b), q(x_3, b)\}$. Opposite to the first case, the number of really deleted instantiations of the head literal will be small, namely at most the number of facts for p_2 $(= 4)$. Hence, we take another exact step finding only one instantiation of $p_2(x_3, b)$ stored in the database which results in the substitutions σ_3 and σ_4 suitable for disproving consistency.

5 Conclusion

A unifying approach to consistency checking has been proposed and verified. This approach avoids certain inefficiencies detected in other procedures, and exhibits more flexibility. However, unlike the methods described in [4] and [2], we did not deal with the insertion or deletion of rules. Nevertheless, an appropriate extension of our theory seems possible. One has to unify the positive literal $r_{i,j}$ of the added (deleted) rule with some $l \in \mathcal{L}_A$, and to proceed in the proposed way.

References

[1] R. Kowalski. A proof procedure using connection graphs. *JACM*, 22, 1975. 572-595.

[2] R. Kowalski, F. Sadri, and P. Soper. Integrity checking in deductive databases. In *Proc. 13th Int. Conf. VLDB*, 1987. 61-69.

[3] J.W. Lloyd. *Foundations Of Logic Programming*. Springer, 1984.

[4] J.W. Lloyd and R.W. Topor. A basis for deductive database systems. *J. Logic Programming*, 2, 1985. 93-109.

[5] J.-M. Nicolas. Logic for improving integrity checking in relational data bases. *Acta Informatica*, 18, 1982. 227-253.

[6] R. Reiter. On closed world data bases. *in: H. Gallaire and J. Minker (eds.)*, Logic and Data Bases, Plenum, New York, 1978. 55-76.

IDEMPOTENT SINGLE-PREDICATE HORN CLAUSES†

Peter T. Wood
Alberto O. Mendelzon

Computer Systems Research Institute
University of Toronto
Toronto, Canada M5S 1A4

Paolo Atzeni

Dipartimento di Informatica e Sistemistica
Universita' di Napoli
Napoli, Italy

ABSTRACT

Previous work has addressed the issues of idempotence and boundedness for various restricted classes of Horn-clause queries. In this paper, we consider queries consisting of a single clause containing a single predicate symbol. As such, these queries are a notational variant of the full, untagged tableau queries with recursive semantics. The study of the idempotence and boundedness for single-clause, single-predicate queries has previously been restricted to the typed case. We generalize these results to obtain syntactic, polynomial-time computable characterizations of idempotence for certain classes of untyped queries.

1. INTRODUCTION

For some time it has been recognized that so-called "relationally complete" [Codd72] query languages are inadequate for expressing a number of reasonable queries [AhUl79]. This limitation has led to proposals for increasing the expressive power of relational query languages by allowing recursive queries to be formulated. As a result, there is currently widespread study on a number of issues concerning recursive queries, such as, their efficient evaluation (e.g. [BaRa86]) and the design of languages in which to express them (e.g. [CMW87]). In this paper we are interested in the more fundamental notion of recognizing which recursive expressions in fact denote non-recursive or first-order queries. This problem, known as *bounded* or *data-independent* recursion, has also been addressed in [Ioan85, CoKa86, Naug86a, NaSa87, Sagi88]. Apart from being of theoretical interest, this problem has practical significance for the optimization of recursive queries.

The bounded recursion problem has been studied for two classes of query languages, one based on *linear recursive Horn clauses* [Ioan85, Naug86a], and the other based on *untagged recursive database tableaux* [CoKa86, Sagi88], which are essentially single-predicate Horn-clauses. These two languages have incomparable expressive power. A linear recursive rule query allows many relations (predicates) to be referenced in the query, while a tableau query can refer to only a single relation. On the other hand, tableau queries permit any number of occurrences of the recursive predicate, thus admitting non-linear queries.

† This research was supported by the Natural Sciences and Engineering Research Council of Canada.

Most work on database tableaux has centred on the *typed* case, where no variable can appear in more than one column of a tableau. Effectively this means that one can consider all the attribute domains of the relation being queried to be disjoint. As a query language, however, typed tableaux are very limited. For example, a query as simple as computing the transitive closure of a relation requires an untyped tableau for its formulation.

A syntactic characterization of *idempotent* typed tableaux is given in [Sagi85]. The problem of *k-boundedness*, where a tableau need be composed with itself at most k times to compute all the answers to a given query on any relation, is studied in [CoKa86, Sagi88]. A necessary and sufficient condition for a typed tableau to be k-bounded is given in these papers. Studying the idempotence and boundedness problems for untyped tableaux seems considerably more difficult. For example, the general boundedness problem for untyped tableaux is still not known to be decidable [CoKa86].

In this paper, we make some progress towards finding a syntactic characterization for idempotent single-predicate Horn clauses or untyped tableaux. Specifically, we generalize typed tableaux to what we call *semi-typed* tableaux and study the idempotence problem for this class. The next section introduces the required background material and definitions. In Section 3, we define semi-typed tableaux and review some properties of typed tableaux that do not hold in general for semi-typed tableaux. We also present the syntactic characterization of idempotent typed tableaux. In Section 4, a number of necessary conditions as well as sufficient conditions for a semi-typed tableau to be idempotent are derived. In addition, we provide exact syntactic characterizations of idempotence for various subclasses of semi-typed tableaux. Some difficulties with generalizing these results to general untyped tableaux are outlined in Section 5. Section 6 contains suggestions for further research in the area.

2. BACKGROUND

We assume that the reader is familiar with the basic definitions of relational database theory as found, for example, in [Ullm83]. In what follows, we will restrict our attention to databases consisting of a single relation, and hence will use the terms *relation* and *instance* interchangeably.

Tableaux can be used to express queries over a given database scheme. Since our database scheme comprises only a single relation scheme, the tableaux we consider are those usually referred to as *untagged* tableaux. Let R be a relation scheme defined over the attributes $A_1, \ldots, A_n$. A *tableau* T is a table with columns $A_1, \ldots, A_n$, and rows that are tuples of *variables* (that is, we consider only *full* tableaux). Each row of T must have variables in all of its columns, and no variable may repeat in a row. The rows of T are partitioned into a special row s, called the *summary* of T, and rows $w_1, \ldots, w_m$ which comprise the *body* of T. The variables appearing in the summary of T, namely $s(A_1), \ldots, s(A_n)$, are called *distinguished variables* (*dv's*), while those that appear only in the body of T are called *nondistinguished variables* (*ndv's*). In our examples, dv's will usually be denoted by $x, y, z, \cdots$, while ndv's will usually be denoted by subscripted b's. Unique ndv's will sometimes be represented by hyphens. An ndv which appears more than once in a tableau T is called a *shared* ndv. Each dv must appear in some row in the body of T. If the dv $s(A)$ appears only in column A and no ndv appears in more than one column of T, then T is said to be *typed*. The class of all typed tableaux is denoted by τ.

A tableau defines a mapping from instances to relations. Let r be a relation over scheme R. A mapping h is a *valuation* of T into r if h maps every row of T to a tuple of r. The tableau T maps relation r to the following relation, denoted $T(r)$,

$$\{h(s) \mid s \text{ is the summary of } T \text{ and } h \text{ is a valuation of } T \text{ into } r\}.$$

Thus, a tableau query can be viewed as a form of *conjunctive query* [ChMe77].

EXAMPLE 2.1: Let T be the following typed tableau:

T:	x	y
w_1:	x	b_1
w_2:	b_2	y

The summary s of T is (x,y), while the body of T consists of two rows, w_1 and w_2, where $w_1=(x,b_1)$ and $w_2=(b_2,y)$. Given a binary relation r, $T(r)$ is the Cartesian product of the sets of constants which appear in the first and second components of r. □

We are interested in when two tableaux are equivalent, that is, when they express the same query. Let T_1 and T_2 be tableaux with summary rows s_1 and s_2 respectively. A *homomorphism* h of T_1 into T_2 is a mapping of the variables of T_1 into the variables of T_2 that preserves summary and rows, that is

(1) if w is a row of T_1, then $h(w)$ is a row of T_2, and

(2) for each column A, $s_1(A)$ is mapped to $s_2(A)$.

Since, in our case, the summaries of T_1 and T_2 are always identical, h is the identity mapping on the dv's of T_1. The mapping of the rows of T_1 into the rows of T_2 induced by a homomorphism h is called a *containment mapping*. A containment mapping $\psi: T_1 \rightarrow T_2$ satisfies the following two conditions:

(1) if rows w_1 and w_2 share a variable in columns A_1 and A_2 respectively, then so do $\psi(w_1)$ and $\psi(w_2)$, and

(2) if row w has a dv x in some column A, then so does $\psi(w)$.

A tableau T_1 *contains* a tableau T_2, written $T_1 \supseteq T_2$, if, for all instances I, $T_1(I) \supseteq T_2(I)$. Tableaux T_1 and T_2 are *equivalent*, written $T_1 \equiv T_2$, if $T_1 \supseteq T_2$ and $T_2 \supseteq T_1$. Given tableaux T_1 and T_2, $T_1 \supseteq T_2$ if and only if there is a containment mapping from T_1 to T_2 [ASU79a]. We call the tableau T' a *subtableau* of T if T' has the same summary row as T and contains a proper subset of the rows of T. The tableau T is *minimal* if there is no subtableau T' of T which is equivalent to T.

Since we wish to interpret a tableau as a recursive query, we are interested in compositions of tableaux. Given two tableaux T_1 and T_2, the *composition* of T_1 and T_2, written $T_2 \circ T_1$, is defined such that for all instances I,

$$T_2 \circ T_1(I) = T_2(T_1(I)).$$

The composition $T \circ T \circ \cdots \circ T$ (i times) is denoted T^i. Given a tableau T with summary s, we will denote by T^0 the *identity tableau for* T, which has summary s and a single row s.

We now show how to construct the tableau T^2 from the tableau T. A slightly different but equivalent construction is given in [BeVa84]. Let T be a tableau with n columns $A_1, \ldots, A_n$, m rows $w_1, \ldots, w_m$, and summary s. For the purpose of compositions of tableaux, each row w_i of T can be viewed as defining a mapping over the variables of T. Suppose there are p nondistinguished variables $b_1, \ldots, b_p$ in T. The mapping associated with w_i, denoted θ_i, is defined as follows:

$$\theta_i(s(A_j)) = w_i(A_j),\ 1 \le j \le n$$

$$\theta_i(b_k) = b_{(i \times p)+k},\ 1 \le k \le p,$$

that is, the dv in column A_j of the summary is mapped to the variable appearing in column A_j of row w_i, and each ndv in T is mapped to a distinct nondistinguished variable not appearing in T.

The mapping θ_i can be extended to a mapping between rows of symbols. Following Sagiv, we will denote by w_j^i the row obtained by applying θ_i to w_j. We also define the result of applying θ_i to each row in the body of a tableau T by

$$\theta_i(T) = \{\ \theta_i(w_j) \mid 1 \le j \le m\ \}.$$

Then T^2 is the tableau with the same summary as T, and with body

$$\bigcup_{i=1}^{m} \theta_i(T).$$

Note that the ndv's appearing in $\theta_i(T)$ are the ndv's of row w_i along with p new ndv's (assuming T has p ndv's). Furthermore, $\theta_i(T)$ and $\theta_j(T)$ share ndv's if and only if rows w_i and w_j do.

EXAMPLE 2.2: Let T be the tableau of Example 2.1:

T:	x	y
w_1:	x	b_1
w_2:	b_2	y

The mapping associated with row w_1 is defined by $\theta_1(x)=x$, $\theta_1(y)=b_1$, $\theta_1(b_1)=b_3$, $\theta_1(b_2)=b_4$. Then $\theta_1(T)$ is given by the two rows (x,b_3) and (b_4,b_1). The tableau T^2, whose body is $\theta_1(T) \cup \theta_2(T)$, is as follows:

T^2:	x	y
w_1^1:	x	b_3
w_2^1:	b_4	b_1
	---	---
w_1^2:	b_2	b_5
w_2^2:	b_6	y

There is a homomorphism h of T into T^2 given by $h(b_1)=b_3$ and $h(b_2)=b_6$. The containment mapping induced by h maps w_1 to w_1^1 and w_2 to w_2^2. Tableau T^2 is not minimal since the subtableau with body $\{w_1^1, w_2^2\}$ is equivalent to T^2. □

By allowing a query to be formulated as a set of tableaux, we introduce disjunction into tableau queries. The mapping associated with a set of tableaux is defined as follows. Let S be a set $\{T_1, \ldots, T_n\}$ of tableaux each with the same summary. Then S defines a mapping from instances to relations as follows:

$$S(I) = \bigcup_{i=1}^{n} T_i(I)$$

Given two sets of tableaux S_1 and S_2, S_1 *contains* S_2, written $S_1 \sqsupseteq S_2$, if for all I, $S_1(I) \supseteq S_2(I)$. The following is a re-wording of a theorem in [SaYa80].

THEOREM 2.1: *Let $S=\{T_1, \ldots, T_n\}$ and $S'=\{T'_1, \ldots, T'_m\}$ be sets of tableaux. Then $S \sqsupseteq S'$ if and only if S and S' have the same summary and, for* each *tableau T_j' of S', there is a containment mapping from* some *tableau T_i of S to T_j'.*

We now define the composition $S \circ S'$ of two sets S and S' of tableaux. Let $S=\{T_1,\ldots,T_n\}$ and $S'=\{T'_1,\ldots,T'_m\}$ be sets of tableaux. The set $S \circ S'$ is a union of n sets $S_1,\ldots,S_n$ of tableaux, where S_i is the set of tableaux $T_i \circ S'$. If T_i has p rows, then the set S_i consists of m^p tableaux, one for each sequence $(j_1,\ldots,j_p)$, $1 \le j_k \le m$. The tableau corresponding to the sequence $(j_1,\ldots,j_p)$ has the same summary as T_i, and has as body

$$\bigcup_{k=1}^{p} \theta_k(T'_{j_k}).$$

A slightly different formulation of the same construction is given in [CoKa86].

A set of tableaux S is *idempotent* if $S \equiv S^2$. The semantics of a set of tableaux, interpreted as a recursive query, is as follows. If I is an instance and S is a set of tableaux, then the result of applying S to I recursively is denoted $S[I]$ and is defined by

$$S[I]=\bigcup_{i=1}^{\infty} S^i(I).$$

3. TYPED AND SEMI-TYPED TABLEAUX

We start by defining the class of semi-typed tableaux and then demonstrate some properties of typed tableaux that are not necessarily exhibited by semi-typed tableaux. These properties help to demonstrate why the idempotence problem for semi-typed tableaux is more complex than that for typed tableaux. We also state the simple syntactic characterization for idempotent typed tableaux.

The class of semi-typed tableaux is obtained by relaxing the second condition in the definition of typed tableaux. A tableau T is *semi-typed* if the dv $s(A)$ appears only in column A. In other words, ndv's may appear in more than one column but dv's may not. This means that if I is an instance with set of values D_i in column i, $1 \le i \le n$, and T is a semi-typed tableau comprising n columns, then $T(I)$ is a subset of $D_1 \times \cdots \times D_n$. Once again, we do not allow repeated variables in a row. The class of all semi-typed tableaux is denoted by σ; clearly, $\sigma \supseteq \tau$. Note that the class σ is closed under composition. From now on, we consider only minimal tableaux.

EXAMPLE 3.1: The following tableau T is semi-typed.

T:	x	y
w_1:	x	b_1
w_2:	b_1	y

T is not typed since the shared ndv b_1 appears in both columns of T. □

Next, we consider a number of properties of typed tableaux.

PROPOSITION 3.1: *For all instances I and any tableau $T \in \tau$, $T(I) \supseteq I$.*

COROLLARY 3.1: *If $T \in \tau$, then $T^2 \supseteq T$ and $T \supseteq T^0$.*

For typed tableaux, one containment mapping θ from T^2 to T is defined by $\theta(w_j^i)=w_j$, $1 \le i,j \le m$ [Sagi85]. In fact, combining the inverse variable mappings θ_i^{-1} for each row w_i produces a homomorphism θ^{-1} which induces the containment mapping θ.

COROLLARY 3.2: *If $T \in \tau$, then T is idempotent if and only if $T \supseteq T^2$.*

A syntactic characterization of idempotent typed tableaux is given below [Sagi85].

THEOREM 3.1: *Let T be a minimal, typed tableau. Then $T \supseteq T^2$ if and only if there are no shared ndv's in T.*

Proposition 3.1 does not necessarily hold for semi-typed tableaux; the tableau T of Example 3.1 provides a counter-example. Given the instance $I=\{(0,1)\}$, $T(I)=\emptyset$. In fact, if T is semi-typed but not typed, then $T \not\supseteq T^0$ since variables cannot repeat in the row of T^0. It is also not necessarily true that $T^2 \supseteq T$ if T is semi-typed. Consider the following example.

EXAMPLE 3.2: Let T be the following semi-typed tableau.

T:	x	y	z
w_1:	x	b_1	b_2
w_2:	x	y	b_1
w_3:	b_3	b_4	z

Tableau T is minimal and contains a shared ndv; yet we will prove in Section 4.3 that applying T once is sufficient to obtain all answer tuples for all instances. That is, $T \supseteq T^2$. However, T is not idempotent since, as we will see, $T^2 \not\supseteq T$. □

The reason we want to test for idempotence is that we would like to be able to interpret the tableau T as a non-recursive query rather than a recursive one. In other words, we would like to compute $T(I)$ rather than $T[I]$. This simplification is safe if and only if T is idempotent. Consequently, for semi-typed tableaux, we assume that the identity tableau T^0 is included with T, and denote the resulting set $T^* = \{T, T^0\}$. The two properties of T^* given below follow directly from the definitions.

PROPOSITION 3.2: *Given a tableau T, $T^*(I) \supseteq I$ and $(T^*)^2 \supseteq T^*$.*

Hence, if $T^* \supseteq (T^*)^2$, then T^* is idempotent. We will say that a semi-typed tableau T is *1-bounded* if T^* is idempotent. For a typed tableau the terms 1-bounded and idempotent are synonymous, but, as we have seen, this is not true for semi-typed tableaux; the semi-typed tableau T of Example 3.2 is not idempotent ($T^2 \not\supseteq T$) but is 1-bounded because T^* is idempotent. The fact that $T^* \supseteq T^2$ but $T^2 \not\supseteq T^*$ motivates our choice of the term 1-bounded.

EXAMPLE 3.3: The set of tableaux $T^* = \{T, T^0\}$, where T is the tableau of Example 3.2, represents the same query as the following set of Horn clauses:

$$C_1: T(x,y,z) \leftarrow R(x,y,z).$$

$$C_2: T(x,y,z) \leftarrow T(x,b_1,b_2), T(x,y,b_1), T(b_3,b_4,z).$$

The clause C_1 corresponds to T^0: the predicate symbol R is the name of the base relation being queried. Clause C_2 corresponds to the tableau T. □

Let T be a tableau with m rows $w_1, \ldots, w_m$, and let $T^* = \{T, T^0\}$. We show how to construct $(T^*)^2$. The set $(T^*)^2$ is a union of two sets S_1 and S_2 of tableaux, where $S_1 = T \circ T^*$ and $S_2 = T^0 \circ T^*$. Since T has m rows and there are two tableaux in T^*, S_1 consists of 2^m tableaux. The tableau T^0 comprises only the identity row, so $S_2 = T^*$. For each $1 \le i \le m$, let us call the set of rows $\theta_i(T)$ (see Section 2) the *expansion* of row w_i. A *partial expansion* of T is a tableau T' in which a nonempty subset of the rows of T, say $w_{i_1}, \ldots, w_{i_l}$ ($l \le m$), has been expanded, this being denoted by $T[\theta_{i_1}, \ldots, \theta_{i_l}]$. Thus, T^2 is the partial expansion $T[\theta_1, \ldots, \theta_m]$. Let the set of all partial expansions of T be denoted P_T. The set S_1 is exactly the set P_T of partial expansions of T along with T itself. Consequently, $(T^*)^2 = P_T \cup T^*$.

EXAMPLE 3.4: Consider the semi-typed tableau T of Example 3.1.

T:

x	y
x	b_1
b_1	y

The set T^* of tableaux computes the transitive closure of a binary relation. The partial expansions of T, namely $T[\theta_1]$, $T[\theta_2]$ and T^2, are as follows:

$T[\theta_1]$:

x	y
x	b_2
b_2	b_1
---	---
b_1	y

$T[\theta_2]$:

x	y
x	b_1
---	---
b_1	b_3
b_3	y

T^2:

x	y
x	b_2
b_2	b_1
---	---
b_1	b_3
b_3	y

Thus, the partial expansion $T[\theta_i]$ comprises the rows $\theta_i(T)$ and $T-\{w_i\}$. Note that there is no containment mapping from T^2 to $T[\theta_1]$, $T[\theta_2]$ or T. In particular, $\underline{\theta}: T^2 \rightarrow T$ is not a containment mapping, since b_1 is forced to map to both y and x. □

PROPOSITION 3.3: *If $T^* \supseteq P_T$, then T is 1-bounded.*

EXAMPLE 3.5: The tableau T from the previous example is not 1-bounded. For instance, $T \not\supseteq T[\theta_1]$, since either x would have to map to b_2 or y to b_1. Similarly, $T \not\supseteq T[\theta_2]$ and $T \not\supseteq T^2$. In fact, it is well-known that T is not k-bounded, for any constant k [AhUl79]. □

4. IDEMPOTENT TABLEAU QUERIES

In this section, we study the problem of idempotence for the class of semi-typed tableaux. Clearly, a semi-typed tableau T is 1-bounded if it contains no shared ndv's, since T is then typed. The absence of shared ndv's, however, is not necessary for a semi-typed tableau to be 1-bounded; Example 3.2 provides a counter-example. We begin by defining certain binary relations between the rows of a tableau, as well as a number of row properties.

Let us say that row w_i is *related to* row w_j, denoted $Rel(w_i,w_j)$, if some ndv appearing in w_i appears in w_j. In addition, if w_i is related to w_j, and w_j is related to w_k, then w_i is related to w_k. So the relation Rel is transitive; clearly, it is also reflexive and symmetric.

PROPOSITION 4.1: *The relation Rel is an equivalence relation.*

We will subsequently find it convenient to denote the equivalence class in which row w_i appears by $Rel(w_i)$, that is, the set of rows related to w_i.

In a semi-typed tableau T, row w_i *subsumes* row w_j, denoted $w_i \geq w_j$, if for each column A of T in which $w_j(A)=s(A)$, it is also true that $w_i(A)=s(A)$. Let E be one of the equivalence classes defined by the relation Rel. A row $w_i \in E$ is called *maximal* if w_i subsumes every row in E, and is called a *source* if w_i subsumes no row $w_j \neq w_i$ in E. We say that row w_i *covers* row w_j (or w_j is *covered*) if $w_i \geq w_j$ and for each column A in which w_j has a shared ndv, $w_i(A)=s(A)$. Row w_i *partially covers* row w_j if $w_i \geq w_j$ and for *some* column A in which w_j has a shared ndv, $w_i(A)=s(A)$. Thus, covering $\rightarrow$ partial covering $\rightarrow$ subsumption.

Since $\geq$ does not define a total ordering on the rows of an equivalence class E, there need not necessarily be a maximal row in E. Obviously, for any equivalence class $E=\{w\}$, w is a maximal row. If there is more than one row in equivalence class E, then no row in E can be both maximal and a source. Alternatively, if all rows in a tableau T are both maximal and a source, then T has no shared ndv's and is hence 1-bounded. Unlike the subsumes relation, both the covering and partial covering relations are irreflexive: row w covers or partially covers itself if and only if w contains no shared ndv's. Both relations are also asymmetric: if a row w_i covers or partially covers row w_j, then w_j covers or partially covers w_i if and only if neither w_i nor w_j contains a shared ndv.

EXAMPLE 4.1: The tableau in Example 3.1 has only a single equivalence class $E = Rel(w_1) = Rel(w_2) = \{w_1, w_2\}$. Both w_1 and w_2 are sources. In the tableau of Example 3.2, there are two equivalence classes: E and $E' = \{w_3\}$. Row w_3 covers both w_1 and w_2. E has no maximal row, whereas w_3 is maximal in E'. □

LEMMA 4.1: *Let $\psi_i : T \to T[\theta_i]$ be a containment mapping. The following results follow directly from the definitions of expansion and containment mapping.*

1. *If $\psi_i(w_j) = w_k$, then $w_k \geq w_j$.*
2. *If $\psi_i(w_j) = w_k^i$, then $w_i \geq w_j$ and $w_k \geq w_j$.*
3. *If $\psi_i(w_j) = w_k^i$, then variable v in column A of w_j maps either to $w_i(A)$ if $w_k(A) = s(A)$ or to an ndv b not in T if $w_k(A)$ is an ndv.*

We begin by developing some simple sufficient conditions for the existence of a containment mapping ψ_i from a semi-typed tableau T to a single row expansion $T[\theta_i]$ of T.

LEMMA 4.2: *Let T be a semi-typed tableau and $w_i \in T$. There is a containment mapping from T to $T[\theta_i]$ if w_i is covered.*

PROOF: It can be shown that a mapping which maps w_i to w_j^i, where w_j is a covering row for w_i, and maps every other row in T to itself in $T[\theta_i]$ is a containment mapping. □

The above result includes the special case when there are no shared ndv's as then each row in T is its own covering row.

LEMMA 4.3: *Let T be a semi-typed tableau and $w_i \in T$. There is a containment mapping from T to $T[\theta_i]$ if w_i is maximal.*

PROOF: For each row $w_j \in T$, let ψ be defined as follows:

$$\psi(w_j) = \begin{cases} w_j^i & \text{if } w_j \in Rel(w_i) \\ w_j & \text{otherwise} \end{cases}$$

It is not hard to prove that ψ is a containment mapping from T to $T[\theta_i]$. □

COROLLARY 4.1: *There is a containment mapping $\psi_i : T \to T[\theta_i]$ in which ψ_i maps each row in $Rel(w_i)$ into $\theta_i(T)$ if and only if w_i is maximal.*

4.1. Sufficient conditions

Next, we consider some conditions which are sufficient for a semi-typed tableau T to be 1-bounded. All of these results also apply trivially to typed tableaux.

LEMMA 4.4: *A semi-typed tableau T is 1-bounded if each row in T is covered.*

PROOF: Follows from a simple extension to Lemma 4.2. □

COROLLARY 4.2: *If the identity row is in T, then T is 1-bounded.*

For a tableau T to be 1-bounded, it is not sufficient that each equivalence class in T have a maximal row, although it will be true that $T \supseteq T^2$. The following example illustrates this fact.

EXAMPLE 4.2:

T:	x	y	z
w_1:	x	y	b_1
w_2:	x	b_1	b_2
w_3:	b_2	y	-
w_4:	b_3	y	z
w_5:	-	b_3	z

$T[\theta_1]$:	x	y	z
	x	y	b_4
	x	b_4	b_5
	b_5	y	-
	b_6	y	b_1
	-	b_6	b_1
	---	---	---
w_2:	x	b_1	b_2
w_3:	b_2	y	-
w_4:	b_3	y	z
w_5:	-	b_3	z

$T[\theta_2]$:	x	y	z
w_1:	x	y	b_1
	---	---	---
	x	b_1	b_7
	x	b_7	b_8
	b_8	b_1	-
	b_9	b_1	b_2
	-	b_9	b_2
	---	---	---
w_3:	b_2	y	-
w_4:	b_3	y	z
w_5:	-	b_3	z

In this example there are two equivalence classes: $E_1 = \{w_1, w_2, w_3\}$ and $E_2 = \{w_4, w_5\}$. In E_1, row w_1 subsumes both w_2 and w_3. As a result, $T \supseteq T[\theta_1]$ and $T \supseteq T^2$, but $T \not\supseteq T[\theta_2]$, so T is not 1-bounded. □

We can combine the results of Lemmas 4.2 and 4.3 to obtain a weaker sufficient condition for T to be 1-bounded.

LEMMA 4.5: *A semi-typed tableau T is 1-bounded if each row in T is either maximal or covered.*

PROOF: Consider a partial expansion T' of T in which a set S of rows has been expanded. Assume that the rows in S are in equivalence classes $E_1, \ldots, E_l$. Note that $S \subseteq E_1 \cup \cdots \cup E_l$. For each equivalence class E_k, $1 \le k \le l$, choose one row in $S \cap E_k$ that is maximal, if such a row exists, and call this row *the* maximal row for E_k. Construct a mapping $\psi: T \to T'$ as follows. For each row $w_i \in T$,

(a) $\psi(w_i) = w_i^j$, if $w_i \in E_k$, $1 \le k \le l$, and some $w_j \in S$ is the maximal row for E_k,
(b) $\psi(w_i) = w_m^i$, if $w_i \in S$, no row in S is the maximal row for $Rel(w_i)$, and w_m covers w_i, or
(c) $\psi(w_i) = w_i$, otherwise.

Once again, it is not hard to show that ψ is a containment mapping. □

COROLLARY 4.3: *A semi-typed tableau T is 1-bounded if the rows comprising each equivalence class have the same dv's.*

PROOF: Every row in T is maximal. □

EXAMPLE 4.3: The following tableau demonstrates that the conditions of Lemma 4.5 are not necessary for a tableau to be 1-bounded.

T:	x	y	z	w
w_1:	b_1	y	b_2	w
w_2:	-	b_1	b_3	w
w_3:	x	-	-	b_3
w_4:	x	-	-	b_2
w_5:	b_4	y	z	w
w_6:	-	b_4	z	w
w_7:	x	-	-	w

Every row in T except w_1 is either maximal (w_5) or covered (w_2, w_3, w_4, w_6, w_7). However, it can be shown that T is 1-bounded. In particular, there are containment mappings $\psi_1: T \rightarrow T[\theta_1]$ and $\phi: T \rightarrow T^2$. The mapping ψ_1 maps the rows of T as follows: $w_1 \rightarrow w_5^1$, $w_2 \rightarrow w_6^1$, $w_3 \rightarrow w_4$, $w_4 \rightarrow w_4$, $w_5 \rightarrow w_5$, $w_6 \rightarrow w_6$, $w_7 \rightarrow w_7$. The mapping ϕ maps the rows of T as follows: $w_1 \rightarrow w_5^1$, $w_2 \rightarrow w_6^1$, $w_3 \rightarrow w_7^4$, $w_4 \rightarrow w_7^4$, $w_5 \rightarrow w_5^5$, $w_6 \rightarrow w_6^5$, $w_7 \rightarrow w_7^7$. □

The conditions in Lemma 4.5 *will* turn out to be necessary for 1-boundedness of a subclass of semi-typed tableaux, namely, the "simple" tableaux. Before proving this, however, we require some additional results.

4.2. Necessary conditions

If a semi-typed tableau T is 1-bounded, we can derive certain properties which T must satisfy. Again, these results generalize those for typed tableaux, in that any idempotent typed tableau also exhibits these properties. It is useful first to investigate the structure of the containment mappings $\psi_i: T \rightarrow T[\theta_i]$ more closely.

Unlike for typed tableaux, it is not always the case that there is a containment mapping from $T[\theta_i]$ to T (see Example 3.4). Let $\psi_i(T)$ denote the image of ψ_i on T, that is, $\psi_i(T) = \{\psi_i(w) \mid w \in T\}$. The following lemma shows under what conditions there is a containment mapping from $\psi_i(T)$ to T.

LEMMA 4.6: *Let T be a semi-typed tableau for which there is a containment mapping $\psi_i: T \rightarrow T[\theta_i]$. The mapping $\phi: \psi_i(T) \rightarrow T$ defined by*

$$\phi(w_l) = w_l, \text{ if } w_l \in \psi_i(T) \cap (T - \{w_i\}), \text{ and}$$

$$\phi(w_l^i) = w_l, \text{ if } w_l^i \in \psi_i(T) \cap \theta_i(T),$$

is a containment mapping if and only if no two rows $w_j, w_k \in Rel(w_i)$ share an ndv b such that

(1) ψ_i maps w_j into $\theta_i(T)$,

(2) ψ_i maps w_k into $T - \{w_i\}$, and

(3) ψ_i maps b to a shared ndv of w_i.

PROOF: Easy. □

LEMMA 4.7: *Let T be a minimal, semi-typed tableau with a containment mapping $\psi_i: T \rightarrow T[\theta_i]$. Either (a) w_i is maximal, or (b) there are rows $w_j, w_k \in Rel(w_i)$ which share an ndv b such that*

(1) ψ_i maps w_j into $\theta_i(T)$,

(2) ψ_i maps w_k into $T - \{w_i\}$, and

(3) ψ_i maps b to a shared ndv of w_i.

PROOF: If both (a) and (b) are false, we can use Lemma 4.6 to show that T cannot be minimal, a contradiction. ☐

We are now in a position to prove some necessary conditions for a semi-typed tableau to be 1-bounded. The first uses the partial covering relation defined earlier.

LEMMA 4.8: *A semi-typed tableau T is 1-bounded only if, for each row $w_i \in T$, either*
(a) w_i is maximal, or
(b) there are rows $w_j \in Rel(w_i)$ and $w_k \in T$ such that $w_i \geq w_j$ and w_k partially covers w_j.

PROOF: We show that if (a) is false, then (b) must be true. Since T is 1-bounded, there is a containment mapping $\psi_i: T \to T[\theta_i]$. If (a) is false, then, by the corollary to Lemma 4.3 and by Lemma 4.7, there are rows $w_j, w_k \in Rel(w_i)$ in which $w_j(A_p) = w_k(A_q) = b$, such that ψ_i maps w_j to some $w_j^i \in \theta_i(T)$, maps w_k into $T - \{w_i\}$, and maps b to a shared ndv b' of w_i. Hence, $w_i \geq w_j$ and $w_l \geq w_j$. Furthermore, $w_j^i(A_p) = b'$ and $w_l(A_p) = s(A_p)$, so w_l partially covers w_j. ☐

We can restate the above lemma in weaker but simpler terms. If T is 1-bounded, then each row in T is maximal, partially covered, or not a source. The tableau T of Example 4.2 shows that the above necessary condition is still too weak: T satisfies the condition but is not 1-bounded. For instance, row w_1 satisfies (a), and row w_2 satisfies (b) since $w_2 \geq w_2$ and w_1 partially covers w_2. Unfortunately, as the following example demonstrates, we cannot strengthen this result to restrict row w_j to be the same row as w_i.

EXAMPLE 4.4:

T:	x	y	z	w
w_1:	b_1	b_2	b_6	w
w_2:	b_2	b_3	z	w
w_3:	b_3	b_2	z	w
w_4:	b_4	b_1	-	-
w_5:	-	-	b_4	-
w_6:	b_5	y	-	-
w_7:	-	-	b_5	-
w_8:	x	-	-	-

$T[\theta_1]$:	x	y	z	w
	b_7	b_8	b_{12}	w
	b_8	b_9	b_6	w
	b_9	b_8	b_6	w
	b_{10}	b_7	-	-
	-	-	b_{10}	-
w_6^1:	b_{11}	b_2	-	-
w_7^1:	-	-	b_{11}	-
	b_1	-	-	-
	---	---	---	---
w_2:	b_2	b_3	z	w
w_3:	b_3	b_2	z	w
w_4:	b_4	b_1	-	-
w_5:	-	-	b_4	-
w_6:	b_5	y	-	-
w_7:	-	-	b_5	-
w_8:	x	-	-	-

In this example, $Rel(w_1) = \{w_1, \ldots, w_5\}$, so w_1 does not subsume each row in $Rel(w_1)$. There is a containment mapping from T to $T[\theta_1]$ in which rows w_1 and w_3 map to w_2, w_2 maps to w_3, and w_4 and w_5 map to w_6^1 and w_7^1 respectively. No row partially covers w_1, although condition (b) of Lemma 4.8 is satisfied since $w_1 \geq w_4$ and w_6 partially covers w_4. ☐

We can also prove that certain types of rows in a tableau T require the existence of other rows if T is 1-bounded.

LEMMA 4.9: *A minimal, semi-typed tableau T is 1-bounded only if every source row in T is covered.*

4.3. Exact characterizations

By considering various subclasses of semi-typed tableaux, we can derive necessary and sufficient conditions for such tableaux to be 1-bounded. Let us say that a semi-typed tableau T is *simple* if at most one shared ndv appears in any column of T. That is, if shared ndv b appears in column A of T, then no shared ndv $b' \neq b$ can appear in A. The tableaux of Examples 3.1 and 3.2 are both simple. This definition of simple is less restricted than the usual definition for typed tableaux [ASU79a], which requires that if a shared ndv appears in column A, then no other *variable* (dv or ndv) can appear more than once in A. As pointed out in [ASU79a], the algebraic expressions corresponding to non-simple tableaux are fairly intricate and hence are less likely to be encountered in practice. For a simple tableau T, the conditions in Lemma 4.5 are both necessary and sufficient for T to be 1-bounded. This generalizes the characterization of idempotent simple typed tableaux. The following lemma is used in the proof of the theorem.

LEMMA 4.10: *Let T be simple and $\psi_i: T \to T[\theta_i]$ be a containment mapping. The mapping $\phi: T \to T$ defined below is a containment mapping. For each row $w \in T$,*
(a) if $\psi_i(w) = w_l$, then $\phi(w) = w_l$, and
(b) if $\psi_i(w) = w_l^i$ and ψ_i maps every shared ndv in w either to itself or to a dv, then $\phi(w) = w_i$, and
(c) if $\psi_i(w) = w_l^i$ and ψ_i maps every shared ndv b in w either to $\theta_i(b)$ or to a dv, then $\phi(w) = w_l$.

PROOF: Because T is simple, a shared ndv b is mapped to itself, $\theta_i(b)$, or a dv. The proof proceeds by cases, considering how a pair of rows can be mapped by ϕ. □

THEOREM 4.1: *Let T be minimal, semi-typed and simple. T is 1-bounded if and only if each row in T is either maximal or covered.*

PROOF: Since T is semi-typed, sufficiency follows from Lemma 4.5. Necessity can be proved using Lemma 4.7 and Lemma 4.10. □

COROLLARY 4.4: *Whether a minimal, simple tableau is 1-bounded or not can be determined in polynomial time.*

EXAMPLE 4.5: Consider again the tableau of Example 3.2:

T:	x	y	z
w_1:	x	b_1	b_2
w_2:	x	y	b_1
w_3:	b_3	b_4	z

Because T is simple, we can now prove that T is 1-bounded by applying Theorem 4.1; row w_1 is covered by row w_2, row w_2 is maximal, and w_3 is both maximal and covered. □

In a sense, the above characterization is a generalization of that for idempotent typed tableaux, in that it is not difficult to show that every row in a typed tableau T is either maximal or covered if and only if T has no shared ndv's. We can also provide exact characterizations of 1-boundedness for other subclasses of semi-typed tableaux.

THEOREM 4.2: *Let T be a minimal, semi-typed tableau in which no row subsumes any other row in its equivalence class. Tableau T is 1-bounded if and only if each row in T is covered.*

PROOF: Sufficiency was proved in Lemma 4.4. Since every row in T is a source row, necessity follows from Lemma 4.9. □

The tableau T of Example 3.4, where T^* computes the transitive closure of a binary relation, is an example of a tableau in which no row subsumes any other row in its equivalence class. We conclude that T is not 1-bounded. It turns out that we can extend the class of tableaux for which the existence of covering rows characterizes 1-boundedness as follows.

THEOREM 4.3: *Let T be a semi-typed tableau in which no row subsumes any row with which it shares an ndv. Then T is 1-bounded if and only if each row in T is covered.*

PROOF: Omitted. □

EXAMPLE 4.6: The following example shows that, when no row in T subsumes any other row with which it shares an ndv, there can be a containment mapping from T to a single row expansion of T, in this case $T[\theta_1]$, even if w_1 does not have a covering row.

T:	x	y	z	w
w_1:	b_1	b_2	z	w
w_2:	x	b_3	z	w
w_3:	b_1	y	b_4	-
w_4:	x	y	b_2	-
w_5:	x	y	b_3	-
w_6:	-	b_4	z	b_5
w_7:	b_5	-	-	w
w_8:	-	y	z	b_6
w_9:	b_6	-	-	w

In the containment mapping, w_1 maps to w_2, w_3 maps to w_4 which maps to w_5, and w_6 and w_7 map to w_8^1 and w_9^1 respectively, while all other rows map to themselves. This does not invalidate the above theorem, however, as T is not 1-bounded. For example, there is no containment mapping from T to $T[\theta_2]$. □

5. UNTYPED TABLEAU QUERIES

For typed tableaux, Theorem 3.1 characterizes the idempotent (or 1-bounded) tableaux as those which do not contain any shared ndv's. In the previous section, we saw that this characterization was sufficient but not necessary for a semi-typed tableau to be 1-bounded. Even so, we had difficulty finding a syntactic characterization of the 1-bounded semi-typed tableaux. In this section, we demonstrate by means of a simple example that the absence of shared ndv's in a general untyped tableau T is no longer a sufficient condition for T to be 1-bounded.

EXAMPLE 5.1: Consider the following tableau T, which has no shared ndv's, and two of its partial expansions, $T[\theta_2]$ and T^2:

T:	x	y	z
w_1:	x	b_1	b_2
w_2:	y	b_3	z
w_3:	b_4	y	z

$T[\theta_2]$:	x	y	z
w_1:	x	b_1	b_2
	---	---	---
w_1^2:	y	b_9	b_{10}
w_2^2:	b_3	b_{11}	z
w_3^2:	b_{12}	b_3	z
	---	---	---
w_3:	b_4	y	z

T^2:	x	y	z
w_1^1:	x	b_5	b_6
	b_1	b_7	b_2
	b_8	b_1	b_2
	---	---	---
	y	b_9	b_{10}
	b_3	b_{11}	z
	b_{12}	b_3	z
	---	---	---
	b_4	b_{13}	b_{14}
w_2^3:	y	b_{15}	z
w_3^3:	b_{16}	y	z

In this example, $T \not\sqsupseteq T[\theta_2]$ because row w_2 in T cannot be mapped to any row in $T[\theta_2]$. Therefore, T is not 1-bounded despite the fact that it contains no shared ndv's. On the other hand, $T \sqsupseteq T^2$ because $w_1 \to w_1^1$, $w_2 \to w_2^3$, and $w_3 \to w_3^3$. Note that both w_2 and w_3 map to rows in $\theta_3(T)$, the expansion of row w_3. □

6. CONCLUSION

We have studied the characterization of idempotent, single-predicate Horn clauses by viewing them as untyped, recursive tableau queries. Although there is a particularly simple characterization for idempotent typed tableaux, this does not carry over to the untyped case. We generalized typed tableaux to what we called semi-typed tableaux, which include those tableaux that we feel would be encountered most often in practice. For this class of tableaux, we derived both sufficient conditions and necessary conditions for idempotence, while for various subclasses of semi-typed tableaux, we characterized exactly the idempotent tableaux.

An obvious topic for further research is to try to characterize those tableaux in these classes which are k-bounded, for some constant k. Another direction for research would be to generalize the classes for which necessary and sufficient conditions for both idempotence and k-boundedness can be found. As pointed out in the introduction, recursive tableau queries are non-linear in nature. It would be interesting if we could extend our results to provide a means for converting non-linear queries to linear queries. We hope to address these issues in future papers.

References

ASU79a.

A.V. AHO, Y. SAGIV, AND J.D. ULLMAN, "Equivalences among Relational Expressions," *SIAM J. Comput.*, vol. 8, no. 2, pp. 218-246, 1979.

AhU179.

A.V. AHO AND J.D. ULLMAN, "Universality of Data Retrieval Languages," *Proc. 6th ACM Symp. on Principles of Programming Languages*, pp. 110-120, 1979.

BaRa86.
F. BANCILHON AND R. RAMAKRISHNAN, "An Amateur's Introduction to Recursive Query Processing Strategies," *Proc. ACM SIGMOD Conf. on Management of Data*, pp. 16-52, 1986.

BeVa84.
C. BEERI AND M.Y. VARDI, "Formal Systems for Tuple and Equality Generating Dependencies," *SIAM J. Comput.*, vol. 13, no. 1, pp. 76-98, 1984.

ChMe77.
A.K. CHANDRA AND P.M. MERLIN, "Optimal Implementation of Conjunctive Queries in Relational Data Bases," *Proc. 9th ACM Symp. on Theory of Computing*, pp. 77-90, 1977.

Codd72.
E. F. CODD, "Relational Completeness of Data Base Sublanguages," in *Data Base Systems*, ed. R. Rustin, pp. 65-98, Prentice-Hall, Englewood Cliffs, N. J, 1972.

CoKa86.
S. COSMADAKIS AND P. KANELLAKIS, "Parallel Evaluation of Recursive Rule Queries," *Proc. 5th ACM SIGACT—SIGMOD Symp. on Principles of Database Systems*, pp. 280-293, 1986.

CMW87.
I.F. CRUZ, A.O. MENDELZON, AND P.T. WOOD, "A Graphical Query Language Supporting Recursion," *Proc. ACM SIGMOD Conf. on Management of Data*, pp. 323-330, 1987.

Ioan85.
Y.E. IOANNIDIS, "A Time Bound on the Materialization of Some Recursively Defined Views," *Proc. 11th Int. Conf. on Very Large Data Bases*, pp. 219-226, 1985.

Naug86a.
J. NAUGHTON, "Data Independent Recursion in Deductive Databases," *Proc. 5th ACM SIGACT—SIGMOD Symp. on Principles of Database Systems*, pp. 267-279, 1986.

NaSa87.
J. NAUGHTON AND Y. SAGIV, "A Decidable Class of Bounded Recursions," *Proc. 6th ACM SIGACT-SIGMOD-SIGART Symp. on Principles of Database Systems*, pp. 227-236, 1987.

Sagi85.
Y. SAGIV, "On Computing Restricted Projections of Representative Instances," *Proc. 4th ACM SIGACT—SIGMOD Symp. on Principles of Database Systems*, pp. 171-180, 1985.

Sagi88.
Y. SAGIV, "On Bounded Database Schemes and Bounded Horn-Clause Programs," *SIAM J. Comput.*, vol. 17, no. 1, pp. 1-22, 1988.

SaYa80.
Y. SAGIV AND M. YANNAKAKIS, "Equivalence among Relational Expressions with the Union and Difference Operators," *J. ACM*, vol. 27, no. 4, pp. 633-655, 1980.

Ullm83.
J.D. ULLMAN, *Principles of Database Systems*, Computer Science Press, Potomac, Md., 1983.

Hypothetical Datalog: Complexity and Expressibility

Anthony J. Bonner
Department of Computer Science
Rutgers University
New Brunswick, NJ 08903

Abstract

We present an extension of Horn-clause logic which can hypothetically add and delete tuples from a database. Such logics have been discussed in the literature, but their complexities and expressibilities have remained an open question. This paper examines two such logics in the function-free, predicate case. It is shown, in particular, that augmenting Horn-clause logic with hypothetical addition increases its data-complexity from PTIME to PSPACE. When deletions are added as well, complexity increases again, to EXPTIME. To establish expressibility, we augment the logic with *negation-by-failure* and view it as a query language for relational databases. The logic of hypothetical additions then expresses all database queries which are computable in PSPACE. When deletions are included, the logic expresses all database queries computable in EXPTIME.

1 Introduction

Several researchers in the logic programming community have pointed out the utility of augmenting Horn-clause logic with the ability to hypothetically add facts to a database [15,14,24,29,21,7]. Others have done as much by investigating the intuitionistic semantics of embedded implications [22,23]. However, the complexity and expressibility of these logics has remained an open question. This paper addresses these issues from a database point of view. In particular, results on data-complexity and expressibility are established for the function-free predicate case.

This paper also examines hypothetical deletion. In contrast to additions, hypothetical deletions have received little, if any, attention in the logic-programming literature, one exception being the work of Manchanda and Warren [21]. As in their work, this paper focuses on deletions from the database, and not from the least fixpoint. Although relatively simple, such deletions nevertheless increase the complexity and expressibility of the logic from PSPACE to EXPTIME.[1,2]

Results are established for two distinct extensions of Horn-clause logic: (i) Horn logic augmented with hypothetical additions (called the *restricted* logic), and (ii) Horn logic augmented with both hypothetical additions and deletions (called the *full* logic).

Hypothetical queries are particularly useful in the context of rule-based systems and deductive databases. For example, one might ask, "If I were to take *eng*423, would I be able to graduate?", or perhaps, "Retrieve those students who could graduate if they took one more course." Gabbay and Reyle have reported a need to augment Prolog with hypothetical rules in order to encode the British Nationality Act. In particular, the act contains rules such as the following: "You are eligible for citizenship if your father would be eligible if he were still alive" [15]. Rules such as these are called *embedded implications* [22].

Embedded implications have an intuitionistic semantics. That is, their models are Kripke structures, consisting of many possible substates [13]. McCarty has developed an intuitionistic fixpoint-semantics for embedded implications and has shown that they have interesting semantical properties analogous to the unique minimal-model property of Horn clauses [22,3]. In particular, he has shown that they have a unique maximal Kripke-model, which in turn, has a unique minimal substate. It is also known that in the propositional case, intuitionistic validity is PSPACE-complete

[1] In this paper, the terms EXPTIME and "exponential time" denote DTIME($2^{n^{O(1)}}$).

[2] The increase is strict iff $PSPACE \neq EXPTIME$, which although considered likely, is an open question.

[25,20]. To our knowledge, however, we are the first to address the questions of the data-complexity and expressibility of intuitionistic reasoning.

In contrast to additions, hypothetical deletions do not appear to have an intuitionistic semantics. The problem is that, like most logics, intuitionistic logic has no concept of database; it sees only the logical closure of the database and the rulebase. Thus, deletions from the database make no sense in intuitionistic logics. One alternative is to view our logic as a dynamic logic of database updates. In fact, our notation for hypothetical updates is reminiscent of dynamic logic, with additions and deletions being the primitive actions [16,21]. This paper introduces a semantics for hypothetical updates which in some sense is "midway" between that of dynamic and intuitionistic logic.

Semantics are introduced, however, mainly as a vehicle for establishing upper complexity bounds. We define a notion of *rulebase interpretation* and introduce a *fixpoint operator*, much like the T-operator of Horn-clause logic [3,26]. A bottom-up, iterative procedure is developed for computing the "least fixpoint" of a database and a set of rules. It is easy to show that this procedure runs in exponential time.

For the restricted logic of hypothetical additions, a mixed top-down/bottom-up algorithm is developed. One way to view this algorithm is as a top-down, recursive algorithm in which bottom-up, least-fixpoint computations occur at each level of recursion. There are polynomially many levels of recursion and each level takes polynomial time. Thus, we have an algorithm which runs in polynomial space.

In this way, EXPTIME and PSPACE upper-bounds on the data-complexity of query processing are established for the full logic and its restriction, resp. To establish these as lower bounds, we use the logics to encode the computations of alternating Turing-machines [11]. In the full logic, the database represents the machine tape and hypothetical updates represent the machine transitions. Hypothetical deletion simulates tape erasure, and hypothetical addition simulates tape writing. In this way, alternating PSPACE machines can be encoded. In the restricted logic, the approach is more familiar: time is represented explicitly and the database encodes an entire computation path. By making time explicit, however, it is possible only to encode alternating PTIME machines. This is why hypothetical additions have a lower complexity than hypothetical additions and deletions combined.

After establishing complexity results, the issue of expressibility is addressed. In particular, we view the two logics as query languages for relational databases, and we ask, "what class of database queries do these logics express?" Because they are monotonic, there are many simple queries that these logics cannot express; so we first augment them with *negation-by-failure* [19]. When augmented in this way, the full logic expresses all database queries which are computable in exponential time; and the restricted logic expresses all database queries computable in polynomial space.

The proofs rely on our simulation of alternating Turing-machines. In this respect they are similar to other expressibility proofs in the literature [18,27]. One difference, however, is that we do not require the data domain to be linearly ordered. Linearly-ordered domains are used to simulate counters, which in turn, are used to simulate tape-head movements. Our approach is to start with unordered domains and assert linear orders hypothetically. This, however, involves some novel technical problems.

2 Examples

This section gives several examples of hypothetical queries and rules. In each example, tuples are hypothetically added or deleted from the database before a least-fixpoint query is made. We express these queries with modal-like operators. In particular, $Q[add : P]$ means, "If P were added to the database, then Q would be true"; and $Q[del : P]$ means, "If P were deleted from the database, then Q would be true." The notation $R, DB \vdash \phi$ means that the query ϕ is true when applied to the rule-based system $[R, DB]$. The next section will be more precise about this. This section provides examples of hypothetical queries and how they are expressed in our logic.

The examples are centered on a rule-based system which describes university policy. For instance, the atomic formula $take(s,c)$ means that student s has taken course c, and $grad(s)$ means that s is eligible for graduation. Thus, the database DB contains facts such as $take(tony, cs250)$, and the rulebase R contains rules such as

$$grad(s) \leftarrow take(s, his101), take(s, eng201).$$

In the following examples, each query is described in three ways: (i) informally, in English, (ii) formally, at the meta-level, and (iii) formally, at the object-level with operators of addition and deletion.[3]

Example 1. Consider the query, "If Tony took cs452, would he be eligible to graduate?" That is, if $take(tony, cs452)$ were added to the database, could we infer $grad(s)$? This query can be formalized at the meta-level as follows:

$$R, DB + take(tony, cs452) \vdash grad(tony)$$

In our language of hypotheticals, it is represented by the expression $grad(tony)[add : take(tony, cs452)]$. This is an object-level level expression ψ such that $R, DB \vdash \psi$ iff the meta-level condition is satisfied.

Example 2. "If Tony had not taken engl01, would he have graduated?" That is, if $take(tony, eng101)$ were deleted from the database, could we infer $grad(tony)$? This query can be formalized at the meta-level as follows:

$$R, DB \sim take(tony, eng101) \vdash grad(tony)$$

At the object-level, it is represented by the expression $grad(tony)[del : take(tony, eng101)]$.

Example 3. "Retrieve those students who could graduate if they took (at most) one more course." i.e., at the meta-level, "Retrieve those s such that

$$\exists c\ [R, DB + take(s, c) \vdash grad(s)]$$

At the object-level, this query is represented by the expression $\psi(s) = \exists c, grad(s)[add : take(s, c)]$. That is, for each value of s, $R, DB \vdash \psi(s)$ iff the meta-level condition is satisfied.

Example 4. "Retrieve those students who have taken $eng201$ but who could have graduated if they had taken $eng250$ instead." i.e., at the meta-level, "Those s such that

$$R, DB \vdash take(s, eng201) \quad \text{and}$$
$$R, DB + take(s, eng250) \sim take(s, eng201) \vdash grad(s)$$

[3] See [19] for a description of meta-level and object-level reasoning.

and at the object-level,[4]

$$take(s, eng201) \ \wedge$$
$$grad(s)\ [add : take(s, eng250)]\ [del : take(s, eng201)]$$

Having introduced hypothetical queries, we can also use them in the premises of rules. These rules have the form $A \leftarrow B[add : C]$, meaning, "A is true if adding C to the database causes B to become true." Such rules turn our query language into a logic for building rulebases.

Example 5. Suppose the university wishes to change its policy on financial aid by enacting the following rule:

> "If a student is within one course of graduation and is not eligible for primary aid, then he is eligible for secondary aid."

This hypothetical rule can be represented by adding the following two rules to the rulebase:[5]

$$aid2(s) \leftarrow \sim aid1(s),\ grad1(s).$$
$$grad1(s) \leftarrow \exists c\ [grad(s, c) \leftarrow take(s, c)]$$

Here, $aid1(s)$ and $aid2(s)$ mean that student s is eligible for primary and secondary aid, resp. $grad1(s)$ means that s is within one course of graduation.

3 Hypothetical Inference

Having provided examples of hypothetical queries and rules, this section now defines a logic for expressing them. First its syntax is defined, and then its meaning is given in terms of an inference system.[6] We use the syntax and terminology of Horn-clause logic augmented with with modal-like operators. In particular, an expression is called *atomic* iff it is an atomic formula of predicate logic. Although the rest of this paper focusses on the function-free case, the definitions of this section do not require this restriction.

Definition 1 *A premise (or query) is an expression having one of the following forms:*

- A *where A is atomic.*

[4] Here we use the convention that $A[B][C]$ means $(A[B])[C]$.

[5] The first rule uses negation-by-failure [19].

[6] Semantics is touched upon only briefly in this paper. But see [4] for a proof that the hypothetical logic of additions has an intuitionistic semantics.

- $A[add : B]$ *where A and B are atomic.*
- $A[del : B]$ *where A and B are atomic.*

Definition 2 *A hypothetical rule is an expression of the form* $A \leftarrow \phi_1, \phi_2, ..., \phi_k$ *where* $k \geq 0$, *A is atomic, and each* ϕ_i *is a premise.*

Notice that hypothetical rules include atomic formulas and definite Horn-rules as special cases. This syntax is therefore an extension of that of Horn logic[19]. The inference system too is an extension of Horn logic, as the following definition shows.

Definition 3 *Suppose R is a set of hypothetical rules and DB is a database. Then hypothetical inference is defined as follows, where A and B are ground atomic formulas:*

1. $R, DB \vdash A$ *if for some rule* $A' \leftarrow \phi_1, ..., \phi_k$ *in R, and for some substitution* θ *such that* $A = A'\theta$, *it is the case that* $R, DB \vdash \phi_i\theta$ *for each i.*
2. $R, DB \vdash A$ *if* $A \in DB$
3. $R, DB \vdash A[add : B]$ *if* $R, DB + \{B\} \vdash A$
4. $R, DB \vdash A[del : B]$ *if* $R, DB \sim \{B\} \vdash A$

It is implicit in the above definition, that all variables in a rule are universally quantified; however, variables that appear in the premise, but not the head of a rule admit a special interpretation. For example, in the rule $A(x) \leftarrow B(x,y)[add : C(x,y)]$, the variable y does not appear in the head. If this rule were to appear in the rulebase R, then inference rule 1 would imply that for any ground term x, it is the case that $R, DB \vdash A(x)$ if $R, DB + \{C(x,y)\} \vdash B(x,y)$ for some ground term y. For this reason, this rule can be interpreted in two ways:[7]

- $\forall x \forall y \; A(x) \leftarrow B(x,y)[add : C(x,y)]$
- $\forall x \; A(x) \leftarrow \exists y B(x,y)[add : C(x,y)]$

It is the latter interpretation which enables our logic to represent the examples given in section 2. In particular, the rule $grad1(s) \leftarrow grad(s)[add : take(s,c)]$ defines those students who are "within one course of graduation."

Example 6. Suppose R contains rules for defining a predicate D and also contains the following rules:

$$\begin{array}{l} A_1 \leftarrow A_2[add : B_1] \\ A_2 \leftarrow A_3[add : B_2] \\ \quad ... \\ A_n \leftarrow A_{n+1}[add : B_n] \\ A_{n+1} \leftarrow D \end{array}$$

Then $R, DB \vdash A_1$ if $R, DB + \{B_1, ..., B_n\} \vdash D$.

In the next two examples, we assume the database DB includes the following atomic formulas, which define a finite sequence $a_1, a_2, ..., a_n, a_{n+1}$:

$$FIRST(a_1),\; NEXT(a_1,a_2),\; NEXT(a_2,a_3),\; ... \; NEXT(a_n,a_{n+1}),\; LAST(a_{n+1})$$

Example 7. Suppose R contains rules defining the predicate D and also contains the following three rules:

$$\begin{array}{l} E \leftarrow FIRST(x),\; A(x). \\ A(x) \leftarrow NEXT(x,y),\; A(y)[add : B(x)]. \\ A(x) \leftarrow LAST(x),\; D. \end{array}$$

Then $R, DB \vdash E$ if $R, DB + \{B(a_1), ... B(a_n)\} \vdash D$.

Example 8. Suppose R contains rules defining the predicate D and also contains the following four rules:

$$\begin{array}{l} E \leftarrow FIRST(x),\; A(x). \\ A(x) \leftarrow NEXT(x,y),\; A(y)[add : B(x)]. \\ A(x) \leftarrow NEXT(x,y),\; A(y)[add : C(x)]. \\ A(x) \leftarrow LAST(x),\; D. \end{array}$$

Then $R, DB \vdash E$ if

$$\begin{array}{rl} & R, DB + \{C(a_1), B(a_2), ..., B(a_n)\} \vdash D \\ or & R, DB + \{B(a_1), C(a_2), ..., B(a_n)\} \vdash D \\ or & R, DB + \{C(a_1), C(a_2), ..., B(a_n)\} \vdash D \\ & ... \\ or & R, DB + \{C(a_1), C(a_2), ..., C(a_n)\} \vdash D \end{array}$$

The last example illustrates that a fixed set of hypothetical rules can express $O(2^n)$ meta-level queries, where n is the database size. Such "blowups" can be viewed as the source of the EXPTIME and PSPACE data-complexity bounds for our hypothetical logics.

4 Bottom-Up Inference

In this section, hypothetical inference is formulated in terms of a bottom-up, iterative operator, much like the T-operator of Horn-clause logic [3,26]. This view of inference forms the basis of algorithms developed in the next section, algorithms whose complexities are easily determined. This section develops enough theory to verify that these algorithms are sound and complete

[7] Similar interpretations also exist in Horn-clause logic.

with respect to the inference system defined in the last section.

We first introduce a rudimentary semantics in which a rulebase is viewed as a mapping $\mathcal{M}$ which takes a database DB as input and returns a larger database $\mathcal{M}(DB)$ as output. For instance, the identity mapping $\mathcal{I}$ corresponds to the empty rulebase, which when given a database DB, does not add any inferences to it. More generally, a set of Horn rules is naturally interpreted as a mapping which takes a database and returns a least fixpoint. However, to justify this semantics on philosophical grounds is not the purpose of this paper. Our motive is purely pragmatic: this semantics is a convenient vehicle for establishing upper complexity-bounds.

Given a rulebase R, we define an operator T_R which represents "one step" inferences. This operator takes a mapping $\mathcal{M}$ as input and returns another mapping $T_R(\mathcal{M})$ as output. For instance, $T_R(\mathcal{I})$ is the mapping which when given a database DB, adds those atomic formulas which can be derived from R and DB in one step. Similarly, $T_R^k(\mathcal{I})$ is the mapping which when given a database DB, adds those atomic formulas which can be derived from R and DB in k or fewer steps.

The rest of this section makes these ideas precise. In particular, we assume that the databases DB are built from a universal domain of constant and predicate symbols and that all mappings $\mathcal{M}$ are defined on these databases.

Definition 4 *A rulebase interpretation is a mapping $\mathcal{M}$ which takes a database DB and returns a larger database $\mathcal{M}(DB)$. That is, $DB \subseteq \mathcal{M}(DB)$. In addition,*

- *$\mathcal{I}$ is the identity interpretation. That is, $\mathcal{I}(DB) = DB$.*
- *$\mathcal{M}_1 \leq \mathcal{M}_2$ iff for each database DB, $\mathcal{M}_1(DB) \subseteq \mathcal{M}_2(DB)$.*
- *$\mathcal{M} = \mathcal{M}_1 \cup \mathcal{M}_2$ iff for each database DB, $\mathcal{M}(DB) = \mathcal{M}_1(DB) \cup \mathcal{M}_2(DB)$.*

Definition 5 *Suppose $\mathcal{M}$ is a rulebase interpretation and DB is a database. If A and B are atomic, then*

- $\mathcal{M}, DB \models A$ *iff* $A \in \mathcal{M}(DB)$
- $\mathcal{M}, DB \models A[add : B]$ *iff* $A \in \mathcal{M}(DB + \{B\})$
- $\mathcal{M}, DB \models A[del : B]$ *iff* $A \in \mathcal{M}(DB \sim \{B\})$

Definition 6 *Suppose R is a set of hypothetical rules. Then T_R is an operator which takes a rulebase interpretation $\mathcal{M}$ as input and returns a rulebase interpretation $T_R(\mathcal{M})$ as output. Furthermore, if DB is a database, then $A \in [T_R(\mathcal{M})](DB)$ iff one of the following are true:*

- *$A \in DB$*
- *for some rule $A' \leftarrow \phi_1, \ldots, \phi_k$ in R, and for some substitution θ such that $A = A'\theta$, it is the case that $\mathcal{M}, DB \models \phi_i$ for each i.*

Loosely speaking, $\mathcal{M}$ represents a set of inferences, and $T_R(\mathcal{M})$ adds to $\mathcal{M}$ those inferences which can be derived from R in one step. Of course, the exact inferences performed depend on the database, which is why $\mathcal{M}$ and $T_R(\mathcal{M})$ are functions of DB.

Lemma 1 *T_R is inflationary and monotonic. i.e.,*

- *$\mathcal{M} \leq T_R(\mathcal{M})$*
- *If $\mathcal{M}_1 \leq \mathcal{M}_2$, then $T_R(\mathcal{M}_1) \leq T_R(\mathcal{M}_2)$.*

Definition 7 *If $\mathcal{M}$ is a rulebase interpretation, then*

- $T_R^0(\mathcal{M}) = \mathcal{M}$
- $T_R^{n+1}(\mathcal{M}) = T_R[T_R^n(\mathcal{M})]$
- $T_R^*(\mathcal{M}) = \cup_{n=0}^{n=\infty} T_R^n(\mathcal{M})$

From these definitions, the following theorem is straightforward [6]. It is the basis of the algorithms introduced in the next section.

Theorem 1 *$R, DB \vdash \phi$ iff $T_R^*(\mathcal{I}), DB \models \phi$.*

Example 9. Suppose R contains exactly two rules, $B \leftarrow C$ and $A \leftarrow B[add : C]$. The following table shows that it takes two applications of T_R to reach a fixpoint and compute $T_R^*(\mathcal{I})$. In this table, each column represents a mapping $T_R^k(\mathcal{I})$ for some k. As k increases form left to right, atoms are added to each column, but never subtracted, reflecting the inflationary character of T_R.

DB	$[T_R(\mathcal{I})](DB)$	$[T_R^2(\mathcal{I})](DB)$	$[T_R^3(\mathcal{I})](DB)$
-	-	A	A
A	A	A	A
B	AB	AB	AB
C	BC	ABC	ABC
AB	AB	AB	AB
AC	ABC	ABC	ABC
BC	ABC	ABC	ABC
ABC	ABC	ABC	ABC

Atoms added by T_R have been highlighted. For instance, the B in the second column/fourth row was added by the Horn rule $B \leftarrow C$. This in turn caused the addition of A to the third column/first row by the rule $A \leftarrow B[add : C]$. Formally, the first application of T_R establishes that $T_R(\mathcal{I}), \{\} \models B[add : C]$, and the second establishes that $T_R^2(\mathcal{I}), \{\} \models A$.

Note that A is eventually inferred for all databases; that is, $T_R^*(\mathcal{I}), DB \models A$ for all DB. Thus, by theorem 1, it should also be the case that $R, DB \vdash A$ for all DB. Using the inference rules of section 3, it is not hard to see that this is indeed the case.

5 Complexity: Upper Bounds

This section establishes upper complexity bounds both for the full logic of hypothetical additions and deletions and for the restricted logic of hypothetical additions. In particular, the data complexity for the full logic is in EXPTIME, and for the restricted logic, it is in PSPACE. *Data complexity* is the complexity of query processing when the database is regarded as input but the arity of all relations is bounded and the rulebase is fixed [28]. For purposes of presentation, we restrict the analysis to the propositional case, but the arguments generalize to the function-free, predicate case in a straightforward way.

5.1 EXPTIME Upper-Bound

Using the analysis of section 4, it is straightforward to show that query processing in the full logic can be done in exponential time. The key points are (i) that a hypothetical interpretation $\mathcal{M}$ can be represented in exponential space, (ii) that each application of operator T_R requires exponential time, and (iii) that at most exponentially many applications of T_R are needed to compute $T_R^*(\mathcal{I})$.

Suppose then that R is a set of hypothetical rules and DB is a database. Let $\mathcal{L}$ be the set of atoms appearing in R and DB. We represent an interpretation $\mathcal{M}$ of R by the set $\{< DB', \mathcal{M}(DB') > \mid DB' \subseteq \mathcal{L}\}$. Indeed, we shall identify $\mathcal{M}$ with this set. To compute $T_R^*(\mathcal{I})$, $\mathcal{M}$ is first initialized to $\mathcal{I}$ by the assignment $\mathcal{M} \leftarrow \{< DB', DB' > \mid DB' \subseteq \mathcal{L}\}$. Next, the assignment $\mathcal{M} \leftarrow T_R(\mathcal{M})$ is executed repeatedly until $\mathcal{M}$ no longer changes, at which point $\mathcal{M} = T_R^*(\mathcal{I})$.

The complexity of this procedure is easily determined. Since there are $2^{|\mathcal{L}|}$ subsets of $\mathcal{L}$, our representation of $\mathcal{M}$ uses exponential space (exponential in the size of $DB \cup R$). Thus, each application of the operator T_R can be done in exponential time. By lemma 1, each such application makes $\mathcal{M}$ larger. Thus, during each application, except the last, there must be some element $< DB', S >$ of $\mathcal{M}$ in which S acquires a new atom. But, for each DB', this can happen at most n times, where $n = |\mathcal{L}|$. And since there are 2^n values of DB', no more changes will be possible after $n \cdot 2^n$ operator applications. Thus $T_R^*(\mathcal{I})$ is computed after exponential time.

Given $T_R^*(\mathcal{I})$, one can then use definition 5 to determine in exponential time whether $DB, T_R^*(\mathcal{I}) \models \phi$ for any query ϕ. Thus, for the full logic of hypothetical additions and deletions, the complexity of query processing is in EXPTIME in the propositional case.

This argument is easily generalized to the function-free, predicate case. In this case, however, we are interested in data-complexity, in which the arity of all predicates is bounded. The hypothetical databases DB' are built from the predicate symbols and constant symbols appearing in DB and R. Because of the bounded arity, the number of possible tuples is polynomial in the size of the data domain; so the number of hypothetical databases DB' is still exponential. Hence, the data-complexity of the full logic is in EXPTIME in the function-free, predicate case.

5.2 PSPACE Upper-Bound

This section shows that for the restricted logic of hypothetical additions, query processing can be done in polynomial space. In particular, because there are no hypothetical deletions, a query ϕ to a rulebase system $[R, DB]$ is answered by referring only to hypothetical databases which contain DB. We exploit this fact to write a mixed top-down/bottom-up procedure $LFP(R, DB)$ which computes $[T_R^*(\mathcal{I})](DB)$ and which runs in polynomial space. This procedure has a single top-down, recursive phase; and at each level of recursion, a bottom-up, iterative computation is performed. Each bottom-up phase computes $LFP(R, DB')$ for some database DB' containing DB. Because there are no hypothetical deletions, DB' grows larger with each level of recursion.

Each bottom-up phase of LFP is analogous to the bottom-up, least-fixpoint computations of Horn-clause logic. Starting with $S = DB$, atoms are added to S by repeatedly applying the rules in R until no more inferences are possible. For each rule, the head of the rule is added to S iff the premise of the rule is satisfied.

To test the premise of a hypothetical rule, LFP calls itself recursively, invoking another bottom-up phase. For instance, to apply the rule $A \leftarrow B[add : C]$, a new (hypothetical) database $DB' = DB + \{C\}$ is created, and the rules in R are applied to DB' in bottom-up fashion. If B is inferred during this phase, then $R, DB \vdash B[add : C]$, and the premise of the hypothetical rule is satisfied.

At each level of recursion, the bottom-up phase takes polynomial time (as in Horn-clause logic). Furthermore, the depth of recursion is polynomial, since only polynomially-many distinct tuples can be added to DB. The entire computation, therefore, is performed in polynomial space.

This description is made precise by the three procedures given below, which for clarity, are restricted to the propositional case. They implement the following inference system, which is equivalent to the inference system of section 3 in the propositional case without hypothetical deletions.

1. $R, DB \vdash A$ if for some rule $A \leftarrow \phi_1, \ldots, \phi_n$ in R, it is the case that $R, DB \vdash \phi_i$ for each i.

2. $R, DB \vdash A$ if $A \in DB$

3. (a) $R, DB \vdash A[add : B]$
   if $B \in DB$ and $R, DB \vdash A$

   (b) $R, DB \vdash A[add : B]$
   if $B \notin DB$ and $R, DB + \{B\} \vdash A$

Inference rule 1 is implemented by the procedures $LFP(R, DB)$ and $T(R, DB)$. T applies each rule in R exactly once, and LFP calls T until $[T_R^*(\mathcal{I})](DB)$ has been computed. Together, LFP and T execute a single bottom-up phase. Inference rules 2 and 3 are implementent by the procedure $MATCH(R, DB, \phi)$, which determines whether $R, DB \vdash \phi$. $MATCH$ tests the premise of a rule, invoking a new level of recursion, and a new bottom-up phase, if necessary.

```
Procedure: LFP(R, DB)
  S1 ← DB;
  S2 ← T(R, DB);
  do until S1 = S2
     S1 ← S2;
     S2 ← T(R, S1);
  return(S1);
  end

Procedure: T(R, DB)
  S ← DB;
  for each rule  A ← φ1, ..., φn  in R   do
     if MATCH(R, DB, φi) is true for each i
        then S ← S + {A};
  return(S);
  end

Procedure: MATCH(R, DB, φ)
  if φ is atomic and φ ∈ DB
     then return(true);
  if φ = A[add : B] and B ∈ DB
                    and A ∈ DB
     then return(true);
  if φ = A[add : B] and B ∉ DB
                    and A ∈ LFP(R, DB + {B})
     then return(true)
     else return(false);
  end
```

It is straightforward to show that if $LFP(R, DB')$ are correctly computed for all $DB' > DB$, then $LFP(R, DB)$ will return the correct answer. By induction, therefore, these three procedures are correct.

To check the complexity, suppose that $MATCH$ were an oracle taking constant time. LFP would then return after polynomial time, as in the Horn-clause case. In fact, $MATCH$ calls LFP recursively; but this recursion can go only to depth n, where n is the number of distinct atoms in R. Thus, there are $O(n)$ levels of recursion, each taking polynomial time; so the entire computation is in PSPACE.

6 Complexity: Lower Bounds

This section establishes lower complexity bounds both for the full logic of hypothetical additions and deletions and for the restricted logic of additions. In particular, the data-complexity for the full logic is EXPTIME-hard, and for the restricted logic, it is PSPACE-hard. Recall that data-complexity is the complexity of query processing when the database is regarded as input but the arity of all relations is bounded and the rulebase is fixed [28].

The main idea is to use our logic to encode the computations of an alternating Turing machine. Like nondeterministic machines, an alternating machine may have many possible transitions at any point in the computation. Alternating Turing machines, however, may require that *all* machine transitions be successful, not just one. This capability gives alternating machines more power than nondeterministic machines [11].

6.1 EXPTIME Lower-Bound

We first show that query processing for the full logic of hypothetical additions and deletions is EXPTIME-hard. Our strategy is to use the logic to encode the computations of an alternating PSPACE machine. Since APSPACE=EXPTIME, the result follows [11]. In addition, these machine encodings are central to the EXPTIME expressiveness result of section 7.

Let M be a one-tape, alternating Turing-machine which runs in polynomial space (an APSPACE machine), and let $\bar{s}$ be an input string. We encode $\bar{s}$ as a database $DB(\bar{s})$, and M as a rulebase $R(M)$, such that

$$R(M), DB(\bar{s}) \vdash ACCEPT \quad \textit{iff} \quad M \textit{ accepts } \bar{s} \qquad (1)$$

where $ACCEPT$ is a 0-ary predicate symbol.

The important point is that the rulebase $R(M)$ is independent of the input $\bar{s}$. This allows us prove that the data-complexity of query processing is EXPTIME-hard. Indeed, let M be an APSPACE machine which recognizes an EXPTIME-complete language[8]. The result then follows immediately. Combining this with the EXPTIME upper-bound of section 5, we have the following result:

Theorem 2 *For the full logic of hypothetical additions and deletions, the data-complexity of query processing is EXPTIME-complete in the function-free, predicate case.*

[8] see [12] for examples of such machines.

6.1.1 Simulating the Machine

The rest of this section establishes formula (1).

Since M is an APSPACE machine, its computations use n^k tape cells for some integer k, where n is the length of the input. A counter is therefore needed to represent these n^k positions. This is easily implemented by placing the following entries in the database $DB(\bar{s})$:

$$FIRST(0),\ NEXT(0,1),\ NEXT(1,2), \\ \ldots NEXT(n^k-2, n^k-1),\ LAST(n^k-1)$$

Given this counter, we can represent machine *id*'s with the following predicates:

- $CELL(c,j)$: the tape cell at position j contains the symbol c.
- $HEAD(q,j)$: the control head is in state q and is scanning the cell at position j.

We need to specify the initial *id* of the machine. This means stating that the control is in state q_0, that the tape head is scanning the first tape cell, and that the input is the string $\bar{s} = < s_0, s_1, \ldots, s_{n-1} >$. We must, therefore, put the symbol s_i in the ith tape cell and *blank* in the rest. This is done by placing the following entries in the database $DB(\bar{s})$:

$$\begin{array}{ll} HEAD(q_0, 0), & \\ CELL(s_0, 0), & CELL(blank, n), \\ CELL(s_1, 1), & CELL(blank, n+1), \\ \cdots & \cdots \\ CELL(s_n, n-1), & CELL(blank, n^k-1). \end{array}$$

We must also simulate read, write and move operations of the machine's control head. This is done by hypothetically adding and deleting entries from the database. That is, we construct a logic program which in moving from one hypothetical database to another, simulates the transition of the machine M from one *id* to another. In particular, at any point in the inference, the database represents an *id* of the machine. This is comparable to the use by Abiteboul and Vianu, of a database update language to simulate non-deterministic Turing machines [1].

Every machine *id* is either *accepting* or *rejecting*. Furthermore, since M is an alternating Turing machine, it has three kinds of states: *accepting*, *universal* and *existential*. Whether an *id* is accepting or not is then determined recursively as follows:

- An *id* is accepting if it has an accepting state.
- An *id* is accepting if it has a universal state and all its successor *id*'s are accepting.
- An *id* is accepting if it has an existential state and at least one of its successor *id*'s is accepting.

This criterion for acceptance can be encoded as a set of hypothetical rules. In particular, we add rules to $R(M)$ so that when DB encodes an *id*,

$R(M), DB \vdash ACCEPT$ iff DB encodes an *accepting id*.

where $ACCEPT$ is a 0-ary predicate.

We define three types of rules, one for each type of machine state. The simplest type is for those *id*'s which have an accepting state. Specifically, for each accepting state, we introduce a constant symbol q_a and add the following rule to $R(M)$:

$$ACCEPT \leftarrow HEAD(q_a, j).$$

That is, an *id* is accepting if it contains the accepting state q_a. (The variable j signifies that the head position is unimportant.)

The rules for universal and existential states are more complex and depend on the transition relation of the machine M. In particular, for each machine transition, there are three pieces of information that may change: q, the state of the control head; j, the position of the control head; and c, the tape symbol that the control head is reading. This information is encoded in the database by the formulas $HEAD(q, j)$ and $CELL(c, j)$. For each machine transition, we delete these two formulas from the database, and add two new ones. The deletions are taken care of by a single rule:

$$ACCEPT \leftarrow HEAD(q, j),\ CELL(c, j),$$
$$TRANS(c, q, j)\ [del: HEAD(q, j),\ CELL(c, j)].$$

where c, q and j are variables.

$TRANS(c, q, j)$ is a predicate which completes the machine transition by adding the new formulas to the database. This depends on the details of the transition relation. Suppose that given c and q, the machine has k possible transitions. Suppose that the ith such transition is given by the triple $< c_i,\ \Delta_i,\ q_i >$, which means *write the symbol* c_i, *move* Δ_i *squares to the right, and go into state* q_i, where Δ_i may be 1, 0 or -1.

If q is a universal state, then a machine *id* containing q is accepting iff each of its k successor *id*'s is accepting. This is expressed by the following rule, which we add to $R(M)$:

$$TRANS(c, q, j) \leftarrow$$
$$j_1 = j + \Delta_1,\ j_2 = j + \Delta_2,\ \dots\ j_k = j + \Delta_k,$$
$$ACCEPT[add: HEAD(q_1, j_1),\ CELL(c_1, j)],$$
$$ACCEPT[add: HEAD(q_2, j_2),\ CELL(c_2, j)],$$
$$\dots$$
$$ACCEPT[add: HEAD(q_k, j_k),\ CELL(c_k, j)].$$

where the c's and q's are constant symbols and the j's are variables.

If q is an existential state, then a machine *id* containing q is accepting iff at least one of its successor *id*'s is accepting. This is expressed by the following k rules, which we add to $R(M)$:

$$TRANS(c, q, j) \leftarrow j_1 = j + \Delta_1,$$
$$ACCEPT[add: HEAD(q_1, j_1),\ CELL(c_1, j)].$$
$$TRANS(c, q, j) \leftarrow j_2 = j + \Delta_2,$$
$$ACCEPT[add: HEAD(q_2, j_2),\ CELL(c_2, j)].$$
$$\dots$$
$$TRANS(c, q, j) \leftarrow j_k = j + \Delta_k,$$
$$ACCEPT[add: HEAD(q_k, j_k),\ CELL(c_k, j)].$$

We can write such rules for each pair of tape-symbols c and control-states q. In this way, we encode both the transition relation of the machine and the criterion for acceptance. That is, we can construct a set of hypothetical rules $R(M)$ such that $R(M), DB \vdash ACCEPT$ iff DB encodes an accepting *id*.

By definition, the machine M accepts its input iff the initial *id* is accepting. Since the initial *id* is represented by the database $DB(\overline{s})$, it follows that $R(M), DB(\overline{s}) \vdash ACCEPT$ iff M accepts the input $\overline{s}$. Thus, we have established formula (1), thereby proving theorem 2.

6.2 PSPACE Lower-Bound

This section shows that query processing for the restricted logic of hypothetical additions is PSPACE-hard. The proof is similar to that of the previous section except that instead of encoding alternating PSPACE machines, we encode alternating PTIME machines. Since APTIME=PSPACE, the result follows [11]. In addition, these machine encodings are central to the PSPACE expressiveness result of section 7.

The main difference between the encodings in this section and the last is that we now represent time explicitly. That is, because tape-erasure can no longer be simulated by database deletion, we introduce a time parameter t into many of the predicates. In particular, we represent machine *id*'s as follows:

- $CELL(c, j, t)$: at time t, the tape cell at position j contains the symbol c.
- $HEAD(q, j, t)$: at time t, the control head is in state q and is scanning the cell at position j.

As before, we store a successor predicate $NEXT(i, j)$ in the database so that we can count from 0 to $n^k - 1$, where n is the length of the machine input. This time, however, we count computation steps (time) as well as tape positions (space). Thus we can simulate only those machines which halt in at most n^k steps, that is, machines which run in polynomial time.

Let M be a one-tape, alternating Turing-machine which runs in polynomial time (an APTIME machine), and let $\overline{s}$ be an input string. We encode $\overline{s}$ as a database $DB(\overline{s})$, and M as a rulebase $R(M)$, such that

$$R(M), DB(\overline{s}) \vdash ACCEPT \quad \textit{iff} \quad M \textit{ accepts } \overline{s} \qquad (2)$$

Again, it is important that the rulebase $R(M)$ is independent of the machine input $\overline{s}$. This allows us to prove that the data-complexity of query processing is PSPACE-hard. Indeed, let M be an APTIME machine which recognizes a PSPACE-complete language.[9] The result then follows immediately. Combining this with the PSPACE upper-bound of section 5 gives the following result:

Theorem 3 *For the restricted logic of hypothetical additions, the data-complexity of query processing is PSPACE-complete in the function-free, predicate case.*

6.2.1 Simulating the Machine

Because we are representing time explicitly, we can now store more than one machine *id* in the database. In fact, we can store a sequence of *id*'s, a computation *path*. In general, an alternating Turing machine has a computation *tree*, containing many such paths. The rulebase $R(M)$ explores this tree one path at a time, asserting each path hypothetically, and then retracting it.

As before, the transition relation of the machine M is encoded as a set of hypothetical rules. This time, however, there is one set of hypothetical additions for each transition, and no hypothetical deletions. For each transition, the rules add a new machine *id* to the database, so that the computation path is "grown" one *id* at a time.

The rules are a simple variation of those in section 6.1 (see [6] for details). They define a predicate $ACCEPT(t)$ which determines whether the *id* at the end of a computation path is accepting. In particular, if DB encodes a computation path ending at time t, then

$R(M), DB \vdash ACCEPT(t)$ iff the last *id* in the path is accepting.

As before, we encode the input string $\overline{s}$ in the database $DB(\overline{s})$ as the initial *id* of the machine. That is, $DB(\overline{s})$ represents a computation path of length 1 ending at time 0. Thus, machine M accepts input $\overline{s}$ iff $R(M), DB(\overline{s}) \vdash ACCEPT(0)$.

We can now establish formula (2) by adding the rule $ACCEPT \leftarrow ACCEPT(0)$ to $R(M)$. This, in turn, proves theorem 3.

7 Expressibility

We have shown that the data-complexity of the full logic of hypothetical updates is EXPTIME-complete, and that for the restricted logic of hypothetical additions, it is PSPACE-complete. This is the price we pay in worst-case performance, for the ability to reason about hypothetical database updates. What do we get for this price? In [7] it is shown that there are some low-complexity, hypothetical queries that cannot be expressed in classical logic unless one assumes the user has full knowledge of the rulebase. Thus we get the ability to express certain hypothetical queries in a rulebase-independent way. This section, however, treats these logics as query languages for a relational

[9] For examples of such languages, see [17].

database and establishs the class of queries that they express.

Section 5 showed that any database query expressible in the full logic is computable is EXPTIME. This section establishes a converse: by augmenting the full logic with *negation-by-failure* [19,14], any database query computable in exponential time can be expressed. Similarly, by augmenting the restricted logic with negation-by-failure, any database query computable in polynomial space can be expressed.

The proofs rely on the simulations of Turing machines as developed in the section 6. In this respect, they are similar to other expressibility proofs in the literature (e.g., [18,27]). One difference, however, is that we do not require the domain of the database to be linearly ordered. Linearly-ordered domains are used to simulate counters, which in turn, are used to simulate the movement of the control head. Our approach is to start with unordered domains and assert linear orders hypothetically. This, however, involves some interesting technical problems.

The main problem is that we cannot select and assert a particular linear order. There is no *a priori* ordering on the domain, and so there is no way for a rulebase to prefer one ordering over another. We can, however, assert all possible linear-orders, one after another, and simulate the Turing machine for each one. This is sufficient as long as the Turing machine simulation is insensitive to the particular linear-order being used. To prove this, we exploit the definition of "generic database queries" as given by Chandra and Harel [8]. This definition requires that a query satisfy a consistency criterion: if the constants in the database are renamed in a consistent way, then the constants in the answer to a query must be renamed in the same way. In our machine simulations, changing the linear order is equivalent to renaming the database constants. Hence, it does not matter which linear order is used. In this way, the consistency criterion is central to our ability to use unorderd domains.

Before proceeding, we define the notions of relational database and of database query. The following definitions are esentially those given in [8].

Definition 8 *Let U be a countable set, called the universal data domain. A relational database DB of type $\overline{\alpha} = (\alpha_1, ..., \alpha_m)$ is a tuple $(D, R_1, ..., R_m)$ where D is a finite subset of U and R_i is an α_i-ary relation over D, i.e., $R_i \subseteq D^{\alpha_i}$. D is called the domain of DB, written $dom(DB)$.*

In logical systems such as ours, a relational database is represented as a set of ground atomic formulas. U is a universal set of constant symbols, and for each relation R_i there is a predicate symbol P_i whose ground atomic formulas represent R_i.

Definition 9 *A database query of type $\overline{\alpha} \rightarrow \beta$ is a partial function ψ which takes a database DB of type $\overline{\alpha}$ and returns a relation $\psi(DB)$ over $dom(DB)$ of arity β. ψ must satisfy the following consistency criterion: if DB' can be derived from DB by renaming constant symbols,*[10] *then $\psi(DB')$ can be derived from $\psi(DB)$ by the same renaming.*

7.1 Negation by Failure

It is clear that in order to express all EXPTIME-computable queries, our logic must be augmented in some way. This is because the logic is *monotonic*: as entries are added to the database, inferences do not disappear. Clearly many low-complexity queries are non-monotonic, such as relational-algebra queries involving complementation. Adding negation-by-failure to a logic makes it non-monotonic as well.

Let R be a hypothetical rulebase, and let DB be a database. *Negation-by-failure* is then defined by adding the following inference rule to those of definition 3:

$$R, DB \vdash \sim \phi \quad \text{if} \quad R, DB \not\vdash \phi$$

Unfortunately, such inferences are not always well-defined when negation appears in the premise of rules which are mutually recursive. This is a familiar problem in Horn-clause logic [2]. For example, given the two rules $A \leftarrow \sim B$ and $B \leftarrow \sim A$ and an empty database, it is not clear whether A is to be inferred, or B, or both, or neither. However, as in the Horn-clause case, as long as there is no recursion through negation, there is no ambiguity. In this paper, we restrict our attention to such "stratified" rulebases.

In the following example, negation-by-failure is used to determine the parity of a monadic relation D. The first two rules select and remove elements of

[10] In this case we say that DB and DB' are *isomorphic*. See [8] for a more precise definition.

D from the database one-by-one. As elements are removed, the rulebase "flips back and forth" between two subqueries, $EVEN$ and ODD, until the relation D is empty. The third rule states that the empty relation has even parity.

It does not matter in which order the elements of D are removed. Every order will give the same answer: either every order will result in a proof of $EVEN$ or every order will result in a proof of ODD.

Example 10. Suppose R is the following collection of rules:

$$EVEN \leftarrow D(x),\ ODD[del : D(x)].$$
$$ODD \leftarrow D(x),\ EVEN[del : D(x)].$$
$$EVEN \leftarrow \sim D(x).$$

Then $R, DB \vdash EVEN$ iff DB contains an even number of entries of the form $D(x)$.

$EVEN$ is clearly a non-monotonic query, since as elements are added to D, the predicate $EVEN$ alternates between true and false. Thus, $EVEN$ cannot be expressed in our hypothetical logic without negation-by-failure. It is also known, however, that $EVEN$ cannot be expressed in Horn-clause logic even with negation-by-failure [10,9].

Using a slightly more sophisticated use of negation-by-failure, $EVEN$ can also be implemented in the restricted logic of hypothetical additions. The trick is to notice that the use of deletion above is particularly simple. In fact, it can be simulated by a combination of addition and negation as follows: (i) instead of deleting the element $D(x)$, add the element $ND(x)$; and (ii) instead of selecting an element $D(x)$ which has not been deleted, select an element $D(x)$ for which $ND(x)$ has not been added. In this way, the deletion of $D(x)$ from the database can be simulated.

Example 11. Suppose R is the following collection of rules:

$$EVEN \leftarrow SELECT(x),\ ODD[add : ND(x)].$$
$$ODD \leftarrow SELECT(x),\ EVEN[add : ND(x)].$$
$$EVEN \leftarrow \sim SELECT(x).$$
$$SELECT(x) \leftarrow D(x),\ \sim ND(x).$$

Then $R, DB \vdash EVEN$ iff DB contains an even number of entries of the form $D(x)$.

7.2 PSPACE Expressibility

This section shows that any database query that can be computed in polynomial space can be expressed in our logic of hypothetical additions augmented with negation-by-failure. i.e.,

Theorem 4 *Suppose that ψ is a database query of type $\overline{\alpha} \rightarrow \beta$ and that DB is a database of type $\overline{\alpha}$. Suppose also that DB has a monadic predicate $D(x)$ which defines the data domain. If ψ is computable in polynomial space, then there is a rulebase $R(\psi)$ of hypothetical additions with negation-by-failure such that*

$$R(\psi), DB \vdash Q(\overline{x}) \quad \textit{iff} \quad \overline{x} \in \psi(DB)$$

where Q is a predicate symbol of arity β.

This theorem assumes that the data domain is accessible via a predicate D. Although this is not necessary according to definition 8, it is a much weaker assumption than that of a linearly ordered domain. Furthermore, for many purposes, the data domain can be defined as the set of constant symbols appearing in the database. In this case, D can be constructed from the database predicates $P_1, ..., P_m$ by adding the following rules to $R(\psi)$ for each i:

$$D(x_1) \leftarrow P_i(x_1, x_2 ... x_{\alpha_i}).$$
$$D(x_2) \leftarrow P_i(x_1, x_2 ... x_{\alpha_i}).$$
$$\cdots$$
$$D(x_{\alpha_i}) \leftarrow P_i(x_1, x_2 ... x_{\alpha_i}).$$

To prove theorem 4, suppose we have a database query ψ which is computable in in polynomial space. Then there is a PSPACE Turing-machine which computes it. That is, if DB is encoded on the input tape, then the machine generates an encoding of $\psi(DB)$ on its output tape after consuming (at most) a polynomial amount of tape.

This machine generates all tuples in $\psi(DB)$; that is, it solves the *generation problem* for ψ. Related to this is the *recognition problem*, recognizing whether a particular tuple is in $\psi(DB)$. It is easy to transform the generation problem into the recognition problem: given a tuple $\overline{x}$ and a database DB, generate the relation $\psi(DB)$, and return *true* iff $\overline{x} \in \psi(DB)$. Since the arity of the output relation $\psi(DB)$ is fixed, there are polynomially many tuples $\overline{x}$ that need to be tested (polynomial in $|dom(DB)|$). Thus, given a PSPACE machine which solves the generation problem for ψ, there is another PSPACE machine which solves the recognition problem. This machine recognizes the language $\{<\overline{x}, DB> \mid \overline{x} \in \psi(DB)\}$.

Since PSPACE=APTIME, there is an alternating PTIME machine M which also recognizes this language [11]. Our main result is to construct a rulebase $R(M)$ which solves the recognition problem for ψ by simulating the computations of M. Specifically, we construct $R(M)$ so that for all databases DB of type $\overline{\alpha}$,

$$R(M), DB + \{P_0(\overline{x})\} \vdash A \quad \textit{iff} \;\; M \textit{ accepts } <\overline{x}, DB> \tag{3}$$

where P_0 is a predicate symbol of arity β.

Given this, it is straightforward to augment $R(M)$ with rules so that it can solve the generation problem for ψ. In particular, we add the following rule to $R(M)$ to form $R(\psi)$:

$$Q(x_1...x_\beta) \leftarrow D(x_1), \ldots D(x_\beta), A[add: P_0(x_1...x_\beta)].$$

where $D(x)$ is true iff $x \in dom(DB)$. This rule generates all possible β-tuples $\overline{x}$ over $dom(DB)$. For each such tuple, $P_0(\overline{x})$ is hypothetically added to the database, and then $<\overline{x}, DB>$ is tested for acceptance by M. Thus, we have the following:

$$\begin{aligned} & R(\psi), DB \vdash Q(\overline{x}) \\ \textit{iff} \quad & R(M), DB + \{P_0(\overline{x})\} \vdash A \\ \textit{iff} \quad & M \textit{ accepts } <\overline{x}, DB> \\ \textit{iff} \quad & \overline{x} \in \psi(DB) \end{aligned}$$

which proves theorem 4.

7.2.1 Constructing R(M)

The above proof is based on construction of the rulebase $R(M)$, which solves the recognition problem fora query ψ according to formula 3. The rest of this section describes this construction.

Recall that M is an alternating PTIME machine which accepts the language $\{<\overline{x}, DB> \mid \overline{x} \in \psi(DB)\}$. Section 6.2 showed how to simulate APTIME machines in the logic of hypothetical additions. To use this construction, two things must be done: (i) encode the pair $<\overline{x}, DB>$ onto M's input tape, and (ii) simulate a counter from 0 to $n^k - 1$, where n is the size of the input and n^k is an upper bound on the amount of time consumed during the computation. Actually, it will be convenient to choose n to be the size of the data domain $dom(DB)$. We can do this because the database size is at most a polynomial function of the domain size.

7.2.2 Counting

If there is a total linear order on the data domain, then by using predicates of arity k, one can construct a counter from 0 to $n^k - 1$, where $n = |dom(DB)|$. The assumption of a linearly ordered domain is common in the literature, especially when expressiblity results are established in terms of complexity classes, as in theorem 4 [18,27]. For hypothetical logics, however, this assumption is unnecessary. Instead, if there is no linear order on the domain, then one can be asserted hypothetically.

The difficulty is in choosing a linear order to assert. Since there is nothing special about any ordering, the rules have no way of selecting one over another. The trick is to hypothetically assert every possible ordering, one at a time, and to note that the Turing-machine simulations will return the same answer for each one. A similar trick was used in expressing the query $EVEN$ in examples 10 and 11. In this way, no *a priori* domain ordering is needed and no distinguished ordering need be selected.

The rules below use the techniques of example 11 to assert all possible linear orderings of the data domain. They select and remove domain elements one-by-one, where deletion is simulated using negation-by-failure. After the first selection, a ground instance of the predicate $FIRST_1(x)$ is added to the database; after each subsequent selection, an instance of $NEXT_1(x, y)$ is added; and after the last selection, an instance of $LAST_1(x)$ is added. These rules assume the existence of a monadic predicate $D(y)$ which defines the data domain.

$$\begin{aligned} & A \leftarrow SEL(x),\; B(x)[add: FIRST_1(x),\; ND(x)] \\ & B(x) \leftarrow SEL(y),\; B(y)[add: NEXT_1(x,y),\; ND(y)] \\ & B(x) \leftarrow \sim SEL(y),\; ACCEPT[add: LAST_1(x)] \\ & SEL(y) \leftarrow D(y),\; \sim ND(y) \end{aligned}$$

After asserting a linear order in this way, the rules try to infer the atom $ACCEPT$, which invokes a Turing-machine simulation. These simulations are constructed so that either $ACCEPT$ is true for all linear orderings, or $ACCEPT$ is false for all linear orderings.

During each of these simulations, there is a (hypothetical) linear-order on the data domain $dom(DB)$. In particular, for the ordering $< a_1, a_2 ... a_n >$, the following entries have been added to the database:

$$FIRST_1(a_1),\ NEXT_1(a_1, a_2),\ NEXT_1(a_2, a_3),$$
$$\ldots NEXT_1(a_{n-1}, a_n),\ LAST(a_n)$$

This is in addition to the original database predicates $P_1, \ldots P_m$.

This ordering on $dom(DB)$ provides a way of counting from 0 to $n-1$. In addition, it induces an ordering on $[dom(DB)]^k$, that is, on the space of k-tuples of the domain elements. This in turn provides a way of counting from 0 to $n^k - 1$. In particular, we can write Horn rules to define the following three predicates: $FIRST(\overline{x})$, $NEXT(\overline{x}, \overline{y})$, and $LAST(\overline{y})$, where $\overline{x}$ and $\overline{y}$ are k-tuples [5]. $FIRST(\overline{x})$ and $LAST(\overline{y})$ are true iff $\overline{x}$ and $\overline{y}$ represent the integers 0 and $n^k - 1$, respectively; and $NEXT(\overline{x}, \overline{y})$ is true iff $\overline{y}$ represents the integer $\overline{x} + 1$.

7.2.3 Representing the Machine

With the above counter, we can use k-tuples to represent n^k distinct points in time and n^k distinct positions on the tape. We can thus simulate APTIME machines much as we did in section 7.2. In particular, we use the following two predicates to represent the machine, where $\overline{p}$ and $\overline{t}$ are k-tuples:

- $CELL(c, \overline{p}, \overline{t})$: at time $\overline{t}$, the tape cell at position $\overline{p}$ contains the symbol c.
- $HEAD(q, \overline{p}, \overline{t})$: at time $\overline{t}$, the control head is in state q and is scanning the cell at position $\overline{p}$.

We must also specify the initial *id* of the machine, that is, the initial tape contents, head position and state of the control head. The control head is initialized by the following rule, which says that at time 0, the control head is in state q_0 and is scanning the tape cell at position 0:

$$HEAD(q_0, \overline{p}, \overline{t}) \leftarrow FIRST(\overline{p}),\ FIRST(\overline{t}).$$

The next section deals with the tape.

7.2.4 Initializing the Machine Tape

Given a database DB and a tuple $\overline{x}$, we must encode them onto the tape of our machine. We are assuming that $\overline{x}$ is of arity β and that DB consists of ground instances of the predicates $P_1, P_2, \ldots P_m$, of arities $\alpha_1, \ldots, \alpha_m$, resp.[11] We are also assuming that DB is augmented by a single instance of a predicate P_0, to represent the tuple $\overline{x}$ (see formula 3). Thus, we are given the set $DB + \{P_0(\overline{x})\}$, and we must write rules which encode it onto the Turing-machine tape.

Any reasonable encoding will do, and it is convenient to use a bit-map representation. We divide an initial segment of the tape into $m+1$ blocks and put a bit-map of P_i in the ith block. In particular, each tape cell in block i corresponds to a possible database entry $P_i(x_1, \ldots, x_{\alpha_i})$, that is, a cell contains a 1 iff the corresponding entry $P_i(x_1, \ldots, x_{\alpha_i})$ is in the database. The use of *negation-by-failure* is crucial to setting the tape cell to 0 when $P_i(x_1, \ldots, x_{\alpha_i})$ is *not* in the database.

It is straightforward to construct a set of Horn rules which set the input tape cells to 0 or 1 and which make all other tape cells blank. In particular, one can define a predicate $INIT(c, \overline{p})$ which is true iff the tape cell at position $\overline{p}$ should be initialized to the symbol c, where $c \in \{0, 1, blank\}$ (see [5] for details). The machine tape is then initialized by the following rule:

$$CELL(c, \overline{p}, \overline{t}) \leftarrow FIRST(\overline{t}),\ INIT(c, \overline{p}).$$

7.2.5 Order Independence

This machine representation depends on the existence of a total linear order on the data domain. If such an order is not provided *a priori*, then the rules of section 7.2.2 can assert one hypothetically. These rules assert every possible linear order, one after the other, simulating the machine M for each one. In most respects, the linear order is a mere implementation detail, and the particular ordering used does not effect the computations which M performs. However, in one respect this is not true: the initialization of the machine tape depends crucially on the linear order. In particular, different linear orders will result in different bit-map representations of the database.

Which of these bit maps actually represents the database? They all do. M either accepts all these bit

[11] That is, we are assuming that the database query ψ which we are trying to express is of type $\overline{\alpha} \rightarrow \beta$, where $\overline{\alpha} = (\alpha_1, \ldots, \alpha_m)$.

maps, or it rejects all these bit maps. This is because M is a special Turing machine: it solves the recognition problem for a database query ψ. As a database query, ψ satisfies the *consistency criterion*: if the constant symbols in a database DB are renamed in a consistent way, then the constant symbols in output relation $\psi(DB)$ are renamed in the same way. It is not hard to see that changing the linear order on the data domain is equivalent to renaming the constants symbols in DB, at least as far as the machine M is concerned. Thus, the different bit maps that M receives for each linear order represent isomorphic databases.

For example, suppose that ψ is a database query which takes a database of two monadic predicates P and Q, and returns a binary relation. Consider the recognition problem, $(a,b) \in \psi[\{P(a),\ Q(b)\}]$. In this case the data domain is $\{a,b\}$, and there are two linear orders on the domain, $a < b$ and $b < a$. The bit-map representations of this problem under these two linear orders are shown in diagrams 1 and 2 below. In each diagram, the sequence of 1's and 0's represents the machine tape, and the tuples beneath represent the interpretation given to the tape cells.

1. Encoding the problem $(a,b) \in \psi[\{P(a),\ Q(b)\}]$ under the linear order $a < b$:

0	1	0	0	1	0	0	1
(a,a)	(a,b)	(b,a)	(b,b)	$P(a)$	$P(b)$	$Q(a)$	$Q(b)$

2. Encoding the problem $(a,b) \in \psi[\{P(a),\ Q(b)\}]$ under the linear order $b < a$:

0	0	1	0	0	1	1	0
(b,b)	(b,a)	(a,b)	(a,a)	$P(b)$	$P(a)$	$Q(b)$	$Q(a)$

3. Encoding the problem $(b,a) \in \psi[\{P(b),\ Q(a)\}]$ under the linear order $a < b$:

0	0	1	0	0	1	1	0
(a,a)	(a,b)	(b,a)	(b,b)	$P(a)$	$P(b)$	$Q(a)$	$Q(b)$

Diagrams 1 and 2 show clearly that changing the linear order changes the input to the machine. Diagrams 1 and 3 show that renaming the constant symbols changes the input in exactly the same way.

In general, a re-ordering of the domain is equivalent to a renaming of the constant symbols. Thus, either M accepts $< \bar{x}, DB >$ under all linear orderings, or M rejects $< \bar{x}, DB >$ under all linear orderings.

7.3 EXPTIME Expressibility

This section shows that any database query which is computable in exponential time can be expressed in the hypothetical logic of additions and deletions augmented with negation-by-failure. The proof is almost identical to that of the previous section. There are two main differences: (i) an APSPACE machine is encoded, not an APTIME machine, and (ii) the process of initializing the machine is more complicated. Section 6.1 showed how to encode APSPACE machines. This section focusses on initializing the machine.

With hypothetical deletions, initializing the machine is less straightforward. If we were to use the technique of section 7.2, we would simply write Horn rules such as the following:

$$HEAD(q_0,\bar{p}) \leftarrow FIRST(\bar{p}).$$
$$CELL(c,\bar{p}) \leftarrow FIRST(\bar{p}),\ INIT(c,\bar{p}).$$

These rules invoke the predicate $INIT(c,\bar{x})$, which is true iff the cell at position $\bar{x}$ should be initialized to c. The main point, however, is that with such rules, the atomic formulas $HEAD(q_0,\bar{p})$ and $CELL(c,\bar{p})$ are not part of the database, but are inferred.

The difficulty with this is that the rules of hypothetical deletion do not delete inferred facts; they only delete facts that are in the database. Furthermore, hypothetical deletion plays a crucial role in our simulation of APSPACE machines. We must therefore store the machine *id* in the database, and in particular, we cannot infer the initial *id* using Horn rules.

The alternative is to add the initial *id* to the database using hypothetical rules. The rules below do precisely this. In trying to prove the atom $ACCEPT$, they first initialize the control head, then they iterate over all k-tuples $\bar{x}$, placing the appropriate symbol in the tape cell at position $\bar{x}$, and finally they try to infer the atom $SIMULATE$, which is meant to invoke a machine simulation , as described in section 6.1.

$$ACCEPT \leftarrow FIRST(\bar{x}),\ E(\bar{x})[add: HEAD(q_0,\bar{x})]$$
$$E(\bar{x}) \leftarrow INIT(c,\bar{x}),\ F(\bar{x})[add: CELL(c,\bar{x})]$$
$$F(\bar{x}) \leftarrow NEXT(\bar{x},\bar{y}),\ E(\bar{y})$$
$$F(\bar{x}) \leftarrow LAST(\bar{x}),\ SIMULATE$$

Given this, and the techniques of 7.2, the following theorem is straightforward.

Theorem 5 *Suppose that ψ is a database query of type $\overline{\alpha} \rightarrow \beta$ and DB is a database of type $\overline{\alpha}$. Suppose also that DB has a monadic predicate $D(x)$ which defines the data domain. If ψ is computable in exponential time then there is a rulebase $R(\psi)$ of hypothetical additions and deletions with negation-by-failure such that*

$$R(\psi), DB \vdash Q(\overline{x}) \quad \textit{iff} \quad \overline{x} \in \psi(DB)$$

where Q is a predicate symbol of arity β.

8 Conclusions

Two modal-like operators have been introduced, $A[add : B]$ and $A[del : C]$, representing hypothetical addition and deletion, resp. $A[add : B]$ means, "adding B to the database allows A to be inferred," and $A[del : C]$ means, "deleting C from the database allows A to be inferred." An extension of Horn-clause logic was then defined in which these operators appear in the premises of rules. Several examples were given of the use of this logic in formulating queries to a rulebase system.

The bulk of the paper, however, was devoted to an analysis of the complexity and expressibility of hypothetical reasoning in the function-free, predicate case. Two cases were examined: (i) the full logic of hypothetical additions and deletions, and (ii) a restricted logic of hypothetical additions only. It was shown, in particular, that the data-complexity of query processing in the full logic is EXPTIME-complete, and that for the restricted logic, it is PSPACE-complete. The complexity comes from the ability of these logics to encode alternating Turing-machines, APSPACE and APTIME machines in particular.

The form of hypothetical deletion that was considered is relatively simple, in that it deletes entries from the database, and not from the least fixpoint. Deletions from the least fixpoint are potentially more complex, in that they would have to be "back propagated" through the rules in order to maintain consistency. We have completely avoided this complication by considering deletions from the database only. Nevertheless, these relatively simple deletions increase the complexity and expressibility from PSPACE to EXPTIME.

Because these two logics are monotonic, there are many queries which they cannot express. Adding *negation-by-failure* solves this problem. Indeed, with negation, the full logic can express any database query which is computable in exponential time; and the restricted logic can express any database query computable in polynomial space.

Acknowledgements

The work of Thorne McCarty on the intuitionistic semantics of embedded implications was the original stimulus for this work, and discussions with Tomasz Imielinski helped provide direction and insight. Thanks go to Jan Chomicki for helpful comments on the paper.

References

[1] S. Abiteboul and V. Vianu. A Transaction Language Complete for Database Update Specification. In *Proceedings of the ACM Symposium on the Principles of Database Systems*, pages 260–268, 1987.

[2] K.R. Apt, H.A. Blair, and A. Walker. Towards a Theory of Declarative Knowledge. In Jack Minker, editor, *Foundations of Deductive Databases and Logic Programming*, chapter 2, pages 89–148, Morgan Kaufmann, 1988.

[3] K.R. Apt and M.H. Van Emden. Contributions to the Theory of Logic Programming. *Journal of the ACM*, 29(3):841–862, 1982.

[4] A.J. Bonner. A Logic for Hypothetical Reasoning. In *Proceedings of the Seventh National Conference on Artificial Intelligence*, American Association for Artificial Intelligence, August 1988.

[5] A.J. Bonner. *Hypothetical Datalog: Complexity and Expressibility.* Technical Report DCS-TR-231, Department of Computer Science, Rutgers university, New Brunswick, NJ 08903, 1988.

[6] A.J. Bonner. Hypothetical Datalog: Complexity and Expressibility. In *Proceedings of the Second International Conference on Database Theory*, Bruges, Belgium, August 31-September 2 1988.

[7] A.J. Bonner. *A Logic for Hypothetical Reasoning.* Technical Report DCS-TR-230, Department of Computer Science, Rutgers University, New Brunswick, NJ 08903, 1988.

[8] A.K. Chandra and D. Harel. "Computable Queries for Relational Databases". *Journal of Computer and Systems Science*, 21(2):156–178, 1980.

[9] A.K. Chandra and D. Harel. "Horn Clauses and the Fixpoint Hierarchy". In *Proceedings of the ACM Symposium on the Principles of Database Systems*, pages 158–163, 1982.

[10] A.K. Chandra and D. Harel. "Structure and Complexity of Relational Queries". In *Proceedings of the Symposium on the Foundations of Computer Science*, pages 333–347, 1980.

[11] A.K. Chandra, D. Kozen, and L.J. Stockmeyer. "Alternation". *Journal of the ACM*, 114–133, 1981.

[12] A.K. Chandra and L.J. Stockmeyer. "Alternation". In *Proceedings of the Symposium on the Foundations of Computer Science*, pages 98–108, 1976.

[13] M.C. Fitting. *Intuitionistic Logic, Model Theory and Forcing*. North-Holland, 1969.

[14] D.M. Gabbay. "N-Prolog: an Extension of Prolog with Hypothetical Implications. II. Logical Foundations and Negation as Failure". *Journal of Logic Programming*, 2(4):251–283, 1985.

[15] D.M. Gabbay and U. Reyle. "N-Prolog: an Extension of Prolog with Hypothetical Implications. I". *Journal of Logic Programming*, 1(4):319–355, 1984.

[16] D. Harel. *First-Order Dynamic Logic*. Volume 68 of *Lecture Notes in Computer Science*, Springer Verlag, 1979.

[17] J.E. Hopcroft and J.D. Ullman. *Introduction to Automata Theory, Languages and Computation*. Addison-Wesley, 1979.

[18] N. Immerman. Relational Queries Computable in Polynomial Time. In *Proceedings of the Symposium on the Foundations of Computer Science*, pages 147–152, 1982.

[19] R. Kowalski. *Logic for Problem Solving*. North-Holland, 1979.

[20] R.E. Ladner. The Computational Complexity of Provability in Systems of Propositional Modal Logic. *SIAM Journal of Computing*, 6(3):467–480, 1977.

[21] S. Manchanda and D.S. Warren. A Logic-based Language for Database Updates. In Jack Minker, editor, *Foundations of Deductive Databases and Logic Programming*, chapter 10, pages 363–394, Morgan Kaufmann, 1988.

[22] L.T. McCarty. "Clausal Intuitionistic Logic. I. Fixed-Point Semantics". *Journal of Logic Programming*, 5(1):1–31, 1988.

[23] L.T. McCarty. Clausal Intuitionistic Logic. II. Tableau Proof Procedures. *Journal of Logic Programming*, 1988. To appear.

[24] D. Miller. A Logical Analysis of Modules in Logic Programming. In *Proceedings of the IEEE Symposium on Logic Programming*, 1986.

[25] R. Statman. Intuitionistic Propositional Logic is Polynomial-Space complete. *Theoretical Computer Science*, 9(1):67–72, 1979.

[26] M.H. Van Emden and R.A. Kowalski. The Semantics of Predicate Logic as a Programming Language. *Journal of the ACM*, 23(4):733–742, 1976.

[27] M. Vardi. Relational Queries Computable in Polynomial Time. In *Proceedings of the Symposium on the Foundations of Computer Science*, pages 137–145, 1982.

[28] M. Vardi. The Complexity of Relational Query Languages. In *Proceedings of the ACM Symposium on the Principles of Database Systems*, pages 137–146, 1982.

[29] D.S. Warren. Database Updates in Pure Prolog. In *Proceedings of the International Conference on Fifth Generation Computer Systems*, pages 244–253, 1984.

ON USING CONDITIONAL ROTATION OPERATIONS TO ADAPTIVELY STRUCTURE BINARY SEARCH TREES

R. P. Cheetham, B. J. Oommen and D.T.H.Ng
School of Computer Science
Carleton University
Ottawa : CANADA : K1S 5B6

ABSTRACT

Consider a set $\mathfrak{A} = \{A_1, A_2, \ldots, A_N\}$ of records, where each record is identified by a unique key. The records are accessed based on a set of access probabilities $\mathfrak{S}=\{s_1, s_2, \ldots, s_N\}$ and are to be arranged lexicographically using a binary search tree. If $\mathfrak{S}$ is known *a priori*, it is well known [7] that an optimal binary search tree may be constructed using $\mathfrak{A}$ and $\mathfrak{S}$. We consider the case when $\mathfrak{S}$ is not known *a priori*. A new restructuring heuristic is introduced that requires three extra integer memory locations per record, and this restructuring of the tree is performed **only** if it decreases the weighted path length of the overall resultant tree. We also present a space optimized version of the latter restructuring mechanism which requires only one extra integer field per record. We show that the cost of the tree is reduced by each restructuring operation, and present experimental results to demonstrate the superiority of our algorithm over all other reported efficient static and dynamic schemes.

I. INTRODUCTION

A binary search tree may be used to store records whose keys are members of an ordered set $\mathfrak{A} = \{A_1, A_2, \ldots, A_N\}$. The records are stored in such a way that a symmetric-order traversal of the tree will yield the records in ascending order. This structure has a wide variety of applications, such as for symbol tables and dictionaries. If we are given $\mathfrak{A}$, the set of records, and their set of access probabilities $\mathfrak{S}=\{s_1, s_2, \ldots, s_N\}$, the problem of constructing an optimal binary search tree has been extensively studied. The most well known scheme, due to Knuth [7], uses dynamic programming techniques and produces an optimal binary search tree using $O(N^2)$ time and space. Alternatively, Walker and Gotlieb [14] have used dynamic programming and divide and conquer techniques to yield a nearly optimal binary search tree using $O(N)$ space and $O(N \log N)$ time. In this paper, we study the problem in which $\mathfrak{S}$, the access probability vector, is **not** known *a priori*. In this case, we seek a scheme which dynamically transforms towards an optimal configuration.

This topic is closely related to the subject of self-organizing lists. A self-organizing list is a linear list that rearranges itself such that the list, after a long enough period of time, tends towards the optimal arrangement, with the most probable element at the head of the list and the rest of the list recursively ordered in the same manner. Many memoryless schemes have been developed to reorganize a linear list dynamically. Among these are the **move-to-front** rule [8], due to McCabe, which moves the record which has been accessed to the front of the list, and the **transposition** rule [12], also due to McCabe and discussed by Rivest, which exchanges the record accessed with the record preceding it.

As well, schemes involving the use of extra memory have been developed. The first scheme, and indeed one of the initial schemes developed for rearranging linear lists to an optimal form [7], is one in which each element of the list contains a counter which records the number of times that that particular element has been accessed. The list is arranged in such a way that the most frequently accessed element becomes the head of the list, and the rest of the list is ordered similarly. By the law of large numbers this scheme will, over a long enough period of time, converge to the optimal ordering. Another scheme which requires extra memory is the stochastic move-to-rear rule [10], due to Oommen and Hansen, which moves the accessed element to the rear with a probability which decreases each time the element is accessed. As well, a stochastic move-to-front [10] and a deterministic move-to-rear scheme [11] were also developed by the same authors. Details of these schemes and others which have been developed may be found in the literature [3,5,6,7,8,10,11,12]. We refer the reader to the latter papers and in particular to the review paper by Gonnet et al. [6], which are excellent surveys of the list organizing strategies that have been researched.

A binary search tree is not quite so simple to reorganize as a linked list for the following reasons. Firstly, the lexicographic ordering property of the binary search tree must be preserved throughout the reorganization of the tree. This can sometimes be in conflict with the request to move a record upwards in the tree. As well, a restructuring operation in a binary search tree may move more than just one record; it could also move an entire subtree either up or down in the tree [15]

In order to preserve the binary search property, **rotation** is the primitive tree restructuring operation. This operation is well known [1], and tree reorganizing schemes using this operation have been developed which are analogous to various list organizing methods discussed in the literature. The description of the operation and its properties is included in all brevity in the appropriate sections of the body of this paper.

A few memoryless tree reorganizing schemes exist in the literature. Allen and Munro presented the first scheme of this type [2], which is analogous to the move-to-front rule. This scheme uses rotations to move the accessed record up to the root of the tree, and the rule is hence called the **move-to-root** scheme. They also developed another scheme called the **simple exchange** rule, which rotates the accessed element one level towards the root, similar to the transposition rule. Contrary to the case of lists, where the transposition rule is better than the move-to-front rule [12], they show that whereas the move-to-root scheme has an expected cost that is within a constant factor of the cost of a static optimum binary search tree, the simple exchange heuristic does not have this property. Due to this property of the latter heuristic, we reckon that it is superfluous to consider this scheme in any further detail. Sleator and Tarjan [13] introduced a third scheme, which also moves the accessed record up to the root of the tree. This scheme, which uses a restructuring move called **splaying**, differs from that of Allen and Munro's in that it uses different variations of single and double rotations (see Bitner [5]), unlike the move-to-root scheme which applies only successive single rotations. Both of these methods require O(N) space for the records of the tree and **no** extra space for the reorganization process. On the average both require O(log N), i.e., $O(\log_2(N))$, time based on the fact that a binary search tree has an average path length of O(log N) if each of the possible binary search trees that can be constructed from N nodes are equally likely.

One interesting and intuitively appealing scheme requiring extra memory is the **monotonic tree** scheme, first proposed by Knuth [7] as a possible method to structure a tree to obtain a nearly optimal tree. The monotonic tree was later analyzed by Bitner [5] as a dynamic reorganization tactic. In a monotonic tree the root of every subtree has the property that it is the most probable node among the nodes of the subtree. Indeed, this definition is recursive. For the dynamic version, each record contains a counter indicating the number of times it has been accessed, and after each access the record is rotated upwards until it reaches the root or until its parent has a larger access count. Over a long enough period of time, due to the law of large numbers, the tree that is obtained converges to the monotonic tree, with the most probable key at the root, and the subtrees ordered in similar fashion.

This strategy is very similar to that used in organizing linear lists, for which the optimal arrangement is that with the most probable element at the front, and the rest of the list ordered recursively in the same manner. Although this arrangement is the optimal one in the case of a linear list, it need not be optimal for a binary search tree. Indeed, Bitner shows that in contrast to the case of reorganizing a linear list, the monotonic tree scheme may be expected to behave quite poorly, especially for distributions which are highly "non-exponential". In such cases a search for a selected item in a monotonic tree may require O(N) time, which is the same time requirement of a linear list.

In this paper we will introduce a new heuristic that attempts to reorganize a binary search tree to an optimal form. It requires three extra memory locations per record. One will count the number of accesses to that record, a second will count the number of accesses to the subtree rooted at that record, and the third will contain the value of the weighted path length of the subtree rooted at that record. After a record is accessed and these values updated, the record will be rotated upwards once **if** the weighted path length of the entire **tree** (and not just the subtree rooted at the node) decreases. We shall show that this implies that the cost of the entire tree decreases as a result. Our experimental results show that this method is far superior to all other dynamic restructuring methods, and produces a tree which is very nearly optimal.

II. PREVIOUSLY KNOWN METHODS

We note first of all that throughout **all** of the binary search tree dynamic restructuring methods, the primitive operation is the rotation, which was introduced first by Adel'son-Velski'i and Landis [1]. To clarify the discussion, we now briefly describe the rotation operation. Suppose that there exists a node i in a binary search tree, and it has a parent node j, a left child i_L, and a right child i_R. Consider the case that i is a left child (see Figure 1a). A rotation is performed on node i as follows. j now becomes the right child, i_R becomes the left child of node j, and all other nodes remain in their same relative position (see Figure 1b). The case that node i is a right child is done symmetrically. This operation has the effect of raising a specified node in the tree structure while preserving the lexicographic order of the elements (refer again to Figure 1b). The properties of this operation will be described in more detail in the next section.

II.1 The Move-to-Root Heuristic

This scheme was historically the first self-organizing binary search tree scheme in the literature. Allen and Munro developed it and attempted to maintain the tree in a nearly optimal form. They assumed that each element of the tree will be requested with a fixed but unknown probability. Furthermore, the access probability of any node is assumed to be independent of the access probabilities of all the other nodes.

Their heuristic is conceptually both simple and elegant. Each time a record is accessed, rotations are performed on it in an upwards direction until it becomes the root of the tree. The idea is that a frequently accessed record will be close to the root of the tree as a result of its being frequently moved to the root, and this will minimize the cost of the search and the retrieval operations. The properties of the move-to-root scheme are explained in detail in [2], but omitted here for the sake of brevity. However, it should be noticed that the advantage of the move-to-root heuristic is that over a long sequence of requests, the average search time will, according to Allen and Munro, "almost certainly" be within a small constant factor of the optimal. Thus, whereas a bad static tree will remain bad, a structure that is self-organizing can emerge out of a bad initial configuration into a less expensive one. Also, since the variance of the number of comparisons is small, the heuristic will **rarely** behave worse than expected.

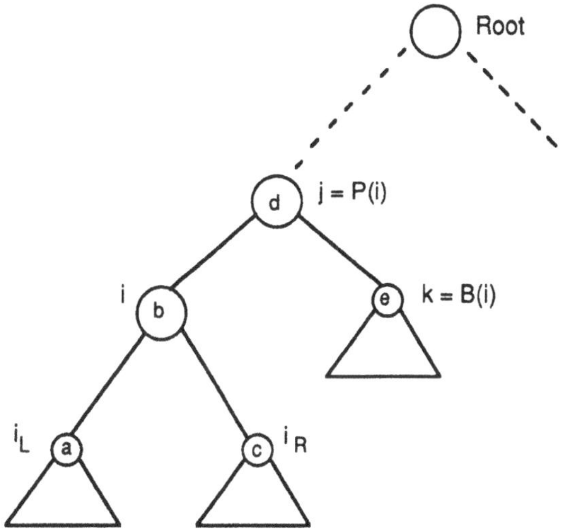

Figure 1a : The tree before a rotation is performed. The contents of the nodes are their data values, in this case the characters {a, b, c, d, e}.

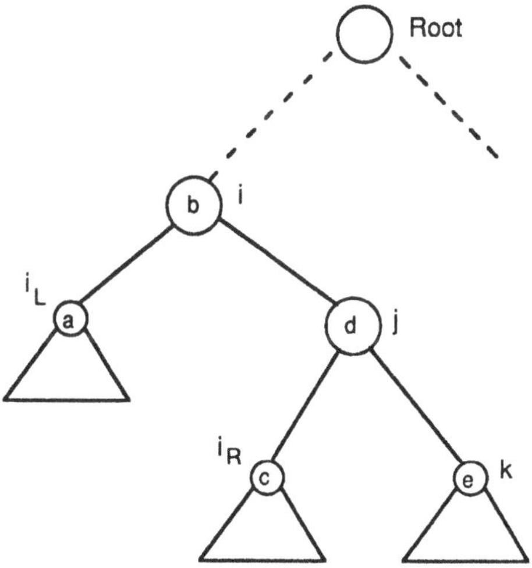

Figure 1b : The tree after a rotation is performed on node i. Observe the properties stated in Lemma II.

II.2 The Splaying Heuristic

Sleator and Tarjan [13] developed a self-organizing tree structure, which is designed in the context of a complete set of tree operations which included insertion, deletion, access, split, and join. Their structure, called the **splay tree**, was shown to have an amortized time complexity of O(log N) for **all** of its operations.

The splaying heuristic is a rather ingenious scheme. It is a restructuring move that brings the node accessed up to the root of the tree, and also keeps the tree in symmetric order (which simply means that an in-order traversal would access each item in order from the smallest to the largest). As well, it has the interesting side effect of tending to keep the tree in a form that is nearly height-balanced, besides capturing the desired effect of keeping the most frequently accessed elements near the root of the tree. The heuristic is somewhat similar to the move-to-root scheme developed by Allen and Munro, but whereas the move-to-root has an asymptotic average access time within a constant factor of optimum under the assumption that the access probabilities are independent and time invariant, the splaying operation yields identical results even if the above assumptions are relaxed.

We shall now describe the splaying operation more explicitly. To do so we use the notation that for a node i in the tree, P(i) is its **unique** parent node. By definition, P(root) is NIL, the null pointer. We distinguish three cases whenever the node i is not the root.

(i) If P(i) is the root of the tree, then rotate the edge joining i with P(i). This is the terminating case of the recursion.

(ii) If P(i) is not the root and i and P(i) are both left or both right children, rotate the edge joining P(i) with P(P(i)) and then rotate the edge joining P(i) with i.

(iii) If P(i) is not the root and i is a left child and P(i) is a right child or vice-versa, rotate the edge joining i with P(i) and then rotate the edge joining i with the new P(i).

These steps are performed from the bottom of the tree towards the root until the record that was accessed is the root of the tree. A more complete description of the heuristic is found in [15].

II.3 The Monotonic Tree Scheme

The scheme which we introduce in this subsection is the only scheme in the literature which requires extra memory. It is a dynamic version of a tree structuring method suggested by Knuth [7] as a means to structure a nearly optimal static tree. The static monotonic tree is arranged such that the most probable key is the root of the tree, and the subtrees are recursively ordered in the same manner. The static version of this scheme, as it turns out, behaves quite poorly as shown in Mehlhorn [9]. Walker and Gotlieb [14] have presented simulation results for static monotonic trees, and these results also indicate that this strategy behaves quite poorly as compared to the other static trees known in the literature.

Bitner suggested a dynamic version of this scheme [5], which could be used in the scenario when the key probabilities are not known *a priori*. Each record has one extra memory location, which contains the total number of accesses to that particular record. The reorganization of the tree after an access is then very straightforward. When a record is accessed, its counter is incremented, and then the record is rotated upwards in the tree until it becomes the root of the tree, or it has a parent with a higher frequency count than itself. Over a long enough sequence of accesses this will, by the law of large numbers, converge to the arrangement described by the static monotonic tree in which the distribution $\mathfrak{S}$ is time invariant and independent. The other properties of the scheme are proven in [5].

II.4 Drawbacks of the existing rules

In spite of all their advantages, all of the schemes given in the preceding sections have drawbacks, some of which are more serious than others. The two memoryless schemes have one major disadvantage, which is that both the move-to-root and splaying rules **always** move the record accessed up to the root of the tree. This means that if a nearly optimal arrangement is reached, a single access of a seldomly-used record will disarrange the entire tree along the access path, as the accessed element is moved up by successive steps along the path. Furthermore, on the average, these two schemes perform O(log N) operations on each access. Note that these operations are not merely computations, but rotations. Thus, performing a move-to-root or splaying operation every time a record is accessed can be **very** expensive. We would like a heuristic that could solve these two problems.

As opposed to these schemes, the monotonic tree rule does not move the accessed element to the root every time. But as we have seen, the monotonic tree rule does not perform well. Our aim is to adopt the strategy taken by this rule, but in doing so, we would like to achieve the restructuring **conditionally**, depending on the access statistics of the nodes of the actual physical tree.

III. THE CONDITIONAL ROTATION HEURISTIC

The new heuristic which we introduce requires that each of the records in the binary search tree contains three integer storage locations. The first location contains the number of accesses to that node, the second contains the total number of accesses to the subtree rooted at that node, and the third contains the weighted path length of the subtree rooted at that node. Every time an access is performed, these fields are updated for the accessed node, and also along the path traversed to achieve the access. The accessed node is rotated upwards (i.e. towards the root) **once** if and only if the weighted path length of the entire tree decreases as a result of the operation.

We first introduce some elementary definitions. Let i be any node in the given tree, whose left and right children are i_L and i_R respectively. T_i is the subtree rooted at node i. The parent of node i is P(i), and its unique brother is B(i), where B(i) would be NIL if it is non-existent. We define $\alpha_i(n)$ as the total number of accesses of node i up to and including the time instant n. Similarly, we define $\tau_i(n)$ as the total number of accesses to the subtree rooted at node i. It is obvious that $\tau_i(n)$ satisfies (7) below.

$$\tau_i(n) = \sum_{j \in T_i} \alpha_j(n) \tag{1}$$

Let $\lambda_i(n)$ be the path length of i from the root. By definition, this quantity is at least unity. Then, $\kappa_i(n)$ is defined as the weighted path length of the tree T_i rooted at node i at time instant 'n', where,

$$\kappa_i(n) = \sum_{j \in T_i} \alpha_j(n) \cdot \lambda_j(n) \tag{2}$$

In future, where no ambiguity results, we shall omit reference to the time instant 'n'. Since the τ and κ values need to be updated each time a record is accessed, we need a method to update them that doesn't require a complete traversal of the tree at every time instant. Obviously such a traversal is not required in order to update α_i. The following lemma yields the recursive properties of τ_i and κ_i, and these properties shall be used to update them without traversing the entire tree.

Lemma I.

For T_i, the subtree rooted at node i, the following are true :

(a) $\tau_i = \alpha_i + \tau_{iL} + \tau_{iR}$ (3)

(b) $\kappa_i = \alpha_i + \tau_{iL} + \tau_{iR} + \kappa_{iL} + \kappa_{iR}$ (4)

Proof : The lemma is proved in [15]. •••

This lemma means that to calculate τ and κ for any node, it is necessary **only** to look at the values stored at the node itself and at the corresponding quantities stored for the **children** of the node. Observe that the recursion does not involve the quantities in the entire tree nor the entire subtree rooted at the node. We shall now state (without proof [15]) the effects that a rotation on node i has on the rest of the tree.

Lemma II. (Rotation properties definition)

The following are the properties of a rotation performed on node i.

(i) The subtrees rooted at i_L and i_R remain unchanged.

(ii) After the rotation has been performed, i and P(i) interchange roles i.e. i becomes the parent of P(i).

(iii) With the exception of P(i), nodes which were ancestors of node i before the rotation remain the ancestors of node i after the rotation.

(iv) Nodes which were not ancestors of node i before the rotation was performed do not become ancestors of node i after the rotation. •••

We now obtain a simple method to calculate the α, τ, and κ fields of the tree after each access. We shall do this for both the case in which a rotation is performed at i and for the case in which no rotation is performed.

Theorem I.

Let j be any arbitrary node in the **entire** tree, T. On accessing $i \in T$, the following updating scheme of α, τ, and κ is consistent whether a rotation operation is performed at i or not.

(a) **Updating of α:**

$\alpha_j = \alpha_j + 1$, $j = i$; $\alpha_j = \alpha_j$, $j \neq i$

(b) **Updating of τ:**

(i) τ values in the subtrees of node i are unchanged.

(ii) τ values in the subtrees not on the access path from the root to node i are unchanged.

(iii) τ values in the nodes on the access path from the root to P(P(i)) are updated according to the following equation :

$$\tau_j = \tau_j + 1.$$

(iv) τ_i and $\tau_{P(i)}$ are updated according to the equation above as well, unless a rotation is performed. If a rotation is performed they are updated by applying

$$\tau_j = \alpha_j + \tau_{jL} + \tau_{jR}, \text{ where } j \in \{i, P(i)\},$$

and $\tau_{P(i)}$ is computed before τ_i.

(c) **Updating of κ :**

(i) κ values in the subtrees of node i are unchanged.

(ii) κ values in the subtrees not on the access path from the root to node i are unchanged.

(iii) κ values in the nodes on the access path from the root to node i are updated by applying (5) from node i **upwards** to the root.

$$\kappa_j = \alpha_j + \tau_{jL} + \tau_{jR} + \kappa_{jL} + \kappa_{jR} \tag{5}$$

Proof : The theorem is proved in [15]. •••

Note that after a rotation has been performed, our notation can be misleading if the reader does not realize that the notation refers to the node identities. We repeat that we refer to the accessed node and its parent, j, before the rotation operation is performed as i and P(i)=j respectively. After the rotation operation has been performed, however, we refer to the **same** nodes as i and j, even though the original relationship between the nodes has been destroyed, and indeed, the relationship between the two nodes is completely reversed. To render the notation consistent, P(i) will refer to j. However, we introduce the notation that post-rotational quantities shall have the superscript '. Thus, P(j)' = i in this particular case.

III.1 Criteria for Performing Rotations

Up to this point we have described the memory locations used for determining whether or not to rotate, and how these locations may be updated after an access of a specified node, both in the case that a rotation is performed and in the case that it is not performed. What we have not addressed yet is the question of a criterion to decide whether a rotation should be performed or not.

The basic condition for rotation of a node is that the weighted path length of the **entire tree** must decrease as a result of the operation. A brute-force method for determining whether or not to rotate is performed as follows. When an access is performed, the record is found, and updating at the record is done. We then retrace our steps back along the access path to the root of the tree, updating the values of τ and κ as we go, at the same time computing the hypothetical values of τ and κ that would be obtained had we performed the rotation operation. Once we have reached the root of the tree, we decide whether to perform the rotation operation or not by comparing the hypothetical κ-value to the actual κ-value. If the hypothetical value is the smaller of the two, then the record is again found, the rotation is performed, and the τ and κ values are again updated upwards along the access path as described in Theorem I.

This method achieves the goal, but is very expensive. In the case that a rotation is actually performed four passes must be made between the accessed node and the root of the tree, which implies that O(4 log N) operations will be required. We now present a method to anticipate **at the level of the rotation itself** whether or not the κ-value of the entire tree will decrease if a rotation operation is performed, and hence determine if the operation should be performed or not. By applying such a method, we can reduce the average time requirements of the access operation to O(2 log N).

Before we describe our new criterion for rotation, the notation we referred to above will be clarified. Any primed quantity (e.g. α',τ',κ') is a **post-rotational** quantity. That is, it is the value of the specified quantity after the rotation has been performed.

We now define our rotation criterion. Let θ_i be $\kappa_{P(i)} - \kappa_i'$. θ_i is a criterion function which tells us whether performing a rotation at node i will reduce the κ-value at P(i) or not. We shall prove that the κ-value of the entire tree is reduced by a rotation if and only if θ_i is reduced by the rotation at i. Such a rotation is called a κ-lowering rotation. The advantages of this scheme over the ones in the literature are described in [15].

Theorem II.

Any κ-lowering rotation performed on any node in the tree will cause the weighted path length of the entire tree to decrease.

Proof : The proof is rather involved but given in [15]. •••

For the sake of completeness, we present below our access and reorganizing algorithm which is based on these results. The algorithm, as seen below, covers the general case for any node j, and covers all possible cases. The τ values are updated on the way down the tree, and the κ values are updated on the path back up.

Algorithm CON_ROT_Access { CONditional ROTation Access }
Input : A binary search tree T and a search key k_i
Output : (i) the restructured tree T'
(ii) a pointer to record i containing k_i
Method : $\tau_j \leftarrow \tau_j + 1$ { increment τ for the present node }
if $k_i = k_j$ **then** { This is the record we want }
$\alpha_j \leftarrow \alpha_j + 1$
calculate $\kappa_{P(j)}$, κ_j' using Lemma I
if $\kappa_{P(j)} - \kappa_j' > 0$ **then**
rotate node j upwards
recalculate $\kappa_{P(j)}$, κ_j, $\tau_{P(j)}$, τ_j
endif
else { Search the subtrees }
if $k_i < k_j$ **then**
perform CON_ROT_Access on j^.Leftchild
else
perform CON_ROT_Access on j^.Rightchild
endif
recalculate κ_j
endif
return record i
end Method
end Algorithm CON_ROT_Access.

IV. THE SPACE-OPTIMIZING CONDITIONAL ROTATION HEURISTIC

Up to this point we have developed a scheme for dynamically restructuring binary search trees by considering whether the weighted path length of the entire tree decreases as a result of performing the operation, and performing any reorganization only if the weighted path length does actually decrease as a result of the operation. We also introduced a method to determine whether or not to rotate based merely on a criterion specified in terms of the path length at the **parent** of the node that was accessed. In this section, we present a scheme which performs tree reorganization using the same heuristic that was used in the preceding section. However, we reduce both the time and the space it requires. If we could eliminate the need for storing and updating the κ values, we could save greatly in both time and space.

As it turns out, not only can we remove the κ values, but we can also eliminate the need for the α values. It is obvious from Lemma I that the information stored in the α values is also stored in the τ values, and may be readily extracted. This means that the

α values do not have to be explicitly stored. What is not quite so obvious is the fact that the information stored in the τ fields is sufficient to determine whether or not a rotation operation should be performed.

We define a new criterion function ψ which is dependent entirely upon the τ values stored in each node, in contrast to the previous criterion function θ, which was dependent upon the α, τ, and κ values. Previously, we performed a rotation operation if the criterion function θ_i took a positive value. Now, we perform the rotation if the new criterion function ψ_i takes a positive value. We will show that indeed, performing a rotation based on the criterion function ψ_i is equivalent to performing a rotation based on the criterion function θ_i.

Theorem III.

Let i be the accessed node of the binary search tree, and let $\kappa_{P(i)}$ be the weighted path length of the tree rooted at the parent P(i) if no rotation is performed on node i. Let κ_i' be the weighted path length of the tree rooted at node i if the rotation is performed. Furthermore, let ψ_i be defined as follows:

$$\psi_i = \alpha_i + \tau_{iL} - \alpha_{P(i)} - \tau_{B(i)} \qquad \text{if i is a left child;}$$

$$\psi_i = \alpha_i + \tau_{iR} - \alpha_{P(i)} - \tau_{B(i)} \qquad \text{if i is a right child.}$$

As defined above, let $\theta_i = \kappa_{P(i)} - \kappa_i'$. Then, $\psi_i \geq 0$ if and only if $\theta_i \geq 0$.

Proof : The proof of the theorem is quite involved and is given in [15]. •••

Unlike θ_i, ψ_i only requires us to use the information stored in the α and τ fields in each record. This implies that we do not need to maintain the κ fields at all, and this in turn implies that after the search for the desired record and after performing any reorganization, we do not need to retrace our steps back up the tree to update the κ values of the ancestors of i. As well, observe that at any node i, the value of α_i obeys,

$$\alpha_i = \tau_i - \tau_{iL} - \tau_{iR}.$$

This implies that the α values may be expressed in terms of the τ values, and so the former are redundant and they too need not be maintained. Thus we need to maintain only one extra memory location per node, and we are not required to make a second pass upwards on the tree. Our modified algorithm, which is a space optimizing version of CON_ROT_Access, requires O(N) extra space and O(log N) time, the latter being the time required to **access** the node i, which would anyway have to be taken in **any** binary search tree scheme. The additional properties of the two Algorithms now follow.

Corollary I.

Algorithm CON_ROT_Access and its space optimizing version SpaceOptCON_ROT_Access are stochastically equivalent. •••

Theorem IV

Any algorithm which reduces the weighted path length of a binary search tree asymptotically reduces the cost of the entire tree. •••

In particular, the algorithms CON_ROT_Access and the space optimizing version SpaceOptCON_ROT_Access achieve the above result, and thus we believe that our method is superior to all the other dynamic schemes presented in the literature, as is demonstrated by our experimental results.

Algorithm SpaceOptCON_ROT_Access
Input : A binary search tree T and a search key k_i.
Output : the restructured tree T', a pointer to record i containing k_i
Method :

```
τj ← τj + 1                 { update τ for the present node }
if ki = kj then             { Found the record in question }
   if node j is a left child then
        ψj ← 2τj - τjR - τP(j)
   else
        ψj ← 2τj - τjL - τP(j)
   endif
   if ψj > 0 then
        rotate node j upwards
        recalculate τj, τP(j)
   endif
   return record j
else
   if ki < kj then          { Search the subtrees }
        perform SpaceOptCON_ROT_Access on j^.Leftchild
   else
        perform SpaceOptCON_ROT_Access on j^.Rightchild
   endif
endif
end Method
```

end Algorithm SpaceOptCON_ROT_Access

V. EXPERIMENTAL RESULTS

A series of experiments was run to compare the asymptotic properties of the various binary search tree structures. The following schemes were used in the simulations :

(i) Allen and Munro's move-to-root scheme [2],
(ii) Sleator and Tarjan's splay tree scheme [13],
(iii) the optimal tree, constructed using Knuth's algorithm [7],
(iv) a height-balanced tree [1],
(v) the monotonic tree rule described by Bitner [5],
(vi) the nearly optimal tree rule due to Walker and Gotlieb [14], and
(vii) CON_ROT, the scheme we have presented in this paper.

Since both of our algorithms are stochastically equivalent, the results we present are results of simulations using the first version of the algorithm, which indeed worked in lock-step with the second, which is the space optimized version of the first. In each simulation, there were 100 parallel experiments run, and each initial tree contained 15 records. The initial tree structure of each experiment was randomly chosen. 30,000 accesses were performed on each tree, each accessed item being randomly chosen, the randomness being specified by a probability distribution vector. Four different types of distributions were used which included the Zipf's distribution, the Exponential distribution, and two distinct types of wedge distributions.

The experimental results and their significance are discussed in [15]. It may be seen quite clearly from the results presented in [15] that our new scheme, CON_ROT_Access, outperforms all of the other static and dynamic binary search tree schemes, excepting the static optimal tree itself. The results obtained for the Zipf's law distribution are typical. In this case, Allen and Munro's move-to-root scheme had a cost which was approximately 20.5% greater than the static optimal tree, Sleator and Tarjan's splay tree had a cost approximately 23.5% greater than the static optimal, and the balanced tree was approximately 17% more expensive than the static optimal tree scheme. The results for the monotonic tree verified the fact that it is a poor scheme, as it proved to have an average cost which was 55% greater than the average cost of the static optimal tree. The nearly optimal tree presented by Walker and Gotlieb was not as nearly optimal as it should have been, giving an average cost which was 16.1% greater than the optimal tree's cost. Our scheme proved to have an average cost that was only 3.6% greater than the average cost of the static optimal tree. These results which are typical for each of the distributions used in the simulations.

VI. CONCLUSIONS AND OPEN PROBLEMS

In this paper we have introduced a new self-organizing tree strategy requiring extra memory which attempts to reorganize a binary search tree to an optimal form. It required three extra memory locations per record. One counts the number of accesses to that record, a second contains the number of accesses to the subtree rooted at that record, and the third contains the value of the weighted path length of the subtree rooted at that record. After a record is accessed and these values updated, the record is rotated one level upwards **if** the weighted path length of the entire **tree** (and not just the subtree rooted at the node) decreases as a result of the rotation operation. We have shown that this implies that the cost of the entire tree asymptotically decreases as a result. But to do this, we anticipate at the level of the rotation whether a rotation will yield this result, and decide accordingly whether to restructure the tree or not. As well, we have presented a space optimizing version of this algorithm which requires us to maintain only one extra memory location per node. We have shown that this space optimizing version of the algorithm and the former version are stochastically equivalent. Both of these rules require O(N) extra memory and O(log N) time. Simulation results demonstrate that overall, our new scheme has an asymptotic expected cost of retrieval

AN O(N^2) EQUIVALENCE ALGORITHM FOR FAN-OUT FREE QUERIES

Pratul Dublish S.N. Maheshwari
Department of Computer Science & Engineering
Indian Institute of Technology, Delhi
New Delhi - 110016, India

Abstract: An equivalence algorithm for fan-out free queries, which form an untyped subclass of conjunctive queries, based on an extension of the implication graph technique is presented. This algorithm runs in O(n^2) time where n is the size of the queries involved. This algorithm subsumes all known equivalence testing algorithms for various subclasses of fan-out free queries.

Introduction

Conjunctive query equivalence problem, besides being of theoretical interest, is commonly faced in environments such as designing heuristics for optimizing queries which are expressed using union or difference operations on conjunctive queries. Optimization of such queries is computationally very hard [SY]. If an efficient equivalence algorithm is available for some class of conjunctive queries then it can be used as a heuristic to identify the redundant subqueries. Furthermore, conjunctive query equivalence algorithms can also be used for eliminating duplicate clauses from Horn clause query programs [CH]. Conjunctive query equivalence was first studied by Chandra and Merlin [CM]. They showed that the problem was NP-complete in general. Since then attempts have been made to identify subclasses of conjunctive queries for which polynomial time equivalence algorithms exist. Johnson and Klug [JK] were first to identify a reasonably expressive untyped subclass, called fan-out free queries, for which they gave an O(n^4) equivalence algorithm. Sagiv [Sag] has presented O(n^2) equivalence algorithms for two typed subclasses of fan-out free queries.

Johnson and Klug have attempted to solve the equivalence problem by checking whether the implication graphs of the two queries are isomorphic. They have reduced the implication graph isomorphism problem to that of testing for isomorphism between certain labelled forests. Their algorithm constructs these forests from the implication graphs of the two queries and then uses the well known labelled tree isomorphism algorithm [AHU] to test for isomorphism between them. This algorithm is fairly complicated and runs in O(n^4) time. However, the "graph isomorphism" approach used in [JK] does not appear to be a natural approach for solving the equivalence problem. A more natural approach is to directly find homomorphisms which map one query onto the other. The O(n^2) equivalence algorithms presented in [Sag] follow which is within a small percentage of the asymptotic expected cost of the **static** optimal tree.

Acknowledgements : This work was partially supported by the Natural Sciences and Engineering Research Council of Canada.

REFERENCES

[1] Adel'son-Velski'i, G. M. and Landis, E.M., "An algorithm for the organization of information", Sov. Math. Dokl., 3(1962), pp. 1259-1262.

[2] Allen, B. and Munro, I., "Self-organizing binary search trees", J.ACM 25(1978), pp.526-535.

[3 Arnow, D. M. and Tenenbaum, A. M., "An investigation of the move-ahead-k rules", Congressus Numerantium, Proceedings of the Thirteenth Southeastern Conference on Combinatorics, Graph Theory and Computing, Florida, Feb. 1982, pp.47-65.

[4] Bayer, P. J., "Improved bounds on the costs of optimal and balanced binary search trees", MAC Technical Memo-69, Nov. 1975.

[5] Bitner, J. R., "Heuristics that dynamically organize data structures", SIAM J.Comput., 8(1979), pp.82-110.

[6] Gonnet, G. H., Munro, J. I. and Suwanda, H., "Exegesis of self-organizing linear search", SIAM J.Comput., 10(1981), pp.613-637.

[7] Knuth, D. E., The Art of Computer Programming, vol. 3, Addison-Wesley, Reading, Ma., 1973.

[8] McCabe, J., "On serial files with relocatable records", Operations Research, 12(1965), pp.609-618.

[9] Mehlhorn, K., "Nearly optimal binary search trees", Acta Informatica, 5(1975), pp.287-295.

[10] Oommen, B.J. and Hansen, E. R., "List organizing strategies using stochastic move-to-front and stochastic move-to-rear operations", SIAM J.Comput., vol.16, No.4, pp. 705-716.

[11] Oommen, B. J., Hansen, E. R. and Munro, J. I., "Deterministic Move-to-Rear List Organizing Strategies with Optimal and Expedient Properties", Proc. of the Twenty-Fifth Allerton Conference, Sept. 1987.

[12] Rivest, R. L., "On self-organizing sequential search heuristics", Comm.ACM, 19(1976), pp.63-67.

[13] Sleator, D. D. and Tarjan, R. E., "Self-adjusting binary search trees", J.ACM, 32(1985), pp.652-686.

[14] Walker, W. A. and Gotlieb, C. C., "A top-down algorithm for constructing nearly optimal lexicographical trees", in Graph Theory and Computing, Academic Press, New York, 1972.

[15] Cheetham,R. P., Oommen, B. J. and Ng, D. T. H.,"Adaptive Structuring of Binary Search Trees Using Conditional Rotations". Submitted for publication.

this approach.

In this paper we present an $O(n^2)$ equivalence algorithm for fan-out free queries. In contrast to the algorithm in [JK], our algorithm works by directly finding an isomorphism which maps one query onto the other. We assume **wlg** that the two given queries are optimized (fan-out free queries can be optimized in $O(n^2)$ time, see [DM]). We construct an extended version of the implication graph using the two given queries. However, the extended implication graph may contain fan-out vertices. This is problematic in that finding self-homomorphisms using implication graphs which contain fan-out vertices is known to be NP-complete [MDM]. Our main contribution is to show that there is sufficient structure in the extended implication graphs, obtained from optimized fan-out free queries, for traditional methods of testing equivalence to be applicable.

Definitions

While we assume familiarity with the theory and results presented in [JK], for the sake of readability and completeness we give certain definitions. Definitions of terms not defined can be found in [JK,Mai,Ull].

A **conjunctive query** is a first order formula of the form

$$(x_1, x_2, \ldots, x_p) \exists\ y_1\ y_2 \ldots y_q\ c_1 \wedge c_2\ \ldots \wedge c_r\ .$$

The free variables x_is are the **distinguished variables** (**DVs**) and the quantified variables y_is are the **non-distinguished variables** (**NDVs**). Each **conjunct** c_i, $1 \leq i \leq r$, is an atomic formula of the form $R_i(c_i[1], c_i[2], \ldots, c_i[m])$ where R_i, also denoted by $R(c_i)$, is some relation from the underlying relation scheme having m attributes and each $c_i[k]$, $1 \leq k \leq m$, is either a DV or a NDV or a **constant**, i.e., an element from the domain of the kth attribute of R_i. Since all queries referred to in this paper are conjunctive, in what follows the word query denotes a conjunctive query. Two queries are said to be **equivalent** if for all databases they produce the same output relation. Given a query Q1, its **optimal equivalent query** is one which has a **minimum** number of conjuncts and is equivalent to Q1. A query is said to be **optimized** if it is its own optimal equivalent query.

For a query **Q**, let C_Q denote the set of its conjuncts and U_Q be the union of DVs, NDVs and constants occuring in **Q**. Let Q1 and Q2 be two queries having the same set of DVs. A **symbol mapping** from Q1 to Q2 is a function **f** : $U_{Q1} \rightarrow U_{Q2}$ which preserves all DVs and constants. We say $c_2 \in C_{Q2}$ **covers** $c_1 \in C_{Q1}$ if $R(c_1) = R(c_2)$ and there is a symbol mapping from Q1 to Q2 which maps c_1 to c_2. A **conjunct mapping** is a function **g** : $C_{Q1} \rightarrow C_{Q2}$ such that $g(c_1)$ covers c_1 for each $c_1 \in C_{Q1}$. A **homomorphism** **h** from Q1 to Q2 is a tuple (**f**,**g**), where **f** is a symbol mapping from Q1 to Q2 and **g** is a conjunct mapping from Q1 to Q2 such that **f** induces **g** and vice versa. The following fact shows that the notion of homomorphism is central to the process of query equivalence.

Fact [CM] : Two queries Q1 and Q2 are equivalent iff there are homomorphisms h_{12} : Q1 $\rightarrow$ Q2 and h_{21} : Q2 $\rightarrow$ Q1. ∎

It follows from the above fact that if Q1 is an optimized query then it has no **shrinking self-homomorphism**, i.e., an homomorphism which maps Q1 to Q2 such that $C_{Q2} \subset C_{Q1}$. If both Q1 and Q2 are optimized then the above fact can be strengthened as follows.

Fact [JK] : Two optimized queries, Q1 and Q2, are equivalent iff there is an isomorphism from Q1 to Q2, i.e., a homomorphism from Q1 to Q2 which is one-one and onto for both conjuncts and NDVs. ∎

Consequently, if Q1 and Q2 are equivalent they satisfy the following conditions :
(i) they have the same number of conjuncts and NDVs, and
(ii) they have the same set of DVs and constants.
For the rest of this paper we assume that the above conditions hold for Q1 and Q2.
We also assume **wlg** that the NDVs occuring in Q1 are distinct from those in Q2.

The **implication graph** of a query **Q** is a bipartite graph G[Q] = (V[Q],E[Q]) defined as follows :
The vertices of G[Q] correspond to the potential elements of homomorphisms. The set of vertices V[Q] consists of $V_C[Q]$, a set of **conjunct-pair vertices** (**CPVs**), and $V_S[Q]$, a set of **symbol-pair vertices** (**SPVs**). $V_C[Q]$ contains a vertex $<c_1,c_2>$ for each pair of conjuncts in C_Q such that c_2 covers c_1 and a special vertex $<\Theta>$, which indicates that no homomorphism is possible. $V_S[Q]$ contains a vertex $<s_1,s_2>$ for each NDV $s_1 \in U_Q$ and each $s_2 \in U_Q$ such that for some CPV $<c_1,c_2>$ and some j, $c_1[j] = s_1$ and $c_2[j] = s_2$. Each edge in E[Q] joins a CPV to a SPV. There is an edge between $<s_1,s_2>$ and $<\Theta>$ iff there is a conjunct c_1 such that $c_1[j] = s_1$ and for each conjunct c_2 covering c_1, $c_2[j] \neq s_2$. There is an edge between $<s_1,s_2>$ and $<c_1,c_2>$ iff for some j, $c_1[j] = s_1$ and $c_2[j] = s_2$.

A SPV $<s_1,s_2>$ is said to be **fan-out free** if either all its neighbours have the same first component or all its neighbours have distinct first components. A SPV which is **not** fan-out free is said to be a **fan-out** SPV. A query is said to be **fan-out free** iff each SPV $<s_1,s_2>$, $s_1 \neq s_2$, in its implication graph is fan-out free.

The notion of implication graph was developed in [JK] for finding shrinking self-homomorphisms. This notion can be extended to check for the existence of an isomorphism from Q1 to Q2. We construct an **extended** implication graph **G** as follows. The vertices of **G** correspond to the potential elements of isomorphisms from Q1 to Q2. The vertex set of **G** consists of a set of CPVs and SPVs. The CPVs of **G** correspond to the conjunct mappings from Q1 to Q2 which **may** be extended to an isomorphism from Q1 to Q2. Note that if an isomorphism from Q1 to Q2 maps conjunct c1 to c2, then c1 and c2 must cover each other. Thus the CPV set of **G** contains, besides <Θ>, **only** those CPVs <c1,c2>, c1 ∈ C_{Q1} and c2 ∈ C_{Q2}, such that c1 and c2 cover each other. <s1,s2>, s1 and s2 are NDVs occuring in Q1 and Q2 respectively, is a SPV in **G** if there exists a CPV <c1,c2> in G with c1[j]=s1 and c2[j]=s2. In this case there is an edge between <c1,c2> and <s1,s2>. There is an edge between a SPV <s1,s2> and <Θ> if one of the following conditions hold

(i) s1 occurs in c1 ∈ C_{Q1} and there is no CPV with c1 as its first component adjacent to <s1,s2>,

(ii) s2 occurs in c2 ∈ C_{Q2} and there is no CPV with c2 as its second component adjacent to <s1,s2>, or

(iii) number of conjuncts in which s1 occurs does not equal the number of conjuncts in which s2 occurs.

Note that if <s1,s2> is adjacent to <Θ> then no isomorphism from Q1 to Q2 mapping s1 to s2 is possible.

The notions of fan-out free and fan-out SPVs, defined previously for implication graphs, remain valid for **G**. Note that **G** may contain fan-out SPVs even when Q1 and Q2 are optimized fan-out free queries. For example, let Q1 be the query

$\exists$ s1 s2 s3 $c_1 \wedge c_2 \wedge c_3 \wedge c_4$ where c_1 = R(c1,s1,s2), c_2 = R(c1,s1,s3), c_3 = R(c2,s1,s2) and c_4 = R(c3,s1,s3). Let Q2 be the query

$\exists$ s4 s5 s6 $\bar{c}_1 \wedge \bar{c}_2 \wedge \bar{c}_3 \wedge \bar{c}_4$ where $\bar{c}_1$ = R(c1,s4,s5), $\bar{c}_2$ = R(c1,s4,s6), $\bar{c}_3$ = R(c2,s4,s5) and $\bar{c}_4$ = R(c3,s4,s6). The extended implication graph of Q1 and Q2, shown in Figure 1(a), contains a fan-out SPV <s1,s4>.

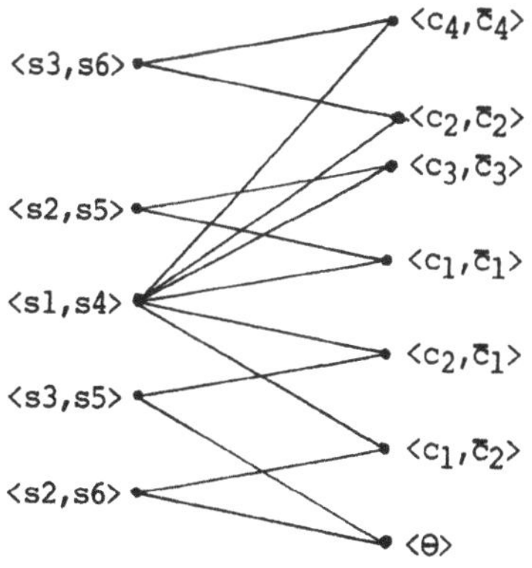

Figure 1(a)

1. <$c_1,\bar{c}_1$>, <$c_2,\bar{c}_2$>, <$c_3,\bar{c}_3$>, <$c_4,\bar{c}_4$>
2. <$c_1,\bar{c}_1$>, <$c_2,\bar{c}_1$>, <$c_3,\bar{c}_3$>, <$c_4,\bar{c}_4$>
3. <$c_1,\bar{c}_2$>, <$c_2,\bar{c}_2$>, <$c_3,\bar{c}_3$>, <$c_4,\bar{c}_4$>
4. <$c_1,\bar{c}_2$>, <$c_2,\bar{c}_1$>, <$c_3,\bar{c}_3$>, <$c_4,\bar{c}_4$>

Figure 1(b)

G can be used to find an isomorphism from Q1 to Q2 as follows. Suppose we wish to know whether an isomorphism mapping c_1 ∈ C_{Q1} to c_2 ∈ C_{Q2} is possible. Let **h** = (**f**,**g**) be such an isomomorphism. Then **g** has the CPV <c_1,c_2> (we shall consider **g** to be a set of CPVs and **f** to be a set of SPVs). Since **f** and **g** induce each other, **f** must contain the NDV mappings induced by mapping c_1 to c_2. Note that these mappings are given by the SPVs adjacent to <c_1,c_2>. We add all such SPVs to **f**. Let <s_1,s_2> be any SPV adjacent to $<c_1,c_2>$. Then all the conjunct mappings induced by $<s_1,s_2>$ must be added to **g**. If $<s_1,s_2>$ is adjacent to $<\Theta>$, then we know that no isomomorphism mapping c_1 to c_2 is possible. We stop after adding $<\Theta>$ to **g**. If $<s_1,s_2>$ is a fan-out free SPV then each CPV adjacent to it must be added to **g**. However, if $<s_1,s_2>$ is a fan-out SPV, i.e., it has CPVs $<c_3,c_4>$ and $<c_3,c_5>$ adjacent to it, $c_4 \neq c_5$ and $c_3 \neq c_1$, then only one of $<c_3,c_4>$ or $<c_3,c_5>$ can be added to **g**. Note that in this case we do not know which choice would eventually lead to an isomorphism.

Based on the above discussion, the concept of **implication** can be introduced to capture the notion of **f** inducing **g** and vice versa. A CPV **implies** all its neighbouring SPVs. A SPV which is adjacent to $<\Theta>$ only implies $<\Theta>$. A fan-out free SPV implies all the CPVs which are adjacent to it. We now define the notion of implication for fan-out SPVs. Recall that a fan-out SPV, encountered while constructing an IC, offers a choice in extending the partial conjunct mapping. Thus the set of CPVs implied by it is not uniquely defined. Let $<s_1,s_2>$ be a fan-out SPV, not adjacent to $<\Theta>$, and let $c_1,c_2,\ldots,c_k$, $k \geq 2$, be the conjuncts which occur as the first component of some CPV adjacent to $<s_1,s_2>$. Let S_i denote the set of CPVs, adjacent to $<s_1,s_2>$, which have c_i as their first component, $1 \leq i \leq k$. Then an **implication set** of $<s_1,s_2>$ is defined to be

$$\bigcup_{i=1}^{k} \textbf{oneof}\ (S_i),$$

where the operator **oneof** applied to a set chooses exactly one element from it. For example, Figure 1(b) shows all possible implication sets of the fan-out SPV <s1,s4> shown in Figure 1(a).

An **implication closure** (IC) containing a CPV $<c_1,c_2>$ can be constructed by initially placing $<c_1,c_2>$ in the IC and repeatedly adding vertices to it until no further additions are possible. Vertices are added to the IC by the following process :

(i) If a CPV $<c_i,c_j>$ is in the IC, add all the SPVs implied by it to the IC

(ii) If the IC contains a SPV which is adjacent to $<\Theta>$, add $<\Theta>$ to the IC and terminate the IC construction.

(iii) If a fan-out free SPV $<s_i,s_j>$ is in the IC, add all CPVs implied by it to the IC.

(iv) If a fan-out SPV $<s_i,s_j>$ is in the IC, add all the CPVs belonging to any implication set of $<s_i,s_j>$, which contains all the CPVs adjacent to $<s_i,s_j>$ already in the IC, to the IC . If no such implication set of $<s_i,s_j>$ exists, then terminate the IC construction.

An IC is said to induce a **partial isomorphism** if it does not contain $<\Theta>$ and no two CPVs in it have the same first or second component. If an IC induces a partial isomorphism then, as shown later, there exists an isomorphism from Q1 to Q2 which contains the IC, provided that Q1 and Q2 are equivalent. Thus to check the existence of an isomorphism from Q1 to Q2 which maps conjunct c_1 to c_2, we must verify whether there exists an IC which contains $<c_1,c_2>$ and induces a partial isomorphism. The presence of fan-out SPVs complicates this task since there may be many ICs containing $<c_1,c_2>$. If we find an IC containing $<c_1,c_2>$ which fails to induce a partial isomorphism, it does not rule out the possibility of another IC which contains $<c_1,c_2>$ and induces a partial isomorphism. Note that the presence of fan-out SPVs in the implication graph of a query causes the problem of finding shrinking self-homomorphisms to become NP-complete [MDM]. However, we shall show later that the problem structure allows us to efficiently find ICs in G which induce partial isomorphisms.

The notion of implication and IC can be similarly defined, with appropriate modifications, for implication graphs of fan-out free queries. A $<\theta>$-adjacent SPV only implies $<\theta>$. A SPV $<s_1,s_1>$ implies nothing (such a SPV cannot occur in **G**). A SPV $<s_1,s_2>$, $s_1 \neq s_2$, implies a neighbouring CPV $<c_1,c_2>$ iff $<c_1,c_2>$ is the only CPV adjacent to it having c_1 as its first component. A CPV implies all SPVs adjacent to it. Since the implication graph does not contain any fan-out SPVs, the IC containing a CPV is uniquely defined. Thus we define the IC **of a CPV** rather than the IC **containing a CPV.** The IC of a CPV $<c_1,c_2>$ can be constructed as in the case of the extended implication graph **G.** The importance of IC, for optimizing fan-out free queries, arises from the following fact [JK]. For a fan-out free query, if an IC does not contain $<\theta>$ and a conjunct (NDV) appears as the first component of atmost one CPV (SPV) in the IC then the IC induces a self-homomorphism on the query. Note that if the query is optimized then the self-homomorphism induced by any IC is an automorphism.

We now define the notion of implication path which is used in the proofs that follow. Given a fan-out free query **Q**, let v_s and v_t be two distinct vertices not adjacent to each other in G[Q]. An **implication path** from v_s to v_t is an alternating sequence of CPVs and SPVs $v_1,v_2,....,v_k$ such that v_s implies v_1, v_i implies v_{i+1}, $1 \leq i \leq k-1$, and v_k implies v_t. If v_s is a CPV (SPV) then v_1 is a SPV (CPV). If v_s and v_t are both CPVs, then by reversing the implication path from v_s to v_t we obtain an implication path from v_t to v_s. Hence there is an implication path between any two CPVs in an IC. The notion of implication path can be defined in a similar fashion for G.

The Equivalence Testing Algorithm

We first establish the relevance of ICs which induce partial isomorphisms to the problem of finding an isomorphism from Q1 to Q2.

Lemma 1 : If there exists an isomorphism from Q1 to Q2 which maps conjunct c1 to conjunct c2 then there exists an IC in **G** which contains <c1,c2> and induces a partial isomorphism. Further for each CPV $<c_i,c_j>$ (SPV $<s_i,s_j>$) in this IC, the isomorphism from Q1 to Q2 maps c_i to c_j (s_i to s_j).

Proof : We prove the lemma by constructing an IC containing <c1,c2> with the desired properties. Since there exists an isomorphism mapping c1 to c2 therefore $\langle c1,c2\rangle$ is a CPV in **G**. We start by placing $\langle c1,c2\rangle$ and all the SPVs implied by it in the IC under construction. Let $\langle s1,s2\rangle$ be any SPV adjacent to $\langle c1,c2\rangle$. Since the isomorphism maps s1 to s2 therefore $\langle s1,s2\rangle$ cannot be $\langle\Theta\rangle$-adjacent. Further, the isomorphism from Q1 to Q2 maps each conjunct in Q1 having an occurence of s1 to a distinct conjunct in Q2 having an occurence of s2. The CPVs corresponding to these conjunct mappings are precisely the CPVs implied by $\langle s1,s2\rangle$, if $\langle s1,s2\rangle$ is fan-out free, or they form an implication set of $\langle s1,s2\rangle$, if $\langle s1,s2\rangle$ is a fan-out SPV. Therefore they can be placed in the IC under construction.

By repeatedly applying the above arguments to the "new" CPVs added to the IC, we can show that each CPV (SPV) in the IC corresponds to some conjunct (symbol) mapping in the isomorphism. Hence this IC cannot contain two CPVs having the same first or second component and therefore induces a partial isomorphism. ▯

Lemma 2 : If Q1 and Q2 are equivalent and there exists an IC containing $\langle c1,c2\rangle$ which induces a partial isomorphism then there is an isomorphism from Q1 to Q2 which maps c1 to c2.

To prove Lemma 2, we make use of the following lemma :

Lemma 3 : Let $\langle s_i,s_j\rangle$ be a fan-out SPV in **G**. Then any SPV $\langle s_i,x\rangle$ in G, $x \neq s_j$, cannot be contained in any IC inducing a partial isomorphism.

Proof : Suppose that some SPV $\langle s_i,x\rangle$ lies in an IC inducing a partial isomorphism. Then $\langle s_i,x\rangle$ is not adjacent to $\langle\Theta\rangle$. Thus each conjunct in Q1 having an occurence of s_i appears as the first component of some CPV adjacent to $\langle s_i,x\rangle$. Since $\langle s_i,s_j\rangle$ is a fan-out vertex, there exist distinct conjuncts c_{i1} and c_{i2} such that $\langle s_i,s_j\rangle$ has, adjacent to it, atleast one CPV with c_{i1} as its first component and atleast two CPVs with c_{i2} as their first component. Let these CPVs be $\langle c_{i1},c_{j1}\rangle$, $\langle c_{i2},c_{j2}\rangle$, and $\langle c_{i2},\bar{c}_{j2}\rangle$, $\bar{c}_{j2} \neq c_{j2}$. Then $\langle s_i,x\rangle$ has some CPVs $\langle c_{i1},c_p\rangle$ and $\langle c_{i2},c_q\rangle$ adjacent to itself. Note that since c_{i1} and c_{j1} cover each other and c_{i1} and c_p cover each other therefore c_{j1} and c_p cover each other. Similarly c_{j2} ($\bar{c}_{j2}$) and c_q cover each other. If $c_p \neq c_q$, then in the implication graph of Q2 the SPV $\langle x,s_j\rangle$ has CPVs $\langle c_p,c_{j1}\rangle$, $\langle c_q,c_{j2}\rangle$ and $\langle c_q,\bar{c}_{j2}\rangle$ adjacent to it. This contradicts the fact that Q2 is a fan-out free query. If $c_p=c_q$ and $\langle c_{i1},c_p\rangle$ and $\langle c_{i2},c_p\rangle$ are the only CPVs adjacent to $\langle s_i,x\rangle$ with c_{i1} and c_{i2} as their first component respectively, then any IC containing $\langle s_i,x\rangle$ cannot induce a partial isomorphism since it will contain $\langle c_{i1},c_p\rangle$ and $\langle c_{i2},c_p\rangle$. ▯

Note that the proof of Lemma 3 holds even if $\langle s_i,s_j\rangle$ is **$\langle\Theta\rangle$-adjacent.** Thus if **G** contains a $\langle\Theta\rangle$-adjacent fan-out SPV then Q1 and Q2 are not equivalent. However, if $\langle s_i,s_j\rangle$ is a non $\langle\Theta\rangle$-adjacent fan-out SPV then each isomorphism from Q1 to Q2 maps s_i to s_j provided that Q1 and Q2 are equivalent. Therefore, it follows that if G contains two or more fan-out SPVs with the **same** first or second component then Q1 and Q2 are not equivalent. Note that as a consequence of the above lemma, if two separate ICs induce partial isomorphisms and both the ICs contain distinct SPVs with the **same** first or second component then these SPVs are fan-out free.

Proof of Lemma 2 : Suppose that there is no isomorphism from Q1 to Q2 which maps c1 to c2. Since Q1 and Q2 are equivalent there is an isomorphism which maps c1 to some other conjunct in Q2, say $\bar{c}2$. From Lemma 1 it follows that there exists an IC containing $\langle c1,\bar{c}2\rangle$ which induces a partial isomorphism. Since c2 covers c1 and c1 covers $\bar{c}2$ therefore c2 covers $\bar{c}2$. Thus $\langle \bar{c}2,c2\rangle$ is a CPV in the implication graph of Q2. Consider the IC of $\langle \bar{c}2,c2\rangle$. Since Q2 is an optimized query, it has no shrinking self-homomorphism. Therefore, IC $\{\langle \bar{c}2,c2\rangle\}$ either induces an automorphism on Q2 or it contains $\langle\Theta\rangle$ or it has two distinct CPVs with the same first component. We shall show that if G has ICs which induce partial isomorphisms and contain $\langle c1,c2\rangle$ and $\langle c1,\bar{c}2\rangle$ respectively, then IC$\{\langle \bar{c}2,c2\rangle\}$ in the implication graph of Q2 **cannot** contain $\langle\Theta\rangle$ or have two distinct CPVs with the same first component. Therefore, IC $\{\langle \bar{c}2,c2\rangle\}$ must induce an automorphism on Q2. But composing the isomorphism from Q1 to Q2, which maps c1 to $\bar{c}2$, with this automorphism would give us an isomorphism from Q1 to Q2 which maps c1 to c2, a contradiction.

We now show that IC$\{\langle \bar{c}2,c2\rangle\}$neither contains $\langle\Theta\rangle$ nor does it contain two distinct CPVs with the same first component.

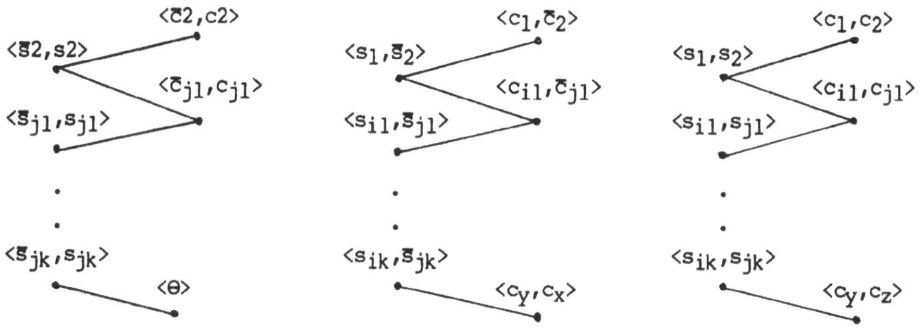

Figure 2(a) **Figure 2(b)** **Figure 2(c)**

Case 1: Assume that IC$\{\langle \bar{c}2,c2\rangle\}$ contains $\langle\Theta\rangle$.
Then there exists an implication path from $\langle \bar{c}2,c2\rangle$ to $\langle\Theta\rangle$ (see Figure 2(a)) such that $\langle \bar{s}2,s2\rangle$ is the SPV implied by $\langle \bar{c}2,c2\rangle$ on this path. Consider the CPVs $\langle c1,\bar{c}2\rangle$ and $\langle c1,c2\rangle$ in G. Note that $\langle c1,\bar{c}2\rangle$ implies a SPV $\langle s1,\bar{s}2\rangle$ (see Figure 2(b)), $s1\neq\bar{s}2$, and $\langle c1,c2\rangle$ implies a SPV $\langle s1,s2\rangle$ (see Figure 2(c)), $s1\neq s2$. Since $\langle \bar{s}2,s2\rangle$ occurs on the implication path from $\langle \bar{c}2,c2\rangle$ to $\langle\Theta\rangle$, therefore $\bar{s}2\neq s2$. Note that any IC containing $\langle c1,\bar{c}2\rangle$ ($\langle c1,c2\rangle$) also contains the SPV $\langle s1,\bar{s}2\rangle$ ($\langle s1,s2\rangle$). Since there exists an IC containing $\langle c1,\bar{c}2\rangle$ ($\langle c1,c2\rangle$) which induces a partial isomorphism therefore $\langle s1,\bar{s}2\rangle$ ($\langle s1,s2\rangle$) cannot be $\langle\Theta\rangle$-adjacent. From Lemma 3 it follows that $\langle s1,\bar{s}2\rangle$ and $\langle s1,s2\rangle$ are fan-out free SPVs. Since the NDV $\bar{s}2$ occurs in the conjunct $\bar{c}_{j1}$ (see Figure 2(a)), $\langle s1,\bar{s}2\rangle$ implies a CPV $\langle c_{i1},\bar{c}_{j1}\rangle$ (see Figure 2(b)). This is so for the following reason. Since $\langle s1,\bar{s}2\rangle$ is not $\langle\Theta\rangle$-adjacent, the

number of conjuncts in which s1 occurs is the same as those in which $\bar{s}2$ occurs. Further each conjunct in which s1 occurs must occur as the first component of some CPV adjacent to <s1,$\bar{s}2$>. If $\bar{c}_{j1}$ does not occur as the second component of any CPV adjacent to <s1,$\bar{s}2$> then atleast two CPVs adjacent to <s1,$\bar{s}2$> have the same second component. Since <s1,$\bar{s}2$> is fan-out free this contradicts the assumption that there exists an IC containing <c1,c2> which induces a partial isomorphism. Similarly we can show that <s1,s2> implies a CPV whose second component is c_{j1}. Let this CPV be <c_x,c_{j1}>. We claim that $c_x=c_{i1}$. To see this consider the case when $c_x \neq c_{i1}$. Since <s1,s2> belongs to an IC which induces a partial isomorphism, it also implies a CPV <c_{i1},c_q>, $c_q \neq c_{j1}$. Since <c_{i1},$\bar{c}_{j1}$> and <c_{i1},c_q> are CPVs in **G**, c_q covers $\bar{c}_{j1}$. Hence the SPV <$\bar{s}2$,s2>, in the implication graph of Q2, has CPVs <$\bar{c}_{j1}$,c_q> and <$\bar{c}_{j1}$,c_{j1}> adjacent to it. This contradicts the fact that Q2 is a fan-out free query. We have shown that corresponding to the CPV <$\bar{c}_{j1}$,c_{j1}> in the implication graph of Q2, every IC in **G** which contains the CPV <c1,$\bar{c}2$> (<c1,c2>) must also contain the CPV <c_{i1},$\bar{c}_{j1}$> (<c_{i1},c_{j1}>). As shown in Figures 2(b) and 2(c), <c_{i1},$\bar{c}_{j1}$> implies the SPV <s_{i1},$\bar{s}_{j1}$> and <c_{i1},c_{j1}> implies the SPV <s_{i1},s_{j1}>.

By repeatedly applying the above arguments we can show that there exist implication paths, devoid of any fan-out SPVs, from <c1,$\bar{c}2$> to the SPV <s_{ik},$\bar{s}_{jk}$> (see Figure 2(b)) and from <c1,c2> to the SPV <s_{ik},s_{jk}> (see Figure 2(c)). Thus any IC containing <c1,$\bar{c}2$> (<c1,c2>) must contain <s_{ik},$\bar{s}_{jk}$> (<s_{ik},s_{jk}>). Since <s_{ik},$\bar{s}_{jk}$> (<s_{ik},s_{jk}>) is a fan-out free SPV belonging to an IC which induces a partial isomorphism, each conjunct in Q1, having an occurence of s_{ik}, appears as the first component of exactly one CPV adjacent to <s_{ik},$\bar{s}_{jk}$> (<s_{ik},s_{jk}>). Similarly each conjunct in Q2 having an occurence of $\bar{s}_{jk}$ (s_{jk}) appears as the second component of exactly one CPV adjacent to <s_{ik},$\bar{s}_{jk}$> (<s_{ik},s_{jk}>). Let c_x be any conjunct in Q2 in which the NDV $\bar{s}_{jk}$ occurs. Then a CPV <c_y,c_x> is adjacent to <s_{ik},$\bar{s}_{jk}$>, $c_y \in C_{Q1}$. There is also a CPV <c_y,c_z> adjacent to <s_{ik},s_{jk}>, $c_z \in C_{Q2}$. Therefore the implication graph of Q2 contains the CPV <c_x,c_z> adjacent to <$\bar{s}_{jk}$,s_{jk}>. Thus <$\bar{s}_{jk}$,s_{jk}> cannot be <Θ>-adjacent, a contradiction.

Case 2: Assume that IC{<$\bar{c}2$,c2>} contains two CPVs with the same first component. The proof is similar to that of Case 1. ∎

To find an isomorphism from Q1 to Q2 we first construct the graph G. If G has a <Θ>-adjacent fan-out SPV or it has more than one non <Θ>-adjacent fan-out SPVs with the same first or second component then it follows from Lemma 3 that Q1 and Q2 are not equivalent. If the above tests fail, we search **G** looking for an an IC, say I_1, which induces a partial isomorphism. If the partial isomorphism induced by I_1 is also an isomorphism from Q1 to Q2 then we are done. Otherwise, if Q1 and Q2 are equivalent, it follows from Lemmas 1 and 2 that G has distinct ICs $I_1,\ldots,I_k$, $2 \leq k \leq$ number of conjuncts in Q1, each one of them inducing a partial isomorphism such that the union of these partial isomorphisms is the desired isomorphism from Q1 to Q2. We use the following method to find the ICs $I_2,\ldots,I_k$. Having found the IC I_i, $1 \leq i \leq k-1$, we delete from G all CPVs <c_i,c_j> such that either <c_i,c_j> is in I_i or there is a CPV in I_i whose first (second) component is c_i (c_j). After the above

CPV deletion is over, we search G for I_{i+1}. The above process is repeated until the ICs $I_2, \ldots, I_k$ are found. We now establish the correctness of this method.

Consider the case when Q1 and Q2 are equivalent. Let I_1 be the IC discovered in the first iteration of the above procedure. Then Lemma 2 assures us that there is an isomorphism from Q1 to Q2 which maps c_i to $\bar{c}_i$ for each CPV $\langle c_i, \bar{c}_i \rangle$ in I_1. The deletion of CPVs ensures that for each CPV $\langle c_i, \bar{c}_i \rangle$ in I_1, no IC discovered in any future iteration will map c_i to $\bar{c}_j$, $\bar{c}_j \neq \bar{c}_i$, or map some c_j to $\bar{c}_i$, $c_j \neq c_i$. Further, since the union of the partial isomorphisms induced by $I_1, I_2, \ldots, I_k$ is an isomorphism from Q1 to Q2, the CPV deletion after the discovery of I_1 will not delete any CPV from $I_2, \ldots, I_k$. However, the CPV deletion process may not delete an IC completely and may cause it to split into several fragments. Formation of such fragments is problematic since a fragment may exhibit the characterstics of a partial isomorphism inducing IC and thus may be mistaken for some I_i, $2 \leq i \leq k$. This would compromise the correctness of our method since the fragment was not present, as an IC, in G to begin with. We now show that the CPV deletion process does not create any fragments.

Lemma 4 : If the CPV deletion process deletes a CPV of some IC then it deletes all the CPVs of that IC.

Proof : Consider the CPV deletion which occurs after the discovery of I_i, an IC which induces a partial isomorphism. Clearly the CPV deletion deletes all the CPVs of I_i. Let I1 be some other IC and let <c1,c2> be a CPV of I1 which gets deleted. Note that due to the presence of fan-out SPVs it is possible that that I_i and I1 share some CPVs. Clearly all such common CPVs are deleted. Let <s1,s2> be a SPV in I1, adjacent to <c1,c2>, such that <s1,s2> implies at least one other CPV besides <c1,c2>.

Case 1 : $\langle c1, c3 \rangle \in I_i$, $c3 \neq c2$.
Note that <c1,c3> has a SPV <s1,s3> adjacent to it. Since Q1 and Q2 have distinct NDVs, $s1 \neq s3$. Since I_i induces a partial isomorphism, <s1,s3> is not $\langle \theta \rangle$-adjacent. Therefore, each conjunct $c_x \in C_{Q1}$, in which s1 occurs, occurs as the first component of some CPV in I_i. Hence for each CPV $\langle c_x, c_y \rangle$ in I1, adjacent to <s1,s2>, there exists a CPV $\langle c_x, c_z \rangle$ in I_i. Therefore all such CPVs in I1 are deleted. By inductively applying the same argument at $\langle c_x, c_y \rangle$ and $\langle c_x, c_z \rangle$, the proof follows.

Case 2 : $\langle c3, c2 \rangle \in I_i$, $c3 \neq c1$.
The proof is similar to that of Case 1. ∎

As a consequence of the above lemma, all partial isomorphism inducing ICs discovered by our method were present in **G** at the beginning, i.e, before any CPV deletion occured. Let I_2' be the IC discovered in the second iteration. Since I_2' also induces a partial isomorphism, it follows from Lemma 2 that there is an isomorphism from Q1 to Q2 which maps c_j to $\bar{c}_j$ for each CPV $\langle c_j, \bar{c}_j \rangle$ in I_2'. To show that I_2' is the same as I_2, the following lemmas are needed.

Lemma 5 : Let the queries Q1 and Q2 be equivalent. Let there be isomorphisms from Q1 to Q2 which map conjuncts c1 to $\bar{c}1$, c1 to $\bar{c}2$ and c2 to $\bar{c}1$ respectively where $c1 \neq c2$ and $\bar{c}1 \neq \bar{c}2$. Then there exists an isomorphism from Q1 to Q2 which maps c2 to $\bar{c}2$.

Proof : Lemma 1 tells us that there exists an IC containing $\langle c1,\bar{c}1\rangle$ ($\langle c1,\bar{c}2\rangle$) which induces a partial isomorphism. By arguments of Lemma 2 we can show that IC $\{\langle\bar{c}1,\bar{c}2\rangle\}$, in G[Q2], induces an automorphism on Q2. The composition of the isomorphism from Q1 to Q2, which maps c2 to $\bar{c}1$, with this automorphism gives us an isomorphism from Q1 to Q2 which maps c2 to $\bar{c}2$. ∎

Lemma 6 : (i) Let I1 be an IC containing the CPV $\langle c1,\bar{c}1\rangle$ and let I2 be an IC containing the CPV $\langle c1,\bar{c}2\rangle$, $\bar{c}2 \neq \bar{c}1$. Let I1 and I2 induce partial isomorphisms. Then a conjunct appears as the first component of some CPV in I1 iff it appears as the first component of some CPV in I2.

(ii) Let I1 be an IC containing the CPV $\langle c1,\bar{c}1\rangle$ and let I2 be an IC containing the CPV $\langle c2,\bar{c}1\rangle$, $c1 \neq c2$. Let I1 and I2 induce partial isomorphisms. Then a conjunct appears as the second component of some CPV in I1 iff it appears as the second component of of some CPV in I2.

Proof : (i) The assertion holds for conjunct c1. Let $\langle s1,\bar{s}1\rangle$ be any SPV implied by $\langle c1,\bar{c}1\rangle$. Then $\langle c1,\bar{c}2\rangle$ implies a SPV $\langle s1,\bar{s}2\rangle$. Clearly $\langle s1,\bar{s}1\rangle$ and $\langle s1,\bar{s}2\rangle$ are not $\langle\Theta\rangle$ adjacent. Therefore, each conjunct in Q1, in which s1 occurs, occurs as the first component of some CPV adjacent to $\langle s1,\bar{s}1\rangle$ and $\langle s1,\bar{s}2\rangle$. Thus the assertion holds for each CPV in I1 (I2) adjacent to $\langle s1,\bar{s}1\rangle$ ($\langle s1,\bar{s}2\rangle$). The proof follows from simple induction.

(ii) The assertion holds for the conjunct $\bar{c}1$. Let $\langle s1,\bar{s}1\rangle$ be any SPV implied by $\langle c1,\bar{c}1\rangle$. Then $\langle c2,\bar{c}1\rangle$ implies a SPV $\langle s2,\bar{s}1\rangle$. Note that if s1=s2 then $\langle s1,\bar{s}1\rangle$ is a fan-out SPV. We now show that the assertion holds for each conjunct appearing as the second component of some CPV in I1 (I2) adjacent to $\langle s1,\bar{s}1\rangle$ ($\langle s2,\bar{s}1\rangle$). The proof follows from simple induction. Since $\langle s1,\bar{s}1\rangle$ ($\langle s2,\bar{s}1\rangle$) is not $\langle\Theta\rangle$-adjacent, the number of conjuncts in Q1, in which s1 (s2) occurs, equals the number of conjuncts in Q2, in which $\bar{s}1$ occurs. Note that for each conjunct in which s1 (s2) occurs $\langle s1,\bar{s}1\rangle$ ($\langle s2,\bar{s}1\rangle$) always implies a CPV whose first component is this conjunct. Since no two CPVs in I1 (I2) can have the same second component, for each conjunct in Q2, in which $\bar{s}1$ occurs, there is a CPV in I1 (I2) adjacent to $\langle s1,\bar{s}1\rangle$ ($\langle s2,\bar{s}1\rangle$) whose second component is this conjunct. ∎

Suppose that $I_2' \neq I_2$. Then there exist CPVs $\langle c1,\bar{c}1\rangle$ and $\langle c2,\bar{c}2\rangle$ in I_1 and I_2' respectively such that no isomorphism from Q1 to Q2 maps c1 to $\bar{c}1$ and c2 to $\bar{c}2$ but **separate** isomorphisms mapping c1 to $\bar{c}1$ and c2 to $\bar{c}2$ respectively do exist. The isomorphism, say h_i, that maps c1 to $\bar{c}1$ must map c2 to c3, $c3 \neq \bar{c}2$, and some other conjunct c3 to $\bar{c}2$, $c3 \neq c2$. From Lemma 1 it follows that there exist ICs I_a and I_b, containing $\langle c2,\bar{c}3\rangle$ and $\langle c3,\bar{c}2\rangle$ respectively, which induce partial isomorphisms. Since I_2' contains $\langle c2,\bar{c}2\rangle$ and it induces a partial isomorphism, from Lemma 5 we have that there exist an IC, say I_c, containing <c3,$\bar{c}$3> which induces a partial isomorphism. From Lemma 6 it follows that a conjunct appears as the first (second) component of some CPV in I_c iff it appears as first (second) component of some CPV in I_b (I_a). Similarly a conjunct appears as the first (second) component of some CPV in I_2' iff it appears as the first (second) component of some CPV in I_a (I_b). Therefore by deleting the conjunct and symbol mappings, corresponding to the CPVs and SPVs in I_b and I_c, from h_i and adding to it the conjunct and symbol mappings corresponding to the CPVs and SPVs in I_2' and I_c, we obtain another isomorphism from Q1 to Q2 which maps c1 to $\bar{c}$1 and c2 to $\bar{c}$2, a contradiction.

A simple induction on the number of iteration establishes that if an isomorphism exists then our method will find it. If our method finds an isomorphism then the two queries are clearly equivalent. Thus, Q1 and Q2 are equivalent iff the union of the partial isomorphisms discovered by this method is an isomorphism from Q1 to Q2.

However, as mentioned earlier, because of the presence of fan-out SPVs searching for ICs inducing partial isomorphisms may be prohibitively expensive. We now consider the problem of efficiently searching for such ICs in the presence of fan-out SPVs. Let the **restricted** IC of a CPV be its IC computed under the assumption that a fan-out SPV, not adjacent to <Θ>, implies nothing. In the absence of fan-out SPVs, the restricted IC of a CPV is the same as its IC. Using the notion of restricted ICs we can prune (reduce the number of choices at fan-out SPVs) G as follows. We delete all the CPVs belonging to restricted ICs which contain <Θ> or which have two CPVs with the same first or second component as such restricted ICs can never be a part of any IC inducing a partial isomorphism. Note that as a consequence of Lemma 3, if <s_i,s_j> is a fan-out SPV in G then every isomorphism from Q1 to Q2 must map s_i to s_j, provided that Q1 and Q2 are equivalent. Therefore, if <s_i,s_j> is a fan-out SPV then we delete all CPVs belonging to restricted ICs which either contain a SPV <s_i,x>, $x \neq s_j$, or a SPV <y,s_j>, $y \neq s_i$. Note that the pruning process does not delete any SPVs. However, if all the CPVs adjacent to a SPV are deleted then that SPV cannot affect the process of finding an isomorphism and can therefore be treated as deleted.

Let **GP** be the subgraph of G obtained by the above pruning process. We now show that making the right choices at a fan-out SPV in **GP** is very simple.

Lemma 7 : Let <s_i,s_j> be a non <Θ>-adjacent fan-out SPV in GP. Let <c1,c2> and <c1,$\bar{c}$2> be two CPVs adjacent to it. Then there exists an isomorphism from Q1 to Q2 mapping c1 to c2 iff there exists an isomorphism mapping c1 to $\bar{c}$2.

Proof : The proof is similar to that of Lemma 2 and we shall only sketch it. Note that since <c1,c2> (<c1,$\bar{c}$2>) was **not** deleted by the pruning process therefore the restricted IC of <c1,c2> (<c1,$\bar{c}$2>) does not contain <Θ> and no two CPVs in it have the same first or second component.

If : We show that IC {<$\bar{c}$2,c2>} in the implication graph of Q2 induces an automorphism on Q2. Suppose that IC {<$\bar{c}$2,c2>} contains <Θ> (see Figure 2(a)). Then <c1,$\bar{c}$2> implies a SPV <s1,$\bar{s}$2> (see Figure 2(b)) and <c1,c2> implies a SPV <s1,s2> (see Figure 2(c)). Since <$\bar{s}$2,s2> lies on the implication path from <$\bar{c}$2,c2> to <Θ> therefore $\bar{s}2 \neq s2$. Note that all vertices in the restricted IC of a CPV are contained in any IC containing that CPV. Since there exists an IC containing <c1,$\bar{c}$2> which induces a partial isomorphism, it follows from Lemma 3 that <s1,s2> is a fan-out free SPV. If <s1,$\bar{s}$2> is a fan-out SPV then since <s1,s2> is not <Θ>-adjacent we can show that either <s1,s2> implies two distinct CPVs with the **same** second component or the SPV <s2,$\bar{s}$2>, in G[Q2], is a fan-out SPV (see the proof of Lemma 3 for details). But this is impossible since <c1,c2> survived the pruning process and Q2 is a fan-out free query. Thus <s1,s2> and <s1,$\bar{s}$2> are fan-out free SPVs. Now by using the arguments of Case 1 of Lemma 2 we can show that IC {<$\bar{c}$2,c2>}, in G[Q2], cannot contain <Θ>. Similarly we can rule out the case when IC {<$\bar{c}$2,c2>} contains two CPVs with the same first component.

The "Only If" part can be proved similarly. ▮

Thus if Q1 and Q2 are indeed equivalent and <s1,s2> is a non <Θ>-adjacent fan-out SPV in G^P, then from Lemma 3 it follows that each isomorphism from Q1 to Q2 must map s1 to s2. Then from Lemma 7 it follows that for each CPV <c_i,c_j> adjacent to <s1,s2> there exists an isomorphism mapping c_i to c_j. Therefore each choice in the neighbourhood of <s1,s2> is a "correct" choice. It only remains to pick up these choices in a consistent fashion. This is done by the following simple strategy. Pick up a CPV <c_i,c_j> adjacent to <s1,s2> and compute its restricted IC. For each CPV <c_x,c_y> in this restricted IC delete all CPVs in G^P whose first (second) component is c_x (c_y). This process is repeated until all CPVs adjacent to <s1,s2> are deleted. If some other fan-out SPV is encountered while constructing the restricted IC of a CPV adjacent to <s1,s2>, the above process is repeated at that fan-out SPV after all CPVs adjacent to <s1,s2> have been deleted. Note that this process of finding whether there exists a partial isomorphism mapping s1 to s2, where <s1,s2> is a fan-out SPV in G^P, is similar to the process of finding whether there exists an isomorphism from Q1 to Q2. The correctness of the above process can also be established in a similar fashion. It can be shown that the CPV deletion, which occurs after the discovery of a restricted IC in G^P, either deletes all the CPVs of a restricted IC or leaves it unaltered (the details are similar to the proof of Lemma 4). By arguments similar to those used in Lemma 5 we can show that if CPVs <c1,$\bar{c}$1> , <c1,$\bar{c}$2> and <c2,$\bar{c}$1> are adjacent to a fan-out SPV <s1,s2> in G^P, then <s1,s2> also has <c2,$\bar{c}$2> adjacent to it. Note that Lemma 6 remains valid even if I1 and I2 are chosen to be the **restricted** ICs of the respective CPVs. Now by arguments similar to those used for justifying the process of finding an isomorphism from Q1 to Q2, we can show that the process of finding a partial isomorphism which maps s1 to s2, <s1,s2> being a fan-out SPV in G^P, is correct.

Based on the preceding lemmas and arguments, the algorithm for testing equivalence of fan-out free queries can be expressed as the following :

Algorithm Fan-Out_Free_Query_Equivalence

1. Optimize Q1 and Q2.
2. Construct G.
3. **if** G contains either a <Θ>-adjacent fan-out SPV or more than one fan-out SPV with the same first or second component
   then report failure ;
4. Prune G to obtain GP.
5. $h_c \leftarrow$ null;
6. **while** $\exists$ a restricted IC I in GP **do**
   begin
   $h_c \leftarrow h_c \bigcup \{<c_i,c_j> : <c_i,c_j> \in I\}$;
   for each CPV $<c_i,c_j>$ in I, delete from GP all CPVs whose first (second) component is c_i (c_j);
   end;
7. **if** h_c is an isomorphic conjunct mapping from Q1 to Q2
   then report success
   else report failure;

Theorem 1 : The above algorithm correctly tests for equivalence of two fan-out free queries in $O(n^2)$ time.

Proof : The correctness of the above algorithm essentially follows from the lemmas and arguments presented in this section. However, step 6 requires some explanation. Note that if the IC of a CPV, say <c1,c2>, does not contain any fan-out SPV, then IC <c1,c2> and the restricted IC of <c1,c2> are the same. Thus, in this case step 6 finds an IC I inducing a partial isomorphism. If an IC, say I_1, contains fan-out SPVs, then I_1 can be expressed as the union of the restricted ICs of those CPVs in I_1 which are adjacent to some fan-out SPV. In this case step 6 may not discover the restricted ICs of I_1 in consecutive iterations. Let step 6 discover two restricted ICs of I_1 in iterations i and j respectively, $j > i+1$, such that no iteration k, $i<k<j$, discovers a restricted IC of I_1. Then the following problems may occur. Since the CPV deletion in the ith iteration is **not** due to a complete IC, fragment formation may occur. Thus there is a possibility of a fragment being chosen as I in k^{th} iteration, $i<k<j$. Further, the CPV deletion in some k^{th} iteration, $i<k<j$, may delete some restricted ICs of I_1. Hence, step 6 may fail to compute I_1. We now show that these problems do not occur.

Let <s1,s2> be a fan-out SPV in I_1. Recall that no other SPV in GP has s1 (s2) as its first (second) component. Thus a CPV adjacent to <s1,s2> can only be deleted due to the restricted IC of some CPV adjacent to <s1,s2>. Since the deletion of a CPV in a restricted IC leads to the deletion of the entire restricted IC, it follows that the restricted IC of a CPV adjacent to <s1,s2> can only be deleted due the restricted IC of some CPV adjacent to <s1,s2>. Let <c1,c2> be a CPV adjacent <s1,s2> and let $<c_i,c_j>$ be a CPV in the restricted IC of <c1,c2>. Then any restricted IC which has a CPV whose first (second) component is c_i (c_j) also has a CPV whose first (second) component is c1 (c2). This CPV must be adjacent to <s1,s2>. Thus deletions due to the restricted IC of a CPV adjacent to <s1,s2> only delete restricted ICs of CPVs which are also adjacent to <s1,s2>.

The time bound of $O(n^2)$ follows from the following observations. Step 1 can be implemented in $O(n^2)$ time by using the optimization algorithm in [DM]. G can be constructed in $O(n^2)$ time [JK]. Step 3 takes time proportional to the number of SPVs in G, i.e., $O(n^2)$. The pruning process in step 4 can be carried out in $O(n^2)$ time since a restricted IC can be constructed and its candidature for deletion determined in time proportional to the size of the restricted IC [JK]. Similarly, step 6 can be implemented in $O(n^2)$ time by maintaining linked lists of CPVs which have the same first (second) component. Step 7 can be easily carried out in O(n) time. ∎

References

[AHU] A.V.Aho,J.E.Hopcroft and J.D. Ullman, The Design and Analysis of Computer Algorithms, Addison-Wesley.

[ASU] A.V.Aho,Y.Sagiv and J.D.Ullman, Equivalences Among Relational Expressions, SIAM Journal on Computing, Vol 8, No 2, May 1979.

[CH] A.K.Chandra and D.Harel,Horn Clause Programs and Generalizations, Journal of Logic Programming, Vol 2, 1985.

[CM] A.K.Chandra and P.M.Merlin, Optimal Implementation of Conjunctive Queries in Relational Databases, Proc. of 9th ACM-STOC, May 1977.

[DM] P.Dublish and S.N.Maheshwari, An $O(n^2)$ Algorithm for Fan-out Free Query Optimization, Proc. of FST&TCS 7, Lecture Notes in Computer Science, Vol 287, Springer-Verlag.

[JK] D.S.Johnson and A.Klug,Optimizing Conjunctive Queries that contain Untyped Variables, SIAM Journal on Computing, Vol. 12, No. 4, Nov 1983.

[MDM] B.N.S.Murthy, P.Dublish and S.N.Maheshwari, Some Negative Results on the Optimization of Conjunctive Queries,Technical Report TR 85/01, Deptt. of Computer Science and Engg., IIT Delhi, Dec 1985.

[Mai] D.Maier, The Theory of Relational Database, Computer Science Press, 1983.

[Sag] Y.Sagiv, Quadratic Algorithms for Minimizing Joins in Restricted Relational Expressions, SIAM Journal on Computing, Vol. 12, No. 2, May 1983.

[SY] Y.Sagiv and M.Yannakakis, Equivalences Among Relational Expressions with Union and Difference Operators, Journal of ACM, Vol 27, No. 4, Oct 1980.

[Ull] J.D.Ullman, Principles of Database Systems, Computer Science Press, 1982.

TWO-WAY JOIN OPTIMIZATION IN PARTITIONED DATABASE SYSTEMS

Fang Li and Lawrence V. Saxton

Department of Computer Science, University of Regina
Regina, Saskatchewan, Canada S4S 0A2
e-mail: SAXTON@UREGINA1.BITNET

ABSTRACT

The optimization of two-way joins is studied in order to minimize the response time in a partitioned database. We assume that the background communication network is capable of parallel transmission, which differentiates the response time measure from the total cost measure. However, we do not make the standard simplifying assumption that communications between different sites is uniform, which results in a nonlinear optimization formulation of the problem. Subsequently, we derive a fast polynomial algorithm to solve the problem. Two less general algorithms are also proposed to explore the effect of local semijoins and remote semijoins as reducers. Finally, computational experiments are carried out to investigate the trade-off between the computation time and the quality of solutions as well as to analyze the sensitivity of the solutions to various parameters of our model.

1. Introduction

One of the important problems in distributed database systems is the optimization of query processing. The objective is to minimize the total cost or the response time in processing queries. Many models based on a variety of assumptions have been developed to characterize and solve this problem. Because of the diversity of distributed processing environments, no model seems to be generally applicable. From the point of view of distribution transparency, the processing environments can be classified into two broad categories, namely, non-fragmented database systems and fragmented database systems. The query optimization for non-fragmented database systems has been extensively studied in [1, 2, 5, 8, 9].

The optimization of query processing in fragmented database systems has received more and more attention recently. However, most of the research is still limited to the simple case where the fragmentation is restricted to partitioning, [3, 7, 17]. In a partitioned database, each relation is horizontally decomposed into non-empty and disjoint subsets, called "fragments", which may be located at different sites in a network. The partitioning of the relation is predetermined by some data allocation strategies. In *SDD*–1, [2], the partitioning is used in the query processing as well.

Most of the models proposed for partitioned databases deal with static optimization of single queries. Sequential data transmission is considered and the site uniform assumption is made. In some earlier models such as System R^*, [15], each fragment was treated as a single relation. This is inefficient in a partitioned environment. A rigorous treatment of partitioning was given by Pelagatti and Manning, [11]. A drawback in this approach is that the resulting mathematical formulation applies only to the case where fragments of one relation have to be assembled at a site. Yu and Chang, [17], proposed an algorithm for partitioned databases based on the premise that there is no benefit in reducing a fragment of a relation by a fragment of another relation. Similarly, Epstein at al., [6], have given an heuristic algorithm used in *INGRES* for both total cost and response time measures based on the same premise. This premise however has been shown to be generally false in the analysis of Segev, [12]. Based on the concept of logical assembly, Segev proposed a more general model in the sense that it overcomes the drawbacks of the above two models. Segev's objective was the minimization of the total cost.

In this paper, the join optimization is considered in a partitioned environment. As in other models, we deal with the static optimization of single queries, but our objective is to minimize the response time. In most networks today, it is reasonable to assume that if data is sent to one node on the network, then all nodes can gain access to the data; as well, two different sites can send data simultaneously to different receiving sites. Thus, most networks allow parallel transmission and the response time measure is more relevant than the total cost measure. The significance of parallel transmission distinguishes this problem from other problems treated. We also discard the site uniform assumption to take into account the changing features of message traffic in the optimization. Based on a set of simplifying assumptions, we develop a mathematical formulation to describe the problem. A polynomial algorithm based on the model is then established to find the minimum response time. Two simplifying algorithms as alternatives are also proposed to study the impact of semijoin strategies on the optimization. Computational experiments have been carried out to evaluate the performance of the algorithms as well as to investigate the trade-off between the computing time and the quality of the solutions. The sensitivity of the solutions to various parameters of the model is also analyzed.

The rest of the paper is organized as follows. Some important definitions, notations and basic assumptions are presented in Section 2. A mathematical model for two-way join optimization and the corresponding algorithm are presented in Section 3. In Section 4, a numerical example as well as the alternative algorithms are given. The computational analysis of the algorithms is presented in Section 5. Finally, we give concluding remarks in Section 6.

2. Definitions and Notations

The total cost and response time are the two commonly used objective functions in query processing. The former is defined as the sum of all the costs used in processing queries while the latter is the time elapsed, [8]. It should be pointed out that the response time is highly sensitive to parallelism, whereas the total cost is not affected by parallelism and the solution can be simply described in terms of sequential processing and transmission.

The two-way join optimization is defined as the problem of processing a class of queries called two-way joins such that the response time is minimized. A two-way join is defined as a relational query which involves the join of two partitioned relations.

In this paper, a distributed database system consists of a relational partitioned database distributed among M sites, together with a collection of M autonomous processors communicating with each other via a remote point-to-point network where parallel transmission is allowed. Each processor, known as a site in the network, is capable of data processing and storage.

The following assumptions are also made in the problem.

a). There is no duplication of relations and/or fragments. Under this assumption, the choice of the best materialization for a query is beyond our discussion.

b). All the fragments are distributed at different sites. If several fragments are allocated to the same site, the site can be split into several sites such that each site has only one fragment and the network parameters can be set to zero among these sites.

c). The sets of tuples resulting from distinct semijoins on fragment r_i are disjoint. This assumption is not essential to the model, but it simplifies the exposition of the problem.

d). The transmission delay is dominant. This is true in most remote networks. Under this assumption, the processing time of computers is ignored, and the solution of the problem becomes a transmission arrangement with minimum response time.

e). Several sites on the network may simultaneously send data to other sites without conflict. Although this assumption restricts the model slightly, the transmission delay can be adjusted to take account of any conflicts.

It should be noted that we do not make the site uniform assumption which restricts the transmission delay between any two sites in the network to be the same, [9]. Without this assumption, the changing features of message traffic such as queuing delays can be considered in the optimization.

In join query processing, a semijoin is known as a powerful reducer, [10]. A semijoin on relation r with relation s, written as $r \ltimes s$, is a project followed by a join; that is, the join result of r and s is projected on the scheme of r. An important property of semijoin is that the join of r and s is equal to the join of $r \ltimes s$ and s. Since the size of $r \ltimes s$ is usually smaller than the size of r, by transmitting $r \ltimes s$ instead of r to the query site to perform the join of r and s, the amount of transmission may be reduced.

There are three possible semijoin approaches in partitioned databases: the relation to relation semijoin; the fragment to relation semijoin; and the fragment to fragment semijoin, [18]. According to the analysis of Segev in [12], the fragment to fragment semijoin is the most beneficial approach. Thus the following studies of optimality are based on this hypothesis.

There exist two strategies to do a semijoin: *local semijoin* and *remote semijoin*. For a semijoin $r \ltimes s$, Under remote semijoin means that the join attributes of r and s are sent to a selected site to do a semijoin and the result is sent back to the location of r to perform the semijoin on r. In contrast using local semijoin means that the join attributes of s are directly sent to the location of r to do the semijoin on r (see [12] for details).

Let the two relations in a two-way join be r and s. The following notation will be used in this paper.

$S1$, $S2$ = The sets of site numbers among which relations r and s are respectively fragmented.

$T = S1 \cup S2$.

$$\Gamma_i = \begin{cases} S2, & \text{if } i \in S1; \\ S1, & \text{if } i \in S2. \end{cases}$$

(We use this notation to conveniently refer to the following: "if i is a fragment of one relation, then Γ_i is the set of fragments of the other relation.")

C_{ij} = The transmission delay rate between site i and site j.

(The delay function is $DT(X) = C_{ij}X$ for the transmission X from site i to site j)

q = The query site.

r_i = The fragment of relation r, stored at site i.

F_i = Size of the fragment stored at site i.

D_i = Size of the projection of fragment i on the join attributes.

$\alpha_{ij} = \dfrac{\text{size of } r_i \ltimes s_j}{\text{size of } r_i}$, which is called the selectivity factor for $r_i \ltimes s_j$.

3. Mathematical Model and Optimization Algorithm for Two-way Join

A mathematical programming formulation for the two-way join optimization is given as problem RT_J. The decision variables used in the formulation are defined as follows:

$$X_i = \begin{cases} 1 & \text{if fragment } i \text{ is reduced by a semijoin,} \\ 0 & \text{otherwise;} \end{cases}$$

$$Y_{ijk} = \begin{cases} 1 & \text{if the remote semijoin } r_i \ltimes s_j \text{ is performed at site } k, \\ 0 & \text{otherwise;} \end{cases}$$

$$W_{ijk} = \begin{cases} 1 & \text{if the join attributes of fragment } r_i \text{ is transmitted from site } j \text{ to site } k, \\ 0 & \text{otherwise;} \end{cases}$$

$$Z_{ijk} = \begin{cases} 1 & \text{if the reduced join attributes at site } i \text{ is transmitted from site } j \text{ to site } k, \\ 0 & \text{otherwise;} \end{cases}$$

Problem RT_J:

$$Min\{ \underset{i \in T}{Max} \{rt(i)\}\} \tag{1}$$

$$rt(i) = F_i C_{iq}(1 - (1 - \sum_{j \in \Gamma_i} \alpha_{ij})\, X_i) + \underset{j \in \Gamma_i}{Max}\{smct(i\ j)\} \tag{2}$$

$$smct(i, j) = \sum_{p \in T} [\ \underset{l = i, j}{Max}\{ \sum_{k \in T} \sum_{n \in T} D_l C_{kn} W_{lkn} \} + D_i \alpha_{ij} Y_{ijp} (\sum_{l \in T} \sum_{n \in T} C_{ln} Z_{pln})] \tag{3}$$

Subject to

$$X_i \le \sum_{k \in T} Y_{ijk} + \sum_{\substack{k \in T \\ k \ne i}} W_{jki} \qquad i \in T,\ j \in \Gamma_i \tag{4}$$

$$Y_{ijk} \le \sum_{t \in T} Z_{kti} \qquad i \in T,\ j \in \Gamma_i,\ k \in T,\ k \ne i \tag{5}$$

$$Y_{ijk} \le \sum_{\substack{t \in T \\ t \ne k}} W_{itk} \qquad i \in T,\ j \in \Gamma_i,\ k \in T,\ k \ne i \tag{6}$$

$$Y_{ijk} \le \sum_{\substack{t \in T \\ t \ne k}} W_{jtk} \qquad i, k, t \in T,\ k \ne t,\ k \ne i,\ i \ne t \tag{7}$$

$$W_{itk} \leq \sum_{\substack{j\in T\\ j\neq t}} W_{ijt} \qquad i, k, t\in T,\ k \neq t,\ k \neq i,\ i \neq t \tag{8}$$

$$Z_{itk} \leq \sum_{\substack{j\in T\\ j\neq t}} Z_{ijt} \qquad i, k, t\in T,\ k \neq t,\ k \neq i,\ i \neq t \tag{9}$$

$$X_i,\ Y_{ijk},\ W_{ijk},\ Z_{ijk} \in \{0, 1\} \qquad i, j, k \in T. \tag{10}$$

In problem RT_J, the first maximum gives the response time for a two-way join query since the reduction and transmission of all the fragments in a query to the query site are done simultaneously. The part $F_iC_{iq}\ (1 -(1 - \sum_{j\in\Gamma_i} \alpha_{ij})X_i)$ in (2) is the transmission delay of fragment r_i. That is, the delay of fragment r_i is F_iC_{iq} if it is not reduced by semijoins, and $F_iC_{iq}\sum_{j\in\Gamma_i}\alpha_{ij}$ if it is reduced. The selectivity factors are added because all fragments F_j, $j \in \Gamma_i$ belong to the same relation and the assumption that the results of distinct semijoins on a fragment are disjoint. The second maximum in problem RT_J gives the delay of the semijoin reduction on fragment r_i. The part $Max_{l=i,j}\{\sum_{k\in T}\sum_{n\in T} D_lC_{kn}W_{lkn}\}$ in $smct(i, j)$ accounts for the delay of transmitting join attributes to the selected site of a remote semijoin and the maximum is due to the possible parallel transmissions. The second part accounts for the delay of transmitting reduced join attributes back to their original sites. Thus formula $smct(i, j)$ contributes the delay of a fragment to fragment semijoin.

Constraint (4) means that if a fragment is to be semijoined, it has to be semijoined by every fragment of the other relation. This is the constraint for recovering the join result from fragment to fragment semijoins, [3]. Constraint (5) states that the result of the remote semijoin must be sent back. Constraints (6) and (7) say that in order for a semijoin to take place at a site, both of the join attribute must be available at that site. Constraints (8) and (9) ensure that a join attribute can be transmitted from site t to site k only if it is available at site t.

Since all the parallel transmission arrangements can be developed independently without increasing the elapsed time, the following two equations hold.

$$Min\{\underset{i\in T}{Max}\{rt(i)\}\} = \underset{i\in T}{Max}\{Min\{rt(i)\}\} \tag{11}$$

$$Min\{\underset{j\in \Gamma_i}{Max}\{smct(i, j)\}\} = \underset{j\in \Gamma_i}{Max}\{Min\{smct(i, j)\}\} \tag{12}$$

The above two equations allow us to break down the problem RT_J into some local optimizations and their proper integration. Consequently, we are able to solve the problem in polynomial time. It should be noted at this point that these equations do not hold for a join involving three relations, and hence these results do not generalize.

We first develop an algorithm, *MINDELAY*, to find the minimum delay for a fragment to fragment semijoin; that is, $Min\{smct(i, j)\}$. In this algorithm, the point-to-point network is considered as a digraph $G = (V, E)$, where V consists of all the sites associated with a query and each $e \in E$ represents the communication link between sites with the delay rate as its weight. The problem is thus related with a graph-theoretic problem. The key point is that every feasible solution to $Min\{smct(i, j)\}$ is based on the composition of the shortest paths from sites i and j to another site k in G and the shortest path from site k to site i. The site k will be the selected site of the semijoin. Since all pair shortest paths can be found in $O(|V|^3)$ time, [14], an enumerative method is used to find the solution of semijoin $r_i \ltimes s_j$ with minimum delay in polynomial time.

The inputs to algorithm *MINDELAY* are the locations of fragments r_i and s_j, selectivity α_{ij} of semijoin $r_i \ltimes s_j$, the size of r_i and s_j, and a $T \times T$ weight matrix M obtained from Floyd's algorithm, [14] for the shortest distance between all pairs of sites. It should be noted that the input to Floyd's algorithm is the matrix of transmission delay rates, $C = \{ C_{ij} \mid i \in T, j \in T \}$.

Algorithm *MINDELAY* $(i, j, M, \alpha_{ij}, D_i, D_j)$

Initialization: $smct(i, j) = \infty$;

Loop for $(k = 1, k = k + 1, k \le T)$

$Max\{D_i M_{ik}, D_j M_{jk}\} \rightarrow temp$;

$Min\{temp + D_i \alpha_{ij} M_{ki}, smct(i, j)\} \rightarrow smct(i, j)$;

Endloop;

Return ($smct(i, j)$).

With the minimum delay of each fragment to fragment semijoin, the following algorithm, *RESPONSE*, is developed to solve the problem RT_J. The inputs to this algorithm are a $T \times T$ weighted matrix M obtained from Floyd's algorithm, a selectivity matrix $\alpha = \{\alpha_{ij} \mid i, j \in T\}$, sets $F = \{F_i \mid i \in T\}$ and $D = \{ D_i \mid i \in T \}$.

Algorithm *RESPONSE* (M, α, F, D)

Loop 1. for $Z \in \{S1, S2\}$

$final = 0$;

Loop 2 for all $i \in Z$

$rt(i) = F_i M_{iq}$;

If $rt(i) > final$ Then

$ct(i) = 0$;

Loop 3 for all $j \in \Gamma_i$

$MINDELAY(i, j, M, \alpha_{ij}, D_i, D_j)$;

If $ct(i) < smct(i, j)$ then

$ct(i) = smct(i, j)$;

Endif;

Endloop 3;

$scost = rt(i) \sum_{j \in \Gamma_i} \alpha_{ij} + ct(i)$;

$Min\{rt(i), scost\} \rightarrow rt(i)$;

$Max\{rt(i), final\} \rightarrow final$;

Endif;

Endloop 2;

Endloop 1;

Return($final$).

It is clear that the time complexity of algorithm *MINDELAY* is linear with respect to $|T|$. Algorithm *RESPONSE* has two major loops, Loop 2 and Loop 3, each of which takes less than $|T|$ steps. Thus the complexity of the algorithm is $O(|T|^3)$.

4. Numerical Example and Alternative Algorithms for Two-Way Joins

To clarify some of the points presented above, we consider an example of a 2-way join of r and s where $r = r_0 \cup r_1$ and $s = s_2 \cup s_3$. The fragment size, selectivity factors, transmission delay rate, and other parameters are given in the following.

i	F_i	D_i
0	17	5
1	12	10
2	18	10
3	14	1

α_{ij}	0	1	2	3
0	1	1	0.2	0.1
1	1	1	0.1	0.3
2	0.4	0.1	1	1
3	0.2	0.1	1	1

C_{ij}	0	1	2	3	q
0	0	1	2	2	3
1	1	0	3	4	2
2	2	3	0	1	3
3	2	4	1	0	4
q	3	2	3	4	0

First of all, Floyd's algorithm can be used to compute the all pair shortest paths with the shortest distance matrix M shown below:

M	0	1	2	3	q
0	0	1	2	2	3
1	1	0	3	<u>3</u>	2
2	2	3	0	1	3
3	2	<u>3</u>	1	0	4
q	3	2	3	4	0

The algorithm *RESPONSE* is then applied to find the minimum response time which is 49.00 unit time for this example.

In order to represent clearly the arrangement of data transmission, a graphical notation is introduced. A digraph, called a transmission schedule, is used in which the nodes are the sites in G and the directed edges represent the data transmission by labeling the data to be transmitted. As an example, the optimal transmission schedule of the above 2-way join obtained from algorithm *RESPONSE* is shown in Figure 4.1. The join attributes of the fragment stored at site i is denoted as J_i.

From Figure 4.1, it can be clearly seen that four types of strategies are considered in algorithm *RESPONSE*: they are local semijoin; simple remote semijoin (that is, the selected site is the location of fragment to be semijoined); direct transmission (that is, no semijoin reduction is used before the fragment transmission); and remote semijoin at a third site (that is, the selected site is not the location of fragment being semijoined). This indicates the generality of our approach to solving the optimization problem of two-way joins. However, in order to consider all these strategies, a substantial amount of time is required. If we disregard some of the strategies, we may be able to reduce the computation time, but the solution may not be optimal. It is desirable to explore the impact of different strategies on 2-way join optimization as well as the trade-off between the computation time and the quality of solutions.

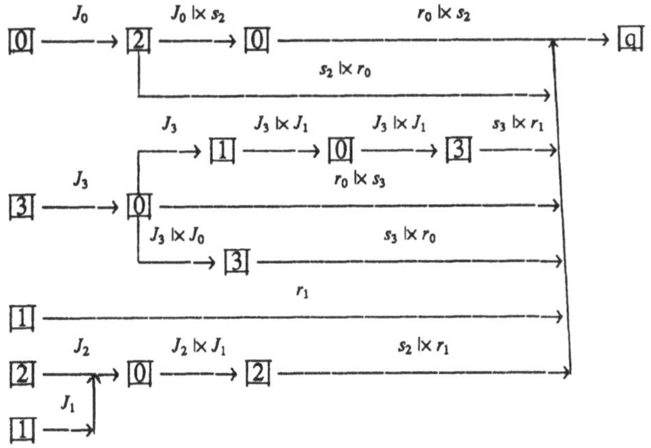

Figure 4.1 Transmission schedule for Algorithm 1.

Two simplifying algorithms as alternatives are proposed for the study. In the first one, Algorithm 2, the remote semijoin strategy is not used. This reduces the time complexity to $O(|T|^2)$. The second alternative, Algorithm 3, is a best sending path algorithm where the best paths for sending the fragments in a two-way join query to the query site are found. No semijoin is allowed as reduction and the time complexity is linear on $|T|$. The minimum response time found by Algorithms 2 and 3 for the above example is 54.00 and 56.00 unit time and the corresponding transmission schedules are shown in Figures 4.2 and 4.3 respectively.

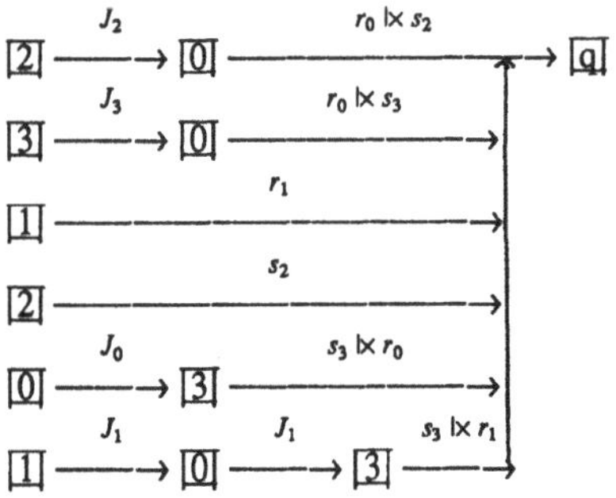

Figure 4.2 Transmission schedule from Algorithm 2.

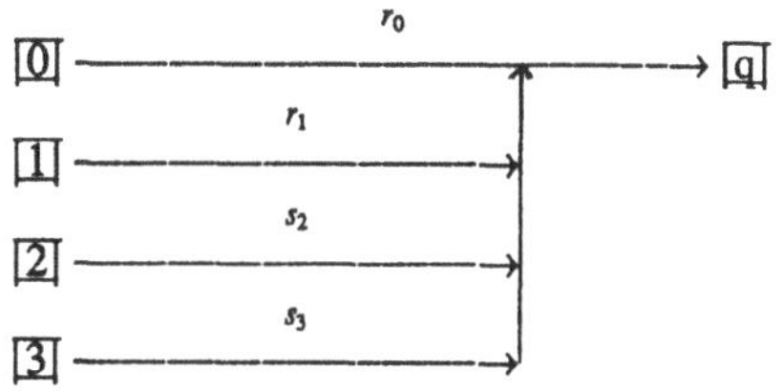

Figure 4.3 Transmission schedule from Algorithm 3.

5. Computational Analysis of Two-way Join Algorithms

In this section, we compare some experimental results of the three algorithms proposed above. The experiments are designed to evaluate numerically the performance of these algorithms and investigate the effect of remote semijoin, local semijoin as reducers. They also allow us to explore the trade-off between the computing time and the quality of the solutions as well as to analyze the sensitivity of the solutions to various parameters of our model.

The three algorithms were programmed and tested in the *C* language. The computational experiments were based on a uniform distribution of the parameter values. Although the actual distributions may be different, it is likely that the major trade-off exhibited in the uniform case will be valid in other environments. Moreover, the methodology presented in this section can be applied to arbitrary environments.

5.1. Comparative Analysis

In the comparative experiments, the three algorithms were applied to 2-way join problems of various size. The results of Algorithms 2 and 3 were compared with the optimal solution of algorithm *RESPONSE* which we will call Algorithm 1 hereafter. The running time of each algorithm was also recorded.

The results summarized in Table 5.1 were based on the following data: the fragment size was drawn from a uniform distribution with the range [10, 20], the size of the join attribute ranged from 2 percent to 50 percent of the fragment size, the transmission delay rates were drawn from a uniform distribution with a range of [0, 5], and the selectivity factors were drawn from a uniform distribution with the range [0, 0.5]. Note that no specific units were assigned to the size and delay rates, because the solution to the problem is affected by the relative rather than the absolute magnitudes. Hence, the range [10, 20] can be interpreted as 10K to 20K, 10M to 20M, and so on.

With each fixed number of fragments, ten set of parameters were generated from uniform distributions. The *MIN* and *MAX* relative response time is respectively the minimum and maximum of the ten solutions. Other values are the average of the ten solutions and the optimal response time is the solution of Algorithm 1. It can be clearly seen from Table 5.1 that the solutions obtained from Algorithm 2 are close to the minimum response time while the running time is substantially reduced. The computation time is further reduced by Algorithm 3 but its solutions are relatively poor.

Table 5.1 Comparative results of three algorithms

		Algorithm 1	relative response time[a] Algorithm 2				Relative response time Algorithm 3			
|T|	|S1|,|S2|	CPU[b]	CPU	MIN.	MAX.	AVG.	CPU	MIN.	MAX.	AVG.
5	2,3	0.019	0.005	1.00	1.41	1.13	0.000	1.69	4.05	2.53
10	2,8	0.122	0.006	1.00	1.71	1.22	0.001	1.56	4.25	2.66
	5,5	0.120	0.006	1.00	1.26	1.08	0.001	1.30	3.84	2.02
15	2,13	0.248	0.006	1.06	1.40	1.24	0.003	1.72	3.91	2.33
	7,8	0.440	0.006	1.00	1.21	1.10	0.002	1.56	2.68	2.10
20	5,15	0.888	0.011	1.06	1.47	1.24	0.003	1.52	2.68	2.09
	10,10	1.146	0.010	1.00	1.42	1.23	0.003	1.54	2.47	1.98
30	5,25	2.316	0.014	1.07	1.34	1.28	0.003	1.52	2.86	2.41
	15,15	3.764	0.019	1.00	1.34	1.19	0.004	1.56	2.15	1.82
40	5,35	4.408	0.026	1.05	1.89	1.31	0.005	1.51	4.13	2.44
	20,20	8.346	0.037	1.03	1.24	1.14	0.005	1.55	2.59	2.03

[a] Relative response time of an algorithm = $\frac{\text{solution of the algorithm}}{\text{minimum response time}}$.

[b] Average CPU time, measured in VAX750 seconds.

5.2. Sensitivity Analysis

The experiments in this section were designed to analyze the sensitivity of solutions, generated by the three algorithms, to various parameters of the model. The model's parameters chosen to be varied and the rationale of their selection are as follows:

(1) *The selectivity factors.* The values of selectivity factors may have a significant effect on the solutions generated by Algorithms 1 and 2. Large selectivity factors may decrease the reduction ability of semijoin operations. As a result, the solutions of Algorithms 1 and 2 will be closer the those of Algorithm 3 in which no semijoin is involved. The semijoin strategies are expected to have more reduction power with small values of selectivity factors.

(2) *The join attribute size versus its fragment size.* The reduction delay is due to the transfer of join attributes. Thus, it is likely that a smaller size of join attributes relative to their fragments will cause Algorithms 1 and 2 to generate solutions with more semijoin operations. When the join attribute size is close to the fragment size, the solutions of Algorithms 1 and 2 will be close to that of Algorithm 3 in which no semijoin is used as reducer. However, if the selectivity is small enough such that the fragment delay saved is larger than the reduction delay, the semijoin strategy will still be beneficial even if the join attribute size is large.

(3) *The variance of the transmission delay rates.* Semijoin is a technique to reduce the fragment size before it is transmitted. When the communication delay rates increase, the transmission delay for

the fragment not reduced by semijoins is likely to increase faster than that for the fragment reduced by semijoins.

(4) *The variance of the size of fragments and join attributes.* The variance of the size of fragments and join attributes were found to make a significant difference between the algorithms with and without remote semijoins for the optimization total cost, [11]. This led us to investigate the effect of this parameter in the case of the response time optimization. We found that the gaps between the three algorithm remain the same when the parameter is changed. Therefore, there is an indication that the variance in fragment size has no impact on the quality of the three algorithms.

The purpose of the sensitivity analysis is to validate the above conjectures and to determine what is "small" and what is "large". In our experiments, the number of fragments of the two relations were fixed, $|S1| = 15$ and $|S2| = 10$. Each fragment size was drawn randomly from a uniform distribution with a range [10, 20], denoted as *fragment size* $\sim U(a, b)$ where a=10 and b=20.

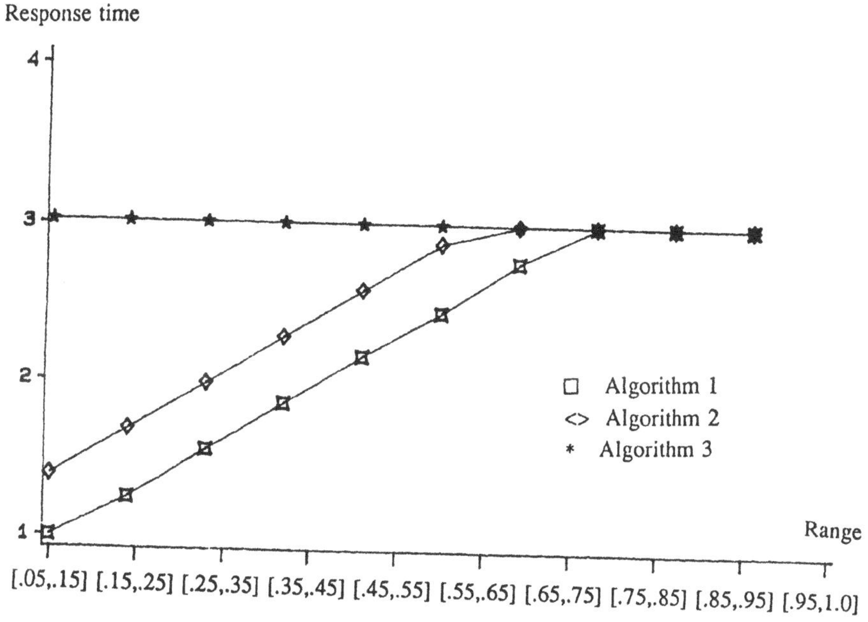

Figure 5.1 Effect of selectivity factors

The effect of changes in the values of the selectivity factors α_{ij} is shown in Figure 5.1. Each point in the graph represents the average response time found by the respective algorithm for ten sample two-way joins. All the response times were normalized by dividing them by the value of minimum response time. The selectivity factors were derived by first generating $\alpha'_{ij} \sim U(a, b)$, where a and b are respectively the lower and upper limits of the range, as specified in Figure 5.1, and then setting $\alpha_{ij} = \alpha'_{ij}/|\Gamma_i|$. Dividing α'_{ij} by $|\Gamma_i|$ ensures that $\sum_{j \in \Gamma_i} \alpha_{ij} \le b$. The size of the join attributes D_i was obtained by generating $d_i \sim U(0.02, 0.5)$ and multiplying it by F_i. The transmission delay rates were $C_{ij} \sim U(0, 5)$.

The results of the experiment validated our conjecture: for large values of the selectivity factors ($a \geq 0.75$ for $\alpha'_{ij} \sim U(a, b)$), the values of all the solutions generated here converged to the values of no semijoin solution. It should be noted that the values of the solutions with only local semijoins converged to the values of no semijoin solution faster than those of the solutions with both local and remote semijoins.

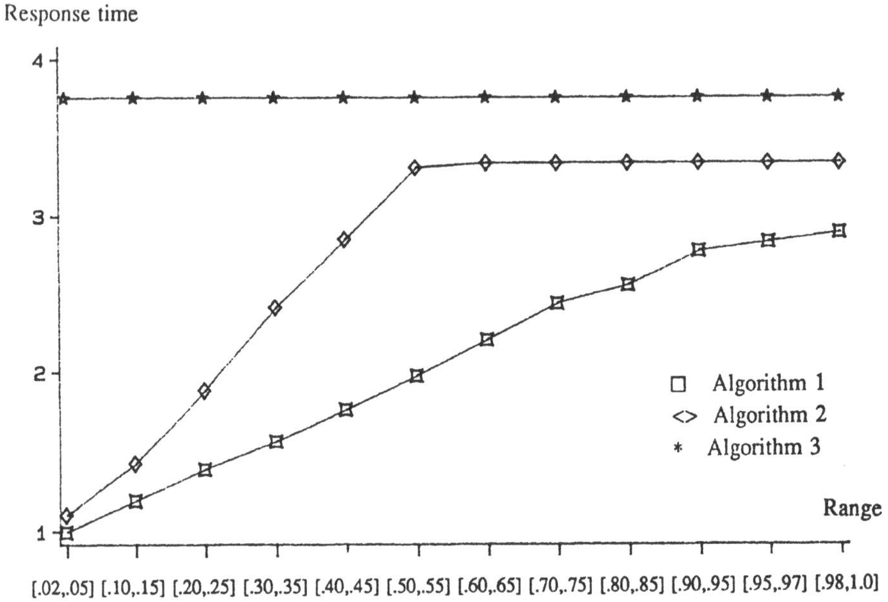

Figure 5.2 Effect of relative sizes

The effect of the join attribute size relative to the fragment size is shown in Figure 5.2. In this experiment, the selectivity factors were drawn from a fixed range ($\alpha'_{ij} \sim U(0, 0.5)$). The transmission delay rates were the same as in the first experiment. The size of the join attributes (as a fraction of the fragment size) was produced by generating $d_i \sim U(a, b)$, where a and b are specified in Figure 5.2, and multiplying it by F_i. It can be seen that the effect of this parameter is very similar to that of selectivity factors. However, the values of the solutions found by Algorithms 1 and 2 do not converge to the values of no semijoin solutions. This is because the selectivity factors used are relatively small.

With the increase of the join attribute size, the values of the solutions without remote semijoin increased much faster than those of the solutions with remote semijoin. After the lower limit $a \geq 0.5$ in $d_i \sim U(a, b)$, the values of the solutions without remote semijoin remain stable at the maximum value, while the values of the solutions with remote semijoin still increased slowly until $a \geq 0.9$. It can also be observed that when the size of the join attributes is small ($b \leq 0.1$), remote semijoin is not very useful.

Figure 5.3 illustrates the effect of variance of the communication delay rates. The communication delay rates C_{ij} were drawn from a uniform distribution with a range of [0, b], where b is specified in the figure. The size of the join attributes and the selectivity factors were respectively the same as in the first and second experiments. It is clear from Figure 5.3 that the solutions generated by Algorithm 3 were sensitive to the variation in the communication delay rates, whereas its impact on Algorithms 1 and 2 were not substantial.

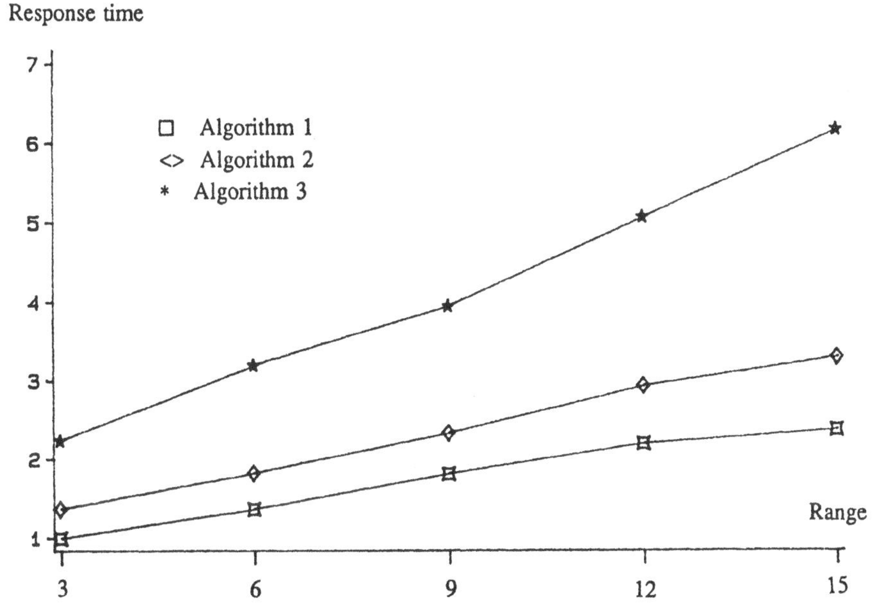

Figure 5.3 Effect of communication delay rates

6. Conclusion

The problem of minimizing response time of two-way joins has a polynomial algorithm in a partitioned environment. This is due to the impact of allowing parallel transmission which allows us to break down the problem into some local optimizations and their proper integration. Semijoin strategies are shown to be powerful tools in the minimization of response time.

Two parameters, the selectivity factors and the size of the join attributes, were found to have major impacts on the solutions of minimum response time. Large values for the selectivity factors and/or the join attribute sizes reduce the benefit of using semijoins.

As we noted in the discussion of the formulation, the local optimization technique used does not generalize, even to three-way joins. We believe, however, that the results obtained for two-way joins will be useful in the investigation of multi-way join optimization.

REFERENCES

[1] Apers, P. M. G., Hevner, A. R. and Yao, S. B., "Optimization Algorithms for Distributed Queries", *IEEE Transactions on Software Engineering,* Vol. SE-9 No. 1, Jan. 1983, 57-68.

[2] Bernstein, P. A. and Goodman, N., "Query Processing in a System for Distributed Database (*SDD*–1)", *ACM Transactions on Database Systems,* Vol. 6, No. 4, Dec. 1981, 602-625.

[3] Ceri, S. and Gottlob, G., "Optimizing Joins between Two Partitioned Relations in Distributed Databases", *Journal of Parallel and Distributed Computing,* Vol. 3, 1986, 183-205.

[4] Ceri, S. and Pelagatti, G., *Distributed database Principle and Systems,* McGraw-Hill Book Company, New York, 1985.

[5] Daniels, D. et al., " An Introduction to Distributed Query Compilation in R^*.", *Distributed Data Bases, H. J. Schneider, ed., North-Holland,* 1982.

[6] Epstein, R., Stonebraker M. and Wong, E., "Distributed Query Processing in a Relational Database", *Proceedings SIGMOD International Conference on Management of Data,* May 1978, 169-180.

[7] Gavish, B. and Segev, A., " Set Query Optimization in Horizontally Partitioned Distributed Database Systems", *ACM Transaction on Distributed Database Management Systems,* Vol. 11, No. 3, 1986, 265-293.

[8] Hevner, A. R. and Yao, S. B., " Query Processing in Distributed Database systems", *IEEE Transaction on Software Engineering,* Vol. SE-5, No. 3, May 1979, 177-187. 69-88.

[9] Lafortune, S. and Wong, E., " A State Transition Model for Distributed Query Processing", *ACM Transactions on Database System,* Vol. 11, No. 3, Sept. 1986, 294-322.

[10] Maier, D., *The Theory of Relational Databases,* Computer Science Press, Rockville, Maryland, 1983.

[11] Pelagatti, G., and Manning, E. D., "A Model of an Access Strategy in a Distributed Database System", *In Proceedings of the IFIP-TC2, Database Architecture,* 1979

[12] Segev, A., "Optimization of Join Operations in Horizontal Partitioned Database Systems", *ACM Transactions on Database Systems,* Vol. 11, No. 1, March 1986, 48-80.

[13] Stonebraker, M. and Neuhold, E., " A Distributed Database Version of INGRES", *In Proceedings of the 3rd Berkeley Workshop on the Distributed Data Management and Computer Networks,* 1977.

[14] Syslo, M. M., Deo, N. and Kowalik, J., "Discrete Optimization Algorithms with Pascal Programs", *Prentice-Hall, Inc., Englewood Cliffs, New Jersey,* 1983.

[15] Williams, R., et al., "R^*: An overview of the architecture", *IBM Res. Rep. RJ3325,* 1981.

[16] Yu, C. T., Chang, C. C. and Chang, Y., "Two Surprising Results in Processing Simple Queries in Distributed Databases", *Proceedings of the IEEE 6th International Computer Software and Application Conference,* 1982, 377-384.

[17] Yu, C. T., Chang, C. C., "On the design of a query processing strategy in a distributed databases", *Proceedings of the ACM SIGMOD Database Week,* 1983, 30-39.

[18] Yu, C. T. and Chang, C. C., "Distributed Query Processing", *Computing Surveys,* Vol. 16, No. 4, December 1984, 399-433.

[19] Yu, C. T. and Chang, C. C. et al., " Query Processing in a Fragmented Relational Distributed Systems: Mermaid", *IEEE Transaction on Software Engineering,* Vol. SE-11, No. 8, August 1985, 795-810.

Deciding whether a production rule is relational computable†

Eric Simon and Christophe de Maindreville
INRIA - Rocquencourt, BP 105
78153 Le Chesnay cedex, France

ABSTRACT : In this paper, we consider the problem of integrating a production rule language, named RDL1, with a relational DBMS. A production rule in RDL1, consists of a condition part which is a relational calculus expression and of an action part which is a sequence of database updates. The main problem addressed in this paper is to determine whether a rule program can be computed as a relational algebra program, i.e., whether the initial semantics of the program is not modified by a set-oriented or relational computation. First, we define the syntax and the semantics of the RDL1 language which is given as the sequence of database states reachable by the computation of the program. We conjecture that deciding if a rule is relational computable is an undecidable problem and then, propose sufficient conditions to decide if a rule is relational computable. We present a general method to check the validity of these conditions. Finally, we propose two algorithms which are derived from the previous method. The first one gave sufficient syntactic conditions for a rule to be relational computable. The second one gave sufficient semantic conditions and leads to check integrity constraints over the database to decide whether a rule is relational computable.

1. Introduction

A deductive database consists of a set of base relations called *extensional database* (EDB), and a set of virtual relations defined using *rules*, called *intentional database* (IDB). In general the rule based language used to express the rules is a set of function-free Horn clauses, called DATALOG, where a clause contains at most one positive literal. Several researchers studied extensions of DATALOG in order to increase the power of the rule language. The introduction of negative literals in the body of a clause leads to DATALOG^{neg}. This language looses a good property of a DATALOG program that is its least fixpoint semantics. However , it has been shown that under some syntactic restrictions called *stratification*, it is possible to assign a least fixpoint semantics to a DATALOG^{neg} program [Apt86].

We proposed in [Gardarin85, Maindreville87, Maindreville88a] an original approach to deductive databases based on the integration of a production rule language, called RDL1, with a relational DBMS (RDBMS). A production rule, in our language, consists of a conditional part which is a relational calculus expression and a consequent part which is a sequence of insertions and deletions of tuples in database derived relations. The main features of this language are the following. First, it captures the operational (or declarative) semantics of stratified DATALOG^{neg} programs but offers more generality and more computational power than a DATALOG^{neg} language since a sequence of database updates can be expressed within a single rule. Second, the operational semantics of the language provides a uniform and clean compromise between declarativity and procedurality. Indeed, the procedural aspects of RDL1 stand upon (i) the use of updates and (ii) the

† Research is supported in part by the Esprit Project ISIDE (under contract P1133).

use of an implicit ordering of rules (stratification-like) combined with an explicit (user given) partial ordering of rules. Notice that stratification in logic programs already introduces procedurality in the language.

In this paper, we define a formal framework to study the properties of production rules in deductive databases. In particular, one theoritical and practical important problem is to determine whether a rule and a rule program can be computed using a relational algebra program, i.e., whether the initial semantics of the program is preserved by a relational (or set oriented) computation. Roughly speaking, it means that we want to characterize production rules which are firable in a set oriented way, instead of in a "one tuple at a time" way. We will see that this problem is closely connected to the problem of controlling forward rule instances. Thus, the findings presented in this paper go beyong the framework of the RDL1 language. Such work addresses problems encountered in any powerfull enough rule language such as *conflict resolution strategies* and managing of *conflict set.*. Furthermore, the findings of this paper provide a characterization of deterministic rules, and then, using a stratification like technique which defines a partial ordering over rules, of deterministic programs. Furthermore, it gives an efficient way to compute production rules in a RDBMS. Indeed, it benefits via the relational algebra, of the efficient RDBMS manipulation of sets of data.

The paper is organized as follows. Section 2 defines the syntax and the semantics of the RDL1 language. Section 3 introduces the notion of relational computability; then, it is conjectured that deciding if a rule is relational computable is an undecidable problem. In Section 4, we propose sufficient conditions to decide if a rule is relational computable. We present a general method to check the validity of these conditions. Finally, we propose two algorithms which are derived from the previous method. Section 5 is the conclusion.

2. The production rule language

The purpose of this section is to present an overview of the production rule language we use.

2.1. A tuple relational calculus

A *relational schema* R is a finite set of attributes $\{A_1, ..., A_n\}$. Let dom (A_i) be the domain of values of attribute A_i. A *constant tuple* $t = (c_1, ..., c_n)$ over a relational schema R is a mapping from R into dom $(A_1) \cup$ dom $(A_2) \cup .... \cup$ dom (A_n) such that for each i in $\{1, \ldots, n\}$ $c_i \in$ dom (A_i). We denote by dom (R) the set of all possible constant tuples over R. An *instance* of a relational schema R, (sometimes called a relation), is a finite set of constant tuples over R. A *database schema* is a finite set of relational schemas. Finally, an *instance* I over a database schema S is a total function from S such that for each R in S, I(R) is an instance over R.

We use an extended version of the relational calculus of [Codd71] based on a multi-sort logic where terms are typed. This relational calculus has two types of predicate symbols : The relational predicates (unary predicates) are those for which an interpretation corresponds to the instances of the relational schemas. The non relational predicates correspond to the usual comparative ones.

A formula is composed of a first part which indicates the type of some tuple variables (the range definition part) and of a second part conjunctively connected to the former (called a *sub-formula*) which states a condition that must be satisfied by the tuple variables.

A *range predicate* is defined as follows :

- If R is a relational predicate name and x is a tuple variable then R (x) is a *(positive) range predicate* and ¬ R (x) is a *(negative) range predicate,*
- Let U and V be two range predicates then U AND V is a range predicate.

Examples :

`PARENTS(x), ¬PENGUIN(x)` are range predicates.

`(∃ x ∈ R) (x.A ≤ y.B)` is a sub-formula.

`PARENT (x) AND x.Child = Jeremie` is a formula.

In the following, we impose that our formulae meet the range restricted property [Nicolas82] initially defined for closed formulae and that we extended to opened formulae. We come now to the interpretation of a formula. Let D be the finite set of sorts composed by all the domains of attributes defined over a database schema *S* and by the domain of each relational schema. Thus, D = {dom (A_1), dom (A_2), ... , dom (R1), dom (R2), ...}. A database DB is the set of instances of all the relational predicates. We call DB an interpretation. Thus, DB = {I (R_1), I (R_2), ... }. Then, a formula is evaluated in the classical way.

2.2. Syntactic definition of rules

The general form of a rule is the sentence : Condition → Action. To define the precise notion of rule, we need the auxiliary concepts of *condition* and *action.* A *condition* over a database schema *S* is a range restricted formula of the relational calculus. There are two *elementary actions*, denoted "+" and "-". The update action "+" takes a ground fact (i.e., a constant tuple) and maps a database state into another state which contains this fact. Thus the action "+" inserts a constant tuple in a relation. On the contrary, the action "-" takes a fact and deletes it from a relation. Complex update actions can be specified in terms of these two primitive actions. *Parameterized actions* are defined using variables as arguments of actions. All these update actions can also be composed into a sequence. An action is then defined as follows :

Definition 2.1: An *action* over a database schema *S* is defined as follows :

(i) For R in *S* and for each tuple t = (t_1, ..., t_n) over R {A_1, ..., A_n} then + R ($A_1 = t_1$, ..., $A_n = t_n$) and - R ($A_1 = t_1$,..., $A_n = t_n$) are (elementary) *actions* (respectively called insertion and deletion in R).

(ii) Let x be a tuple variable ranging over an instance of T, for R in *S* , + R (x) and - R (x) are (parametrized) *actions* provided the two relational schemas R and T are identical.

(iii) If A1 and A2 are two actions then A1• A2 is an *action* over a database schema *S*. The symbol "•" is the concatenation operation over actions.

Examples :

```
- ANCESTOR (Asc = Cati, Desc = Sarah)
+ ANCESTOR (Asc = x.Father, Desc = x.Child)
```

are respectively an elementary action and a parametrized action over ANCESTOR.

Let C be a condition, we call *Free (C)* the set of free variables appearing in C. These variables appear in the range predicate of the formula representing the condition of the rule. We call *Free*$^+$ *(C)* the set of free variables of C only appearing in positive range predicates. Let A be an action, we call *Var (A)* the set of variables appearing in A. There is no notion of free or bounded variable in an action. A *rule* is defined as follows:

If C is a condition and A is an action and Free$^+$ (C) $\supseteq$ Var (A) then C $\rightarrow$ A is a rule.

In our context, this means that the only values of tuples that can be deleted or inserted by a rule are values coming from the instances of the database.

Examples :

The two following sentences obey to the definition of a rule :

```
PARENT(x)  →+ ANCESTOR(x)
EMPLOYEE(x)  AND  x.Name  =  Jules  →- EMPLOYEE(Name  =  Jules,  Dept.  =  toys)  +
EMPLOYEE(Name = Jules, Dept = sports)
```

The sentence below <u>is not</u> a rule : y appears in the action and is existentially quantified in the condition. Thus y is not a free variable

```
PARENTS(x) →+ANCESTOR(y)
PARENTS(x) AND (∃ y ∈ EMPLOYEE)(y.Name = Jules)
        →+EMPLOYEE (Name = y.Name, Dept = toys)
```

A finite set of rules defines a *rule program* .

2.3. Semantics of rules

In order to define the semantics of rules, we need the auxiliary concepts of valuation of conditions and actions. Let C be a condition over a database schema *S*. A *valuation* θ is given by an assignment to the constants, functions and free variables of C. A *valued condition* is obtained by replacing in C each free variable x over R by a constant tuple chosen in the domain of R. A valued condition θ (C) interpreted by an interpretation $\Im$ (that is a database) is denoted $\Im$ (θ (C)) and is called an *interpreted condition*. Therefore, an interpreted condition takes a value which is either true or false.

Example :

The valued condition θ [PARENT (x) AND x.Child = Jeremie] is obtained by replacing x by a constant tuple chosen in the domain of PARENT. Given an interpretation $\Im$, that is an instance of PARENT and an instance of the equality predicate, we can assign a value to the interpreted condition. For instance, suppose PARENT = {(Father = Nestor, Child = Franck), (Father = Samuel, Child = Max)}, then the interpreted condition takes always the value false. A particular valued condition would be PARENT (x/(Father = Nestor, Child = Franck)) AND x.Child/Franck = Jeremie where the second conjunction takes the value false.

A valued action θ (A) is defined as follows. For each parametrized action of A, + R (u) or - R (u), where u is either a tuple variable or a tuple over R, u is replaced by a constant tuple over R.

Definition 2.2 : Let P : C $\rightarrow$ A be a rule. A *valued rule*, noted θ (P), by a valuation θ is an expression θ (C $\rightarrow$ A) that is θ (C) $\rightarrow$ θ (A).

The semantics of a rule is defined using a binary relation, noted Γ_P, over the instances I of a database schema *S* (i.e. a subset of I (*S*) x I (*S*)). Intuitively, Γ_P (I) is the set of immediate consequences of I using a production rule P, that is the set of database states reachable by applying the valued rule P only once. We first define the semantics of an elementary action, that is a simple insertion or deletion into a relation. We then give the semantics of a general action. Finally, we describe the semantics of a general rule.

Definition 2.3 : Let R be a relational schema of *S* and t be a constant tuple over R. Let I and J denote two instances of *S*. Then :

(1) The rule P : TRUE $\rightarrow$ + R (t) defines a binary relation Γ_P such that (I, J) $\in \Gamma_P$ iff J (R) = I (R) $\cup$ {t} and J (T) = I (T) for each T in *S* such that T $\neq$ R.

(2) The rule P : TRUE $\rightarrow$ - R (t) defines a binary relation Γ_P such that (I, J) $\in \Gamma_P$ iff J (R) = I (R) - {t} and J (T) = I (T) for each T $\in$ *S* such that T $\neq$ R

The semantics of a general action is now given.

Definition 2.4 : Let I and J denote two instances of a database schema *S*. A rule P : TRUE $\rightarrow$ A, where A = $(((A_1 \bullet A_2) \bullet \ldots) \bullet A_n)$ is a valued action over *S*, and the A_i are elementary actions, defines a binary relation Γ_P such that for each R appearing in A, (I, J) $\in \Gamma_P$, or equivalently

$J = \Gamma_P (I)$, iff $J (R) = [(I (R) \cup I (R^+)) - I (R^-)] \cup [I (R) \cap I (R^+) \cap I (R^-)]$

where I (R^+) is the set of all the constant tuples t appearing in the elementary actions + R (t) and I (R^-) is the set of all the constant tuples t' appearing in the elementary actions - R (t').

Thus, an action is seen as an *atomic database update*. To illustrate, figure 1 below represents the sets I (R), I (R^+) and I (R^-). The effect of the action A is described by the dashed part which represents the instance of R after executing the action A.

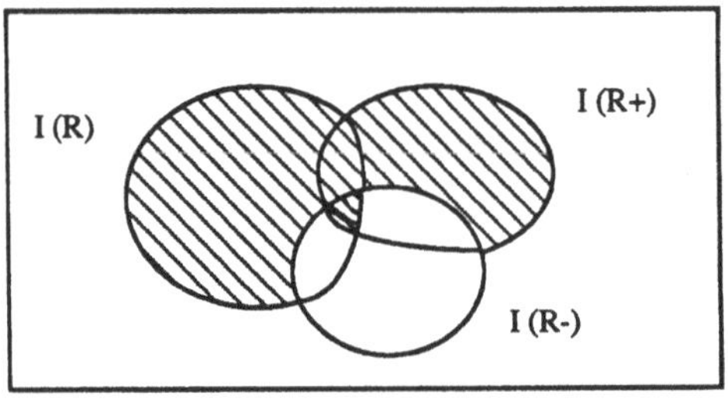

Figure 2.1 : result of an action over R

This definition has several consequences. First, it guarantees that the order of insertions and deletions in an action is irrelevant. Second, it nullifies an action which inserts and deletes the same constant tuple. More formally, we have :

Theorem 2.1: Let A_1, A_2 and A_3 be actions of any kind then :

(i) $A_1 \bullet A_2 = A_2 \bullet A_1$

(ii) $A_1 \bullet (A_2 \bullet A_3) = (A_1 \bullet A_2) \bullet A_3$

(iii) there exists a particular action called *null action* s.t. $A_1 \bullet$ null action $= A_1$

(iv) for each action A_1, there always exists A_1' such that $A_1 \bullet A_1' =$ null action

Proof : Omitted; it easily derives from definition 2.4.

Examples :

Let R {A} be a relational schema then the following rules have no effect on R

```
R(x) AND x.A = a →+ R(A = a) - R(A = a)
R(x) AND x.A = a →+ R(A = a) - R(A = a) + R(A = a) + R(A = a)
```

The following rule changes the value of attribute A from a to b.

```
R(x) AND x.A = a →+R(A = b) - R(x)
```

Finally, the semantics of a general rule is given.

Definition 2.5 : Let I and J denote two instances of *S*. A rule P : C → A defines a binary relation Γ_P such that $J = \Gamma_P$ (I) iff there exists $n \geq 0$, $I = J_0, \ldots, J_n = J$ and some valuations $\theta_1, \theta_2, \ldots, \theta_n$ of P such that :
for each $i \in \{0, \ldots, n\text{-}1\}$, $J_{i+1} = \Gamma_{\theta i\,(P)}\,(J_i)$ that is, $J_i \models \theta_i$ (C) and $J_{i+1} = \Gamma_{\theta i\,(A)}\,(J_i)$.

The semantics we give to rules is very closed to the one defined in [Abiteboul87] for a database Transaction Language (TL). In fact this semantics in the spirit of the semantics given in [Kripke63] for modal logic. We now precise two fundamental notions for rules which are the notion of fixpoint and determinism.

Definition 2.6 : Let P : C → A be a rule over *S*. Γ_P has a *fixpoint* (or equivalently P has a *stable state*) if and only if for each database state I there exists J such that :

- $J = \Gamma_P$ (I) and
- J is such that for each valuation θ, $(J' = \Gamma_{\theta\,(P)}\,(J))$ implies $(J' = J)$

J is called a *stable state* for P.

Examples :

Let R {Int : integer}, Q {Int : integer} and S {A : integer, B : integer} be two relational schemas. Then the two following rules have a stable state.

```
R(x) and ¬ Q(x) → + Q(Int = x.Int)
R(x) and R(y) and x ≠ y → -R(x) - R(y) + R(Int = x.Int + y.Int)
```

The two following rules have not a stable state :

```
R(x) → + R(Int = x.Int + 1)
S(x) → + S(A = x.B, B = x.A) - S(x)
```

Definition 2.7: Let P be a rule. P is said to be *deterministic*, iff Γ_P has a unique fixpoint.

We come now to the semantics of a rule program.

Definition 2.8: Let I and J denote two instances of *S*. A *rule program* P = $\{P_1, P_2, \ldots, P_q\}$ over a database schema *S* defines a binary relation Γ_P. Then, J = Γ_P (I) iff there exists $n \geq 0$, I = $J_0, \ldots, J_n$ = J such that : for each $i \in \{0, \ldots, n-1\}$ there exists $k \in \{1, \ldots, q\}$ such that : $J_{i+1} = \Gamma_{P_k}(J_i)$.

Let P = $\{P_1, \ldots, P_n\}$ be a rule program over a database schema *S*. Γ_P has a fixpoint (or equivalently P has a stable state) if and only if for each database state I, there exists J such that : J = Γ_P(I) and J is such that for each valuation θ , J = $\Gamma_{\theta(P)}(J)$.

2.4. Properties of RDL1 programs

The first property is the expressiveness power of RDL1. By expressiveness, we refer to the set of computable queries (in the sense of [Chandra80]) that can be expressed with the language. As a result, it can be proved, using techniques described in [Abiteboul87], that RDL1 has more expressive power than stratified DATALOG^{neg}. A generic example of a deterministic RDL1 program that cannot be expressed in stratified DATALOG^{neg} is :

```
NOT DONE ('1') →+ DONE('1') + EVEN('1')
EVEN ('1') AND R(x)  →+ ODD('1') - R(x) - EVEN('1')
ODD ('1') AND R(x)  →+EVEN('1') - R(x) - ODD('1')
```

This program returns '1' in the relation ODD if the number of tuples in relation R is odd and returns '1' in the relation EVEN otherwise.

Another way of looking at this result is to study the programming primitives provided by RDL1. Indeed, the additional (procedural) primitives in RDL1 with respect to DATALOG^{neg} are the updates in the action part of a rule. We are strongly convinced that such an update facility is fundamental for programming real deductive database applications. Another primitive, namely explicit ordering, was introduced in the language but is not studied in this paper.

The second property is that RDL1 is a non deterministic language. This point will be further discussed in section 3.

2.5. Examples of rule programs

We conclude the presentation of the language with one example of rule programs. Each program is introduced under the form of a rule *module*. A module takes some input relations which are either base or derived relations and produces in output some *target* relations defined using a set of rules. *Temporary* relations can be used to compute intermediate results in a module.

Let us assume a base relation EDGE (N° : integer, Orig. : char, Ext. : char, Label : integer), which represent oriented arcs in a graph. We can compute the "serial reduction" of the EDGE relation into the EDGE* relation with the following rule module. The first rule copies all the tuples of EDGE into EDGE* and memorizes this operation by marking the tuples in DONE. The second rule replaces two serial edges x and y from EDGE* by one new resulting edge whose label is a certain function f applied to the labels of x and y.

```
MODULE  REDUCTION
 target
EDGE* (N° : integer; ORIG. : char ; EXT : char; LABEL : integer),
 Rules
P1 : EDGE(x) AND NOT DONE(x) →+EDGE*(x) + DONE(x)

P2 : EDGE*(x) AND EDGE*(y) AND x.Ext = y.Orig AND (∀z ∈ EDGE*)[(z.N° ≠y.N°)
   OR (z.Origin ≠x.Ext AND z.Ext ≠x.Ext)]
   →-EDGE*(x) - EDGE*(y) + EDGE*(N° = x.N°, Orig. = x.Orig., Ext = y.Ext,
   label = f (x.label, y.label)),
end.
```

3. Relational computation of rules

3.1. Definition

In this section we first introduce the notion of relational computation of rules. We show that this corresponds to assign a different semantics to an RDL1 program, namely $RDL1^{rc}$ semantics ("rc" stands for *relational computation*). Intuitively, a relational computation of a rule means that the condition of the rule is first evaluated as a relational algebra program which returns all the valuations that satisfy the condition. The action is then globally computed for this set of valuations as a second relational algebra expression only containing project, union and difference operations. This notion is formalized below.

Auxiliary definitions are first needed.

Definition 3.1 : Let P : C → A be a rule and I be a database state. We call *relevant set of tuples for P and I*, noted $Rel_I(P)$, the set of all the valuations $\theta_1, \dots, \theta_n$ that make C true in I, and such that $\Gamma_{\theta i}(A)(I) \neq I$.

Example :

Consider the rule P : PARENT (x) → + ANCESTOR (x)

and I = {I (PARENT) = {(father = Adam, child = Bill), (father = Bill, child = Caïn)},

I (ANCESTOR) = ∅ }.Then, Rel_I (P) = {x / (Adam, Bill), x / (Bill, Caïn)}.

Definition 3.2 : Let P : C → A be a rule, I be a database state, and $Rel_I(P) = \{ \theta_1, \dots, \theta_n \}$ the relevant set of tuples for P and I. The relational computation of P, noted $RDL1^{rc}$ (P) defines a new meaning relation Γ^{rc}_P as follows.

$J = \Gamma^{rc}_P$ (I) iff there exists $n \geq 0$, $I = J_0, \dots, J_n = J$ and some sets $Rel_{J_0}(P), \dots, Rel_{J_{n-1}}(P)$ s. t. : $\forall i \in \{0,\dots, n-1\}$, $J_{i+1} = \Gamma_{\theta 1(A) \bullet \dots \bullet \theta n(A)}(J_i)$ where $\theta_1, \dots, \theta_n \in Rel_{J_i}(P)$. (Note that $\theta_1(A) \bullet \dots \bullet \theta_n(A)$ is a valued action.)

Definition 3.3 : Let $P = \{P_1, \dots, P_n\}$ be a rule program. A relational computation of P consists of firing each rule using a relational computation.

Example :

Considering the previous example, there are two valuations in Rel_I (P). Thus, there exists J_1 s. t. $J_1 = \Gamma_{\theta 1(A) \bullet \theta 2(A)}(I)$ where :

θ1(A) = + ANCESTOR (Adam, Bill) and θ2 (A) = + ANCESTOR (Bill, Caïn).

Thus, J_1 = I (ANCESTOR) ∪ {(Adam, Bill), (Bill, Caïn)} = Γ^{rc}_P (I).

Now consider the example of rules defining the EDGE* relation. Let I be a database instance of a database schema *S*.

I (*S*) = {I (EDGE) = {(A, B, a), (B, C, b), (C, D, c)}, I (EDGE*) = ∅, I (DONE) = ∅}. We compute successively the relevant sets for each one of the three rules.

$Rel_I(P_1)$ = {x / (A, B, a), x / (B, C, b), x / (C, D, c)}

$Rel_I(P_2)$ = {[x / (A, B, a), y / (B, C, b)], [x / (B, C, b), y / (C, D, c)]}

$Rel_I(P_2)$ = ∅

There are three valuations in $Rel_I(P_1)$, thus the relational computation of P_1 gives :

$J_1 = \Gamma^{rc}_{P1}(I) = \Gamma_A(I)$ where A is the valued action :

A = + EDGE* (A, B, a) + EDGE* (B, C, b) + EDGE* (C, D, c) and thus J_1 is :

J_1(*S*) = {J_1 (EDGE) = I (EDGE), J_1 (EDGE*) = I (EDGE), J_1 (DONE) = I (EDGE)}.

There are still exactly the same valuations in $Rel_{J1}(P_2)$ than in $Rel_I(P_2)$. Thus the relational computation of P_2 gives:

$J_2 = \Gamma^{rc}_{P2}(J_1) = \Gamma_{A'}(J_1)$ where A' is the valued action :

A' = - EDGE* (A, B, a) - EDGE* (B, C, b) + EDGE* (A, C, f (a, b))

- EDGE* (B, C, b) - EDGE* (C, D, c) + EDGE* (B, D, f (b, c)).

According to the meaning of an action given in definition 2.4, J_2 is :

J_2 (*S*) = {J_2 (EDGE) = I (EDGE), J_2 (EDGE*) = {(A, C, f (a, b)), (B, D, f (b, c))},

J_2 (DONE) = I (EDGE)}

Finally, the computation stops since J_2 is a stable state. []

We showed that under certain syntactic restrictions [Maindreville88b], a program computed using a relational computation can be guaranteed to be deterministic. One condition is to use a meta-semantics similar in essence to the idea of stratification described in [Apt86].

3.2. Characterization of relational computable rules

In general, given a program P, the original RDL1 computation of P (noted RDL1 (P)), differs from the relational computation of P (noted $RDL1^{rc}$ (P)). however, for a certain class of programs P (that correspond to fixpoint queries), there always exists a program P' such that RDL1 (P) ≡ $RDL1^{rc}$ (P). In this paper, we restricted ourselves to study the following "SiRuP" problem (Single Rule Program) : Given a single rule P, how to determine whether RDL1 (P) ≡ $RDL1^{rc}$ (P) ?. Let us precise more formally this last notion.

Definition 3.4. Let P be a single rule then P is said to be *relational computable* iff for any database instance I, Γ^{rc}_P and Γ_P have the same fixpoints.

The notion of relational computability presents two major features. First, it provides sufficient conditions to determine whether a production rule is deterministic. This can be further used to elaborate conditions under which a rule program is deterministic. The interest of this feature is related to the fact that in general, determining if a program is deterministic is undecidable. The second feature is that among all the possible sufficient characterizations of determinism of a single rule, relational computability also provides an efficient way of computing the stable state of the rule. Indeed, it enables to compute the effect of a rule as a relational algebra program. A large discussion about the use of relational computability for optimizing query evaluation is given in [Maindreville88b].

Unfortunately, we conjecture the following result.

Conjecture : It is recursively unsolvable to determine, for an arbitrary rule P, whether P is relational computable.

In the following, we describe a sufficient semantic characterization of a relational computable rule. The intuitive idea is to start from the relational computation of a rule and to impose conditions that guarantee that the stable state computed in this way is exactly the stable state computed by the RDL1 semantics. Two conditions are provided.

The first condition states that given a set of valuations in the relevant set of tuples for a rule, firing the rule with a particular valuation does not remove the other valuations from the relevant set. More formally :

Condition 1 : Let P be a rule and I be a database instance. Let $Rel_I(P) = \{\theta_1, \ldots, \theta_n\}$ then $Rel_I(P)$ is *rel_preserving* iff :

$$\text{for each } i,\ 1 \leq i \leq n,\ Rel_I(P) - \{\theta_i\} \subseteq Rel_{\Gamma\theta i(A)(I)}(P)$$

The second condition states that composition over actions is equivalent to concatenation over actions. The *composition* of two valued actions A and A' (denoted by A o A') is defined as the application of the action A over the result of performing A'.

Condition 2 : Let P : C → A be a rule and I be a database instance. Let $Rel_I(P) = \{\theta_1, \dots, \theta_n\}$ then $Rel_I(P)$ is *rel_endomorph* iff :
for each i and j, $1 \le i, j \le n$, $i \ne j$, $\theta i(A) \circ \theta j(A) = \theta i(A) \bullet \theta j(A)$
or equivalently : $\Gamma_{\theta i(A)}(\Gamma_{\theta j(A)}(I)) = \Gamma_{\theta i(A) \bullet \theta j(A)}(I)$

Remark that this condition only makes sense if $Rel_I(P)$ is rel_preserving.

Theorem 3.1. : Let P : C → A be a rule. If for any database instance I, $Rel_I(P)$ is *rel_endomorph* and *rel_preserving* then P is relational computable.
Sketch of proof :
Let $Rel_I(P) = \{\theta_1, \dots, \theta_n\}$. It is sufficient to prove that :
$\Gamma^{TC}{}_P(I) = \Gamma_{\theta 1(A) \bullet \dots \bullet \theta n(A)}(I) = \Gamma_{\theta 1(P)}(\Gamma_{\theta 2(P)}(\dots(\Gamma_{\theta n(P)})))(I)$.
This follows from the two previous conditions: the first condition says that the right hand side of the previous equation can be defined and the equality is proved by application of the condition 2 and by induction on the number of valuations θi.

4. Sufficient conditions for relational computability

4.1. Syntactic sufficient conditions

We present in this section two lemmas which provide sufficient conditions to decide if a rule is relational computable. These conditions are purely syntactic ones, i.e., they do not depend on the database state. Hence, they can be checked at compile time. We distinguish two cases depending on whether the action part of a rule contains deletions or insertions. For both cases, we first need technical lemmas which state the validity of formula of the relational calculus when the database instance is uptaded. The proofs of all these lemma can be found in [Simon88].

Notation : In the following, C(x1, ..., xn) denotes a rule condition, i.e., a relational calculus formula as :
$R_1(x_1)$ and ... and $R_n(x_n)$ and SF where $R_1, \dots, R_n$ are range predicates, $x_1, \dots, x_n$ are the free variables of C and SF is a sub-formula.

Lemma 4.1 : Let I be an instance of a database schema S = {R1, ..., Rn} and C be a condition. Let θ_i a valuation such that $I \models \theta_i(C)$. Let J be another instance of S such that $I(R_j)$ $J(R_j)$.
If - the range predicates appear positively in C and
- there is no j such that :
(i) $I(R_j) \ne J(R_j)$
(ii) SF contains a universally quantified range coupled predicate of the form $(\forall t \in R_j)$
then $J \models \theta_i(C)$.

Example 4.3 :

Let I be an instance of S = {R, Q} as defined in example 4.1 and C be :
`R(x) and (∀ y ∈ Q, y.C > 10)` such that I $\models \theta_i(C)$ for a valuation θ_i. Then, due to the form of C,we have :
$\forall J, I \subseteq J \Rightarrow J \models \theta_i(C)$.

Now let us consider C' : `R(x) and (∀ y ∈ Q, y.C > 10)`. Then, due to the universal range coupled quantifier over Q , inserting the constant tuple t = (9, 1) in the relation T invalidates a substitution θ_i such that I $\models \theta_i(C)$, i.e $I \cup \{t\} \not\models \theta_i(C)$. []

We now consider rules having only insertions in their action part :

Lemma 4.2 : Let P : C → A be a rule such that :
(i) C verifies the hypothesis of the lemma 4.1.
(ii) A is only composed of insertions.
Then the rule P is relational computable.

Example 4.4 :

- Consider the ancestor rule P1 :

```
ANCESTOR (x) and PARENT (x) and x.desc = y.par
        → + ANCESTOR (Asc = x.asc, Desc = y.child)
```

Lemma 4.2 yields that P1 is relational computable.

- Consider the following rule :

P2 : `R (x) and (∀ y ∈ Q, y.C > 10) → + R (C = x.A, D = x.B)`

The rule P2 is relational computable because the predicate Q does not appear in the action part of the rule.

- Finally let us consider the rule :

P3 : `R (x) and (∀ y ∈ Q, y.C > 10) → + Q (C = x.A, D = x.B)`

Then P3 is not relational computable because the variable y is universally quantified and Q appears in the action part of the rule. For instance, let I(P) = {(1,2), (12,7)}, I(Q) ={∅} be two instances of the relations P and Q. A relational computation of P3 leads to the following instances : I(P) = {(1,2), (12,7)}, I(Q) = {(1,2), (12,7)}. A one tuple-at-a-time computation leads to one of the two different instances : I(P) = {(1,2), (12,7)}, I(Q) ={(1,2)} and I(P) = {(1,2), (12,7)}, I(Q) ={(12,7), (1,2)}. []

We now present a technical lemma similar to lemma 4.1.

Lemma 4.3 :

Let I(R) be an instance of a relation R and let C = (R(x) and SF) be a condition. Let $\Theta = \{\theta_1,..., \theta_n\}$ be a set of valuations such that I $\models \theta_i$(R(x) and SF). Let J (R) be another instance of R such that :

J(R) = I(R) - $\{\theta_k(R(x))\}$.

Then, if there is no variable existentially quantified over R in SF, we have :

J $\models \theta_i$(R(x) and SF) for each $i \neq k$.

Lemma 4.4 :

Let P : C → A be a rule such that :

(i) C verifies the hypothesis of the lemma 4.3.

(ii) A is composed of only one deletion whose argument is a tuple variable.

Then the rule P is relational computable.

Example 4.4 :

Let us consider the following rule :

P4 : `R(x) and x.C > 10 and (∃ y∈ Q, y.C > 10) → - R(x).`

The rule P4 is detected as relational computable.

Consider the following rule :

P5 : `R(x) and x.C > 10 and (∃ y ∈ Q, y.C > 10) → - Q(x).`

Due to the presence of the existential quantifier over the variable y, the rule P5 is not relational computable.

Let B denote the relational schema BROTHER = {Name1,Name2}.

Then the following rule is not relational computable:

`B (x) →- B (Name1 = x.Name2, Name2 = x.Name1)`

Indeed, assume I(B) = {(John, Paul), (Paul, John)}. A relational computation of the rule leads B to have I(B) = {∅} as instance and a one-tuple-at-a-time one leads to one of the different instances: I(B) = {(John, Paul)}, I(B) = {(Paul, John)}. []

4.2 An algorithm to detect a relational computable rule.

In the previous section we gave sufficient syntaxic conditions for a rule to be set oriented. As it will be shown on the following example, these conditions are not optimal. Consider the rule P6 over the relational schemas R {A, B} and Q {C, D}:

P6 : `R (x) and (∀ y ∈ Q, y.C > 10) →+ Q (C = 11, D = x.B) .`

This rule is not detected as relational computable by application of the lemma 4.2 since there exists a universal quantifier over a relation which is updated by an insertion. Hence, according to the action part of the rule, and if we suppose Q empty before any firing of the rule the closed formula (`∀ y ∈ Q, y.C > 10`) is always true. So, this rule is obviously relational computable. Thus, it is interesting to provide weaker conditions to decide if a rule is relational computable. The algorithm we present uses the two previous semantic conditions of section 3 to detect a relational computable rule. We first give an intuitive description of the algorithm using examples and then give its general form.

Example 4.1.

Let R {A, B} and Q {C, D} be two relational schemas. Consider the rule :

`P0 : R (x) and (∀y ∈ Q, y.C < 10) → + Q (C = x.A, D = x.B)`

Consider two valuations θi and θj that map x into x_i (resp. x_j) and such that θi (A) and θj (A) are satisfied in a current database state I. Thus, θi and θj ∈ Rel_I (P0). Our objective is to decide if

Rel $_I$ (P0) is rel_preserving and rel_endomorph.

Let us explicit that Rel $_I$ (P0) is rel_endomorph :

$\theta i\ (A) \bullet \theta j\ (A) = + Q\ (C = x_i.A, D = x_i.B) + Q\ (C = x_j.A, D = x_j.B)$ [1]

$\theta i\ (A) \circ \theta j\ (A) = (+ Q\ (C = x_i.A, D = x_i.B)) \circ (+ Q\ (C = x_j.A, D = x_j.B))$ [2]

We want to decide if $\theta i\ (A) \circ \theta j\ (A) = \theta i\ (A) \bullet \theta j\ (A)$. Now, using the two above expressions, we can derive formulae that are implicitly satisfied.

From [1], as : $\theta i \in$ Rel $_I$ (P0) and $\theta j \in$ Rel $_I$ (P0),

then we derive : $\varphi_1 \equiv x_i \in R$ and $x_j \in R$ and $(\forall\ y \in Q, y.C < 10)$

From [2], as : $\theta j \in$ Rel $_I$ (P0)

we first derive : $\varphi_2 \equiv x_j \in R$ and $(\forall\ y \in Q, y.C < 10)$

then, if Rel $_I$ (P0) is rel_preserving : $\theta i \in$ Rel $_J$ (P0) where $J = \Gamma_{\theta i\ (A)}$ (I)

we also derive : $\varphi_3 \equiv x_i \in R$ and $(\forall\ y \in Q \cup \{(x_j.A, x_j.B)\}, y.C < 10)$

Now, Rel $_I$ (P0) is rel_preserving and rel_endomorph means that : $\varphi_1 \equiv \varphi_2 \wedge \varphi_3$. This last equivalence can be further simplified by eliminating the expressions that are common to φ_1 and $\varphi_2 \wedge \varphi_3$ and we are led to examine whether the formula $(\forall\ y \in Q \cup \{(x_j.A, x_j.B)\}, y.C < 10)$ is satisfiable. This formula can be transformed into :

$(\forall\ y \in Q, y.C < 10) \wedge (\forall\ y \in \{(x_j.A, x_j.B)\}, y.C < 10)$

The first conjunctive member is always true by hypothesis and the second member is equivalent to test $x_j.A < 10$. Since the property must be true for any database state I and any valuation θj, if the formula $(\forall\ x \in R, x.A < 10)$ is valid for any I then we infer that $\varphi_1 \equiv \varphi_2 \wedge \varphi_3$ is valid and then that Rel $_I$ (P0) is rel_preserving and rel_endomorph. Since R is never modified by the rule, it is sufficient to enforce the formula $(\forall\ x \in R, x.A < 10)$ for any *initial* database state I. This means that this formula is viewed as an integrity constraint on which the relational computability of P0 relies. []

Example 4.2 :

Consider the same relational schemas as above and the rule :

```
P : R (x) and Q (y) and x.A = y.D → - R (x) + Q (x)
```

Consider two valuations θi and θj that map x and y into x_i and y_i (resp. x_j and y_j) and such that θi (A) and θj (A) are satisfied in a current database state I.

Let us explicit that Rel $_I$ (P) is rel_endomorph :

$\theta i\ (A) \bullet \theta j\ (A) = - R\ (x_i) + Q\ (x_i) - R\ (x_j) + Q\ (x_j)$ [1]

$\theta i\ (A) \circ \theta j\ (A) = (- R\ (x_i) + Q\ (x_i)) \circ (- R\ (x_j) + Q\ (x_j))$ [2]

We want to decide if $\theta i\ (A) \circ \theta j\ (A) = \theta i\ (A) \bullet \theta j\ (A)$. Now, using the two above expressions, we can derive formulae that are implicitly satisfied.

From [1], as : $\theta i \in$ Rel $_I$ (P) and $\theta j \in$ Rel $_I$ (P), then we derive :

$\varphi_1 \equiv x_i \in R$ and $x_j \in R$ and $y_i \in Q$ and $y_j \in Q$ and $x_i.A = y_i.D$ and $x_j.A = y_j.D$

From [2], as : $\theta j \in$ Rel $_I$ (P) we first derive :

$\varphi_2 \equiv x_j \in R$ and $y_j \in Q$ and $x_j.A = y_j.D$

then, if Rel $_I$ (P) is rel_preserving : $\theta i \in$ Rel $_J$ (P) where $J = \Gamma_{\theta i\ (A)}$ (I)

we also derive : $\varphi_3 \equiv x_i \in R - \{x_j\}$ and $y_i \in Q \cup \{(x_j)\}$ and $x_i.A = y_i.D$

Now, Rel $_I$ (P) is rel_preserving and rel_endomorph means that : $\varphi_1 \equiv \varphi_2 \wedge \varphi_3$. This last equivalence can be further simplified by eliminating the expressions that are common to φ_1 and $(\varphi_2 \wedge \varphi_3)$ and we are led to examine whether the formula :

$x_i \in R$ and $y_i \in Q$ and $x_i.A = y_i.D \equiv x_i \in R - \{x_j\}$ and $y_i \in Q \cup \{(x_j)\}$ and $x_i.A = y_i.D$
is valid. The second member of the equivalence can be rewritten as :

$((x_i \in R$ and $x_i \neq x_j))$ and $((y_i \in Q$ and $x_i.A = y_i.D)$ or $(x_i.A = x_j.B))$

and further as:

$(x_i \in R$ and $x_i \neq x_j$ and $y_i \in Q$ and $x_i.A = y_i.D$) or $(x_i \in R$ and $x_i \neq x_j$ and $x_i.A = x_j.B)$
The first disjunctive member is a valid formula. Thus, we can infer that P is relational computable.

The general form of the algorithm is now given.

```
algorithm  detect_rel_comput.
input : a rule P : C → A
output : a formula whose satisfiability attests the relational computability
        of P
begin
   1. Let θi and θj be two valuations that map each free variable x^1, ..., x^p of
      C into some constants c_i^1,..., c_i^p (resp. c_j^1,..., c_j^p).
   2. Explicit respectively the expressions θi (A) • θj (A)  [1]
                                         and θi (A) o θj (A)  [2]
   3. From [1], use that θi ∈ Rel_I (P) and θj ∈ Rel_I (P) to derive φ1
      From [2], use that θj ∈ Rel_I (P) and derive φ2
           then use that  θi ∈ Rel_J (P) where : J = Γθi (A) (I) to derive φ3
   % this step uses the rel_preserving property of Rel_I (P) %
   4. Built the formula :    φ1 ≡ φ2 ∧ φ3.
   % uses the rel_endomorphism and the rel_preserving property of Rel_I (P) %
   5. Find the simplest form φ of the above formula (i.e., eliminate
      redundancies)
   6. if φ is valid then P is relational computable
        else if φ is unsatifiable then P is not relational computable
          else φ is an integrity constraint on which relies the rel. comp. of P
end.
```

Algorithm 4.1

4.3 Semantic characterization of set oriented rules

In this subsection, we present a more restricted but more applicable algorithm than the one presented in the previous section. This algorithm applies to a subset of RDL1 rules that consists of rules having only one elementary action in their action part. Moreover, we only consider deletion actions having a tuple variable as argument. The motivation for this is the following : we know that for such rules, the first condition of the theorem 3.1 (rel_preserving) is sufficient to ensure the relational computation of a rule. Remark that this result has already been used in the proof of the lemmas 4.2 and 4.4. Hence, in this case the general algorithm can be simplified.

Before introducing the new algorithm, we define the notion of connection graph.

Definition 4.1 : The *connection graph* of a rule P is a graph where :

(i) nodes are terms figuring in the rule P and

(ii) two nodes t1 and t2 are connected in the graph by an oriented arc from t1 to t2 iff the equality (t1 = t2) appears in the action part of the rule.

Example 4.5 :

Consider the above rule P6 :

`R(x) and (∀ y ∈ Q, y.C > 10) →+ Q (C = 11, D = x.B)`

Its connection graph is portrayed on *Figure 4.1*.

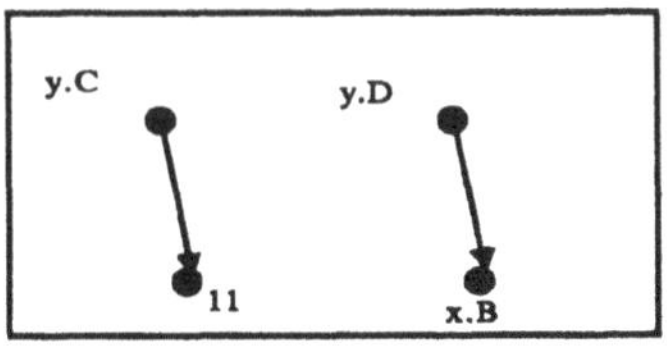

Figure 4.1 : Connection graph for P.

The aim of our method is first to rewrite any sub-formula figuring in the condition part of the rule into a formula which contains no variable ranging over relations appearing in the action part of the rule. This rewriting is done using the connection graph of the rule. Then, as the general algorithm does, the free variables appearing in the formula are universally quantified. Finally, the validity of a resulting closed formula is checked against the database.

Let P be a rule of the following form : P : RP **and** FF **and** CF →± R (t) where RP is a conjunction of range predicates, FF is an opened relational calculus sub-formula and CF a closed relational calculus sub-formula put in prenex form.

In the following, we note CFF the formula FF where all the variables are universally quantified.

```
Relational checking algorithm :
input: A rule P: RP and FF and CF → A
output: a formula whose satisfiability attests the relational computability
        of P
begin
  1. Built the connection graph of P.
  2. Rewrite the formula appearing in the action part of the rule
     according to the connection graph.
  3. Quantify universally the free variables figuring in the action
     part of the rule.
  If the action is an insertion then
     If the formula CFF ⇒ CF
           is true over the database then the rule is relational
           computable.
  If the action is a deletion then
     If the formula CFF ⇒ ¬CF
           is true over the database then the rule is relational
           computable.
end.
```

Algorithm 4.2

We now illustrate the algorithm with several characteristic examples.

Example 4.6 :

Consider the rule P7: `R(x) and (∀ y ∈ Q, y.C < 10) →+ Q (C = 11, D = x.B)`

Then, according to the connection graph portrayed on *Figure 4.1* the formula (R(x) **and** ∀ y ∈ Q, y.C < 10) is rewritten into : (∀ x ∈ R ∀ y ∈ Q TRUE ⇒ 11 < 10), (we assume here that the relation Q is empty before firing P). This closed formula is trivially always false. Thus, this rule is not relational computable.

Consider the rule P6. The previous algorithm leads to check the formula (∀ x ∈ R ∀ y ∈ Q TRUE ⇒ 11 > 10). This closed formula is always true. Thus, this rule is detected as relational computable .

Consider now the rule P0 defined in example 4.1 :

P0 : R (x) **and** (∀ y ∈ Q, y.C < 10) →+ Q (C = x.A, D = x.B) .

The connection graph of P0 is portrayed on the figure 4.2.

Then, the formula (R(x) **and** ∀ y ∈ Q, y.C < 10) is rewritten into :

(∀ x ∈ R TRUE ⇒ x.A < 10). If this closed formula is true, the rule P0 is relational computable. Then we obtain the same result than the one expressed in the example 4.1.

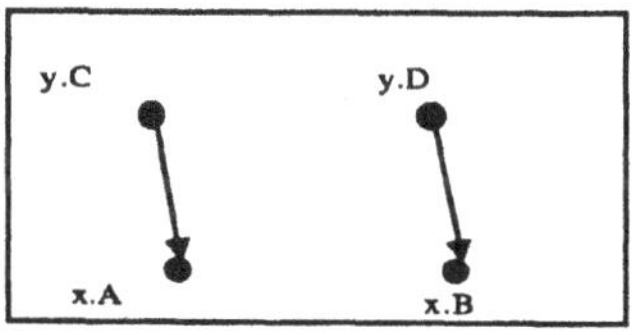

Figure 4.2

Consider the rule

P8 : R(x) **and** (∀ y ∈ Q, y.D > x.A) → + Q (C = x.A, D = x.B) .

The connection graph of P8 is portrayed on *Figure 4.2*. The formula (R(x) **and** ∀ y ∈ Q, y.D > x.A) is rewritten into : (∀ x ∈ R ∀ x' ∈ R TRUE ⇒ x'.B > x.A) . Remark that two quantified variables are ranging over the predicate R. The validity of this formula determines the relationality of P.

Finally, consider the following rule :

P9 : R(x) **and** (∃ y ∈ Q, y.C > 10) →- Q (C = x.A, D = x.B) .

Here, the deletion in the action part of the rule leads to rewrite the sub-formula into: ⌉ (∃ x ∈ R, x.A > 10) which is equivalent to (∀ x ∈ R, x.A ≤ 10). Hence, the relational computability of P9 depends to the validity of this last formula.[]

This method permits to detect at run time if a rule is relational computable or not. Let us point out that the method leads to check the validity of closed formulae over the database. These formulae can be viewed as *integrity constraints* over database relations. In particular, they can be automatically maintained during the life of the database. As soon as one integrity constraint is violated the corresponding rule is set to a non relational computation. One of the most interesting feature of the proposed method is to benefit of works which have been done for efficiently enforcing integrity constraints [Simon87a, Simon87b].

5. Conclusion

In this paper, we presented a general framework to study production rule language for relational databases, called RDL1. After introducing the syntax and semantics of RDL1, we gave a formal definition of a subset (relational computable rules) of the language which can be processed by relational algebra programs. This class of rules corresponds to deterministic rules. Furthermore, these rules can be efficiently processed over a relational DBMS. We introduced sufficient conditions which ensured the relational computability of rules. We derived from these conditions two algorithms to check the relational computability of a rule. The first one can be used at compile time and gives sufficient syntactic conditions for a rule to be relational. The second one must be used at run time and gives semantic sufficient conditions. This last method leads to check integrity constraints over database relations. A lot of work remains to be done to improve the proposed methods: (i) to store semantic information about the database relations in order to have a more efficient control of the integrity constraints, (ii) the checking of the integrity constraints must also be used to improve the performance of the rule's firing.

Acknowledgements

We wish to thank Serge Abiteboul for fruitful discussions on the rule language.

References :

[Abiteboul87] S. Abiteboul, V. Vianu : "*Transaction languages for database update and specification*", INRIA Research Report, N° 715, 64 pages, Sept. 1987.

[Apt86] K.R. Apt, H. Blair, A. Walker : "*Towards a Declarative Knowledge*" IBM Research Report RC 11681, April 1986.

[Codd71] E.F. Codd : " *A Data Base Sublanguage founded on the relational calculus.*" Proc. of ACM-SIGFIDET, 1971.

[Chandra80] K.A Chandra, D. Harel : "*Computable Queries for Relational Databases*", Journal of Computer and Systems Science, 1980.

[Maindreville87] C. de Maindreville, E. Simon : " *A Predicate Transition Net for Evaluating Queries against Rules in a DBMS.*" INRIA Research Report N° 604, Feb 1987. Also Extended abstract in Adavances in Data Bases, Port Camargue, France May 1987.

[Maindreville88a] C. de Maindreville, E. Simon : " *A Production Rule based approach to Deductive Databases.*" . Proc of 4th Int.Conf. on Data Engineering, Los Angeles 1988.

[Maindreville88b] C. de Maindreville, E. Simon : "*Modelling Non Deterministic Queries and Updates in Deductive Databases*", Proc. Int. Conf. on VLDB, Los Angeles, 1988.

[Nicolas82] J.M. Nicolas, R. Demolombe : "*On the stability of relational queries*", Proc of Int Workshop : Logical bases for Databases, CERT, Toulouse, 1982.

[Simon87a] E. Simon, P. Valduriez : "*Design and Analysis of a Relational Integrity Subsystem.*" MCC Technical Report DB-O15, 51 pages, Austin, Texas, Jan. 87.

[Simon87b] E. Simon : "*Simplifying integrity constraints by generating differential pre-tests*", INRIA Research Report N° 742, 54 pages, Nov. 1987.

[Simon88] E. Simon, C. de Maindreville : "*Deciding whether a production rule is relational computable*", Research Report INRIA.

Modeling Inheritance and Genericity in Object Oriented-Databases

C. Lécluse and P. Richard

GIP Altaïr, BP 105
78153 Le Chesnay Cédex
France

Abstract

This paper formalizes inheritance and genericity in the context of object oriented databases. We present a uniform view for objects and types. We model, in the same framework, multiple inheritance and unconstrained genericity. We plan to use this model as the theoretical foundation for the O_2 object-oriented database system.

1 Introduction

The object concept is acquiring a great importance in the database field. Standard database systems based on data models such as the relational model provided a good solution for business applications. However they fall short of solving problems introduced by new applications such as CAD, CASE and office automation. Moreover, relational systems are well suited for ad hoc querying, but not for application development. Programming applications implies a communication between the query language of the system and an external programming language. This has a lot of drawbacks: the programmer needs to learn two different languages, the communication is tuple at a time and the two languages generally have different type system (impedance mismatch).

The object-oriented paradigm is a good way of solving these problems. Following [Wegner 87], the characteristics of object-oriented languages are the notions of objects, classes and inheritance. As opposed to tuples in the relational model, objects have an identity which is independent of their value. This is useful for sharing and updating objects. Classes factorize common structure of objects, and inheritance is a good modeling tool. It allows to reuse existing objects or classes, and to define new specialized objects or classes [Goldberg 83,Lécluse 87,Maier 85].

Theoretical foundations for object-oriented languages [Bruce 86,Cardelli 85,Milner 78] already exist. These models formalize standard object-oriented features such as inheritance and genericity (type polymorphism). However, they do not take into account many important database issues. Databases objects are highly structured and built using constructors such as the set and tuple. Data models manipulating highly structured values have been proposed [Abiteboul 87] and [Pistor 85,Schek 85]. These models do not consider the notion of object identity nor the inheritance (subtyping) mechanism. Other models exist for object-oriented databases. FAD [Bancilhon 87] is a data model with tuple and set constructors and object identity. However, FAD does not model types inheritance. Another interesting approach is proposed in LOGIN [Ait-Kaci 86] where the inheritance relationship is introduced in a logic programming framework. However, objects of this model are limited to tuples, and there is no object identity although object sharing is achieved through the introduction of variables.

The main features of our model are the following:

- A uniform view of type structures and objects: there is no distinction between objects and type structures. Objects are seen as single-value types.
- The construction of generic types: as said in [Meyer 86], some applications are not easily handled using inheritance, but are easily developed using unconstrained genericity.
- A set inclusion semantics for the inheritance relationship which apply to both non-generic and generic types.
- Multiple inheritance.

In this paper, we further extend the data model of [Lécluse 88] which incorporated set and tuple constructors, object identity altogether with inheritance and genericity. However, the model of [Lécluse 88] only deals with the static aspect of types, that is the type structures. We consider here, both static and behavioural aspects of types.

We first introduce informally the main notions of this model, using examples. Entities represent our computer world. They consist of an identifier (a name for the entity) and a value. Values can be basic values, such as **-2, 0, 3.1415, 'the sky is blue'**, but also **integer, real, string**. Note that the symbol **integer** is considered as a basic value just as the symbol **1**. Intuitively, the value **integer** represents the set of all integers (in the database), whereas **1** represents only one of these integers, namely 1. They can be both considered as types (type structures), because **1** can be seen as a single-value type, and as objects. This is why we introduce the notion of entity which covers both the notions of type structures and objects. We construct more complex entities using the set and tuple constructors. A set value is a term like $\{i_1, i_2\}$ where i_1 and i_2 are entity identifiers. Given entities (i_1, 1) and (i_2, -2), the term $\{i_1, i_2\}$ represents a(all) set(s) containing the integers 1 and -2. We can build tuple values in the same way: [name: i_3, age: i_4] is a tuple term. Note that the fields of a tuple term are named. We can thus construct arbitrarily complex entities, as we show below. We shall adopt the following conventions in the following of the paper: basic entity values (such as **1**) are written bold-faced, whereas entity identifiers are written in italics. We are listing below a set of entities.

(*integer* , **integer**)

(*string* , **string**)

(*person* , [name: *string* , age: *integer*])

(*employee* , [name: *string* , age: *integer* , salary: *integer*])

(*department* , {*employee* })

(*john_name* , **'John Smith Jr.'**)

(*bill_name* , **'Bill Smith.'**)

(*fourty* , **40**)

(*fiveK* , **5000**)

(*john* , [name: *john_name* , age: *fourty*])

(*bill* , [name: *bill_name* , age: *fourty* , salary: *fiveK*])

Although we define (and use) all these entities in a uniform way, we can distinguish intuitively between the first five entities (*integer*, ..., *department*) and the last ones (*john_name*, ..., *bill*). Entities such as *person* represents the set of all persons in the database, that is the set of all tuple entities having the corresponding fields. *john* is such an entity. Similarly, the entity *john* represents the set of all tuple entities having name *john_name* and age *fourty*, that is, itself in this example. As explained before, we can consider *person* as a type structure and *john* as an object, but we can also consider *john* as a type structure representing, here, only one value. This approach will give a uniform semantics for types and objects.

We define the notion of *refinement* between values. We denote this ordering by $\leq$. Examples of refinements are:

1. **30** $\leq$ **integer**. This means that every entity with value 30 is also an entity with an integer value.

2. **'John Smith Jr.'** $\leq$ **string**, for the same reason.

3. [name: *string* , age: *integer* , salary: *integer*] $\leq$ [name: *string* , age: *integer*]. This relationship is more "classical" than the previous ones. It means that triples such as employees can be seen as special cases of pairs, such as persons. We shall see that our interpretation for tuples is similar to that of Cardelli in [Cardelli 84].

We can see on these examples that we identify, intuitively, the membership and subset relationships. Indeed, the inequalities 1 and 2 above are membership relations. The last one is a subset relation.

We also want to model a kind of genericity, namely unconstrained genericity. To this end, we introduce variables in the terms defining entities. The following expressions are examples of generic entities:

- (*ab_tuple* , [a: x, b: y])
- (*ab_=_tuple* , [a: x, b: x])

Intuitively, the entity of name *ab_tuple* represents the entities of value $[a : x, b : y]$, for all possible entities x and y in the database. The variables x and y are abstractions for entity identifiers. We can think of *ab_tuple* as a notation for all tuple entities having two fields 'a' and 'b'. The generic entity *ab_=_tuple* is a notation for all tuple entities with two fields 'a' and 'b' having the same value.
To a generic entity can be applied a *substitution*. That is, identifiers can be substituted to variables in the entity. For example, applying the substitution ⟨x/*real*, y/*real*⟩ to the entity of name *ab_tuple* leads to the entity (*ab_tuple*(*integer, real*), [a:*integer*, b:*real*]).

The paper is organized as follows. Section 2 formally defines all the notions that we just introduced. In Section 3, we gives a syntactical characterization of the refinement relationship, and Section 4 contains some concluding remarks.

2 Entities and their Semantics

In this section, we define the syntax and the semantics of entities.

2.1 Syntax

We consider some basic values (**1, 2, ..., 3.4, 'the sky is still blue', ..., integer, real, string**) and we use the set and tuple constructors to build structured values from the basic ones.
We suppose given the following four disjoint sets:

- A countable set $\mathcal{D}$, the union of the set N of integers, the set R of (computer) reals, the set S of strings, and the set {**nil, any, integer, real, string**}. Formally, N (resp R and S) are sets of numerals which represent the integers (the reals and the strings). For the sake of simplicity, we do not distinguish values from their representation.
- A countably infinite set $\mathcal{A}$ of symbols, the *attributes*. The elements of $\mathcal{A}$ are names for tuple fields.
- A countably infinite set $\mathcal{V}$ of symbols, the *variables*. The elements of $\mathcal{V}$ range over entities. They are denoted by the letters x, y and z with or without subscripts.
- A countably infinite set $\mathcal{I}$ of symbols called *ground identifiers*. We extend ground identifiers as follows: A *valuated identifier* is an expression $i(\epsilon_1, \ldots, \epsilon_n)$ where i is a ground identifier of $\mathcal{I}$ and $\epsilon_1, \ldots, \epsilon_n$ are either variables, or ground identifiers or valuated identifiers. The ground identifier i is called the *root* of the valuated identifier We shall note $\mathcal{I}^*$ the set of all identifiers and we shall write them in italics.

Note: In the following, the term "identifier" will refer to either ground or valuated identifiers.
We can now define the notion of *term*.

Definition 2.1 We denote by $\mathcal{T}$ the set of all terms defined as follows:

- Every element v of $\mathcal{D}$ is a term, called a *basic term*.
- *Set-structured* terms are expressions of the form: $\{\epsilon_1, \ldots, \epsilon_n\}$[1], where the ϵ_i's are either variables or identifiers.
- *Tuple-structured* terms are expressions of the form: $[a_1 : \epsilon_1, \ldots, a_n : \epsilon_n]$[2], where a_1, ..., a_n are attributes in $\mathcal{A}$ and the ϵ_i's have the same meaning as above.

We call *degree*(t) the number of variables which appear in the term t. A term t is *generic* if its degree is greater than 0, otherwise it is *ground*. □

Examples of ground terms are:

- **integer**
- [name: *string*, age: *integer*]
- {*integer*, *set(real)*}

The first term represents the set of all integers. The second one represents the set of all tuples having an attribute name whose values are strings and an attribute age whose values are integers. The last one represents all (heterogeneous) sets containing integers and sets of reals. Examples of generic terms are:

- {x}
- {*integer*, x}
- [a: x, b: x]
- [name: *string*, children: *set*(x)]

The first term represents the generic homogeneous "set". Intuitively, applying substitutions to this term will produce all possible homogeneous sets. The second represents a generic heterogeneous set containing integers. The third one represents a generic tuple having two fields of the *same* value. Note that expressions like {*integer*, *integer*} are valid terms. However, as we shall see later, the semantics of {*integer*, *integer*} is the same as the semantics of {*integer*}.
We can now define the notion of entity.

---

[1]or {} if n=0

[2]or [] if n=0

Definition 2.2 An *entity* is a pair e = (*id*, t), where *id* is an identifier and t is a term of $\mathcal{T}$ such that:

- either t is a ground term and id is a ground identifier of $\mathcal{I}$, in this case, e is called a ground entity,
- or t is a generic term and id is a valuated identifier i(ϵ_1, ..., ϵ_p) such that every variable appearing in t also appear in id. In this case, e is called a generic entity.

We define, in a natural way, the notion of ***basic***, ***set-structured*** and ***tuple-structured*** entities. If e=(id, t) is an entity then *identifier*(e) denotes the identifier id and *term*(e) denotes the term t. □

Figure 1 gives several examples of entities. We shall use variable ***substitutions***. A substitution σ is an expression $\langle x_1/i_1, \ldots, x_n/i_n\rangle$ where the x_j's are variables and the i_j's are identifiers. As usual, if t is a generic term and σ a substitution, we note t.σ the term obtained by replacing in t the variables by the corresponding identifiers of σ. If i is an identifier and σ a substitution, we note i.σ the identifier obtained by replacing in i the variables by the corresponding identifiers of σ. Finally, if e=(i, t) is an entity and σ is a substitution, we note e.σ=(i.σ, t.σ). The following are examples of such substitutions.

- (*set*(x), {x}).⟨x/*integer*⟩ = (*set(integer)*, {*integer*})
- (*set*(x), {x}).⟨x/*real*⟩ = (*set(real)*, {*real*})
- (*age_tuple*(x), [age: x]).⟨x/*integer*⟩ = (*age_tuple(integer)*, [age: *integer*])

We now introduce the notion of ***consistents set of entities.***

Definition 2.3 Let $\mathcal{E}$ be a set of entities. $\mathcal{E}$ is *consistent* iff the following conditions hold:

- There are no two entities with the same identifier root.
- For every entity e in $\mathcal{E}$, and for every identifier id of root i appearing in term(e), there is an entity in $\mathcal{E}$ having i as identifier root.
- For every entity (*id*, t) in $\mathcal{E}$, if *id* is a valuated identifier, then *id* only contains distinct variables.

□

Intuitively, in a consistent set of entities, each entity has a unique identifier, there are no "dangling pointers" in it, and the generic entity identifiers only contain variables. For example, (set(x), {x}) is a generic entity which can appear in a consistent set of entities. However, (set(*integer*), {*integer*}) is not legal in a consistent set of entities, because it does not "completely" define the entity ***set***. It is the result of the substitution ⟨x/*integer*⟩ in the entity (set(x), {x}).
Figure 1 is an example of a consistent set of entities. Note that our construction allows self-referencing entities. As entities are used to model both types and objects, we can define self-referencing types (such as *person* in Figure 1) but also self-referencing objects.

1. (*nil*, nil)
2. (*integer*, integer)
3. (*string*, string)
4. (*person*, [name: *string*, age: *integer*, married_to: *person*])
5. (*employee*, [name: *string*, age: *integer*, married_to: *person*, salary: *integer*])
6. (*department*, {*employee* })
7. (*company*, {*department* })
8. (*age_tuple(x)*, [age: x])
9. (*set(x)*, {x})
10. (*aName*, 'John Smith Jr.')
11. (*bad_weather*, 'The sky is not blue any more')
12. (*anotherName*, 'Bill Smith.')
13. (*thirty*, 30)
14. (*fourty*, 40)
15. (*fiveK*, 5000)
16. (*john*, [name: *aName*, age: *thirty*, married_to: *nil*])
17. (*bill*, [name: *anotherName*, age: *fourty*, married_to: *nil*, salary: *fiveK*])
18. (*aDepartment*, {*bill* })
19. (*aBag*, {*thirty*, *fourty*, *bad_weather*})

Figure 1: A consistent set of entities

An important aspect of our definition of entities is genericity. For example, the entity (set(x), {x}) of Figure 1 is a generic entity which represents any kind of (homogeneous) sets. Moreover, ground and generic terms are manipulated in a uniform way. The main originality of this model, is that we do not distinguish between type structures and objects. These two notions are subsumed by the notion of entity. For example, (one, 1) and ($integer$, integer) are treated in the same way.

In the following paragraph, we define the semantics of terms, using consistent sets of entities.

2.2 Semantics

In this section, we define the semantics of our model. In what follows, in order to distinguish between set-structured terms and sets in the meta-language, we note the latter with bold curly brackets. Let $\mathcal{E}$ be a consistent set of entities. To define the interpretation of terms in $\mathcal{E}$, we use an extension of $\mathcal{E}$ with all possible substitutions of the entities of $\mathcal{E}$. We define $\mathcal{E}^*$ as follows:

$$\mathcal{E}^* = \mathcal{E} \cup \Big\{ \text{e}.\sigma, \text{ where e} \in \mathcal{E} \text{ and } \sigma \text{ is a substitution} \Big\}.$$

A term t is *defined on* $\mathcal{E}$, if it contains only identifiers [3] of entities of $\mathcal{E}$. In the following definition, we give an interpretation for all terms defined on $\mathcal{E}$. The interpretation of a ground term is a subset of $\mathcal{E}^*$. For a generic term t, the interpretation of t is a function mapping all substitutions σ on the interpretation of the corresponding substitution of t.

Definition 2.4 Let $\mathcal{E}$ be a consistent set of entities. Let t be a term defined on $\mathcal{E}$. The interpretation $I_{\mathcal{E}}(\text{t})$ is defined as follows:
Ground terms:

- Basic terms:

$$\begin{array}{lll}
I_{\mathcal{E}}(\text{nil}) & = & \Big\{ (i, \text{nil}) \in \mathcal{E} \Big\}. \\
I_{\mathcal{E}}(\text{any}) & = & \mathcal{E}^*. \\
I_{\mathcal{E}}(\text{v}) & = & I_{\mathcal{E}}(\text{nil}) \cup \Big\{ (i, \text{v}) \in \mathcal{E} \Big\}, \text{ if v is a symbol of } \mathcal{D}. \\
I_{\mathcal{E}}(\text{integer}) & = & I_{\mathcal{E}}(\text{nil}) \cup \Big\{ (i, \text{n}) \in \mathcal{E} \ \wedge \text{n} \in \text{N} \Big\}. \\
I_{\mathcal{E}}(\text{real}) & = & I_{\mathcal{E}}(\text{nil}) \cup \Big\{ (i, \text{r}) \in \mathcal{E} \ \wedge \text{r} \in \text{R} \Big\}. \\
I_{\mathcal{E}}(\text{string}) & = & I_{\mathcal{E}}(\text{nil}) \cup \Big\{ (i, \text{s}) \in \mathcal{E} \ \wedge \text{s} \in \text{S} \Big\}. \\
I_{\mathcal{E}}(\text{boolean}) & = & I_{\mathcal{E}}(\text{nil}) \cup \Big\{ (i, \text{b}) \in \mathcal{E} \ \wedge \text{b} \in \text{B} \Big\}.
\end{array}$$

- Set-structured terms: if t = $\{i_1 \ldots, i_n\}$, where i_α is an identifier.
$I_{\mathcal{E}}(\text{t}) = I_{\mathcal{E}}(\text{nil}) \cup \Big\{ (i.\sigma, \text{v}.\sigma) \in \mathcal{E}^* \text{ where v}.\sigma = \{j_1, \ldots, j_q\} \text{ and } j_k \in \bigcup_{l=1}^{n} I_{\mathcal{E}}(term(i_l)) \Big\}$.
- Tuple-structured terms: if t = $[a_1\text{: } i_1, \ldots, a_n\text{: } i_n]$, where i_α is an identifier.
$I_{\mathcal{E}}(\text{t}) = I_{\mathcal{E}}(\text{nil}) \cup \Big\{ (i.\sigma, \text{v}.\sigma) \in \mathcal{E}^*$ where v.σ is a tuple-structured term
$[a_1\text{: } j_1, \ldots, a_n\text{: } j_n, \ldots, a_{n+p}\text{: } j_{n+p}]$ such that for all k in 1, …, n, $j_k \in I_{\mathcal{E}}(\text{term}(i_k)) \Big\}$.

[3] or substitutions of such identifiers

Generic terms:

- If t is a generic term of degree p, $I_{\mathcal{E}}(\mathrm{t})$ is a function from the set of all substitutions, into $2^{\mathcal{E}^*}$ such that:

$$I_{\mathcal{E}}(\mathrm{t})(\sigma) = I_{\mathcal{E}}(\mathrm{t}.\sigma).$$

□

Let us consider the consistent set defined in Figure 1. The following table gives the interpretation of a few terms.

	t	$I_{\mathcal{E}}(\mathrm{t})$
1	**30**	$\{$*nil, thirty*$\}$
2	**integer**	$\{$*nil, thirty, fourty, fiveK*$\}$
3	**string**	$\{$*nil, aName, anotherName, bad_weather*$\}$
4	[name: *string*, age: *integer*]	$\{$*nil, john, bill*$\}$
5	$\{$*person*$\}$	$\{$*nil, aDepartment, set(bill), set(john)*$\}$
6	$\{$*integer, string*$\}$	$\{$*nil, aBag, set(thirty), set(aName), ...*$\}$
7	[age: x]	$\{$ ⟨x/*integer*⟩ → $\{$*nil, john, bill, age_tuple(nil), age_tuple(thirty), age_tuple(fourty), age_tuple(fiveK)*$\}$ ⟨x/*real*⟩ → $\{$*nil, age_tuple(nil)*$\}$ ⋮ $\}$

This table shows that for basic ground terms such as **integer**, the interpretation is simply the set of identifiers of $\mathcal{E}$ which represent entities with an integer value. The fourth row shows that we interpret tuples with every entity which is *at least* defined on the attributes of the term. This is why an 4-tuple like *bill* is in the interpretation of the 2-tuple "[name: *string*, age: *integer*]". As shown in rows 5 and 6, substitutions of generic entities are in the interpretation of terms. Indeed, the substitution of the entity *set(x)*[4] with ⟨x/*bill*⟩ gives an element of the interpretation of $\{$*person*$\}$ identified by *set(bill)*. Another interesting point of this model is that we allow *heterogeneous* sets like: $\{$*integer, string*$\}$. The above table shows that such a set-structured term is interpreted by set-entities like "*aBag*" having both integers and strings as elements. Row 7 shows the interpretation of a generic term. In this case, the interpretation is a set of functions which associates to a substitution such as ⟨x/*integer*⟩ the interpretation of [age: *integer*]. Recall that [age: *integer*] is obtained by applying the substitution ⟨x/*integer*⟩ to the generic term [age : x].

Note that, in the case of self-referencing entities such as *person*, our definition of interpretation is circular. The interpretation of such terms can be formally defined as the largest set verifying the equations given in definition 2.4. See [Lécluse 87] for such a formal fixpoint construction.

---

[4]formally, the entity identified by set(x)

2.3 Ordering on terms

In this subsection, we introduce an ordering on terms, called *refinement*. This refinement relationship allows us to say that 1 is an integer, or that an employee is a person. Our interpretation for tuples, similar to that of [Cardelli 84] allows us to say that a tuple [a: *i*, b: *j*] is a refinement of the tuple [a: *i*]. This property is very important, in our approach, because we define the refinement relationship (for ground terms) as the inclusion of interpretations.

Definition 2.5 Let $\mathcal{E}$ be a consistent set of entities. Let v and w be two terms defined on $\mathcal{E}$. We define the refinement relationship v $\leq_{\mathcal{E}}$ w as follows:
Ground terms:

v $\leq_{\mathcal{E}}$ w if and only if $I_{\mathcal{E}}(\text{v}) \subseteq I_{\mathcal{E}}(\text{w})$

Generic terms: Let $x_1, \ldots, x_p$ be the variables of v and $y_1, \ldots, y_q$ be the variables of w.

v $\leq_{\mathcal{E}}$ w if and only if there is a partial injective function θ from $\{1, \ldots, q\}$ to $\{1, \ldots, p\}$ such that for all identifiers $i_1, \ldots, i_p, j_1, \ldots j_q$, verifying $i_{\theta(\alpha)}=j_\alpha$ whenever $\theta(\alpha)$ is defined, we have $I_{\mathcal{E}}(\text{v}.\langle x_1/i_1, \ldots, x_p/i_p\rangle) \subseteq I_{\mathcal{E}}(\text{w}.\langle y_1/j_1, \ldots, y_q/j_q\rangle)$.

□

In the case of ground terms, the refinement relationship corresponds exactly to the inclusion of the interpretations. The definition for generic entities can be explained as follows: v is a refinement of w if we can map some variables of w on some variables of v such that, when applying substitutions to both terms with the same entities in the corresponding variables, the ordering holds. This mapping is a *variable mapping associated to v and w.* The definition of refinements for ground terms is just a special case of the definition for generic terms. We have separated the two cases to make the definition clearer.

The ordering defined in Definition 2.5 depends on the set $\mathcal{E}$. We need a general ordering on terms , independent from the underlying consistent set of entities. This ordering will be used to model the subtyping relationship. If $\mathcal{E}$ is a consistent set of entities and t is a term, the closure of t in $\mathcal{E}$ (noted $\bar{t}$) is the smallest consistent subset $\mathcal{E}$' of $\mathcal{E}$ such that every identifier appearing in t identifies an entity of $\mathcal{E}$'. For example, the closure $\overline{\{person\}}$ in the set of entities of Figure 1 is:
{(*integer*, integer), (*string*, string), (*person*, [name: *string*, age: *integer*, married_to: *person*])}

Definition 2.6 Let $\mathcal{E}$ be a consistent set of entities, let v and w be two terms defined on $\mathcal{E}$. v *refines* w (denoted v $\leq$ w) iff for all consistent set of entities $\mathcal{E}$' containing the closures of t and t', we have: v $\leq_{\mathcal{E}'}$ w. □

Let us now consider some examples of refinement relationships.

1. **3.1415** $\leq$ **real**

2. [a: *thirty*, b: *real*] $\leq$ [a: *thirty*]

3. [a: *thirty*] $\leq$ [a: *integer*]

4. {*int*} $\leq$ {*int, real*}

5. {*employee*} $\leq$ {*person*}

6. [a: x, b: *thirty*] $\leq$ [a: y]

7. [a: x, b: y] $\leq$ [a: y]

8. [a: *integer*, b: x] $\leq$ [a: *integer*]

9. {x} $\leq$ any

10. {z} $\leq$ {x, y}

These examples show that the refinement relationship represents both set membership and set inclusion. Indeed, Example 1 means that 3.1415 is a real, whereas Example 5 means that all sets of employees are sets of persons. Example 7 illustrates the refinement of generic entities. The corresponding variable mapping θ associates y to x. The variable mapping corresponding to the inequality 10 is partial and maps z on x. Note that it is not unique because we could equally map y on z.
There are some false refinement relations that we could be tempted to consider as true, such as:

1. [a: *integer*] $\not\leq$ [a: x]

2. [a: *integer*, b: y] $\not\leq$ [a: x, b: y]

The relationship between the terms [a: *integer*] and [a: x] is not a refinement relationship, but a substitution, and we have [a: *integer*] = [a: x].$\langle$x/*integer*$\rangle$. The last example is also a substitution because we have [a: *integer*, b: y] = [a: x, b: y].$\langle$x/*integer*$\rangle$.

An alternative choice for the definition of the interpretation of generic terms could be the following:

$$I_{\mathcal{E}}(t) = \bigcup_{\sigma} I_{\mathcal{E}}(t.\sigma)$$

In this case, substitution would be a subcase of refinement and the above relationships would be true. On the other hand, the variables in terms would have the same meaning as *any*. For example, {any} and {x} would have the same interpretation ! Similarly, one could not distinguish between {x, y} and {z}.

Figure 2 gives a graphical representation of some refinement and substitution links. The simple arrows represent refinement links and the double arrows represent substitution links. An important feature of this model, is that generic and ground terms are manipulated in the same way. Thus, the refinement relationship deals with generic terms exactly in the same way as with ground ones. This leads us to general refinement and substitution graphs such as that of Figure 2. In this figure, several paths go from the term "[a: x]" to the term "[a: integer, b: real]". One path first substitutes *integer* to x "[a: x]" and then refines it

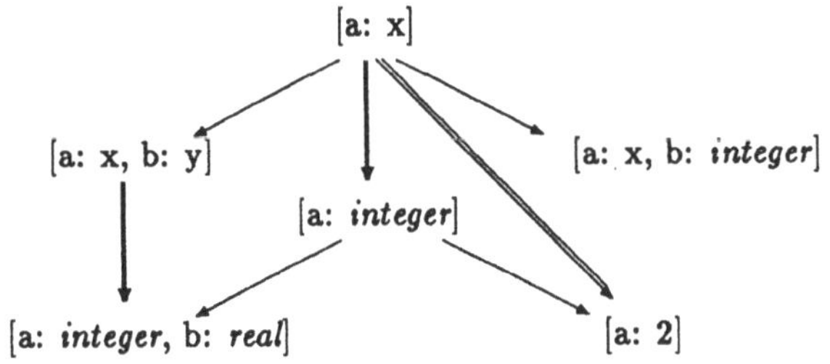

Figure 2: Refinement versus substitution

in "[a: integer, b: real]". The other path first refines the generic term [a: x] in the generic term "[a: x, b: y]" and then substitutes *integer* to x and *real* to y.

Note also that we model multiple inheritance. In fact, a term can be a refinement of several terms. Figure 3 gives a graphical representation of an example of multiple inheritance. The term PhD_student is a refinement of the terms Student *and* Assistant. Both terms are themselves refinements of the term person.

3 Syntactical Characterization of Refinement

In this section, we give a syntactical characterization of the refinement relationship. We first consider the case of ground terms.

Theorem 3.1 Let $\mathcal{E}$ be a consistent set of entities.

- *Basic* ground terms:

  nil $\leq$ t for all term t,
  t $\leq$ **any** for all term t,
  n $\leq$ **integer** for all n in N,
  r $\leq$ **real** for all r in R,
  s $\leq$ **string** for all s in S,

- *Set-structured* ground terms:
  Let t=$\{\epsilon_1, \ldots, \epsilon_n\}$ and t'=$\{\epsilon'_1, \ldots, \epsilon'_p\}$ be two terms defined on $\mathcal{E}$.
  t $\leq$ t' iff for all i in $\{1, \ldots, n\}$ there exists j in $\{1, \ldots, p\}$ such that term(ϵ_i) $\leq$ term(ϵ'_j).
- *Tuple-structured* ground terms:
  Let t and t' be two terms defined on $\mathcal{E}$.
  t $\leq$ t' iff for all field a_i of value ϵ_i in t, there is a field a_i of value ϵ'_i in t' such that term(ϵ_i) $\leq$ term(ϵ'_i).

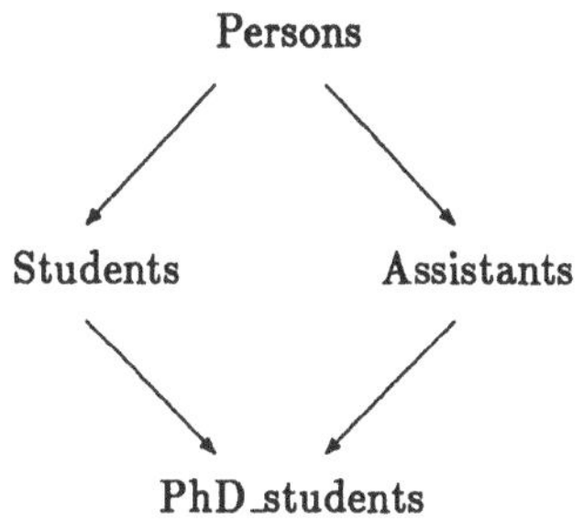

- Persons = [name: *string*, age: *integer*]
- Students = [name: *string*, age: *integer*, grade: *string*]
- **Assistants** = [**name:** *string*, **age:** *integer*, **courses:** *set*(x/*string*)]
- **PhD_students** = [**name:** *string*, **age:** *integer*, **grade:** *string*, **courses:** *set*(x/*string*)]

Figure 3: multiple inheritance

□

Proof: The reader interested in the proof can find it in [Lécluse 88].
Theorem 3.1 shows that our refinement relationship for tuples follows that of [Cardelli 84]. The following theorem extends it in the case of generic terms. As for the refinement definition, Theorem 3.2 subsumes Theorem 3.1, which was given for the sake of clarity.

Theorem 3.2 Let $\mathcal{E}$ be a consistent set of entities.

- *Set-structured* terms:
  Let t= $\{\epsilon_1, \ldots, \epsilon_n\}$ and t'= $\{\epsilon'_1, \ldots, \epsilon'_m\}$ be two terms defined on $\mathcal{E}$.
  t $\leq$ t' iff there exists a variable mapping θ as in 2.5 such that, for all ϵ in term(t):
  - either ϵ is a variable x_k and there exists a variable ϵ'=y_l in term(t') such that θ(l)=k,
  - or ϵ is an identifier i(x_1, ..., x_p) and there exists ϵ' = j(y_1, ..., y_p) in term(t') such that y_k is mapped on x_k by θ and term(i) $\leq$ term(j).
- *Tuple-structured* terms:
  Let t and t' be two terms defined on $\mathcal{E}$.
  t $\leq$ t' iff there exists a variable mapping θ as in 2.5 such that, for all field a of value ϵ in t, there is a field a of value ϵ' in t' such that
  - either ϵ is a variable x_k and ϵ' is a variable y_l such that θ(l)=k,
  - or ϵ is an identifier i(x_1, ..., x_p), ϵ' is an identifier j(y_1, ..., y_p) such that y_k is mapped on x_k by θ and we have term(i) $\leq$ term(j).

□

The proof of this theorem can be found in [Lécluse 88].
Let us apply this theorem on the following refinement:

$$\{set(\mathrm{x}),\ employee\} \leq \{person,\ set(\mathrm{y})\}$$

We consider a variable mapping θ such that θ(y)=x and we know, from theorem 3.2, that the refinement holds if and only if

1. $\{\mathrm{x}\} \leq \{\mathrm{y}\}$ (since term(set(x))={x}), and

2. $\begin{array}{l}\text{[name: } \textit{string}, \\ \text{age: } \textit{integer}, \\ \text{married\_to: } \textit{person}, \\ \text{salary: } \textit{integer}]\end{array} \leq \begin{array}{l}\text{[name: } \textit{string}, \\ \text{age: } \textit{integer}, \\ \text{married\_to: } \textit{person}]\end{array}$

We use Theorem 3.2 once more on the two refinements above. The first one is trivial, with a mapping of y on x. The last refinement holds if and only if

1. **string** $\leq$ **string**, and

2. **integer** $\leq$ **integer**, and

3. term($person$) $\leq$ term($person$).

All these statements are obviously true, and we can conclude that all the refinements actually hold.

This theorem leads to a syntactical characterization of refinements. The only difficulty in deriving a test algorithm from the theorem is the case of self-referencing entities. The test algorithm must include a cycle detection mechanism.

4 Conclusion

We have presented an object-oriented data model which incorporates set and tuple constructions, object identity altogether with inheritance and genericity. The main features of our model are a uniform view of types and objects, the construction of generic types, a set inclusion semantics for inheritance relationship and multiple inheritance.

We do not distinguish between data objects and type structures. We define a uniform framework where these concepts are viewed as entities constructed from basic values and the set and tuple constructors. The terms are interpreted using consistent sets of entities. Furthermore, we allow the use of variables in the construction of entities in order to model genericity. Due to the uniformity of this model, the *refinement* relationship over entities (the so-called inheritance link) is applied to generic entities as well as to ground entities. This model embodies every step between ground entities such as "1" or "[name: bill, age: 40]" to generic entities such as "[name: x, age: y]" including entities such as "[name: string, age: integer]" or partially instanciated entities such as "[name: string, age: 40]".

The semantics of tuple-structured entities is unusual in the database world and follows the original proposal of [Cardelli 84]. It allows to give a simple set inclusion semantics to the refinement relationship among tuple structured entities. Furthermore, this refinement relationship models multiple inheritance. This model extends the work of [Lécluse 87] and leads to a formal type system for generic typed object-oriented languages.

This work is a formal basis for an object-oriented system called O_2currently under development in the Altair group. In this paper, we only considered the structural aspects of types. In the object-oriented paradigm, types encapsulate both the structure and behaviour of the objects. This work can be easily extended in the way of [Lécluse 87] in order to take into account the behavioural aspects of types. However in [Lécluse 87], functions (methods in object-oriented terminology) are not objects of the model which is thus first order. We intend to extend this work to functions by adding a function constructor. This will allow us to consider functions as entities and thus to deal with second order.

References

[Abiteboul 87] S. Abiteboul and C. Beeri, *On the Power of Languages for Manipulating Complex Objects*, International Workshop on Theory and Applications of Nested Relations and Complex Objects, Darmstadt, 1987.

[Ait-Kaci 86] H. Ait-Kaci and R. Nasr, *LOGIN: A Logic Programming Language with Built-in Inheritance*, Journal of Logic Programming, 1986.

[Albano 85] A. Albano et al., *GALILEO, A Strongly Typed, Interactive, Conceptual Language*, ACM TODS, vol 10:2, 1985.

[Bancilhon 87] F. Bancilhon et al., *FAD, a Powerful and Simple Database Language*, Proc of the 13th Conference on Very Large Databases, Brighton, 1987.

[Bancilhon 86] F. Bancilhon and S. Khoshafian, *A Calculus for Complex Objects*, ACM PODS, 1986.

[Barbedette 87] G. Barbedette et al., *Connecting the* O_2 *Data Model to Programming Languages, Version V0*, Technical Report, 13-87, GIP Altaïr, 1987.

[Bruce 86] K.B. Bruce, *An Algebraic Model of Subtypes in Object Oriented Languages*, SIGPLAN Notices, vol 21:40, 1986.

[Cardelli 84] L. Cardelli, *A Semantics of Multiple Inheritance*, Semantics of Data Types, Lecture Notes in Computer Science, 1984.

[Cardelli 85] L. Cardelli and P. Wegner, *On Understanding Types, Data Abstraction, and Polymorphism*, ACM Computing Surveys, Vol 17:4, 1985.

[Goldberg 83] A. Goldberg and D. Robson, *Smalltalk 80, the Language and Implementation*, Addison Wesley, 1983.

[Lécluse 87] C. Lécluse , P. Richard and F. Velez, O_2, *an Object Oriented Data Model*, Technical Report, 10-87, GIP Altaïr, 1987, to appear in Proc of the ACM-SIGMOD Conference, Chicago, 1988.

[Lécluse 88] C. Lécluse and P. Richard, *Modeling Inheritance and genericity in Object-Oriented Databases*, Altaïr Technical Report No 18-88, 1988, submitted for publication.

[Maier 85] D. Maier A. Otis and A. Purdy, *Development of an Object Oriented DBMS*, in *a Quaterly Bulletin of the IEEE Computer Society Technical Committee on Database Engeneering*, Special issue on Object Oriented Systems, Vol 8:4, 1985.

[Meyer 86] B. Meyer, *Genericity versus Inheritance*, OOPSLA, Portland, Oregon, 1986.

[Milner 78] R. Milner, *A Theory of Type Polymorphism in Programming Languages*, JCSS, Vol 17, 1978.

[Pistor 85] P. Pistor, *A Database Language for Sets, Lists, and Tables*, IBM Wiss. Zentr. Heidelberg, Technical Report TR 85.10.004, 1985.

[Schek 85] H. Schek, *A Basic Relational* NF^2 *Algebra Processor*, Proceedings of the International Conference on Foundations of Data Organization, Kyoto, Japan, pp 173-182, may 1985.

[Wegner 87] P. Wegner, *The Object-Oriented Classification Paradigm*, Research Directions in Object-oriented Programming, ed. B. Schiver and P. Wegner, MIT Press, Cambridge, 1987.

Semantics of Types for Database Objects*

Atsushi Ohori†

Department of Computer and Information Science,
University of Pennsylvania,
Philadelphia, PA 19104-6389, U.S.A.

Abstract

This paper proposes a denotational semantics of types for database objects. A simple typed language to represent database objects is defined and its denotational semantics is given. In this language, sets are first-class values and a join and a projection are available as typed operations on general data structures including sets.

For database objects, individual types correspond to partially ordered sets, which we shall call *description domains*. In order to type-check expressions involving joins and projections, an ordering is defined on the set of types in the language. This ordering is interpreted as a relation on description domains induced by embedding-projection pairs. A semantic space of types is then defined as a set of description domains partially ordered by that relation.

The type system is shown to be sound and complete with respect to the semantics. It is also shown that the semantic space of types for database objects can be embedded in a semantic domain of an ML-like programming language. This guarantees that the type system for database objects can be safely integrated in a type system of an ML-like strongly typed programming language.

1 Introduction

A database can be regarded as a collection of descriptions of real-world objects. In last few years, there have been a number of attempts to develop data models to represent these complex descriptions beyond the first-normal-form relational model. Examples include nested relations [FT83, OY85, RKS84] and complex object models [BK86, AH86]. The motivation of this study is to establish a firm basis to integrate these data models into an ML-like strongly typed programming language, whose type system can *infer* all possible types of legal expressions yielding flexible yet robust programs.

As suggested by Cardelli [Car84a], one way to represent complex descriptions in a programming language is to use labeled records found, for example in Standard ML [HMM86], Amber [Car84b] and Galileo [ACO85]. The following is an example of a record expression:

$$[Name = [Firstname = 'Joe', Lastname = 'Doe'], Dept = 'Sales', Office = 278]$$

Types for expressions can be easily defined. For example, the above record is given the following type:

$$[Name : [Firstname : string, Lastname : string], Dept : string, Office : int]$$

Tuples in the relational model can be regarded as a special case of labeled records that contain only atomic values. Assuming computable equality on each atomic type, equality on records that do not contain functions is also computable and it is straightforward to introduce set expressions on those records. A database can then be represented as a set of records.

In practice, however, both records and set are very large and contain a great deal of redundancy. In the relational model, this problem is solved by first *projecting* descriptions onto various small partial descriptions and then representing a database as a collections of sets of these small partial descriptions.

*This research was supported in part by grants NSF IRI86-10617, ARO DAA6-29-84-k-0061, and by funding from AT&T's Telecommunications Program at the University of Pennsylvania and from OKI Electric Industry Co., Japan.

†Network mail address : ohori@cis.upenn.edu

Larger descriptions are obtained by *joining* these partial descriptions when needed. In order to support complex descriptions in a programming language, it is therefore essential to generalize a join and a projection to expressions that represent complex descriptions.

The *natural join* in the relational model is defined on sets (relations), which is based on the underlying operation that computes a join of two tuples. We regard the latter as a basic operation. One way to generalize such an operation to complex descriptions is to consider it as an operation that *combine* information of consistent descriptions. For example, the join of $[Name = [Firstname = 'Joe']]$ and $[Name = [Lastname = 'Doe']]$ yields $[Name = [Firstname = 'Joe', Lastname = 'Doe']]$ but the join of $[Name = [Firstname = 'Joe']]$ and $[Name = [Firstname = 'Susan']]$ does not exists. If we regard expressions as elements in a space of descriptions *ordered* by the "goodness" of descriptions, then this operation is formalized as the least upper bound operation under the ordering. The following is an example of the ordering on a space of descriptions:

$$\begin{aligned}&[Name = [Firstname = 'Joe'], Dept = 'Sales'] \\ &\quad \sqsubseteq \; [Name = [Firstname = 'Joe', Lastname = 'Doe'], Dept = 'Sales', Office = 278]\end{aligned}$$

This ordering was first observed by Zaniolo [Zan84] in connection with null values and was studied in detail in [BO88]. Later we shall see that sets of database objects can be also regarded as descriptions and the *natural join* on sets (relations) can be treated as a special case of the least upper bound operation.

A projection, on the other hand, *throws away* information. In order to define projection, we need to specify what part of descriptions should be retained. In the relational model this is done by specifying a set of labels. For complex descriptions, however, we need to specify a structure that should be retained. A description can be projected onto a structure if it has a *larger* structure. Since, in a programming language, structures are specified by types, a projection should therefore be defined by specifying a type onto which values are to be projected. For example, $[Name = [Firstname = 'Joe', Lastname = 'Doe']]$ can be projected onto the type $[Name : [Firstname : string]]$ yielding $[Name = [Firstname = 'Joe']]$ but the projection of the above record on the type $[Dept : string]$ should not be allowed since the record does not contain the structure specified by the type.

In order to support these generalized join and projection in an ML-like strongly typed programming language, a type system should be able to infer types of expressions that contain joins and projections and to detect all type errors without evaluating expressions. It is not straightforward to do this in a conventional type system for records and sets. To see this, consider the join of two expressions e_1, e_2, for which we write $e \bowtie e'$ following the conventional notation in the relational model. The type of $e \bowtie e'$ depends on those of e and e' and inferring it requires non trivial computation on types. For example, the type of

$$[Name = [Firstname = 'Joe']] \bowtie [Name = [Lastname = 'Doe']]$$

is $[Name : [Firstname : string, Lastname : string]]$ which is computed from $[Name : [Firstname : string]]$ and $[Name : [Lastname : string]]$.

It is shown in [OB88] that by defining an ordering on types that reflects the ordering on values, an ML-like type system can be extended to support generalized join and projection without sacrificing its useful property of the decidability of the type inference problem. Intuitively, the ordering relation $\tau_1 \leq \tau_2$ on types represents the fact that the structure specified by the type τ_2 is *larger* than that specified by the type τ_1. For example, if

$$\begin{aligned}\tau_1 &= [Name : [Firstname : string]] \\ \tau_2 &= [Name : [Lastname : string]] \\ \tau_3 &= [Name : [Firstname : string, Lastname : string]]\end{aligned}$$

then $\tau_1 \leq \tau_3$ and $\tau_2 \leq \tau_3$. Moreover, the structure specified by τ_3 is the *smallest* among those that are larger than both of those specified by τ_1 and τ_2, i.e. τ_3 is the least upper bound of τ_1 and τ_2 under the ordering $\leq$. A type system can then type-check expressions involving joins and projections by using the following properties:

1. If e_1 has a type τ_1 and e_2 has a type τ_2 and τ_3 is the least upper bound of τ_1 and τ_2 then the type of the join $e_1 \bowtie e_2$ (if exists) is τ_3.

2. If e has a type τ_1 and $\tau_2 \leq \tau_1$ then the type of the projection of e onto the type τ_2 is τ_2.

In this paper, we propose a denotational semantics for a type system with the above ordering. Since our main purpose is to define precise semantics of data structures that represent database objects, we do not completely define the semantics of a surrounding programming language. Instead, we show that the type system can be safely integrated in an ML-like strongly typed programming language by showing that a semantic model proposed here can be embedded in a semantic domain of a programming language.

In section 2 we define a simple language to represent database objects. In section 3 we construct a semantic domain of the language. We first characterize domains of values that correspond to individual types. We then show that the ordering relation $\tau_1 \leq \tau_2$ is modeled by the property that there is an embedding-projection pair between the domains corresponding to τ_1, τ_2. Based on this property, we construct a semantic space of types as a set of domains ordered by a set of embedding-projection pairs. In section 4, we define a complete denotational semantics of the language. In section 5, we show that the semantic space constructed in this paper can be embedded in a Scott domain of a programming language.

2 A Simple Typed Language for Database Objects

In this section we define a simple typed language to represent database objects. We first informally introduce the language and then give a formal definition.

2.1 Expressions and Types for Database Objects

Expressions for database objects that do not contain joins and projections are constructed from atomic constants (on which we assume computable equality) by labeled record constructors $[l_1 = \_, \ldots, l_n = \_]$ and set constructors $\{\_, \ldots, \_\}$, where labeled records are unordered associations of labels and values. The following is an example of an expression:

$$\begin{aligned} r_1 \ = \ \{ & [Pname = 'Nut', Supplier = \{ [Sname = 'Smith', City = 'London'], \\ & \qquad\qquad\qquad\qquad\qquad\quad [Sname = 'Blake', City = 'Paris']\}], \\ & [Pname = 'Bolt', Supplier = \{ [Sname = 'Blake', City = 'Paris'], \\ & \qquad\qquad\qquad\qquad\qquad\quad [Sname = 'Adams', City = 'Athens']\}]\} \end{aligned}$$

In database programming, it is often necessary to represent non informative values, usually called *null* values. For this purpose we include a special constant $null^b$ for each base type b. For example, $[Name = 'Joe\ Doe', Age = null^{int}]$ is a record whose *Age* attribute is unknown.

Types of these expressions represent their structures and are constructed from base types by record type constructors $[l_1 : \_, \ldots, l_n : \_]$, and the set type constructor $\{\_\}$. Typing rules for expressions that do not contain joins and projections are similar to those in conventional programming languages such as Pascal:

1. If the types of $e_1, \ldots, e_n$ are respectively $\tau_1, \ldots, \tau_n$ then the type of $[l_1 = e_1, \ldots, l_n = e_n]$ is $[l_1 : \tau_1, \ldots, l_n : \tau_n]$.

2. If the type of $e_1, \ldots, e_n$ is τ then the type of $\{e_1, \ldots, e_n\}$ is $\{\tau\}$.

For example, the type of r_1 is given as:

$$\tau_1 = \{[Pname : string, Supplier : \{[Sname : string, City : string]\}]\}$$

One distinguishing property of these expressions is that they denote partial descriptions of real-world objects and are ordered by how well they describe real-world objects. We formalize this property by defining a syntactic relation $\sqsubseteq$ on expressions. The join operation $\bowtie$ is then defined as the least upper bound operation under this ordering. To get such an ordering, we first define a pre-order $\preceq$:

$$
\begin{array}{rcl}
c & \preceq & c \text{ for all atomic values } c \\
null^b & \preceq & c \text{ for all } c \text{ of type } b \\
[R_1] & \preceq & [R_2] \text{ if for each } (l = e) \in R_1 \text{ there is } (l = e') \in R_2 \text{ such that } e \preceq e' \\
S_1 & \preceq & S_2 \text{ if for each } s \in S_2 \text{ there is } s' \in S_1 \text{ such that } s' \preceq s
\end{array}
$$

The rule for sets, the fourth rule, is defined to capture the ordering on sets in database programming. Readers are referred to [BO88] for the relevance of this ordering to database programming.

$\preceq$ fails to be anti-symmetric because of the fourth rule. However we can use the induced equivalence relation $\{(a,b) | a \preceq b \text{ and } b \preceq a\}$ as the equality relation for database expressions. We then define $\sqsubseteq$ as the partial ordering on equivalence classes. This ordering has the *pairwise bounded join* property:

Prop. 1 *For any two $\overline{e_1}, \overline{e_2}$, if there is some $\overline{e}$ such that $\overline{e_1} \sqsubseteq \overline{e}$ and $\overline{e_2} \sqsubseteq \overline{e}$ then the least upper bound of $\overline{e_1} \sqcup \overline{e_2}$ exists, where $\overline{e}$ is the equivalence class containing e.*

Proof. By induction on the structure of e_1. We only show the case for sets. Other cases are simpler. Suppose $e_1 = \{a_1, \ldots, a_n\}$. By the existence of e, e_2 must be of the form $e_2 = \{b_1, \ldots, b_m\}$. Define $e' = \{a_i \sqcup b_j | 1 \le i \le n, 1 \le j \le m \text{ and } a_i \sqcup b_j \text{ exists }\}$. By induction hypothesis, any pair a_i, b_j has the bounded join property. Then by definition of the ordering, $\overline{e_1} \sqsubseteq \overline{e'}$, $\overline{e_2} \sqsubseteq \overline{e'}$ and for any e'' if $\overline{e_1} \sqsubseteq \overline{e''}$ and $\overline{e_2} \sqsubseteq \overline{e''}$, then $\overline{e'} \sqsubseteq \overline{e''}$. This means $\overline{e'}$ is the least upper bound of $\overline{e_1}$ and $\overline{e_2}$. ∎

Now for each equivalence class, we can define a unique canonical representative satisfying the property that if it contains a set expression S then there are no $s, s' \in S$ such that $s \preceq s'$. This property taken with computable equality associated with each atomic value domain guarantees that equality, the ordering predicate and the least upper bound operation are all computable. The computable equality also allows usual set theoretic operations on set expressions including union, intersection and difference. We define $e_1 \bowtie e_2$ to denote the canonical representative of the least upper bound of equivalence classes $\overline{e_1}, \overline{e_2}$ containing e_1, e_2 (if exists). The pairwise bounded join property and the uniqueness of the canonical representative guarantee that this definition is well defined. This operation, when applied to sets, is a generalization of the natural join in the relational model. Indeed, it is shown in [BO88] that if r_1, r_2 are first-normal-form relation instances then $r_1 \bowtie r_2$ is the natural join of r_1 and r_2. The following is an example of a generalized join of nested set expressions:

$$
\begin{aligned}
r_2 = \{&[Pname = 'Nut', Supplier = \{[City = 'Paris']\}, Qty = 100], \\
&[Pname = 'Bolt', Supplier = \{[City = 'Paris']\}, Qty = 200]\}
\end{aligned}
$$

$$
\begin{aligned}
r_1 \bowtie r_2 = \{&[Pname = 'Nut', Supplier = \{ [Sname = 'Blake', City = 'Paris'], Qty = 100], \\
&[Pname = 'Bolt', Supplier = \{ [Sname = 'Blake', City = 'Paris']\}, Qty = 200]\}
\end{aligned}
$$

Note that $\bowtie$ is defined on not only sets but also on records and atomic values.

Along with the join on expressions, we also define the join on types as the least upper bound operation under the partial ordering of their structures:

$$
\begin{array}{rcl}
b & \le & b \text{ for all base types } b \\
[T_1] & \le & [T_2] \text{ if for each } (l : \tau) \in T_1 \text{ there is } (l : \tau') \in T_2 \text{ such that } \tau \le \tau' \\
\{\tau\} & \le & \{\tau'\} \text{ if } \tau \le \tau'
\end{array}
$$

The following is an example of a join of two types:

$$
\begin{array}{rcl}
\tau_2 & = & \{[Pname : string, Supplier : \{[City : string]\}, Qty : int]\} \\
\tau_1 \sqcup \tau_2 & = & \{[Pname : string, Supplier : \{[Sname : string, City : string]\}, Qty : int]\}
\end{array}
$$

Between the ordering on expressions and the ordering on types, we have the property that if $e_1 : \tau_1, e_2 : \tau_2$ and the join of e_1, e_2 exists then $e_1 \bowtie e_2 : \tau_1 \sqcup \tau_2$. This property allows us to type-check statically expressions containing joins. Note, however, that the lease upper bound of e_1, e_2 may not exists even if $\tau_1 \sqcup \tau_2$ exists. In such a case, $e_1 \bowtie e_2$ does not denote any proper value and we define it to generate *run time exception*.

Projections are also generalized to projections on types. π_τ is a mapping from any expressions of type τ' such that $\tau \leq \tau'$ to expressions of type τ. The following is an example of a projection:

$$\pi_{\{[Pname:string, Supplier:\{[Sname:string]\}]\}}(r_1) =$$
$$\{[Pname = 'Nut', Supplier = \{\,[Sname = 'Smith'], [Sname = 'Blake']\}],$$
$$[Pname = 'Bolt', Supplier = \{\,[Sname = 'Blake'], [Sname = 'Adams']\}]\}$$

In order to illustrate how these data structures can be used in a programming language, we show a simple programming examples using standard operations on these data structures:

1. *Field selection from records*
   If e is a record expression containing an l field then $e.l$ is a value of the l field in e.

2. *Mapping of a function to a set*
   If f is a function expression of type $\tau_1 \to \tau_2$ then *map* f is a function of type $\{\tau_1\} \to \{\tau_2\}$ that taking a set expression $\{e_1, \ldots, e_n\}$ returns the set expression $\{f(e_1), \ldots, f(e_n)\}$.

We use the syntax of ML to define functions. $f\ x_1\ x_2 \cdots$ is the function application $(\cdots((f\ x_1)\ x_2)\cdots)$. Other expressions are self-explanatory. The first example is a selection by a value. *select*1 takes an expression e and a set expression S and returns the set expression containing all expressions in S that *match* with e. *select_age_21* selects records whose *Age* field is 21.

```
fun select1 e S = {e} ⋈ S

fun select_age_21 S = select1 [Age = 21] S
```

The next is a general selection function. The function *select* takes a boolean valued function p and a set expression S and returns the set expression containing all expressions in S that are true of p, i.e. expressions e such that $p\ e = true$. *select_minors* selects records whose *Age* field is less than 21.

```
fun select p S =
 let
   fun mark p x = [Mark = p x, Value = x]
   fun get_value x = x.Value
 in
   map get_value ((map (mark p) S) ⋈ {[Mark = true]})
 end

fun is_minor x = (x.Age) < 21

fun select_minors S = select is_minor S
```

Note that in the above examples, the join plays a crucial role. Using the method described in [OB88], a type system can infer correct typings for all such expressions.

2.2 Definition of the Language

In this section, we formally define the language for database objects. We assume that we are given sets $B_1, \ldots, B_n$ of atomic values corresponding to base types $b_1, \ldots, b_n$ and a set of labels $\mathcal{L}$. The set of types of the language is defined by the following abstract syntax:

$$\tau ::= b \mid [l_1 : \tau_1, \ldots, l_m : \tau_m] \mid \{\tau\}$$

The set of expressions of the language is defined by the following abstract syntax:

$$e ::= c^b \mid null^b \mid [l_1 = e_1, \ldots, l_m = e_m] \mid \{e_1, \ldots, e_k\} \mid e_1 \bowtie e_2 \mid \pi_\tau(e)$$

where c^b stands for constants of type b, $null^b$ for the null value of type b and $l_1, \ldots, l_m \in \mathcal{L}$.

The complete set of typing rules for this language is defined by the following deduction system $\vdash$ for typing $e : \tau$.

Axioms

$$(const) \qquad \vdash c^b : b$$

$$(null) \qquad \vdash null^b : b$$

$$(\{\}) \qquad \vdash \{\} : \{\tau\} \quad \text{for any } \tau$$

Inference Rules

$$(record) \qquad \frac{\vdash e_1 : \tau_1 \ \cdots \ \vdash e_n : \tau_n}{\vdash [l_1 = e_1, \ldots, l_n = e_n] : [l_1 : \tau_1, \ldots, l_n : \tau_n]}$$

$$(set) \qquad \frac{\vdash e_1 : \tau \ \cdots \ \vdash e_m : \tau}{\vdash \{e_1, \ldots, e_m\} : \{\tau\}}$$

$$(join) \qquad \frac{\vdash e_1 : \tau_1 \qquad \vdash e_2 : \tau_2 \qquad \tau = \tau_1 \sqcup \tau_2}{\vdash e_1 \bowtie e_2 : \tau}$$

$$(\pi) \qquad \frac{\vdash e_1 : \tau_1 \qquad \tau_2 \leq \tau_1}{\vdash \pi_{\tau_2}(e_1) : \tau_2}$$

From this definition, it is straightforward to define a type-checking function *type* that taking an expression e returns its type if e is well typed and otherwise reports type error.

It is not hard to extend this language to include various operations associated with these data structures and function expressions using λ abstraction. We refer the reader to [OB88] for a complete definition of a programming language containing these operations, for equation rules between expressions which provide an operational semantics of the language and for its complete type inference algorithm. But now we turn our attention to semantics of this language.

3 Semantic Domain

Since the meanings of expressions depend on the meanings of types, we first construct the set of values $\mathcal{T}[\![\tau]\!]$ denoted by each type τ and interpret the relation $\tau_1 \leq \tau_2$ as a relation between the sets $\mathcal{T}[\![\tau_1]\!]$ and $\mathcal{T}[\![\tau_2]\!]$. The semantics $\mathcal{E}[\![e]\!]$ of an expression e is then defined in such a way that it preserves types, i.e. $\mathcal{E}[\![e]\!] \in \mathcal{T}[\![type(e)]\!]$.

3.1 Semantics of Individual Types

We define the meaning of a type as the set of all values having that type. Such a set should be partially ordered to represent the ordering of the goodness of descriptions and should be able to give semantics to the syntactic relation $\sqsubseteq$ on expressions. As a model of a type of database objects, we require a partially ordered set D to have the following properties:

(1) D is countable.

(2) D has a bottom element $null^D$ such that for any $d \in D, null^D \sqsubseteq d$.

(3) D has the pairwise bounded join property.

As we shall see in section 5, condition (1) is needed to embed a semantic domain of database objects into a semantic domain of programming language. Condition (2) allows us to represent non informative value which is essential for partial descriptions. Condition (3) states that if we have two consistent descriptions then the combination of the two is also representable as a description. We call a partially ordered set satisfying these conditions a ***description domain***. It should be noted that description domains are models of types of database objects and not models of general types in programming languages such as function types. Orderings associated with description domains are just computable predicates like the lexicographical ordering on strings and have nothing to do with the orderings associated with domains that are used to give semantics to programming languages [Sch86]. We shall discuss more about the relationship between description domains and semantic domains of programming languages later.

Description domains are closed under the following constructions that correspond to type constructors:

1. *Flat description domains*
   Let V be any countable set of atomic values such as the set of integers. Define $V_{null} = V \cup \{null^V\}$ with the ordering $x \sqsubseteq y$ iff $x = null^V$ or $x = y$.

   Prop. 2 *V_{null} is a description domain.* ▮

2. *Records*
   Let $L = \{l_1, \ldots, l_n\}$ be a finite set of labels and $(D_1, \sqsubseteq_1), \ldots, (D_n, \sqsubseteq_n)$ be description domains. Define $[l_1 : D_1, \ldots, l_n : D_n] = \{[l_1 = d_1, \ldots, l_n = d_n] | d_i \in D_i, 1 \le i \le n\}$ with the ordering $[l_1 = d_1, \ldots, l_n = d_n] \sqsubseteq [l_1 = d'_1, \ldots, l_n = d'_n]$ iff for all $i, d_i \sqsubseteq_i d'_i$.

   Prop. 3 *$[l_1 : D_1, \ldots, l_n : D_n]$ is a description domain.* ▮

3. *Database Sets*
   Let D be a description domain. We first define a pre-order $\preceq$ on finite subsets of D as $X \preceq Y$ iff for all $y \in Y$ there is some $x \in X$ such that $x \sqsubseteq y$. Now define $\mathcal{S}(D)$ as the set of all equivalence classes of all finite subsets of D induced by $\preceq$ with the ordering $\overline{S_1} \sqsubseteq \overline{S_2}$ iff $S_1 \preceq S_2$ where $\overline{S}$ is an equivalence class containing S.

   Prop. 4 *$\mathcal{S}(D)$ is a description domain.*

   Proof. For $X \subseteq D$, define $\uparrow X = \{d \in D | \exists x \in X . x \sqsubseteq d\}$, the *upper set* of X. Let $\mathcal{U}(D)$ be the poset $\{\uparrow X | X \subseteq D$ and X finite$\}$ ordered by inverse inclusion, i.e. $X \sqsubseteq Y$ iff $X \supseteq Y$. Then $\mathcal{S}(D)$ is isomorphic to $\mathcal{U}(D)$ with the isomorphism $\overline{S} \mapsto \uparrow S$. But by the property of $\supseteq$, $\mathcal{U}(D)$ has the pairwise bounded join property. $\mathcal{U}(D)$ clearly satisfies the other two conditions of description domains. ▮

Note that the record and set domain constructions correspond exactly to the record and set expression constructors defined in the previous section and the associated orderings are also same. Using these description domain constructions, we are ready to give semantics to types and expressions that do not contain joins and projections. However, expressions that contain joins and projections depend on an interpretation on the ordering relation on types. In order to define complete semantics of the language, we therefore need to define a semantics of the ordering on types as a relation on description domains in such a way that the ordering relation on types is preserved by the semantic mapping of types. In the next section, we construct a semantic space of an ordered set of types as a space of description domains with such a relation.

3.2 Semantics of the Ordering on Types

Intuitive meaning of the relation $\tau_1 \le \tau_2$ is that the structure specified by τ_2 *contains* the structure specified by τ_1. This intuitive idea is formalized by using the notion of *embedding-projection* pairs.

Let D_1, D_2 be description domains. A monotone function $\phi : D_1 \rightarrow D_2$ is an *embedding* if there exists $\phi^R : D_2 \rightarrow D_1$ such that $\phi \circ \phi^R \le id_{D_2}$ and $\phi^R \circ \phi = id_{D_1}$ where $f \circ g$ is a function composition defined as $f \circ g(x) = f(g(x))$, id_X is the identity function on X and the ordering on functions $\le$ is the pointwise ordering. The function ϕ^R is called *projection* and is uniquely determined by ϕ. The proof of the uniqueness of ϕ^R is essentially same as the case of complete lattices and continuous functions

[GHK*80]. The following is an example of an embedding-projection pair. Let $D_1 = [Name : Str_{null}]$ and $D_2 = [Name : Str_{null}, Age : Int_{null}]$ then

$$\phi([Name = s]) = [Name = s, Age = null^{int}]$$

is an embedding with the associated projection

$$\phi^R([Name = s, Age = i]) = [Name = s]$$

where Str_{null}, Int_{null} are flat description domains of strings and integers respectively.

As the above example suggests, if a pair of description domains (D_1, D_2) has an embedding then D_2 contains an isomorphic copy $D_1' = \phi(D_1)$ of D_1 and for any element d in D_2 there is a unique maximal element $d' \in D_1'$ such that $d' \sqsubseteq d$. We regard this property as the meaning of the ordering relation on types and interpret an ordered space of types as a set of description domains connected with a set of embedding-projection pairs. This is a refinement of one of the characterizations of subtypes proposed by Bruce and Wegner [BW86], who characterized the notion of subtypes in three ways; one of them being that the larger set contains an isomorphic copy of the smaller.

We say that a set of description domains associated with a set of embeddings between them (Dom, Emb) is a ***database domain*** if it satisfies:

(1) For any two domains $D_1, D_2 \in Dom$, there is at most one $\phi \in Emb$ such that $\phi : D_1 \to D_2$, Under this condition, each $\phi \in Emb$ is identified by its domain and co-domain. In what follows, we write $(D_1 \trianglelefteq D_2)$ for the element $\phi : D_1 \to D_2 \in Emb$.

(2) For any domain $D \in Dom$, $(D \trianglelefteq D) \in Emb$.

(3) Emb is closed under composition.

(4) For any two domains $D_1, D_2 \in Dom$, if there is some $D \in Dom$ such that $(D_1 \trianglelefteq D) \in Emb$ and $(D_2 \trianglelefteq D) \in Emb$ then there is a unique $D' \in Dom$ depending only on D_1, D_2 such that $(D_1 \trianglelefteq D') \in Emb, (D_2 \trianglelefteq D') \in Emb$ and for any $D'' \in Dom$ if $(D_1 \trianglelefteq D'') \in Emb$ and $(D_2 \trianglelefteq D'') \in Emb$ then $(D' \trianglelefteq D'') \in Emb$.

The condition (1) means that the set of embeddings defines a relation on Dom. Moreover,

Prop. 5 *The relation defined by Emb is a partial ordering with the pairwise bounded join property.*

Proof. From (2) and (3), the relation is reflexive and transitive. For anti-symmetricity, suppose $(X \trianglelefteq Y)$ and $(Y \trianglelefteq X)$ for some $X, Y \in Dom$. Since $(X \trianglelefteq X)$ and $(Y \trianglelefteq Y)$, the uniqueness of D' in the condition (4) implies $X = Y$. The pairwise bounded join property is an immediate consequence of the condition (4). ▮

This property correctly reflects the structure of the ordering on types and we therefore define a semantic space of types as a database domain. Let $(Type, \leq)$ be a set of types ordered by $\leq$. Also let (Dom, Emb) be a database domain and μ be a mapping from $Type$ to Dom. We say that (Dom, Emb) is a ***model of*** $(Type, \leq)$ ***under the interpretation*** μ if for any $\tau_1, \tau_2 \in Type, \tau_1 \leq \tau_2$ iff $(\mu(\tau_1) \trianglelefteq \mu(\tau_2)) \in Emb$.

A more intuitive way of understanding these definition is to consider $(D_1 \trianglelefteq D_2) \in Emb$ as a *coercer* from D_1 to D_2 which maps an element $d \in D_1$ to the least element $d' \in D_2$ such that d' contains all information in d. The corresponding projection $(D_1 \trianglelefteq D_2)^R$ maps an element $d \in D_2$ to a unique maximal element $d' \in D_1$ that contains only information in d and is regarded as a database projection from D_2 to D_1.

3.3 A Semantic Domain of the Language

We now construct a database domain $(DBdom, DBemb)$ for the type system of our language. $DBdom$ is the smallest set satisfying:

1. $B_{null} \in DBdom$ for each primitive set of values B,

2. If $D_1, \ldots, D_n \in DBdom$ and $l_1, \ldots, l_n \in \mathcal{L}$ then $[l_1 : D_1, \ldots, l_n : D_n] \in DBdom$.
3. If $D \in DBdom$ then $\mathcal{S}(D) \in DBdom$.

In order to define $DBemb$ we define the embedding constructions corresponding to domain constructions defined earlier:

1. *Records*
   Let $\phi_1 : D_1 \to D'_1, \ldots, \phi_n : D_n \to D'_n$ be embeddings and $l_1, \ldots, l_n, l_{n+1}, \ldots, l_{n+m} \in \mathcal{L}$. Define $[l_1 : \phi_1, \ldots, l_n : \phi_n, l_{n+1} : null^{D_{n+1}}, \ldots, l_{n+m} : null^{D_{n+m}}]$ as the function ϕ from $[l_1 : D_1, \ldots, l_n : D_n]$ to $[l_1 : D'_1, \ldots, l_n : D'_n, l_{n+1} : D_{n+1}, \ldots, l_{n+m} : D_{n+m}]$ such that $\phi([l_1 = d_1, \ldots, l_n : d_n]) = [l_1 = \phi_1(d_1), \ldots, l_n : \phi_n(d_n), l_{n+1} = null^{D_{n+1}}, \ldots, l_{n+m} = null^{D_{n+m}}]$.

   Prop. 6 $[l_1 : \phi_1, \ldots, l_n : \phi_n, l_{n+1} : null^{D_{n+1}}, \ldots, l_{n+m} : null^{D_{n+m}}]$ *is an embedding from* $[l_1 : D_1, \ldots, l_n : D_n]$ *to* $[l_1 : D'_1, \ldots, l_n : D'_n, l_{n+1} : D_{n+1}, \ldots, l_{n+m} : D_{n+m}]$. *The corresponding projection is the function* ϕ^R *defined as* $\phi^R([l_1 = d_1, \ldots, l_{n+m} = d_{n+m}]) = [l_1 = \phi_1^R(d_1), \ldots, l_n = \phi_n^R(d_n)]$. ▮

2. *Sets*
   Let $\phi : D_1 \to D_2$ be an embedding. Define $\{\phi\}$ as the function from $\mathcal{S}(D_1)$ to $\mathcal{S}(D_2)$ such that $\{\phi\}(\overline{\{d_1, \ldots, d_n\}}) = \overline{\{\phi(d_1), \ldots, \phi(d_n)\}}$.

   Prop. 7 $\{\phi\}$ *is an embedding from* $\mathcal{S}(D_1)$ *to* $\mathcal{S}(D_2)$. *The corresponding projection is the function* $\{\phi\}^R$ *defined as* $\{\phi\}^R(\overline{\{d_1, \ldots, d_n\}}) = \overline{\{\phi^R(d_1), \ldots, \phi^R(d_n)\}}$.

   Proof. Since mappings ϕ and ϕ^R are monotone, $\{\phi\}$ and $\{\phi\}^R$ are well defined, i.e. if $\overline{\{a_1, \ldots, a_n\}} = \overline{\{b_1, \ldots, b_m\}}$ then $\overline{\{f(a_1), \ldots, f(a_n)\}} = \overline{\{f(b_1), \ldots, f(b_m)\}}$ for $f \in \{\phi, \phi^R\}$. Then the desired property of $\{\phi\}$ and $\{\phi\}^R$ is shown by using the isomorphism defined in the proof of the proposition 4. ▮

$DBemb$ is then defined as the smallest set containing id_D for each $D \in DBdom$ and closed under function composition and the above two embedding constructions.

Theorem 1 $(DBdom, DBemb)$ *is a database domain.*

Proof. By definition, $(DBdom, DBemb)$ satisfies the conditions (1) – (3) of database domains. The property of the condition (4) is proved by induction on the structure of D_1. Here we only show the case of records. Let $D_1 = [a_1 : D_1^1, \ldots, a_n : D_n^1]$. Then, by the existence of a bound of D_1 and D_2, D_2 must be of the form: $D_2 = [b_1 : D_1^2, \ldots, b_m : D_m^2]$. Suppose there is some $D \in DBdom$ such that $(D_1 \trianglelefteq D)$ and $(D_2 \trianglelefteq D)$. Without loss of generality we assume that $a_1 = b_1 = l_1, \ldots, a_k = b_k = l_k$ for some $k, k \leq n, k \leq m$. Then by definition of $DBemb$, D must be a domain of the form $[l_1 : D_1, \ldots, l_k : D_k, \ldots]$ and for each $1 \leq i \leq k$, $(D_i^1 \trianglelefteq D_i)$ and $(D_i^2 \trianglelefteq D_i)$. Let D'_i be the domain satisfying the condition (4) for D_i^1 and D_i^2. It is then shown that the domain $[l_1 : D'_1, \ldots, l_k : D'_k, a_{k+1} : D_{k+1}^1, \ldots, a_n : D_n^1, b_{k+1} : D_{k+1}^2, \ldots, b_m : D_m^2]$ satisfies the condition (4). ▮

One advantage of our semantics of the ordering on types is that it not only defines the meaning of the ordering but it also defines the associated embedding-projections explicitly as computable functions. This means that, in developing a practical programming language for databases, once we define types for databases based on our semantic model then the required projections and embeddings are readily available. Using these embeddings and projections, we are now ready to define a complete denotational semantics of the language.

4 Semantics of the Language

Let $(DBtype, \leq)$ be the set of all types and $TypedExpr$ be the set of all expressions that have a typing. In this section, we define two semantic mappings $\mathcal{T} : DBtype \to DBdom$ and $\mathcal{E} : TypedExpr \to \bigcup DBdom$ such that $(DBdom, DBemb)$ is a model of $(DBtype, \leq)$ under the mapping $\mathcal{T}$ and if e does not yield an exception then $\vdash e : \tau$ iff $\mathcal{E}[\![e]\!] \in \mathcal{T}[\![type(e)]\!]$.

4.1 Semantics of Types

The semantic mapping $\mathcal{T}$ of types is inductively defined as:

$$\begin{aligned}\mathcal{T}[\![b]\!] &= B_{null}\\ \mathcal{T}[\![[l_1:\tau_1,\ldots,l_n:\tau_n]]\!] &= [l_1:\mathcal{T}[\![\tau_1]\!],\ldots,l_n:\mathcal{T}[\![\tau_n]\!]]\\ \mathcal{T}[\![\{\tau\}]\!] &= \mathcal{S}(\mathcal{T}[\![\tau]\!])\end{aligned}$$

By the definition of *DBdom* it is easy to check that this definition is well defined. Moreover,

Theorem 2 *(DBdom, DBemb) is a model of (DBtype, $\leq$) under the semantic mapping $\mathcal{T}$.*

Proof. By inductions on the structures of types τ_1, τ_2 such that $\tau_1 \leq \tau_2$. ∎

4.2 Semantics of Join and Projection

In order to define the semantic mapping $\mathcal{E}$, we need to define the semantics of the operators $\bowtie$ and π_τ; the only operators we have included in the language.

Intuitively, the join operator is a least upper bound operator under the ordering of the goodness of descriptions. If the join is applied to two expressions of a same type then the semantics of the join is just the least upper bound operator associated with the description domain of that type. For example, if

$$\begin{aligned}e_1 &= [Name = {}'Joe\ Doe', Age = 21, Office = null^{int}]\\ e_2 &= [Name = {}'Joe\ Doe', Age = null^{int}, Office = 278]\end{aligned}$$

then the join $e_1 \bowtie e_2$ is exactly the least upper bound in the description domain $[Name : Str_{null}, Age : Int_{null}, Office : Int_{null}]$. However, we also compute joins of different types. For example, we compute the join $e_1' \bowtie e_2'$ where

$$\begin{aligned}e_1' &= [Name = {}'Joe\ Doe', Age = 21]\\ e_2' &= [Name = {}'Joe\ Doe', Office = 278]\end{aligned}$$

Such a join cannot be directly interpreted as a least upper bound on a description domain. This problem is solved by first *coercing* e_1', e_2' to e_1, e_2 using the embeddings

$$\phi_1 : [Name : Str_{null}, Age : Int_{null}] \rightarrow [Name : Str_{null}, Age : Int_{null}, Office : Int_{null}]$$

and

$$\phi_2 : [Name : Str_{null}, Office : Int_{null}] \rightarrow [Name : Str_{null}, Age : Int_{null}, Office : Int_{null}]$$

respectively and then computing the join by the least upper bound operator on $[Name : Str_{null}, Age : Int_{null}, Office : Int_{null}]$. The fact that (*DBdom*, *DBemb*) is a model of (*DBtype*, $\leq$) guarantees that ϕ_1, ϕ_2 exist if $e_1' \bowtie e_2'$ is well typed. The semantics of a join expression is then define as

$$\mathcal{E}[\![e_1 \bowtie e_2]\!] = (\mathcal{T}[\![type(e_1)]\!] \trianglelefteq \mathcal{T}[\![\tau]\!])(\mathcal{E}[\![e_1]\!]) \sqcup (\mathcal{T}[\![type(e_2)]\!] \trianglelefteq \mathcal{T}[\![\tau]\!])(\mathcal{E}[\![e_2]\!])$$

where $\tau = type(e_1) \sqcup type(e_2)$, which exists iff $e_1 \bowtie e_2$ is well typed.

We already defined projections. For any type τ, the expression $\pi_\tau(e)$ is well typed iff $\tau \leq type(e)$. In the semantics of types, this means that there is an embedding $(\mathcal{T}[\![\tau]\!] \trianglelefteq \mathcal{T}[\![type(e)]\!]) : \mathcal{T}[\![\tau]\!] \rightarrow \mathcal{T}[\![type(e)]\!]$ and therefore the corresponding projection $(\mathcal{T}[\![\tau]\!] \trianglelefteq \mathcal{T}[\![type(e)]\!])^R : \mathcal{T}[\![type(e)]\!] \rightarrow \mathcal{T}[\![\tau]\!]$. As we mentioned earlier, the semantics of a database projection is a projection between description domains. We therefore define:

$$\mathcal{E}[\![\pi_\tau(e)]\!] = (\mathcal{T}[\![\tau]\!] \trianglelefteq \mathcal{T}[\![type(e)]\!])^R(\mathcal{E}[\![e]\!])$$

This definition is faithful to the relational projections. The type of a relation scheme $\{l_1, \ldots, l_n\}$ in the relational model can be defined in our language as $\{[l_1 : v, \ldots, l_n : v]\}$ where v is a constant type denoting the set V of all possible atomic values that can appear in tuples. Then a relational projection $\pi_{\{l_1,\ldots,l_n\}}$ can be applied to a relation instance of a scheme that contains $\{l_1,\ldots,l_n\}$. Let r be a relation instance of a scheme $\{l_1,\ldots,l_n,\ldots,l_{n+m}\}$ then the projection $\pi_{\{l_1,\ldots,l_n\}}(r)$ is $\{\phi(d)|d \in r\}$ where ϕ is the function defined as $\phi([l_1 = d_1,\ldots,l_{n+m} = d_{n+m}]) = [l_1 = d_1,\ldots,l_n = d_n]$. This is exactly our definition of the projection $\{[l_1 : id_V,\ldots,l_n : id_V, l_{n+1} : null^V,\ldots,l_{n+m} : null^V]\}^R$ from the type $\{[l_1 : v,\ldots,l_n : v,\ldots l_{n+m} : v]\}$ to $\{[l_1 : v,\ldots,l_n : v]\}$.

4.3 Semantics of Expressions

The semantic mapping $\mathcal{E}$ is now inductively defined as:

$$\begin{aligned}
\mathcal{E}[\![c]\!] &= c\\
\mathcal{E}[\![null^b]\!] &= null^{\mathcal{T}[\![b]\!]}\\
\mathcal{E}[\![[l_1 = e_1,\ldots,l_n = e_n]]\!] &= [l_1 = \mathcal{E}[\![e_1]\!],\ldots,l_n = \mathcal{E}[\![e_n]\!]]\\
\mathcal{E}[\![\{e_1,\ldots,e_n\}]\!] &= \overline{\{\mathcal{E}[\![e_1]\!],\ldots,\mathcal{E}[\![e_n]\!]\}}\\
\mathcal{E}[\![e_1 \bowtie e_2]\!] &= (\mathcal{T}[\![type(e_1)]\!] \trianglelefteq \mathcal{T}[\![\tau]\!])(\mathcal{E}[\![e_1]\!]) \sqcup (\mathcal{T}[\![type(e_2)]\!] \trianglelefteq \mathcal{T}[\![\tau]\!])(\mathcal{E}[\![e_2]\!])\\
&\quad \text{where } \tau = type(e_1) \sqcup type(e_2)\\
\mathcal{E}[\![\pi_\tau(e)]\!] &= (\mathcal{T}[\![\tau]\!] \trianglelefteq \mathcal{T}[\![type(e)]\!])^R(\mathcal{E}[\![e]\!])
\end{aligned}$$

We can then show the soundness of the type system.

Theorem 3 (Semantic Soundness) *If* $\vdash e : \tau$ *and* e *does not yield an exception then* $\mathcal{E}[\![e]\!] \in \mathcal{T}[\![\tau]\!]$.

Proof. By induction on the structure of e. For cases other than $e_1 \bowtie e_2$ and $\pi_\tau(e)$ are immediate consequences of the definitions. We only show the case of $e_1 \bowtie e_2$. The case of $\pi_\tau(e)$ is simpler. Suppose $\vdash e_1 \bowtie e_2 : \tau$ and $e_1 \bowtie e_2$ does not yield an exception. Then the least upper bound of e_1 and e_2 exists and there are τ_1, τ_2 such that $\vdash e_1 : \tau_1, \vdash e_2 : \tau_2$ and $\tau_1 \sqcup \tau_2 = \tau$. By induction hypothesis, $\mathcal{E}[\![e_1]\!] \in \mathcal{T}[\![\tau_1]\!]$ and $\mathcal{E}[\![e_2]\!] \in \mathcal{T}[\![\tau_2]\!]$. It is easily shown by induction that if the least upper bound of e_1 and e_2 exists then there are e_1', e_2' such that (1) e_1', e_2' do not contain $\bowtie$, (2) the least upper bound of e_1', e_2' exists, (3) $\vdash e_1' : \tau, \vdash e_2' : \tau$,and (4) $(\mathcal{T}[\![\tau_1]\!] \trianglelefteq \mathcal{T}[\![\tau]\!])\mathcal{E}[\![e_1]\!] = \mathcal{E}[\![e_1']\!]$, $(\mathcal{T}[\![\tau_2]\!] \trianglelefteq \mathcal{T}[\![\tau]\!])\mathcal{E}[\![e_2]\!] = \mathcal{E}[\![e_2']\!]$. It is also easily shown by induction that if $\vdash e_1' : \tau, \vdash e_2' : \tau$ and the least upper bound of e_1', e_2' exists then the least upper bound of $\mathcal{E}[\![e_1']\!]$ and $\mathcal{E}[\![e_2']\!]$ exists. Then $\mathcal{E}[\![e_1 \bowtie e_2]\!] = \mathcal{E}[\![e_1']\!] \sqcup \mathcal{E}[\![e_2']\!] \in \mathcal{T}[\![\tau]\!]$. ∎

The converse of this theorem, semantic completeness, is rather trivial because of the lack of function expressions.

Theorem 4 (Semantic Completeness) *For any* $e \in TypedExpr$*, if* $\mathcal{E}[\![e]\!] \in \mathcal{T}[\![\tau]\!]$ *for some* τ *then* $\vdash e : \tau$.

Proof. It is easily shown that for any e there is at most one τ such that $\vdash e : \tau$. Then the theorem is an immediate consequence of the fact that for nay τ_1, τ_2, $\mathcal{T}[\![\tau_1]\!] \cap \mathcal{T}[\![\tau_2]\!] = \emptyset$. ∎

5 Database Domains and Domains of Programming Languages

We have defined a language and its semantics for data structures representing database objects. In order to develop a practical programming language including theses data structures, we need to embed the database domain defined in the previous section into a semantic domain of a programming language.

Milner [Mil78] showed that a semantic domain of ML can be constructed as a solution of a domain equation over a special class of partially ordered set, called *complete partial orders* (cpos) and the semantics of types is defined as *ideals* in a cpo. MacQueen et.al. [MPS86] extended this to recursive polymorphic types. For definitions and constructions of cpos and ideals, readers are referred to [MPS86]. The ordering associated with a semantic domain is the approximation ordering on computable functions introduced by Scott [Sco72]. The bottom element corresponds to non-terminating computation. This ordering is nothing to do with the ordering we used to give semantics to data structures for database objects. As mentioned earlier, our ordering is just a computable predicate.

All element in a domain of descriptions including *null*'s are incomparable elements with respect to Scott ordering and should be interpreted as *compact* (or *finite*) elements in a Scott domain. Once we understand this relationship, we can easily construct a Scott domain of database objects as follows.

Let $\mathcal{D}$ be the union of all description domains in $DBdom$, i.e. $\mathcal{D} = \bigcup DBdom$. Since each $D \in DBdom$ is countable and $DBdom$ is countable, $\mathcal{D}$ is countable. From the observation above, the countable set $\mathcal{D}$ is regarded as a set of atomic values with respect to Scott ordering. We can then simply *lift* $\mathcal{D}$ with Scott bottom element $\perp$ to get a flat Scott domain of database objects $\mathcal{D}_\perp$ with the ordering defined as $x \sqsubseteq y$ iff $x = y$ or $x = \perp$. By including $\mathcal{D}_\perp$ in a desired domain equation for a semantic domain of a programming language, we immediately get a semantic domain of a programming language that contains our language. The semantics of types for database objects is also consistent with the ideal model of types. Let $\mathcal{V}$ be the desired solution of the domain equation containing $\mathcal{D}_\perp$. In our semantics, a type is interpreted as a description domain $D \in DBdom$. In $\mathcal{V}$, D is a subset of the set of maximal elements and induces the ideal $D \cup \{\perp\}$. This means that all types in our language are indeed types in the extended programming language containing our language. Moreover, it can also be shown that the extended type system is also sound. This guarantees that the type system we have defined can be embedded in a type system of an ML-like programming language.

6 Conclusion and Future Works

We regard a database as a set of descriptions of real-world objects. Data structures for complex descriptions including sets, join and projection can be represented as typed expressions by defining an ordering on expressions and an ordering on types.

In this paper, we have proposed a semantic model of types of data structures for those complex descriptions. We have shown that individual types are interpreted in a special class of partially ordered sets, which we called *description domains*, and the ordering relation on types is interpreted as the property that there is an embedding-projection pair between the description domains denoted by types. An ordered space of types is then interpreted as a set of description domains ordered by embedding-projection pairs. Based on this semantic model, we have defined a denotational semantics of a simple typed language representing database objects and shown that the type system is sound and complete with respect to the semantics. We have also shown that the type system can be safely integrated in an ML-like strongly typed programming language by showing that a semantic model proposed here can be embedded in a semantic domain of such a language.

It is reasonable to expect complex descriptions to be extended to recursive or cyclic structures. In semantics, such a description should be interpreted in a domain of infinite trees. It seems rather difficult to extend complex descriptions to include general infinite trees, because many necessary properties of general infinite trees may be undecidable. However, there is a particularly simple class of infinite trees, called *regular trees* [Cou83], which can be represented by finite state automata. It seems not hard to extend the theory developed here to a domain of regular trees. For example, if we restrict only to labeled record constructors with recursive definitions, then the appropriate ordering is to be the inclusion relation on regular sets, which is shown to be decidable. It is also possible to extend this ordering to set constructors. A more challenging thing is to develop a type inference algorithm for such a extended system.

Acknowledgement

I would like to thank Peter Buneman for discussions and many helpful comments on this paper.

References

[ACO85] A. Albano, L. Cardelli, and R. Orsini. Galileo: A Strongly Typed, Interactive Conceptual Language. *ACM Transactions on Database Systems*, 10(2):230–260, 1985.

[AH86] S. Abiteboul and R. Hull. Restructuring of Complex Objects and Office Forms. In *Proc. International Conference on Database Theory, Lecture Notes in Computer Science 243*, Springer-Verlag, Rome, Italy, September 1986.

[BK86] F. Bancilhon and S. Khoshafin. A Calsulus for Complex Objects. In *Proc. ACM Conference on Principles of Database Systems*, 1986.

[BO88] P. Buneman and A. Ohori. Using Powerdomains to Generalize Relational Databases. *Theoreical Computer Science*, To Appear, 1988. Available as a technical report from Department of Computer and Information Science, University of Pennsylvania.

[BW86] K. B. Bruce and P. Wegner. An Algebraic Model of Subtypes in Object-Oriented Languages. *SIGPLAN Notices*, 21(10):163–172, October 1986.

[Car84a] L. Cardelli. A Semantics of Multiple Inheritance. In *Semantics of Data Types, Lecture Notes in Computer Science 173*, Springer-Verlag, 1984.

[Car84b] L. Cardelli. *Amber*. Technical Memorandum TM 11271-840924-10, AT&T Bell Laboratories, 1984.

[Cou83] B. Courcelle. Fundamental Properties of Infinite Trees. *Theoretical Computer Science*, 25:95–169, 1983.

[FT83] P.C. Fischer and S.J. Thomas. Operators for Non-First-Normal-Form Relations. In *Proc. IEEE COMPSAC*, 1983.

[GHK*80] G. Gierz, H.K. Hofmann, K. Keimel, J.D. Lawson, M. Mislove, and D.S. Scott. *A Compendium of Continuous Lattices*. Springer-Verlag, 1980.

[HMM86] R. Harper, D. B. MacQueen, and R. Milner. *Standard ML*. LFCS Report Series ECS-LFCS-86-2, Department of Computer Science, University of Edinburgh, March 1986.

[Mil78] R. Milner. A Theory of Type Polymorphism in Programming. *Journal of Computer and System Sciences*, 17:348–375, 1978.

[MPS86] D.B. MacQueen, G.D. Plotkin, and Sethi. An ideal model for recursive polymorphic types. *Information and Control*, 71(1/2):95–130, 1986.

[OB88] A. Ohori and P. Buneman. Type Inference in a Database Programming Language. In *Proc. ACM Conference on LISP and Functional Programming*, Snowbird, Utah, July 1988.

[OY85] Z. Özsoyoğlu and L. Yuan. A Normal Form for Nested Relations. In *Proceedings of the ACM SIGACT-SIGMOD Symposium on Principles of Database Systems*, pages 251–260, Portland, March 1985.

[RKS84] A.M. Roth, H.F. Korth, and A. Silberschatz. *Extended Algebra and Calculus for ¬1NF Relational Databases*. Technical Report TR-84-36, Department of Computer Sciences, The University of Texas at Austin, 1984. revised 1985.

[Sch86] D.A. Schmidt. *Denotational Semantics, A Methodology for Language Development*. Allyn and Bacon, 1986.

[Sco72] D. Scott. Continuous Lattices. In *Toposes, Algebraic Geometry and Logic, Lecture Notes in Mathematics*, pages 97–136, Springer-Verlag, 1972.

[Zan84] C. Zaniolo. Database Relation with Null Values. *Journal of Computer and System Sciences*, 28(1):142–166, 1984.

Towards Abstracting Complex Database Objects: Generalization, Reduction and Unification of Set-type Objects (Extended Abstract)

Katsumi Tanaka

Dept. of Instrumentation Engineering
Kobe University
Kobe 657, Japan

Masatoshi Yoshikawa

Institute of Computer Sciences
Kyoto Sangyo University
Kyoto 603, Japan

Abstract

Representing and manipulating complex (database) objects are important issues in the semantic database models and object-oriented database models, most of which have a rich expressive power for complex objects. In this paper, we will focus on the manipulation of complex objects, and introduce the notions and the operations for abstracting complex objects. We introduce the notion of "element-based" generalization relationships between complex objects, and two new abstraction operators: reduction and unification. Their algebraic properties are then formally investigated especially for "set-type" complex objects.

1. Introduction

Recently, much attention has been paid both to semantic data models[HuKi87] which try to directly represent semantic structures of real world data, and to object-oriented databases[OODB86][MSOP86][BCGKWBK87] which, in addition, try to capture behavioral aspects of real world data.

One of the major features of these data models is the direct representation of complex database objects. Arbitrary complex database objects which represent, for example, cars or VLSI circuits can be stored in databases by themselves without being forced to be decomposed into several records which is typically observed in conventional record-oriented data models. Large amount of such complex objects give a precise description of real world data on one hand. However, their whole image or profile tends to be difficult to understand for users on the other. Therefore, in databases allowing complex objects, functions for data abstraction or summarization have much important role than in conventional databases storing only "flat" records.

There are, in general, several different kinds of data abstraction. Generalization and aggregation are two widely accepted types of data abstraction[SmSm77]. Since the generalization (or IS-A) relationship between objects is an important semantic construct in semantic database models or object-oriented data models, we will focus our attention to the abstraction of complex objets utilizing generalization hierarchies. In this paper, we will study the mechanism for abstracting complex objects based on generalization hierarchies and give a formal discussion on this mechanism. The major contribution of this paper is as follows:

(1) Introduction of the notion of "element-based" generalization relationship among complex objects.

(2) Introduction of two new abstraction operators: reduction and unification.

(3) Formal definition of the above (1) and (2), and discussions of several algebraic properties of them for set-type complex objects.

Set and tuple are widely recognized in literature[Hull87][BaKh86] as important structural constructs of complex objects. In Section 2, the basic concepts and motivating examples of the (1) and (2) are given both for set-type and tuple-type objects. We believe that these notions and operations are fundamentally important for the theoretical investigations of complex objects. And, in this first paper, we start our investigations by concentrating on the formal discussion of them especially for set-type objects.

Although the generalization relationship between atomic objects is extensively studied, there is no widely accepted concept of generalization between sets of objects. In Section 3, we newly introduce the notion of generalization between sets of objects. When multiple inheritances are allowed in IS-A hierarchy, there are (at least) two plausible interpretations of generalization of sets of objects. Therefore, we have defined two versions of "is-a" relationship, strong-isa (s-isa) and weak-isa (w-isa), both of which are natural extension of conventional is-a relationship. These notions provide the foundation of the following discussion on abstraction of complex objects. In Section 4, using these extended notions of generalization, new operators, which give the minimal common generalization objects of given two objects, are defined. These operators can be regarded as the abstraction-based unification of the two objects. Also, reduction operators, which picks most generic (or specific) objects out of a given set-object, are introduced and several algebraic properties of these operators are presented.

There are some related works. Survey of theoretical research on query languages and comparisons of information capacity of complex database objects is given in [Hull87]. In [AtPa86], generalization relationships are discussed in the context of integrity constraints, and inference rules and satisfiability problems are discussed. Bancilhon et. al.[BaKh86] introduced a mathematical formalism and a calculus for complex objects. Also, in [BBKV87], they developed a database language FAD based on their calculus. However, they are not incorporating generalization relationships into their calculus or language. To the knowledge of the authors, there is no study on the generalization relationships in which structural constructs such as sets or tuples are explicitly incorporated.

2. Basic Concepts and Motivating Examples

In semantic database modeling[HuKi87] and object-oriented databases[BBKV87], the basic constructs to represent "complex database objects" are (1)set-type objects and (2)tuple-type objects. Also, one of the most fundamental tools to abstract database objects is a generalization relationship[SmSm77] (is-a relationship) among objects. For example, in Smalltalk-80[GoRo83] or many object-oriented DBMSs, both the subclass-superclass relationship and the instance-class relationship are used to construct a generalization hierarchy (which also permits some classes to have their multiple superclasses). In these systems, each set-type object is considered to belong to the "Collection" class or some of its subclasses. Each tuple-type object is regarded just as an instance object because each instance object consists of multiple attribute values (the values of instance variables).

Consider the following sentence:

(s1) "There is a software package of the category ProductionSystem, which is developed by Bill using Turbo-C and Lisp."

This sentence is represented by the following tuple-type object

(Bill, {Turbo-C, Lisp})

This object is an instance of the class ProductionSystem. If we use the instance-class relationship, the given sentence can be abstracted into the following sentence:

(s2) "There is a software package of the category ProductionSystem."

In the similar manner, if the set-type object {Turbo-C, Lisp} is an instance of the LanguageSet class, it can be abstracted into a LanguageSet.

However, when we focus our attention on the generalization hierarchy of the elements contained inside the tuple-type object or the set-type object, many variations of their abstracted versions are obtained. For example, if Bill is an instance of the AssociateProfessor class and Turbo-C is an instance of the C class, then the given sentence can be abstracted into the following:

(s3) "There is a software package of the category ProductionSystem, which is developed by an AssociateProfessor using C and Lisp."

This sentence is represented by the following tuple-type object:

(AssociateProfessor, {C, Lisp})

Suppose that the generalization hierarchy in Fig. 2.1 and the following three tuple-type objects are given:

(1) (Bill, {Turbo-C, Lisp})

(2) (John, {C, CommonLisp})

(3) ({Bill, John}, {Turbo-C, Lisp, C, CommonLisp})

The meaning of these three objects are of the same kind. That is, there are three software packages. The first one was developed by Bill using Turbo-C and Lisp, where it is not known what kind of Lisp was actually used. The second one was developed by John using C and CommonLisp, where it is not known what kind of C was actually used. Note that in this example, the class objects C and Lisp appear as elements of complex objects. In general, several interpretations of these class objects exist when they are used as elements of complex objects. Here, we adopt the 'existential and no-information' interpretation, that is, for example, we know that the first software package object was developed partially by a programming language of type C, but we have no information about deciding what kind of C was actually used. As for the third object, we assume that this software package is an

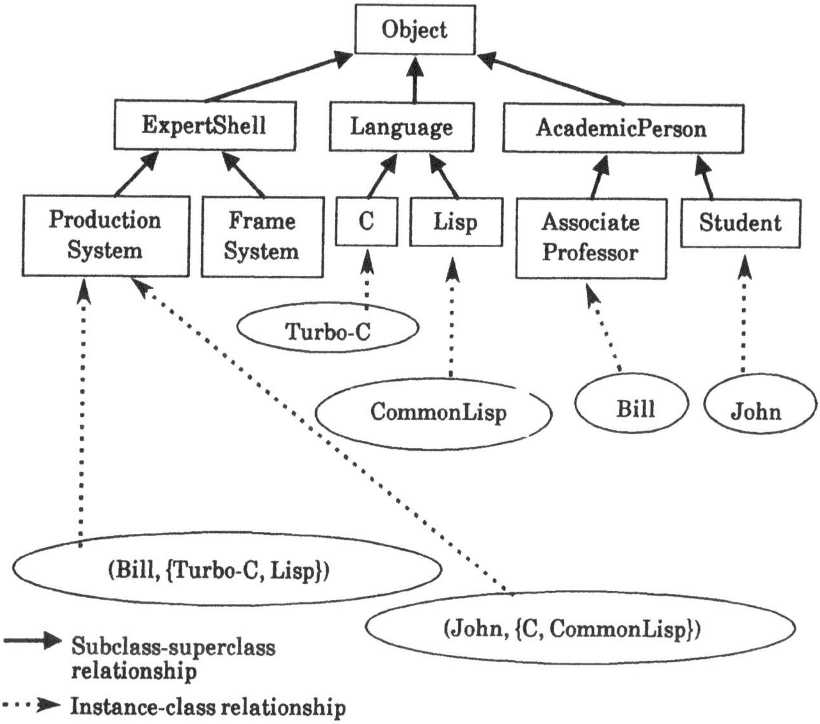

Fig.2.1 An example generalization hierarchy

integrated version of the first and the second software packages. Therefore, The developer of this software is the set-type object {Bill, John}, and the used languages are represented by the union of {Turbo-C, Lisp} and {C, CommonLisp}. Then, several types of abstractions for these three tuple-type objects are obtained by (a combination of) the following abstraction operations:

(a) *Generalization of objects by a given class hierarchy:* This is a usual abstraction operation using only a given class hierarchy. For example, (Bill, {Turbo-C, Lisp}) can be abstracted into ProductionSystem, and further into ExpertShell.

(b) *Element-based generalization of set-type objects:* This is an abstraction operation by replacing an element of a set-type object by the element's class or the element's superclass. For example, {Turbo-C, Lisp} can be abstracted into {C, Lisp}, and further, into {ProgrammingLanguage}.

(c) *Element-based generalization of tuple-type objects:* This is an abstraction operation by replacing an element of a tuple-type object by the element's class or the element's superclass. For example, (Bill, {Turbo-C, Lisp}) can be abstracted into (AssociateProfessor, {Turbo-C, Lisp}), and further, into (AssociateProfessor, {Language}).

(d) *Generic reduction of set-type objects:* This is an operation to remove "redundant" elements from a set-type object. Here, the redundant elements mean that those are generalized into at least one element in the set-type object. For example, the set-type object {Turbo-C, Lisp, C, CommonLisp} (which appeared as an element of the third tuple-type object above) can be reduced into the set-type object {Lisp, C}. This is because the object Turbo-C can be generalized into C and the object CommonLisp can be generalized into Lisp.

(e) *Specific reduction of set-type objects:* This is an operation to remove "redundant" elements from a set-type object. Here, the redundant elements mean that those are obtained by generalizing some element in the set-type object. For example, the set-type object {Turbo-C, Lisp, C, CommonLisp} can be reduced into the set-type object {Turbo-C, CommonLisp}.

(f) *Unification of two set-type objects:* This is an operation to unify two set-type objects into a more generic set-type object by generalizing two set-type objects. For example, the set-type objects {Turbo-C, Lisp} and {C, CommonLisp} are unified into the set-type object {C, Lisp}.

(g) *Unification of two tuple-type objects:* This is an operation to unify two tuple-type objects into a more generic tuple-type object by generalizing these two tuple-type objects. For example, the two tuple-type objects (Bill, {Turbo-C, Lisp}) and (John, {C, CommonLisp}) are unified into the tuple-type object (AcademicPerson, {C, Lisp}).

The example of the above abstraction operations is shown in Fig. 2.2. Each of (a)-(g) in Fig. 2.2 corresponds to one of the operations (a) to (g) described above.

In this paper, we will focus our attention especially on (a), (b), (d), (e) and (f).

3. Element-based Generalization Concepts for Set-type Objects

In this section, we will define the "objectbase" and two versions of generalizations for set-type objects, and show their properties.

Let U_{id} be a countably infinite set of symbols called *object identifiers*. Also, let U_{att} be a countably infinite set of symbols called *attributes*.

[Definition 3.1] (Object)

(1) A number, a character, a string or an image is an object called an *atomic object*.

(2) If $O_1,...,O_n$ $(n \geq 0)$ are objects, then the set $\{O_1,...,O_n\}$ is an object called a *set-object*.

(3) If f is a partial mapping that maps each attribute in U_{att} to an object and i is an object identifier in U_{id}, then the ordered pair (i, f) is an object called a *mapping-object*.

Throughout this paper, we use O, O', X and Y (possibly with subscripts) to denote objects. Also, we use o, x, y and z (possibly with subscripts) to denote atomic- or mapping-objects, and use R, R', S, S' and T (possibly with subscripts) to denote set-objects.

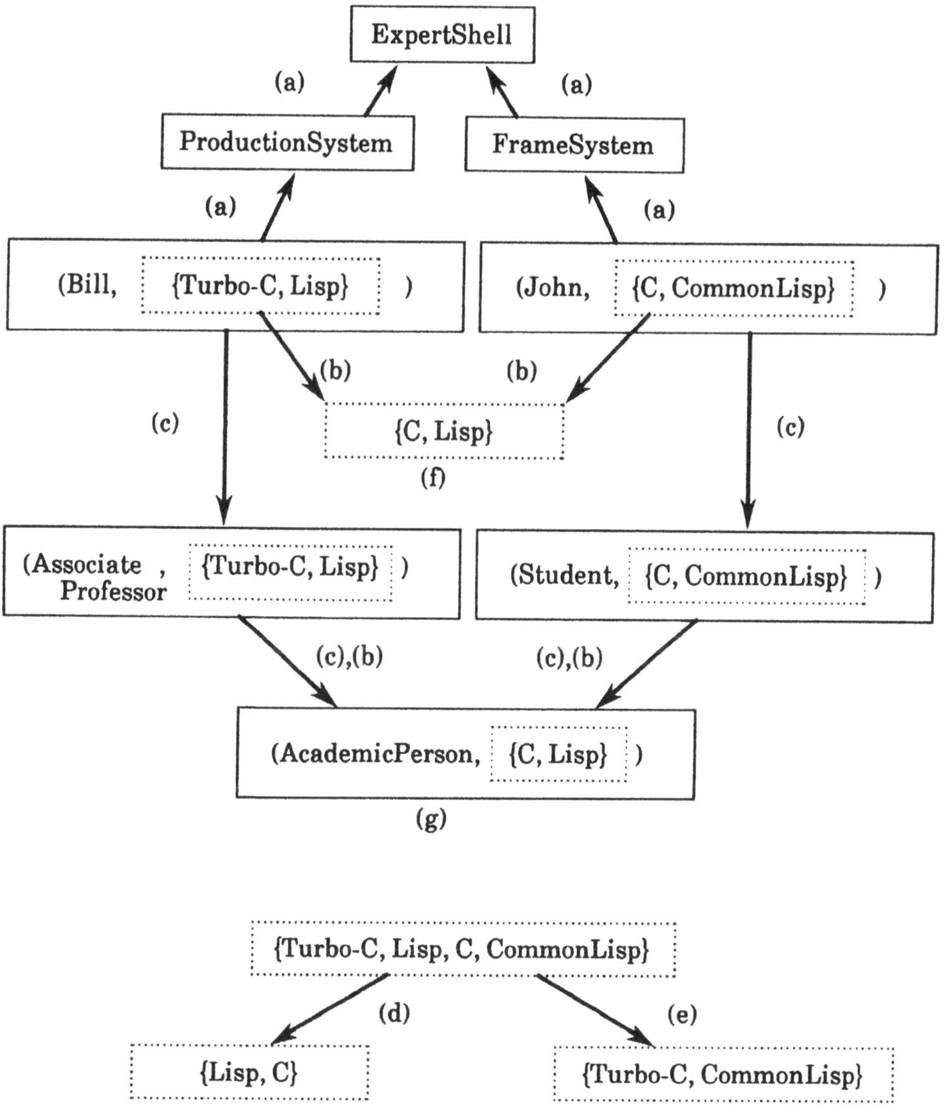

Fig.2.2 An example of abstractions of complex database objects

Let U_∞ be the set of all the possible objects defined in the above. We assume that U_{id}, U_{att} and U_∞ are mutually disjoint. Given a mapping-objet o=(i, f) and an attribute $A \in U_{att}$, f(A) (if defined) is also denoted by o.A.

A *database instance* is the contents of a database at a certain time. In this paper, a database instance is said to be an *objectbase*. To formally define the notion of objectbases, first, we define the notion of *closed set-objects*.

[Definition 3.2] (Closed set-objects) For a given set-object S, an object O is said to be *closed with respect to S* if O satisfies one of the following conditions:

(i) O is an atomic object and $O \in S$.

(ii) O is a set-object and $O \in S$. Also, each element of O is closed with respect to S.

(iii) O is a mapping-object (i, f) and $O \in S$. Also, for each attribute $A \in U_{att}$, if f(A) is defined then f(A) is closed with respect to S.

If each element of a set-object O is closed with respect to O, then O is said to be a *closed set-object*.

Intuitively, an objectbase consists of a closed set-object and an IS-A relationship between objects. Formally, we have

[Definition 3.3] (Objectbase) An *objectbase* is an ordered pair (O_{base}, IS-A), where

(1) O_{base} is a finite, closed set-object such that for each mapping-object $o_1=(i_1, f_1)$ and $o_2=(i_2, f_2)$ in O_{base}, if $i_1=i_2$, then $f_1=f_2$.

(2) IS-A is a nonreflexive, non-symmetric binary relation over O_{base} such that

  (i) if x IS-A y then each of x and y is either an atomic object or a mapping-object.

  (ii) if x_1 IS-A x_2, ..., x_{n-1} IS-A x_n ($n \geq 3$) then x_1 IS-A x_n does not hold.

  (iii) if x_i IS-A x_{i+1} holds for each i (i = 1, ..., n-1, $n \geq 2$) then x_n IS-A x_1 does not hold.

Note that the condition (i) of (2) in the above Definition 3.3 implies that no set-object has its belonging class in the IS-A hierarchy. That is, for example, we are not interested in abstracting the set-object {Turbo-C, Lisp} into the LanguageSet class, which it belongs to.

Given a set-object S, let S' = (S - {x}) ∪ {y} be another set-object such that x IS-A y holds. Then, intuitively, we say that S' is a more abstract version of S and that there is a generalization relationship between S and S'. Formally, we have:

[Definition 3.4] (Strong generalization) For a given objectbase (O_{base}, IS-A), *strong-isa* (abbreviated by *s-isa*) is a binary relation defined over U_∞, which satisfies the following:

(1) For each object O in U_∞, O s-isa O.

(2) For arbitrary atomic- or mapping-objects O_1, O_2 in U_∞ such that O_1 IS-A O_2, O_1 s-isa O_2.

(3) For each set-object $S = \{O_1, ..., O_{i-1}, X, O_{i+1}, ..., O_n\}$ ($n \geq 0$) and each object Y in U_∞ such that X s-isa Y, S s-isa $(S-\{X\}) \cup \{Y\}$.

Also, the transitive closure of s-isa is denoted by *s-isa**.

By the above definition, for example, if both of x IS-A y and x IS-A z hold, then {x} s-isa {y} and {x} s-isa {z} hold. However, {x} s-isa {y, z} does not hold. The following is a little weaker version of 'isa', which allows {x} 'isa' {y, z}.

[Definition 3.5] (Weak generalization) For a given objectbase (O_{base}, IS-A), *weak-isa* (abbreviated by *w-isa*) is a binary relation defined over U_∞, which satisfies the following:

(1) For each object O in U_∞, O w-isa O.

(2) For arbitrary atomic- or mapping-objects O_1, O_2 in U_∞ such that O_1 IS-A O_2, O_1 w-isa O_2.

(3) For each set-object $S = \{O_1, ..., O_{i-1}, X, O_{i+1}, ..., O_n\}$ ($n \geq 0$) and each object $Y_1, ..., Y_k$ ($k \geq 1$) in U_∞ such that X w-isa Y_j for all j ($k \geq j \geq 1$), S w-isa $(S-\{X\}) \cup \{Y_1, ..., Y_k\}$.

Also, the transitive closure of w-isa is denoted by *w-isa**.

[Example 3.1] Let (O_{base}, IS-A) be an objectbase defined as

O_{base} = {Tom, Jerry, 20, 21, Product, Game, IntelligentGame, VideoGame, Chess, Go, TVOthello, VideoHockey, Packman, {Chess, VideoGame}, {IntelligentGame, Packman}}

and IS-A is a binary relation shown in Fig. 3.1.

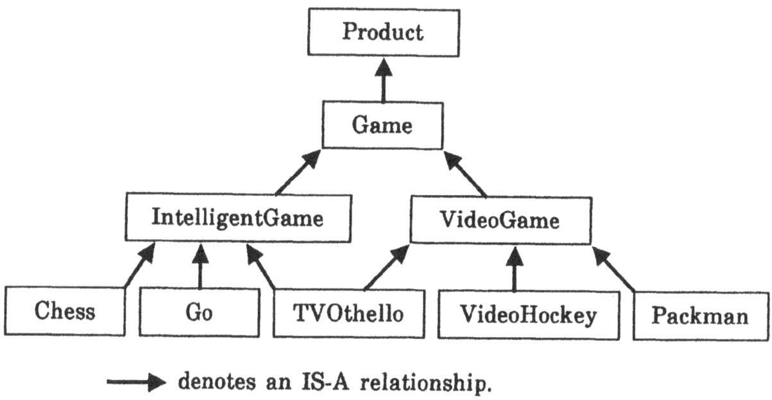

Fig.3.1 An IS-A hierarchy about products

Here, 20 and 21 are atomic objects, {Chess, VideoGame} and {IntelligentGame, Packman} are set-objects. All the other elements in O_{base} are assumed to be mapping-objects such that Tom.age = 20, Jerry.age = 21, Tom.developingProduct = {Chess, VideoGame}, Jerry.developingProduct = {IntelligentGame, Packman}. Clearly, O_{base} is a closed set-object.

Since Chess IS-A IntelligentGame,

{Invader, {Othello, Chess}} s-isa {Invader, {Othello, IntelligentGame}}.

Also, note that

{TVOthello} w-isa {IntelligentGame, VideoGame}

holds, but

{TVOthello} s-isa {IntelligentGame, VideoGame}

does not hold.

Clearly, we have the following relationship between s-isa and w-isa.

[Proposition 3.1] Given an objectbase (O_{base}, IS-A), if O_1 s-isa O_2 then O_1 w-isa O_2 for arbitrary objects O_1, O_2 in U_∞.

As for the transitive closure s-isa*, we have the following property.

[Theorem 3.1] The binary relation s-isa* is a partial order.

As for the proof, the reflexivity and transitivity of s-isa* is obvious. The anti-symmetricity is proved by the induction of the set-height of given objects.

Note that the binary relation w-isa* is not a partial order in general (see Section 4). Also, the following fundamental properties hold.

[Proposition 3.2] Let R, R_1, R_2, S, S_1, S_2 and T be arbitrary set-objects. For a given objectbase (O_{base}, IS-A), we have

(1) If R w-isa* S then ($R \cup T$) w-isa* ($S \cup T$).

(2) If R_1 w-isa* S and R_2 w-isa* S then ($R_1 \cup R_2$) w-isa* S.

(3) If R w-isa* S_1 and R w-isa* S_2 then R w-isa* ($S_1 \cup S_2$).

(4) If R_1 w-isa* S_1 and R_2 w-isa* S_2 then ($R_1 \cup R_2$) w-isa* ($S_1 \cup S_2$).

4. Unification and Reduction of Objects

In this section, we will introduce unification and reduction operations which are based on the "element-based" generalization of set-objects, and will describe their algebraic properties.

4.1 Unification of set-objects

As shown in the motivating example in Section 2, fully utilizing the 'element-based' generalization, we can unify two given set-objects into a more abstract one, even if the intersection of these two set-objects is empty. For example, the two set-objects {Turbo-C, Lisp} and {C, CommonLisp} are unified into the more abstract set-object {C, Lisp} although the intersection of the two is empty. For two atomic or mapping-objects, the notion of the unification directly corresponds to the notion of the least common ancestor of them in an IS-A hierarchy. However, since an attribute values in databases can be a set-object as well as a single atomic or mapping-object, it is desired that the same notion as the "least common ancestor" is extended to cope with set-objects as well.

[Definition 4.1] (Least generic unified objects) Given an objectbase $B=(O_{base}, \text{IS-A})$ and two objects O_1, O_2 ($\in O_{base}$), an object O which satisfies the following two conditions (1) and (2) is called a *least strongly-generic (s-generic) unified object* (*least weakly-generic (w-generic) unified object,* respectively) of O_1 and O_2.

(1) O_1 s-isa* O and O_2 s-isa* O
    (O_1 w-isa* O and O_2 w-isa* O)

(2) There is no object O' (O' $\neq$ O) that satisfies
    O_1 s-isa* O', O_2 s-isa* O' and O' s-isa* O.
    (O_1 w-isa* O', O_2 w-isa* O' and O' w-isa* O.)

The least s-generic (w-generic, respectively) unified object of O_1 and O_2 is denoted by $O_1 \wedge_s O_2$ ($O_1 \wedge_w O_2$, respectively) if and only if it uniquely exists.

The above definition subsumes the notion of least common ancestors of two atomic or mapping-objects in an IS-A hierarchy. The following is a relationship between the least s-generic unified object and the least w-generic unified object for two given objects.

[Proposition 4.1] For any two objects O_i and O_j, and for any least s-generic unified object $O_{s\text{-}generic}$ of O_i and O_j, ($O_i \wedge_w O_j$) w-isa* $O_{s\text{-}generic}$ holds.

If the least s-generic unifier of O_i and O_j is unique,

$$(O_i \wedge_w O_j) \text{ w-isa* } (O_i \wedge_s O_j)$$

holds from Proposition 4.1.

Note that the least generic unifiers are not always uniquely determined (see Example 4.1).

[Example 4.1] In the IS-A hierarchy in Fig. 3.1,

{VideoGame, Chess} $\wedge_s$ {Packman, IntelligentGame}

= {VideoGame, Chess} $\wedge_w$ {Packman, IntelligentGame}

= {VideoGame, IntelligentGame}

However, the least s-generic unified objects of {TVOthello, Chess} and {Packman, TVOthello} are not uniquely determined, and they are {VideoGame, IntelligentGame} or {Game, TVOthello}. On the other hand, the least w-generic unified object of {TVOthello, Chess} and {Packman, TVOthello} is unique, and

{TVOthello, Chess} Λ_w {Packman, TVOthello}

= {TVOthello, VideoGame, IntelligentGame}

Note that, as Proposition 4.1 says, both of the following relationships hold:

{TVOthello, VideoGame, IntelligentGame} w-isa* {VideoGame, IntelligentGame}

{TVOthello, VideoGame, IntelligentGame} w-isa* {Game, TVOthello}

In the following, we show some algebraic properties about the least s-generic unified objects.

[Proposition 4.2] For any objects O_1, O_2 and O_3, each of the following properties hold.

(i) $O_1 \Lambda_s O_1 = O_1$

(ii) $O_1 \Lambda_s O_2 = O_2 \Lambda_s O_1$

(iii) $(O_1 \Lambda_s O_2) \Lambda_s O_3 = O_1 \Lambda_s (O_2 \Lambda_s O_3)$.

In general, the distribution law between Λ_s and $\cup$ or between Λ_w and $\cup$ does not hold. However, we have the following proposition.

[Proposition 4.3] For any set-objects S_i, S_j and S_k, each of the following relationships holds.

(1) $(S_i \cup S_j) \Lambda_w S_k$ w-isa* $(S_i \Lambda_w S_k) \cup (S_j \Lambda_w S_k)$

(2) $(S_i \cup S_j) \Lambda_w S_k$ w-isa* $(S_i \Lambda_s S_k) \cup (S_j \Lambda_s S_k)$

For each pair of set-objects R and S such that $O_r \Lambda_w O_s$ exists for each O_r in R and each O_s in S, $\{ O \mid O = O_r \Lambda_s O_s, O_r \in R, O_s \in S\}$ is called a *pairwise s-generic unified object,* and is denoted by pair-Λ_s(R, S). Similarly, $\{ O \mid O = O_r \Lambda_w O_s, O_r \in R, O_s \in S\}$ is called a *pairwise w-generic unified object,* and is denoted by pair-Λ_w(R, S). Next we will discuss the relationships between least s-generic (w-generic) unified objects and pairwise s-generic (w-generic) unified objects of two set-objects. It is important to examine this relationship, since once we have obtained R Λ_s S (R Λ_w S) for set-objects R and S, this relationship might reduce the cost for recomputing R' Λ_s S' (R' Λ_w S') for other set-objects R' and S'.

It should be noted that it is possible to prove that the following two statements are independent each other for set-objects R and S.

(i) The least s-generic (w-generic, respectively) unified object of R and S is uniquely determined.

(ii) The least s-generic (w-generic, respectively) unified object of O_r and O_s is uniquely determined for each $O_r \in R$ and $O_s \in S$.

Also, it is possible to find an example of set-objects R and S for R Λ_s S $\neq$ pair-Λ_s(R, S) and an example for R Λ_w S $\neq$ pair-Λ_w(R, S) for set-objects R and S. However, we have the following properties.

[Lemma 4.1] For any set-objects R and S such that R Λ_w S exists,

R Λ_w S $\subseteq$ pair-Λ_w(R, S)

[Lemma 4.2] For any set-objects R and S such that R Λ_w S exists,

R Λ_w S w-isa* pair-Λ_w(R, S)

[Example 4.2] Consider the IS-A hierarchy in Fig. 3.1, and let R and S be set-objects {TVOthello, Chess} and {Packman, TVOthello}, respectively. The least s-generic and w-generic unified objects of R and S are given in Example 4.1. Also, pair-Λ_s(R, S) = pair-Λ_w(R, S) = {TVOthello, VideoGame, IntelligentGame, Game}. Check to see Lemmas 4.1 and 4.2 hold.

4.2 Reduction of objects

In this section, first we will define unary operators $\downarrow$ and $\uparrow$ which selects most specific objects and generic objects, respectively, from a given set object. Then we will give some algebraic properties of these operators. Finally we will show that a simple relationship holds between the least w-generic unified object and pairwise w-generic unified object of two set-objects by taking into account the operator $\downarrow$.

[Definition 4.2] (Specific and generic reduction of an object) Given an objectbase B=(O_{base}, IS-A) and an object O $\in$ O_{base}, a *specific reduction* (*generic reduction*) of O is defined as follows.

(1) If O is an atomic object or a mapping-object, a specific reduction (generic reduction) of O is O.

(2) If O is a set-object, a specific reduction of O is a set-object O_s such that both of $O_s \subseteq O$ and O_s w-isa* O hold, and for each object O_s' such that $O_s' \subsetneq O_s$, O_s' w-isa* O does not hold. Similarly, a generic reduction of O is a set-object O_g such that both of $O_g \subseteq O$ and O w-isa* O_g hold, and for each object O_g' such that $O_g' \subsetneq O_g$, O w-isa* O_g' does not hold.

The specific reduction (generic reduction) of O is denoted by $\downarrow$O ($\uparrow$O) if and only if it is uniquely determined.

[Definition 4.3] (Reduction of an object) Given an objectbase B=(O_{base}, IS-A) and an object O $\in$ O_{base}, a *reduction* of O is defined as follows.

(1) If O is an atomic object or a mapping-object, a reduction of O is O.

(2) If O is a set-object, a reduction of O is the union of a specific reduction of O and a generic reduction of O.

The reduction of O is denoted by $\updownarrow$O if and only if it is uniquely determined.

[Example 4.3] (example of $\downarrow$, $\uparrow$ and $\updownarrow$) Consider the IS-A hierarchy shown in Fig. 3.1, and let S be a set-object {Game, Chess, TVOthello, VideoGame, Packman}. From the definition, $\downarrow$S = {Chess, TVOthello, Packman}, $\uparrow$S = {Game} and $\updownarrow$S = {Game, Chess, TVOthello, Packman}.

It should be noted that for each object O in U_∞,

(1) O w-isa* $\uparrow$O and O w-isa* $\updownarrow$O hold. (by Definitions 4.2, 4.3 and Proposition 3.1)

(2) $\downarrow$O s-isa* O and $\updownarrow$O s-isa* O do not hold in general.

(3) $\downarrow$O w-isa* O and $\updownarrow$O w-isa* O hold. (by Definitions 4.2, 4.3 and Proposition 3.1)

The binary relation w-isa* is not a partial order in general. For example, if x IS-A y and y IS-A z hold, two set-objects {x, y, z} and {x, z} do not satisfy the antisymmetric law of w-isa*. However, as shown in the following theorem, if we allow only reduced set-objects, we can assure that w-isa* is a partial order.

[Theorem 4.1] The binary relation w-isa* for a given objectbase B=(O_{base}, IS-A) is a partial order if $\updownarrow$S = S holds for each set-object S $\in$ O_{base}.

The unary operator $\downarrow$ picks out most "specific" objects in a given set-object. It is important to investigate what kind of generalization relationships between two given set-objects R and S are preserved under the $\downarrow$ operator. To discuss this problem, first we need to define a more general notion than the least w-generic unified object.

[Definition 4.4] (Partial weak-isa) For a given objectbase (O_{base}, IS-A), *partial weak-isa* (abbreviated by *pw-isa*) is a binary relation defined over U_∞, which satisfies the following:

(1) For arbitrary objects O_1, O_2 in U_∞, if O_1 w-isa O_2 then O_1 pw-isa O_2.

(2) For each set-objects S in U_∞ and each object O ($\in$ S), S pw-isa S - {O}.

Also, the transitive closure of pw-isa is denoted by pw-isa*.

In general, each of the following statements (1), (2) and (3) does not hold:

(1) If R s-isa* S then $\downarrow$R s-isa* $\downarrow$S.

(2) If R s-isa* S then $\downarrow$R w-isa* $\downarrow$S.

(3) If R w-isa* S then $\downarrow$R w-isa* $\downarrow$S.

However, the following proposition holds.

[Proposition 4.4] For arbitrary set-objects R and S such that both $\downarrow$R and $\downarrow$S exist, if R pw-isa* S then $\downarrow$R pw-isa* $\downarrow$S.

Therefore, the relationship pw-isa* is, in a sense, closed under the specific reduction operation $\downarrow$. From the definition of pw-isa, R pw-isa* S holds if and only if there exists a set-object R' such that R' $\subseteq$ R and R' w-isa* S. Since R' $\subseteq$ R means that R contains more objects than R', and R' w-isa* S means that R' has more specific objects than S, R pw-isa* S can be interpreted that R is more informative set-object than S. So, Proposition 4.4 can be rephrased as:

If R is more informative set-object than S, then $\downarrow$R is more informative set-object than $\downarrow$S.

From Proposition 4.4, the following corollaries hold.

[Corollary 4.1] For any set-objects R and S such that R $\subseteq$ S and both of $\downarrow$S and $\downarrow$R exist,
$\downarrow$S pw-isa* $\downarrow$R.

[Corollary 4.2] For any set-objects R and S such that S w-isa* R and both of $\downarrow$S and $\downarrow$R exist,
$\downarrow$S pw-isa* $\downarrow$R.

A stronger result than Proposition 4.4 holds if R and S satisfy some conditions as shown in the following theorem.

[Theorem 4.2] If R w-isa* S and R $\subseteq$ S hold and if both of $\downarrow$R and $\downarrow$S exist, then $\downarrow R = \downarrow S$.

Finally, let us examine the interaction of the specific reduction and the least s-generic (w-generic) unified object.

[Proposition 4.5] For set-objects S_1 and S_2, the following properties hold.

(i) $\downarrow(\text{pair-}\Lambda_s(R, S_1 \cup S_2)) = \downarrow(\downarrow(\text{pair-}\Lambda_s(R, S_1)) \cup \downarrow(\text{pair-}\Lambda_s(R, S_2)))$

(ii) $\downarrow(\text{pair-}\Lambda_w(R, S_1 \cup S_2)) = \downarrow(\downarrow(\text{pair-}\Lambda_w(R, S_1)) \cup \downarrow(\text{pair-}\Lambda_w(R, S_2)))$

In general, $\downarrow R \ \Lambda_s \downarrow S \neq \text{pair-}\Lambda_s(R, S)$, and
$\downarrow R \ \Lambda_w \downarrow S \neq \text{pair-}\Lambda_w(R, S)$.

Also, as stated in Section 4.1, in general, $R \ \Lambda_w \ S \neq \text{pair-}\Lambda_w(R, S)$.

However, from Lemmas 4.1, 4.2 and Theorem 4.2, we can obtain the following:

[Theorem 4.3] For any set-objects R and S such that $R \ \Lambda_w \ S$, $\downarrow(R \ \Lambda_w \ S)$ and $\downarrow\text{pair-}\Lambda_w(R, S)$ exist,
$\downarrow(R \ \Lambda_w \ S) = \downarrow\text{pair-}\Lambda_w(R, S)$

From Proposition 4.5 and Theorem 4.3, it is shown that once we have obtained $\downarrow(R \ \Lambda_w \ S)$ for some set-objects R and S, $\downarrow(R' \ \Lambda_w \ S')$ can be computed differentially for other set-objects R' and S'.

Acknowledgement

This work is partially supported by the Science Foundation Grant #63750359 and #63780049 of the Ministry of Education, Science and Culture of Japan. The authors are grateful to Mr. K. Takeda at IBM Japan for valuable discussion at the early stage of this study.

References

[AtPa86] Atzeni, P. and Parker, D. S. Jr., "Formal Properties of Net-based Knowledge Representation Schemes", *Proc. the 2nd IEEE Intl. Conf. on Data Engineering,* pp. 700-706, Feb. 1986.

[BaKh86] Bancilhon, F. and Khoshafian, S., "A Calculus for Complex Objects", *Proc. 5th ACM SIGACT-SIGMOD Symposium on Principles of Database Systems,* pp. 53-59, Mar. 1986.

[BBKV87] Bancilhon, F., Briggs, T., Khoshafian, S. and Valduriez, P., "FAD, a Powerful and Simple Database Language", *Proc. of the 13th International Conference on VLDB,* pp. 97-105, Sept. 1987.

[BCGKWBK87] Banerjee, J., Chou, H. -T., Garza, J. F., Kim, W., Woelk, D., Ballou, N. and Kim, H. -J., "Data Model Issues for Object-Oriented Applications", *ACM Trans. on Office Information Systems,* Jan. 1987.

[GoRo83] Goldberg, A. and Robson, D., *Smalltalk-80: The Language and Its Implementation,* Addison Wesley Reading, Mass., 1983.

[HuKi87] Hull, R. and King, R., "Semantic Database Modeling: Survey, Applications, and Research Issues", to appear in *ACM Computing Surveys,* Aug. 1987.

[Hull87] Hull, R., "A Survey of Theoretical Research on Typed Complex Database Objects", in *DATABASES* (J. Paredaens ed.), pp. 193-256, Academic Press, 1987.

[MSOP86] Maier, D., Stein, J., Otis, A. and Purdy, A., "Development of an Object-Oriented DBMS", *Tech. Report CS/E-86-005, Oregon Graduate Center,* April 1986. (Also, appeared in *Proc. of 1986 ACM Conference on Object-Oriented Programming Systems, Languages and Applications*).

[OODS86] *International Workshop on Object-Oriented Database Systems,* ACM-SIGMOD and IEEE TC on Database Engineering, Pacific Grove, CA, Sept. 23-26, 1986.

[SmSm77] Smith, J. M. and Smith, D. C. P., "Database Abstractions: Aggregation and Generalization", *ACM Trans. Database Systems,* Vol. 2, No. 2, pp. 105-133, June 1977.

[Stone86] Stonebraker, M., "Object Management in POSTGRES Using Procedures", in [OODS86], pp. 66-72, Sept. 1986.

[ZABCKM86] Zaniolo, C., Ait-Kaci, H., Beech, D., Cammarata, S., Kerschberg, L. and Maier, D., "Object Oriented Database Systems and Knowledge Systems", in *Expert Database Systems* (L. Kerschberg ed.), Benjamin/Cummings Pub. Co. Inc., pp. 49-65, 1986.

On the Complexity of Queries in the Logical Data Model

Extended Abstract

Gabriel M. Kuper
IBM Watson Research Center

Moshe Y. Vardi
IBM Almaden Research Center

Abstract

We investigate the complexity of query processing in the *logical data model* (LDM). We use two measures: *data complexity*, which is complexity with respect to the size of the data, and *expression complexity*, which is complexity with respect to the size of the expressions denoting the queries. Our investigation shows that while the operations of product and union are essentially first-order operations, the power set operation is inherently a higher-order operation and is exponentially expensive. We define a hierarchy of queries based on the depth of nesting of power set operations and show that this hierarchy corresponds to a natural hierarchy of Turing machines that run in multiply exponential time.

1 Introduction

Research in database theory during the 1970's and the early 1980's has focused mainly on the relational model [Co70], probably due to its elegance and mathematical simplicity. This very simplicity, however, has gradually been recognized as one of the major disadvantages of the relational model: it forces the stored data to have a flat structure that real data does not always have [SS77,Co79]. This has motivated a great deal of research during the past decade on *structured* data models: the so-called *semantic data models* (cf. [AH87, HM81, Sh81]), *nested relations* (cf. [FT83,JS82]), and *complex objects* (cf. [BK86]).

Continuing in this spirit, we introduced in [KV84,Ku85] the *Logical Data Model* (LDM), which combines and extends Jacobs' *database logic* [Ja82] and Hull and Yap's *format model* [HY82]. This model uses three basic operations to structure data: *product*, *union*, and *power set*.[1] These operations can be combined not only hierarchically but also in a cyclic manner; LDM allows cyclicity both at the schema level and at the data level. An essential feature of the model is the separation between the *data space* and the *address space*. This separation guarantees that cyclic data has a well-defined semantics. The model also consists of a logic, in which integrity constraints can be specified, and a query facility, consisting of equivalent *procedural* (algebraic) and *nonprocedural* (calculus-like) query languages. An attractive feature of this query facility is that answers to queries need not be flat, i.e., relations, but can have semantically motivated structure as well. Thus, for example, the answer to a query over a network database can also have a network structure.

[1] The product operation is called *aggregation* in [SS77] and *composition* in [HY82]. The union operation is called *generalization* in [SS77] and *classification* in [HY82]. The power set operation is called *collection* in [HY82].

Recognizing that the expressiveness of LDM may not come for free, we set in a [KV85] to investigate the expressive power of the model. We showed there that even though the model is semantically powerful, it is not overly powerful so as to be intractable. This was demonstrated from three aspects. First, we studied the complexity of checking integrity constraints, and showed that it is no more difficult than checking integrity constraints in the relational model. Secondly, we showed that the logic of integrity constraints is essentially first-order. Finally, we proved the somewhat surprising result that in a certain precise sense, the ability to define cycles does not add any power to the model. Thus, any cyclic schema can be converted to an "equivalent" acyclic schema.

In this paper we continue our investigation of the expressiveness of LDM by studying the complexity of query processing. We use the two measures defined in [Va82]: *data complexity*, which is complexity with respect to the size of the data, and *expression complexity*, which is complexity with respect to the size of the expressions denoting the queries. Our investigation shows that while the operations of product and union are essentially first-order operations, the power set operation is inherently a higher-order operation and is exponentially expensive. We define a hierarchy of queries based on the depth of nesting of power set operations and show that this hierarchy corresponds to a natural hierarchy of Turing machines that run in multiply exponential time.

Our result here should be contrasted with the results in [KV85], where it is shown that the logic of integrity constraints is essentially first-order even in the presence of power nodes. The reason for the contrast is that the logic of integrity constraints deals with existing values of power nodes, whereas the logical query language tries to create new values of power nodes.

Our investigation is independent but closely related to that of Hull and Su [HS88]. They defined a hierarchy of queries similar to ours and established upper complexity bounds, but provided lower complexity bounds only to the lower levels of the hierarchy. We completely characterize the complexity of our hierarchy in terms of tight lower and upper bounds. Our investigation is also loosely related to that of Bennet [Be62], who characterized the models of higher-order logic in terms of constructive arithmetics.

2 Basic Definitions

2.1 LDM Schemas and Instances

In the *Logical Data Model* (LDM), *schemas* are directed labeled multigraphs, where there is an additional ordering imposed on the multiset of *children* for each node (y is a *child* of x if there is an edge from x to y). Each node is labelled by a *type*. There are four types: *basic*, denoted graphically by □, *product*, denoted graphically by ⊗, *union*, denoted graphically by Ⓤ, and *power*, denoted graphically by ⊛. The domains of basic nodes are the basic data domains of the database. The domains of product nodes are the cross product of the domains of successor nodes. The domains of union nodes contain disjoint unions of the domains of child nodes. The domains of power nodes contain the power sets of the domains of child nodes. Accordingly, basic nodes must be *leaves*, i.e., they have no children, union nodes must have distinct children, and power nodes must have unique children.

An *instance* of a schema is an assignment of a finite set of addresses to each node. We use the notation $I(u)$ for the set of addresses assigned to a node u by an instance I. The addresses are taken from a set A, which is disjoint from the set D of atomic data elements. We require that the instances of distinct nodes be disjoint. Every address l points to a data value, denoted $data(l)$. We require that the data value be of the correct form, depending on the type of the node, as follows. If $l \in I(v)$, then

1. if v is a basic node, then $data(l)$ has to be an element of D,
2. if v is a product node with successors $v_1, \ldots, v_n$, $data(l)$ has to be a tuple $\langle l_1, \ldots, l_n \rangle$, where $l_j \in I(v_j)$, for $1 \leq j \leq n$,
3. if v is a union node with successors $v_1, \ldots, v_n$, then $data(l)$ has to be a member of $\cup_{j=1}^{n} I(v_j)$, and
4. if v is a power node with successor w, then $data(l)$ has to be a subset of $I(w)$.

For more formal definitions and several examples the reader is referred to [KV84,Ku85].

2.2 LDM Logic

Let S be a schema. We define a many-sorted logic $\mathcal{L}(S)$ over S. Each variable in $\mathcal{L}(S)$ has a *sort*, where the sorts are the nodes of S. The sorts restrict the possible values that the variables can take. For example, if x is a variable of type v, then x can assume values only from $I(v)$. We shall usually subscript a variable with its sort, e.g., x_v. We also use the elements of D as constants of $\mathcal{L}(S)$, with the convention that these constants always denote themselves.

The *atomic formulas* of $\mathcal{L}(S)$ are of the following types:

1. $x_v \pi_t y_w$, where w is a product node and v is its t-th child, meaning that x_v is the t-th component of y_w's data value,
2. $x_v \rho y_w$, where w is a union node and v is one of its children, meaning that x_v is y_w's data value,
3. $x_v \in y_w$, where w is a power node and v is its meaning that x_v is a member of y_w's data value,
4. $x_v = y_v$, with the obvious meaning,
5. $x_v =_d y_w$, meaning that x_v and y_w have the same data value, and $x_v =_d c$, where v is a basic node and $c \in D$, meaning that c is the data value of x_v.

Formulas are defined from atomic formulas by means of propositional connectives and individual quantifiers. The semantics is defined in the standard way. If $\varphi(x_{v_1}, \ldots, x_{v_n})$ is a formula, then $I \models \varphi(l_1, \ldots, l_n)$ means that φ is satisfied by I when l_i is assigned to x_{v_i}.

2.3 Logical Query Language

In the relational model the result of a query is a relation. By analogy, we expect in LDM the result of a query to be an LDM instance. The definitions to follow are guided by this intuition.

For the result of the query to be an LDM instance, the query has to have a schema. Let S and S' be schemas with node sets V and V', respectively. We say that S' *extends* S if V is a subset of V', and the restriction of S' to V is equal to S (i.e., S' does not contain "new" edges between nodes of S). Also, an instance I' on S' *extends* an instance I on S if it agrees with I on V. A *query* Q over a schema S with node set V consists of a schema S' with node set V' that extends S, a linear order $\prec$ on $V' - V$ and an assignment of a formula φ_v to each node v in $V' - V$ such that:

1. if v is a child of w. where v and w are nodes in $V' - V$. then $v \prec w$.

2. φ_v has precisely one free variable and its sort is v, and
3. if φ_v contains a bound variable y_w, then either w is a node in V or w is a node in V' and $w \prec v$.

We call the nodes in $V' - V$ the *new* nodes. The intuition is that the order $\prec$ is the order in which we define the result of the query on the new nodes. Each formula φ_v defines the set content of v in terms of database nodes and nodes that precede v. Note that the requirement that edges between nodes in $V' - V$ respect the order $\prec$ implies that cycles are impossible in the "query schema". For a discussion of this see [KV84,Ku85]. To define the semantics of queries, we first define the semantics of *simple* queries. Simple queries are queries where the schema contains only a single new node.

Let Q be a simple query with a schema S', node set V', where $V' - V = \{v\}$, and a formula $\varphi_v(x_v)$ associated with v. Let I be an instance of S. We say that r is a *candidate data value* for Q and I if the following holds: Let I' be an extension of I to S' where $I(v) = \{l\}$ and $data(l) = r$. Then $I' \models \varphi(l)$. Note that the choice of l is quite arbitrary, and it is $data(l)$ that is important. We now define $Q(I)$ as an instance I' of S that extends I such that all elements of $I(v)$ have distinct data values and the set of data values for addresses in $I(v)$ is precisely the set of candidate data values for Q and I. In other words, the result of the query is a minimal set of addresses that point to all candidate data values.

To define the semantics of non-simple queries we use the fact that, because of the order $\prec$ that is part of the query, we can view a non-simple query as a chain of simple queries. The result of the query can now be defined by induction on the length of the chain.

We define several measures for syntactic complexity of queries. For simplicity we assume that the formulas associated with nodes in the query schema are in prenex normal form. The *alternation depth* of a formula φ is the number of alternations of quantifiers in the formula. (e.g., the sequence $\exists$ has one alternation, and the sequence $\exists\forall\exists\exists$ has three alternations). Let $v_1, \ldots, v_n$ be the new nodes of a query Q, and let v_k be the top power node (i.e., $v_1, \ldots, v_{k-1}$ are not power nodes). The alternation depth of Q is the sum of the alternation depths of $\varphi_{v_1}, \ldots, \varphi_{v_{k-1}}$. Q is *existential* if the quantifier prefix of φ_{v_1} starts with an existential quantifier, and it is *universal* if the quantifier prefix of φ_{v_1} starts with a universal quantifier. The *product depth* of Q is the number of product nodes among the new nodes. The *power depth* of Q is the number of power nodes among the new nodes. Let $power(l)$ denote the class of queries with power depth at most l. Let $\exists - power(k,l)$ denote the class of existential queries of alternation depth at most k and power depth at most l, and analogously for $\forall - power(k,l)$. Similarly, let $\exists - power - product(k,l,m)$ denote the class of existential queries of alternation depth at most k, power depth at most l, and product depth at most m, and analogously for $\forall - power - product(k,l,m)$.

2.4 Alternating Turing Machines

An *alternating Turing Machine* (ATM) [CKS81] is a Turing machine where every state is either *existential* or *universal*.[2] Intuitively, a state is existential if it is sufficient that there is some move from that state that leads to acceptance, and it is universal if it necessary that all moves from that state lead to acceptance. Formally, an *acceptance* of an input by an ATM M is a tree of configurations in which the following holds.

1. The root is the initial configuration.
2. All leaves are accepting configurations.

[2] For a basic introduction to machine-based complexity theory see [HU79].

3. If an interior node is an existential configuration, then it has one child that is a successor configuration.
4. If an interior node is a universal configuration, then it has several children, one for each successor configuration.

The *depth* of the acceptance is the length of the longest branch. The *alternation depth* of the acceptance is the maximal number of alternations between existential and universal states along a branch.

We say that M accepts *in time* $g(n)$, for a function g, if for every x accepted by M there is an acceptance of depth at most $g(|x|)$. We say that M accepts *in* k *alternations* if for every x accepted by M there is an acceptance of alternation depth at most k. We say that M accepts in *a linear number of alternations* if there is a constant c such that for every x accepted by M there is an acceptance of alternation depth at most $c|x|$.

A *computation* of M is a sequence of successive configurations. A *starting* computation is a computation such that the first configuration is the starting configuration. An *accepting* computation is a computation such that the last configuration is an accepting configuration.

We define a sequence of families of functions G_l as follows: G_0 is the family of all polynomial functions. Inductively, G_{i+1} is the family of all functions 2^g where $g \in G_i$. Thus, G_1 is the family of all exponential functions, G_2 is the family of all doubly exponential functions, etc.. Let Σ_k^l denote the class of languages accepted by alternating Turing machines in time $g(n)$ for some $g \in G_l$ and in k alternations starting from an existential configuration. Analogously, let Π_k^l denote the class of languages accepted by alternating Turing machines in time $g(n)$ for $g \in G_l$ and in k alternations starting from a universal configuration. In particular, the sequences Σ_i^0, $i \geq 1$ and Π_i^0, $i \geq 1$ are known as the *polynomial hierarchy* [St76]. It is known that Σ_1^l is strictly contained in Σ_1^{l+1}, and, similarly, Π_1^l is strictly contained in Π_1^{l+1} [HU79]. Thus, the hierarchies Σ_k^l and Π_k^l are at least of height ω. Let Alt_{lin}^l denote the class of languages accepted by alternating Turing machines in time $g(n)$ for $g \in G_l$ in a linear number of alternations [Vo83].

3 Complexity of Queries

The complexity of query evaluation can be measured in three different ways [Va82]. First, one can fix a query Q and ask about the complexity of evaluating Q on different databases, where the complexity is measured with respect to the size of the data. This complexity measure is called *data complexity*. (We assume some standard encoding for database instances so it is meaningful to talk about the size of an instance.) Second, one can fix an instance I and ask about the complexity of evaluating different queries on I, where the complexity is measured with respect to the size of the expressions denoting the queries. This complexity measure is called *expression complexity*. Finally, *combined complexity* is measured with respect to the combined size of the data and the expressions denoting the queries. We focus here on data and expression complexity.

As an illustration, let us first focus on evaluation of simple queries. To study the data complexity we fix a simple query Q with new node v. We then consider the set

$$cand(Q) = \{\langle r, I\rangle : r \text{ is a candidate data value for } Q \text{ and } I\}.$$

The following proposition follows from the results in [KV85] (see also [CH82]).

Proposition 3.1: *For every simple query Q, the set $cand(Q)$ is in LOGSPACE.*

Thus, the data complexity of simple queries is LOGSPACE.

To study expression complexity we fix a database schema S and an instance I. We then consider the set

$$cand(I) = \{\langle r, Q\rangle : Q \text{ is a simple query and } r \text{ is a candidate data value for } Q \text{ and } I\}.$$

The following proposition follows from the results in [KV85].

Proposition 3.2: *For every database schema S and every instance I, the set $cand(I)$ is in PSPACE. Furthermore, there is a database schema S and an instance I such that $cand(I)$ is PSPACE-complete.*

Thus, the expression complexity of simple queries is PSPACE.

Note that by considering the sets $cand(Q)$ and $cand(I)$ we have converted the query evaluation problem to a language membership problem. This enables us to talk about the complexity of query evaluation independently of the size of the result of the query. For general queries, we cannot use the same technique, since candidate data values for new nodes are defined in terms on values of preceding nodes. Thus, it is not meaningful to talk about the sets $cand(Q)$ and $cand(I)$. To be able to talk about the complexity of query evaluation independently of the size of the result of the query, we restrict our attention to *Boolean* queries [CH82] The result of a Boolean query is a yes/no answer. Every query can be viewed as a Boolean query in the following manner. Let Q be a query, and let v be the maximal new node. If I' is the result of applying Q to an instance I and $I'(v)$ is nonempty, then we say that the result is *positive*. If $I'(v)$ is empty, then the result is *negative*.

Let Q be a query. We define $answer(Q)$ to be the set of instances I such that the result of applying Q to I is positive. Let Ψ be a class of queries and let C be a complexity class. We say that the data complexity of Ψ is in C if if for every Q in Ψ the set $answer(Q)$ is in C. We say that Ψ is *data-complete* for C if the data complexity of Ψ is in C and in addition there is a query Q in Ψ such that $answer(Q)$ is logspace-complete for C. Let I be an instance, and let Ψ be a class of queries. We define $answer_\Psi(I)$ to be the set of queries in Ψ such that the result of applying Q to I is positive. We say that the data complexity of Ψ is in C if for every instance I the set $answer_\Psi(I)$ is in C. We say that Ψ is *expression-complete* for C if the expression complexity of Ψ is in C and in addition there is an instance I such that $answer_\Psi(I)$ is logspace-complete for C.

3.1 Data Complexity

We first consider queries without power nodes.

Theorem 3.3: *The data complexity of the class $power(0)$ is in LOGSPACE.*

Thus, product and union nodes do not increase the data complexity of query evaluation; essentially, both product and union are first-order operations.

We now consider queries with power nodes.

Theorem 3.4: *For any $l > 0$ and $k > 0$ the class $\exists - power(k,l)$ is data-complete for Σ_k^{l-1} and the class $\forall - power(k,l)$ is data-complete for Π_k^{l-1}.*

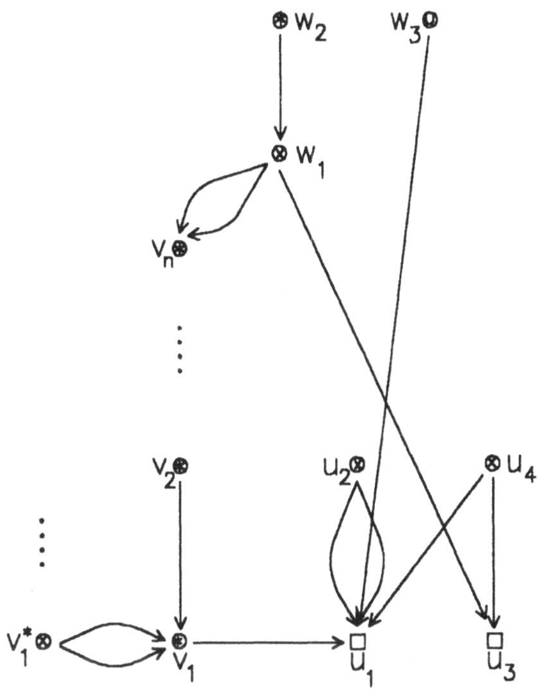

Figure 1: Query Schema

Proof: We focus here on the lower bound for $\exists - power(k, l)$.

We define a family of functions $f_l(n)$ as follows: $f_0(n) = n$, and $f_{l+1}(n) = 2^{f_l(n)}$. Let M be an ATM that runs in time $f_l(n)$ and in k alternations, such that the language accepted by M is Σ_k^l-complete. Let $x = x_1, \ldots, x_n$ be an input of length n.

To describe computations of M we need the following notation. A *symbol* is either a tape symbol or a composite symbol, which is a pair consisting of a state of M and a tape symbol. A configuration of M can be described by a sequence of $f_l(n)$ symbols, one of which is a composite symbol representing the state of M and the location of its head. It is known that computations of Turing machines are local. More formally, there is a 4-ary relation R_M over symbols, such that if $\mathbf{a} = a_1, \ldots, a_{f_l(n)}$ and $\mathbf{b} = b_1, \ldots, b_{f_l(n)}$ encode configurations of M, then $\mathbf{b}$ is a successor of $\mathbf{a}$ if and only if $\langle a_{i-1}, a_i, a_{i+1}, b_i \rangle R_M$ for $1 < i < f_l(n)$ [St74].

We construct an LDM schema and query, together with a (polynomial-time) mapping of the input tape into an instance of the schema, such that the result of the query is nonempty precisely when the ATM accepts the given input.

The LDM schema consists of the nodes u_1, u_2, u_3 and u_4 in Figure 1. The query schema consists of the remaining nodes in the figure. We first show how to map the input x into an instance I of S.

The set D contains the numbers $0, \ldots, n-1$ and all the symbols of M. The node u_1 contains addresses with the data values $0, \ldots, n-1$. The nodes u_2 contains the obvious linear order on the elements of u_1. The node u_3 contains addresses with the symbols of M as data values. Finally, the node u_4 encodes x, i.e., it contains addresses with data values $\langle i, x_i \rangle$.

We now define the query formulas. For each node we also show what the result of the query means in terms of the original ATM.

We first need some way to count up to the maximum number of steps $(f_l(n))$ that M is allowed to take, which is therefore also a bound on the size of the tape. By defining v_1 as the powerset of u_1, and v_{i+1} as the powerset of v_i, it is clear that v_l has the desired number of elements. We also need a total order on the elements of $I(v_l)$, and this is constructed as follows. A total order on v_i is stored at the node v_i^*, and is based on the order stored at the node v_{i-1}^*. For uniformity, we shall use v_0 and v_0^* to refer to the nodes u_1 and u_2.

We use the following abbreviation:

$$x_{v_i}^1 < x_{v_i}^2 \text{ means } (\exists x_{v_i^*})((x_{v_i}^1 \pi_1 x_{v_i^*} \wedge (x_{v_i}^2 \pi_2(x_{v_i^*})).$$

Then $\varphi_{v_{i+1}^*}(x_{v_{i+1}^*})$ is:

$$(\forall y_{v_{i+1}}^1)(\forall y_{v_{i+1}}^2)(y_{v_{i+1}}^1 \pi_1 x_{v_{i+1}^*} \wedge y_{v_{i+1}}^2 \pi_2 x_{v_{i+1}^*}) \rightarrow$$
$$(\exists y_{v_i})((\forall y_{v_i}^*)(y_{v_i}^* < y_{v_i} \rightarrow (y_{v_i}^* \in y_{v_{i+1}}^1 \iff y_{v_i}^* \in y_{v_{i+1}}^2) \wedge (y_{v_i} \in y_{v_{i+1}}^2) \wedge (y_{v_i} \notin y_{v_{i+1}}^1)))$$

Intuitively, this formula says that a pair (l_1, l_2) is in $I(v_i^*)$ (i.e. l_1 "<" l_2) whenever (a) the sets that they represent are equal for all elements less than y_{v_i} and (b) the first element for which they differ is in the first set, but not in the second. It can then be shown that the relation < defined above is a total order on each $I(v_i^*)$ and that the empty set in each such instance is the first element under this order.

We now use the nodes w_1 and w_2 to encode all possible computations of length at most $f_l(n)$. We first define w_1 as the cross product of v_l (which represents $0, \ldots, f_l(n) - 1$), v_l, and u_3 (the alphabet). An element of w_1 encodes a triple (i, j, c), which means that cell j contains the symbol c at time i.

The elements of $I(w_2)$ represent valid computations of length at most $f_l(n)$. This means that $I(w_2)$ is the set of all values l such that there exist i_1 and i_2, $1 < i_1 < i_2 < f_l(n)$, for which the following holds: following:

1. for all i between i_1 and i_2 and for all j between 1 and $f_l(n)$ there is a unique symbol c such that the triple $\langle i, j, c \rangle$ is in $data(l)$,
2. for all triples $\langle i, j, c \rangle$ in $data(l)$ we have that i is between i_1 and i_2,
3. if for some i and j, $i_1 \leq i < i_2$ and $1 < j < f_l(n)$ we have that the triples $\langle i, j-1, a \rangle$, $\langle i, j, b \rangle$, and $\langle i, j+1, c \rangle$ are in $data(l)$, then there is a symbol d such that $\langle a, b, c, d \rangle \in R_M$ and $\langle i+1, j, d \rangle$ is also in $data(l)$.
4. Either all the states along the computation encoded by l are existential or they are all universal.

In the full paper we will show that these conditions can be expressed by an LDM formula.

Finally, we want to assert that the node w_3 will be nonempty if and only if the machine M accepts the input x in time $f_l(n)$ in k alternations. The formula $\varphi_{w_3}(x_{w_3})$ has the form

$$(\exists y_{w_2}^1)(\forall y_{w_2}^2) \cdots (\mathbf{Q} y_{w_2}^k)\psi(x_{w_3}, y_{w_2}^1, \ldots, y_{w_2}^k),$$

($\mathbf{Q}$ is $\exists$ if k is odd and it is $\forall$ if k is even), where ψ asserts that

1. $y^1_{w_2}$ encodes a starting computation,
2. $y^k_{w_2}$ encodes an accepting computation,
3. $y^{i+1}_{w_2}$ encodes a computation that continues the computation encoded by $y^i_{w_2}$, and
4. $y^{i+1}_{w_2}$ encodes an existential computation if and only if the computation encoded by $y^i_{w_2}$ is universal, and vice versa.

Note that in order to say that a computation is a starting configuration the formula φ_{w_3} has to refer to the node u_4, which encodes the input x. ∎

Corollary 3.5: *For any $k > 0$, $l > 0$, and $m \leq l$ the class $\exists - power - product(k,l,m)$ is data-complete for Σ^{l-1}_k and the class $\forall - power - product(k,l,m)$ is data-complete for Π^{l-1}_k.*

It follows from the above theorem and corollary that product depth does not have a significant impact on data complexity.

3.2 Expression Complexity

Again, we first consider queries without power nodes.

Theorem 3.6: *The class $power(0)$ is expression-complete for Alt^1_{lin}.*

Proof: We prove that for any $k > 0$ the class $\exists - power(k, 0)$ is expression-complete for Σ^1_k.

Let M be an ATM that runs in time $f_1(n)$ and in k alternations, such that the language accepted by M is Σ^1_k-complete. Let $x = x_1, \ldots, x_n$ be an input of length n. We construct an LDM schema and an instance together with a (polynomial-time) mapping of the input tape into a query such that the result of the query is nonempty precisely when the ATM accepts the given input.

The LDM schema consists of the nodes u_1 and u_2 in Figure 2.

We first define an instance I of S. The set D contains the numbers 0 and 1 and all the symbols of M. The node u_1 contains addresses with the data values 0 and 1. The node u_2 contains addresses with the symbols of M as data values.

The query schema consists of the remaining nodes in the figure. The nodes $v_1, \ldots, v_{n-1}$ form a stack of product nodes of height n, where v_1 is a product of u_1 with itself, and v_i is a product of u_1 and v_{i-1} for $1 < i < n$. Thus, an element in $I(v_m)$ can be viewed as a $m+1$-tuple over $0, 1$, i.e., a binary number between 0 and $2^{m+1} - 1$. The nodes $w_1, \ldots, w_{2n}$ form a stack of product nodes of height $2n$, where w_1 is a product of u_2 with itself, and w_i is a product of w_{i-1} with itself for $1 < i \leq 2n$. Thus, an element in $I(w_m)$ can be viewed as a 2^m-tuple of symbols of M. Since a configuration of M can be described by a sequence of 2^n symbols, we can view an element in $I(w_{n+m})$ as a sequence of 2^m configurations.

The nodes $p_1, \ldots, p_n$ are meant to describe the content of the configurations described by $w_1, \ldots, w_n$. The node p_1 is a product node of w_1, u_1, and u_2, and p_i, $1 < i \leq n$ is a product node of w_i, v_{i-1}, and u_2. Intuitively, if $l \in I(p_m)$ and $data(l) = (\alpha, \beta, \gamma)$, where $\alpha \in I(w_m)$, $\beta \in I(v_{m-1})$ and $\gamma \in I(u_2)$, then the configuration α contains the symbol γ in position β.

The node w is meant to describe legal transitions of M. Intuitively, if $l \in I(w)$ and $data(l) = (\alpha, \beta)$ then the configuration β is a legal successor to the configuration α.

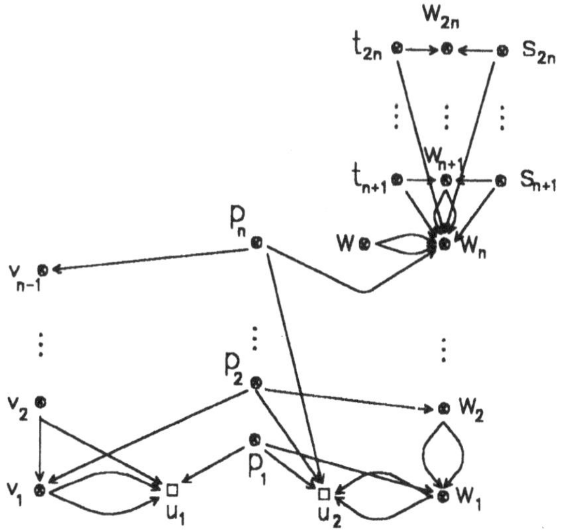

Figure 2: Query Schema

The nodes $s_{n+1},\ldots,s_{2n}$ are meant to describe the first configurations of the configuration sequences described by $w_{n+1},\ldots,w_{2n}$. The node s_i a product of w_i and w_n. Intuitively, if $l \in I(s_i)$ and $data(l) = (\alpha,\beta)$, where $\alpha \in I(w_i)$, $\beta \in I(w_n)$, then β is the first configuration in the configuration sequence α. Analogously, the nodes $t_{n+1},\ldots,t_{2n}$ are meant to describe the last configuration of the configurations described by $w_1,\ldots,w_n$.

We now define the query formulas. For each node we also show what the result of the query means in terms of the original ATM.

First we need formulas that guarantee that the p_i's "perform" correctly. For the node p_1 we define $\varphi_{p_1}(x_{p_1})$ to be

$$(\exists x_{w_1}, x_{u_1}, x_{u_2}, y^0_{u_2}, y^1_{u_2})(x_{w_1}\pi_1 x_{p_1} \wedge x_{u_1}\pi_2 x_{p_1} \wedge x_{u_2}\pi_3 x_{p_1} \wedge y^0_{u_2}\pi_1 x_{w_1} \wedge y^1_{u_2}\pi_2 x_{w_1} \wedge \\ ((x_{u_1} =_d 0 \rightarrow y^0_{u_2} = x_{u_2}) \wedge (x_{u_1} =_d 1 \rightarrow y^1_{u_2} = x_{u_2}))).$$

For nodes p_i, $1 < i \leq n$, we define $\varphi_{p_i}(x_{p_i})$ to be

$$(\exists x_{w_i}, x_{v_{i-1}}, x_{u_2}, y^0_{w_{i-1}}, y^1_{w_{i-1}}, z^0_{u_1}, z^1_{v_{i-2}}) \\ (x_{w_i}\pi_1 x_{p_i} \wedge x_{v_{i-1}}\pi_2 x_{p_i} \wedge x_{u_2}\pi_3 x_{p_i} \wedge y^0_{w_{i-1}}\pi_1 x_{w_i} \wedge y^1_{w_{i-1}}\pi_2 x_{w_i} \wedge z^0_{u_1}\pi_1 x_{v_{i-1}} \wedge z^1_{v_{i-2}}\pi_2 x_{v_{i-1}} \wedge \\ (z^0_{u_1} =_d 0 \rightarrow (\exists r_{p_{i-1}})(y^0_{w_{i-1}}\pi_1 r_{p_{i-1}} \wedge z^1_{v_{i-2}}\pi_2 r_{p_{i-1}} \wedge x_{u_2}\pi_3 r_{p_{i-1}})) \wedge \\ (z^0_{u_1} =_d 1 \rightarrow (\exists r_{p_{i-1}})(y^1_{w_{i-1}}\pi_1 r_{p_{i-1}} \wedge z^1_{v_{i-2}}\pi_2 r_{p_{i-1}} \wedge x_{u_2}\pi_3 r_{p_{i-1}}))).$$

We leave the complete description of $\varphi_w(x_w)$ to the full paper. Intuitively, the formula asserts that if $l \in I(w)$, where $data(l) = (\alpha,\beta)$, $l_1,\ldots,l_4 \in I(p_n)$, where $data(l_i) = (\alpha,\gamma_i,a_i)$, for $1 \leq i \leq 3$, and $data(l_4) = (\alpha,\gamma_2,b)$, and $\gamma_1,\gamma_2,\gamma_3$ represent successive integers, then $\langle a_1,a_2,a_3,b\rangle \in R_M$.

We now describe formulas that guarantee that the s_i's "perform" correctly. For the node s_{n+1} we define $\varphi_{s_{n+1}}(x_{s_{n+1}})$ to be

$$(\exists x_{w_{n+1}}, x_{w_n}, y^1_{s_n}, y^2_{s_n})(x_{w_{n+1}}\pi_1 x_{s_{n+1}} \wedge x_{w_n}\pi_2 x_{s_{n+1}} \wedge y^1_{s_n}\pi_1 x_{w_{n+1}} \wedge y^2_{s_n}\pi_2 x_{w_{n+1}} \wedge y^1_{s_n} = x_{w_n}).$$

For the node s_i, $n+1 < i \leq 2n$, we define $\varphi_{s_i}(x_{s_i})$ to be

$$(\exists x_{w_i}, x_{w_n}, y^1_{w_{i-1}}, y^2_{w_{i-1}}, x_{s_{i-1}})$$
$$(x_{w_i}\pi_1 x_{s_i} \wedge x_{w_n}\pi_2 x_{s_i} \wedge y^1_{w_{i-1}}\pi_1 x_{w_i} \wedge y^2_{w_{i-1}}\pi_2 x_{w_i} \wedge y^1_{w_n}\pi_1 x_{s_{i-1}} \wedge x_{w_n}\pi_2 x_{s_{i-1}}).$$

We now describe the formulas that force $w_{n+1}, \ldots, w_{2n}$ to encode legal configuration sequences. For the node w_{n+1} we define $\varphi_{w_{n+1}}(x_{w_{n+1}})$ to be

$$(\exists x_w, y^1_{w_n}, y^2_{w_n})(y^1_{w_n}\pi_1 x_{w_{n+1}} \wedge y^2_{w_n}\pi_2 x_{w_{n+1}} \wedge y^1_{w_n}\pi_1 x_w \wedge y^2_{w_n}\pi_2 x_w).$$

For the node w_i, $n+1 < i \leq 2n$, we define $\varphi_{w_i}(x_{w_i})$ to be

$$(\exists x_{s_{i-1}}, x_{t_{i-1}}, y^1_{w_{i-1}}, y^2_{w_{i-1}}, z^1_{w_n}, z^2_{w_n}, x_w)$$
$$(y^1_{w_{i-1}}\pi_1 x_{w_i} \wedge y^2_{w_{i-1}}\pi_2 x_{w_i} \wedge y^1_{w_{i-1}}\pi_1 x_{t_{i-1}} \wedge y^2_{w_{i-1}}\pi_1 x_{s_{i-1}} \wedge$$
$$z^1_{w_n}\pi_2 x_{t_{i-1}} \wedge z^2_{w_n}\pi_2 x_{s_{i-1}} \wedge z^1_{w_n}\pi_1 x_w \wedge z^2_{w_n}\pi_2 x_w).$$

The rest of the construction is similar to the construction in the previous section and is left to the full paper. ∎

The reader should contrast the above theorem with Proposition 3.2 and Theorem 3.3. The theorem shows that even though product nodes do not increase the data complexity of query evaluation, since product is essentially a first-order operation, they increase the expression complexity, since they enable us to write very succinct queries.

We now consider queries with power nodes. Unlike the situation with data complexity, product depth does have a significant impact on expression complexity.

Theorem 3.7: *For any $k > 0$, $l > 0$, and $m \geq l+2$ the class $\exists - power - product(k,l,m)$ is expression-complete for Σ^l_k and the class $\forall - power - product(k,l,m)$ is expression-complete for Π^l_k.*

Proof: Again we focus here on the lower bound. Let M be an ATM that runs in time $f_l(n)$ and in k alternations, such that the language accepted by M is Σ^l_k-complete. Let $x = x_1, \ldots, x_n$ be an input of length n.

We construct an LDM schema and an instance together with a (polynomial-time) mapping of the input tape into a query such that the result of the query is nonempty precisely when the ATM accepts the given input.

The LDM schema consists of the nodes u_1 and u_2 in Figure 3. The query schema consists of the remaining nodes in the figure. The node v_1 is a product node with n edges to u_1. This is the only dependence of the query schema on x.

We first define an instance I of S. The set D contains the numbers 0 and 1 and all the symbols of M. The node u_1 contains addresses with the data values 0 and 1. The node u_2 contains addresses with the symbols of M as data values.

We now define the query formulas. For each node we also show what the result of the query means in terms of the original ATM.

As in the previous section, we first need some way to count up to the maximum number of steps ($f_l(n)$) that M is allowed to take, which is therefore also a bound on the size of the tape. By defining v_1 as the the n-th power of u_1, and v_{i+1} as the powerset of v_i, it is clear that v_n has the desired number of elements. We also need a total order on the elements of $I(v_n)$, and

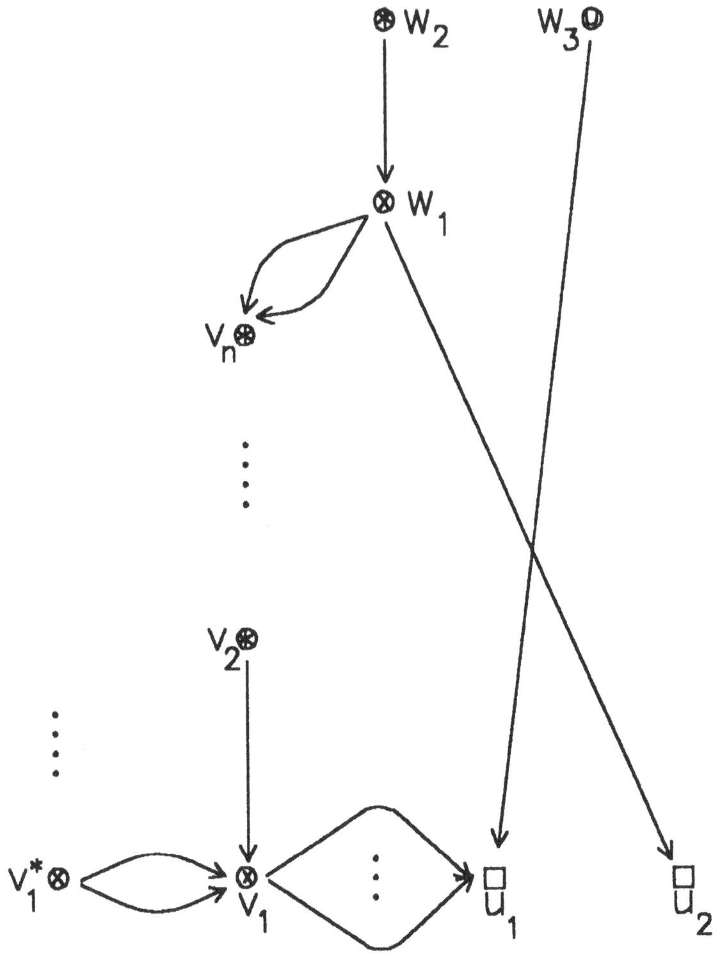

Figure 3: Query Schema

this constructed as follows. A total order v_i is stored at the node v_i^*, and is based on the order stored at the node v_{i-1}^*. The difference from the proof in the previous section is in the formula for $\varphi_{v_1^*}(x_{v_1^*})$:

$$(\forall y_{v_1}^1, y_{v_1}^2)(\forall w_{u_1}^1 \dots w_{u_1}^n)(\forall z_{u_1}^1 \dots z_{u_1}^n)(y_{v_1}^1 \pi_1 x_{v_1^*} \wedge y_{v_1}^2 \pi_2 x_{v_1^*} \wedge \bigwedge w_{u_1}^i \pi_i y_{v_1}^1 \wedge \bigwedge z_{u_1}^i \pi_i y_{v_1}^2) \Rightarrow$$
$$(\bigvee_{i=1}^{n})((\bigwedge_{j=1}^{i-1})(w_{u_1}^j =_d z_{u_1}^j) \wedge w_{u_1}^i =_d 0 \wedge z_{u_1}^i =_d 1).$$

Intuitively, the addresses in v_1 encode n-bits, and $\varphi_{v_1^*}(x_{v_1^*})$ defines the standard order on n-bits.

The rest of the construction is analogous to the construction in the previous section. The only difference is that to talk in φ_{w_3} about starting computation we have to refer directly to the input x (in the previous proof x was encoded by the database). Thus, this formula also depends on the input. ∎

We now look at expression complexity for queries with unbounded product depth.

Theorem 3.8: *For any $k > 0$ and $l > 0$, the class $\exists - power(k, l)$ is expression-complete for Σ_k^{l+1} and the class $\forall - power(k, l)$ is expression-complete for Π_k^{l+1}.*

Proof: The proof combines the ideas from Theorems 3.6 and 3.7. Intuitively, using a stack of l power nodes on top of a stack of n product nodes we can count up to $f_{l+2}(n)$. Details are left to the full paper. ∎

In [Va82] it was observed that expression complexity tends to be exponentially higher than data complexity. Here we see that the situation can be more complicated. For the classes $\exists - power - product(k, l, m)$ and $\forall - power - product(k, l, m)$ we indeed have an exponential gap. But for the classes $\exists - power(k, l)$ and $\forall - power(k, l)$ we have a doubly exponential gap.

Acknowledgements. We are grateful to R. Hull and an anonymous reviewer for helpful comments.

4 References

[AH87] Abiteboul, S., Hull, R.: IFO, a formal semantic database model. *ACM Trans. on Database Systems*, Dec. 1987.

[Be62] Bennet, J.H.: *On Spectra*, Ph.D. Dissertation, Princeton University, 1962.

[BK86] Bancilhon, F., Khoshafian, S.: A calculus for complex objects. *Proc. ACM Symp. on Principles of Database Systems*, 1986.

[CH82] Chandra, A., Harel, D.: Structure and Complexity of Relational Queries. *J. Computer and Systems Sciences* 25(1982), pp. 99–128.

[CKS81] Chandra, A.K., Kozen, D.C., Stockmeyer, L.J.: Alternation. *J. ACM* 28(1981), pp. 114–133.

[Co70] Codd, E.F.: A relational model of data for large shared data banks. *Comm. ACM* 13(1970), pp. 377–387.

[Co79] Codd, E.F.: Extending the database relational model to capture more meaning. *ACM Trans. on Database Systems*, 4(1979), pp. 397–434.

[FT83] Fischer, P.C., Thomas, S.J.: Operators for non-first-normal-form relations. *Proc. IEEE Computer Software Applications Conference*, 1983, pp. 464–475.

[**HM81**] Hammer, M., McLeod, D.: Database description with SDM: a semantic database model. *ACM Trans. on Database Systems*, 6(1981), pp. 351–386.

[**HS88**] Hull, R., Su, J.: On the expressive power of database queries with intermediate types. *Proc. ACM Symp. on Principles of Database Systems*, 1988.

[**HU79**] Hopcroft, J.E., Ullman, J.D.: *Introduction to Automata Theory, Languages, and Computation*, Addison-Wesley, 1979.

[**HY82**] Hull, R., Yap, C.K.: The format model: a theory of database organization. *Proc. ACM Symp. on Principles of Database Systems*, 1982.

[**Ja82**] Jacobs, B.E.: On database logic. *J. ACM* 29(1982), pp. 310–322.

[**JS82**] Jaeschke, B., Schek, H.J.: Remarks on the algebra of non-first-normal-form relations. *Proc. ACM Symp. on Principles of Database Systems*, 1982.

[**Ku85**] Kuper, G.M.: *The logical data model: a new approach to database logic*. Ph.D. Dissertation, Stanford University, 1985.

[**KV84**] Kuper, G.M., Vardi, M.Y.: A new approach to database logic. *Proc. ACM Symp. on Principles of Database Systems*, 1984.

[**KV85**] Kuper, G.M., Vardi, M.Y.: On the expressive power of the logical data model. *Proc. SIGMOD*, 1985.

[**Sh81**] Shipman, D.: The functional model and the data language DAPLEX. *ACM Trans. on Database Systems*, 6(1981), pp. 140–173.

[**SS77**] Smith, J.M., Smith, D.C.P.: Database abstractions: aggregation. *Comm. ACM* 20(1977), pp. 405–413.

[**St74**] Stockmeyer, L.J.: *The complexity of decision problems in automata theory and logic*. Ph.D. Dissertation, MIT, 1974.

[**St76**] Stockmeyer, L.J.: The polynomial time hierarchy. *Theoretical Computer Science* 3(1977), pp. 1–22.

[**Va82**] Vardi, M.Y.: The complexity of relational query language. *Proc. ACM Symp. on Theory of Computing*, 1982.

[**Vo83**] Volger, H.: Turing machines with bounded alternation. *Theoretical Computer Science* 23(1983), pp. 333–337.

ON DOMAIN INDEPENDENT DISJUNCTIVE DATABASES

E. A. Sonenberg
R. W. Topor

Department of Computer Science
University of Melbourne
Parkville, Vic. 3052
Australia

Abstract

We extend the concept of domain independence from queries and databases to disjunctive databases. Informally, a domain independent disjunctive database is one for which the set of correct answers to any domain independent query is independent of the domains of variables in the database statements. We prove that every allowed stratified disjunctive database is domain independent and that every domain independent disjunctive database has an equivalent allowed disjunctive database. We also discuss a generalization and properties of two alternative definitions.

1. Introduction

It has long been recognized that only certain formulas make reasonable queries for a relational database [3,8]. Such queries have been called domain independent, or stable, and have been extensively studied in, for example, [4,10]. Informally, a query is reasonable if, for each assignment of relations to the predicates in the query, it has the same answers whatever the domains of the variables in the query. Simple examples of unreasonable queries are $\forall x\, p(x)$, whose truth depends on the domain of x, and $\sim p(x,a)$, whose set of answers depends on the domain of x.

In [15,16], it was observed that, for similar reasons, only certain deductive databases could be regarded as reasonable, and the concept of domain independent formulas was extended to that of domain independent databases. A simple example of an unreasonable deductive database is $\{p(a)\leftarrow,\ q(a)\leftarrow \sim p(x)\}$, for which the (reasonable) query $q(a)$ is true if and only if a is the only constant in the domain of x. In [16], a class of allowed databases was defined, and it was proved that every allowed stratified database is domain independent and that every domain independent stratified database has an equivalent allowed database. Other properties of domain independent databases have been studied in [7].

Here we extend the observations and results of [16] to a class of disjunctive databases.

A disjunctive database consists of a set of formulas of the form $A_1 \vee \cdots \vee A_m \leftarrow L_1 \wedge \cdots \wedge L_n$, where each A_i is an atom and each L_j is a literal. Such databases are useful for representing indefinite and incomplete information, and their properties have been studied in, for example, [9,12,13]. A simple example of an unreasonable disjunctive database is $\{p(x) \vee q(a) \leftarrow\}$, for which the (reasonable) query $(p(x) \vee q(x)) \wedge x \neq a$ has an answer if and only if a is not the only constant in the domain of x.

One of our main aims is to study the way in which the set of correct answers to a query depends on the particular language used. We propose a definition of domain independence for disjunctive databases and introduce a class of allowed disjunctive databases. Our main results are that every allowed stratified disjunctive database is domain independent and that every domain independent disjunctive database has an equivalent allowed disjunctive database.

Section 2 contains our definitions of disjunctive databases and correct answers for queries. Section 3 contains our definition of a domain independent disjunctive database and the proofs of the main results. Section 4 discusses various alternative definitions, contains variants and extensions of the main results, and suggests problems for further research.

2. Disjunctive Databases

In this section we define disjunctive databases, perfect models, stratified disjunctive databases, and correct answers for queries with respect to disjunctive databases. Our presentation follows that of Przymusinski [12].

Each database and query is assumed to be expressed in a first order function-free language with equality. In practice, typed languages should be used, but, for simplicity, we restrict our attention to type-free languages throughout. We assume that each such language contains only finitely many constants and predicates, and at least one constant. For languages L and L', we say L' extends L if L' contains the same predicates as L and at least all the constants of L.

The concepts of interpretation, model, Herbrand model, logical consequence, and so on, are defined in the usual way for first order theories. We only consider Herbrand interpretations throughout. We denote the Herbrand base of a language L by B_L.

Definition A *database clause* is a first order formula $\forall(A_1 \vee \cdots \vee A_m \leftarrow L_1 \wedge \cdots \wedge L_n)$, where each A_i is an atom other than an equality and each L_j is a literal. $A_1 \vee \cdots \vee A_m$ (resp., $L_1 \wedge \cdots \wedge L_n$) is called the *head* (resp., *body*) of the clause. We assume that $m \geq 1$ and $n \geq 0$. A database clause C is *positive* if the body of C is a conjunction of atoms. We conventionally denote $\forall(A_1 \vee \cdots \vee A_m \leftarrow L_1 \wedge \cdots \wedge L_n)$ by $A_1 \vee \cdots \vee A_m \leftarrow L_1 \wedge \cdots \wedge L_n$.

Although every database clause is logically equivalent to a positive clause, Przymusinski [12] shows that a (non-positive) clause contains more information than its positive form, and introduces the perfect model semantics for disjunctive databases which exploits this difference.

Definition A *disjunctive database* D is a finite set of database clauses. A disjunctive database is *positive* if each database clause in D is positive. A disjunctive database is called simply a *database* if $m=1$ in each database clause in D. The language L_D of D is the language whose constants and predicates are those that occur in D. We denote the Herbrand base of L_D by B_D.

Example 2.1 Here is a simple disjunctive database D_{ex}.

knows(x, Dutch) $\vee$ knows(x, French) $\leftarrow$ ~child(x)
female(Alice) $\leftarrow$
male(Bob) $\leftarrow$
child(Alice) $\leftarrow$

□

Definition A *query* is a first order formula.

Unless indicated otherwise, we assume that every query for a database is in the language of the database.

Definition An *answer set* for a query Q is a set of ground substitutions for all free variables in Q. We denote an answer set $\{\theta_1, \ldots, \theta_n\}$ by $\theta_1 + \cdots + \theta_n$.

To define when an answer set is correct, we use the concept of a perfect model. Other approaches to the definition of a correct answer are discussed below.

Definition Let D be a disjunctive database. The *dependency graph* $G(D)$ of D is the directed graph whose vertices are the predicates in D and whose edges are the pairs $q \rightarrow p$ such that, for some database clause $A_1 \vee \cdots \vee A_m \leftarrow L_1 \wedge \cdots \wedge L_n$ in D, p is the predicate in some A_i and q is the predicate in some A_j $(i \neq j)$, in which case the edge $q \rightarrow p$ is positive, or q is the predicate in some L_k, in which case the edge $q \rightarrow p$ has the same sign as L_k. An edge may be both positive and negative.

Let p and q be predicates in L_D. We write $q < p$ if there is a path from q to p in $G(D)$ passing through a negative edge.

The relation $<$ is well-defined and transitive. It induces a relation between atoms as follows: $p(s_1, \ldots, s_m) < q(t_1, \ldots, t_n)$ if $p < q$.

The relation $<$ between atoms is used to define a class of perfect models for D as follows.

Definition Let D be a disjunctive database, L a language extending L_D, and $M \neq N$ interpretations for L that are models for D. Then N is *preferable to* M (written $N \ll M$) if for every ground atom A in $N \setminus M$ there exists a ground atom B in $M \setminus N$ such that $B < A$. We write $N \leq M$ if $N = M$ or $N \ll M$. A model M for D is *perfect* if there are no models for D preferable to M. We write $PERF(D, L)$ for the set of interpretations for L that are perfect models for D.

Informally, the relation $<$ between predicates describes the relative priority for minimizing the corresponding relations in models for D. If $q < p$, then q has a higher priority for minimization than p. If M and N are models such that, for all pairs of predicates $q < p$, (the relation assigned to) q is smaller in N than in M, even if (the relation assigned to) p is larger in N than in M, then N is preferable to M.

Example 2.2 Let D be the following database.

$$p(x) \leftarrow \neg p(x) \wedge q(x)$$
$$q(a) \leftarrow$$

Then $\{p(a), q(a)\}$ is the unique perfect model for D. □

Example 2.3 The models for D_{ex} in Example 2.1 include:

$M_1 = S \cup$ {child(Bob)}
$M_2 = S \cup$ {knows(Bob, Dutch)}
$M_3 = S \cup$ {knows(Bob, French)}
$M_4 = S \cup$ {knows(Bob, Dutch), knows(Bob, French)}

where S = {female(Alice), male(Bob), child(Alice)}. $PERF(D_{ex}, L_{D_{ex}}) = \{M_2, M_3\}$, M_1 is minimal but not perfect, and M_4 is not minimal. □

Note that $PERF(D, L)$ can depend on the language L.

Example 2.4 After inserting into D_{ex} the database clause female(Carol) ←, say, the perfect models for D_{ex} are:

$M_5 = S' \cup$ {knows(Bob, Dutch), knows(Carol, Dutch)}
$M_6 = S' \cup$ {knows(Bob, Dutch), knows(Carol, French)}
$M_7 = S' \cup$ {knows(Bob, French), knows(Carol, Dutch)}
$M_8 = S' \cup$ {knows(Bob, French), knows(Carol, French)}

where S' = {female(Alice), male(Bob), child(Alice), female(Carol)}. □

We can now define a correct answer set for a query with respect to a disjunctive database and a language.

Definition Let D be a disjunctive database, L a language extending L_D, and Q a query in L. An answer set $\theta_1 + \cdots + \theta_n$ for Q is a *correct answer set* for Q wrt D and L if $PERF(D, L) \models Q\theta_1 \vee \cdots \vee Q\theta_n$, i.e. if $Q\theta_1 \vee \cdots \vee Q\theta_n$ is true in every perfect model for D wrt L. We write $ans(Q, D, L)$ for the set of all minimal correct answer sets for Q wrt D and L.

Example 2.5 Consider the queries Q_1 = knows(Alice, y), Q_2 = knows(Bob, y), and Q_3 = knows(x, Dutch) ∨ knows(x, French). Let L_1 be the language with constants {Alice, Bob, Dutch, French} and L_2 the extension of L_1 with the additional constant Carol. Then:

$ans(Q_1, D_{ex}, L_i) = \emptyset, \quad i = 1,2$
$ans(Q_2, D_{ex}, L_i) = \{y/\text{Dutch} + y/\text{French}\}, \quad i = 1,2$
$ans(Q_3, D_{ex}, L_1) = \{x/\text{Bob}\}$
$ans(Q_3, D_{ex}, L_2) = \{x/\text{Bob}, x/\text{Carol}\}$

Note that x/Bob + x/Carol is a correct answer set for Q_3 wrt D and L_2 but is not minimal. □

When $PERF(D, L)$ is empty, every answer set for Q is correct. Accordingly, we restrict attention to a class of disjunctive databases for which $PERF(D, L)$ is not empty.

Definition A *level mapping* for a database is a mapping from its set of predicates to the natural numbers. The level of a literal L is the level of the predicate in L. If M is a model for D, we write M_j for the restriction of M to atoms of level at most j and D_j for the set of database clauses in D defining predicates of level at most j.

Definition Let D be a disjunctive database. Then D is *stratified* if it has a level mapping such that, for every database clause $A_1 \vee \cdots \vee A_m \leftarrow L_1 \wedge \cdots \wedge L_n$ in D, each A_i has the same level, the level of each positive literal L_j is less than or equal to the level of the A_i, and the level of each negative literal L_k is less than the level of the A_i.

The disjunctive database in Example 2.1 is stratified but the database in Example 2.2 is not. Without loss of generality, we assume that the predicate levels in a stratified database are $0, 1, \ldots, k$, for some k.

Note that, if D is stratified, the preference relation $\ll$ is transitive and hence a partial order [12].

The following result states that stratified disjunctive databases have the desired property.

Theorem 2.1 (Przymusinski [12]) *For every model N for a stratified disjunctive database D, there exists a perfect model M for D such that $M \leq N$. In particular, every stratified disjunctive database has at least one perfect model. Moreover, if D is a stratified database, D has a unique perfect model, which coincides with the standard model M_D in* [1].

Theorem 2.1 justifies our emphasis on stratified disjunctive databases in the remainder of the paper. It also shows that our definition of a correct answer set generalizes the definition of a correct answer for a query with respect to a stratified database and a language given in [16].

3. Domain Independence

Just as not all queries or databases are reasonable, not all disjunctive databases are reasonable. As the set of perfect models, $PERF(D, L)$, for a stratified disjunctive database can depend on the language L, the set of correct answer sets for a perfectly reasonable query can also depend on L. When the language L is not given explicitly, this situation should be regarded as unacceptable. When the language L is identified with the language of D, this language can change after an update to D, causing the set of correct answer sets to change after a database update that is apparently irrelevant to the query. Again, this situation should be regarded as unacceptable.

Example 3.1 Let Q be the (reasonable) query knows(x, Dutch) $\vee$ knows(x,French) and D_{ex} the disjunctive database of Example 2.1 in language L. If the only constants in L are Alice and Bob, then the only correct answer for Q wrt D_{ex} and L is x/Bob. But, for every additional constant Carol, say, in an extension L' of L, x/Carol is also a correct answer for Q wrt D_{ex} and L'. Thus, D_{ex} should not be considered a reasonable database. □

We now attempt to characterize the class of reasonable disjunctive databases. There are several ways in which this might be done; we present one way here, and discuss some other ways later. First, we recall the definition of a domain independent query.

Definition. Let Q be a query with k free variables, L a language extending that of Q, U the set of constants in L, and I a Herbrand interpretation for L. If $k>0$, $val(Q,I)$ is the set of elements of U^k for which Q is true in I. If $k=0$, $val(Q,I)$ is *true* (resp., *false*) if and only if Q is true (resp., false) in I.

Definition. A query Q is *domain independent* if, for all languages $L \neq L'$ extending that of Q, and for all Herbrand interpretations I for L and I' for L' that assign the same relations to the predicates in Q, $val(Q,I) = val(Q,I')$.

We now define when a stratified disjunctive database is domain independent.

Definition A disjunctive database D is *domain independent* if, for all languages $L \neq L'$ extending L_D, $PERF(D,L) = PERF(D,L') \neq \emptyset$.

Lemma 3.1 *Let D be a domain independent disjunctive database. Then, for all languages $L \neq L'$ extending L_D, and for all domain independent queries Q in L and L', $ans(Q,D,L) = ans(Q,D,L')$.*

Proof Immediate. □

We believe that this definition captures the informal concept of a reasonable disjunctive database as discussed above. In particular, it generalizes the definition of a (relatively) domain independent database given in [7,16]. The disjunctive database D_{ex} in Example 2.1 is not domain independent according to this definition, but the database in Example 2.2 is domain independent.

It is not possible in general to determine whether a given query is domain independent [3,17], but it is possible to determine whether a given database is domain independent [7,16]. We do not yet know if it is possible to determine whether a given disjunctive database is domain independent. Even if it is possible to determine whether a given disjunctive database is domain independent, the decision procedure is likely to be computationally expensive. Thus, we would like to find a decidable subclass of the domain independent disjunctive databases with a simpler decision procedure. To this end we introduce the class of allowed disjunctive databases.

Definition A variable x is *allowed in* a conjunction $L_1 \wedge \cdots \wedge L_n$ of literals if x occurs in a positive literal L_i such that either

(a) L_i is not an equality, or

(b) L_i is an equality $x=c$, where c is a constant, or

(c) L_i is an equality $x=y$, where y is allowed in $L_1 \wedge \cdots \wedge L_{i-1} \wedge L_{i+1} \wedge \cdots \wedge L_n$.

A database clause C is *allowed* if every variable x in C is allowed in the body of C. A disjunctive database D is *allowed* if every database clause in D is allowed.

Example 3.2 The database clause

knows(x, Dutch) $\vee$ knows(x, French) $\leftarrow$ ~child(x)

in D_{ex} is not allowed, but the database clause

knows(x, Dutch) $\vee$ knows(x, French) $\leftarrow$ Belgian(x) $\wedge$ $x=y$ $\wedge$ ~child(y)

is allowed. □

The above definition is a variant of the one in [16]. It follows from (generalizations of) results in that paper that the body of an allowed database clause is a domain independent query.

Theorem 3.1 below shows that a particular decidable class of disjunctive databases is domain independent. The proof of this result requires the following definitions and lemmas.

Definition A model M for a disjunctive database D is *causal* if, for every ground atom A in M, there exists a ground instance C of a database clause in D such that A occurs in the head of C and the body of C is true in M [2].

The model M_1 for D_{ex} in Example 2.3 is not causal.

Lemma 3.2 *Every perfect model for an allowed stratified disjunctive database is causal.*

Proof Clearly, every perfect model of a stratified disjunctive database is minimal. We use induction on the maximum predicate level k in D.

Basis. Suppose k=0. Then D is a positive disjunctive database. Let M be a perfect and hence minimal model for D. If M is not causal, there exists a ground atom A in M such that A is not an instance of a disjunct of the head of any database clause in D. As A can only occur positively in (instances of) the bodies of database clause in D, $M \setminus \{A\}$ is also a model for D, contradicting the minimality of M.

Induction step. Suppose the maximum predicate level in D is k+1 and the lemma holds for all allowed stratified disjunctive databases of maximum predicate level k. Let M be a perfect and hence minimal model for D. From [12], M_k is a perfect model for D_k. By the induction hypothesis, M_k is causal. As before, if M is not causal, there exists a ground atom A of level k+1 in M such that A is not an instance of a disjunct of the head of any database clause in D. Again, A can only occur positively in (instances of) the bodies of database clauses in D, so $M \setminus \{A\}$ is also a model for D, and the result follows. □

Lemma 3.3 *Let D be an allowed stratified disjunctive database and L a language extending L_D. Then every perfect model for D wrt L is a subset of B_D.*

Proof Let M be a perfect model for D and A a ground atom in M. By Lemma 3.2, there exists a ground instance $C\theta$ of a database clause C in D such that A occurs in the head of $C\theta$ and the body of $C\theta$ is true in M. By assumption, C is an allowed database clause. Hence, by (a generalization of) Lemma 4(a) in [16], θ is a ground substitution in L_D, and A is in B_D. □

Example 3.3 Let D be the (non-allowed) database $\{p(a) \vee q(x) \leftarrow\}$ and L the language extending L_D with constants a and b. Then the perfect models for D wrt L are $\{p(a)\}$ and $\{q(a), q(b)\}$, and $\{q(a), q(b)\}$ is not a subset of B_D. □

Theorem 3.1 *Every allowed stratified disjunctive database is domain independent.*

Proof Let D be an allowed stratified disjunctive database and $L \neq L'$ languages extending L_D. We prove that $PERF(D,L) \subseteq PERF(D,L')$, and the result follows from symmetry. Let $M \in PERF(D,L)$ be a perfect model for D wrt L. We want to show that $M \in PERF(D,L')$. By Lemma 3.3, M is a subset of B_D. Let C be an (allowed) database clause $A_1 \vee \cdots \vee A_m \leftarrow L_1 \wedge \cdots \wedge L_n$ in D and $C\theta$ a ground instance of C in L' such that $(L_1 \wedge \cdots \wedge L_n)\theta$ is true in M wrt L'. By (a generalization of) Lemma 4(a) in [16], θ is a ground substitution in L_D and hence in L, and $(L_1 \wedge \cdots \wedge L_n)\theta$ is thus true in M wrt L. As $C\theta$ is true in M wrt L, some $A_i\theta$ is true in M, and hence $C\theta$ is true in M wrt L'. That is, M is a model for D wrt L'. Finally, suppose $M \notin PERF(D,L')$. Then there exists a model N' for D wrt L' such that $N' \ll M$. By Theorem 2.1, there exists a perfect model N for D wrt L' such that $N \leq N'$. By Lemma 3.3, $N \subseteq B_D$, so, regarded as models for D wrt L, $N \ll M$, contradicting the assumption that $M \in PERF(D,L)$. □

We now show that no expressive power is lost by restricting attention to allowed disjunctive databases, as every domain independent disjunctive database is equivalent to some allowed disjunctive database in the following sense.

Theorem 3.2 *Let D be a domain independent disjunctive database. Then there exists an allowed disjunctive database D' in L_D such that, for every language L extending L_D, $PERF(D,L) = PERF(D',L)$.*

Proof Let D' be the set of all ground instances in L_D of database clauses in D. Then it is easy to see that $PERF(D,L) = PERF(D,L_D) = PERF(D',L_D) = PERF(D',L)$. □

This construction greatly increases the number of clauses in the database. An alternative construction is the following. Let $c_1, \ldots, c_p$ be the constants in L_D and DOM_D a predicate not in L_D. For each c_i in L_D, add to D' the database clause $DOM_D(x) \leftarrow x = c_i$. Then, for each database clause $A_1 \vee \cdots \vee A_m \leftarrow L_1 \wedge \cdots \wedge L_n$ in D, add to D' the database clause

$$A_1 \vee \cdots \vee A_m \leftarrow DOM_D(x_1) \wedge \cdots \wedge DOM_D(x_q) \wedge L_1 \wedge \cdots \wedge L_n,$$

where $x_1, \ldots, x_q$ are the variables in the database clause in D that are not allowed in $L_1 \wedge \cdots \wedge L_n$. This construction introduces a new predicate, slightly increases the size of the clauses, and increases the number of clauses by the number of constants in the database.

4. Discussion

In this section, we consider some extensions and alternatives to the above results, and draw some conclusions.

First, it is straightforward to prove that Lemmas 3.2 and 3.3 and Theorems 3.1 and 3.2 also hold for the class of locally stratified disjunctive databases defined in [12]. As every stratified disjunctive database is locally stratified, this characterizes a larger (decidable) class of domain independent disjunctive databases.

Second, we consider other approaches to the definition of a correct answer for a query with respect to a disjunctive database. One approach is the Generalized Closed World Assumption (GCWA) [9]. In this approach an answer set $\theta_1 + \cdots + \theta_n$ for Q is *correct* with respect to database D and language L if $Q\theta_1 \vee \cdots \vee Q\theta_n$ is true in every *minimal* model for D wrt L. The use of minimal models in this definition does not enable the GCWA to exploit the information present in a non-positive database clause that is additional to the information in its (logically equivalent) positive form. As a model for a positive disjunctive database is minimal if and only if it is perfect, the GCWA coincides with the perfect model approach for positive disjunctive databases.

Another approach is the Disjunctive Database Rule (DDR). This approach was proposed and studied only recently [14], so we briefly summarize it here.

Let D be a stratified disjunctive database and L a language extending L_D. We start by defining a mapping $T_{D,L}$ from the lattice of interpretations for L into itself.

Definition Let I be an interpretation for L. Then $T_{D,L}(I) = \{A \in B_L$: C is a ground instance of a database clause in D such that A occurs in the head of C and every positive literal in the body of C is true in $I\}$. We also define $T_{D,L}\uparrow 0 = \emptyset$, $T_{D,L}\uparrow n{+}1 = T_{D,L}(T_{D,L}\uparrow n)$ and $T_{D,L}\uparrow\omega = \cup_{n\geq 0} T_{D,L}\uparrow n$.

We can then define a correct answer for a query and a domain independent disjunctive database using the DDR as follows.

Definition Let D be a stratified disjunctive database, L a language extending L_D, and Q a query in L. Let $DDR(D,L) = \{\sim A : A \in B_L \setminus T_{D,L}\uparrow\omega\}$ and $MOD(D,L)$ be the set of models for $D \cup DDR(D,L)$ wrt L. An answer set $\theta_1 + \cdots + \theta_n$ for Q is *correct* with respect to D and L if $MOD(D,L) \models Q\theta_1 \vee \cdots \vee Q\theta_n$, i.e. if $Q\theta_1 \vee \cdots \vee Q\theta_n$ is true in every model for $D \cup DDR(D,L)$ wrt L.

Definition A stratified disjunctive database D is *(DDR) domain independent* if, for all languages $L \neq L'$ extending L_D, $MOD(D,L) = MOD(D,L')$.

It is then straightforward to prove the following analogues of Lemma 3.3 and Theorems 3.1 and 3.2.

Lemma 4.1 *Let D be an allowed stratified disjunctive database and L a language extending L_D. Then every model for $D \cup DDR(D,L)$ wrt L is a subset of B_D.*

Theorem 4.1 *Every allowed stratified disjunctive database is (DDR) domain independent.*

Theorem 4.2 *Let D be a (DDR) domain independent disjunctive database. Then there exists an allowed disjunctive database D' in L_D such that, for every language L extending L_D, $MOD(D,L) = MOD(D',L)$.*

We draw the following conclusions from this investigation. First, only domain independent disjunctive databases should be used, to ensure the correct answers for a query are independent of the (implicit) language in which the database and query are expressed and hence predictable. Otherwise, the correct answers may vary when an apparently irrelevant relation is updated and a new constant is thereby added to the language of the database.

Second, only allowed (locally) stratified disjunctive databases should be used, to ensure that disjunctive databases are domain independent. This property of disjunctive databases holds for various definitions of domain independence. Whether a disjunctive database is (locally) stratified or allowed can easily be checked when the disjunctive database is entered.

This investigation has been restricted to declarative properties of disjunctive databases. The most important remaining research problem is to find efficient procedures for evaluating queries with respect to disjunctive databases. Initial steps towards this goal are reported in [5, 6, 11].

Acknowledgement

We thank Teodor Przymusinski for helpful communications on topics in this paper.

References

1. Apt, K. R., H. A. Blair and A. Walker, "Towards a Theory of Declarative Knowledge", in *Foundations of Deductive Databases and Logic Programming*, Minker, J. (ed.), Morgan Kaufmann, Los Altos, Ca., 1988, 89-148.

2. Bidoit, N. and R. Hull, "Positivism vs. Minimalism in Deductive Databases", *Proc. Fifth ACM Symp. on Principles of Database Systems*, Cambridge, Mass., 1986, 123-132.

3. Di Paola, R. A., "The Recursive Unsolvability of the Decision Problem for the Class of Definite Formulas", *J. ACM* **16**, 2 (1969), 324-327.

4. Fagin, R., "Horn Clauses and Database Dependencies", *J. ACM* **29**, 4 (1982), 952-985.

5. Grant, J. and J. Minker, "Answering Queries in Indefinite Databases and the Null Value Problem", in *Advances in Computing Research, Vol. 3*, JAI Press, 1986, 247-267.

6. Henschen, L. J. and H.-S. Park, "Compiling the GCWA in Indefinite Deductive Databases", in *Foundations of Deductive Databases and Logic Programming*, Minker, J. (ed.), Morgan Kaufmann, Los Altos, Ca., 1988, 395-438.

7. Kifer, M., "On Safety, Domain Independence, and Capturability of Database Queries", *Proc. 3rd Int. Conf. on Data and Knowledge Bases*, Jerusalem, 1988.

8. Kuhns, J. L., "Answering Questions by Computer: A Logical Study", RM-5428-PR, Rand Corp., Santa Monica, Ca., 1967.

9. Minker, J., "On Indefinite Databases and the Closed World Assumption", in *6th Conf. on Automated Deduction*, Loveland, D. W. (ed.), Lecture Notes in Computer Science 138, Springer-Verlag, 1982, 292-308.

10. Nicolas, J.-M. and R. Demolombe, "On the Stability of Relational Queries", Research Report, ONERA-CERT, Toulouse, 1983.

11. Przymusinski, T. C., "An Algorithm to Compute Circumscription", manuscript, Department of Mathematical Sciences, University of Texas, El Paso, 1986. To appear in *Artificial Intelligence*.

12. Przymusinski, T. C., "On the Declarative Semantics of Deductive Databases and Logic Programs", in *Foundations of Deductive Databases and Logic Programming*, Minker, J. (ed.), Morgan Kaufmann, Los Altos, Ca., 1988, 193-216.

13. Reiter, R., "On Closed World Data Bases", in *Logic and Data Bases*, Gallaire, H. and J. Minker (eds), Plenum Press, New York, 1978, 55-76.

14. Ross, K. A. and R. W. Topor, "Inferring Negative Information from Disjunctive Databases", Technical Report 87/1, Department of Computer Science, University of Melbourne, 1987. To appear in *J. Automated Reasoning*.

15. Topor, R. W., "Domain Independent Formulas and Databases", *Theoretical Computer Science* **52**, 3 (1987), 281-307.

16. Topor, R. W. and E. A. Sonenberg, "On Domain Independent Databases", in *Foundations of Deductive Databases and Logic Programming*, Minker, J. (ed.), Morgan Kaufmann, Los Altos, Ca., 1988, 217-240.

17. Vardi, M. Y., "The Decision Problem for Database Dependencies", *Inf. Proc. Letters* **12**, 5 (1981), 251-254.

UPDATE IN HIERARCHICAL DATA BASES

M.E. Iofinova, E.A. Komissartschik
Institute for System Studies
Academy of Sciences of the USSR
9, Prospekt 60-Let Oktyabria
117312, Moscow, USSR

Abstract

Usually information comes into a data base by input of documents with fixed structure. In this paper, the process of input in hierarchical data base is formally described. A data base is considered as a result of input of documents and its update is considered as an update of some of the documents with corresponding update of the state of the data base. An algorithm of decomposition of the data base to the source documents is given. The algorithm works in a time that is linear in a volume of input information. Basing upon this algorithm, an algorithm of update with the same time of complexity is obtained.

1. Introduction

The problems of update play the foremost role in the life of information systems. It is known that in such systems up to 90% of time spends on update, i.e. input and correction of information. The problems of update are discussed in many papers (see, for instance [1,2,4,5,7,9,10]). This paper analyses update under the proposed in [6] documental approach. This approach is based upon the idea, that a data base is a union of images of a sequence of information quanta (input documents). One can suppose each document to be a description of some object of external world, and the data base itself to be an integrated description of the corresponding set of objects. From this point of view it is natural to understand an update of the data base as an update of some subset of the documents. We differ input and correction of a data base. Under the input we mean a particular case of update, namely, addition of information to the data base without any deletion. And the correction is a process connected with deletion and changing of information in the data base. In this paper under the update we mean the correction.

It was shown in [6], that under the proposed point of view the update can be done only in the case of uniqueness of decomposition of the data base to images of input documents. The problem of uniqueness of decomposition in slightly different context was discussed in the literature on relational data bases. For instance, one can consider the problem of uniqueness of universal relation as the problem of decomposition of the data base in the case of trivial input mapping, where input document is a tuple in a universal relation, and input is a projection of this tuple to relations in the data base. In the book [8, Ch. 8] the problem of uniqueness of reconstruction of a universal relation from a state of a data base is considered, and the possibility of such a reconstruction is discussed in the case of functional and join dependencies.

In section 2 of this paper a formal machinery for dealing with hierarchical data base is described. Basing upon this machinery the problem of invertibility of an input mapping α of a set U of documents in a data base $B=\alpha(U)$, i.e. the problem of reconstruction source information from a data base, is discussed.

In section 3 an algorithm for construction of the mapping $\alpha^{-1}(B)$ is given. This algorithm works in linear time in number $|U|$ of input documents.

The algrorith from the section 3 is used in section 4 to solve the problem of update of a data base. The algorithm for update, which is presented in this section, has the same time of comlexity. For an important case the upper bound is linear not in the number of all documents but in the number of documents, which are subject to update.

2. Formal model

Marked trees play the same role for the hierarchical model as relations play for relational one. We begin this section from the definition of marked tree. The model considered in this paper is closed to the model from [3, Ch.8].

A *root tree* is an acyclic undirect graph with unique so called root vertex in each connected component. Evidently, every vertex of a root tree is in one to one correspondence with the path to it from appropriate root vertex.

A root tree R is called *A-tree* for arbitrary set A (or *tree*, if A is fixed), if each vertex of R is marked by some element of A, and vertices-brothers have different marks. It is clear that different paths in a tree have different sequences of marks and every tree R is in one to one correspondence with the set of all (root) paths p(R) in it. Relatively to standard set theoretic operation all A-trees form a lattice, which will be denoted as L^A.

Example 2.1.

```
      . a             . a   . d              . a      . d
     / \              |     |               / \       |
  b .   . c    U      . b   . e    =     b .   . c    . e
         \            |                       /    \
          . d         . c                  c .      . d
```

Let $A=A_1\times\ldots\times A_n$, $B=\underset{i\in M}{\times} A_i$ $C=\underset{i\notin M}{\times} A_i$ for some $M\subseteq[1..n]$. A natural projection π_B of A onto B induces the projection of paths from L^A to paths from L^B: if $r=(a_1,\ldots a_k)$ is a path, then $\pi_B(r) = (\pi_B(a_1),\ldots\pi_B(a_k))\in L^B$; if $R\in L^A$, then let $\pi_B(R)=\bigcup_{r\in p(R)}\pi_B(r)$. Let $\sigma_A(R)$ (or simply $\sigma(R)$) denotes the set of all marks of vertices from R. Let $\sigma_B(R)=\pi_B(\sigma_A(R))$.

Let $R\in L^B$. One can connect with R a set $\tilde{L}_R^C = \{S \mid S\in L^A, \pi_B(S)\subseteq R\}$. Evidently, that $\tilde{L}_R^C$ is a sublattice in L^A. If $T\in\tilde{L}_R^C$, then we shall write $\pi_R(T)$ instead of $\pi_B(T)$ below.

Now we can define a lattice of data bases. In hierarchical models each vertex has a type. In the simplest case there are only two types - "array" and "elementary". Let each vertex in a tree R have one of these two types. Consider a lattice $\tilde{L}_R^C$. Denote $L_R^C = \{T\in\tilde{L}_R^C \mid$ for any vertices-brothers u, v from T such that $\pi_R(u)=\pi_R(v)$, $\pi_R(u)$ is a vertex of type "array" in $R\}$. The partial lattice L_R^C is called *the lattice of the data bases with the scheme R.*

Notice, that the operation "U" is partially defined on L_R^A. Really, if $T_1, T_2\in L_R^A$ and r_i is a path from T_i, $i=1,2$, and $r_1=(a_1,\ldots,a_k)$, $r_2=(b_1,\ldots,b_k)$, where $a_i=b_i$, $i=1,\ldots,k-1$, $a_k\neq b_k$, and $\pi_R(a_k)=\pi_R(b_k)$ is an elementary vertex of R, then $T_1\cup T_2\in L^A\setminus L_R^A$. Such a situation is called a *collision*.

We shall consider data bases with fixed scheme D and common domain V for all attributes. These data bases form a lattice L_D^V. D is a tree with unary marks.

We consider as a main example the following already classical

Example 2.2.

The data base "Suppliers-Parts" ("S-P") has the following structure D_{S-P} :

```
            S#  *                            P#  *
         /    |    \                           /   \
     P# *  Name·  City·                    Name·  City·
        |
     Qty·
```

Here "*" denotes array type and "·" denotes elementary one.

Below an instance of the data base is presented.

```
                          (S#,S1)
            /          /          \            \
    (P#,P1)    (P#,P2)    (Name,Smith)  (City,London)
        |          |
    (Qty,300)  (Qty,200)

              (P#,P1)                      (P#,P2)
              /      \                     /      \
    (Name,Nut)  (City,London)     (Name,Bolt)  (City,Paris)
```

The data base from the example belongs to the lattice $L^{V}_{D_{S-P}}$ for $V \supseteq \{S_1, P_1, P_2, 200, 300, \text{Smith}, \text{London}, \text{Paris}, \text{Nut}, \text{Bolt}\}$.

Input documents are vectors of $W=V^n$ for some integer n. Denote $N=[1,\dots,n]$. Input of elements from W in a data base B over D is given by a mapping α: $W \to L^V_D$ and then union $B \cup \alpha(w)$. Let $E \in L^N_D$. Then one can connect E with a mapping β: $W \to L^V_E$ by the following manner. If $w=(w_1,\dots,w_n) \in W$, then $\beta_E(w)$ is made from E by ascribing to each vertex $e \in E$ a ternary mark $(m_D(e), m_N(e), w_{m_N}(e))$ instead of the binary mark $(m_D(e), m_N(e))$. Since $E \in L^N_D$, one has $L^V_E \subseteq L^{N,V}_D$. Hence there exists a natural projection π: $L^V_E \to L^V_D$.

As in [6], we suppose that

$$(*) \quad \alpha = \beta_E \circ \pi$$

for some $E \in L^N_D$. Till the end of the paper we fix α and E and we shall write simply β instead of β_E. So we have the following commutative diagram

$$\begin{array}{ccc} & L^V_E & \\ \beta \nearrow & & \searrow \pi \\ W & \xrightarrow{\alpha} & L^V_D \end{array}$$

The equality $\alpha(w)=\pi(\beta(w))$ allows us to consider E as a structural description of the input mapping α. Spread β to partially defined vectors from W by the following way. Let $u=w|_M$ for some $w\in W$ and $M\subseteq N$. Then define $\beta(u)=\{s \mid s$ is a path in $\beta(w)$, and $\sigma_N(s)\subseteq M\}$. (Since elements of considered lattices are defined uniquelly by sets of their paths, we shall identify a tree and the set of its paths). Notice, that if $M=\sigma_N(E)\neq N$ then $\beta(u)=\beta(w)$ for all w. So, without loss of generality one can suppose $\sigma_N(E)=N$ and $\pi_D(E)=D$.

Define also the restriction of α and β on $F\subseteq E$. For $w\in W$ denote $\beta_F(w)=\{s \mid s$ is a path in $\beta(w)$ and $\pi_E(s)\subseteq F\}$, $\alpha_F(w)=\pi(\beta_F(w))$. It is clear, that $\beta_F(w)=\beta_F(w|_{\sigma_N(F)})$. The same is valid for α_F.

We say that $B\in L_D^V$ is *the result of input of a set $U\subseteq W$*, if $B=\bigcup_{u\in U}\alpha(u)$. In this case we shall write $B=\alpha(U)$.

A set $U\subseteq W$ is called ***α-admissible***, if for any $u,v\in U$ there exists a union $\alpha(u)\cup\alpha(v)$.

It is clear, that if $U\subseteq W$ is an α-admissible set then there exists $\alpha(U)=\bigcup_{u\in U}\alpha(u)$.

A subset $K\subseteq N$ is called a *key* for a subset $U\subseteq W$, if $u|_K\neq v|_K$ for any $u\neq v\in U$.

Consider a set of keys $\mathbf{K}=\{K_1,\ldots,K_l\}$. Without loss of generality one can suppose, that $K_i\not\subseteq K_j$ for $i\neq j$.

A set $U\subseteq W$ is called ***(α,K)-admissible*** if it is α-admissible and every element from $\mathbf{K}$ is a key for U.

It is evident, that each subset of $\alpha,\mathbf{K}$-admissible set is $\alpha,\mathbf{K}$-admissible.

Fix α, E and $\mathbf{K}$ till the end of the paper. We shall omit $(\alpha,\mathbf{K})$ in the definition of admissibility.

Let Ω be a set of all admissible subsets in W.

In the rest part of this section we discuss the following problem:

Let a set $\mathbf{K}$ of keys be fixed. Under which E the mapping α is an injection on Ω? The interest to this problem is explained by the fact, that injectivity of α is a necessary condition for the existence of the inverse mapping α^{-1}. We introduce below the notion of sound subtree in E. Lemma 2.4 declares that soundness of E is a sufficient condition for injectivity of α. In its turn, Proposition 2.10 shows that under some additional assumptioms on $\mathbf{K}$ and α soundness of E is necessary too.

Example 2.3. After input of the following input document

1	2	3	4	5	6	7
S_2	Jones	Paris	P_1	300	Nut	London

under input mapping E_{S-P}

```
                (S#,1)                      (P#,4)
            /     |     \                  /     \
     (P#,4)  (Name,2) (City,3)     (Name,6) (City,7)
        |
     (Qty,5)
```

the data base "S-P" looks like this:

```
                         (S#,S1)
         /          /          \            \
     (P#,P1)   (P#,P2)    (Name,Smith)   (City,London)
        |            |
     (Qty,300)   (Qty,200)

                         (S#,S2)
                  /          |          \
          (P#,P1)    (Name,Jones)   (City,Paris)
              |
          (Qty,300)

     (P#,P1)                         (P#,P2)
     /       \                        /      \
 (Name,Nut)  (City,London)    (Name,Bolt)  (City,Paris)
```

Now if we try to input the document

1	2	3	4	5	6	7
S_2	Blake	Paris	P_1	300	Nut	London

it would be a collision in the vertex Name of supplier, since its type is elementary.

Let the set $\{1,4\}$ be a key for a set of input documents of our data base "S-P".

Let F be a subtree in E. Call $B \in L_D^V$ *evaluation of F*, if $B=\alpha_F(w)$ for some $w \in W$.

Evidently, each evaluation of a path is a path too.

A subtree F in E is called *sound*, if for any $U \in \Omega$ and $w \in W$ such that $\alpha_F(w) \subseteq \alpha_F(U)$, $\beta_F(w)=\beta_F(u)$ for some $u \in U$.

One has immediately from the definition:

Lemma 2.4. Let $F \subseteq E$ be a sound subtree. Then α_F is injective on the set $\Omega|_{\sigma_N(F)}$.

The following lemmas allow us to find sound subtrees in E constructively.

Lemma 2.5. Let r be a path in E. If $\pi_D(r) \neq \pi_D(s)$ for each path $r \neq s \in E$, then r is sound.

Proof. Let $w \in W$, $\alpha_r(w) \in \alpha(U)$. It is clear that there exists $u \in U$ such that $\alpha_r(w) \subseteq \alpha(u)$. From the hypothesis of the Lemma it follows that there is only one path r^* in $\beta(u)$ with $\pi_D(r^*) = \pi_D(\alpha_r(w)) = \pi_D(r)$. Hence, $r^* = \beta_r(w) = \beta_r(u)$.

Let $T \in L_R^A$, $S \subseteq T$ and $\tilde{S}$ be the maximal subtree in T, which contains S, and such that all its vertices outside S are elementary. The subtree $O_T(S) = \{r \mid r \text{ is a path in } T, \sigma_N(r) \subseteq \sigma_N(\tilde{S})\}$ is called the *neighbourhood* of S in T.

Lemma 2.6. If R is a sound subtree in E and $S \subseteq O_E(R)$, then $R \cup S$ is sound too.

Proof. Let $u \in U$ and $w \in W$ such that $\alpha(w) \subseteq \alpha(U)$ and $\beta_R(u) = \beta_R(w)$. Let S be a subtree in E such that all vertices from $S \setminus R$ are elementary. Evidently, $\pi_D(R) \subseteq \pi_D(\alpha(u) \cap \alpha(w))$. Since $\alpha(u) \cup \alpha(w) \subseteq \alpha(U)$, then the set $\{u, w\}$ is α-admissible, and we obtain $\beta_S(u) = \beta_S(w)$ immediately. Further, $\sigma_N(u \cap w) \supseteq \sigma_N(S)$. Hence $\beta_{\tilde{S}}(u) = \beta_{\tilde{S}}(w)$, where $\tilde{R}$ is the neighbourhood of R in E.

Lemma 2.7. If R and S are sound subtrees and $\sigma_N(R) \cap \sigma_N(S)$ contains a key, then $R \cup S$ is sound too.

Proof. Let $u_1, u_2 \in U$ and $w \in W$ with $\alpha(w) \subseteq \alpha(U)$, $\beta_R(u_1) = \beta_R(w)$ and $\beta_S(u_2) = \beta_S(w)$. So, $u_1|_{\sigma_N(R) \cap \sigma_N(S)} = u_2|_{\sigma_N(R) \cap \sigma_N(S)}$. By the hypothesis $\sigma_N(R) \cap \sigma_N(S) \supseteq K$, where K is a key. Hence, $u_1 = u_2$ and $\beta_{R \cup S}(w) = \beta_{R \cup S}(u_1)$.

A path in E is called *constructively sound*, if it satisfies hypothesis of Lemma 2.5. A tree is called constructively sound, if it could be obtained from constructively sound paths from E using two operations: extending (Lemma 2.6) and union (Lemma 2.7).

Lemma 2.8. E could be represented by the unique way as a union $E = F_0 \cup F_1 \cup \ldots \cup F_k$, where $F_1, \ldots, F_k$ are maximal constructively sound subtrees in F, $p(F_0) = p(E) \setminus p(\bigcup_{i \le k} F_i)$, and every path in $p(F_0)$ is not constructively sound.

Proof. Let $E = F_0 \cup \ldots \cup F_k$ be such a union and R be a constructively sound subtree in E. Show that $R \subseteq F_i$ for suitable i, $1 \le i \le k$. Denote by $p^*(R)$ the set of all constructively sound paths in R. If $p^*(R) \subseteq p(F_i)$, then $R \subseteq F_i$. Hence for some F_i, $1 \le i \le k$, $p^*(R) \cap p^*(F_i) \neq \emptyset$ and $p^*(R) \not\subseteq p^*(F_i)$. Certainly, an operation $S_1 \cup S_2$ must appear in the construction of R, where S_1, S_2 are some constructively sound subtrees from E, $S_1 \subseteq F_i$, $S_2 \not\subseteq F_i$ and $\sigma_N(S_1) \cap \sigma_N(S_2) \supseteq K$, $K \in \mathbf{K}$. But then $\sigma_N(F_i) \cap \sigma_N(S_2) \supseteq K$, and consequently $F_i \cup S_2$ is a constructively sound tree - a contradiction with the maximality of F_i.

Lemma 2.9. For any $E \in L_D^N$ there exist $D^* \supseteq D$ and $E^* \supseteq E$, $E^* \in L_{D^*}^N$ such that E^* is constructively sound.

Notice that the input mapping E_{S-P} from Example 2.3 is sound and the set of input documents for the last instance of the data base is

1	2	3	4	5	6	7
S_1	Smith	London	P_1	300	Nut	London
S_1	Smith	London	P_2	200	Bolt	Paris
S_2	Jones	Paris	P_1	300	Nut	London

Proposition 2.10. Let $|K|=1$ for every $K\in\mathbf{K}$, $|V|>1$, each maximal path in E is constructively sound, and each path in E with elementary terminal vertex contains a key. Then α is injective on Ω iff E is constructively sound.

Corollary 2.11. Under the hypothesis of Proposition 2.10 every sound tree is constructively sound.

We concern in this paper only with constructively sound trees. rollary 2.11 allow us to hope that the class of all constructively sound trees is not so far from the class of all sound trees.

3. Construction of inverse mapping

The goal of this section is an algorithm of construction of a mapping α^{-1}, i.e. a reconstruction of the set of input documents from a data base. A necessary condition for this is injectivity of α on the set Ω of all admissible (relatively to α and $\mathbf{K}$) subsets from $\mathbf{W}$. Since constructive soundness of a subtree $F\subseteq E$ provides injectivity of α (see Lemmas 2.4-2.7), it will be convenient to introduce a hypergraph Γ. Some subsets of N corresponding to constructively sound subtrees from E will be vertices of Γ.

Let F be a subtree in E. Consider a series $F=F_0\subseteq F_1\subseteq\ldots$, where F_i is a neighbourhood of F_{i-1} for $i>0$. It follows from the finiteness of N that the series is stabilized, i.e. for some k, $F_k=F_{k+1}=\ldots$ The subtree $\overline{F}=F_k$ is called the *closure* of F. Let $M\subseteq N$. Denote $E_M=\{r \mid r$ is a path in E, $\sigma_N(r)\subseteq M\}$. It is clear, that $\overline{F}=E_{\sigma_N(\overline{F})}$.

It follows immediately from the definition of $\overline{F}$ that the closure of $\overline{F}$ coincides with $\overline{F}$.

Let the vertices of the hypergraph Γ be $\sigma_N(F)$ for all closed constructively sound subtrees $F\subseteq E$. A triple (a,b,c) is an arc of the hypergraph Γ if $a\cap b$ contains a key from $\mathbf{K}$, and the closure of $E_a\cup E_b$ coincides with E_c.

We shall build the hypergraph Γ as an inductive limit of an ascending series of hypergraphs $\Gamma_0 \subseteq \Gamma_1 \subseteq \ldots$

Let $V(\Gamma_0)=\{\sigma_N(\bar{r}) \mid r$ is a maximal constructively sound path from E, there exists $K \in \mathbf{K}$ such that $K \subseteq \sigma_N(\bar{r})$ and $\sigma_N(\bar{r})$ is maximal under inclusion relatively to the first two properties$\}$ be the set of vertices of the hypergraph Γ_0. The set of arcs $E(\Gamma_0)=\emptyset$.

Let for some $i>0$ $\Gamma_0,\ldots,\Gamma_{i-1}$ be constructed already. Then let $V(\Gamma_i) = V(\Gamma_{i-1}) \cup \left(\left\{\sigma_N(\bar{E}_{L_1 \cup L_2} \mid L_1, L_2 \in V(\Gamma_{i-1}),\ L_1 \not\subseteq L_2,\ L_2 \not\subseteq L_1\right.\right.$ and for some $K \in \mathbf{K}$, $\left.\left. K \subseteq L_1 \cap L_2 \right\}\right)$ be vertices of the hypergraph Γ_i; $E(\Gamma_i) = E(\Gamma_{i-1}) \cup \left(\left\{(L_1, L_2, M) \mid M=\sigma_N(\bar{E}_{L_1 \cup L_2})\right.\right.$ for some $K \in \mathbf{K}$, $K \subseteq L_1 \cap L_2$, where (L_1, L_2) is considered as an unordered pair$\left.\left.\right\}\right)$ be arcs of the hypergraph Γ_i.

This process is stabilized, since $|V(\Gamma_i)|<2^{|N|}$. So, $\Gamma_k=\Gamma_{k+1}=\ldots$ for some k. Denote $\Gamma=\Gamma_k$.

Vertices a and b are called the *sources*, and vertex c is called the *target* of an arc $(a,b,c) \in E(\Gamma)$. We shall say also that (a,b,c) comes out from a (or b) and comes in c. Nonisolated vertices without any coming in arcs are called *sources*, and nonisolated vertices without any coming out arcs are called *targets* of the hypergraph Γ. Denote the set of sources of a hypergraph Δ by $S(\Delta)$, and the set of its targets by $T(\Delta)$.

If there is at least one arc in a hypergraph $\Delta \subseteq \Gamma$, then there is at least one arc in Δ which comes out from $S(\Delta)$. In particular, $|S(\Delta)| \geq 2$.

Time complexity of an algorithm described below is linear in the number of arcs in a subhypergraph Δ, which connects $V(\Gamma_0)$ with a vertex $x \in V(\Gamma)$. Since the number of arcs in Γ can be estimated only by 2^{n^2}, then it is natural to choose a hypergraph with minimal possible number of arcs as Δ. An algorithm for construction of a hypergraph R with $|V(E(R))| \leq |V(E)|$ is given below.

Definition 3.1. Let $A,B \subseteq V(\Gamma)$. A subhypergraph $R \subseteq \Gamma$ is called a *road* from A to B if the following conditions hold:

(1) $S(R)=A$.

(2) $T(R)=B$.

(3) If $a \in V(R) \setminus S(R)$, then exactly one arc of R comes in a.

(4) If $a \in V(R) \setminus T(R)$, then exactly one arc of R comes out from a.

A road with unique target is similar to direct path without selfcrossing in conventional direct graph.

Lemma 3.2. If R is a road, then $|V(R)|=2 \cdot |S(R)|-|T(R)|$ and $|E(R)|=|S(R)|-|T(R)|$.

Now we give an outline of an algorithm of construction of a road R from $S(R) \subseteq V(\Gamma_0)$ to $\{x\}$ for arbitrary $x \in V(\Gamma) \setminus V(\Gamma_0)$. The algorithm works in three steps:

1. Construct a hypergraph $R_1 \subseteq \Gamma$ such that $S(R_1) \subseteq V(\Gamma_0)$, each vertex v of R_1 belongs to x (remind, that each vertex in Γ is a subset in N), and at most one arc comes in v. We construct R_1 iteratively, starting from x and adding at each step an arc of Γ that comes in a source vertex of current hypergraph.

2. Now, transform R_1 into a hypergraph R_2 such that x would be a target of R_2, $S(R_2) \cap V(\Gamma_0) \neq \emptyset$, each vertex v of R_2 would belong to x, and at most one arc comes out from v. R_2 is constructed by iteratively using the following operation. Let (v,a,b) and (v,c,d) are arcs that come out from v. Change (v,c,d) by an arc (b,c,e), where $e=\sigma_N(\bar{E}_{b \cup c})$. Further, change arcs that come out from v by ones that come out from e.

3. At last, construct a hypergraph R from R_2 by the same way as R_1 from Γ. R_2 has the property that at most one arc comes out from each vertex of it. The same holds for R. Besides of that at most one arc comes in each vertex of R. Thus, R is a road.

One can show that the algorithm described above has time complexity linear in the number of arcs of Γ.

Now we can describe an algorithm IM (Inverse Mapping) of construction of a mapping α_F^{-1} for subtrees $F \subseteq E$ which correspond to vertices of Γ (i.e. $F=E_{\sigma_N(F)}$). We shall write α_F^{-1} instead of $\alpha^{-1}{}_{\sigma_N(F)}$.

Let $x \in V(\Gamma)$ and R is a road in {x} with $S(R) \subseteq V(\Gamma_0)$. The algorith constructs α_y^{-1} inductively, starting from $y \in V(\Gamma_0)$ and moving through arcs of R. Namely, if $y \in S(R) \subseteq V(\Gamma_0)$ then some constructively sound path r of E corresponds to the vertex y of Γ by the construction. Because of soundness of r, we fill all columns in U with numbers from y by searching of all possible evaluations of r in the data base $\alpha(U)$, and then constructing the closure $\bar{r}$. By this way we obtain the relations, which correspond to vertices of S(R). Further, if (a,b,c) is an arc of R, and the relations for a and b are already constructed, then by join we shall obtain a relations for c. At the very end after |E(R)| joins we obtain a relation for x, i.e. we construct $\alpha_x^{-1}(\alpha(U))$.

For $F \subset E$ denote $\hat{F}=\{s \mid$ s is a path in E and there exists a path t in F, such that $\pi_D(s) \cap \pi_D(t)$ is a maximal subpath in $\pi_D(s)\}$.

Proposition 3.3. The algorithm IM can be realized in $O(|U| \cdot |V(\hat{E}_x)| \cdot |S(R)|) \leq O(|U| \cdot |V(\hat{E}_x)|^2)$ operations, where one operation is a move along an edge of a tree.

In some cases (see, for example, next section) we are interested not in U as a whole, but in some subset of U satisfying some conditions. Suppose, that a subset $M \subseteq N$ and $w \in W$ are fixed and we want to build

$U_1 \subseteq U$ from $\alpha(U)$ such that $U_1|_M \equiv w|_M$. In particular, if M contains a key, then $|U_1|=1$. It is clear that one can construct U by the algorithm IM and then delete unnecessary vectors. But if, say, M contains a key then one have to delete all but one elements. The following proposition shows, that in some cases it is possible to construct U_1 cheaper.

Proposition 3.4. Let R be a road from $S(R)\subseteq V(\Gamma_0)$ to $x\in V(\Gamma)$, $M\subseteq x$, $w\in W$, U be admissible subset in W and $U_0=\left\{u\in U \mid u|_M=w|_M\right\}$. Moreover, suppose that if $y\in S(R)$ and $r=r(y)$, then $\sigma_N(s)=\sigma_N(r)\cap M$ for appropriate path $s\subseteq r$, and $u|\sigma_N(s)=w|\sigma_N(s)$ implies $u|_M=w|_M$. Then it is possible to construct U_0 by $\leqslant O(|U_0|\cdot|V(\hat{E}_x)|\cdot|S(R)|) \leqslant O(|U_0|\cdot|V(\hat{E}_x)|^2)$ steps.

4. Update

In this section we shall consider the problem of update of a data base. Let U be an admissible subset in W. Speaking on update of a data base $\alpha(U)$, we mean a change of "incorrect" admissible U by a "correct" admissible $U'\subseteq W$, and, as a consequence, a transformation of $\alpha(U)$ to $\alpha(U')$. A change of U by U' is defined by the following way. Let a context of a change, i.e. a pair of partially defined vectors $a=(a_1,\dots,a_n)$ and $b=(b_1,\dots,b_n)$ from W, be given. We tell that a vector $u\in U$ goes through the context if $u|_{\{i\}}=a_i$ for any $i\in N$ such that $a_i\neq\emptyset$. So, $a_i=\emptyset$ means indifferent value. A vector b in its turn defines new values for elements from U gone through the context. In this paper, we consider the input of completely defined vectors from W only. Because of that, $b_i=\emptyset$ for some i means that either $a_i=\emptyset$ and a value of i-th coordinate is unchangeable, or $b_j=\emptyset$ for all $j\in N$, i.e. a change consists of deletion of all vectors from U gone through the context.

Let $C_1=\left\{i\in N \mid \emptyset\neq a_i\neq b_i\right\}$, $C_2=\left\{i\in N \mid \emptyset\neq a_i=b_i\right\}$. C_1 defines correction part of the context, and C_2 defines its indicating part.

Definition 4.1. Say that a subtree $F\subseteq E$ *contains the context C*, if the following conditions hold:

(a) If r is a path in E and $\sigma_N(r)\cap C_1\neq\emptyset$, then $r\subseteq F$.

(b) $C_2\subseteq\sigma_N(F)$.

It follows immediately from the definition, that if $F\subseteq G\subseteq E$, then G contains the context C as well as F.

Suppose now that E_x contains the context C, where $x\in V(\Gamma)$, and R is a road from $S(R)\subseteq V(\Gamma_0)$ to $\{x\}$. Such R exists by Lemma 3.2. Let U_a be a set of all vectors from U gone through the context C, and U_b be an image of U_a under the substitution $a\mapsto b$. Evidently $U'=(U\setminus U_a)\cup U_b$.

Consider the following algorithm of update.

Algorithm 4.2.

(a) Using of Algorithm IM, construct U from $\alpha(U)$.

(b) Searching of U, construct two sets U_a and $U \setminus U_a$.

(c) Construct U_b from U_a.

(d) Construct $U' = (U \setminus U_a) \cup U_b$.

(e) Construct $\alpha(U')$ from U'.

It follows immediately from Proposition 3.3, that the algorithm 4.2 needs $\leqslant O(|U| \cdot |V(\hat{E}_x)| \cdot |S(R)|)$ moves.

As follows from the following trivial example this bound can not be improved, i.e. it is not always possible to update a data base without considering all its elements.

Example 4.3. Now, let we have the following context of change

1	4	5	6	7
(S_1, S_1)	(P_1, P_3)	$(\emptyset, 100)$	$(\emptyset, \text{Cog})$	$(\emptyset, \text{Athens})$

i.e. the supplier S_1 supply P_3 instead of P_1. After the update we obtain the following instance of the data base "S-P":

$(S\#, S_1)$
/ / \ \
$(P\#, P_3)$ $(P\#, P_2)$ (Name, Smith) (City, London)
| |
(Qty, 100) (Qty, 200)

$(S\#, S_2)$
/ | \
$(P\#, P_1)$ (Name, Jones) (City, London)
|
(Qty, 300)

$(P\#, P_1)$
/ \
(Name, Nut) (City, London)

$(P\#, P_2)$
/ \
(Name, Bolt) (City, Paris)

$(P\#, P_3)$
/ \
(Name, Cog) (City, Athens)

In some cases it is possible to replace $|U|$ by $|U_a|$ in upper bound. The proposition 3.4 allows us to do this under some additional assumptions.

Algorithm 4.4. Let there exist a counter in each vertex of $\alpha(U)$, which indicates the number of moves down through this vertex during input, i.e. the number of vectors from U, whose image contains this vertex. Moreover, suppose the hypotesis of Proposition 3.4 hold. Consider the following operations:

(a) Construction of U_a from $\alpha(U)$.

(b) For each $u \in U_a$ construct $\alpha_{E_x}(u)$ and subtract 1 from the counter of every vertex of $\alpha(U)$ belonging to $\alpha_{E_x}(u)$. Furthermore, if the counter of some vertex becomes 0, then delete this vertex together with its subtree. At last, by the substitution $a \mapsto b$ construct $\tilde{u}$ and $\alpha_{E_x}(\tilde{u})$ from u. Then, add $\alpha_{E_x}(\tilde{u})$ to the current data base and add 1 to every vertex of $\alpha_{E_x}(\tilde{u})$ counter.

Proposition 4.5.

(i) The algorithm 4.4 build $\alpha(U')$.

(ii) An upper bound of the algorithm 4.4 is $O(|U_a|\cdot|V(\hat{E}_x)|\cdot|S(R)|)$.

Proof.

(i) follows immediately from $U'=(U\setminus U_a)\cup U_b$.

(ii) For proving of (ii) notice, that if the value of the counter of a vertex equals to 1, then there was only one vector, say w, whose image moves through this vertex. Consequently, the volume of its subtree $\leq |V(\alpha_{\hat{E}_x}(w))| = |V(\hat{E}_x)|$.

Since we consider admissible subsets of W only, then it is necessary to check admissibility of U'. If U' is not admissible, then by the addmissibility of U, either a collision between $\alpha(u)$ and $\alpha(v)$ arises in some elementary vertex, or $u|_K = v|_K$ for some key K, where $u \in U\setminus U_a$, $v \in U_b$, $u \neq v$. The presence of the first alternative can be checked during the realization of the algorithms 4.2 or 4.4. Below an algorithm that checks the absence of two elements in U' with the same key is given.

Let $K_i = (k_1, \ldots k_m) \in \mathbf{K}$. Define the following tree D_i with unary mark:

```
             .k1
              |
   Di        .k2
              :
             .km
            /|  \
           1 2...n
```

Let $K_i \subseteq M \subseteq N$, $w \in W = V^n$, and $u = w|_M$ be a partially defined vector. Associate with D_i a mapping $\alpha_i : u \to \alpha_i(u) \in L^V_{D_i}$, which ascribe to each $a \in V(D_i)$ a value $u|\{a\}$. Evidently, if $U \subseteq W$ and K_i is a key for U, then $\alpha_i(U)$ is well-defined, i.e. there are no collisions in simple nodes of D_i. Immediately from the definition of D_i one obtains that a presentation of U as an element of the lattice $L^V_{D_i}$ is equivalent to its presentation as a relation, i.e α_i is invertible, and it is easy to reconstruct U from $\alpha_i(U)$.

Algorithm 4.6.

(a) Construct $U \backslash U_a$.

(b) Construct U_b.

(c) For each $K_i \in \mathbf{K}$ construct a tree D_i and a mapping α_i: $U \rightarrow \alpha_i(U) \in L^V_{D_i}$. Further, construct $\alpha_i(U \backslash U_a) \cup \alpha_i(U_b)$ and check the presence of collisions in simple vertices.

Proposition 4.7.

(i) The algorithm 4.6 indicates the presence of two elements in U' having the same key.

(ii) An upper bound of the algorithm 4.6 is
$O(|U| \cdot |V(\hat{E}_x)| \cdot |S(R)| \cdot |\mathbf{K}|)$.

Proof.

(i) follows from the definions of D_i and α_i.

(ii) For every $K_i \in \mathbf{K}$ one should make all steps of the algorithm 4.2.

As in the case of the update algorithm one can obtain more efficient algorithm under some additional assumptions.

Algorithm 4.8. Let for every $K_i \in \mathbf{K}$ there exist a path $r_i \subseteq E_x$ such that $\alpha_N(r_i) = K_i$. Moreover, suppose that the hypotheses of the algorithm 4.4 hold. Then

(a) Construct U_a from $\alpha(U)$.

(b) For every $u \in U_a$ and every $K_i \in \mathbf{K}$ construct $\alpha_{r_i}(\tilde{u})$, where $\tilde{u}$ is the image of u under the substitution $a \mapsto b$.

Proposition 4.9.

(i) The algorithm 4.8 indicates the presence of two elements in U' with the same key.

(ii) An upper bound of the algorithm 4.8 is
$O(|U_a| \cdot |V(\hat{E}_x)| \cdot |S(R)|)$.

Proof.

(i) If $\alpha_{r_i}(\tilde{u}) \subseteq \alpha(U)$, then there exists $w \in U$ such that $\tilde{u}|_K = w|_K$. In that case we say that the update is not admissible.

(ii) For constructing all of $\alpha_{r_i}(\tilde{u})$ one needs $< |V(\hat{E}_x)|$ moves. The rest follows from the proposition 4.5(ii).

Remark 4.10. The checking of $\mathbf{K}$-admissibility of U' is not needed at all if $a|_L = b|_L$, where $L = \bigcup_{K \in \mathbf{K}} K$.

In conclusion, let us discuss time complexity of construction of a road R and of finding some vertex $x \in V(\Gamma)$ such that E_x goes through the context. It could be shown that the finding of a minimal (up to cardinality) vertex x is NP-hard. We can construct the road R only by using the whole hypergraph Γ, i.e. in exponential time on |N| in the worst case. However, suitable x and R could be found rather quickly. Moreover, the most frequent x and R can be stored. And at last, we can take x=N and construct the road R from $S(R)\subseteq V(\Gamma_0)$ in N only once during the process of construction of the hypergraph Γ.

We wish to thank A.V. Karzanov for helpful discussions and the unknown referees for making numerous excellent suggestions for improving this paper.

References

1. Abiteboul S., Vianu V., Transaction languages for database update and specification. Preprint I.N.R.I.A., 1987.

2. Blakeley J.A., Larson P.-A., Tompa F.W. Efficiently updating matherialized views. ACM SIGMOD Record, v. 15, 1986, N2, 61-71.

3. Delobel C., Adiba M. Relational Database Systems. North-Holland, 1985.

4. Fagin R.,Ullman J.D.,Vardi M.Y. On the semantics of updates in databases. Proc. 2nd ACM Symp. on the Principles of Database Syst., 1983, 362-365.

5. Fagin R., Kuper G.M., Ullman J.D., Vardi M.Y. Updating logical databases. Advances in Computing Research, v.3, 1986, 1-18.

6. Iofinova M.E., Komissartschik E.A. Data base consistency and the input information flow. Automatics and Telemechanics, N 3, 1988, 155-167. [In Russian].

7. Jajodia S. Universal and representative instances using unmarked nulls. Lect Notes Comp. Sci., v. 181, 1984, 367-378.

8. Maier D. Theory of Relational Data Bases. Computer Science Press, 1983.

9. Mark L., Roussopoulos N., Chu B. Update dependencies. Database Semantics (DS-1), T.B. Steel, jr. and R. Meersman (Eds.), North-Holland, 1986, 303-319.

10. Sagiv Y. A characterization of globally consistent databases and their correct paths. ACM Trans. Database Syst., v. 8, 1983, N 2, 266-286.

Parallel Update Transactions

(Extended Abstract)

by
Dino Karabeg† Victor Vianu

Dept. of Computer Science and Engineering‡
Mail Code MC-014
University of California at San Diego
La Jolla, California 92093
U. S. A.

1. Introduction

While query languages have been extensively studied in the framework of the relational model, database updates and transactions have only recently become the object of formal investigation. Indeed, most studies of transactions have focused on concurrency issues [BG, PBR]. In [AV, KKPV], a formal model for sequential update transactions in relational databases was introduced, and several basic results on transaction equivalence and optimization were obtained. In the present paper we introduce a model for *parallel* update transactions, which is an extension of the model developed in [AV] for sequential transactions. Our results focus on the problem of maximizing the degree of parallelism within parallel transactions, and producing optimal parallelizations of sequential transactions.

Parallel transactions are viewed here as partially ordered sets of atomic database updates forming a semantic unit. We consider a widely accepted class of atomic updates. These consist of insertions, deletions, and modifications, where the selection of tuples (to be deleted or modified) involves the inspection of individual attribute values for each tuple. We first look at the specification of parallel transactions. Since specifying a parallel transaction by a partially ordered set of updates can be awkward, we propose a more convenient syntax, called "in-line", and examine its relationship to partially ordered sets of updates. While the "in-line" syntax is more restrictive, we show that it is powerful enough to capture the same relevant information on the degree of parallelism as arbitrary partial orders of updates.

The main results of the paper focus on algorithms for maximizing the degree of parallelism within parallel transactions. The algorithms can be used to optimize given parallel transactions, or to parallelize given sequential transactions. First, a notion of optimal parallel transaction is introduced. While it is shown that the optimization problem for parallel transactions is NP-complete, we exhibit efficient approximation algorithms which produce parallelizations close to the optimum -- within a constant factor in general, and within absolute constants (1 or 2) in special cases. The results for the special cases are of particular interest, since they provide new examples of NP-complete problems with very good polynomial approximations. We argue that the same type of problem is likely to occur in other contexts as well.

The paper consists of four sections. Section 2 summarizes the model for sequential transactions of [AV]. In Section 3, parallel transactions are defined and the optimization problem is shown to be NP-complete. In Section 4 we present the approximate polynomial-time optimization algorithms.

2. Background on Sequential Transactions

In this section we review the model of sequential transactions and some results previously obtained in [AV].

---

† On leave from Rudjer Boskovic Institute, Zagreb, Yugoslavia.
‡ The authors were supported in part by the National Science Foundation, under grant number IST-8511538.

We assume knowledge of the basic concepts and notation of relational databases, as in [M, U].

The sequential transactions we consider are finite sequences of insertions, deletions, and modifications. We focus on the large class of "domain-based" transactions, where the selection of tuples to be deleted or modified involves the inspection of individual attribute values of a tuple, independently of other attribute values in the tuple and of other tuples in the relation.

The following is a simple example of a domain-based transaction in SQL [D].

2.1 Example. Suppose a relation EMP (employee) has been defined (its attributes are NAME, DEPT, RANK, and SALARY). The following transaction hires Moe as the new manager of the parts department, with a salary of 30K, then fires all managers from the parts department other than Moe. Finally, all employees from the parts department who are not managers are transfered to the service department. The rank remains unchanged. The new salary is 20K:

```
insert into EMP values ('moe','parts','manager',30K)
delete from EMP where NAME ≠ 'moe' and DEPT = 'parts'
        and RANK = 'manager'
update EMP set DEPT = 'service', SALARY = 20K
      where DEPT = 'parts' and RANK ≠ 'manager'.□
```

We now define the notions of a "condition" and satisfaction of a condition by a tuple.

Definition. Let U be a set of attributes. A *condition* over U is an expression of the form A=a or A≠ a, where $A \in U$ and $a \in dom(A)$. A tuple u over U *satisfies* a condition A=a (A≠ a) iff u(A) = a (u(A) ≠ a). A tuple u *satisfies* a set C of conditions if it satisfies every condition in C. We do not explicitly use logical connectors to build up complex conditions. It can be easily seen that this would not add power to our transactions. In the following, only *satisfiable* sets of conditions are considered, that is, sets of conditions with no mutually exclusive conditions. Although the conditions use only equality and inequality, this assumption is not central to the development (it is straightforward to extend the conditions so that comparisons of the form A>a, A<a are allowed).

A set of conditions over U is used to specify a set of tuples over U (those satisfying the conditions). Due to the form of our conditions, we use the intuitively suggestive term "hyperplane" to identify such sets of tuples:

Definition The *hyperplane* H(U,C) defined by a (satisfiable) set C of conditions over U is the set $\{t \in Tup(U) \mid t \text{ satisfies } C\}$.

For simplicity, we sometimes use the same notation for a set C of conditions over U and for the hyperplane H(U,C) defined by C. Thus, we say "hyperplane C" instead of "hyperplane H(U,C)", whenever U is understood. The *support* of a hyperplane H(U,C) is the set of attributes {A | A = a is in C for some a}. Thus the suppport of the hyperplane defined by {A=0, B=1, C≠5} is AB.

We now define the updates used to build our transactions. An *insertion* over a database schema **R** is an expression $i_X(C)$ where **X** is a relation schema in **R** and C is a set of conditions specifying a complete tuple over X. A *deletion* over **R** is an expression $d_X(C)$, where X is a relation schema in **R** and C is a set of conditions over **X**. Finally, a modification over **R** is an expression $m_X(C_1; C_2)$, where X is a relation schema in **R**, C_1 and C_2 are sets of conditions over X and, for each A in X, either(1) $C_1|_A = C_2|_A$ or $A = a \in C_2$. (The equalities present in C_2 but not in C_1 indicate how tuples in $H(X, C_1)$ are modified.) Note that, if m(C_1; C_2)

(1) If C is a set of conditions over U and A ∈ U, then $C|_A$ denotes the set of conditions in C involving attribute A.

is a modification, then support(C_1) $\subseteq$ support(C_2). An *update* is an insertion, deletion, or modification. Following is an example of updates.

2.2 Example. Consider again the database of Example 2.1. The following are updates over U, corresponding to the SQL updates in Example 2.1:

1) i_U (<moe, parts, manager, 30K>),
2) d_U (NAME ≠ moe, DEPARTMENT = parts, RANK = manager)
   (this deletes all managers in the parts department whose names are not Moe),
3) m_U (DEPARTMENT = parts, RANK ≠ manager;
   DEPARTMENT = service, RANK ≠ manager, SALARY = 20K)

This transfers all employees who are not managers from the parts department to the service department. The rank remains unchanged. The new salary is 20K. □

In the following we sometimes omit the subscripts in writing updates. For instance, we write i(C) instead of $i_X(C)$, whenever X is understood.

A *transaction* over a database schema **R** is a finite sequence of updates over **R** (the empty sequence is denoted by ε). The semantics of a transaction t is defined by a mapping associating old instances and new instances, called the *effect* of t and denoted by eff(t) (see [AV] for formal definition of effect). Two transactions are *equivalent* if they have the same effects.

Since the effects of updates over different relation schemas are independent, we will consider from now on only transactions over uni-relational schemas.

We next introduce a non-procedural method for describing the effect of a transaction on a database. The effect is described at the tuple level using the notion of a "transition". Transitions can be specified in an intuitively appealing manner and are useful tools. For each tuple, a transition indicates whether the tuple is deleted or, if not, how it is updated. In addition, a transition gives a finite set of inserted tuples. A transition will be specified by first partitioning the space of tuples into sufficiently many hyperplanes, so that all tuples in each hyperplane of the partition are either deleted or updated to yield another hyperplane in the partition. This is specified using a "transition graph" whose vertices are the hyperplanes in the partition. If H_1 is updated to H_2, there is an edge from H_1 to H_2. If H_1 is deleted there is no edge leaving H_1. The set of inserted tuples cannot be conveniently specified using the graph, and is given separately. A *transition specification (spec)* is a pair <G, Insert>, where G is a transition graph and Insert is a set of newly inserted tuples (called the insert set of the transition spec). A transition specification <G,Insert> is *normalized* if its vertices are disjoint hyperplanes whose union is the domain of the relation, and if there is no edge (C1,C2) in G such that $C2 \in Insert$.

We now give a simple example of a transition spec (see [AV] for the formal definition of transition specs and for more elaborate examples).

2.3 Example. Let U = AB and G be the transition graph represented below (Figure 2.1).

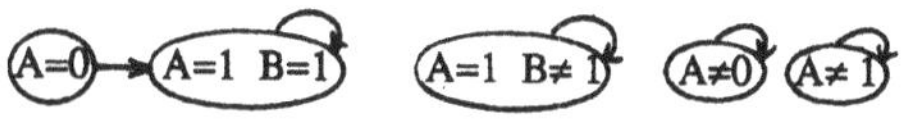

Figure 2.1

Let Insert = {<1,1>}. Then (G,Insert) is a transition specification over AB. The transition specified by (G,Insert) consists of replacing all tuples t where t(A) = 0 by the tuple <1,1>. All other tuples remain unchanged. The tuple <1,1> is inserted. □

We next look at the relation between transactions and transitions. For each transaction there exists a corresponding transition spec which represents the final effect of the transaction. In order to construct the transition spec corresponding to a transaction, it is first necessary to perform some "preprocessing" of the transaction. Specifically, the transaction is modified so that all hyperplanes corresponding to distinct sets of conditions occurring in the transaction are disjoint. A transaction having this property is said to be in *First Normal Form* (1NF). The 1NF property simplifies considerably our algorithms and results. It is shown in [AV] that every transaction can be transformed into an equivalent 1NF transaction by "splitting" every hyperplane occurring in it into sufficiently small hyperplanes.

2.4 Examples

(i) Consider the transaction over AB:
i(<0,3>) m ({A=0} ; {A=1, B=1}). The corresponding transition specification is the one of Example 2.3.

(ii) The transition specification corresponding to the transaction over A:
d({A=2}) m({A=0}; {A=2}) m({A=1} ; {A=0}) m{(A=2} ; {A=1}) is $<G, \phi>$, where G is represented in Figure 2.2.□

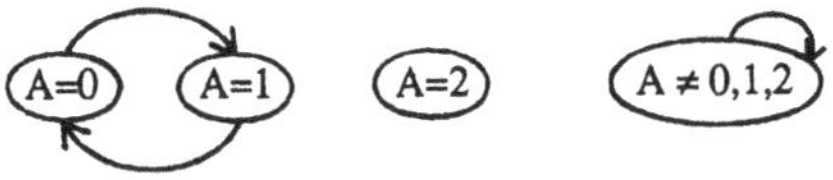

Figure 2.2

Note that the transition graph in Fig. 2.2 has a cycle. A transaction whose transition graph has no cycles is called *acyclic*. Thus, the transaction (i) is acyclic. Transaction (ii) is cyclic. Note that transaction (ii) implements the cycle by using the hyperplane {A=2} as "temporary storage". It is shown in [AV] that a transaction must always use some temporary storage to implement a cycle. It follows that transition graphs where no hyperplanes are "available" for use as temporary storage cannot be realized by any transaction. For instance, if hyperplane {A=2} in Fig. 2.2 is left unchanged rather than deleted, the transition graph is not realizable. A formal characterization of realizable transition specifications is given in [AV]. A *syntactic cycle* is a transaction of the form $m(C_1;C_T)m(C_k;C_1)m(C_{k-1};C_k)...m(C_2;C_3)m(C_T;C_2)$. Note that a syntactic cycle implements a cycle involving hyperplanes $C_1, \ldots, C_k$, using C_T as temporary storage.

In [KKPV], a sound and complete set of axioms for proving transaction equivalence is exhibited. Of these, we only need in this paper axioms indicating when two updates commute. For example, $d(C_1)\,i(C_2) \approx i(C_2)\,d(C_1)$ $(C_1 \neq C_2)$ is a commutativity axiom.

3. Parallel Transactions

In this section the notion of a parallel transaction is introduced. The "in-line" syntax for specifying parallel transactions is defined and compared to the specification using partial orders of updates. Some technical properties of parallel transactions are established, which help to understand the factors limiting parallelism within a transaction.

Definition. A *parallel transaction* is a partially ordered set of updates (A,<) such that two updates e_i and e_j in A are incomparable with respect to the ordering relation "<" only if e_i and e_j commute.

We will represent a parallel transaction using the Hasse diagram of its partial order, defined next.

Definition. A *Hasse diagram* of a partially ordered set (S, <) is a directed graph (V,E) where the vertex set V = S, and $(e_1, e_2) \in$ E if and only if

(i) $e_1 < e_2$ and

(ii) there is no e_3 in S such that $e_1 \neq e_3, e_2 \neq e_3$ and $e_1 < e_3 < e_2$.

The Hasse diagram representing the partial order of a parallel transaction t = (A, <) is called the *parallel transaction graph* of t (PTG(t)). The *effect* eff(t) of a parallel transaction t is the effect of any sequential transaction t' which is a linear extension of t. The *transition specification* of t is the transition specification of any linear extension of t. Two parallel transactions t_i and t_j are *equivalent* ($t_i \approx t_j$) if and only if $eff(t_i) = eff(t_j)$.

It is clear that parallel transactions include the sequential transactions as a special case. It follows from the definition of a parallel transaction that all the sequential transactions that are linear extensions of a given parallel transaction t have the same effect and the same transition specification. Hence, the effect and the transition specification of a parallel transaction are well defined.

We now introduce a measure of complexity of parallel transactions, called the "length". The length of a parallel transaction indicates the maximum number of updates of the transaction which must be performed sequentially. The length of a parallel transaction t is equal to the time required for the execution of t on a parallel computer assuming that the number of available parallel processors is sufficiently large and that each update is performed by a processor in one unit of time.

Definition. Let $t=(A, <)$ be a parallel transaction. The *parallel time* of update e in t, denoted ptime(e), is the length of a longest sequence of updates $e_1, e_2, \cdots, e_k$ such that $e_i < e_{i+1}$ $(1 \le i < k)$ and $e_k = e$. The *length* $|t|$ of t is the maximum of ptime(e) over all updates e in A. For each positive integer τ, the transaction $t^{(\tau)}$ is the parallel transaction defined as the restriction of t = (A, <) to the updates e in t such that ptime$(e) \le \tau$. The transaction $t^{(>\tau)}$ is the restriction of (A, <) to the updates e in t such that ptime(e) > τ. A parallel transaction t^* is *optimal* if there is no parallel transaction t such that $t \approx t^*$ and $|t| < |t^*|$.

The above definition of a parallel transaction has the disadvantage that specifying a parallel transaction involves specifying a parallel transaction graph, which is impractical. To remedy this difficulty we introduce a restricted class of parallel transactions, called the "in-line parallel transactions", which can be specified using a more pleasant syntax.

Definition: The set IPTrans(U) of *in-line parallel transactions* over a set of attributes U is the set of all expressions obtained by a finite number of applications of the following rules (note that the effect and length of in-line parallel transactions are defined concomitantly):

(i) Each sequential transaction over U is also in IPTrans(U).

(ii) If t_1 and t_2 are in IPTrans(U) then $t_1;t_2$ is in *IPTrans* (*U*), $eff(t_1;t_2) = eff(t_1) \circ eff(t_2)$, and $|t_1;t_2| = |t_1| + |t_2|$.

(iii) If $t_1, \ldots, t_n$ are in IPTrans (U) and for each i, j, $1 \le i < j \le n$, each update in t_i commutes with each update in t_j, then
$(t_1 | t_2 | \cdots | t_n)$ is in IPTrans(U),
$eff((t_1 | t_2 | \cdots | t_n)) = eff(t_1 \cdots t_n)$ and(2)
$|(t_1 | t_2 | \cdots | t_n)| = \max\{|t_i| : 1 \le i \le n\}$.

The following algorithm produces an in-line transaction that is equivalent to the parallel transaction t given as input.

Algorithm IN-LINE
Input: A PTG G of parallel transaction t.
Output: An in-line transaction equivalent to t.
Set i=0 and repeat until there are no more vertices in G

(2) Note that, due to the condition required of the t_i's, $eff(t_1 \cdots t_n) = eff(t_{\sigma(1)} t_{\sigma(2)} \ldots t_{\sigma(n)})$ for every permutation σ of n.

```
begin
increment i;
set j=0;
repeat for each vertex e in G that has indegree zero
      begin
      increment j;
      set e_ij = e;
      remove e from G;
      end
set n_i = j
end
output (e_11 | e_12 | ··· | e_1n_1); ··· ;(e_i1 | ··· | e_in_i)
```

It is easy to verify that Algorithm IN-LINE runs in polynomial time. The correctness of the algorithm follows from the easily verifiable fact that the partial order of the input transaction t is contained in the partial order induced by the output in-line transaction t'. It is also easy to see that the length of t' is equal to the length of the input parallel transaction t. Indeed, if the updates (e_1, e_2) form an edge in the parallel transaction graph of t, and if that edge belongs to some maximum path in the graph, then e_1 and e_2 are assigned the labels (i,j) and (i+1,k) for some i, j and k. Hence, we have the following.

3.1 Proposition. Algorithm IN-LINE runs in polynomial time. For any parallel transaction t the algorithm IN-LINE produces an in-line transaction t' such that $t' \approx t$ and $|t'|=|t|$.

Remark. Although the output of Algorithm IN-LINE is equivalent to the input parallel transaction and has equal length, it is clear that some loss of information occurs when a parallel transaction is represented by a corresponding in-line transaction produced by the algorithm. For example, consider the transaction t whose parallel transaction graph is $(\{e_1,e_2,e_3\},\{(e_1,e_3)\})$. The in-line parallel transaction corresponding to t produced by Algorithm IN-LINE is $t'=(e_1 | e_2);e_3$. In the transition from t to t' the information that e_2 and e_3 can be performed concurrently is lost. Note that, in this case, the complete information can be captured by a different in-line transaction: $(e_1;e_3 | e_2)$. However, there are parallel transactions for which there is no in-line transaction capturing precisely the same information. For instance, consider the parallel transaction graph G = $(\{e_1,e_2,e_3,e_4\}, \{(e_1,e_3),(e_1,e_4),(e_2,e_4)\})$. It is easily seen that, in every in-line transaction consistent with G, either e_3 precedes e_4, or e_2 precedes e_3. It is straightforward to modify Algorithm IN-LINE so that the output in-line transaction captures the same information as the input, if such an in-line transaction exists. We do not do this because the information lost when applying Algorithm IN-LINE does not affect the length of the output, which we use here as a measure of parallelism. The additional information may become relevant if a more refined measure of parallelism is used. □

Given a sequential, or, more generally, a parallel transaction, it is desirable to find an equivalent parallel transaction of minimal length. This gives rise to an optimization problem that is the focus of this paper. We first present an example of a parallel transaction and its corresponding optimal parallel transaction.

3.2 Example. Figure 3.1 exhibits (a) a PTG of a transaction t, (b) the PTG of a corresponding optimal parallel transaction t^* and (c) the in-line parallel transaction that corresponds to t^*. Intuitively, t^* is obtained by "cutting" the long path in the PTG of t into segments. This is accomplished by implementing some of the updates on the long path by pairs of modifications, using the empty hyperplanes corresponding to the leaves of short paths as temporary storage.□

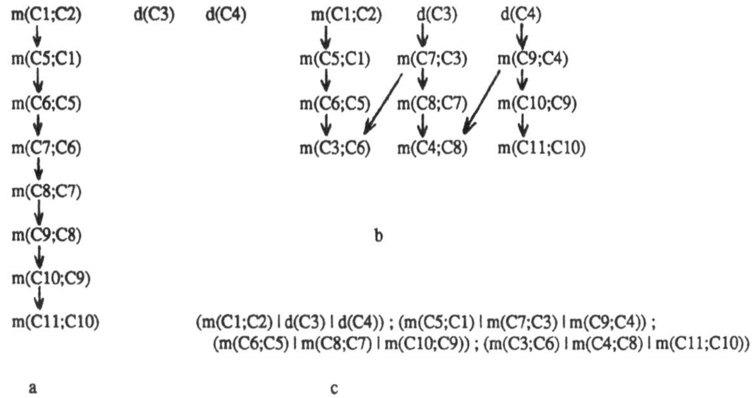

Figure 3.1.

We next present some technical concepts and results that will help understand the factors that limit parallelism within a parallel transaction. These results will then be used to evaluate the complexity of the optimization problem and, in the next section, to develop parallelization algorithms.

We use normalized transition specifications to represent effects of transactions to be parallelized. Recall that the normalized transition specification of transaction t is obtained from a transition specification of t by removing all directed edges (C_1,C_2) from G that end at hyperplanes that are inserted by t. Intuitively, the reason for using the normalized transition specifications is the following. If the removed edge is a loop, then deleting the corresponding hyperplane does not change the effect of the transaction. This increases the number of deleted hyperplanes that can subsequently be used as temporary storage to speed up the computation. On the other hand, increasing the number of deletions does not in general increase the length of a parallel transaction since all deletions can be performed in parallel. If $C_1 \neq C_2$ then the corresponding edge in the transition graph has to be implemented by modifications, hence deleting the edge is likely to reduce the number of modifications. Notice that such an edge can be removed (and the corresponding modification turned into a deletion) and the effect will not change.

We say that the hyperplane C is *deleted* by transaction t if C has no outgoing edges in the normalized transition graph G of t. Hyperplane C is *emptied* by t if C has no ingoing edges in G. Hyperplane C_1 is *stored in* hyperplane C_2 by t if there is an edge (C_1,C_2) in G.

It is clear (see Example 3.1) that if many hyperplanes are deleted by a transaction t, then t will be likely to have an equivalent parallel transaction of a small length. Indeed, it is easy to see that if the number of hyperplanes that are deleted by a transaction t is as large as half of the total number of hyperplanes of t, and if all the hyperplanes have the same support, then there always exists a parallel transaction equivalent to t whose length does not exceed the constant four (the deletions are done in the first parallel step, all the modifications required to implement the edges in the transition graph of t are done in the second and third step, and the insertions are done in the last, fourth step). Of course, an arbitrary transaction t will in general not have such an efficient parallelization even if all its hyperplanes have the same support. We now discuss the factors that limit parallelism within a parallel transaction.

To begin with, it is clear that the number of hyperplanes that can be deleted and then used as temporary storage to speed up the computation is limited. Indeed, when a hyperplane is deleted, its contents are permanently lost. Hence only those hyperplanes that are deleted by t can be deleted. This gives rise to the following technical result.

3.3 Lemma. Let $e=d(C)$ be a deletion in a parallel transaction t, let (G,I) be the transition specification of t. Then each hyperplane that is stored in C by $t^{(ptime(e)-1)}$ is deleted by t.□

Intuitively, since all the deletions as well as all the insertions can be performed concurrently, the number of modifications will provide a measure of the essential part of "work" that needs to be done by any parallel transaction that is equivalent to some given transaction t. We focus on modifications that are likely to contribute to the effect of the transaction.

Definition. A modification $e=m(C_1;C_2)$ of a parallel transaction t is *active* if

(i) $C_1 \neq C_2$ and

(ii) if $t^{(ptime(e)-1)}$ stores some hyperplane C in C_1 then C is not deleted by t.

Note that a non-active modification can either be removed (i) or replaced by a deletion (ii). In particular, a non-active modification does not contribute towards implementing an edge in the normalized transition graph.

The number of active modifications in a transaction t is related to the number of edges (excluding loops) in a normalized transition graph of t, as those edges have to be implemented by modifications. Cycles require one additional modification for using the temporary storage, unless there is a "natural" storage for that cycle (i.e., a hyperplane adjacent to the cycle, with the same support as the hyperplanes in the cycle). The set of cycles in a transition graph G which have *no* natural storage is denoted Cyclesadj(G). The following result formalizes the connection between active modifications in a parallel transaction and edges in its normalized transition graph. It is a direct consequence of Lemma 6.1 in [AV].

3.4 Lemma. Let (G,I) be the normalized transition specification of some parallel transaction t, where G = (V(G), E(G)), and M the number of active modifications in t. Then $M \geq |\{(A,B) \in E(G) : A \neq B\}| + |Cyclesadj(G)|$.□

Modifications can not always be performed in parallel due to precedence constraints that exist between modifications. The next result follows from the observation that if two hyperplanes are stored in a common hyperplane, they can not be subsequently separated.

3.5 Lemma. Let t be a parallel transaction, and let C_1, C_2, C be any hyperplanes such that (C_1,C) and (C_2,C) are edges in the transition graph of $t^{(\tau)}$ for some τ. Then either C_1 and C_2 are both deleted by t or C_1 and C_2 are stored in some common hyperplane by t.

We are now ready to define and discuss the parallel transaction optimization problem.

Definition. An algorithm solves the *Parallel Transaction Optimization (PTO)* problem if, given as input a parallel transaction t, it produces as output an optimal parallel transaction t' such that $t' \approx t$.

The following shows that the PTO problem is intractable even in a simplified version.

3.6 Theorem. The parallel transaction optimization problem is NP-complete even when the input transactions consist only of deletions and modifications, all the hyperplanes in the input transaction have the same support, and all vertices in the transition specification graph have indegrees no greater than one.

Proof. As customary, we prove NP completeness using the "language recognition" version of the PTO problem. We say that an algorithm solves the (language recognition) PTO problem if, given a parallel transaction t and an integer K as input, it decides whether there exists a parallel transaction t' such that $t' \approx t$ and $|t'| < K$.

It is easy to see that the language recognition PTO is in NP, since a nondeterministic Turing machine can "guess" a parallel transaction t', verify that $t' \approx t$ by comparing the corresponding transition specifications, and then verify if $|t'| < K$, all in polynomial time. The proof that the PTO is NP-hard is by reduction from 3-PARTITION.

An instance of 3-PARTITION consists of a finite set A of $3m$ elements, a bound $B \in Z^+$, and a "size" $s(a) \in Z^+$ for each $a \in A$, such that each $s(a)$ satisfies $B/4 < s(a) < B/2$ and the sum of the sizes of all elements in A is equal to mB. An algorithm solves the 3-PARTITION problem if it decides whether A can be partitioned into m disjoint sets $S_1, S_2, \cdots, S_m$ such that, for each set S_i, the sum of sizes of the elements of S_i is equal to B. It is known that the 3-PARTITION problem is NP-complete even when all the element sizes are bounded by a polynomial function of the total number of elements (see the discussion in [GJ], p.99).

We now show that the PTO problem is NP-hard by exhibiting a polynomial-time reduction of the 3-PARTITION with element sizes bounded from above by a polynomial in the number of set elements, to the restricted version of the PTO. Given an instance of the 3-PARTITION problem, the corresponding instance (t,K) of the PTO is constructed as follows. The input parallel transaction t is actually sequential and consists of m deletions of the form d(C1), ..., d(Cm), where Ci = {A = i}, followed by a sequence of $3m$ syntactic cycles, one for each element of the set A. The syntactic cycle for each element a_i of A consists of a sequence of M=$s(a_i)$ modifications of the form $m(C_{i1};C_1)m(C_{i2};C_{i1}) \cdots m(C_{iM-1};C_{iM-2})m(C_1;C_{iM-1})$, where C_{ij} = {A = iB + m + j} (this guarantees that the C_{ij}'s are disjoint). Note that each such syntactic cycle implements a cycle of length s(a_i)-1, using C_1 as temporary storage. The constant K is set to B+1.

It is clear that this transformation can be done in time that is polynomial in the size of the 3-PARTITION instance. It is left to show that the instance of the PTO has an affirmative solution if and only if the instance of 3-PARTITION has an affirmative solution. The idea of the proof is that the PTO has an affirmative solution iff the 3m syntactic cycles can be equally distributed among the m empty hyperplanes C_i in groups of three, such that the three syntactic cycles assigned to C_i use C_i as temporary storage. Clearly, this can be done iff the instance of 3-PARTITION has a solution. We now sketch the proof. Notice that the normalized transition graph G of the transaction t consists only of cycles and vertices with no incident edges. Consider an arbitrary parallel transaction t_1 that is equivalent to t. By Lemma 3.4, t_1 contains at least mB active modifications. It is easy to verify, using the Lemmas 3.3 and 3.5 and the fact that all the indegrees in in the transition graph G of t are at most one, that for any τ there are at most m active modifications e in t_1 such that ptime(e)=τ. There are exactly k active modifications in the parallel step τ only if at least k hyperplanes are empty at the beginning of τ. Since no hyperplanes are empty prior to the first parallel step, no modifications can be performed in the first parallel step. Hence if $|t_1|$=B+1 then the first parallel step of t_1 consists of m deletions, and then mB modifications are performed in the following B parallel steps, m of them at a time in parallel. It is easy to see that this is possible if and only if the syntactic cycles can be partitioned into m subsets of three syntactic cycles each, such that the number of modifications in each subset is equal to B. (The three syntactic cycles in the same subset must use the same hyperplane C_i as temporary storage.) This is equivalent to existence of a solution to the 3-PARTITION instance. □

Although the above NP-completeness proof uses an instance of the PTO corresponding to a cyclic transaction, the NP-completeness result holds even if the input instances are restricted to contain only acyclic transactions. A proof similar to the above exists for this version of the PTO problem.

4. Approximate Optimization Algorithms

Since the PTO problem can be solved in polynomial time only in the highly unlikely case that P=NP, practically feasible approximate algorithms are needed for solving the problem. In this section we consider several such algorithms. We first introduce polynomial-time algorithms for two special cases, and show that they approximate the exact solutions within an absolute constant (one and two, respectively). Finally, we use these algorithms to develop a polynomial-time algorithm for the general case, which approximates the exact solution within a constant factor.

The two special cases we consider involve transactions using only hyperplanes with the same support. It is helpful to think of the problem in this case in terms of the following intuitively suggestive problem. Suppose m boxes B1,...,Bm are given. Initially, each box Bi is either empty or contains some balls. Balls can be moved among boxes by any sequence of *moves*, m(Bj, Bk) each of which consists of putting the entire content of box Bj into box Bk. Suppose that the balls must be re-distributed among boxes according to a given mapping f from boxes to boxes (f(Bj)=Bk means that the content of box Bj must wind up in box Bk after the re-distribution). The PTO problem in this case is to find a parallel schedule of moves which accomplish the re-distribution in minimal time (assuming that each move takes one unit of time). Theorem 3.6 shows that this problem is NP-complete. However, as we shall see next, this problem has a very good polynomial-time approximte algorithm, which produces a solution differing from the optimal at most by the absolute constant 1. Clearly, the problem described above is fairly general and is likely to occur in other situations as well.

We now exhibit our approximate algorithm for the restricted PTO where the transition graph of the input transaction contains hyperplanes with the same support and in-degree at most one. The algorithm first generates a parallel transaction graph that corresponds directly to the transition graph of the input transaction. Because of the indegree restriction, the parallel transaction graph consists only of paths and isolated vertices. The paths in the PTG are subsequently equalized by "cutting" the long paths and "pasting" to them short paths.

Algorithm FIRST APPROXIMATION

Input: A transaction t whose normalized transition specification is (G, ∅) such that all the hyperplanes in G have the same support and indegree no larger than one.

Output: A PTG P of parallel transaction t' such that $t' \approx t$.

1. Compute the normalized transition specification (G,∅) of t.

2. Set P=COMPUTE-PTG(G).

3. Set $K = \left\lceil \frac{|P|}{q} \right\rceil + 1$, where $|P|$ is the number of updates in P and q is the number of connected components in P.

4. Repeat while there exists an update e in P s.t. ptime(e)=K and outdegree of e is not equal to zero.

begin

CUT-AND-PASTE(e);

end

6. Output P.

Procedure COMPUTE-PTG(G)

1. Set P=(∅,∅).

2. For each hyperplane C in G that has no outgoing edges add a deletion d(C) to P.

3. For each directed path in G that does not belong to a cycle add a corresponding sequence of modifications (directed path) to P, and an edge from the first modification to the appropriate deletion.

4. For each cycle in G add to P a syntactic cycle S that implements the cycle by using an arbitrary empty hyperplane C as temporary storage. Add an edge from the update that empties C to the first update of S.

5. Return P.

Procedure CUT-AND-PASTE(e)

1. Find an update e_1 in P with outdegree equal to zero s.t. ptime(e_1) $\leq K-2$. Then either e_1=d(C1) or e_1=m(C1;C2) for some hyperplanes C1,C2. Let e = m(C3;C4), for some hyperplanes C3 and C4.

2. Add a new vertex e_2 = m(C1,C4) to P.

3. Replace the unique edge from the ancestor of e to e by an edge from the same ancestor to e_2.

4. Replace e by e_3= m(C3,C1) in both the vertex set and in the edge set of P.

5. Add edges (e_3,e_2) and (e_1,e_3) to P.

Remark. The empty hyperplane used for temporary storage in Step 4 of COMPUTE-PTG exists by Lemma 5.5 in [AV].

4.1 Theorem. (i) Algorithm FIRST APPROXIMATION runs in polynomial time.
(ii) Let t be a transaction that consist of only deletions and modifications, such that all the hyperplanes in t have the same support and the vertices in the transition specification graph of t have the indegrees no larger than one. Let t' be the parallel transaction produced by FIRST APPROXIMATION under input t. Then $|t'| \leq |t^*|+1$, where t^* is the optimal parallel transaction corresponding to t.

Proof (outline). It is easy to verify that FIRST APPROXIMATION runs in polynomial time, hence we focus on (ii). The proof of (ii) is in two steps:

(*) $|t'| \leq K$.

(**) $|t^*| \geq K-1$.

The proof of (*) consists of showing that CUT-AND-PASTE can always be performed (i.e., if there exists an update e with ptime(e) ≥ K and non-zero outdegree, then there exists another update f with out-degree zero such that ptime(f) ≤ K-2) and proving that the algorithm terminates. This is clearly sufficient due to the termination condition of the main loop (step 4).

To see (**), consider an arbitrary active modification e = m(C1;C2) in the optimal parallel transaction t^*. Since all the indegrees in the transition specification graph of the input transaction are no larger than one, it follows by Lemma 3.5 that if ptime(e) = τ then (i) C2 is empty at the beginning of parallel step τ and (ii) there is no active modification m(C3,C2), for some hyperplane C3, that can be performed concurrently with e. Hence, at any time τ, t^* can perform at most as many modifications as there are emptied hyperplanes after parallel step $\tau-1$. By Lemmas 3.3 and 3.5 there are at most as many empty hyperplanes in t^* at any time as there are zero-outdegree hyperplanes in G. By construction, the number of zero-outdegree hyperplanes in G equals the number q of connected components of P (step 2). Thus, t^* can perform at most q active modifications in each parallel step. On the other hand, from Lemma 3.4 it follows that any parallel transaction equivalent to t must perform at least as many active modifications as in P, that is, |P| - q. Additionally, only deletions can be performed in the first parallel step of t^*. Thus, $|t^*| \geq 1 + \left\lceil \frac{|P|-q}{q} \right\rceil$ = K - 1.□

The above result suggests that there may exist good approximation algorithms even for more general PTO problems. We now show that that is indeed the case. The following algorithm computes a nearly optimal parallel transaction for any transaction in which all the hyperplanes have the same support.

We first explain the intuitive idea behind the algorithm, and then define the algorithm in detail. It is clear that, if a certain hyperplane has several ingoing edges in the transition graph, then the modifications that correspond to those edges can be executed in parallel. Then not only multiple active modifications are done at a time, but also empty hyperplanes are created, which can subsequently be used as temporary storages to speed up the computation.

The algorithm has two phases. The first phase (Steps 1 to 10) divides the hyperplanes into equivalence classes of hyperplanes that are stored into the same hyperplane by the input transaction t. It then generates the first parallel step of the output parallel transaction in which all the hyperplanes that are deleted by t are deleted by deletions, and all the hyperplanes for each equivalence class are joined together into one member of the class by modifications.

The problem that remains to be solved after the first phase is exactly the one solved by Algorithm FIRST APPROXIMATION, hence FIRST APPROXIMATION is called to finish the job. All insertions are performed in the last parallel step. The algorithm is defined in detail below, and illustrated by an example in Figure 4.1.

Algorithm SECOND APPROXIMATION
Input: A transaction t such that all the hyperplanes
in t have the same support.
Output: A PTG P of a a parallel transaction t' such that $t' \approx t$.

1. **Compute the normalized transition specification (G,I) of t.**
2. **Set $P=(\emptyset,\emptyset)$.**
3. **Repeat for each vertex C in G that has no outgoing edges:**
    4. **Add a vertex d(C) to P.**
5. **Divide the vertices of G that have outdegrees greater than zero into equivalence classes such that a vertex C_j is in the equivalence class $S(C_i)$ if (C_j,C_i) is an edge in G.**
6. **Repeat for each equivalence class $S(C_i)$**
    begin

if $S(C_i)$ has more than one element then
begin
7. Set C_i^0=SELECT-ELEMENT($S(C_i)$).
8. Repeat for each $C_j \in S(C_i)$ such that $C_j \neq C_i^0$:
9. Add vertex m(C_j, C_i^0) to P.
10. Remove edge (C_j, C_i) from G.
end
end
11. Run FIRST APPROXIMATION on G and P omitting Steps 1 and 2.
12. Repeat for each vertex e in P created in Steps 4 and 9:
13 Repeat for each vertex e_1 created in Step 11:
if e_1 has no ingoing edges in P then
14 Add edge (e, e_1) to P.
13. Repeat for each hyperplane C such that $C \in I$
begin
14. Add vertex e=i(C) to P.
15. Repeat for each vertex $e_1 \neq e$ in P:
if e_1 has no outgoing edges in P then
14. Add edge (e_1, e) to P.
end

16. Output P.
Procedure SELECT-ELEMENT($S(C_i)$)
if $C_i \in S(C_i)$ then
1. Set $C = C_i$.
else if C_i belongs to a cycle in G and there exists
a $C_j \in S(C_i)$ that is not on the cycle and
that has the same support as C_i then
2. Set $C = C_j$.
else
3. Set $C = C_k$ where C_k is an arbitrary
element of $S(C_i)$.
4. Return(C).

4.2 Theorem. (i) Algorithm SECOND APPROXIMATION is polynomial-time in the number of updates of the input. (ii) Let t' be the parallel transaction produced by SECOND_APPROXIMATION on input t, let t^* be an optimal parallel transaction equivalent to t. Then $|t'| \leq |t^*|+2$. If t has no insertions then $|t'| \leq |t^*|+1$.

The proof is similar to that of Theorem 4.1.

So far we considered a restricted version of the PTO problem, where all hyperplanes have the same support. We next consider the general case, where hyperplanes may have different supports. In that case we can divide the hyperplanes into equivalence classes of hyperplanes with the same support. Intuitively, since the number of different equivalence classes is fixed and relatively small, most of the computation still occurs within individual equivalence classes. This suggests that a reasonable approximation algorithm can be obtained simply by applying the SECOND APPROXIMATION algorithm to each equivalence class independently. This gives rise to the following algorithm (G/S denotes the subgraph of G spanned by a subset S of the vertices).

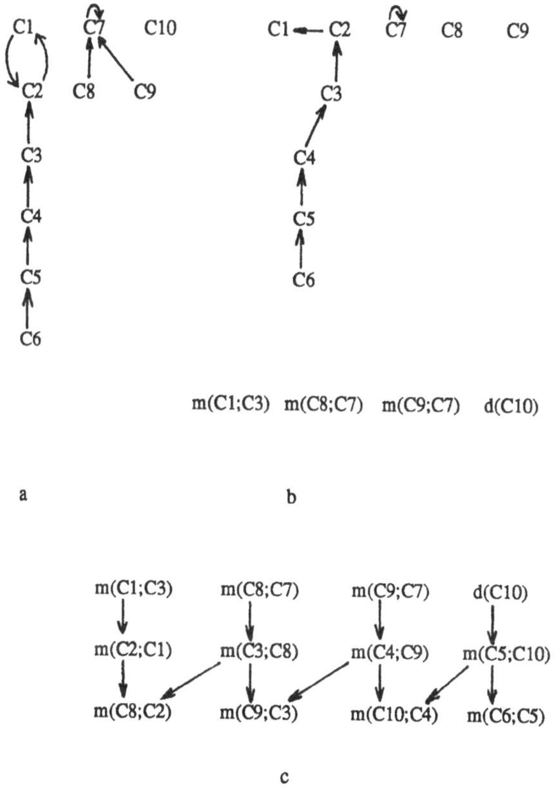

Figure 4.1. (a) Normalized transition graph G of the input transaction, (b) G and P before Step 11, and (c) the output PTG.

Algorithm THIRD APPROXIMATION

Input: A transaction t over a set U of attributes.

Output: A PTG P of a parallel transaction t', $t' \approx t$.

1. **Set $P=(\emptyset,\emptyset)$.**
2. **Compute the normalized transition specification (G,I) of t.**
3. **Divide the vertices in G into equivalence classes of hyperplanes with equal support.**
4. **Repeat for each equivalence class S:**
   5. **Apply SECOND APPROXIMATION to P and $(G/S,\emptyset)$ if support $(S) \neq U$, or $(G/S,I)$ if support $(S)=U$, omitting Steps 1 and 2.**
6. **Repeat for each equivalence class S:**
   7. **Repeat for each edge (C_i, C_j) in G such that $C_i \in S$, $C_j \in S'$ and $S \neq S'$:**
      begin

8. Replace the vertex d(C_i) in the subgraph
of P that corresponds to S by e=m(C_i;C_j).
if there exists a vertex e' in the subgraph of P
corresponding to S' such that e'=d(C_j)
or e'=m(C_j;C_k) for some
hyperplane C_k and e' has no outgoing
edges in P then
9. Add edge (e',e) to P.
end
10. Output P.

4.3 Theorem. (i) Algorithm THIRD APPROXIMATION runs in polynomial time.
(ii) Let t' be the transaction produced by THIRD_APPROXIMATION under input t and let t^* be the optimal parallel transaction that corresponds to t. Then $|t'| \leq K|t^*|+K+1$, where K is the number of attributes in t.

Proof (outline). It is easy to see that THIRD APPROXIMATION is a polynomial-time algorithm. To prove (ii), it is first shown that, intuitively, any optimal t^* must also be optimal within each equivalence class of updates using the same support. Next, consider any sequence $S=e_1,e_2, \cdots ,e_m$ of updates in the PTG of t' such that $e_i<e_{i+1}$ and the number of updates in S is equal to $|t'|$. Since the existence of m(C1; C2) implies support (C1) $\subseteq$ support (C2), the hyperplanes in S belong to at most K distinct equivalence classes of hyperplanes with the same support. Consider the segments $s_1,s_2, \cdots ,s_m$ (m $\leq$ K) of S consisting of updates within the same equivalence class, in the order in which they appear in S. The length of segment s_1 is at most that of the output of SECOND-APPROXIMATION on the equivalence class of s_1. The length of each s_i, i > 1, is at most the length of the output of SECOND-APPROXIMATION on the equivalence class of s_i, minus one (it is easy to see that updates from the first parallel step produced by SECOND-APPROXIMATION on the equivalence class of s_i, i > 1, do not occur in the path considered). Thus, $|s_1| \leq |t^*| + 1$ and $|s_i| \leq |t^*|$. Thus, the maximum number of updates in S involving hyperplanes within the same equivalence class is $K|t^*|+1$. Additionally, S may contain at most $K-1$ modifications m(C_1;C_2), where support(C_1)$\subset$support(C_2). Thus, at most $K-1$ modifications in the sequence S involve hyperplanes from different equivalence classes. Finally, S contains at most one insertion. Hence, the length of S is at most $K|t^*|+K+1$. □

In practice the number K of attributes in a relational database is a small constant, hence the worst case behavior of THIRD APPROXIMATION will differ at most by a constant factor from the optimum. However, it is clear that the worst case occurs only in very unusual circumstances, and that the practical or expected behavior of the algorithm will be much better.

Remark. The behavior of the algorithm in practice can be improved by using some global information about the PTG of the input, rather just information local to each equivalence class of hyperplanes. Specifically, a modified version of the procedure FIRST APPROXIMATION can be used, which takes into account information about the *total* length of chains in the PTG, rather than just the length of chains within a given equivalence class. However, this approach does not improve the worst-case behavior of the algorithm. Indeed, we conjecture that approximating the solution of the PTO in the general case within an absolute constant is NP-complete.

References (1985).

[AV] Abiteboul, S., V. Vianu. Equivalence and Optimization of Relational Transactions, JACM 35, 1 (January 1988).

[BG] Bernstein, P., N. Goodman. Concurrency control in distributed database systems. Computing Surveys, Vol. 13, No. 2 (June 1981).

[D] Date, C.J. *A Guide to DB2*. Addison-Wesley (1984).

[GJ] Garey, M. R. and D. S. Johnson. *Computers and Intractability*. Freeman (1979).

[KKPV] Karabeg, A. D. Karabeg, K. Papakonstantinou, V. Vianu. Axiomatization and Simplification Rules for Relational Transactions, Proc. PODS (1987).

[M] Maier, D. *The theory of relational databases*. Computer Science Press (1983).

[PBR] Papadimitriou, C. H., B. A. Bernstein, J. B. Rothnie. Computational problems related to database concurrency control. Proc. Conf on Theoretical Computer Science, Waterloo, Ontario, Canada (1977).

[U] Ullman, J., *Principles of database systems*. Computer Science Press (1982).

Transformation of Dynamic Integrity Constraints into Transaction Specifications

Udo W. Lipeck
Informatik, Abteilung Datenbanken
Technische Universität Braunschweig
Postfach 3329, D-3300 Braunschweig, Fed. Rep. Germany

Abstract: Dynamic database behaviour can be specified by dynamic integrity constraints, which determine *admissible* sequences of database states, and by transaction specifications, which induce *executable* sequences. Constraints are expressed by formulae of temporal logic, whereas transactions are defined by pre/postconditions in predicate logic. This paper presents concepts and rules for transforming dynamic constraints into transaction specifications in order to prepare integrity monitoring by transactions. At first, such transition graphs must be constructed from temporal formulae that have paths corresponding to admissible sequences. Then these graphs are utilized to refine and to simplify pre/postconditions systematically, so that every executable state sequence becomes admissible, too.

Keywords: integrity, dynamic constraints, temporal logic, transition graphs, transactions, pre/ postconditions, monitoring, constraint simplification

1. Introduction

An essential aspect of database design is specification of dynamic database behaviour [BrMS84]. To this end, dynamic integrity constraints defining correctness of state sequences are stated as well as transaction specifications defining basic state changes. These two kinds of information will usually complement each other at an early stage of design. Together they restrict possible sequences of database states to sequences which are "admissible" *and* "executable", i.e. sequences which obey the constraints and are induced by transactions.

In order to ensure correct database behaviour, integrity constraints must be monitored explicitly or preserved by transactions implicitly. The first way needs a universal runtime monitor, which normally is expensive because of application independence and which has been avoided by most of today's DBMS even for static constraints. The other one relies on specifying all basic database accesses of application programs already at design time: It requires to verify transactions with respect to constraints, i.e., to prove that every executable state sequence is admissible, too.

To obtain such desirable transaction specifications systematically, integrity constraints should be incorporated into them by means of suitable transformations. Then verification often gets superfluous. A direct transformation of static constraints would be adding complete checks of all constraints (and possible compensating actions) to the end of every transaction; this method, however, only imitates a non-optimizing monitor. Considering constraints during transaction design offers the chance of adapting necessary checks to the objects and conditions affected by each transaction, so that an efficient implicit monitoring is prepared. Such transformations and simplifications should be done as far as possible during the design phase to obtain complete and final, but still implementation-independent specifications. Of course, some of the techniques might also be utilized for optimizations done by a runtime monitor.

In contrast to static integrity, dynamic constraints raise fundamental problems how to monitor such long-term conditions by single short-term state transitions and, as a consequence, how to transform them into transaction specifications. Since they may refer to entire intervals within a state sequence by relating several states (in one condition) including past and future states, a naive monitor would store complete database history and predict database future. A realizable approach, however, should allow to judge correctness (at least partially) from database behaviour up to a present state, and it should need only minimal historical information to check the constraints. In addition, simplifications should be made possible, too.

This paper proposes solutions to these problems within a framework of logical specifications. Dynamic integrity constraints can indeed be transformed into transaction specifications, so that all necessary checks are done by the transactions and are tailored to them. Here, constraints are expressed by formulae of temporal logic, whereas transactions are defined by pre/postconditions in ordinary predicate logic.

As far as dynamic integrity as a generalization of transitional integrity has been addressed in the literature, most of the approaches have favoured specifications based on temporal logic [Se80, CaCF82, CaF84, Ku84, LiEG85, FiS86]. Such a formalism allows to express conditions on state sequences, since predicate logic is extended by temporal operators like **always**...**until** or **sometime**... **before**; thus, arbitrary states within a sequence can be related, and explicit quantification over states or subsequences is avoided. Concerning transactions, pre/postconditions are a very widespread means of specification; for a comparison with other formalisms see, e.g., [VeCF81].

Requirements and methods of verifying given transaction specifications wrt dynamic constraints have been analyzed by several of the mentioned authors, too [CaCF82, CaVF84, Ku84, FiS86, CaS87]. All approaches, however, handle only examples or restricted patterns of temporal formulae. Example proofs and (automatable) proof-theoretic techniques for verifications wrt static constraints can be found in [GaM79] and [StS84, ShS85], respectively. Although the idea of transformation has been applied to static constraints in [FuSC81, WaS81] already, transformation methods for dynamic constraints have not yet been discussed by other authors. Only [VeF85] give recommendations *that* specification (and selection) of transactions should be refined to consider those constraints. Our former paper [Li86] contains ad-hoc transformation rules for simple temporal formulae, which are special cases of the theory presented here.

The important step of simplifying constraint formulae by exploiting knowledge about transactions has been inspired by [Ni82, HeMN84]. Their work concentrates on single or multiple relational updates, whereas our approach includes arbitrarily specified transactions.

Transformation of dynamic integrity constraints will rest on two key concepts for a transitional handling: First, it is made precise what partial admissibility of a state sequence up to a present state means. Taking this notion as the goal of monitoring, different procedures can be applied to temporal formulae in order to construct so-called transition graphs, whose paths correspond to (partially) admissible state sequences. A universal monitor would have to interpret these transition graphs by following paths, so that graph structure and reached nodes are the only informations needed apart from the present state. Pertinent theoretic foundations of monitoring dynamic integrity have been introduced in our papers [LiS87, SaL87]. Here, we aim at transforming transition graphs into refinements of pre/postconditions, such that each executable sequence becomes admissible, and at simplifying transformation results systematically.

The rest of the paper is structured as follows. The next two sections briefly introduce syntax and semantics of dynamic integrity constraints and transaction specifications. Section 4 summarizes results needed for the transitional interpretation of temporal formulae. Then Section 5 presents and verifies the transformation rules. This work is based on a detailed elaboration in the recent thesis [Li87].

2. Dynamic Integrity Constraints

Static constraints, which are to describe properties of database states, can usually be expressed by formulae of first order predicate logic. As a prerequisite, the structural elements of states (e.g., relations, tuples, and attributes) must have been represented by nonlogical predicate or function symbols and by some axioms, the so-called inherent constraints. To be independent from specific data models, we assume that such a functional description of objects is given. Thus the syntactic structure of states is defined by a signature as follows:

Definition 2.1: Let a fixed set of data types like Bool, Int, Text, and Year be given. An ***object signature*** OBJ = $\langle S_O, F_O \rangle$ consists of a set S_O of object sorts and a set F_O of function symbols together with their arities given by lists of object or data sorts. □

Example 2.2: In a signature for an "automobile registration authority" database the following object sorts and functions appear:

sorts	CAR, MODEL, CAR-OWNER		
functions	manuf[acturer]:	CAR ⟶ CAR-OWNER	
	registered:	CAR ⟶ Bool	
	reg[istration-]no:	CAR ⟶ Int	
	model:	CAR ⟶ MODEL	
	owner:	CAR ⟶ CAR-OWNER	
	[is-]approved:	MODEL ⟶ Bool	
	is-MANUF[ACTURER],		
	is-GARAGE, is-PERSON:	CAR-OWNER ⟶ Bool	/* types of car-owners */
	this-year:	⟶ Year	/* current year */ □

First order ***formulae*** are built from terms over function symbols (including data operators) and over variables by using equations, logical connectives (∧,∨,¬,...), and quantifications (∀, ∃) over object or data sorts. They are interpreted in ***states*** σ where each object sort s is mapped to a finite set σ(s) of ***actual objects*** and each function symbol f is mapped to an ***actual function*** σ(f) involving the specified sets of objects or data. For each object sort s, we assume to have a common superset Π(s) of ***possible objects***, the so-called "universe of discourse". Data types form a fixed part of the universe and of every state.

In order to specify properties of state sequences, we make use of temporal logic that extends predicate logic by special operators relating states within sequences. Temporal formulae are built from nontemporal, i.e. first-order formulae by using logical connectives and

- quantification over actual objects (∀,∃) and over possible objects ($\underline{\forall}$,$\underline{\exists}$)
- temporal quantification by **always** and **sometime**,
- bounded temporal quantification by **always/sometime** ... **before/until** and **from**,
- and temporal succession operators **next** and **onnext**.

Specification and transformation of dynamic constraints are restricted to ***propositional-temporal***

formulae avoiding object quantifications outside basic parts, which, however, may be arbitrary nontemporal formulae. Temporal formulae are interpreted in infinite or finite sequences of states $\underline{\sigma} = \langle\sigma_0, \sigma_1, \ldots\rangle$ or $\underline{\sigma} = \langle\sigma_0, \ldots, \sigma_{n-1}\rangle$, $n \geq 0$, for substitutions θ of their free variables by data or possible objects.

Notation 2.3: If a formula φ is ***valid*** in $\underline{\sigma}$ for θ, we write "$[\underline{\sigma},\theta] \models \varphi$". The same notation "$[\sigma,\theta] \models \rho$" is used for conventional validity of a nontemporal formula ρ in a state σ. "$\underline{\sigma} \models \varphi$" means that φ is valid in $\underline{\sigma}$ for arbitrary substitutions; in this case, $\underline{\sigma}$ is called ***admissible*** wrt φ. □

Subsequently, validity is defined by induction on formula structure:

Definition 2.4: Let α,ψ,τ be temporal formulae, ρ an atomic nontemporal formula, $\underline{\sigma}$ a state sequence, and θ a substitution. $I(\underline{\sigma})$ denotes the index range of $\underline{\sigma}$, i.e. $I(\langle\sigma_0,\sigma_1,\ldots\rangle) = \mathbb{N}$ and $I(\langle\sigma_0,\ldots,\sigma_{n-1}\rangle) = \{0,\ldots,n-1\}$; $\underline{\sigma}_i$, $i \in I(\underline{\sigma})$, denotes the i-th tail sequence $\langle\sigma_j \mid j \geq i \wedge j \in I(\underline{\sigma})\rangle$, and the index $\mu\tau$ stands for the first occurrence of τ, i.e. $\mu\tau = \min(\{j \in I(\underline{\sigma}) \mid [\underline{\sigma}_j,\theta] \models \tau\} \cup \{\infty\})$.

(0) $[\underline{\sigma},\theta] \models \rho$ iff all variables in ρ are substituted by actual objects of σ_0 and $[\sigma_0,\theta] \models \rho$.
(1) Logical connectives $\wedge,\vee,\neg,\ldots$ are interpreted as usual.
(2) The quantors $\forall/\exists$ refer to actual objects of σ_0, $\underline{\forall}/\underline{\exists}$ to possible objects (Π).
(3a) $[\underline{\sigma},\theta] \models$ **always** ψ iff for all $i \in I(\underline{\sigma})$: $[\underline{\sigma}_i,\theta] \models \psi$
(3b) $[\underline{\sigma},\theta] \models$ **sometime** ψ iff there exists $i \in I(\underline{\sigma})$, such that $[\underline{\sigma}_i,\theta] \models \psi$
(4a) $[\underline{\sigma},\theta] \models$ **always** ψ **before** τ iff for all $i \in I(\underline{\sigma})$: $i < \mu\tau$ implies $[\underline{\sigma}_i,\theta] \models \psi$
(4b) $[\underline{\sigma},\theta] \models$ **sometime** ψ **before** τ iff there exists $i \in I(\underline{\sigma})$, such that $i < \mu\tau$ and $[\underline{\sigma}_i,\theta] \models \psi$
(5) $[\underline{\sigma},\theta] \models$ **always/sometime** ψ **until** τ like (4a/b), with $i \leq \mu\tau$ instead of $i < \mu\tau$
(6) $[\underline{\sigma},\theta] \models$ **from** α [**holds**] ψ iff $[\underline{\sigma}_{\mu\alpha},\theta] \models \psi$ (if $\mu\alpha < \infty$) / **true** (otherwise)
(7a) $[\underline{\sigma},\theta] \models$ **onnext** ψ iff $1 \in I(\underline{\sigma})$ implies $[\underline{\sigma}_1,\theta] \models \psi$
(7b) $[\underline{\sigma},\theta] \models$ **next** ψ iff $1 \in I(\underline{\sigma})$ and $[\underline{\sigma}_1,\theta] \models \psi$

Thus, nontemporal formulae are evaluated in the first state σ_0 of a given state sequence $\underline{\sigma}$. Temporal quantification by **always** or **sometime** requires the argument formula ψ to be valid in every or some tail sequence of $\underline{\sigma}$. This requirement can be restricted by a **before** or **until** clause to those tail sequences which start before the first occurrence of a "termination" condition τ (excluding or including it). **from** instead involves a "start" condition α. The operators **onnext** and **next** uniquely affect the first tail sequence $\underline{\sigma}_1$. If ψ is a nontemporal formula, the conditions simply refer to states σ_i instead of tail sequences $\underline{\sigma}_i$.

Facts 2.5:
- By analogy to quantors $\forall/\exists$ the above pairs of temporal operators are dual to each other:
  $\neg$ **sometime** ψ [**before/until** τ] $\Leftrightarrow$ **always** $\neg\psi$ [**before/until** τ] $\qquad \neg$ **next** ψ $\Leftrightarrow$ **onnext** $\neg\psi$
- **next** and **onnext** coincide on infinite sequences.
- Logical connectives, **next** and one arbitrary operator from { **always** ... **before**, **sometime** ... **before**, **always** ... **until**, **sometime** ... **until**, **from** ... **holds** } suffice to derive all other operators. □

When specifying dynamic integrity, we consider the complete behaviour of a database to be characterized by an infinite sequence consisting of an initial state, the past states, the present state, and a possible or imaginary future. Thus constraints are meant as restrictions on infinite sequences. According to the definition of admissibility, the formulae have to be interpreted in these sequences for all substitutions with arbitrary possible objects. Without formalizing it in this paper, we additionally assume that integrity constraints affect only such objects that exist in the database and only such states that contain the respective objects.

Example 2.6: The following formulae give typical constraints on the automobile registration database, using variables c: CAR, co: CAR-OWNER, and y: Year.

(C1) ¬registered(c) ∧ (this-year=y ⇒ **sometime** registered(c) **before** this-year>y+1)
∧ **from** registered(c) **holds** (owner(c)=manuf(c) ∧ **always** registered(c))

/* When a car c has been entered into the database is not yet registered. It must be registered sometime in the same or in the next year (with its manufacturer as owner), whereupon it always remains registered (possibly with changing owners). */

(C2) **from** owner(c)≠manuf(c) **always** ¬is-MANUF(owner(c))
∧ **always** ((owner(c)=co ∧ is-GARAGE(co)) ⇒ **always** owner(c)=co **before** is-PERSON(owner(c)))

/* From the moment when a car c is no longer owned by its manufacturer, it may never be passed to any manufacturer again. Whenever it belongs to a garage co, it must remain in this property before it is sold to a person. */ □

With the exception of **next** and **onnext**, the temporal operators guarantee a useful property of formulae which allows to restrict monitoring to true state changes only.

Lemma 2.7: Two state sequences $\underline{\sigma}$ and $\underline{\sigma}'$ are called ***iteration-equivalent*** if they differ only in the number of local iterations of each state (between one and infinitely many at the end of a sequence). Every formula φ with temporal operators only from {**always/sometime**...[**before/until**], **from** ...**holds**} is ***iteration-invariant***, i.e., if φ holds in a state sequence $\underline{\sigma}$, then it holds in every iteration-equivalent sequence, too. □

3. Transaction Specifications

Transactions are specified essentially by pre- and postconditions in the style of Hoare's assertions. These conditions may be arbitrary formulae in predicate logic. To separate aspects mixed up in many other approaches, we differ between an applicability condition, one or several pairs of pre/postconditions, and frame conditions for each transaction. The applicability condition says when the transaction may be executed. Then any state following execution must satisfy all postconditions corresponding to the preconditions satisfied before execution. Additionally, valid frame conditions have to be preserved. The formal definition reads as follows:

Definition 3.1: A ***transaction specification*** is denoted by

t(P):	**on**	α	
	case 1:	**pre** π_1	**post** ρ_1
	⋮		
	case c:	**pre** π_c	**post** ρ_c
	frame	Δ	

It consists of a ***name*** t, a set P of ***parameter variables***, an ***applicability condition*** α, ***cases*** of ***pre/postconditions*** π_j/ρ_j, $1 \le j \le c$ (often written as $\{\pi_j\}$ t(P) $\{\rho_j\}$) and a set Δ of ***frame conditions***. All conditions are formulae in predicate logic with free variables from P and from an implicit set L of ***local variables***. A ***parameter*** is any substitution θ_P of the parameter variables; a substitution θ_L of the local variables by data or objects from a given state is called ***local substitution***.

t is ***applicable*** in a state σ for a parameter θ_P iff there exists a local substitution θ_L in σ, such that $[\sigma, \theta_P + \theta_L] \models \alpha$. t ***transfers*** a state σ into a state σ' for a parameter θ_P iff t is applicable in σ and for all local substitutions θ_L in σ, all cases j $(1 \leq j \leq c)$, and all frame conditions $\delta \in \Delta$, the following holds:

(i) $[\sigma, \theta_P + \theta_L] \models \pi_j$ implies $[\sigma', \theta_P + \theta_L] \models \rho_j$ (ii) $[\sigma, \theta_P + \theta_L] \models \delta$ implies $[\sigma', \theta_P + \theta_L] \models \delta$ □

Thus, a relation "transfers" is defined between states. Any program realizing the transaction t has to construct a poststate σ' from a given state σ according to that relation. Such a poststate may not exist (if the applicability condition fails or relevant postconditions evaluate to **false**) or it may be determined not uniquely. The first case indicates an error, the latter leaves room for refinements and implementation decisions. To facilitate understanding and correct realization of a transaction specification, error situations should be made explicit within the applicability condition as far as possible (in negated form).

Entire sequences of states are restricted by transaction specifications to "executable" ones.

Definition 3.2: Let $\mathcal{T}$ be a set of transaction specifications. A finite or infinite state sequence $\underline{\sigma}$ is called ***executable*** wrt $\mathcal{T}$ iff, for each state transition (σ_{i-1}, σ_i) $(i \geq 1)$ with $\sigma_{i-1} \neq \sigma_i$, a transaction $t \in \mathcal{T}$ und a parameter θ_P exist, such that σ_{i-1} is transferred into σ_i by t for θ_P. □

As far as executability is concerned, errors of transaction application may simply be realized by not changing the current state $(\sigma_{i-1} = \sigma_i)$. Other useful reactions like warnings or even error recovery are not relevant to our discussion.

Definitions 3.2 and 3.1 can be reformulated in temporal logic, using the operators **always** (once) and **onnext** only; we will refer to this sublogic as ***transitional logic***.

Lemma 3.3: Let P_t, α_t, etc. be the various components of a transaction t. Expressions like "$\forall X$", "f(X)", etc. involving a set X of variables $x_1,\ldots,x_n$ are abbreviations of "$\forall x_1 .. \forall x_n$", "$f(x_1,\ldots,x_n)$", etc. Then a state sequence $\underline{\sigma}$ is executable wrt to $\mathcal{T}$ iff:

$$\underline{\sigma} \models \textbf{always} \Big(\Xi \vee \bigvee_{t \in \mathcal{T}} \exists P_t \, \big((\exists L_t \, \alpha_t) \wedge (\forall L_t \bigwedge_{j=1,\ldots,c} (\pi_{t,j} \Rightarrow \textbf{onnext } \rho_{t,j}) \wedge \bigwedge_{\delta \in \Delta} (\delta \Rightarrow \textbf{onnext } \delta) \big) \Big)$$

$$\text{where } \Xi \equiv \bigwedge_{\substack{f \text{ object} \\ \text{function} \\ \text{in OBJ}}} \forall X_f \, \forall y_f \, (f(X_f) = y_f \Rightarrow \textbf{onnext } f(X_f) = y_f)$$

The formula Ξ specifies that two successive states are identical. (X_f, y_f denote appropriate variables for arguments/results of f.) □

Example 3.4: Typical transactions in our example database are registration and sale of a car and updating the current year. (Let y,y" : Year; c": CAR; co",mf": CAR-OWNER; etc. be local variables.)

(T1) **next-year:**

on true **pre** this-year = y **post** this-year = y+1

frame manuf(c")=mf", registered(c"), ¬registered(c"), owner(c")=co" , etc.

(by analogy for all other object functions except this-year)

(T2) **sell** (c: CAR, newco: CAR-OWNER):

on owner(c) ≠ newco **pre** true **post** owner(c) = newco

frame c"≠c ⇒ owner(c")=co", manuf(c")=mf", [¬] registered(c"), this-year=y", etc.

(T3) **register** (c: CAR, m: MODEL, co: CAR-OWNER, ...):

on ¬registered(c) ∧ approved(md)

pre true

post registered(c) ∧ ¬∃c' (c'≠c ∧ regno(c')=regno(c)) ∧ model(c) = m ∧ owner(c) = co ∧ ...

frame registered(c"), c"≠c⇒¬registered(c"), c"≠c⇒regno(c")=r", etc.

/* A car c may be registered if the model m has been approved. Then a unique registration number is assigned and the parameter information is stored. */ □

So far, the transactions need not necessarily respect the constraints of example 2.6. Thus the specifications of admissible and executable state sequences really complement each other.

Later transformations of pre/postconditions, in particular simplifications, will utilize formulae whose validity is preserved under a transaction.

Definition 3.5: The ***frame (closure)*** $\bar{\Delta}(t)$ of a transaction t is constituted by *all* formulae δ which satisfy the following condition for all states σ,σ' and parameters θ_P such that t transfers σ into σ', and for all local substitutions θ_L: $[\sigma,\theta_P+\theta_L] \models \delta$ implies $[\sigma',\theta_P+\theta_L] \models \delta$. (We assume that P+L contains all free variables of δ.) Then δ is called ***invariant*** under t. An object function f is ***invariant*** iff the formula $f(x_1,...,x_n)=y$ is so. □

The examples might suggest that frame conditions can easily be derived from postconditions. At least, all functions not mentioned there are usually required to be invariant, and thus all formulae involving these functions only. Complications arise if, e.g., conditional or disjunctive formulae are used as postconditions; then purely syntactic frame assumptions do not exclude all undesirable state changes. To be more flexible, we have listed frame conditions explicitly.

4. Transitional Interpretation of Dynamic Integrity Constraints

Before we can transform dynamic integrity constraints into transaction specifications, we have to tackle two basic problems of monitoring. Constraints are temporal formulae interpreted in infinite state sequences. Thus their validity may depend on (1) unknown future states and (2) entire subsequences. Concerning (1), we introduce notions of partial validity up to a present state in order to get a realizable goal of monitoring. Concerning (2), we make use of so-called transition graphs that can be constructed from temporal formulae and that reduce analysis of constraints in state sequences to local tests in state transitions.

4.1 Partial Validity

During runtime, only a finite prefix of database behaviour is known, namely the sequence from an initial state up to the present state, whereas future continuations depend on the user's choice of state transitions. Integrity monitoring, however, has to judge correctness at each moment from such a finite sequence. For this purpose, the following degrees of partial validity seem to be reasonable:

Definitions 4.1: Let a finite state sequence $\underline{\sigma} = \langle\sigma_0, \sigma_1, ..., \sigma_{n-1}\rangle$, $n \geq 0$, a substitution θ and a temporal formula φ be given.

(a) φ is ***strictly valid*** in $\underline{\sigma}$ (for θ) iff it is valid according to def. 2.4 ($[\underline{\sigma},\theta] \models \varphi$).

(b) φ is ***stationarily valid*** in $\underline{\sigma}$ (for θ) iff it is valid in the constantly continued sequence $(\underline{\sigma} \circ \langle\sigma_{n-1}, \sigma_{n-1}, \ldots\rangle)$.

(c) φ is ***potentially valid*** in $\underline{\sigma}$ (for θ) iff there exists some infinite continuation $\underline{\sigma}' = \langle\sigma'_1, \sigma'_2, \ldots\rangle$, such that $[\underline{\sigma} \circ \underline{\sigma}', \theta] \models \varphi$.

(d) φ is ***provisionally valid*** in $\underline{\sigma}$ iff it is valid in $(\underline{\sigma} \circ \underline{\lambda})$ according to def. 2.4, where $\underline{\lambda}$ is a distinguished tail sequence assumed to satisfy arbitrary formulae. (Please note that this is only an observational characterization of a technical definition not needed in this paper.)

$\underline{\sigma}$ is called ***strictly/... admissible*** wrt φ iff φ is valid in the respective sense for all substitutions. □

Lemma 4.2: Notions (a) and (b) are equivalent for an iteration-invariant formula φ. For an arbitrary formula φ, the implication (b) $\Rightarrow$ (c) $\Rightarrow$ (d) holds. □

Strict and stationary admissibility (a/b) say that database manipulation can be finished after the present state without invalidating the constraint. In many situations, only the weaker requirement of potential admissibility (c) can be satisfied, since future manipulations are expected to handle pending constraint parts like **sometime**-arguments. Thus this notion seems to be most desirable as the goal of monitoring; it guarantees at least one correct continuation. Provisional admissibility (d), however, is sufficient, if one optimistically assumes that every constraint can be become valid at some future time. It excludes exactly all definitive constraint violations that have occurred up to the present state, e.g. by exceeding a termination condition.

4.2 Transition Graphs

Definition 4.3: Let φ be a propositional-temporal formula over nontemporal basic formulae BF. A ***transition graph*** $T=\langle V,E,\nu,\eta,v_0\rangle$ ***for*** φ consists of

- a directed graph $\langle V,E\rangle$ with a finite set V of nodes and edges $E \subseteq V \times V$,
- a node labelling ν by propositional-temporal formulae over BF,
- an edge labelling η by propositional formulae (i.e. logical combinations) over BF,
- and a root node $v_0 \in V$ with $\nu(v_0)=\varphi$. □

Transition graphs shall be used to analyse state sequences by searching corresponding paths, whose edge labels successively hold in the states of a sequence. Such computations require to "mark" the nodes that have been reached at each moment.

Definition 4.4: The ***marking*** $M_T(\underline{\sigma},\theta)$ of T for a finite state sequence $\underline{\sigma}=\langle\sigma_0,\ldots,\sigma_{n-1}\rangle$ with length n and for a substitution θ of the free variables in the labels (i.e. in φ) is defined as the following sets of nodes:

for $n=0$: $M_T(\underline{\sigma},\theta)=\{v_0\}$ for $n>0$: $M_T(\underline{\sigma},\theta) = tr(\, M_T(\langle\sigma_0,\ldots,\sigma_{n-2}\rangle,\theta)\, , \sigma_{n-1}\,)$

where $tr(M,\sigma) = \{\, v' \in V \mid \exists v \in M\ \exists e=(v,v') \in E\colon [\sigma,\theta] \models \eta(e)\,\}$ for any $M \subseteq V$ □

The definition of tr is called ***transition rule*** and formalizes the stepwise processing of the graph: A node v' is marked after passing a state σ iff there exists an edge e from a marked node v to v' such that the label $\eta(e)$ is valid in σ. If no edge starting from the old marking applies, tr yields the empty set, and the inspected state sequence is no longer "accepted".

Definition 4.5: A finite state sequence $\underline{\sigma}$ is ***accepted*** by T iff the marking $M_T(\underline{\sigma},\theta)$ is nonempty for every substitution θ. □

If the transition graph is to be used for monitoring the temporal formula φ in state sequences, it has to obey a semantic restriction on its labels:

Definition 4.6: T is ***correct*** iff the following equivalence holds in infinite state sequences for each node v with outgoing edges $e_k = (v, v_k)$, $k=1,\dots,d$ $(d \geq 0)$:

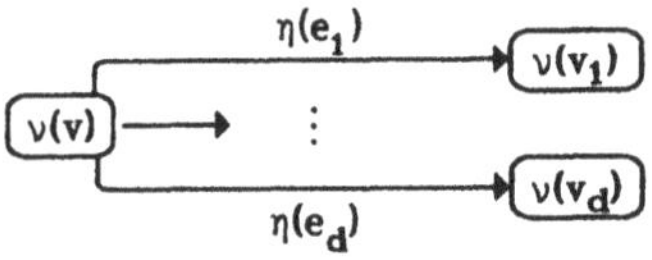

$$\nu(v) \Leftrightarrow \bigvee_{k=1}^{d} (\, \eta(e_k) \wedge \textbf{next}\ \nu(v_k))$$

□

A node label is valid in a state sequence (for an arbitrary substitution) iff at least one outgoing (nontemporal!) edge label holds in the first state and the label of the corresponding target node is valid in the first tail sequence. Thus node labels in a graph for a given constraint must be constraint parts or modifications that remain to be monitored in the future.

Example 4.8: The following transition graphs for not nested temporal operators (α,ψ,τ nontemporal) are correct, since these equivalences ("temporal recursions") hold:

always $\psi \Leftrightarrow (\psi \wedge$ **next always** $\psi)$, **sometime** $\psi \Leftrightarrow (\psi \vee (\neg\psi \wedge$ **next sometime** $\psi))$, etc.

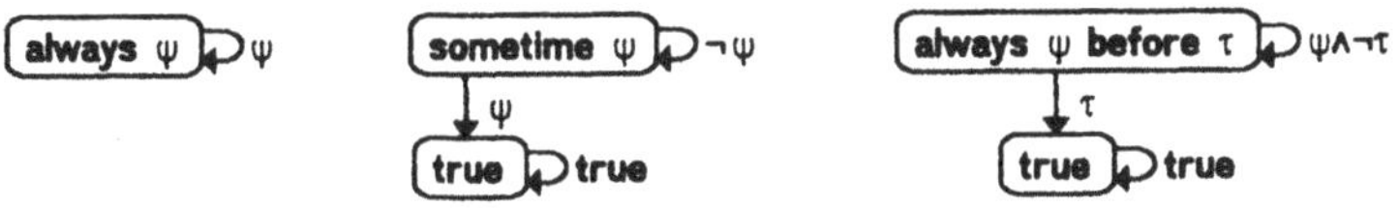

□

By induction on length of state sequences, the following theorem can be concluded from correctness. It states the basic relationship between the validity of a formula φ in an infinite sequence $\underline{\sigma}$ and the acceptance of $\underline{\sigma}$ by a correct transition graph T for φ.

Theorem 4.8: For each substitution θ and each $n \in \mathbb{N}$ holds:

$$[\underline{\sigma},\theta] \models \varphi \text{ iff T accepts } \underline{\sigma}^{(n)} = \langle \sigma_0,\dots,\sigma_{n-1} \rangle \text{ and } [\underline{\sigma}_n,\theta] \models \bigvee_{v \in M_T(\underline{\sigma}^{(n)},\theta)} \nu(v) \quad (*)$$

□

Corollary 4.9: φ is potentially valid in a finite sequence $\underline{\sigma}^{(n)}$ (for θ) iff T accepts $\underline{\sigma}^{(n)}$ and the formula (*) is satisfiable. □

Thus acceptance up to a present state is only a necessary, but not a sufficient condition for potential admissibility. In addition to that, the formula represented by the marked nodes must be satisfiable in some future continuation. If, e.g., all nodes are labelled with satisfiable formulae only, the notions are equivalent; in this case, the graph is called ***reduced***.

In other papers we have presented several algorithms to construct transition graphs from temporal formulae. Originally, transition graphs have been constructed by, e.g., [Wo83,MaW84], to obtain a decision procedure for satisfiability of purely propositional-temporal formulae (only with boolean variables as basic formulae); there a tableau-driven method has been used. Our higher level and more direct algorithm in [LiS87, SaL87] allows arbitrary nontemporal basic formulae and utilizes a conversion of temporal formulae into a disjunctive normalform like that in def. 4.6 (correctness). By iteration, the label of each new node must be normalized to derive further edges and nodes. A completely different algorithm in [FeL87, Li87] composes subgraphs in a bottom-up manner corresponding to the formula structure. It essentially is a recursive system of graph operations, one for each logical or temporal operator.

Starting from an extended propositional-temporal formula φ, both algorithms deliver correct transition graphs T that satisfy the implication:

$$(4.10)\quad \left\{ \begin{array}{l} \underline{\sigma} \text{ potentially admissible wrt } \varphi \Rightarrow \underline{\sigma} \text{ accepted by T (by cor. 4.9)} \\ \qquad\qquad\qquad\qquad\qquad\quad \Rightarrow \underline{\sigma} \text{ provisionally admissible wrt } \varphi \end{array} \right.$$

Such graphs detect all errors in database behaviour up to the present state (violations of provisional admissibility), but not all inevitable errors in the future behaviour (violations of potential admissibility) at the earliest possible moment. In addition to the constructions above, further reductions can be applied [Wo83, LiS87] to delete nodes and paths with unsatisfiable labels. If the basic formulae of φ may be interpreted independently (like boolean variables), the resulting graph is reduced so that exactly all potentially admissible sequences are accepted.

Particularly useful for monitoring and transformation are special transition graphs:

- In "deterministic" graphs, at most one outgoing edge applies in each state, so that markings consist of single nodes only.
- In "iteration-invariant" graphs, markings do not change on a state iteration.

These properties are guaranteed by following defining conditions on edge labels:

Definition 4.11: A transition graph is called ***deterministic*** iff for each node v with outgoing edges $e_k = (v, v_k)$, k=1,...,d holds: $\eta(e_k) \wedge \eta(e_l) \Leftrightarrow$ **false** for all $k \neq l$. □

Definition 4.12: A transition graph is called ***iteration-invariant*** iff there exists a loop e'=(v',v') for each edge e=(v,v'), such that $\eta(e) \Rightarrow \eta(e')$.

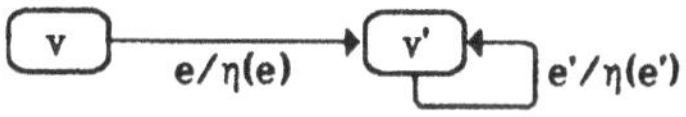

□

The mentioned bottom-up algorithm directly constructs deterministic and iteration-invariant graphs from iteration-invariant formulae as in lemma 2.7.

Example 4.13: Below we give transition graphs for the integrity constraints of example 2.8 that are correct, reduced, deterministic, and iteration-invariant.

(C1) $\varphi_1 \equiv \neg\text{registered(c)} \wedge (\text{this-year=y} \Rightarrow \varphi_{11}) \wedge \varphi_{12}$

$\varphi_{11} \equiv$ **sometime** registered(c) **before** this-year>y+1

$\varphi_{12} \equiv$ **from** registered(c) **holds** (owner(c)=manuf(c) $\wedge$ **always** registered(c))

T_1:

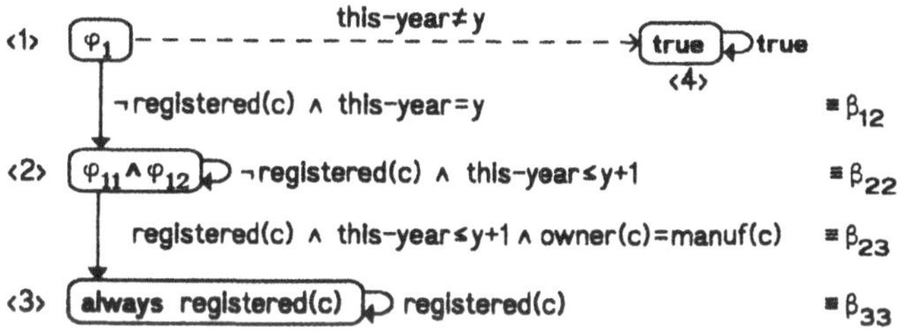

(C2) $\varphi_2 \equiv$ (**from** owner(c)≠manuf(c) **always** ¬is-MANUF(owner(c))) $\wedge\ \varphi_{21}$

$\varphi_{21} \equiv$ **always** (γ(c,co) $\Rightarrow$ **always** owner(c)=co **before** is-PERSON(owner(c)))

where γ(c,co) stands for (owner(c)=co $\wedge$ is-GARAGE(co))

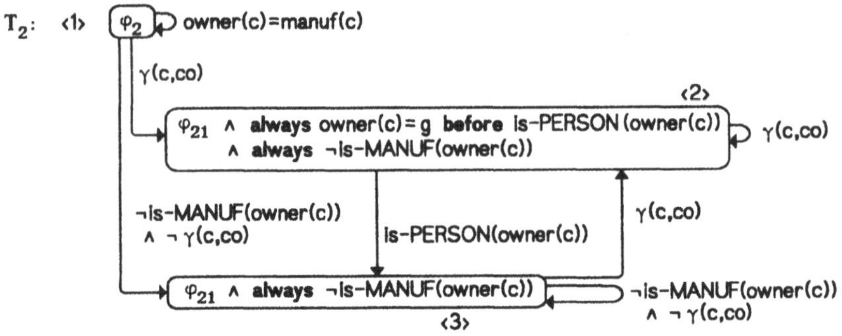

It can easily be recognized that both graphs describe life-cycles of database objects (or object combinations) with respect to the integrity constraints. Intuitively, the nodes correspond to following situations:

T_1: ‹1› ≙ car c before insertion
‹2› ≙ car c between insertion in year y and timely registration
‹3› ≙ car c after registration
‹4› ≙ year y other than the year of insertion (irrelevant)

T_2: ‹1› ≙ car c owned by its manufacturer
‹2› ≙ car c owned by a garage co
‹3› ≙ car c owned by a person or a garage ≠ co

Missing edges indicate possible constraint violations: E.g., T_1 forbids late registrations since no edge starts from node ‹2› in the case "this-year›y+1", and T_2 excludes sales to manufacturers. □

To summarize, monitoring constraints in state sequences can be reduced to passing through transition graphs with the properties discussed above. These graphs determine the degree of admissibility to be guaranteed at runtime; it lies between provisional and potential admissibility.

5. Transformation into Transaction Specifications

The task of transforming dynamic integrity constraints into transaction specifications has been redefined by the last section: It remains to consider corresponding transition graphs such that each executable finite state sequence becomes accepted, too.

Let a finite set $\mathcal{T}$ of transaction specifications and a finite set of integrity constraints C together with corresponding correct transition graphs T_φ for each $\varphi \in C$ be given. To simplify the presentation in this paper, we proceed on several more or less restrictive assumptions:

- The constructed graphs are deterministic and iteration-invariant.
- Markings need to be considered for actual objects only.
  (This holds for all so-called "existence-restricted" constraints like those above [Li87].)
- Transactions do not insert or delete objects.

The following transformation steps have to be applied for each constraint φ, first to the original transaction specifications, then to the already transformed specifications. The first two steps describe which modifications have to be done without considering transactions individually. Only the third step will show how specific knowledge about transactions can be utilized to simplify transformation results.

Since transactions have to decide about the acceptance of state sequences by the given transition graph (T_φ), the database must be extended by a representation of node markings.

Transformation 5.1: (Step I: signature extension)

Let X be the set of free variables $x_1, \ldots, x_p$ in φ with associated sorts $s_1, \ldots, s_p$. Then extend the object signature OBJ to OBJ^+ by adding a data sort Node denoting the set of nodes in T_φ and an object function marking: $s_1 \times \ldots \times s_p \rightarrow$ Node. □

This function should be manipulated in such a way that it always represents the marking $M_T(\underline{\sigma},\theta)$ which is reached after passing a sequence prefix $\underline{\sigma}$ for a substitution θ of X. The extension introduces that (minimal) information into database schema and states which is necessary to monitor the dynamic constraint; no previous states need to be analysed. The additional information may even be helpful for a user at runtime, since it indicates which situation in the life-cycle of an object has been reached and which conditions remain to be satisfied.

Example 5.2: Formally, the graph T_1 of example 4.13 leads to a function

$$\text{marking}_1: \text{ CAR} \times \text{Year} \rightarrow \{1,2,3,4\}.$$

Closer analysis of graph processing shows that it is sufficient to have

$$\text{marking}_1: \text{ CAR} \rightarrow (\{2\} \times \text{Year}) \cup \{1,3\},$$

since only one year, the year of insertion, has to be remembered for each car, and that only in connection with node ‹2›. To improve readability, the name "marking_1" (and the node numbers) might be replaced by more application oriented names like "registration-status". □

The main task of transformation is to incorporate the computation of markings in the transition graph into the pre/postconditions of transactions. As a preparation, we reformulate acceptance like executability in transitional logic:

Lemma 5.3: A finite state sequence $\underline{\sigma}$ wrt the object signature OBJ is accepted by the deterministic transition graph $T_\varphi = \langle V,E,\nu,\eta,v_0\rangle$ iff there is a state sequence $\underline{\sigma}^+$ wrt OBJ^+ that has $\underline{\sigma}$ as its OBJ-reduct (i.e. it coincides with $\underline{\sigma}$ on OBJ sorts and functions) and that satisfies the following condition:

$$\underline{\sigma}^+ \models \ \forall X\ \Phi_{v_0} \ \wedge \ \textbf{always}\Big(\forall X \bigwedge_{v \in V} (\text{marking}(X)=v \Rightarrow \textbf{onnext}\ \Phi_v)\Big)$$

$$\text{where } \ \Phi_v \equiv \Big(\bigvee_{\substack{e \in E \\ e=(v,v')}} \eta(e)\Big) \ \wedge \ \Big(\bigwedge_{\substack{e \in E \\ e=(v,v')}} (\eta(e) \Rightarrow \text{marking}(X)=v')\Big)$$

□

Proof: The condition formalizes definitions 4.4/4.5 and requires $\underline{\sigma}^+$ to satisfy for each substitution θ and each $n \in I(\underline{\sigma})$:

$$[\sigma_n^+,\theta] \models (\text{marking}(X) = v) \quad \text{iff} \quad M_T(\langle\sigma_0,\ldots,\sigma_n\rangle,\theta)=\{v\}$$

Thus, existence of such a sequence $\underline{\sigma}^+$ equivalently characterizes acceptance of $\underline{\sigma}$. □

A comparison of lemmata 3.3 and 5.3 suggests the following refinement of pre/postconditions.

Transformation 5.4: (Step II: refinement)

It is necessary that the sets of variables in φ (X) and in the specifications $\mathcal{T}$ are disjoint or have been renamed appropriately. Besides, the implication $(\exists L\ \alpha) \Rightarrow (\exists L \bigvee \pi_j)$ must hold, i.e., applicability should imply at least one precondition.

Then transform each case $\{\pi_j\}\ t(P)\ \{\rho_j\}$ $(1 \le j \le c)$ of each transaction specification t in as many cases as the graph T_φ has nodes:

$$\left(\{\pi_j \wedge \text{marking}(X)=v\}\ t'(P)\ \ \{\rho_j \wedge \Phi_v\} \;\middle|\; v \in V\right)$$

So the set of local variables is extended by X, whereas applicability and frame conditions are not changed. Let $\mathcal{T}'$ denote the set of resulting transaction specifications. □

The next theorem verifies that this transformation guarantees acceptance of executable state sequences, provided the sequences have been initialized correctly.

Theorem 5.5: For each finite state sequence $\underline{\sigma}$ wrt OBJ^+ holds:

$$\underline{\sigma} \text{ executable wrt } \mathcal{T}' \text{ and } \sigma_0 \models \forall X\ \Phi_{v_0} \implies \underline{\sigma} \text{ accepted by } T_\varphi$$ □

Proof (Sketch): Lemma 3.3 (executability) applied to the refined specifications yields:

$$\underline{\sigma} \models \textbf{always}\left(\Xi \vee \bigvee_{t' \in \mathcal{T}'} \exists P_{t'} \cdot \left((\exists L_{t'} \cdot \alpha_t) \wedge \forall L_{t'} \cdot \bigwedge_{\substack{j=1,\dots,c\\ v \in V}} (\pi_{t',j,v} \Rightarrow \textbf{onnext}\ \rho_{t',j,v}) \wedge \bigwedge_{\delta \in \Delta_t} (\delta \Rightarrow \textbf{onnext}\ \delta)\right)\right)$$

where $L_{t'} = L_t + X$, $\pi_{t',j,v} \equiv (\pi_{t,j} \wedge \text{marking}(X)=v)$, $\rho_{t',j,v} \equiv (\rho_{t,j} \wedge \Phi_v)$.

Thus state changes $(\neg\Xi)$, where a transaction t' must have been applicable, satisfy

$$(**) \qquad \forall X \bigwedge_{v \in V} (\text{marking}(X)=v \Rightarrow \textbf{onnext}\ \Phi_v).$$

If a state (wrt OBJ^+) is only repeated (Ξ), its function marking remains unchanged. This corresponds to the invariance of markings within an iteration-invariant graph (def. 4.13), so that (**) holds in this case, too. For the sequence $\underline{\sigma}$ as a whole, we get $\underline{\sigma} \models$ **always**(**) as required in lemma 5.3, i.e., its OBJ-reduct and thus $\underline{\sigma}$ itself is accepted. □

Example 5.6: The following pre/postconditions result from the refinement step for constraint (C1), its transition graph T_1, and the transaction register (T3) of examples 2.6, 3.4, and 4.13:

case 2: **pre** [**true** ∧] $\text{marking}_1(c')=(2,y)$
post registered(c) ∧ ...
∧ $(\beta_{22} \vee \beta_{23}) \wedge (\beta_{22} \Rightarrow \text{marking}_1(c')=(2,y)) \wedge (\beta_{23} \Rightarrow \text{marking}_1(c')=3)$
≡ registered(c) ∧ ...
∧ (this-year ≤ y+1 ∧ registered(c') ⇒ owner(c')=manuf(c'))
∧ $(\neg\text{registered}(c') \Rightarrow \text{marking}_1(c')=(2,y)) \wedge (\text{registered}(c') \Rightarrow \text{marking}_1(c')=3)$

case 3: **pre** $\text{marking}_1(c')=3$
post registered(c) ∧ ... ∧ registered(c') ∧ $\text{marking}_1(c')=3$

The initial node ‹1› is not considered here, since it cannot be reached by state transitions. Note that the variable c of the constraint has been renamed into c', so that the additions of pre/postconditions apply to arbitrary objects c' independently from the parameter c; this renaming, however, can be withdrawn in the next (simplification) step. □

Example 5.7: Static constraints ψ are represented by formulae (**always** ψ). Since the corresponding graphs have only one node (see ex. 4.8), the function marking is constant, so that each case $\{\pi\}\ t\ \{\rho\}$ is simply changed into $\{\pi\}\ t\ \{\rho \wedge \psi\}$. □

Although we have reached our formal goal as confirmed by theorem 5.5, transformation results often read rather complicated and induce inefficient implementations. (Additional postconditions are usually realized by additional manipulations and tests.) Therefore, postconditions should be simplified to such "subconditions" that are really affected by the respective transaction. These subconditions may be original subformulae or specializations to certain substitutions.

Apart from standard simplifications according to equivalence laws of predicate logic, underlying data types, and transitional logic, invariants of transactions (def. 3.5) can be utilized. Obviously, they may be deleted from a postcondition, if they can be concluded from the associated precondition. Monitoring static constraints additionally exploits the inductive assertion that the constraint itself must have been valid in the prestate. For dynamic constraints, again the corresponding transition graphs offer an appropriate analogy: Each state of an accepted sequence must satisfy one ingoing edge label of the node marked for that state. Thus the following ***graph invariant*** $\overline{\Phi}$ may inductively be assumed for prestates:

Lemma 5.8: For the transition graph T_φ as above, let $\overline{\Phi} = \left(\overline{\Phi}_v \equiv \bigvee_{\substack{e \in E \\ e=(\overline{v},v)}} \eta(e) \;\middle|\; v \in V \right)$.

Then all accepted state sequences (wrt OBJ^+) satisfy: **always** $(\forall X \bigwedge_{v \in V} \text{marking}(X)=v \Rightarrow \overline{\Phi}_v)$ □

If the graph invariant itself is invariant under a transaction, at least for some nodes or some substitutions, the marking will not change in an iteration-invariant graph. Then the corresponding refinements of postconditions may be omitted completely. Now we can compile several simplification rules that preserve executability of state sequences (without proof).

Transformation rules 5.9: (Step III: simplification)

- In each case (j,v), $j \in \{1,..,c\}$, $v \in V$, of a transaction specification $t' \in \mathcal{T}'$, i.e. in

  $$\{\pi_j \wedge \text{marking}(X)=v\} \;\; t' \;\; \{\rho'_{j,v}\},$$

  those subformulae δ of the postcondition may be replaced by **true** which are implied by $(\pi_j \wedge \overline{\Phi}_v)$ and are invariant under t (note: $\Delta_{t'} = \Delta_t$).
- If $\overline{\Phi}_v$ is invariant under t for some node v, the additions of postconditions as introduced in transformation 5.4 (refinement) may be dropped in all cases (...,v), provided the frame is extended by the formula (marking(X)=v).
- If only $(X \neq \theta \Rightarrow \overline{\Phi}_v)$ is invariant for some constant substitution θ (e.g. the transaction parameters), the variables of those additions may be replaced by the objects or data of θ, provided the frame is extended by the formula $(X \neq \theta \Rightarrow \text{marking}(X)=v)$.
- If $\overline{\Phi}_v$ and the applicability condition α contradict each other (**false** $\Leftrightarrow (\exists L \alpha) \wedge \overline{\Phi}_v$), all cases (...,v) may be deleted. □

Finally, new error situations introduced by refinements should be put into the applicability condition (α). Intuitively, these errors are just the possible constraint violations.

Transformation rule 5.10: (Step IV: restriction)

If a transaction specification contains a case $\{\pi\}$ t $\{\rho \wedge \beta\}$ where β consists of free variables, data operators, invariant object functions, and logical connectives only, the following pairwise replacements are allowed: (L local variables)

$$\alpha \longrightarrow \alpha \wedge (\forall L\, \pi \Rightarrow \beta) \qquad \{\pi\}\; t\; \{\rho \wedge \beta\} \longrightarrow \{\pi\}\; t\; \{\rho\}$$ □

Example 5.11: The last rules essentially simplify the transformation of graph T_1 (ex. 4.13) into the specifications of register (T3) and next-year (T1). By utilizing the graph invariant $\overline{\Phi}$,

$$\overline{\Phi}_2 \equiv (\neg\text{registered(c')} \wedge \text{this-year} \leq y+1) \qquad \overline{\Phi}_3 \equiv \text{registered(c')} ,$$

following results can be obtained: (Compare examples 3.4 and 5.6.)

register (c: CAR, m: MODEL, co: CAR-OWNER):

on $\neg$registered(c) $\wedge$ approved(m) $\wedge$ *$marking_1(c)=(2,y)$* $\wedge$ *co=manuf(c)*

pre true **post** registered(c) $\wedge$ owner(c)=co ... $\wedge$ *$marking_1(c)=3$*

frame ... *$c' \neq c \Rightarrow marking(c')=v$* (v variable for nodes)

next-year:

on *($\forall c'$: CAR $marking_1(c')=(2,y) \Rightarrow$ this-year$\neq y+1$)*

pre this-year = y **post** this-year = y+1

frame ... *$marking_1(c')=v$*

These formally derivable specifications [Li87] correspond with the intuitive understanding of the transactions: **register** only fits with the transition from node ‹2› to ‹3› and needs the manufacturer as the first owner. **next-year** is only applicable if node ‹2› is not marked for any car and the year before, since otherwise timely registrations would be made impossible. □

Example 5.12: Transforming the other constraint (C2) into the specification of **sell** (T2) shows an additional simplification. Here, even **always** ($\forall X \bigwedge_{v \in V}$ marking(X)=v $\overset{!}{\Leftrightarrow} \bar{\Phi}_v$) holds in accepted sequences, so that markings can be expressed by means of existing object functions. Thus no signature extension (step I) is necessary. At the end, steps II-IV have only changed the applicability condition by listing legal transitions of ownerships:

co $\neq$ newco $\wedge$ *(owner(c)$\neq$manuf(c) $\Rightarrow$ $\neg$is-MANUF(newco))*

$\wedge$ *$\forall$co (owner(c)=co $\wedge$ is-GARAGE(co) $\Rightarrow$ is-PERSON(newco))* □

6. Conclusions

In this paper we have presented concepts and rules for transforming dynamic integrity constraints into transaction specifications. Finally, transactions guarantee integrity in the sense that every executable finite state sequence is partially admissible wrt to the constraints. The transformation consists of two main parts:

(A) construction of transition graphs from temporal formulae

(B) incorporation of graph processing into pre/postconditions

Since then transactions simulate computation of node markings, executable sequences must be accepted by the graphs; acceptance in turn implies at least provisional admissibility (i.e. correctness of present database behaviour) and at most potential admissibility (i.e. correctness of present and possible future behaviour).

Essential steps of this transformation can be automated by using graph construction algorithms (presented elsewhere) and the refinement rule for pre/postcondition (given here). Further manipulations like graph reduction and, above all, simplifications of transaction specifications need support by automated theorem proving techniques for the respective logics. E.g., the resolution method [HeMN84] for simplifying static constraints in relational updates might be be a candidate for adaptation to our setting of dynamic constraints and arbitrary transactions. Our simplification rules show how invariants of transactions and of transition graphs can be utilized therein.

In any case, however, interactions with the database designer will be needed to direct proofs, to exploit further knowledge, and to control readability of results. Since stepwise transformation helps to recognize the impacts of global constraints on local transactions, sometimes parts of specifications have to be revised in that process.

Thus, the theory presented lays a foundation for a reliable design method that not only delivers a correct specification of database behaviour, but also prepares an efficient implicit monitoring of dynamic integrity.

References

[ADBT84] Advances in Database Theory, Vol. II (H.Gallaire et al., eds.), Plenum Press, 1984

[BrMS84] Brodie,M.L./Mylopoulos,J./Schmidt,J.W(eds.): On Conceptual Modelling. Springer, 1984

[CaCF82] Castilho,J.M.V.de/ Casanova,M.A./ Furtado,A.L.: A Temporal Framework for Database Specifications. VLDB 1982, 280-291

[CaF84] Casanova,M.A./Furtado,A.L.: On the Description of Database Transition Constraints Using Temporal Languages. In [ADBT84], 211-236

[CaS87] Carmo,J./Sernadas,A.: A Temporal Logic Framework for a Layered Approach to Systems Specification and Verification. In: [TAIS87], 31-46

[CaVF84] Casanova,M.A./Veloso,P.A.S./Furtado,A.L.: Formal Database Specification - An Eclectic Perspective. PODS 1984, 110-118

[FeL87] Feng,D.S./ Lipeck,U.W.: Monitoring Temporal Formulae Deterministically (in German). Informatik-Bericht Nr. 87-06, Techn. Univ. Braunschweig 1987

[FiS86] Fiadeiro,J./Sernadas,A.: The INFOLOG Linear Tense Propositional Logic of Events and Transactions. Information Systems 11 (1986), 61-85

[FuSC81] Furtado,A.L./ Santos,C.S.dos/ Castilho,J.M.V.de: Dynamic Modelling of a Simple Existence Constraint. Information Systems 6 (1981), 73-80

[GaM79] Gardarin,G./Melkanoff,M.: Proving Consistency of Database Transactions. VLDB 1979, 291-298

[HeMN84] Henschen,L.J./McCune,W.W./Naqvi,S.A.: Compiling Constraint Checking Programs from First-Order Formulas. In: [ADBT84], 145-169

[Ku84] Kung,C.H.: A Temporal Framework for Database Specification and Verification. VLDB 1984, 91-99

[Li86] Lipeck,U.W.: Stepwise Specification of Dynamic Database Behaviour. SIGMOD 1986,387-397

[Li87] Lipeck,U.W.: On Dynamic Integrity of Databases: Fundamentals of Specification and Monitoring (in German). Habilitation Thesis, Informatics, Techn. Univ. Braunschweig, 1987

[LiEG85] Lipeck,U.W./Ehrich,H.-D./Gogolla,M.: Specifying Admissibility of Dynamic Database Behaviour Using Temporal Logic. In: [TFAIS85], 145-157

[LiS87] Lipeck,U.W./Saake,G.: Monitoring Dynamic Integrity Constraints Based on Temporal Logic. Information Systems 12 (1987), 255-269

[MaW84] Manna,Z./Wolper,P.: Synthesis of Communicating Processes from Temporal Logic Specifications. ACM TOPLAS 6 (1984), 68-93

[Ni82] Nicolas,J.-M.: Logic for Improving Integrity Checking in Relational Data Bases. Acta Informatica 18 (1982), 227-253

[SaL87] Saake,G./Lipeck,U.W.: Foundations of Temporal Integrity Monitoring. In: [TAIS87], 235-249

[Se80] Sernadas,A.: Temporal Aspects of Logical Procedure Definition. Inf.Systems 5(1980), 167-187

[ShS85] Sheard,T./Stemple,D.: Coping with Complexity in Automated Reasoning about Database Systems. VLDB 1985, 426-435

[StS84] Stemple,D./Sheard,T.: Specification and Verification of Abstract Database Types. PODS 1984, 248-257

[TAIS87] Proc. IFIP Work. Conf. on Temporal Aspects in Information Systems 1987 (C.Rolland et al., eds.), North-Holland, Amsterdam 1988

[TFAIS85] Proc. IFIP Work. Conf. on Theoretical and Formal Aspects of Information Systems (A.Sernadas et al., eds.), North-Holland, Amsterdam 1985

[VeCF81] Veloso,P.A.S./Castilho,J.M.V.de/Furtado,A.L.: Systematic Derivation of Complementary Specifications. VLDB 1981, 409-421

[VeF85] Veloso,P.A.S./Furtado,A.L.: Towards Simpler and Yet Complete Formal Specifications. In: [TFAIS85], 175-189

[WaS81] Walker,A./Salveter,S.C.: Automatic Modification of Transactions to Preserve Data Base Integrity. Techn.Report 81/026, Comp. Science, State Univ. of New York, Stony Brook 1981

[Wo83] Wolper,P.: Temporal Logic Can Be More Expressive. Inform.and Control 56 (1983), 72-99

View Update Translation via Deduction and Annotation

Anthony Tomasic

European Computer-Industry Research Centre
Arabellastr. 17, D-8000 Munich 81, West Germany

Abstract

First steps are taken in examining the view update problem in deductive databases. The class of recursive definite deductive databases is examined. A view update is defined as a statement of factual logical consequence of the deductive database. A translation is a minimal update on the facts of a deductive database such that the view update holds. The number of translations for a view update is exponential in the size of the database. Algorithms for view updates are presented and proven correct. They are based on *SLD*-resolution and are independent of the computation rule. Finally, as an example of a method for reducing the number of possible translations of a view update, rule annotations are introduced. A small number of unique annotations (proportional to the size of the database) is shown to produce unique translations of view updates.

1. Introduction

In this paper, the framework of deductive databases (**ddb**) is applied to the view update problem. In particular, the monotonic nature of this class of databases is used extensively (i.e. the addition of data always results in more implied data). We include a set of test predicates whose interpretation is a generalization of the relational *select* operator.

Taking a general translation [9] approach to this problem in a deductive database context, a general translation procedure (a *translator*) will, given an update of an implied fact (a *view update*), provide to the user several sets of updates (several *translations* of the update) on the explicit facts of the **ddb**. Exactly which translations are generated depends on the *update policies* enforced by the translator. A universally accepted update policy requires every translation to correctly update D for a view update. By correct, we mean that **ddb** will (will not) derive the fact after the insertion (deletion) view update.

For example, consider the following database consisting of two relations: *ed(employee,department)* which associates employees and departments and *dm(department,manager)* which associates departments and managers; with the following data:

ed(employee,department)

employee	*department*
John	Sales
William	Production
Fred	Finance

dm(department,manager)

department	*manager*
Sales	Sally
Production	Patricia

Consider the (join-projection) view *em(employee,manager)* which defines the relationship between employees and managers for the above database

$$em(X,Y) \leftarrow ed(X,Z) \wedge dm(Z,Y)$$

The facts which appear in view are *em(John,Sally)* and *em(William,Patricia)*.

Consider a view update:

Delete the fact (*John,Sally*) from this view.

Without considering side-effects of a translation on other views, there are several alternative translations: the deletion of *ed(John,Sales)*, the deletion of *dm(Sales,Sally)*, or (non-minimally) the deletion of both facts.

We impose a simple second view update policy based on minimality of translations which excludes translations from having extra unnecessary updates. Thus, the third translation is not allowed. The translator however cannot decide between the first two alternatives without more information. This decision we call the *choice problem*. We show below that in general the number of translations of a view update is exponential in the length of the database because of the choice problem. We do not consider side-effects of translations on any view in this paper.

This paper addresses the choice problem in a novel way by providing a mechanism for application dependent information to restrict the possible translations. This is done by having the user mark syntactic parts of view definitions to disambiguate view updates. For deletion, this amounts to marking predicates appearing in the bodies of clauses. For insertion, markings are done to clauses of a view definition. These special markings are termed *annotations* and correspond to a simple form of view update policy. In the above example, if the predicate *ed(X,Z)* in the body of the above view is annotated for deletion (desirable for instance when *Sally* is requesting the view update), the translator will always select this predicate for a deletion translation i.e. the only translation will be to delete *ed(John,Sales)*. This is a dynamic annotation because it occurs at the time of the view update translation. If the same deletion annotation was statically added when the view was defined, it would implement a view update policy of "When effectively deleting an employee-manager fact, delete the appropriate employee-department fact." For simplicity, we consider only static annotations of views in this paper.

One major advantage of these markings is their exact control over ambiguous translations and direct computational effect of controlling which subsets of the possible translations are available for consideration to the user. Given a small number of *unique* annotations, in proportion to the depth of the search tree for a fact, a unique translation can be generated.

The approach taken in this paper is to express the update translators in terms of *SLD* resolution. In particular, local variables appearing in view definitions (the variable *Z* in this example) can admit new constants as a possible translation. For example, consider the view update:

Insert the fact (*Fred,Jane*) into the above *em(X,Y)* view.

Since we consider only virtual views, a direct insertion of the fact *em(Fred,Jane)* is not allowed (such an update would violate the logical independence of the database). One translation of this view update is:

Insert the fact (*Finance,Jane*) into the *dm* relation.

View update algorithms appearing in the relational literature admit only this translation for this view. By considering the minimal view update policy, we argue that this assumption is overly restrictive (intuitively since *Fred* could work in more than one department) and that the translation

Insert the facts *ed(Fred,X)* and *dm(X,Jane)* for some given department *X*.

is equally admissible. The translators defined in this paper implement such a more general assumption about new data. The work done here builds upon some related works in several areas.

The generation-based deductive database *BDGEN* [22] provides for two types of deletion: the deletion of an explicit fact, and the deletion of an implied fact. In the later case, this system computes the (minimal) combinations of explicit fact deletions which will effectively delete the implied fact and allows the user to select one of these combinations. This approach is similar to the one presented here. For insertion, since no distinction is made between derived and base facts, insertion updates are translated only by explicit insertion of facts.

An alternate approach to the choice problem is to provide a language to the database administrator to express view update semantics. This approach is taken for the language *DLP* [17]. The syntactic approach to specifying translators of *DLP* is similar to our annotation approach. However, correctness of a translation is left to the view designer. In this regard *view update design tools*, which compute possible side effects of a given translation, are relevant [19]. The general translation approach taken here always generates correct translations.

Other methods and related issues (e.g. integrity constraints, exact translations, unknown values) are addressed in the view update literature [1, 2, 3, 4, 5, 6, 10, 13, 14, 15, 24]. While considering more factors for reducing the number of possible translations to a view update, this body of work is generally restricted to a smaller class of view definitions. The various ambiguities of relational view updates are classified in [18].

Finally, various kinds of update semantics are presented in [8, 11, 12, 23, 26]. Some of the problems we consider here are a result of requiring a single complete resulting state of the update, however multiple translations can be viewed as various partial states of an incomplete information database. This relationship deserves further study.

The remainder of this paper is organized as follows. We assume the reader is familiar with logic programming theory (for more details see [16]). The next sections provide a semantics for updates in terms of correctness and (subset) minimality of the translations and describes translators to implement these semantics. We prove that these algorithms hold for the correctness property. The following section address the control of translation generation by introducing rule annotations and some basic results are proven. Some future directions of this work are discussed in the conclusion.

2. Semantics of Updates

Let L be a first-order language with finite non-empty sets of predicates and functions (constants) and is fixed over all states of the deductive database. Let W be the set of well formed formulae (wffs) constructed from L. Let $D,D' \subset W$ be (consistent) finite subsets of wffs restricted to the class of Horn clauses. We recognize a special set of test predicates (<,>, etc.) in L.

Definition: Let D be a finite set of wffs of the language L such that the elements of D are clauses of the form

$$A_0 \leftarrow A_1 \wedge \ldots \wedge A_n \qquad (n \geq 0)$$

where A_i are atoms. A_0 is termed the *head* of the clause. $A_1 \wedge \ldots \wedge A_n$ is termed the *body* of the clause. We require variables (if any) appearing in any atom to appear in a non-test predicate atom in the body of the clause. Then D is said to be a *deductive database* (**ddb**).

The standard fix-point semantics are associated with the **ddb** and are extended with test predicates which, having a fixed semantics, only test the validity of derivations. The computational implementation of such semantics can be accomplished by a resolution based system which handles test predicates properly e.g. wait mechanism [20].

The restriction on variables is part of *range restriction* [7] and is imposed because update translations are then independent of the domain. There are no *additional* problems with accepting functions in our framework, but see the comments on recursion in section 3. The clauses of the **ddb** are partitioned into two classes, the intensional database definition which contains the views

Definition: Let L be a language with an **ddb** D. Then the set $V=\{e \mid e \in D$ *and* $e=A_0 \leftarrow A_1 \wedge \ldots \wedge A_n$ *and* $n \geq 1\}$ is termed the *intensional database definition* (**idb**). An *intensional database predicate* of L is any predicate appearing in the head of a clause in the **idb**.

and the extensional database containing the facts.

Definition: Let D be a **ddb** in the language L with an **idb** V. Then the set $E \subseteq D$ of (ground) unit clauses is termed the *extensional database* (**edb**). Note that by our restrictions, all unit clauses are ground, and so $V \cup E = D$.

When updating the **ddb**, it will be convenient to distinguish updates on the **edb**.

Definition: Let D be a **ddb** in the language L with an **idb** V. Then any non-intensional database predicate in L is termed an *extensional database predicate*. The set EDP is the set of all extensional database predicates in L.

Definition: Let D be an **ddb**. Then a predicate appearing in the head of a clause is a *view*. The set of clauses with the same predicate name in the head is the *definition* of the view. The definition of a view may depend on the definitions of other views.

Definition: Let D be a **ddb** with an **edb** E and **idb** V. Then a view with a definition containing clauses appearing in both the **edb** and the **idb** is termed a *hybrid view*.

We consider the **ddb** having disjoint **edb** and **idb** predicates (i.e. no hybrid views). This restriction enforces a logical independence between the view and the **edb**.

A *fact* (tuple) is a *ground* unit clause of W. An update u of a fact g is written **ins**(g) for an *insertion update* and a *deletion update* is written **del**(g). Translations are sets of updates.

Definition: Let L be a language with wffs W. Then a *translation* U is a set of insertion and deletion updates.

Thus, only facts appear in translations. Updates of the **edb** are defined by addition and deletion of facts in a translation in a classical (relational) way.

Definition: Let D be a **ddb** with an **edb** E and **idb** V, and U a translation. Then $\Upsilon(D,U)$ is defined to be $V \cup E'$ such that E' is constructed by *removing* every fact appearing in a deletion request in U from E, and *adding* every fact appearing in an insertion request in U to E. That is, $E'=(E-\{g \mid \mathbf{del}(g) \in U\}) \cup \{g \mid \mathbf{ins}(g) \in U\}$

This definition will always be used to update the **ddb** with disjoint insertion and deletion sets of updates in a translation. Note that redundant insertion updates are ignored, and that facts occurring in translations are instantiations of extensional database predicates. Thus the update of the **ddb** is always well defined.

To characterize the derivation of facts and logical consequence, we introduce some notation for an extended *SLD*-resolution.

Definition: Let D be a **ddb**, G a goal of the form $\leftarrow A_1, \ldots, A_k$. We write $D \vdash (A_1, \ldots, A_k)\theta$ if θ is a computed answer substitution of $D \cup \{G\}$. We write $D \models (A_1, \ldots, A_k)\theta$ if θ is a correct answer substitution for $D \cup \{G\}$.

The declarative part of the above definition of updates can be expressed as a very weak correctness view update policy.

Definition: Let D be a **ddb**, u an update on a fact g and U a translation. Then U is said to be *correct* when

- $\Upsilon(D,U) \models g$ for insertion updates
- $\Upsilon(D,U) \not\models g$ for deletion updates

The correctness update policy for view updates implies that update translations must affect at least the EDP which the updated fact depends on (i.e. the predicates which appear in a SLD tree of the fact appearing in the view update), otherwise no change will take place in the existing (deletion) or possible (insertion) derivations of the (fact appearing in the) view update.

In an **idb** with functions or test predicates, no correct translation may exist. For example, $u=$ **ins**$(p(10))$, $D=\{p(X)\leftarrow q(X)\wedge X>10, p(X)\leftarrow q(X)\wedge X<10, p(f(a))\leftarrow q(X)\wedge X=10\}$ (selection- union) has no correct translation since $p(10)$ is not derived from the **ddb** given any state of the **edb**. The translators described in this paper reject such a view update as "impossible".

Correctness is very general in that it admits irrelevent facts in a translation. Thus we define a *minimal* translation.

> **Definition:** Let D be a **ddb** with u an update, and U a correct translation. Then the translation U is said to be *minimal* iff there does not exist a correct translation U' such that $U'\subset U$.

Clearly, there can be several incomparable minimal translations. For example, $u=$**ins**$(p(a))$, $D=\{p(X)\leftarrow q(X), p(X)\leftarrow r(X)\wedge s(X)\}$ which has the correct and minimal translations $U=\{$**ins**$(q(a))\}$ and $U=\{$**ins**$(r(a))$, **ins**$(s(a))\}$. We believe this reflects a more desirable semantics than an update policy based on a more restrictive criteria (e.g. minimality based on cardinality).

The minimal view update policy implies that a translator need not consider updates to EDP predicates which the view update does not depend on. Also, if an insertion view update is already derivable, then the minimal translation is the empty set (i.e. do nothing). The minimal view update policy interacts with insertion updates in various ways.

The minimal policy will, in the case of redundancy, ignore the structure of the views. For example, $u=$**ins**$(p(a))$, $D=\{p(X)\leftarrow q(X), p(X)\leftarrow q(X)\wedge r(X)\}$ has only one correct and minimal translation $U=\{$**ins**$(q(a))\}$, the translation $U=\{$**ins**$(q(a))$, **ins**$(r(a))\}$ associated with the redundant second rule is not a minimal one. We believe this is a reasonable way of handling this view.

One problem which arises is the need for extra constants, not appearing in the view, to make an insertion translation sensible. For example, $u=$**ins**(p), $D=\{p\leftarrow q(Y)\}$. Clearly, some constant c must be provided for correct and minimal translation $U=\{$**ins**$(q(c))\}$. Note that all updates where c is an arbitrary constant are equally minimal. Instead of randomly selecting any constant, we request a value from the user [18]. We denote this requested value as a ground substitution σ applied to the clauses appearing in a translation. A view update can have multiple correct and minimal translations, some or all of which require constants. One way of handling this situation is to present the possible translations with variables, have the user select one and then supply the extra constants. (Another possibility not explored here is the introduction of unknown value semantics, as is typically done in the relational case.)

The handling of redundant views and the acceptance of new values can conflict with a minimal view update policy. For example, $u=$**ins**$(p(a))$, $D=\{p(X)\leftarrow q(X), p(X)\leftarrow q(Y)\wedge r(Y,X)\}$. Here, two correct translations are considered, $U=\{$**ins**$(q(a))\}$ and $U=\{$**ins**$(q(Y))$, **ins**$(r(Y,a))\}$ for some value Y. Now, if the value supplied by the user for Y is a, expressed as the substitution $\sigma=\{Y/a\}$, then there is only one minimal translation: the singleton set $\{$**ins**$(q(a))\}$. We accept this situation and accept only this minimal translation in this case. Perhaps the user should be informed that while specifying a constant for the insertion of two facts, only one fact was actually inserted.

One assumption in relational view updates is that local variables (i.e. variables appearing only in the body of a clause) *necessarily* bind with data in the extensional database. For example, given the view update $u=$**ins**$(em(e,m))$, $V=\{em(E,M)\leftarrow ed(E,D)\wedge dm(D,M)\}$ (join-projection), four possibilities for minimal insertions present themselves, depending on the state of the **edb**:

	edb	$ed(e,D)$	$dm(D,m)$	translation U
(i)	$\{ed(e,d),dm(d,m)\}$	true	true	$\emptyset$
(ii)	$\{ed(e,d)\}$	true	false	$\{$**ins**$(dm(d,m))\}$
(iii)	$\{dm(d,m)\}$	false	true	$\{$**ins**$(em(e,d))\}$
(iv)	$\emptyset$	false	false	$\{$**ins**$(ed(e,D))$,**ins**$(dm(D,m))\}\sigma$ (for some ground substitution σ)

The relational approach assumes in this example that the department in the **edb** is the desired one and that the intended update is not to add the new employee or manager to a new department. That is, that the translation of (iv) is not admissible for cases (i)-(iii).

This assumption is not necessarily desirable. In general, with any local variables in the body of a clause, there is a choice between adding new data and using data in the **edb**. We call this fact the *new-data assumption* problem. We say there is a *strict* new-data assumption if data in the **edb** is always used, and a *general* new-data assumption when translations accept constants from the user in all cases. Our approach is to admit a *general* new-data assumption because it is implied by the minimal view update policy. Note that given the minimal view update policy, the translations admitted will be a superset of the translations admitted under a strict new-data update policy. There are, of course, policies which fall between these two alternatives. With rule annotations a complete range of policies, dependent on each atom or clause in the **idb**, is allowed.

The view update policies for insertion updates do not eliminate the choice problem. This problem occurs for views with two or more clauses in its definition. For example, u=**ins**$(p(a))$, $D=\{p(X)\leftarrow q(X), p(X)\leftarrow r(X)\}$ (union) gives two possible correct and minimal translations $U=$ $\{$**ins**$(q(a))\}$ or $U=\{$**ins**$(r(a))\}$. In particular, the structure of the **edb** presents the extreme case of the choice problem for insertion since the **edb** is assumed to be large. For example, u=**ins**(p), $D=\{p\leftarrow q(X)\wedge r(X)\}$ (join-projection) will have a correct and minimal translation for every element in q and r. In general the number of translations can be exponential in the size of the database. We prove it for the deletion case here:

Lemma 1: Let D be a **ddb**, u a deletion update. Then the number of correct and minimal translations of u can be exponential in the length of D.

Proof: (Sketch) Let D_n be the database $\cup_{i=1}^{n}\{p\leftarrow q_i\wedge r_i, q_i, r_i\}$ where $q_1, q_2, \ldots, r_1, r_2 \ldots$ are unique predicates. For each increment of i the number of translations is doubled since $\{$**del**(q_i),**del**$(r_i)\}\times\{$translations of $D_{i-1}\}$ are all correct and minimal translations. Thus the number of translations is 2^i. Proof by induction on the length of the database follows directly.•

3. Procedural Description

The section describes algorithms which examine *SLD* trees constructed from a query of the fact appearing in the update and the **ddb**. In the deletion case, this is the tree associated with the query constructed from the fact appearing in the deletion view update. In the insertion case, the **ddb** first is extended with a set of special predicates, and then the tree associated with the query constructed from the fact appearing in the insertion view update is examined.

In practice, deductive databases (and logic programming systems) must deal with control problems in computing the answer to recursive queries. This problem is dealt with by requiring ground queries to terminate when *all* possible refutations are explored (i.e. there must be a good halting condition on the *SLD* refutation procedure). This former problem has been solved in the function free case [25]. Since translators are implemented using resolution, they inherit all these problems. However, allowing functions does not introduce additional problems beyond ones considered for recursive query processing.

This approach is based on the class of **ddb** considered and the fact that positive queries are evaluated on a **ddb**. This class of deductive databases is monotonic in the following sense: deletion updates can only remove (implied) facts from the **ddb**, and insertion updates can only add (implied) facts. Thus, deletion view updates need only have translations consisting of deletion updates on the **edb**, and insertion view updates need only have translations consisting of insertion updates on the **edb**. This considerably simplifies the construction of correct translators. Note that view updates are *typed* (e.g. deletions translate to deletions) as a consequence of monotonicity, instead of being imposed as an update policy as in [6].

We introduce a notation for translators.

> **Definition:** Let D be a **ddb** and u an update. Then $\Delta(D,u)$ is a *translator* which computes a correct and minimal translation of u with respect to the **ddb**. There is an insertion translator $\Delta_{ins}(D,u)$ if u is an insertion and a deletion translator $\Delta_{del}(D,u)$ if u is a deletion.

3.1. Deletion

Our approach is to evaluate a query constructed from the fact appearing in the view update and simultaneously to record the clauses of the **edb** which appear in the refutation of the query. Since for our class of **ddb**, every refutation of a view update depends on the presence of an element in the **edb** (see lemma 2), this element can be removed and, by monotonicity, the refutations which used that element will no longer be computed. Of course, the fact in the view update may still be proved by some other refutation. To account for this situation, translations are constructed by selecting one element from of the **edb** from each refutation. To generate all possible translations, we first collect together into a set all the clauses of the **edb** participating in a *single* refutation.

> **Definition:** Let D be a **ddb** (with **edb** E), u a deletion update of a fact g. Let $S=C_1\theta_1, \ldots, C_n\theta_n$ be the sequence of input clauses and mgu's (most general unifiers) for $D \vdash g$ (see figure 3-1). Then the (finite) set of clauses $EDS_{del}=S \cap E$ is termed the *deletion extensional dependency set* (**eds-del**) of a refutation of g with respect to D.

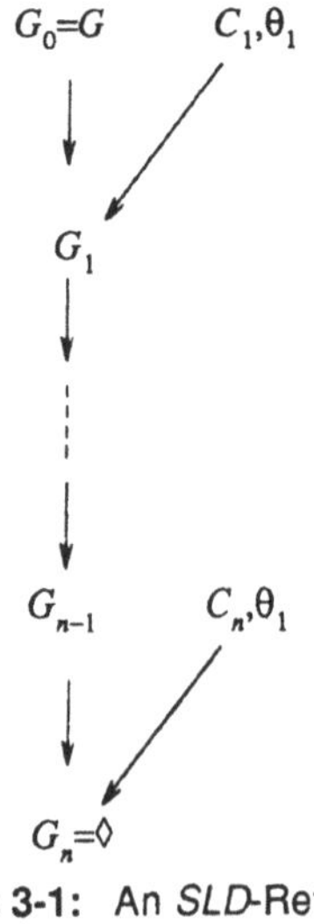

Figure 3-1: An *SLD*-Refutation

In general there are m **eds-del** for a goal, one for each m different refutations of the goal (some of which may be identical). The basic idea of this naive deletion translator is to generate all such (minimal) possible combinations of selecting elements from each of these m sets.

Definition: Let D be a **ddb**, u=**del**(g) a deletion update of a fact g. Then the naive translator $\Delta_{del}^{naive}(D,u)=U$, whose result is a translation U, is defined as

phase 1: (pre)compute every eds

Let $EDS_{del}^{\times}=EDS_{del_1},\ldots,EDS_{del_m}$ be the set of **eds** of g with D for every m *SLD* refutations. Note that by our restrictions on refutation procedures, the set of sets $EDS_{del}^{\times}$ is finite.

phase 2: construct sets of deletions

Let $U^{\times}=\{\{$**del**$(t_1),\ldots,$**del**$(t_m)\}\mid t_i\in EDS_{del_i}\}$

phase 3: choose a minimal set

Select any $U\in U^{\times}$ such that there is no $U'\in U^{\times}$ and $U'\subset U$. (This selection is not unique).

Note that the translation generated by the naive translator is always well defined for updating the **edb**. Next we prove that the naive translator is correct by first demonstrating that every refutation involves the **edb**.

Lemma 2: Let D be a **ddb** (with an **edb** E and **idb** V), u a deletion update of a fact g. Suppose $D\vdash g$, then at least one element of the **edb** is selected in this refutation of g.

Proof: Let $G=G_0,\ldots,G_n$ be the sequence of goals, and $C_1,\ldots,C_n$ be the sequence of selected input clauses of the refutation of G. This sequence is finite and $G_n=\Diamond$ (empty clause) because the refutation is successful. Therefore, G_{n-1} is of the form $\leftarrow A_{n-1}$, where A_{n-1} is an atom. Since no unit clauses are elements of V, the definition of the **Idb** implies $C_n\in E$.•

Corollary: There is at least one element of the **edb** selected in the refutation for every element which appears in a view.

Lemma 3: Let D be a **ddb**, and u=**del**(g) a deletion update of a fact g. Then $\Delta_{del}^{naive}(D,u)=U$ is correct.

Proof: Let $\Upsilon(D,U)=D'$. We must demonstrate that $\Upsilon(D,U)\nvdash g$. The proof rests on the fact that there is an element from every refutation in any generated translation. This is demonstrated by contradiction. Let $G=G_0,\ldots,G_n$ be the sequence of goals, and EDS_{del} the **eds-del**, for any successful refutation of $D\vdash g$. Let $t_i\in EDS_{del}$ such that **del**$(t_i)\in U$ (which exists by phase 2 of the naive translator). The clause t_i is ground. Then $t_i\in E'\subseteq D'$ by definition of a selected positive literal. However, $t_i\notin D'$ by definition of $\Upsilon(D,U)$.•

The central problem with this method is that it generates an exponential in $\prod_{i=1}^{m}|EDS_{del_i}|$ (i.e. the product of the cardinalities of the **eds-del**) number of possible translations, one of which the user must select.

3.2. Insertion

We describe a practical translator which implements correct and minimal translations and which is independent of the computation rule. This independence is crucial when designing methods of restriction the number of translations of a view update, since the semantics of such a method can be independent of the way in which an answer is computed.

The key element to the translator is the temporary addition of clauses, termed insertion clauses, which represent any insertion which could appear in an insertion translation. Thus the semantics of an insertion view update translator is defined to be any set of clauses which satisfy the insertion clauses and which compute a correct and minimal translation. The general idea is to compute a refutation of the fact appearing in an insertion view update and record a trail of the unifications used with the sequence of insertion clauses. The insertion clauses are kept on a list and the refutation proceeds by applying substitutions to the resolvent goal (as usual) and the trail until the search tree is exhausted. Another way of looking at the same process is to imagine a extended concept of the computation rule which never selects insertion clauses [21], and when such a derivation "fails" (i.e. none of the conjuncts in a goal are an insertion clause), then this final goal represents a translation (modulo input by the user).

> **Definition:** Let p be a predicate with arity n. Let $\vec{x}$ denote n unique variable arguments to a predicate of arity n. Then the clause $p(\vec{x})\leftarrow$ (universally quantified) is termed the *most general unit clause* of p.

> **Definition:** Let L be a language with a **ddb** D and extensional database predicates $EDP=e_1,...,e_n$. Let c_i be the most general unit clause of e_i. Then the (finite) set of clauses $IC=\{c_1,...,e_n\}$ is termed the *insertion clauses* of D. Note that because of our restrictions, $D\cap IC=\varnothing$. In addition, we define the *insertion* **ddb** $D^+=D\cup IC$.

The central part of the insertion view update translator is defined as an extension of *SLD* derivations. We assume the existence of a delay mechanism [20] for handling instantiations of test predicates. When evaluating queries on a insertion **ddb**, some test predicates may not be evaluated. For example, with $D=\{p\leftarrow q(X)\wedge X>10\}$ gives the insertion **ddb** $D^+=\{p\leftarrow q(X)\wedge X>10, q(X)\}$, evaluating $D^+\vdash p$ will cause the delay of the test predicate, and the termination of the query. These delayed predicates will be used to check the input data of the user.

> **Definition:** Let D^+ be an insertion **ddb**, u an insertion update of a fact g. Let $C_1,...,C_n$ be the sequence of input clauses, $\theta=\theta_1,...,\theta_n$ the sequence of mgu's for the computed answer substitution (if any), and T the set of delayed test predicates for $D^+\vdash g$, then the set $EDS_{ins}=\{l \mid l=t\theta$ *and t is selected from IC* $\}\cup T$ is termed the *insertion extensional dependency set* (**eds-ins**).

> **Definition:** Let D^+ be an insertion **ddb**, u=**ins**(g) an insertion fact update. Let $EDS^{\times}_{ins}= EDS_{ins_1},...,EDS_{ins_m}$ be the **eds-ins** of the m *SLD* refutations of $D^+\vdash g$. Then
>
> (i) Let $\sigma_1,...,\sigma_m$ be the user specified ground substitutions of the translations. (In practice, the identity substitution can frequently be supplied automatically.)
>
> (ii) An element s_i is chosen by the user from $EDS^{\times}_{ins}$.
>
> If $s_i\sigma_i$ is ground or empty, then the translation is *accepted* and $\Delta^{naive}_{ins}(D,u)=s_i\sigma_i$. Otherwise the translation is rejected. Note that these two steps can be reversed so that at most one input substitution need be supplied by the user.

Returning to the example in section 2, with u=**ins**($em(e,m)$), $V=\{em(E,M)\leftarrow ed(E,D)\wedge dm(D,M)\}$, we have $IC=\{ed(X,Y),dm(X,Y)\}$. The various insertion translations are listed below

edb	translation U
$\{ed(e,d_1),ed(e,d_2),dm(d_1,m)\}$	$\varnothing$ or
	{**ins**($dm(d_1,m)$)} or
	{**ins**($dm(d_2,m)$)} or
	{**ins**($ed(e,d_1)$)} or
	{**ins**($ed(e,D)$),**ins**($dm(D,m)$)}σ
$\{ed(e,d)\}$	{**ins**($dm(d,m)$)} or
	{**ins**($ed(e,D)$),**ins**($dm(D,m)$)}σ
$\{dm(d,m)\}$	{**ins**($ed(e,d)$)} or
	{**ins**($ed(e,D)$),**ins**($dm(D,m)$)}σ

Thus all possible translations are computed via backward chaining and irrespective of the computation rule. Note also that the translator computes redundant insertion updates as part of a translation.

An example in which test predicates are used is u=**ins**(p), $D^+=\{p\leftarrow q(X)\wedge X<10, p\leftarrow r(X)\wedge X\geq 10,$

$q(X), r(X)\}$ the possible translations are $\{q(X) \wedge X<10\}\sigma_1$ and $\{r(X) \wedge X \geq 10\}\sigma_2$. Given that the user supplied substitutions for both translations are the same, say $\sigma_1 = \sigma_2 = \{X/5\}$, then the only possible translation is {**ins**($q(5)$)} because the test predicate of the second translation fails. If the substitutions are different for each translation, then either 0, 1 or 2 translations result, and in the last case the user must select a translation.

In the relational view update literature, view updates which did not satisfy a selection operator were generally rejected. However, with the addition of union views, more flexibility is required. For example, u=**ins**($p(10)$), $D = \{p(X) \leftarrow q(X) \wedge X<10, p(X) \leftarrow r(X) \wedge X \geq 10\}$ (selection-union) where the test predicate is used to control refutations, and not to check the input data. The translator defined above handled this type of view by allowing the test predicates to control which translations are generated.

To prove the correctness of the insertion translator, one preliminary lemma will be useful.

Lemma 4: (Specific Instance Theorem) Let D be a **ddb** and $G = \leftarrow A_1, \ldots, A_k$ a goal. Let $C_1\theta_1, \ldots, C_n\theta_n$ be a sequence of input clauses and mgu's for $D \vdash (A_1, \ldots, A_k)\theta$ where $\theta = \theta_1 \cdots \theta_n$. Then $C_1\theta, \ldots, C_n\theta \models (A_1, \ldots, A_k)\theta$.

Proof:

(i) $D \vdash (A_1, \ldots, A_k)\theta$	By assumption.
(ii) $C_1, \ldots, C_n \vdash (A_1, \ldots, A_k)\theta$	Since the proof of a goal depends only on its input clauses.
(iii) $\vdash C_1, \ldots, C_n \rightarrow (A_1, \ldots, A_k)\theta$	Deduction Theorem of First-Order Logic.
(iv) $\models C_1, \ldots, C_n \rightarrow (A_1, \ldots, A_k)\theta$	Soundness of *SLD* Resolution.
(v) $\models (C_1, \ldots, C_n \rightarrow (A_1, \ldots, A_k)\theta)\theta$	Since variables are $\forall$ quantified.
(vi) $\models C_1\theta, \ldots, C_n\theta \rightarrow (A_1, \ldots, A_k)\theta$	Since the substitution θ is idempotent (input clauses are variants).
(vii) $C_1\theta, \ldots, C_n\theta \models (A_1, \ldots, A_k)\theta$	

•

Theorem 5: (Correctness of the Insertion Translator) Let D^+ be the insertion **ddb** of **ddb** D, u an insertion update of a fact g, and $\Delta_{ins}^{naive}(D,u)$ the insertion translator of u on D. Then $\Delta_{ins}^{naive}(D,u) = U$ is correct.

Proof: We must show $\Upsilon(D,U) \models g$ Let $C_1\theta_1, \ldots, C_n\theta_n$ be the sequence of input clauses and mgu's of the refutation of $\Delta_{ins}^{naive}(D,u)$. Since there is a correct answer, $D \cup IC \vdash g$. By the specific instance theorem, $D \cup IC \vdash g \Rightarrow C_1\theta, \ldots, C_n\theta \models g$. Next, the input clauses are split into two disjoint sets depending on whether the clause matched in the **ddb**, or IC. Let $D^- = \{l \mid l \in \{C_1, \ldots, C_n\}$ *and l is selected from* $D\}$ and let EDS_{ins} be the **eds-ins** for this view update. Since $D^- \subseteq D$ and $EDS_{ins} \cap D^- = \emptyset$ and the grounding substitution in EDS_{ins} insures that the refutation succeeds, we can write $D^- \cup EDS_{ins} \models g$. Clearly, $D \cup EDS_{ins} \models g$ because *SLD*-resolution is monotonic, and $\Upsilon(D,U) \models g$ for the same reason.•

Note that this translator suffers from a limitation of never terminating on the insertion into any recursive views. This is a consequence of the decision to accept new data and the lack of an adequate halting condition. For example, u=**ins**($tc(a,b)$), $D^+ = \{tc(X,Y) \leftarrow p(X,Y), tc(X,Y) \leftarrow p(X,Z) \wedge tc(Z,Y), p(X,Y)\}$ (transitive closure) causes $\Delta_{ins}^{naive}(D,u)$ to loop infinitely computing the translations {**ins**($p(a,b)$)}, {**ins**($p(a,Z_1)$), **ins**($p(Z_1,b)$)}, {**ins**($p(a,Z_1)$), **ins**($p(Z_1,Z_2)$), **ins**($p(Z_2,b)$)} etc. Work continues on this problem for the general case. Rule annotations, described in the next section, can be used to force the translator to consider only non-recursive clauses (at the price of some completeness in the set of translations considered).

Finally, the translator can produce impossible answers since a test predicate, when selected with an unbound variable, is delayed and then eventually added to the final translation. Let u= **ins**(p), $D^+=\{p \leftarrow q(X), X>10,\ q(X) \leftarrow r(X) \wedge X<10,\ r(X)\}$. Since no translation is possible, the view update should be rejected. However, $\Delta_{ins}^{naive}(D,u)=\{$**ins**($r(X)$)$, X<10, X>10\}$, which will always be rejected after accepting any value from the user for X since the constraints are mutually exclusive. A general satisfiability testing program can correct this problem.

4. Rule Annotations

In this section, we provide an example of a method for specifying additional information to the translator to reduce the number of translations. Additional information is expressed as simple markings of predicates, which are termed *annotations*. The annotations guid the search process of the translators.

The general idea is to explore only the branches which are permitted by the annotations. Thus, in a **ddb** where all clauses are annotated in all ways, the annotation view update translator would produce exactly the same translations as the naive translator of the last section. In a **ddb** with no annotations, the annotated translator would always reject the translation as "impossible".

Deletion annotations are denoted by underlining the appropriate predicates. Insertion annotations are denoted by an arrow "→" pointing to the head of an annotated clause. For example, the view

(i) $\rightarrow p(X) \leftarrow \underline{q(X,Y)} \wedge r(Y)$

(ii) $p(X) \leftarrow \underline{s(X)} \wedge \underline{t(X)}$

has a (unique) insertion annotation on the (i) clause of the view and a (unique) deletion annotation of $q(X,Y)$ in that clause. The second clause (ii) has both $s(X)$ and $t(X)$ annotated for deletion. Informally, an insertion update of, say, **ins**($p(a)$) will be translated into {**ins**($q(a,Y)$), **ins**($r(Y)$)}. A deletion update of **del**($p(a)$) will be translated into {**del**($q(a,Y)$), **del**($s(a)$)} or {**del**($q(a,Y)$), **del**($t(a)$)}. By extension to derivations, any subsequent possible translations of an insertion on clause (ii), or deletions of $r(X)$ will be ignored.

Definition: A *deletion annotation* of a clause is a function from a clause to a (possibly empty) set of non-test predicate atoms, such that the value of the function for a clause is always a set of atoms appearing in the body of that clause. If the resulting set has a single element, then the clause is said to have a *unique deletion annotation.* A view definition which is annotated is a *deletion annotated view.*

Definition: An *insertion annotation* of a view is a function from the view's definition to a set of clauses such that the value of the function for a view is always a (possible empty) subset of the view definition. If the resulting set has a single element, then the view is said to have a *unique insertion annotation.*

Definition: An annotated **ddb** D^q is a **ddb** which has annotated clauses (insertion, deletion, or both).

Definition: A *unique annotation* **ddb** is a **ddb** where every clause has a unique deletion annotation and every view has a unique insertion annotation.

The above method can be expressed as a simple extension to *SLD*-resolution. For deletion, the extension is to maintain the annotations of an input clause in the resolvent goal, when appropriate.

Definition: An *deletion annotated atomic goal* is an atomic goal constructed from a deletion annotated atom appearing in an input clause or query.

Definition: Let G_i be a goal, C_{i+1} be an input clause for the selected atom of G_i. Then a *deletion SLD derivation* is an *SLD* derivation using an extended notion of resolvent. Two cases occur:

- The selected atom is a deletion annotated atomic goal. Then the delete annotations of the input clause are maintained in the resolvent goal G_{i+1} i.e. an annotated atom in the input clause will be recognized as annotated when selected from a goal the atom appears in.
- The selected atom is not annotated. Then the deletion annotations of the input clause do not appear (are dropped) in the resolvent goal G_{i+1}.

Using this notion of resolvents, deletion annotated extensional dependency sets are defined by direct extension. They are the subset of the **eds-del** containing selected deletion annotated input clauses.

For insertion, the extension is simply to restrict resolution to consider only clauses with input annotations.

Definition: Let D^q be an annotated **ddb**. Let $Q \subseteq D$ be the subset of the **ddb** containing only insertion annotated clauses. Then an *insertion SLD derivation* is a *SLD* derivation on Q.

Again by direct extension, insertion annotated extensional dependency sets are the subset of the **eds-ins** containing insertion annotated clauses (from the input clauses). The previous translators operate with annotations.

Definition: Let D^q be an annotated **ddb**. Then the translator $\Delta^q_{del}(D,u)$ is the same as the deletion translator $\Delta^{naive}_{del}(D,u)$, except that deletion *SLD* derivations, and annotated **eds-del**, are used. The query constructed from u is annotated.

Definition: Let D^q be an annotated **ddb**. Then the translator $\Delta^q_{ins}(D,u)$ is the same as the deletion translator $\Delta^{naive}_{ins}(D,u)$, except that insertion *SLD* derivations, and annotated **eds-ins**, are used. The query constructed from u is annotated.

Clearly in general the number of translations decreases as the number of annotations decreases since the annotations permit fewer derivations of facts. In fact, with uniquely annotated **ddb**, for each view update a unique correct translation is produced.

Theorem 6: Let D^q be a *uniquely* annotated **ddb**. Then the translators $\Delta^q_{ins}(D,u)$ and $\Delta^q_{del}(D,u)$ each produce a most a single translation for any view update.

Proof: (Sketch) Straightforward since unique annotations imply for deletion only one annotated atomic goal for each step of the refutation and imply for insertion only one refutation.•

Corollary: The number of unique annotations required for a unique translation of an insertion update is worst case $O(n)$ where n is the depth of the *SLD* tree.

Corollary: The number of unique annotations required for a unique translation of a deletion update is worst case $O(m)$ where m is the number of success branches of the *SLD* tree (i.e. the number of refutations).

We see that insertion annotations restrict the possible translations, but when unique translations are desired, some difficulties arise. For example, u=**ins**$(p(5))$,$V=\{p(X) \leftarrow q(X) \wedge X<10, \rightarrow p(X) \leftarrow q(X) \wedge X \geq 10\}$ (selection-union). Since only the second rule is annotated in this example, the translator will fail to produce a translation. When the test predicates for a view check for independent subsets of a domain across all clauses of a view, then such views can be insertion annotated on every clause while still producing unique translations, since the test predicates will only succeed on one of the clauses.

Even considering such restrictions, annotations provide a powerful means of controlling possible translations. For example, the complete range of strict to general new-data assumptions present themselves, simply by annotations of the predicates in *IC* in which new-data is desired. Insertion into (mutually) recursive views can be handled in a limited way by annotation of the nonrecursive clauses in the views. Clearly, a language for relating domain dependent information to annotations is desirable and deserves further research.

5. Conclusion

We have taken some steps towards allowing view updates in deductive databases. A declarative semantics of view updates was presented which considers correct and subset minimal translations. These semantics admit an exponential number of different translations for a view update. Algorithms based on *SLD*-resolution were presented for computing translations. The algorithms are independent of the computation rule, thus providing a basis for methods which reduce the number of translations. An example of such a method, view annotations, is presented. A small number of unique annotations (for insertion, proportional to the depth of the *SLD* tree; for deletion, proportional to the number of refutations) was shown to produce a unique view update translation.

A meta-interpreter written in MU-PROLOG [20] has been written which implements the algorithms and annotations described in this paper.

Acknowledgements
I would like to thank Hervé Gallaire and Jean-Marie Nicolas for the opportunity to do research; Mark Wallace for following this work closely and contributing to it with many interesting discussions; the anonymous referees for numerous improvements; and the following people for providing valuable comments on earlier drafts of this paper: Hendrik Decker, J. Christoph Freytag, Hervé Gallaire, Jean-Marie Nicolas, Volker Küchenhoff, Laurent Vieille, and Mark Wallace.

References

[1] F. Bancilhon, N. Spyratos.
Update Semantics of Relational Views.
ACM TODS 6(4):557-575, 1981.

[2] C. R. Carlson, A. K. Arora.
The Updatability of Relational Views Based on Functional Dependencies.
In *Proceedings COMPSAC 79*, pages 415-420. 1979.
Reprinted in *Tutorial: Database Management in the 1980's*, J. A. Larson, H. A. Freeman (editors), IEEE Computer Society Press, 1981.

[3] S. S. Cosmadakis, C. H. Papadimitriou.
Updates of Relational Views.
Journal of the ACM 31(4):742-760, 1984.

[4] C. J. Date.
Relational Database: Selected Writings.
Addison-Wesley, Reading, Massachusetts, 1986.

[5] J. E. Davidson.
Interpreting Natural Languiage Database Updates.
PhD thesis, Stanford University, 1984.

[6] U. Dayal, P. A. Bernstein.
On the Correct Translation of Update Operations on Relational Views.
ACM TODS 8(3):381-416, 1982.

[7] H. Decker.
Integrity Enforcement on Deductive Databases.
In *Proceedings of the First International Conference on Expert Database Systems.* Charleston, South Carolina, 1986.

[8] R. Fagin, G. M. Kuper, J. D. Ullman, M. Y. Vardi.
Updating Logical Databases.
In *Advances in Computing Research*, pages 1-18. JAI Press, 1986.

[9] A. L. Furtado, M. A. Casanova.
Updating Relational Views.
In W. Kim, D. S. Reiner, D. S. Batory (editors), *Query Processing in Database System*, pages 127-142. Springer-Verlag, Berlin, 1985.

[10] A. L. Furtado, K. C. Sevcik, C. S. Dos Santos.
Permitting Updates through Views of Data Bases.
Information Systems 4:269-283, 1979.

[11] S. J. Hegner.
Specification and Implementation of Programs for Updating Incomplete Information Databases.
In *PODS '87*, pages 146-158. 1987.
(Preliminary Report).

[12] B. E. Jacobs.
Application of database logic to the view update problem.
Technical Report TR 960, University of Maryland, College Park, 1980.

[13] A. M. Keller.
Algorithms for Translating View Updates to Database Updates for Views Involving Selections, Projections, and Joins.
In *PODS '85*, pages 154-163. 1985.

[14] A. M. Keller.
Choosing a View Update Translator by Dialog at View Definition Time.
In *Proceedings of VLDB*, pages 467-474. Kyoto, 1986.

[15] A. M. Keller, J. D. Ullman.
On Complementary and Independent Mappings on Databases.
In *Proceedings of VLDB*, pages 143-148. 1984.

[16] J. W. Lloyd.
Foundations of Logic Programming.
Springer-Verlag, Berlin, 1984.

[17] S. Manchanda, D. S. Warren.
Towards a Logical Theory of Database View Updates.
In J. Minker (editor), *Workshop on Foundations of Deductive Databases and Logic Programming*, pages 27-52. Washington, D.C., 1986.
(preprint).

[18] Y. Masunaga.
A Relational Database View Update Translation Mechanism.
In *Proceedings of VLDB*, pages 309-320. Singapore, 1984.

[19] C. B. Medeiros, F. Wm. Tompa.
Understanding the Implications of View Update Policies.
Algorithmica 1:337-360, 1986.

[20] L. Naish.
MU-PROLOG 3.1db Reference Manual
Department of Computer Science, University of Melbourne, 1984.

[21] L. Naish.
Heterogeneous SLD Resolution.
Journal of Logic Programming 4:297-303, 1984.

[22] J.-M. Nicolas, K. Yazdanian.
An Outline of BDGEN: a Deductive DBMS.
In R. E. A. Mason (editor), *Proceedings of IFIP 83*, pages 711-717. 1983.

[23] B. Ross.
View Updates on Deductive Databases.
Honours Report, Department of Computer Science, University of Melbourne, 1985.

[24] S. Todd.
Automatic Constraint Maintenance and Updating Defined Relations.
In B. Gilchrist (editor), *Proceedings of IFIP 77*, pages 145-148. 1977.

[25] L. Vieille.
Recursive Query Processing: The Power of Logic.
Technical Report TR-KB-17, ECRC, 1987.
Submitted to Theoretical Computer Science.

[26] A. Weber.
Updating Propositional Formulas.
In *Proceedings of the First International Conference on Expert Database Systems*, pages 373-386. Charlston, South-Carolina, 1986.

Conceptual Level Concurrency Control of Relational Update Transactions
(Extended Abstract)

Victor Vianu †
Department of Computer Science and Engineering
University of California, San Diego
La Jolla, California 92093, USA
and
Gottfried Vossen ‡
Lehrstuhl fuer angewandte Mathematik
Technische Hochschule Aachen
Ahornstr. 55, D-5100 Aachen, FRG

Abstract

The concurrency control problem is examined for transactions as they appear at the conceptual level in a concrete database model. Specifically, a class of widely accepted update transactions in relational databases is studied with respect to concurrency control. It is shown how static serializability testing, as well as dynamic scheduling, can be improved by making use of the semantic information available at the conceptual level on transactions and database constraints.

1. Introduction

The concurrency control problem for database systems is traditionally investigated using a simple model for transactions which reflects the sequence of read and write operations performed at the internal level. Schedulers based on such a model allow limited concurrency, because they do not have available any information on the meaning of the transactions. Recently, there has been considerable interest in looking at transaction models capturing more semantic information, and using this information to increase the amount of concurrency allowed by schedulers. The work in this area includes widely different approaches, such as enriching the read/write model with additional operations [12, 5], using models based on abstract data types [18, 21, 17], and using semantic information provided by the users [8]. However, none of these approaches considers transactions as they appear at the conceptual level in a concrete database model. This paper is a first effort in this direction. Specifically, we investigate the concurrency control problem for a widely accepted class of update transactions in relational databases.

The model for transactions used in this paper is that developed in [1, 2]. A transaction is viewed as a sequence of insertions, deletions, or modifications, forming a semantic unit. The selection of tuples (to be deleted or modified) involves the inspection of individual attribute values for each tuple. Several features of this model are particularly desirable in the context of concurrency control. First, equivalence of transactions can be tested effectively and efficiently (see [1, 2]). This enables us to look at serializability of schedules in semantic terms, rather than syntactic, and leads to a scheduling algorithm that allows increased concurrency. Second, efficient techniques are available for simplifying transactions [1, 2, 10] and extracting internal parallelism from

† This author was supported in part by the National Science Foundation, under grant number IST-8511538.
‡ This author was supported by the NATO Science Committee under a Postdoctoral Fellowship, Grant No. DAAD 300/402/508/7; this work was done while the author was visiting at UCSD.

transactions [10, 11]. These techniques can be used in conjunction with scheduling algorithms to obtain simple schedules and to further increase concurrency.

We start by looking at various notions of schedules and serializability, which are natural in the context o our model. Schedules are distinguished based on the connection between the updates occurring in the schedul and those in the transactions. The simplest type of schedule is an interleaving of all updates occurring in th transactions. However, other types of schedules are considered, where the updates in the schedule are connecte to those in the transactions in a less straightforward fashion. Serializability of a schedule is defined entirel semantically: a schedule for a set of transactions is serializable if it has the same *effect* as the execution of th transactions in some serial order. Our results concern static serializability testing, as well as dynamic scheduling We first look at the complexity of testing serializability and show that it is NP-complete. However, we exhib an infinite sequence of increasingly powerful polynomial-time testing algorithms which approximate, in som sense, exact serializability testing. Intuitively, the exact algorithm requires looking at the effect of the schedu as a whole. The approximate algorithms are obtained by restricting, in various ways, the "amount" of context the schedule examined at a time. The least powerful of the approximate algorithms examines only conflict between pairs of updates. (Note that this corresponds to the use of compatibility tables [9, 12] for our updates We also show that efficient, exact serializability testing algorithms exist for less powerful transactions. Fo instance, serializability can be tested in polynomial time if the transactions contain only inserts and deletes (n modifications).

Finally, we briefly look at concurrency control using constraint information. Specifically, we show how ou serializability testing algorithms can use information on the functional dependencies satisfied by the database t allow more concurrency in schedules.

The paper consists of six sections. The model for transactions is briefly outlined in section 2. In section the notions of schedule and serializability are discussed. Our results on testing serializability are presented in se tion 4. Section 5 contains our results on concurrency control in the presence of functional dependencies. In Se tion 6, we summarize our work and review some problems that deserve further study.

This paper is an extended abstract of [20]; due to space limitations, some concepts and results a presented informally, and many details are omitted.

2. The Model for Transactions

The model for transactions used in this paper is that developed in [1, 2]. In this section we review th model and some previously obtained results. We assume familiarity with basic terminology for relational dat bases, as in [14, 19].

Informally, a transaction is a sequence of instructions viewed as a semantic unit. As in most commerci database management systems, three types of atomic instructions are used to build up (update) transaction insertion, deletion, and modification. We focus on a tractable and widely used class of transactions. Specificall we consider the important class of "domain-based" transactions, where the selection of tuples (to be deleted modified) only involves the inspection of each individual attribute value of a tuple, independently of other att bute values in the tuple and of other tuples in the instance. To formally define these instructions, we need t concept of a condition:

2.1 Definition. Let U be a set of attributes. A *condition* over U is an expression of the form A=a or A≠ where A ∈ U and a ∈ dom(A).[1] A tuple μ over U *satisfies* a condition A=a (A≠ a) iff $\mu(A) = a$ ($\mu(A) \neq a$).

[1] The model can easily be extended to include other comparison operators as well.

uple μ *satisfies* a set C of conditions if it satisfies every condition in C. We do not explicitly use logical connec-ors to build up complex conditions. It can be easily seen that this would not add power to our transactions. In he following, only *satisfiable* sets of conditions are considered, that is, sets of conditions with no mutually xclusive conditions.

A set of conditions over U is used to specify a set of tuples over U (those satisfying the conditions). Due to he form of our conditions, we use the intuitively suggestive term "hyperplane" to identify such sets of tuples:

.2 Definition. The *hyperplane* H(U,C) defined by a set C of conditions over U is the set $\{\mu \mid \mu$ is a tuple over J satisfying C$\}$.

For simplicity, we sometimes use the same notation for a set C of conditions over U and for the hyperplane I(U,C) defined by C. Thus, we say "hyperplane C" instead of "hyperplane H(U,C)", whenever U is understood.

We now define the syntax of the atomic instructions ("updates") used to build our transactions. An *inser-ion* over a database schema **R** is an expression $i_X(C)$ where X is a relation schema in **R** and C is a set of condi-ions specifying a complete[2] tuple over X. A *deletion* over **R** is an expression $d_X(C)$, where X is a relation chema in **R** and C is a set of conditions over X. Finally, a modification over **R** is an expression $m_X(C_1 ; C_2)$, vhere X is a relation schema in **R**, C_1 and C_2 are sets of conditions over X and, for each A in X, either[3] $C_1|_A = C_2|_A$ or $A = a \in C_2$ for some a. (The equalities present in C_2 but not in C_1 indicate how tuples in $H(X,C_1)$ are modified.) An *update* is an insertion, deletion, or modification. Following are examples of updates.

2.3 Example. Let EMP be a relation with attributes U = { NAME, DEPT, RANK, SALARY }. The following are updates over U:

1) i_U (<moe, parts, manager, 30K>)
(this hires Moe as the new manager of the parts department),

2) d_U (NAME $\neq$ moe, DEPT = parts, RANK = manager)
(this deletes all managers in the parts department whose names are not Moe),

3) m_U (DEPT = parts, RANK $\neq$ manager;
DEPT = service, RANK $\neq$ manager, SALARY = 20K)

(this transfers all employees who are not managers from the parts department to the service department; the rank remains unchanged; the new salary is 20K). □

In the following we sometimes omit the subscripts in writing updates. For instance, we write i(C) instead of $i_X(C)$, whenever X is understood.

A *transaction* over a database schema **R** is a finite sequence of updates over **R** (the empty sequence is denoted by ϵ). The semantics of a transaction t is defined by a mapping associating old instances and new instances, called the *effect* of t and denoted by eff(t) (see [1] for the formal definition). Two transactions t and t′ are *equivalent*, denoted $t \approx t'$, if they have the same effect.

Since the effects of updates over different relation schemas are independent, we will usually consider transactions over uni-relational schemas; our results can be easily extended to multi-relational schemas.

We next introduce a non-procedural method for describing the effect of a transaction on a database, which is used in our serializability testing and dynamic scheduling algorithms. The effect is described at the tuple level

[2] If $X = A_1 \cdots A_n$, then $C = \{ A_1 = a_1, ..., A_n = a_n \}$ for some $a_i \in dom(A_i)$, $1 \leq i \leq n$.

[3] If C is a set of conditions over U and $A \in U$, then $C|_A$ denotes the set of conditions in C involving attribute A.

using the notion of a "transition". Transitions can be specified in an intuitively appealing manner and are usefu tools. For each tuple, a transition indicates whether the tuple is deleted or, if not, how it is modified. In addi- tion, a transition gives a finite set of inserted tuples. A transition will be specified by first partitioning the spac of tuples into sufficiently many hyperplanes. It is assumed that all tuples in each hyperplane of the partition ar either deleted or updated to yield another hyperplane in the partition. This is specified using a "transitior graph" whose vertices are the hyperplanes in the partition. If H_1 is updated to H_2, there is an edge from H_1 t H_2. If H_1 is deleted there is no edge leaving H_1.

The set of inserted tuples cannot be conveniently specified using the graph, and is given separately. A *tran- sition specification (spec)* is a pair <G, Insert>, where G is a transition graph and Insert is a set of newl inserted tuples (called the *insert set* of the transition spec).

We now give a simple example of a transition spec:

2.4 Example. Let U = AB and G be the transition graph represented below (Figure 2.1).

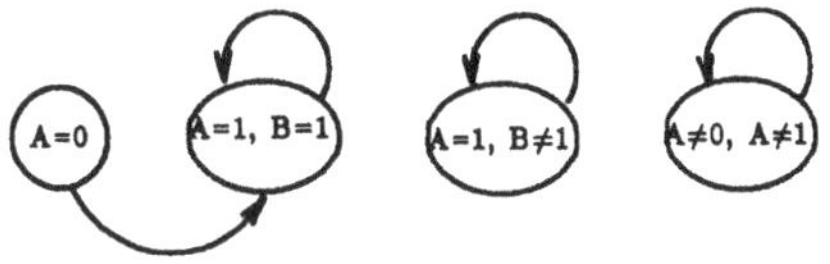

Figure 2.1

Let Insert = {<1,1>}. Then <G,Insert> is a transition specification over AB. The transition specified b <G,Insert> consists of replacing all tuples μ where $\mu(A) = 0$ by the tuple <1,1>. All other tuples remai unchanged. The tuple <1,1> is inserted. □

For each transaction there exists a corresponding transition spec which represents the final effect of th transaction. In order to construct the transition spec corresponding to a transaction, it is first necessary to per form some "preprocessing" of the transaction. Specifically, the transaction is modified so that all hyperplane corresponding to distinct sets of conditions occurring in the transaction are disjoint. A transaction having thi property is said to be in First Normal Form (1NF). The 1NF property simplifies considerably our results. Eac transaction can be transformed into an equivalent 1NF transaction by "splitting" every hyperplane occurring i it into sufficiently small hyperplanes (see [1]).

2.5 Example. Consider the transaction over AB: i(<0,3>) m({A=0};{A=1, B=1}). The corresponding tran sition specification is the one of Example 2.4.

As is shown in [1, 2], transition specs are useful tools for studying transaction equivalence and optimiza tion. In particular, it is shown that transaction equivalence can be decided in polynomial time[4] by reducing th question to deciding whether their associated transition specs describe the same effect. A different method fo deciding equivalence is to use the sound and complete axiomatization described in [10]. Of particular interest t our investigation are rules indicating when two given updates commute. We now list these rules, called *commu tativity rules* (C_1,C_2,C_3,C_4 are from a set of pairwise disjoint hyperplanes):

[4] Here and in the following, we say that an algorithm whose input is a set T of transactions is polynomial-time, if it is polynomial-time in the total number of updates and constants occurring in T.

1) $d(C_1)i(C_2) \approx i(C_2)d(C_1)$ $(C_1 \neq C_2)$

2) $i(C_1)i(C_2) \approx i(C_2)i(C_1)$

3) $d(C_1)d(C_2) \approx d(C_2)d(C_1)$

4) $m(C_1;C_2)i(C_3) \approx i(C_3)m(C_1;C_2)$ $(C_1 \neq C_3)$

5) $m(C_1;C_2)m(C_3;C_4) \approx m(C_3;C_4)\, m(C_1;C_2)$ $(C_3 \neq C_1, C_2$ and $C_1 \neq C_4)$

6) $m(C_1;C_2)d(C_3) \approx d(C_3)m(C_1;C_2)$ $(C_3 \neq C_1, C_2)$

The commutativity rules generate a relation $\leftrightarrow$ on transactions in the natural fashion. The reflexive and transitive closure of $\leftrightarrow$ is denoted $\overset{*}{\leftrightarrow}$. Thus, $t_1 \overset{*}{\leftrightarrow} t_2$ indicates that the transaction t_1 can be proven equivalent to the transaction t_2 using just the commutativity rules.

3. Schedules and Serializability

In this section we discuss several notions of schedule for a set of transactions, and define serializable schedules. The situation we model is that where several transactions are executed concurrently on a single processor. A schedule represents the sequence of updates executed by the processor. Traditionally, a schedule for a finite set $T = \{t_1, \cdots t_n\}$ of transactions is defined as a sequence consisting of all updates in T, such that the updates of a given transaction t_i appear in the schedule in the same order as in t_i. Furthermore, the updates of a transaction t_i are identifiable in the schedule.

As stated earlier, the main purpose of this paper is to develop concurrency control techniques which take into account the semantics of relational transactions at the conceptual level. In this context, the classical notion of a schedule has several limitations. Specifically, the assumption that the updates actually executed by the processor are the same as those in the original transactions is no longer realistic in all cases. Indeed, the additional semantic information available can be used to improve such schedules in several respects. We distinguish several kinds of improvements, and then define extensions to the notion of schedule corresponding to each such improvement. The most general notion of schedule used in this paper is based on semantics rather than syntax alone. Traditional schedules will be viewed as special cases within this more general framework. We next give the formal definition of our notion of schedule:

3.1 Definition. Let T be a finite set of transactions over a database schema **R**.

(i) The *shuffle* of T, denoted shuffle(T), is the set of all sequences that have the elements of T as subsequences and contain no other elements.

(ii) A *schedule* s for T is a transaction for which there exists some sequence s' ∈ shuffle(T) s.t. $s \approx s'$.

In order to distinguish traditional schedules from our, more general schedules, we will refer to them as *strict schedules.* A strict schedule for a set T of transactions is an element of shuffle(T), where the updates of a given transaction are identifiable in the sequence. We will identify updates from transaction t_i by superscripting them with i.

Rather than giving a formal definition, we illustrate the notion of strict schedule using the following example. For simplicity, in this and other examples we denote a hyperplane {A=a} by "a".

3.2 Example. Consider the transactions over a single relation with one attribute A:

$t_1 = d(3)m(1;2)m(3;4)$, and $t_2 = d(3)m(2;3)$.

The following is a strict schedule for t_1 and t_2: $s = d^2(3)d^1(3)m^1(1;2)m^2(2;3)m^1(3;4)$. □

Following the traditional approach, we will consider a schedule for a set T of transactions to be correct i and only if it is *serializable*, that is, the effect of the execution of the schedule is the same as the effect of execut ing the transactions of T consecutively, in some order. In particular, this condition guarantees that the databas state will be consistent after the execution of the schedule, assuming that the input transactions are consistenc preserving. Formally we have:

3.3 Definition. A schedule s for a set $T = \{t_1, \cdots t_n\}$ of transactions over a given database schema **R** is *seri alizable* iff $s \approx t_{\sigma(1)} \cdots t_{\sigma(n)}$ for some permutation σ of $\{1 ,..., n\}$.

Consider the schedule s for $\{t_1, t_2\}$, from Example 3.2. The transition graph of s is exhibited in Figure 3.1

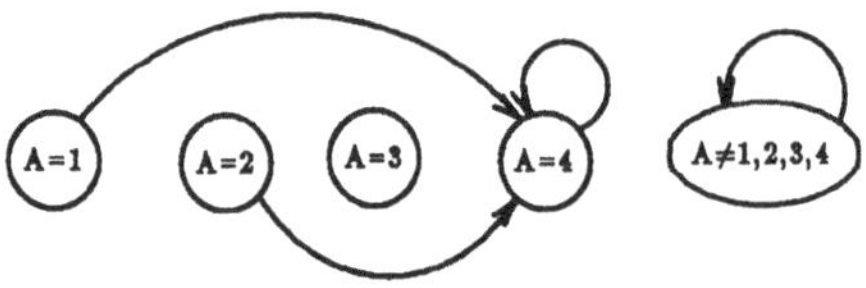

Figure 3.1

The transition graphs for t_1t_2 and t_2t_1 are represented in Figures 3.2 and 3.3, respectively.

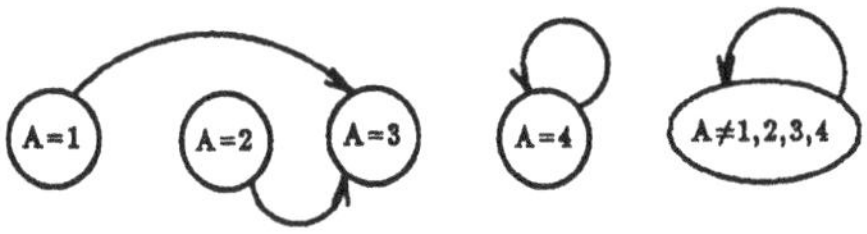

Figure 3.2

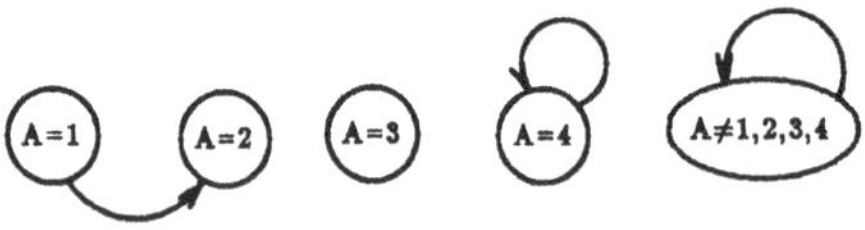

Figure 3.3

Clearly, $s \not\approx t_1t_2$ and $s \not\approx t_2t_1$. Thus, s is not serializable. On the other hand, the schedule

$$s^{\sim} = d^1(3)m^1(1;2)d^2(3)m^1(3;4)m^2(2;3)$$

for $\{t_1,t_2\}$ is equivalent to t_1t_2, and therefore is serializable.

We next look at two kinds of improvements to strict schedules, which result from the use of semantic info mation available within our framework. The first improvement results from processing of individual transa tions, conducted before, or while, the schedule is being generated. Indeed, each transaction can be simplifi sing the optimization techniques of [1, 2]. This results in a simpler overall execution sequence. Moreover, eliminating redundant updates decreases the potential for conflicts. Indeed, a redundant update may make the difference between serializability and non-serializability for the schedule. To see this, consider again Example .2. Clearly, the last update ("m(3;4)") of transaction t_1 is redundant. Thus, t_1 is equivalent to $t_1' = d(3)m(1;2)$. Now consider the non-serializable schedule s. If $m^1(3;4)$ is dropped from s, then the resulting xecution sequence

$$s' = d^2(3)d^1(3)m^1(1;2)m^2(2;3)$$

s serializable (equivalent to t_1t_2). Thus, s′ is an acceptable execution sequence of updates for t_1 and t_2. However, s′ is not a strict schedule for $\{t_1,t_2\}$, since not all updates of t_1 occur in s′. Note that s′ is a strict chedule for $\{t_1', t_2\}$.

We now define an extension to the notion of strict schedule, called "separable schedule", which allows for xecution sequences such as s′.

.4 Definition. A sequence s of updates is a *separable schedule* for a set of transactions $\{t_1, \cdots, t_n\}$, iff s is a trict schedule for some $\{t_1', \cdots, t_n'\}$ where $t_i \approx t_i'$, $1 \leqslant i \leqslant n$.

For instance, s′ above is a separable schedule for $\{t_1, t_2\}$. Intuitively, the term "separable" indicates that or each individual transaction, there is a separate sub-sequence of the schedule which is equivalent to the transaction. In particular, all strict schedules are special instances of separable schedules.

A second kind of improvement of schedules consists of simplifying a schedule using the interaction of updates from *distinct* transactions within the schedule, and results in non-separable schedules. Indeed, consider once more the transactions t_1 and t_2 and the schedule s of Example 3.2. As noted earlier, the last update of the schedule s can be dropped, and this yields a serializable, although non-strict schedule s′. Note that s′, viewed as a single transaction, can be further simplified by using the optimization techniques from [1, 2]. Indeed, s′ is equivalent to the transaction $s'' = d(3)m(1;3)m(2;3)$. In simplifying s′, several updates from different transactions were replaced by new updates. For instance, $m^1(1;2)m^2(2;3)$ was replaced by the simpler (see [1]) $m(1;3)m(2;3)$. As a result, updates in s″ can no longer be associated individually with the original transactions. In other words, s″ is not a separable schedule for $\{t_1,t_2\}$.

Note that non-strict schedules are useful primarily in the framework of dynamic scheduling, where the simplification of the input transactions and the output schedule may not be easily distinguished from the scheduling process itself.

We finally look at the assumption made so far concerning the finiteness of schedules. We claim that this assumption is not always appropriate. Indeed, in a dynamic framework, a scheduler may receive an uninterrupted stream of updates from arbitrarily many transactions. In the course of time, the scheduler generates an infinite schedule which may not be reducible to a sequence of consecutive finite schedules. Thus, it appears useful to extend the earlier definition of (strict) schedules to the infinite case. This can be done straightforwardly, and the details are omitted. Next, a notion of correctness for infinite schedules must be defined. We now propose such a definition. Intuitively, we require that, if the infinite schedule is interrupted at an arbitrary point, the finite schedule obtained by retaining only the transactions completed so far must be serializable. (Given a strict schedule s, a transaction t_i is *completed* in s if all updates of t_i appear in s.) Formally, we have:

3.5 Definition. (i) Let T' be a set of transactions, s a strict schedule for T', and $T \subseteq T'$. The *projection* of s onto T, denoted $\pi_T(s)$, is the sub-sequence of s containing only updates from transactions in T. If $T = \{t_i\}$ we also write $\pi_i(s)$ instead of $\pi_T(s)$.

(ii) A (possibly infinite) strict schedule s is *instantaneously serializable* iff for each prefix s_0 of s, $\pi_T(s_0)$ is serializable, where T is the set of transactions completed in s_0.

3.6 Remark. Clearly, the notion of instantaneous serializability is stronger than usual serializability in the case of finite schedules. This suggests an alternative way to define serializability for possibly infinite schedules weaker than the one given above:

A (possibly infinite) strict schedule s is *eventually serializable* iff for each prefix s_0 of s there exists a prefix p_0 of s containing s_0 s.t. $\pi_T(p_0)$ is serializable, where T is the set of transactions completed in p_0.

Note that instantaneous serializability implies eventual serializability, but the converse does not hold.

4. Checking Serializability of Schedules.

In this section, we investigate the complexity of checking the serializability of a given finite schedule, an propose several algorithms for testing serializability. We will be looking at a static situation, where the com plete schedule, as well as the set of transactions, are available. We will only consider strict schedules, sinc non-strict schedules are of interest primarily when the schedule is dynamically generated. The set of stric schedules over a database schema **R** which are serializable is denoted by SER. (The database schema in questio will always be clear from the context, so that we will not use a special parameter to denote that context expli citly.)

Clearly, testing if a strict schedule s for a set $\{t_1 ,..., t_n\}$ of transactions is serializable can be done by try ing out all permutations σ of $\{1 ,..., n\}$ and checking whether $s \approx t_{\sigma(1)} \cdots t_{\sigma(n)}$. Unfortunately, our first resul suggests that no significantly better testing algorithm exists:

4.1 Theorem. It is NP-complete to determine, given a strict schedule s for a finite set of transactions over database schema **R**, whether or not s is serializable.

The proof of Theorem 4.1 is based on reducing the Hamiltonian circuit problem to serializability testing Note that a result similar to Theorem 4.1 holds in the theory of "internal level" concurrency control. Indeed our notion of serializability is related to "final-state serializability", for which testing was shown to be NP complete [16].

Intuitively, Theorem 4.1 suggests that testing for serializability in the general case cannot be don efficiently. One way to cope with this complexity result is to look for restricted notions of serializability, whic are decidable in polynomial time (such as "conflict serializability" [23] in the theory of internal level concurrenc control). A second approach is to consider less powerful transactions. We explore both approaches in th remainder of this section.

We start by looking at restrictions to the notion of serializability. The first notion we consider is, in som sense, the most restricted. Intuitively, it requires that serializability of the schedule can be determined base just on the interaction of pairs of updates in the schedule. In particular, the serializability of such a schedule ca be proven using just the commutativity axioms of [10], which involve only pairs of updates (see Section 2). Th class of schedules, called "locally serializable", is defined next.

4.2 Definition. A schedule s for a set of transactions $\{t_1, \cdots ,t_n\}$ over a database schema **R** is *locally seriali able* iff $s \overset{*}{\leftrightarrow} t_{\sigma(1)} \cdots t_{\sigma(n)}$ for some permutation σ of $\{1 ,..., n\}$. The class of locally serializable schedules ov **R** is denoted by LSER.

The commutativity rules alone do not provide a convenient way to verify local serializability, since it is n clear which rule should be applied at any given time. We next describe a polynomial-time algorithm for testi ocal serializability, based on a "local conflict graph" associated with the schedule. Given some set T of transactions and a schedule s for T, the *local conflict-graph* G(s) = (V,E) associated with s is the following: V consists of all transactions appearing in s, i.e. V = T. For t_i, $t_j \in V$, $j \neq i$, the directed edge (t_i,t_j) is in E, if s contains a pair (a,b) of updates such that a is from t_i, b is from t_j, a occurs before b in s, and a and b do not commute. The following can now be proven:

.3 Theorem. A schedule s for a set T of transactions over a database schema **R** is locally serializable iff its local conflict graph G(s) is acyclic.

.4 Remark. It is easy to verify that local serializability can be tested in polynomial time. Also, by definition, each locally serializable schedule is serializable. However, the converse is not true, i.e. there are serializable schedules are which are not locally serializable. Intuitively, this is so because conflicts between pairs of updates are sometimes "compensated" by the context. For instance, let $s = m^2(1;2)m^1(2;3)m^2(3;2)$. For this schedule, G(s) is cyclic. Thus, $s \notin$ LSER. However, $s \approx m^1(2;3)m^2(1;2)m^2(3;2)$, so $s \in$ SER.

In some sense, local serializability is the most restricted notion of serializability because it only takes into account local conflicts, without regard for the context. At the other extreme, unrestricted serializability takes into account the entire context. Intermediate notions of serializability can be obtained by looking at some of the context in various ways. We next exhibit one such notion, called "intermediate serializability". Intuitively, intermediate serializability takes into account conflicts detectable by looking at individual updates occurring in a schedule and the prefixes of transactions occurring in the schedule before that update. This type of conflict detection is particularly suited for dynamic scheduling, where only prefixes of the transactions and the schedule are available at any given time. Indeed, intermediate serializability will be used as a basis for our dynamic scheduling algorithm in Section 6. As in the case of local serializability, recognizing intermediately serializable schedules involves constructing a conflict graph, defined next.

4.5 Definition. Let s be a strict schedule for the set of transactions $\{t_1, \cdots, t_n\}$ over database schema **R**. The *intermediate conflict graph* $G_I(s)$ for s is the directed graph (V,E), where:

(i) V = T, and

(ii) $(t_i,t_j) \in E$ iff there exists an update u of t_j such that $s = s'us''$ and $\pi_i(s')u \not\approx u\pi_i(s')$.

Obviously, the commutativity rules for pairs of updates are not sufficient to check whether $\pi_i(s')$ and u commute, since $\pi_i(s')$ and u may commute even if u does not commute with every single update in $\pi_i(s')$. Testing whether $\pi_i(s')$ and u commute is easily done using the transition spec of $\pi_i(s')$.

4.6 Definition. A strict schedule s is ***intermediately serializable*** iff its intermediate conflict graph $G_I(s)$ is acyclic. The set of intermediately serializable schedules over a database schema **R** is denoted ISER.

Clearly, LSER $\subseteq$ ISER for each database schema; also, it can be proven that ISER $\subseteq$ SER. To see that the inclusions are strict, consider the schedules

$$s' = d^1(0)m^1(0;1)m^2(1;2)m^1(2;3) \quad \text{and}$$
$$s'' = m^1(0;1)m^2(1;2)m^1(2;3)d^1(1)d^1(3).$$

It is easily seen that $s' \in$ ISER−LSER and $s'' \in$ SER − ISER. Thus, LSER $\underset{+}{\subset}$ ISER $\underset{+}{\subset}$ SER. Note that intermediate serializability can be tested in polynomial time.

We next show that infinitely many approximate serializability testing algorithms can be obtained by combining in various "doses" local serializability testing with unrestricted serializability testing. These algorithms are polynomial-time and define an infinite hierarchy of serializability classes which, in some sense, converge to SER. Following is an outline of these algorithms; the "tune-up" parameter k is used to determine the amount of exact serializability testing to be performed. The higher k is, the closer the algorithm is to the exact serializability testing algorithm, and the higher its complexity (polynomial in n, with exponent k).

Algorithm SER(k):

Input: a strict schedule s for a set T of n transactions.

Output: YES or NO.

begin

1. for each subset T_k of T of size k such that[5] coalesce(T_k, G(s)) is acyclic do
    2. if $\pi_{T_k}(s)$ is serializable then
        begin
        3. output YES;
        4. halt
        end;
5. output NO

end.

Note that, if coalesce(T_k, G(s)) is acyclic, then s $\approx$ s'π_{T_k}(s)s" (where s' and s" are serial schedules), so s i serializable if $\pi_{T_k}(s)$ is serializable. The algorithm performs exact serializability testing in step 2 on a schedul for k transactions. This step takes time O(k!), which is constant since k is fixed; step 1 takes time O(n^k), so tha the running time of Algorithm SER(k) is polynomial in n. Let SER_k be the set of schedules recognized by Algorithm SER(k). The following result shows that the SER_k constitute an infinite hierarchy of classes of serializable schedules; part (iii) of the theorem shows that the SER_k converge to SER in a certain sense.

4.7 Theorem. For each database schema **R**, the following hold:

(i) $SER_0 = SER_1 = LSER$

(ii) For each $k \geqslant 1$, $SER_k \underset{+}{\subset} SER_{k+1} \underset{+}{\subset} SER$

(iii) For each strict, serializable schedule s there exists some $k \geqslant 0$ such that $s \in SER_k$.

The class ISER of intermediately serializable schedules is, in some sense, "orthogonal" to the SER_k hierar chy; specifically, ISER $\not\subseteq$ SER_k and SER_k $\not\subseteq$ ISER for each $k > 1$.

As seen above, Algorithm SER(k) takes time polynomial in n (with exponent k). We next briefly describe more sophisticated method for approximate serializability testing, which takes time linear in n. In the modifie algorithm, exact testing is applied only to certain connected components[6] of the local conflict graph. Unfor tunately, it can be shown that the "smarter" algorithm converges only for transactions without insertions. W now outline the algorithm.

Algorithm CSER(k):

Input: a strict schedule s for a set T of n transactions

Output: YES or NO

begin

---

[5] By coalesce(T_k, G(s)) is meant the graph obtained from G(s) by coalescing all vertices in T_k into a single vertex.

[6] By the connected components of G(s) we mean the connected components of the underlying undirected graph of G(s).

1. construct the local conflict graph G(s);
2. if G(s) is cyclic then

begin

3. find the connected components of G(s);

(* let the result be $C_1, \cdots, C_m$ *)

4. if there exists some i, $1 \leqslant i \leqslant m$, s.t. $|C_i| > k$ and C_i is cyclic then

begin

5. output NO;
6. halt

end;

7. for i := 1 to m do

8. if C_i is cyclic then

9. if $\pi_{C_i}(s)$ is not serializable then

begin

10. output NO;
11. halt

end;

end;

12. output YES

end.

In the algorithm given above, local testing is applied in step 2, while exact testing is performed in step 9. Now suppose that G(s) has m cyclic connected components of size $k_i \leqslant k$, $1 \leqslant i \leqslant m$, resp. Then the for-loop of step 7 is executed m times, and for the i-th execution step 9 takes time $O(k_i!)$. The worst case occurs if each component has maximal size k, in which steps 7-9 take time $O(m \cdot k!)$. However, since there are at most $\left\lceil \frac{n}{k} \right\rceil$ cycles of size k in a graph with n vertices, this reduces to $O(\left\lceil \frac{n}{k} \right\rceil \cdot k!)$, which is linear in n since k is fixed.

Let $CSER_k$ denote the set of schedules recognized by Algorithm CSER(k). $CSER_i$ and SER_j are incomparable for i, j $\geqslant$ 2. However, the $CSER_k$, like the SER_k, form an infinite hierarchy, for which a theorem similar to Theorem 4.7 holds. However, convergence is no longer guaranteed if the transactions are allowed to contain insertions. The convergence of the CSER(k) can be restored by using a modified test in step 9, which takes into account the insert-sets of all connected components; unfortunately, this test takes time exponential in k, like the original SER(k) algorithms.

Another approach to cope with the complexity result of Theorem 4.1 is to consider less powerful transactions. To this end, it can be shown that exact serializability testing can be done efficiently if the transactions are restricted to contain only inserts and deletes. (A polynomial-time serializability testing algorithm for such transactions is provided in [20].) In this restricted model, some power of the transactions is lost, since in general a modification cannot be simulated by insertions and deletions. This result is similar in spirit to results of [4], where it was shown that certain undecidable questions concerning transactional schemas[7] become decidable if the transactions do not contain modifications. Thus, our results and the results of [4] concur in indicating that

[7] A transactional schema specifies the set of admissible transactions on a database (see [3]).

modifications add considerable power and complexity to transactions. We also note that, even for the restricted transactions, a schedule may be serializable without being locally serializable. Thus, unrestricted serializability remains more complicated than local serializability even when no modifications are allowed in transactions.

We also note that, contrary to expectations, other natural restrictions on transactions do not lead to significantly more efficient serializability testing algorithms. For instance, the proof of Theorem 4.1 shows that testing serializability remains NP-complete even if the input transactions are optimal and in Second Normal Form[8].

Finally, we mention that in [20] an approach to the dynamic generation of schedules for transactions is described. The scheduling algorithm uses the technique developed for intermediate serializability testing adapted to the dynamic situation. Intermediate serializability testing is appropriate in the dynamic framework since only prefixes of transactions are available at any given time. The set of finite sequences of updates generated by the scheduler without performing aborts[9] equals ISER; the infinite schedules produced are instantaneously serializable.

5. Concurrency Control in the Presence of Functional Dependencies

The concurrency control mechanisms developed so far do not make use of semantic information about the valid database states. In this section we show how concurrency control can be improved by taking into account functional dependencies (fd's) satisfied by a database. To simplify the exposition, we only consider unirelational databases. Our results can be extended straightforwardly to multirelational databases.

We first recall that our original definition of serializability of a schedule s for $\{t_1, \ldots, t_n\}$ requires that it be equivalent to executing the t_i's in a *fixed* order, which is independent of the instance on which the schedule is applied. We now argue that this definition must be relaxed in order to take advantage of fd's.

Intuitively, in considering the serializability of a schedule in the presence of fd's, we only need look at the effect of the schedule on instances satisfying the fd's. This leads to the following straightforward extension of our original definition of serializability:

5.1 Definition. Let R be a relation schema and Σ a set of fd's over R. A strict schedule s for a set $\{t_1, \ldots, t_n\}$ of transactions over R is *serializable with respect to* Σ iff there exists a permutation σ of $\{1, \ldots, n\}$ such that $\mathrm{eff}(s)(I) = \mathrm{eff}(t_{\sigma(1)}, \ldots, t_{\sigma(n)})(I)$ for each instance I of R satisfying Σ.

Unfortunately, it can be easily seen that the class of schedules which are serializable wrt Σ is no larger than our old class of serializable schedules. Indeed, we have:

5.2 Proposition. Let Σ be a set of fd's over a relation schema R, and s a strict schedule over R. Then s is serializable wrt Σ iff s is serializable.

In order to take advantage of the extra information provided by fd's, we must relax our definition of serializability with respect to a set of fd's. The following example suggests how this can be done.

5.3 Example. Let R = AB, and $\Sigma = \{A \to B\}$. Let

$$t_1 = m(A{=}0,B{=}0;\ A{=}0,B{=}2)m(A{=}0,B{=}1;\ A{=}0,B{=}2) \quad \text{and}$$
$$t_2 = m(A{=}0,B{=}0;\ A{=}0,B{=}3)m(A{=}0,B{=}1;\ A{=}0,B{=}3)$$

[8] Second Normal Form is a desirable syntactic form for transactions, defined in [1, 2].

[9] Note that this set of schedules is our scheduler's "fixed-point set". Fixed-point sets are defined in [11] and are used to measure the performance of a scheduler.

e two transactions over R and consider the following strict schedule for $\{t_1,t_2\}$:

$$s = m^1(A=0,B=0;\ A=0,B=2)m^2(A=0,B=0;\ A=0,B=3)$$
$$m^2(A=0,B=1;\ A=0,B=3)m^1(A=0,B=1;\ A=0,B=2)$$

is easily seen that s is not serializable. Let us now look closer at the source of conflicts in the schedule s. The onflict edge (t_1, t_2) is due to the first two modifications of the schedule, which affect the tuple <0,0>. The econd conflict edge, (t_2, t_1), is due to the last two modifications, which affect the tuple <0,1>. Note that the rst conflict is relevant only to instances containing the tuple <0,0>, while the second conflict is relevant only to stances containing <0,1>. Next, note that there is no instance satisfying $A \to B$ which contains *both* <0,0> nd <0,1>. It follows that for each instance satisfying $A \to B$, only one of the conflict edges may be relevant. ndeed, there are two disjoint categories of instances I satisfying $A \to B$:

i) $I \cap \{<0,0>, <0,1>\} \subseteq \{<0,0>\}$; then the conflict graph relevant to I consists of the edge (t_1, t_2) only, and $\text{eff}(s)(I) = \text{eff}(t_1t_2)(I)$.

ii) $I \cap \{<0,0>, <0,1>\} \subseteq \{<0,1>\}$; then the conflict graph relevant to I consists of the edge (t_2, t_1) only, and $\text{eff}(s)(I) = \text{eff}(t_2t_1)(I)$. Thus, the execution of the schedule s on each instance is always equivalent to a serial execution of t_1 and t_2 on that instance. However, the order of the serial execution of t_1 and t_2 depends on the instance.

The above example suggests a definition of serializability of a schedule with respect to fd's, which makes he equivalent order of execution of transactions state-dependent. Formally, we have:

.4 Definition. Let R be a relation schema and Σ a set of fd's over R. A strict schedule s for a set $t_1, \ldots, t_n\}$ of transactions over R is ***state-serializable wrt*** Σ iff for each instance I of R satisfying Σ there xists a permutation σ of $\{1, \ldots, n\}$ such that $\text{eff}(s)(I) = \text{eff}(t_{\sigma(1)}, \ldots, t_{\sigma(n)})(I)$. The class of state-serializable chedules wrt Σ is denoted by $SSER^{\Sigma}$.

As shown in Example 5.3, there are non-serializable schedules which are state-serializable wrt a set of fd's. Aore generally, it can be shown that $SER \underset{+}{\subset} SSER^{\Sigma}$ for each set Σ containing at least one non-trivial fd.

We next present an informal description of how our local serializability testing algorithm can be modified o take into account fd's. The modification of the algorithm proceeds along the lines of Example 5.3. Suppose hat a strict schedule s and a set Σ of fd's are given. As before, our algorithm constructs a local conflict graph or s. Additionally, while the conflict graph is being constructed, a record is kept of which hyperplanes are relevant" to each conflict edge. Intuitively, if an instance I does not intersect any of the relevant hyperplanes or an edge (t_i,t_j), then the conflict between t_i and t_j does not occur when the schedule s is executed on state I, nd the edge (t_i,t_j) can be ignored for this particular state. If a cycle occurs, the algorithm checks whether there xists an instance satisfying Σ which intersects at least one relevant hyperplane for each edge in the cycle. This s done by associating a partial tuple with each relevant hyperplane and applying a (polynomial time) procedure imilar to the Chase w.r.t. fd's [15], to relations containing tuples associated with different relevant hyperplanes. f such an instance does not exist for any cycle in the conflict graph, then the schedule is state-serializable wrt Σ. Iowever, the converse is not true. That is, some schedules which are state-serializable wrt Σ are rejected by the lgorithm. A schedule accepted by the modified local serializability testing algorithm is called ***state-locally seri-lizable wrt*** Σ ; the corresponding set of schedules is denoted by $SLSER^{\Sigma}$.

Finally, note that our intermediate serializability testing algorithm as well as our SER(k) algorithms can lso be modified using the above technique. (The portion of the SER(k) algorithm which is modified is that vhere local serializability testing is used, i.e. step 2.) The set of schedules accepted by the modified intermediate serializability testing [SER(k)] algorithm is denoted by $SISER^{\Sigma}$ [$SSER_k^{\Sigma}$], respectively. Each schedule in $SISER^{\Sigma}$ or $SSER_k^{\Sigma}$ is state-serializable wrt Σ; however, the converse is not true in general.

We now describe the relationship between the various classes of state-serializable schedules wrt Σ, as wel as the relationship between the old classes of serializable schedules and the corresponding new classes of state serializable schedules wrt Σ.

5.5 Theorem. For each relation schema R and set Σ of fd's over **R** containing at least one non-trivial fd, th following hold:

(i) $LSER \underset{+}{\subset} SLSER^{\Sigma}$,

$ISER \underset{+}{\subset} SISER^{\Sigma}$,

$SER_k \underset{+}{\subset} SSER_k^{\Sigma}$,

$SER \underset{+}{\subset} SSER^{\Sigma}$,

(ii) $SLSER^{\Sigma} \underset{+}{\subset} SISER^{\Sigma} \underset{+}{\subset} SSER^{\Sigma}$,

(iii) $SSER_0^{\Sigma} = SSER_1^{\Sigma} = SLSER^{\Sigma}$,

$SSER_k^{\Sigma} \underset{+}{\subset} SSER_{k+1}^{\Sigma} \underset{+}{\subset} SSER^{\Sigma}$ for each $k \geqslant 1$.

Finally, note that the dynamic scheduler described in [20] can also be modified to take into account fd' along the same lines as above. The schedules generated are then state-intermediately serializable with respect t the fd's.

6. Conclusions

The present paper provides a theoretical foundation for understanding how semantic information availab at the conceptual level can be used to increase concurrency of transactions. Specifically, we introduced a notic of serializability that is based on semantics rather than syntax. We investigated static serializability testing ar pointed out applications of our techniques to dynamic scheduling of transactions. With respect to static seria izability testing, we showed that the problem is NP-complete in general, and exhibited a variety of polynomia time approximate algorithms. The algorithms make use of semantic information available at the conceptu level that goes beyond simple commutativity of updates, and provide a reasonable basis for a dynamic schedule We also showed that exact serializability testing can be done in polynomial time for a restricted class of transa tions. Finally, we considered a new notion of serializability which is state-dependent, and is natural when co straint information is available.

Clearly, the increase in concurrency obtained by our approach is achieved at the cost of additional ove head. Whether this tradeoff is worthwhile in practice depends on the characteristics of the transaction and dat We plan to evaluate experimentally our approach in future work. Finally, an important related problem is hc conceptual-level concurrency control interacts with internal-level concurrency control. The emerging theory multilevel concurrency control [22] is likely to be useful in understanding this issue.

Acknowledgement. The authors would like to thank D. Karabeg and M. Roesler for useful discussions on t material presented in this paper.

References

[1] Abiteboul, S., V. Vianu. Transactions in Relational Databases. Proc. 10th VLDB (1984) 46-56.

[2] Abiteboul, S., V. Vianu. Equivalence and Optimization of Relational Transactions. JACM 35 (1988) 70-120.

[3] Abiteboul, S., V. Vianu. Transactions and Integrity Constraints. Proc. 4th ACM PODS (1985) 193-204.

[4] Abiteboul, S., V. Vianu. Deciding Properties of Transactional Schemas. Proc. 5th ACM PODS (1986) 235-239.

[5] Bernstein, P. A., N. Goodman, M. Y. Lai. Analyzing Concurrency Control Algorithms When User and System Operations Differ. IEEE Trans. on Software Eng. 9 (1983) 233-239.

[6] Bernstein, P. A., V. Hadzilacos, N. Goodman. *Concurrency Control and Recovery in Database Systems.* Addison-Wesley (1987).

[7] Date, C. J. *A Guide to DB2.* Addison-Wesley (1984).

[8] Garcia-Molina, H. Using Semantic Knowledge for Transaction Processing in a Distributed Database. ACM TODS 8 (1983) 186-213.

[9] Gray, J. Notes on Data Base Operating Systems. in: R. Bayer, M. R. Graham, G. Seegmuller (eds.). *Operating Systems - An Advanced Course.* Springer LNCS 60 (1978) 393-481.

[10] Karabeg, A., D. Karabeg, K. Papakonstantinou, V. Vianu. Axiomatization and Simplification Rules for Relational Transactions. Proc. 6th ACM PODS (1987), 254-259.

[11] Karabeg, D., V. Vianu. Parallel Update Transactions, this proceedings.

[12] Korth, H.F. Locking Primitives in a Database System. JACM 30 (1983) 55-79.

[13] Kung, H. T., C. H. Papadimitriou. An Optimality Theory of Concurrency Control for Databases. Acta Informatica 19 (1983) 1-11.

[14] Maier, D. *The Theory of Relational Databases.* Computer Science Press (1983).

[15] Maier, D., A. O. Mendelzon, Y. Sagiv. Testing Implications of Data Dependencies. ACM TODS 4 (1979) 455-469.

[16] Papadimitriou, C. H. The serializability of concurrent database updates. JACM 26 (1979) 631-653.

[17] Roesler, M., W. A. Burkhard. Concurrency Control Scheme for Shared Objects: A Peephole Approach Based on Semantics. Proc. 7th IEEE Int. Conf. on Distributed Computing Systems (1987), 224-231.

[18] Schwarz, P. M., A. Z. Spector. Synchronizing Shared Abstract Data Types. ACM Trans. on Computer Systems 2 (1984) 223-250.

[19] Ullman, J. *Principles of Database Systems.* Computer Science Press (1982), 2nd ed.

[20] Vianu, V., G. Vossen. Conceptual Level Concurrency Control of Relational Update Transactions. Techn. Rep. CS 87-105, UCSD (October 1987).

[21] Weihl, W., B. Liskov. Specification and Implementation of Resilient Atomic Data Types. ACM TOPLAS 7 (1985) 244-269.

[22] Weikum, G. A Theoretical Foundation of Multi-Level Concurrency Control. Proc. 5th ACM PODS (1986) 31-42.

[23] Yannakakis, M. Serializability by Locking. JACM 31 (1984) 227-244.

VERSION CONSISTENCY AND SERIALIZABILITY IN DESIGN DATABASES

K. Vidyasankar
Department of Computer Science
Memorial University of Newfoundland
St. John's, Newfoundland
Canada A1C 5S7

C.N.G. Dampney
School of Mathematics, Physics, Computing and Electronics
Macquarie University
North Ryde, N.S.W. 2113
Australia

Abstract

A database used by engineering or manufacturing applications for analysis and design purposes i called a *design database* . Here data items represent the actual physical structure of engineering part and components. A design process can be thought of as starting with certain *base* data items or desig objects, and deriving others from them. Several alternate designs may be tried from the same set c base objects. Designs with several sets of base objects may also be tried. Hence several versions c various data items may exist in the system simultaneously. Then "consistent" versions must be used i each derivation. Also a concurrency control mechanism for design database systems must allow keepin various versions until the end of the design process.

In this paper we propose a formal definition of version consistency expressed in terms of transactio histories. This allows checking version consistency from a history graph constructed from transactio processing. The version consistency checking algorithm takes polynomial time. We also demonstrat that a notion called τ_*-serializability is an appropriate correctness criterion for concurrent executions i design databases. This is distinct from view-serializability which is accepted as the appropriate criterio for databases used for business and administrative transaction processing. We show that τ_*-serializabilit of a version consistent history can be checked in polynomial time. In contrast checking τ_*-serializabilit of a not necessarily version consistent history is NP-complete. It turns out that both version consistenc and τ_*-serializability can be checked using the same history graph.

1. Introduction

A database used by engineering or manufacturing applications for analysis and design purposes is alled a *design* or *workbench* database. Unlike in business and administrative database applications here data is required for simply monitoring and tracking what is happening (and hence we will call iem *tracking* databases in this paper), data items in design databases are used to represent the actual hysical structure of engineering parts and components. These data items are likely to have complex epresentations on the computer, not easily broken down into simple sub-items.

A design process can be thought of as starting with certain *base* data items (corresponding to design bjects) and computing (deriving) other objects using the base objects and possibly some additional ata input by the designer. Different input data may be tried with the same base objects to get desired id results. Designs with different base objects could also be tried. Thus several versions of various ata items may exist in the system simultaneously. Then "consistent" versions must be used in each erivation.

Each of the data items may also be represented in several alternate ways, to serve the needs of various rocesses for efficiency. For example, an electronic circuit can have the following representations in a atabase [NH]:

- circuit diagram;
- description in the form of text;
- components list;
- connections description;
- layout diagram; and
- files for controlling the manufacturing tools.

enoting each representation as a distinct data item, consistency among the various versions of these ata items must also be kept track of.

Several papers (for example, [D, K, KSUW, NH]) have dealt with mechanisms for maintaining several rsions of data items in design databases and checking consistency of the versions. They usually talk out users "telling" the system about creation of new versions, updating existing versions, merging two more versions and also deleting some versions. The relation among the various versions is recorded in version graph which is used to detect version (in)consistency. Such mechanisms seem to be inherently imbersome and require user interaction.

A formal definition of version consistency that will enable designing automatic version consistency ntrol mechanisms is attempted in [D]: two data items are version consistent if they are derived from the same versions of their common predecessors, and a database is consistent if no data item has bee derived from data items that are version inconsistent with respect to each other. The version consistenc notion in [NH] is also based on a similar "derived from" property. But the "derived from" property itse. is not formally defined in either of [D, NH]. This introduces some ambiguity. For example, consider dat items X, Y and Z. Suppose version X_2 is derived from version X_1, and Y_3 is derived from X_2. The it is not clear (for the above version consistency definition) whether Y_3 should be considered as derive from X_1 also. Hence if Z_4 is derived from X_1, it is not clear whether Z_4 and Y_3 are version consister or not. Another ambiguous situation is the following. Suppose transaction T_1 has no read steps an writes (only) version X_1 of X, and T_2 has no read steps and writes (only) version Y_2 of Y. Then a X_1 and Y_2 version consistent? If the above T_1 writes version Y_1 of Y also, then are X_1 and Y_2 versio consistent?

Our aim in this paper is to resolve such ambiguity. We define version consistency in terms transaction histories, using a notion called "extended read" which is also formally defined. This notion related to "derived from" property. Our definition allows for checking version consistency by constructin an (extended) history graph from a given history. The same graph can also be used for checkin serializability, which is another topic of this paper.

Some of the factors that must be taken into account in designing a concurrency control mechanis for design database systems are the following.

(i) Transactions in design databases are typically long. They may run for several hours, even day especially if we allow a transaction to include a prolonged session with overnight pauses whil the designer interacts with a design. Hence methods like two phase locking protocol that requi transactions to lock data items and thus make those data items unavailable to other transactior for long periods are not attractive.

(ii) A design is the result of cooperative effort of several people (transactions). Each transactio may be aware of the work of the others well enough and may take proper measures to ensur the correctness of the concurrent executions that the executions need not be view-serializable, a they are expected to be in tracking databases.

(iii) The design process typically involves trying several alternate designs from each set of base object for several such sets. The final design will be decided only at the end, at which time the othe alternate designs will be discarded. Then the concurrent execution need only be view-serializab (assuming that view-serializability is taken as the correctness criterion) with respect to the ster of those transactions which contribute to the final design, for each possible final choice, and no neccessarily with respect to the steps of all the transactions.

New concurrency control mechanisms have been proposed [BKK, KSUW] addressing (i) and (ii) ove. These involve use of "nested transaction" concept, public/private database concept with check-it/checkin facility, relaxing the correctness criteria (for example, allowing arbitrary interleaving of the ub)transactions of a group of designers), etc. But they do not address the factor (iii) above. In this per, we address (iii) and, for simplicity, ignore (i) and (ii). Our proposal can certainly be adopted in njunction with those for (i) and (ii).

We demonstrate that a notion called τ_*-serializability [B, V] is appropriate for design databases. Here r each transaction, the concurrent execution appears to be equivalent to some serial execution. For fferent transactions, the corresponding serial executions, equivalent to the same concurrent execution, ay be different.

The problem of checking τ_*-serializability of a general history is NP-complete. We show that when e history is version consistent, τ_*-serializability can be checked in polynomial time. This involves ecking acyclicity of the (extended) history graph, which can be constructed in polynomial time. Thus e extended history graph can be used to check both version consistency and τ_*-serializability. (We note at our version consistency definition treats all data items as corresponding to design objects. We also ggest a modified definition for the case where some data items do not correspond to design objects. a history is version consistent only according to the modified definition, then checking whether it is -serializable may take exponential time.)

Version consistency is dealt with in section 2, and τ_*-serializability in section 3. Section 4 deals with -serializability of version consistent histories. Section 5 concludes the paper.

2. Version Consistency

In this section we propose a formal definition of version consistency. Each value (written by some ansaction) of each data item is a *version* for our purposes. (In general, some data items may not rrespond to design objects, and version consistency may not be a relevant issue for them. Extension our theory to this general situation is discussed later in this section.) Several versions of a data item ay be created and kept in the database. At some later stage, some versions may be found useless for e "final" design and discarded. For simplicity, we assume that all the versions are kept in the database til the very end of the design process, that is, until all the transaction processing is complete, at which ne, appropriate versions of the various data items are chosen as contributing to the final design. Then any stage, a transaction reading a data item may read any of the already created versions of that ta item. Thus the history of execution of the transaction steps is a *multiversion* history [BG, PK]. e develop a formal notion of histories in the following.

A database system consists of a set of data items and a set $T = \{T_0, T_1, ..., T_n\}$ of transactions. *transaction* is a finite partially ordered set of steps. Each step is either a *read step* reading (exactly one data item, or a *write step* writing (exactly) one data item. We assume each data item is accesse by at most one read step and at most one write step in a transaction; and if both steps do occur, the the read step precedes the write step in the partial order. A transaction is a *write-only* transactio if it does not have any read steps. It is a *read-only* transaction if it does not have any write step The transaction T_0 is a fictitious write-only *initial transaction* with unordered write steps, writing th initial values of some data items.

The version of a data item X written by a transaction T_j is denoted X_j. Then a write step of T writing X is denoted $W_j[X_j]$. A read step of T_j reading Y is denoted $R_j[Y_i]$, where Y_i is the versio of Y read in this step. The set of versions read by a transaction constitutes its *read set*, also referre to as its *input set*, and the set of versions written by a transaction its *write set* or *output set*.

A (*multi-version*) *history* h of T is a sequence of the steps of T representing the executio of the transactions, in a possibly interleaved fashion, starting with the write steps of T_0 (in any order such that (i) the steps of each transaction in h satisfy the partial order specified among them, and (i for each $R_j[X_i]$, $W_i[X_i]$ occurs before $R_j[X_i]$ in h, that is, only the versions that have already bee created can be read.

From a history h, we obtain a history graph of h as follows.

Definition 2.1. Let h be a history of $T = \{T_0, T_1, ...T_n\}$. The *history graph* of h, denoted $H(h$ is a directed graph whose vertex set is T and edge set consists of:

(a) an edge labelled X_i from T_i to T_j for each $R_j[X_i]$ in h and

(b) an unlabelled edge from T_0 to each write-only transaction other than T_0. □

We use T_i to refer to transaction T_i and also the vertex T_i in the graph. An edge α from T_i to T is denoted (T_i, T_j). Here T_i is the *positive end* $p\alpha$ of α, and T_j is the *negative end* $n\alpha$ of α. W also refer to α as an *outdirected* edge of T_i and an *indirected* edge of T_j. A *source* is a vertex wit no indirected edges, and a *sink* is a vertex with no outdirected edges. An *X_i-edge* refers to an edg labelled X_i. We also use the notation *X-edge* to refer to an X_i-edge for some i.

Proposition 2.1. A history graph has the following properties.

(a) It is a one-source multi-sink graph.

(b) No two indirected edges of any vertex have labels X_i, X_j for any X and i, j such that $i \neq$

□

We now consider version consistency. There are two different aspects of version consistency. One is the *internal consistency* of a version. Informally, internally consistent versions are those that "make sense". For example, a version of a layout diagram of a circuit is internally consistent only if it describes the circuit completely. The second aspect is the *mutual consistency* of two versions. For example, versions of a layout diagram and a components list will be mutually consistent only if they both correspond to the same circuit. In the following, we state some properties that motivate our formal definition of version consistency.

VC1. Two distinct versions X_i and X_j, $i \neq j$, of any data item X are mutually inconsistent.

VC2. If Y_k is "derived from" X_i and Z_l is "derived from" X_j, $i \neq j$, then Y_k and Z_l are mutually inconsistent.

VC3. If each version in the read set of a transaction is internally consistent and any two versions in the read set are mutually consistent, then each version in the write set of the transaction is internally consistent and any two versions in the write set are mutually consistent.

In VC3 we are assuming, essentially, that all transactions are "correct". As long as the input versions are (internally and mutually) consistent, the output versions are also consistent. In particular, output versions of all write-only transactions are consistent; we call them *base* versions. The output versions of any other transaction are *derived* ones; derived from the base or other derived versions in the read set of that transaction. The following two examples elaborate mutual consistency.

(i) If T_i and T_j are write-only transactions, writing (only) X_i and X_j respectively, and T_k reads X_j and writes Y_k, then X_i and Y_k are mutually inconsistent (since Y_k is derived from X_j and not X_i).

(ii) Suppose X_i and Y_j are mutually consistent, and T_k reads (only) Y_j and writes (only) Y_k, then X_i and Y_k are mutually consistent.

Note in (ii) above that the pairs Y_j, X_i and X_i, Y_k are mutually consistent, but Y_j, Y_k is not. Thus mutual consistency is not a transitive property.

The following definition captures the "derived from" property. Here "eread" is used as a word similar to "read".

Definition 2.2. A transaction T_k ***extended-reads*** (abbreviated ***ereads***) the following in h : for each T_j such that T_k reads some version written by T_j, T_k ereads

(i) all the versions written by T_j, and

(ii) all the versions eread by T_j, except those of the data items written by T_j. □

The justification for Definition 2.2 is the following. Suppose Y_j is in the read set of T_k. Then Y "influences" (the versions written by) T_k. We take this as the transaction T_j itself influences T_k, or indirectly, all the versions written by T_j influence T_k. Further we assume that all the versions that influence T_j, also influence T_k. If X_i influences T_j, and T_j writes X_j , then X_i influences X_j which in turn influences T_k; only X_j which "directly" influences T_k is taken into account in the definition.

Definition 2.3. Let h be a history of $T = \{T_0, T_1, ...T_n\}$. The *extended history graph* of h denoted $EH(h)$, is a directed graph whose vertex set is T and edge set consists of:

(i) an edge labelled X_i from T_i to T_j for each X_i eread by T_j, and

(ii) an unlabelled edge from T_0 to each write-only transaction other than T_0. □

The eread definition is illustrated through (parts of) several extended history graphs in Figure 1 The broken lines correspond to the eread edges *not* in the read sets.

We are now ready to define version consistency. First we define version consistency of histories. Internal consistency of a version and mutual consistency of two versions will be defined later on. We want a version consistent history to be one in which

(i) each version of each data item is internally consistent, and

(ii) any two versions in the read set of each transaction are mutually consistent.

We note that (ii) implies (i), by VC3, but not vice versa : some read-only transactions may read mutually inconsistent versions, even when each version of each data item in the history is internally consistent. The following definition captures (ii).

Definition 2.4. A history h is *version consistent* if no transaction ereads more than one version of any data item in h . □

The histories corresponding to Figures 1(d) and (f) are not version consistent. We note that in both (e) and (f), T_j reads X_i and writes X_j, that is, it reads one version of X and writes another version of X . This is called *revision* of a version in [K]. In (e), Y_k is mutually consistent with both X_i and X_j but in (f) Y_i is mutually consistent with X_i, but not its revision X_j. If T_j that revises X_i revises Y_i also producing Y_j, and T_k reads Y_j instead of Y_i, then it will be acceptable. That is, our definition will allow revisions of the versions only under the condition that *all the versions in the output set of a transaction are revised together* .

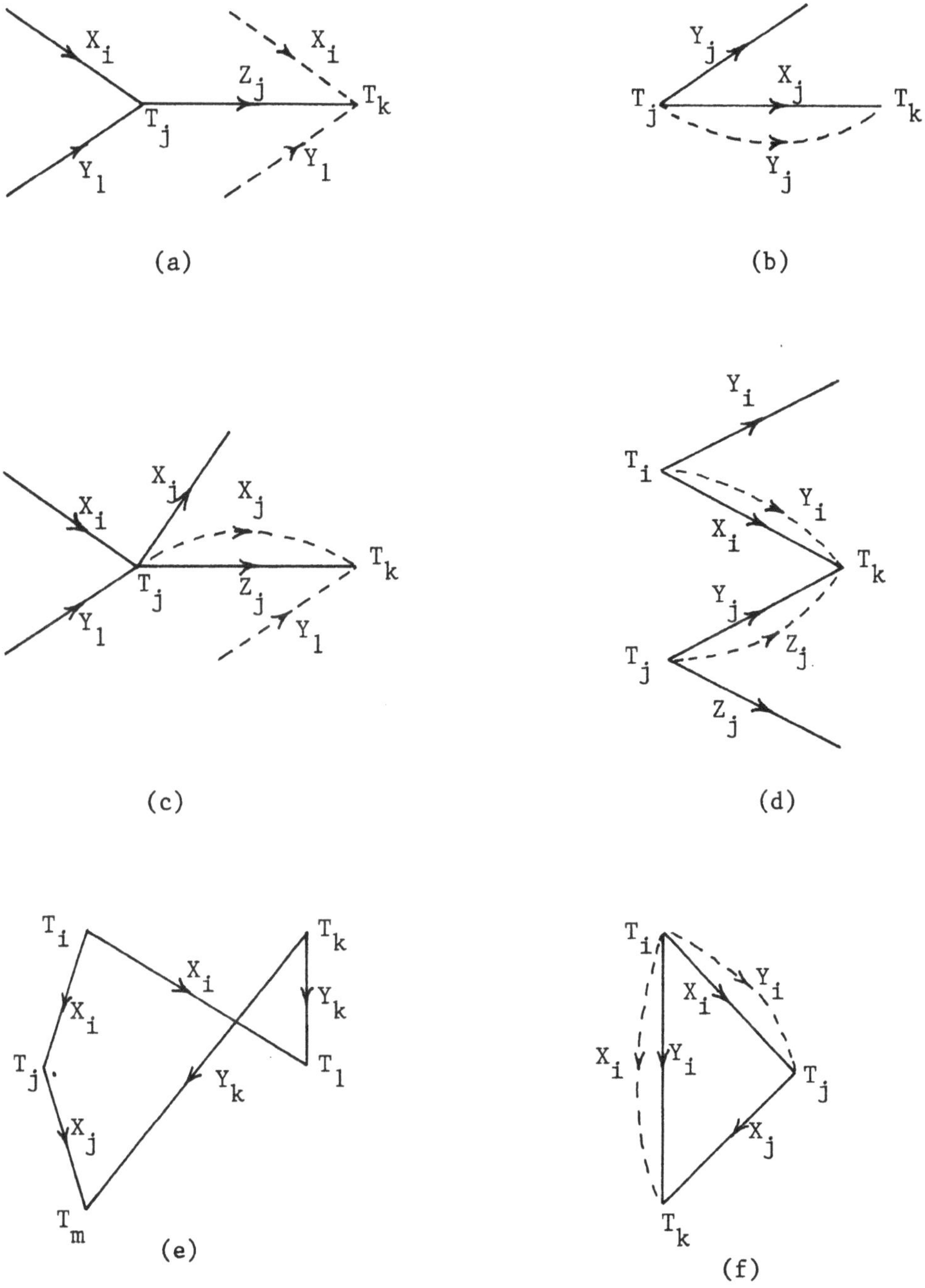
X_i
Z_j
X_i
T_k
T_j
Y_l
Y_l
(a)
Y_j
X_j
T_j
T_k
Y_j
(b)
X_j
X_i
X_j
T_k
T_j
Z_j
Y_l
Y_l
(c)
Y_i
T_i
Y_i
X_i
T_k
Y_j
T_j
Z_j
Z_j
(d)
T_i
T_k
X_i
X_i
Y_k
T_j
T_l
Y_k
X_j
T_m
(e)
T_i
Y_i
X_i
X_i
Y_i
T_j
X_j
T_k
(f)

Figure 1

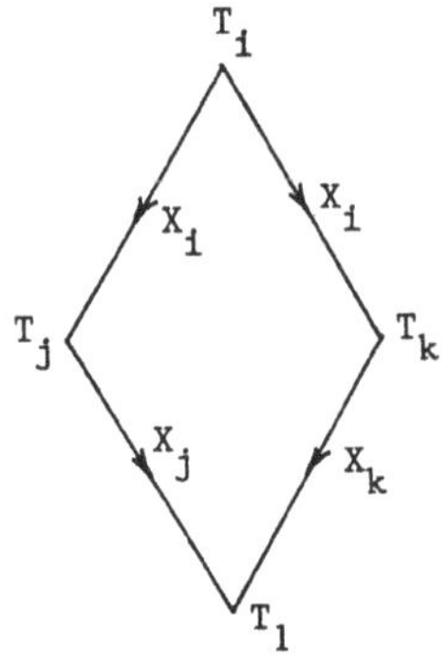

Figure 2

The situation depicted in Figure 2 is also not allowed in a version consistent history, according to ou definition. That is, merging of concurrent revisions is not allowed. The merging of concurrent revisior implies that a data item Z_i is a set of components $(Z_{i_n}, n = 1, N)$ which are revised and selectivel merged. Such merges are common in design databases [K, KSUW] (though [KSUW] considers merge as an advanced feature that need not be supported by an automatic version control mechanism). Ou model is not sufficiently powerful to show subset selection and union (merge) to derive a new versior We rely on the transaction that merges concurrent revisions to maintain internal consistency within th data item. We call this process *consistently merge*. We could revise our definition of version consistenc to:

> A history is version consistent if no transaction (i) ereads more than one version of any data item in h which it does not consistently merge, and (ii) ereads (other than reads) any data item it consistently merges.

Likewise, if some of the data items do not correspond to design objects and version consistency is not relevant issue for them, then only reads (not ereads) may be considered for those data items in Definitic 2.4. We will not consider such extensions in this paper.

Proposition 2.2. A history h is version consistent iff its extended history graph $EH(h)$ is suc that no two indirected edges of any vertex have labels X_i, X_j for any X, and i, j such that $i \neq j$. □

We can now define internal consistency of a version and mutual consistency of two versions. W first define two binary relations on the transactions in a history h : a transaction T_i is *immediatel useful-to* transaction T_j if T_j reads a version written by T_i; the *useful-to* is the transitive closure c mmediately-useful-to. With respect to a specified subset S of T, a transaction T_i is *S-useful* if it useful-to some transaction in S; otherwise it is *S-useless*. The *restriction of* h *with respect to* , denoted $h[S]$, is the history obtained from h by deleting the steps of all *S-useless* transactions, xcluding T_0.

Definition 2.5. A version X_i written by T_i is *internally consistent* if $h[\{T_i\}]$ is version consistent. ∎

Definition 2.6. Given versions X_i and Y_j, let T_a be a new read-only transaction with unordered teps $R_a[X_i]$ and $R_a[Y_j]$, and h' be the history obtained by appending the steps of T_a in any order at ne end of h. Then X_i and Y_j are *mutually consistent* if the history $h'[\{T_a\}]$ is version consistent. □

We conclude this section with a property that will be useful in section 4.

Lemma 2.3. Let h be a history of $T = \{T_0, T_1, ..., T_n\}$. The graph $H(h)$ is acyclic iff $EH(h)$ is cyclic.

Proof: The graph $H(h)$ is a subgraph of $EH(h)$, and hence the "if" part is obvious. For the "only " part, consider an ordering of the transactions corresponding to a topological sort of $H(h)$. Each ransaction may be "influenced" only by the transactions that occur before that transaction in this rdering. Then all eread edges are from "left to right" with respect to this ordering. Thus no directed ycle is possible in $EH(h)$. □

3. Serializability

In this section we discuss the notion of correctness of concurrent executions in design databases.

Definition 3.1. A (multi-version) history h is *serial* if

(i) there is no interleaving of the steps of the transaction in h, that is, once a transaction starts executing, it finishes all its steps without any other transaction executing some step in between, and

(ii) for each $R_j[X_i]$, $W_i[X_i]$ is the last write X step occurring before $R_j[X_i]$ in h. □

A history (corresponding to a concurrent execution) is normally accepted as *correct* if it behaves like serial history. Several correctness criteria have been proposed for different interpretations of "behaves" 3, V, Y]. The notion commonly used in tracking databases is view-serializability [Y] defined below.

Let T be $\{T_0, T_1, ..., T_n\}$ and h be a history of T, as defined in section 2. Let T_f be a hypothetical inal) read-only transaction with unordered read steps, one for each data item. Let h_f be the history obtained by appending the read steps of T_f, in any order, at the end of h such that, for each data iter X , T_f reads the version X_j, where $W_j[X_j]$ is the last write X step in h. The *reads-from* relation of h is defined as:

$$rf(h) = \{(T_i, X_i, T_j) : T_j \text{ has } R_j[X_i] \text{ step in } h_f, \text{ for } T_i,\ T_j \text{ in } T \cup \{T_f\}\}.$$

Two histories h and h' of T are *equivalent* if $rf(h) = rf(h')$. A history h is *view-serializable* there exists a serial history h' equivalent to h .

The view-serializability notion does not seem appropriate for design databases. For example, th following history, denoted h_1, is not view-serializable. (This can be checked easily.)

$$W_0[X_0]R_1[X_0]W_1[X_1]R_3[X_1]W_3[Y_3]R_2[X_0]W_2[X_2]R_4[X_2]W_4[Y_4].$$

Yet h_1 seems to make sense in a design database. Here T_1 revises X_0 to get a new version X_1, which used by T_3 to create version Y_3 of Y . Likewise T_2 revises X_0 to get X_2, which is used by T_4 to creat version Y_4 of Y . Thus X_1 and Y_3, and X_2 and Y_4 may constitute two alternate designs derived fro the same base version of X , namely X_0. One of these designs may be chosen at the end, and the oth discarded. For example, X_2 and Y_4 may be discarded. This amounts also to discarding the transactio T_2 and T_4 that created these versions. We note that once the steps of the discarded transactions a deleted from h_1, the resulting history is view-serializable. This suggests that the correctness notion f concurrent executions in design databases must be such that

(i) several alternate designs are allowed, and

(ii) for each alternate design, the history restricted to the steps of just those transactions usef to that design is view-serializable.

The τ_*-serializability notion defined in [B, V] satisfies the above requirement, and hence is propose for design databases in this paper. We define this notion in the following. The definition given he is slightly different from that in [V], but is more appropriate for design databases, especially when w consider along with version consistency.

Let h be a history of $T = \{T_0, T_1, ..., T_n\}$ and S a subset of T . The *reads-from relation of with respect to S*, denoted $rf(h,S)$, is as follows:

$$rf(h,S) = \{(T_i, X_i, T_j) : T_j \text{ has } R_j[X_i] \text{ step in } h \text{, and } T_j \text{ is } S\text{-useful}\}.$$

Two histories h and h' are *S-equivalent* if $rf(h,S)=rf(h',S)$. A history h is *S-serializable* if there exis a serial history h' S-equivalent to h .

Definition 3.2 . A history is *τ_*-serializable* if it is $\{T_i\}$-serializable for each T_i in T . □

The following lemma will be useful in the next section.

Lemma 3.1. If $H(h)$ is not acyclic, then h is not τ_*-serializable.

Proof: If $H(h)$ has a directed cycle, let T_i be a transaction in that cycle. Clearly T_i is not T_0. Now ll the transactions in that cycle are $\{T_i\}$-useful. Then no serial history can be $\{T_i\}$-equivalent to h. hat is, h is not $\{T_i\}$-serializable, and hence not τ_*-serializable. □

4. Version Consistency and Serializability

In this section we study the τ_*-serializability of version consistent histories. The main result is the llowing.

Theorem 4.1. Let h be a version consistent history of $T = \{T_0, T_1, ..., T_n\}$. Then h is τ_*-serializable f $H(h)$ is acyclic.

Proof: By Lemma 3.1, for any h, if $H(h)$ is not acyclic, then h is not τ_*-serializable. For the onverse, consider a version consistent history h such that $H(h)$ is acyclic. Let T_i be an arbitrary ransaction in T. We will show h is $\{T_i\}$-serializable. For T_i equal to T_0, the result is obvious. uppose T_i is different from T_0.

By Lemma 2.3, since $H(h)$ is acyclic, $EH(h)$ is also acyclic. Let G be the subgraph of $EH(h)$ hose vertex set consists of all the transactions from which there is a directed path to T_i, and edge set onsists of all the edges whose both ends lie in this vertex set. Then G contains exactly the $\{T_i\}$-useful ansactions and T_0, whether T_0 is $\{T_i\}$-useful or not. Clearly G is a 1-source 1-sink acyclic graph, here the source is T_0 and the sink is T_i.

We first show the following lemma.

Lemma 4.2. Let α be an X_j-edge and β an X_k-edge, for $j \neq k$, in G. Then there is a directed path hat contains both α and β in G.

Proof: Clearly $n\alpha$ and $n\beta$ are different, since otherwise h cannot be version consistent. By definition f G, there is a directed path from $n\alpha$ to T_i. Let R_α be a maximal such path, that is, there is no ther path from $n\alpha$ to T_i whose vertex set properly includes that of R_α. Likewise there exists a maximal irected path R_β from $n\beta$ to T_i. If either R_α contains T_k (that is, $p\beta$) or R_β contains T_j (that is, $p\alpha$), en clearly there is a directed path in G that contains both α and β. In the remaining case, let T_m be e first common vertex in these paths. Such a vertex exists since both paths end in T_i. Let R'_α denote the segment of R_α from $n\alpha$ to T_m, and R'_β the segment of R_β from $n\beta$ to T_m. Clearly both R'_α and R are also maximal.

Consider R'_α first. All the edges in this path are labelled, by construction of $EH(h)$. Let T_a be an arbitrary vertex in this path, and T_b be the vertex occurring immediately after T_a in this path. Sinc $n\alpha$ and $n\beta$ are different, such T_a, T_b exist.

Claim 1. T_b reads a version written by T_a.

For, otherwise, the edge from T_a to T_b, that is, (T_a, T_b), has to be an eread edge, obtained becaus of some other transaction T_c which has an eread edge from T_a and whose output version is read by T_b The vertex T_c cannot be in the path R'_α (nor in R_α), otherwise a directed cycle will result in G. The by substituting (T_a, T_c);(T_c, T_b) in place of (T_a, T_b) in R'_α, we get a directed path from $n\alpha$ to T_m whos vertex set includes that of R'_α, thus contradicting the maximality of R'_α.

Claim 2. Both T_a and T_b have an indirected X-edge. The X-edge indirected at T_b has the sam label as the one indirected at T_a if T_a does not write X, and label X_a otherwise.

This follows from the definition of eread, and the fact that the origin of R'_α, namely $n\alpha$, has th indirected X-edge α.

Claim 3. Each vertex in R'_α has an indirected X_p-edge whose positive end, namely T_p, is in $\{p\alpha\}$ $(V(R'_\alpha) - \{T_m\})$, where $V(R'_\alpha)$ is the vertex set of R'_α.

This follows from claim 2.

It follows similarly that each vertex in R'_β has an indirected X-edge whose positive end is in $\{p\beta$ $\cup$ $(V(R'_\beta) - \{T_m\})$. Since T_m is the only common vertex of $V(R'_\alpha)$ and $V(R'_\beta)$, and $p\beta \neq p\alpha$ since $\neq \beta$, it follows that T_m has two indirected X-edges with different labels. This contradicts the versio consistency of h. The proof of the lemma is complete. □

We continue with the proof of the theorem. Let $(T_0, T_{i_1}, T_{i_2}, \ldots, T_i)$ be a topological sort of G. Suppos there are read steps $R_{i_l}[X_{i_m}]$ and $R_{i_p}[X_{i_q}]$ for $i_m \neq i_q$. Then G has an X_{i_m}-edge from T_{i_m} to T_{i_l} an X_{i_q}-edge from T_{i_q} to T_{i_p}. By Lemma 4.2 , there is a directed path that contains both these edge Hence both T_{i_m} and T_{i_l} appear either before or after both T_{i_q} and T_{i_p} in the topological sort. Hence noninterleaved history corresponding to the above topological sort is indeed (i) a serial history and (ii $\{T_i\}$-equivalent to h.

The proof of the theorem is complete. □

From Proposition 2.2, Lemma 2.3 and Theorem 4.1, it follows that both version consistency and τ serializability can be checked by constructing $EH(h)$. The construction of the graph as well as checkin ersion consistency and acyclicity can be done in polynomial time.

We note that $EH(h)$ is needed for checking version consistency, but $H(h)$ suffices for checking τ_*-erializability. Also, for the latter, the labels on the directed edges are not needed. Hence if version onsistency can be checked without constructing $EH(h)$ *explicitly*, the graph required for checking τ_*-erializability can be simplified.

If all the transactions are *two-phase* transactions, that is, all the read steps precede all the write teps, then it can be verified that $H(h)$ is always acyclic. Then only version consistency needs to be hecked.

In section 2 we mentioned that if some data items do not correspond to design objects and version onsistency is not a relevant issue for them, then Definition 2.4 (of version consistency) can be modified consider only reads, and not ereads, of those data items. For histories which are version consistent nder such modified definition, Theorem 4.1 may not hold, since the problem of checking τ_*-serializability f a general history is NP-complete. Then some constraints (like those in classes D, Q and 2PL of [P]) ay be applied with respect to those data items, to get a polynomial test for τ_*-serializability.

We had assumed for simplicity that all the versions that are created are kept until the very end of he design process. This can be relaxed easily. With our version consistency definition, discarding a ersion amounts to discarding the entire transaction which wrote that version. Then all the transactions hat were influenced by this transaction must also be discarded. In other words, any sink vertex in the partial) history graph can be deleted. By repeating this several times, any vertices can be deleted.

5. Conclusion

We have studied version consistency and serializability issues in design databases in this paper.

(i) We have proposed a formal definition of verison consistency in terms of transaction histories. This enables checking version consistency by constructing an (extended) history graph from a given history. This can be done in polynomial time.

(ii) We have argued that τ_*-serializability is the appropriate notion of correctness for concurrent executions in design databases. For business and administrative databases, the commonly accepted criterion is view-serializability.

(iii) We have shown that τ_*-serializability of version consistent histories can be checked in polynomial time. With general histories the problem is NP-complete.

(iv) We have also shown that the graph in (i) above itself can be used to check τ_*-serializability also.

Our results seem to suggest that an on-line automatic integrated version consistency and concurrency control mechanism is feasible. We are investigating this problem currently.

Acknowledgement : Fruitful discussions with Richard Foster in the early stages of this research are gratefully acknowledged.

This research is supported in part by the Natural Sciences and Engineering Research Council of Canada Individual Operating Grant A-3182 of the first author.

References

[BKK] F. Bancilhan, W. Kim and H.F. Korth, A model of CAD transactions, *Proc. VLDB '85* pp. 25-33, 1985.

[BG] P.A. Bernstein and N. Goodman, Multiversion concurrency control - theory and algorithms, *ACM TODS* Vol.8, No.4, pp. 465-483, 1983.

[B] J.A. Brzozowski, On models of transactions, Technical Report No.84001, Department of Applied Mathematics and Physics, Kyoto University, Japan, 1984.

[D] C.N.G. Dampney, Precedency control and other semantic integrity issues in a workbench database, *IEEE 1983 Proceedings of Annual Meeting - Database Week* , pp. 97-104 1983.

[K] U. Kelter, Concurrency control for design objects with versions in CAD databases, *Inform. Systems* Vol.12, No.2, pp. 137-143, 1987.

[KSUW] P. Klahold, G. Schlageter, R. Unland and W. Wilkes, A transaction model supporting complex applications in integrated information systems, *Proc. SIGMOD '85* , pp. 388-401, 1985.

[NH] T. Neumann and C. Hornung, Consistency and transactions in CAD database, *Proc VLDB '82*, pp. 181-188, 1982.

[P] C.H. Papadimitriou, The serializability of concurrent database updates, *J.ACM* , Vol.26 No.4, pp. 631-653, 1979.

[PK] C.H. Papadimitriou and P.C. Kanellakis, On concurrency control by multiple versions *ACM TODS* Vol.9, No.1, pp. 89-99, 1984.

[V] K. Vidyasankar, Generalized theory of serializability, *Acta Informatica* Vol.24, No.1, pp 105-119, 1987.

[Y] M. Yannakakis, Serializability by locking, *J.ACM* Vol.31, No.2, pp. 227-244, 1984.

OBJECT-HISTORY AND SPREADSHEET P-SIMULATION*

(Extended Abstract)

Seymour Ginsburg and Stephen Kurtzman
Computer Science Department, University of Southern California
Los Angeles, California 90089-0782

Introduction

In [GT], a record-based model was introduced for describing object histories. The model consists of sequences of *computation tuples* defined by a *computation-tuple sequence scheme* (CSS). The CSS specifies computational relationships which hold between the tuples in a sequence. Another structure using computational relationships to connect computation tuples in a sequence is the well-known spreadsheet [CSRM, GOUM, R123]. This paper presents a formal description of spreadsheets and compares the relative expressive capabilities of the two models. It then introduces a property, p-simulatability, based on an analogue to the relational database projection operation, which formalizes the notion of when two CSS or spreadsheets represent the same set of histories. Conditions under which a spreadsheet or object-history can be p-simulated are then given.

The paper is divided into three sections. In Section 1, the formal model for object histories is presented. In Section 2, the formal model for spreadsheet histories is introduced and compared to object histories. In the last section the question of spreadsheet and object-history p-simulation is addressed.

Section 1. Preliminaries

In this section we present a terse description of a simplified version of the object-history model introduced in [GT]. The model presented here omits the state attributes and state functions included in the original model. The result is a simplified, essentially equivalent, object-history model.

Informally, an object history is a historical record of an object, such as a person's checking account. It is a sequence of occurrences, each occurrence consisting of input data and some calculation. For example, in the income history of a business, an occurrence might be the monthly totals for inventory acquisitions, inventory on hand, sales, and expenses, together with a computation of the gross and net

* This work was supported in part by the National Science Foundation under grant CCR-86-18907.

profits. In the model, each object history is represented as a sequence of tuples (over the same attributes) called a "computation-tuple sequence". A "computation-tuple sequence scheme" (CSS) is a construc which defines all "valid" computation-tuple sequences. Hence, a CSS for objects of the type "income history" specifies all "valid" income histories. A CSS consists of: ($\Delta 1$) A set of attributes partitioned into input and evaluation attributes according to their roles; ($\Delta 2$) Functions which calculate the value for the evaluation attributes; ($\Delta 3$) Semantic constraints whose satisfaction holds uniformly throughout a computation-tuple sequence; and ($\Delta 4$) A set of computation-tuple sequences of bounded length with which to start a valid computation-tuple sequence until all evaluation functions can be applied. A computation-tuple sequence is valid if it starts with one of the sequences in ($\Delta 4$), uses the functions in ($\Delta 2$) to calculate the values for the evaluation attributes, and satisfies the semantic constraints of ($\Delta 3$).

Formally, Dom_∞ is an infinite set of *domain* elements and U_∞ an infinite set of *attribute*. U_∞ is partitioned into two infinite disjoint sets, I_∞ and E_∞, called *input* and *evaluation* attributes resp. There is a total order, $\leq_\infty$, over U_∞ such that $A \leq_\infty B$ for A in I_∞ and B in E_∞. For A in U_∞, Dom(A) is a subset of Dom_∞ of at least two elements. All attributes are elements of U_∞. A, B, and C (possibly subscripted) denote attributes and U, V, and W (possibly subscripted) nonempty finite sets of attributes.

Let X be a finite nonempty subset of U_∞ and $A_1, \ldots, A_n$ of the elements of X according to $\leq_\infty$. Then $\langle X \rangle$ denotes the sequence $A_1 \ldots A_n$ and $Dom(\langle X \rangle)$ the cartesian product $Dom(A_1) \times \cdots \times Dom(A_n)$. For $i \geq 2$, $\langle X | A_i \rangle$ denotes the prefix $A_1 \ldots A_{i-1}$.

Consistent with ($\Delta 1$) we have:

Definition. An *attribute scheme* over $\langle U \rangle$ is an ordered pair $(\langle I \rangle, \langle E \rangle)$, where[1] $\langle U \rangle = \langle I \rangle \langle E \rangle$, $I = I_\infty \cap U \neq \emptyset$, and $E = E_\infty \cap U \neq \emptyset$.

We now formalize the notions of occurrence and sequence of occurrences using the terms "computation tuple" and "computation-tuple sequence".

Definition. A *computation tuple* over $\langle U \rangle$ is an element in $Dom(\langle U \rangle)$. A *computation-tuple sequence* over $\langle U \rangle$ is a finite, nonempty sequence of computation tuples over $\langle U \rangle$. The set of all computation-tuple sequences over $\langle U \rangle$ is denoted by $SEQ(\langle U \rangle)$.

The symbols u, v, and w, possibly subscripted or primed, represent computation tuples and $\overline{u}$, $\overline{v}$ and $\overline{w}$ computation-tuple sequences.

To formalize the components ($\Delta 1$) and ($\Delta 2$) of a CSS, we have:

---

[1] Given sequences $\langle U_1 \rangle = A_1 \ldots A_{m_1}$ and $\langle U_2 \rangle = B_1 \ldots B_{m_2}$, $\langle U_1 \rangle \langle U_2 \rangle$ denotes the concatenation of the sequences, i.e. $A_1 \ldots A_{m_1} B_1 \ldots B_{m_2}$.

efinition. A *computation scheme* (CS) over $\langle U \rangle$ is a triple $\mathcal{C} = (\langle I \rangle, \langle E \rangle, \mathcal{E})$, where

- $(\langle I \rangle, \langle E \rangle)$ is an attribute scheme over $\langle U \rangle$; and
- $\mathcal{E} = \{e_C | C \text{ in } E, e_C$ is a partial function from $\text{Dom}(\langle U \rangle)^{\rho_C} \times \text{Dom}(\langle U|C \rangle)$ to Dom(C) for some non-negative integer $\rho_C\}$.

he functions in $\mathcal{E}$ are called *evaluation* functions. For each C in E, the integer ρ_C is the *rank* of e_C; d $\rho(\mathcal{C}) = \max\{\rho_C | e_C \text{ in } \mathcal{E}\}$ is the *rank* of $\mathcal{C}$.

Intuitively, the rank of a computation scheme is the minimum number of previous computation ples on which each computation tuple computationally depends.

A CS selects those computation-tuple sequences whose evaluation attributes values are determined the corresponding evaluation functions.

otation. Let $\mathcal{C} = (\langle I \rangle, \langle E \rangle, \mathcal{E})$ be a CS over $\langle U \rangle$. For each C in E, let VSEQ(e_C) = $u_1 \ldots u_m \mid m \geq 1, u_h(C) = e_C(u_{h-\rho_C}, \ldots, u_{h-1}, u_h[\langle U|C \rangle])$ for each h, $\rho_C < h \leq m\}$; and for each $'$, $\emptyset \neq E' \subseteq E$, let VSEQ($\{e_C \mid C \text{ in } E'\}$) = $\bigcap_{C \text{ in } E'}$ VSEQ(e_C). Let VSEQ($\emptyset$) = SEQ($\langle U \rangle$) and SEQ($\mathcal{C}$) = VSEQ($\mathcal{E}$).

$\overline{u}$ is in VSEQ(e_C) iff each interval of $\overline{u}$ of length at least $\rho_C + 1$ is also in VSEQ(e_C). [For $\mathcal{S} \subseteq$ EQ($\langle U \rangle$), Interval($\mathcal{S}$) = $\{\overline{u'} \mid \overline{u'}$ an interval of some $\overline{u}$ in $\mathcal{S}\}$. If $\mathcal{S}$ = Interval($\mathcal{S}$) then $\mathcal{S}$ is *interval osed.*] Thus VSEQ(e_C), whence VSEQ($\mathcal{C}$), is interval closed.

Turning to constraints, i.e. (Δ3), we have:

efinition. A *constraint* σ over SEQ($\langle U \rangle$) is a mapping from SEQ($\langle U \rangle$) into {true, false}. If $\sigma(\overline{u})$ = true, en $\overline{u}$ *satisfies* σ. For a set Σ of constraints, let VSEQ(Σ) = $\{\overline{u}$ in SEQ($\langle U \rangle$) $\mid$ satisfies each σ in $\Sigma\}$. A constraint σ is *uniform* if VSEQ(σ) is interval closed.

Only uniform constraints will used in the model.

The initialization (see (Δ4)) is the set of computation-tuple sequences that are used to start the lid computation-tuple sequences.

efinition. Given a CS $\mathcal{C}$ over $\langle U \rangle$ and a finite set Σ of constraints over SEQ($\langle U \rangle$), an *initialization* (*with spect to* $\mathcal{C}$ *and* Σ) is any prefix-closed subset $\mathcal{I}$ of

$$\{\overline{u} \text{ in VSEQ}(\mathcal{C}) \cap \text{VSEQ}(\Sigma) \mid |\overline{u}| \leq \max\{1, \rho(\mathcal{C})\}\}.$$

iven an initialization $\mathcal{I}$, VSEQ($\mathcal{I}$) denotes

$$\mathcal{I} \cup \{\overline{u} \text{ in SEQ}(\langle U \rangle) \mid \overline{u} = \overline{u}_1\overline{u}_2 \text{ for some } \overline{u}_1 \text{ in } \mathcal{I} \text{ of length } \max\{1, \rho(\mathcal{C})\}\}.$$

Each VSEQ($\mathcal{I}$) is prefix closed but not necessarily interval closed.

Definition. A *computation-tuple sequence scheme* (CSS) over $\langle U \rangle$ is a triple $T = (\mathcal{C}, \Sigma, \mathcal{I})$, where (1) $\mathcal{C}$ is a computation scheme over $\langle U \rangle$; (2) Σ is a finite set of uniform constraints over SEQ($\langle U \rangle$); and (3) $\mathcal{I}$ is an initialization with respect to $\mathcal{C}$ and Σ. Let $\rho(T)$, called the *rank* of T, be $\max\{1, \rho(\mathcal{C})\}$.

For $T = ((\langle I \rangle, \langle E \rangle, \mathcal{E}), \Sigma, \mathcal{I})$, let $\text{VSEQ}(T) = \text{VSEQ}(\mathcal{E}) \cap \text{VSEQ}(\Sigma) \cap \text{VSEQ}(\mathcal{I})$. A computation-tuple sequence is said to be *valid* (*for* T) if it is in VSEQ(T).

We shall assume the following:

Computability Assumption: If $T = (\mathcal{C}, \Sigma, \mathcal{I})$, with $\mathcal{C} = (\langle I \rangle, \langle E \rangle, \mathcal{E})$, is a CSS, then (1) e_B is partially recursive for each B in E; (2) VSEQ(σ) is recursively enumerable for each σ in Σ; and (3) VSEQ($\mathcal{I}$) is recursively enumerable.

Clearly, VSEQ($\mathcal{C}$) and VSEQ(T) are recursively enumerable.

Section 2. Spreadsheet and Object Histories

In this section a formal model for spreadsheets is introduced and compared to CSS.

Spreadsheet programs, such as C-Calc and Lotus 1-2-3, are one of the most widely used types of small-business data-processing software [WS]. In simple terms, a spreadsheet is a finite set of related data. Each datum occupies a unique location and is either specified directly, using a constant value, or indirectly, using a function. In Lotus 1-2-3, each datum location is called a *cell*. The cells are arranged in a 256 column by 8192 row rectangle, and are addressed by row and column indices. The functions are written in terms of the data locations in the spreadsheet. The expressive power of the functions provided by spreadsheet programs vary. In principle, these may be arbitrary computable functions.

Example 2.1. Consider a spreadsheet representation for a business income history. Figure 2.1 shows a possible history displayed as it would appear using Lotus 1-2-3. Column A describes the data in each row. Column B contains the data for the first month. The data in cells B1 through B6 are entered into the spreadsheet as constant values. Because of the application, the value in B6 must be zero. The numbers in B7 through B9 are calculated using the formulas[2] +B6 + B2 − B3, +B4 − B7, and +B8 − B5 resp. and in the specified order. The value in B10 is entered as a constant and must be the same as that in B9.

The data in column C represents the second month of the income history. The information in C1 through C5 is specified directly. The data in C6 through C10 are calculated from the formulas[3] +B…

[2] We adopt the notation used by the Lotus 1-2-3 program for formula specification. See [R123].

[3] The Lotus 1-2-3 formula @IF(*cond*,*expr1*,*expr2*) returns the value of *expr1* if the logical expressio…

	A	B	C	D	E	F
1	Month	Nov-86	Dec-86	Jan-87	Feb-87	Mar-87
2	Inventory Added	12,000	500	1,200	1,200	4,000
3	Closing Inventory	10,000	8,000	8,000	8,500	10,000
4	Sales	5,000	6,000	3,000	2,000	5,000
5	Expenses	1,500	1,800	1,400	1,600	1,800
6	Opening Inventory	0	10,000	8,000	8,000	8,500
7	Sales Cost	2,000	2,500	1,200	700	2,500
8	Gr. Profit	3,000	3,500	1,800	1,300	2,500
9	Net Profit	1,500	1,700	400	- 300	700
10	Net Profit To Date	1,500	3,200	400	100	800

Figure 2.1

C6 + C2 – C3, +C4 – C7, +C8 – C5, and @IF(@MONTH(C1) = 1 , C9 , C9 + B10), respectively nd in the specified order. The information in column B is entered and calculated before the values in 6 through C10. The formulas for C7 through C9 are relativized versions of the formulas used for B7 rough B9. (Most spreadsheet programs provide a command to copy the formulas from one column to nother in this relativized fashion – see the "copy" and related commands in [CSRM, GOUM, R123].)

For columns D, E, and F, the values in rows 1 through 5 are input as constants and 6 through 10 e calculated using relativized versions of the formulas in column C. The calculations are performed for lumns B, C, D, E, and F in that order. □

Example 2.1 shows that there is considerable similarity between spreadsheets and computation ples. Informally, the display in Figure 2.1 is called a spreadsheet. Formally, however, each of the lumns B through F is a separate spreadsheet and the entire figure shows a spreadsheet history. This pe of spreadsheet history also occurs in many other applications. In the checkbook management plications found in [CA,CSRM], each spreadsheet is a checkbook entry. In the sales, cash flow, and dget forecasting[4] applications found in [CA,GOUM], each spreadsheet contains the data for a single me period.

cond is true, and *expr2* if *cond* is false. The function @MONTH(C1) returns the month (1 through 12) of the year of the date stored in cell C1.

[4] Forecasting is also referred to as projection and "what-if" models. See [J] for example.

To model this type of use, we must consider sequences of spreadsheets. One aspect of each of the applications mentioned in the last paragraph is regularity of form. To capture this behavior we restrict our attention to sequences in which each spreadsheet is defined over a fixed set of attributes. As in object histories, we partition the attributes into input and evaluation attributes to separate the roles of input and derived data. That is, we view each spreadsheet in the sequence as a computation tuple. This leads to the first component of the spreadsheet history model, namely, the spreadsheet scheme. Before proceeding to its definition, we introduce convenient symbolism.

Notation. For each $\langle U \rangle$ and $\rho \geq 1$, let $SEQ(\langle U \rangle, \rho) = \{\overline{u} \text{ in } SEQ(\langle U \rangle) \mid |\overline{u}| \geq \rho\}$. Let[5] $SEQ(\langle U \rangle, 0) = \{\Lambda\} \cup SEQ(\langle U \rangle, 1)$.

Definition. A *spreadsheet scheme* (SS) over $\langle U \rangle$ is a triple $S = (\langle I \rangle, \langle E \rangle, \mathcal{S})$, where

- $(\langle I \rangle, \langle E \rangle)$ is an attribute scheme over $\langle U \rangle$; and
- $\mathcal{S} = \{s_C \mid C \text{ in } E, s_C \text{ is a partial recursive function from } SEQ(\langle U \rangle, \rho_{s_C}) \times Dom(\langle U|C \rangle) \text{ to } Dom(C), \text{ where } \rho_{s_C} \geq 0\}$.

The functions in $\mathcal{S}$ are called *spreadsheet functions.* The number ρ_{s_C} is called the *rank* of s_C and $\rho(S) = \max\{\rho_{s_C} \mid C \text{ in } E\}$ is called the rank of S.

As in a CSS evaluation function, the rank of a spreadsheet function determines the number of previous computation tuples needed before the spreadsheet function can be applied. The role of the rank differs in that it does not limit the number of tuples used in the calculation of a spreadsheet function. Intuitively, evaluation functions may only look back at a fixed portion of the history whereas spreadsheet functions are allowed to search back through the entire history. This difference is used later to show that spreadsheet histories are more expressive than object histories. (See Proposition 2.1.) However, in real-life applications, a spreadsheet function often is determined by a bounded number of previous tuples. We call such a spreadsheet function *history bounded.*

Definition. Let s_B be a spreadsheet function in the SS S over $\langle U \rangle$, and τ a non-negative integer. If $s_B(\overline{u}\,\overline{v}, w[\langle U|B \rangle]) = s_B(\overline{v}, w[\langle U|B \rangle])$ for all sequences $\overline{u}\,\overline{v}w$ in $SEQ(\langle U \rangle)$, where $|\overline{v}| = \tau$, then s_B is τ-*history bounded.* A spreadsheet function is *history bounded* if it is τ-history bounded for some τ. If all spreadsheet functions in S are τ-history bounded, then S is τ-*history bounded.* S is *history bounded* if it is τ-history bounded for some τ.

The purpose of an SS is to define a set of spreadsheet sequences which are consistent with the functions in the spreadsheet. This leads to the following symbolism:

---

[5] The symbol Λ denotes the empty sequence.

Notation. Let $S = (\langle I\rangle, \langle E\rangle, \mathcal{S})$ be an SS over $\langle U\rangle$. For each C in E let

$$\mathrm{VSEQ}(s_C) = \{u_1 \ldots u_n \mid u_i(C) = s_C(u_1 \ldots u_{i-1}, u_i[\langle U|C\rangle]) \text{ for } i > \rho_{s_C}\},$$

and for each E′, $\emptyset \neq E' \subseteq E$, let $\mathrm{VSEQ}(\{s_C \mid C \text{ in } E'\}) = \bigcap_{C \text{ in } E'} \mathrm{VSEQ}(s_C)$. Let VSEQ(S) = VSEQ($\mathcal{S}$).

Note that VSEQ(S) is recursively enumerable, hence membership in VSEQ(S) is partially decidable. And since the VSEQ of each spreadsheet function is prefix closed, VSEQ(S) is prefix closed.

To complete the spreadsheet-history model, we must have a mechanism which provides the values for the evaluation attributes at the beginning of a spreadsheet sequence. This is accomplished using a prefix-closed set of sequences of length at most $\rho(S)$, the rank of the spreadsheet.

Definition. Given an SS S over $\langle U\rangle$, an *initialization (with respect to* S) is a recursively enumerable, prefix-closed subset $\mathcal{I}$ of $\{\overline{u} \text{ in } \mathrm{VSEQ}(S) \mid |\overline{u}| \leq \max\{1, \rho(S)\}\}$. Let

$$\mathrm{VSEQ}(\mathcal{I}) = \mathcal{I} \cup \{\overline{u} \text{ in } \mathrm{SEQ}(\langle U\rangle) \mid \overline{u} = \overline{u}_1\overline{u}_2 \text{ for some } \overline{u}_1 \text{ in } \mathcal{I} \text{ of length } \rho(S)\}.$$

Clearly, VSEQ($\mathcal{I}$) is recursively enumerable and prefix closed.

Definition. A ***spreadsheet history scheme*** (SHS) over $\langle U\rangle$ is an ordered pair $H = (S, \mathcal{I})$, where (1) S is a spreadsheet scheme over $\langle U\rangle$ and (2) $\mathcal{I}$ is an initialization with respect to S. Let $\rho(H)$, called the ***rank*** of H, be $\max\{1, \rho(S)\}$.

Definition. For each SHS $H = ((\langle I\rangle, \langle E\rangle, \mathcal{S}), \mathcal{I})$ let $\mathrm{VSEQ}(H) = \mathrm{VSEQ}(S) \cap \mathrm{VSEQ}(\mathcal{I})$. A spreadsheet sequence is said to be *valid (for* H) if it is in VSEQ(H).

Clearly, VSEQ(H) is recursively enumerable.

Example 2.1 (continued). We now present the income history using the spreadsheet model. We ignore column A since it does not affect the calculations. Each of the other columns is a spreadsheet. An SHS for the history is $H = ((\langle I\rangle, \langle E\rangle, \mathcal{S}), \mathcal{I})$, where

- $I = \langle \mathrm{MONTH}, \mathrm{INVADD}, \mathrm{CLOINV}, \mathrm{SALES}, \mathrm{EXPENSE}\rangle$,
  $E = \langle \mathrm{OPINV}, \mathrm{COST}, \mathrm{GRPROF}, \mathrm{NET}, \mathrm{NPCY}\rangle$, and $\langle U\rangle = \langle I\rangle\langle E\rangle$.
- The domains of the attributes are the obvious ones.
- s_{OPINV} is rank one and defined for $u_1 \ldots u_n$ in $\mathrm{SEQ}(\langle U\rangle, 1)$ and v in $\mathrm{Dom}(\langle U\rangle)$ by:

$$s_{\mathrm{OPINV}}(u_1 \ldots u_n, v[\langle U|\mathrm{OPINV}\rangle]) = u_n(\mathrm{CLOINV})$$

if $v(\mathrm{MONTH}) = u_n(\mathrm{MONTH}) + 1$ and it is undefined otherwise.

- s_{COST}, s_{GRPROF}, and s_{NET} are rank-zero and defined for $u_1 \ldots u_n$ in SEQ(⟨U⟩, 0) and v in Dom(⟨U
  by

$$s_{COST}(u_1 \ldots u_n, v[\langle U|COST\rangle]) = v(OPINV) + v(INVADD) - v(CLOINV)$$

$$s_{GRPROF}(u_1 \ldots u_n, v[\langle U|GRPROF\rangle]) = v(SALES) - v(COST)$$

$$s_{NET}(u_1 \ldots u_n, v[\langle U|NET\rangle]) = v(GRPROF) - v(EXPENSE).$$

- s_{NPCY} is rank one and defined for $u_1 \ldots u_n$ in SEQ(⟨U⟩, 1) and v in Dom(⟨U⟩) by:

$$s_{NPCY}(u_1 \ldots u_n, v[\langle U|NPCY\rangle]) = \begin{cases} v(NET) & \text{if } v(MONTH) \text{ is a January} \\ u_n(NPCY) + v(NET) & \text{otherwise.} \end{cases}$$

- $\mathcal{I} = \{u$ in Dom(⟨U⟩) | $u(OPINV) = 0$ and $u(NPCY) = u(NET)\}$. □

Example 2.2. To illustrate the similarity between SHS and CSS, we recast the income history as a CS Let U, I, and E be the attribute sets in Example 2.1. A computation scheme for the history is $\mathcal{C} = ((\langle$ ⟨E⟩, $\mathcal{E}$), with $\mathcal{E}$ containing the following functions:

- e_{OPINV} is the rank-one function defined for u and v in Dom(⟨U⟩) by[6]

$$e_{OPINV}(u, v[\langle U|OPINV\rangle]) = u(CLOINV).$$

- e_{COST}, e_{GRPROF}, and e_{NET} have rank zero and are defined for u in Dom(⟨U⟩) by

$$e_{COST}(u[\langle U|COST\rangle]) = u(OPINV) + u(INVADD) - u(CLOINV).$$

$$e_{GRPROF}(u[\langle U|GRPROF\rangle]) = u(SALES) - u(COST).$$

$$e_{NET}(u[\langle U|NET\rangle]) = u(GRPROF) - u(EXPENSE).$$

- e_{NPCY} is the rank-one function defined for u and v in Dom(⟨U⟩) by

$$e_{NPCY}(u, v[\langle U|NPCY\rangle]) = \begin{cases} v(NET) & \text{if } v(MONTH) \text{ is a January} \\ u(NPCY) + v(NET) & \text{otherwise.} \end{cases}$$

---

[6] Let ⟨U⟩ = $A_1 \ldots A_n$ and ⟨V⟩ be a subsequence of ⟨U⟩. For each computation tuple u over ⟨U $u[\langle V\rangle]$ is the computation tuple v over ⟨V⟩ defined by $v(A) = u(A)$ for each A in V.

For information on the formulas used, see a first-year accounting text, e.g. [McQ].

The income history CSS has one constraint, σ. It requires that consecutive tuples represent consecutive months and is defined by

$$\text{VSEQ}(\sigma) = \{u_1 \ldots u_m \text{ in SEQ}(\langle U \rangle) \mid u_{i+1}(\text{MONTH}) \text{ is the month following } u_i(\text{MONTH}) \text{ for each i, } 1 \leq i \leq m-1\}.$$

The initialization for the income history CSS is the same as in Example 1.1. That is, $\mathcal{I} = \{u$ in Dom(U) | u(OPINV) = 0 and u(NPCY) = u(NET)$\}$. □

The similarities between CSS and SHS are obvious but the differences are subtle. The first two results show some of the connections between the two.

Proposition 2.1. The class of computation-tuple sequence sets defined by CSS is properly contained in the class defined by SHS.

The proof of Proposition 2.1 relies on the fact that spreadsheet functions may be defined with respect to the entire preceding computation-tuple sequence. This permits the construction of an SHS whose VSEQ is equal to that of a given CSS. Because evaluation functions may only be defined with respect to a bounded number of previous computation tuples, the converse is not true.

We now compare a subclass of the SHS with a subclass of the CSS.

Definition. An SHS H = (S, $\mathcal{I}$) is *τ-history bounded*, resp. *history bounded*, if S is τ-history bounded, resp., history bounded.

Definition. A (uniform) constraint σ over SEQ($\langle$U$\rangle$) is *k-local*, $k \geq 1$, if, for all $\overline{u}$ of length at least k, $\sigma(\overline{v})$ = true for all intervals $\overline{v}$ of $\overline{u}$ of length k implies $\sigma(\overline{u})$ = true. A CSS is *local* if each of its constraints is k-local for some k.

The k-local constraints have the property that satisfaction by a sequence under the addition of a computation tuple can be verified by checking satisfaction of just the last k tuples in the new sequence. Local constraints have been studied in [DG,GG,GT].

Proposition 2.2. The class of computation-tuple sequence sets defined by local CSS is the same as that defined by history-bounded SHS.

Because the number of previous tuples which may be used by a history-bounded spreadsheet function is bounded, it is possible to construct evaluation functions which perform equivalent computations. Thus, given a history-bounded SHS an equivalent CSS may be constructed. By incorporating the constraints for a local CSS into the definition of the spreadsheet functions, a reverse construction is also possible.

In [GT] it was shown that there exist sets of computation-tuple sequences which are defined by CS but not by local CSS. Thus, by Proposition 2.2, there exist CSS that describe sets of computation-tupl sequences which cannot be defined by history-bounded SHS.

In summary, SHS are strictly more expressive than CSS, which in turn are strictly more expressiv than history-bounded SHS; which in turn are expressively equivalent to local CSS.

Section 3. Object History and Spreadsheet P-Simulation

In this section the general question of when two CSS or SHS describe the same set of histories i considered. To study this problem, the notion of "sameness" must be formalized. This question ha been partially addressed in two papers [GT,DG], using other concepts of sameness. A new notion o sameness, one based on the object-history analogue to the relational-database projection operation, i now presented and examined.

Definition. Let $\langle U\rangle$ be a sequence of attributes, $\langle V\rangle$ a subsequence of $\langle U\rangle$, and u a computation tupl over $\langle U\rangle$. The tuple $u[\langle V\rangle]$ is called the *projection* of u into SEQ($\langle V\rangle$) and is frequently written a $\Pi_V(u)$. For each $\overline{u} = u_1 \ldots u_m$ in SEQ($\langle U\rangle$), let $\Pi_V(\overline{u}) = \Pi_V(u_1)\ldots\Pi_V(u_m)$. For each $S \subseteq$ SEQ($\langle U\rangle$) let $\Pi_V(S) = \{\Pi_V(\overline{u}) \mid \overline{u} \text{ in } S\}$.

We now formalize the notion of sameness (called "p-simulation") employed in this paper.

Definition. Let T_1 be a CSS (resp. SHS) over $\langle U\rangle = \langle I\rangle\langle E\rangle$ and T_2 be a CSS (resp. SHS) ove $\langle V\rangle = \langle I\rangle\langle E'\rangle$, with[7] $E' \subset E$. Then T_2 *p-simulates* T_1 if the projection Π_V maps VSEQ(T_1) one-to-on onto VSEQ(T_2).

Informally, each history in T_2 is modeled by the same set of inputs as in T_1. Furthermore, th evaluation attributes in T_2 are a (nonempty) subset of those in T_1. In a sense, the roles played by th attributes in T_2 are identical to those played by the same attributes in T_1. Note that any historic information carried by the attributes in $E - E'$ is redundant in the sense that no (historical) informatio is lost by removing those attributes.

Our first major result shows that for SHS, p-simulation is equivalent to the simpler property c one-to-one mapping. (The analogous result for CSS is false.)

Theorem 3.1 Let $H = ((\langle I\rangle, \langle E\rangle, \mathcal{S}), \mathcal{I})$ be an SHS, $\emptyset \neq E' \subset E$, and $\langle V\rangle = \langle I\rangle\langle E'\rangle$. Then there exists a SHS over $\langle V\rangle$ which p-simulates H iff Π_V maps VSEQ(H) one-to-one.

The following proposition simplifies the property of mapping a VSEQ one-to-one by reducing it t

---

[7] The symbol $\subset$ is used to indicate proper inclusion, i.e. $A \subset B$ is equivalent to $A \subseteq B$ and $A \neq B$.

ıe property of mapping a portion of the initialization one-to-one.

roposition 3.2. Let $T = (((\langle I\rangle, \langle E\rangle, \mathcal{E}), \Sigma, \mathcal{I})$ be a CSS or $T = (((\langle I\rangle, \langle E\rangle, \mathcal{S}), \mathcal{I})$ be an SHS, $\emptyset \neq E' \subset E$, nd $\langle V\rangle = \langle I\rangle\langle E'\rangle$. Then Π_V maps VSEQ(T) one-to-one iff it maps[8] $\text{prefix}^r(\text{VSEQ}(T))$ one-to-one, where $= \max\{1, \rho_{e_B} \mid B \text{ in } E - E'\}$.

xample 3.1. Let $H = (((\langle I\rangle, \langle E\rangle, \mathcal{S}), \mathcal{I})$ be the SHS over $\langle U\rangle$ from Example 1.1, $E' = \{\text{OPINV}\}$, and $V\rangle = \langle I\rangle\langle E'\rangle$. It is easily seen that Π_V maps $\mathcal{I}$ one-to-one. Thus, by Proposition 3.2, Π_V maps VSEQ(H) ne-to-one. Hence, by Theorem 3.1, there exists an SHS H′ over $\langle V\rangle$ which p-simulates H. One such HS is $H' = (((\langle I\rangle, \langle E'\rangle, \{s'_{\text{OPINV}}\}), \Pi_V(\mathcal{I}))$, where s'_{OPINV} is the rank-one function defined in a similar ıanner to s_{OPINV}. □

Note that the SHS H′ in Example 3.1 is 1-history bounded. This example is very well behaved. The ıllowing theorem shows that a history-bounded SHS H may be p-simulatable, but there may not exists n SHS which p-simulates H and is also history bounded.

heorem 3.3. SHS history boundedness is not preserved by p-simulation.

We now turn to the conditions under which a CSS may be p-simulated. It can be shown (argument mitted) that one-to-one mapping is not sufficient to insure that the projection of a CSS can be de-ribed by another CSS. Specifically, we need additional hypotheses to assure the existence of evaluation ınctions.

efinition. Let $T = (((\langle I\rangle, \langle E\rangle, \mathcal{E}), \Sigma, \mathcal{I})$ be a CSS over $\langle U\rangle$, X a non-empty, proper subset of E, and $V\rangle = \langle U - X\rangle$. The set X is said to be *ancillary* (*in* T) if for each B in $E - X$ there exists an evaluation ınction e'_B of rank $\rho_{e'_B} \geq \rho(T)$ such that

$$e'_B(u_1[V], \ldots, u_{\rho_{e'_B}}[V], u_{\rho_{e'_B}+1}[\langle V|B\rangle]) = e_B(u_{\rho_{e'_B}-\rho_{e_B}+1}, \ldots, u_{\rho_{e'_B}}, u_{\rho_{e'_B}+1}[\langle U|B\rangle])$$

ır each sequence $u_1 \ldots u_{e'_B+1}$ in VSEQ(T).

It is often simple to identify sets of ancillary attributes. Evaluation functions are formally defined ver a computation-tuple sequence (plus a partial tuple). However, in practice, a function usually epends only on the values of a few of the attributes in the sequence. This information can aid in lentifying some sets of ancillary attributes.

xample 3.2. Let T be the CSS from Example 2.2. Let $X = \{\text{OPINV}, \text{COST}, \text{GRPROF}, \text{NET}\}$ and $V\rangle = \langle U - X\rangle$. The only evaluation attribute in V, NPCY, can be calculated by a rank-one evaluation ınction. This function can be constructed by substitution using the definitions for the evaluation ;tributes in X. Thus, X is ancillary in T. □

[8] The notation $\text{prefix}^r(X)$ denotes the set $\{\overline{u} \text{ in } X \mid |\overline{u}| \leq r\}$.

Definition. Let $T = (((\langle I\rangle, \langle E\rangle, \mathcal{E}), \Sigma, \mathcal{I})$ be a CSS over $\langle U\rangle$, X a set of attributes ancillary in T, and $\langle V\rangle = \langle U - X\rangle$. The *removal of* X *from* T, denoted $\mathcal{R}_X(T)$, is the CSS $(((\langle I\rangle, \langle E - X\rangle, \mathcal{E}'), \{\sigma'\}, \mathcal{I}')$ where:

- $\mathcal{E}' = \{e'_B \mid B \text{ in } E - X\}$, each e'_B being the evaluation function of least rank equal to or greater than $\rho(T)$ such that

$$e'_B(u_1[V], \ldots, u_{\rho_{e'_B}}[V], u_{\rho_{e'_B}+1}[\langle V|B\rangle]) = e_B(u_{\rho_{e'_B}-\rho_{e_B}+1}, \ldots, u_{\rho_{e'_B}}, u_{\rho_{e'_B}+1}[\langle U|B\rangle])$$

  for each sequence $u_1 \ldots u_{\rho_{e'_B}+1}$ in VSEQ(T);
- $\text{VSEQ}(\sigma') = \Pi_V(\text{Interval}(\text{VSEQ}(T)))$; and
- $\mathcal{I}' = \Pi_V(\text{prefix}^r(\text{VSEQ}(T)))$, where $r = \max\{1, \rho_{e'_B} \mid B \text{ in } E - X\}$.

Theorem 3.4. Let $T = (\mathcal{C}, \Sigma, \mathcal{I})$ be a CSS over $\langle U\rangle$, X a set of attributes ancillary in T, $\theta = \max\{1, \rho_{e_B} \mid B \text{ in} X\}$, and $\langle V\rangle = \langle U - X\rangle$. Then $\mathcal{R}_X(T)$ p-simulates T iff (1) Π_V maps $\text{prefix}^\theta(\text{VSEQ}(T))$ one-to-one and (2) $\text{VSEQ}(\sigma') \cap \text{VSEQ}(\mathcal{I}') \subseteq \Pi_V(\text{VSEQ}(T))$.

Example 3.2 (continued). For each u in $\mathcal{I}$, $u(\text{NPCY}) = u(\text{NET})$ and $u(\text{OPINV}) = 0$. Since the evaluation functions e_{COST}, e_{GRPROF}, and e_{NET} have zero rank, the values of $u(\text{COST})$, $u(\text{GRPROF})$, and $u(\text{NET})$ are uniquely determined by $u[I]$. Thus, Π_V maps $\mathcal{I} = \text{prefix}^1(\text{VSEQ}(T))$ one-to-one, i.e., (1) of Theorem 3.4 is satisfied. Now let $\mathcal{R}_X(T) = (\mathcal{C}', \{\sigma'\}, \mathcal{I}')$. Consider a sequence $\overline{v} = v_1 \ldots v_n$ in $\text{VSEQ}(\sigma') \cap \text{VSEQ}(\mathcal{I}')$. Let $\overline{u} = u_1 \ldots u_n$ be the sequence in $\text{VSEQ}(e_{COST}) \cap \text{VSEQ}(e_{GRPROF}) \cap \text{VSEQ}(e_{NET})$ such that $\Pi_V(\overline{u}) = \overline{v}$, $u_1(\text{OPINV}) = 0$, $u(\text{NPCY}) = u(\text{NET})$ and $u_i(\text{OPINV}) = u_{i-1}(\text{CLOINV})$ for each i, $1 < i \leq n$. Clearly, $u_1 \ldots u_n$ is in VSEQ(T). Hence $\overline{v}$ is in $\Pi_V(\text{VSEQ}(T))$. Thus,(2) of Theorem 3.4 is satisfied. Therefore, $\mathcal{R}_X(T)$ p-simulates T.

Our last result demonstrates the special role that rank-zero evaluation functions play.

Theorem 3.5 Let $T = (((\langle I\rangle, \langle E\rangle, \mathcal{E}), \Sigma, \mathcal{I})$ be a CSS over $\langle U\rangle$, and X a set of evaluation attributes such that $E - X \neq \emptyset$. If $\rho_{e_B} = 0$ for each B in X, then X is ancillary in T. Furthermore, $\mathcal{R}_X(T)$ p-simulates T

References

[CA] Cobb, D. and L. Anderson, "1-2-3 For Business," Que Corporation, Indianapolis, In.

[CSRM] "C-Calc Spreadsheet Reference Manual," DSD Corporation, Kirkland, Wa.

[DG] Dong, G. and S. Ginsburg (1986), "Localizable Constraints for Object Histories," *Technical Report* TR-86-217, Computer Science Dept., University of Southern California.

[GG] Ginsburg, S. and M. Gyssens (1987), "Object Histories Which Avoid Certain Subsequences," *Information and Computation* 73, 174 – 206.

[GOUM] "Graphic Outlook User's Manual," Stone Mountain Computing Corporation, Santa Barbara, Ca.

[GT] Ginsburg, S. and K. Tanaka (1986), "Computation-Tuple Sequences and object Histories," *ACM TODS* 11, 186 - 212.

[GTa] Ginsburg, S. and C. Tang (1986), "Projection of Object Histories," *Theoret. Comput. Sci.* 48, 297 - 328.

[McQ] McQuaig, D. (1981), "College Accounting Fundamentals," Houghton Mifflin, Boston, Ma.

[R123] "1-2-3 Reference Manual," Lotus Development Corporation, Cambridge, Ma.

[WS] Wolfe, C. and L. Smith (1986) "Recommending a Microcomputer System to a Small-Business Client" *The Ohio CPA Journal* Spring 1986.

Efficient Management of Replicated Data

Jehan-François Pâris

Computer Systems Research Group
Department of Computer Science and Engineering
University of California, San Diego
La Jolla, CA 92093

ABSTRACT

We propose in this paper a protocol aimed at managing replicated data with many copies more efficiently. Our protocol, called *Majority Consensus Voting with Tokens* generalizes the *primary copy* approach by allowing for more than one primary copy. Since primary copies are identified by the ownership of a token, the protocol allows for easy transfer of tokens from one copy to another to respond to changing access patterns. Tokens owned by failed primary copies can also be reassigned to some live copy to enhance data availability.

Upper and lower bounds for the availability of replicated data objects managed by the MCVT protocol are derived under very general probabilistic hypotheses. We show that MCVT significantly improves upon the availability and reliability offered by the primary copy protocol without incurring the high overhead of most other extant protocols.

1. INTRODUCTION

Data are sometimes replicated to improve their read access times or increase their availability in the presence of system malfunctions. Current trends towards decentralized computing environments and continuing advances in memory technology favor this solution. Data will be replicated more often and replicated data will have many more replicas as larger and cheaper memories will allow the local caching of more files or data base fragments.

This evolution towards replicated files with a larger number of replicas affect the protocols used to guarantee the consistency of the replicated data. All consistency protocols must make a trade-off between data availability and access time. Primary copy protocols, like the one used for Distributed INGRES [Ston79], allow fast updates since the primary copy is the only one that has to record writes in real time. These protocols fair very poorly in terms of data availability since a failure of the primary copy can result in the loss of the most recent version of the replicated data. Other protocols, such as voting and available copy protocols, provide much better data object availabilities but greatly increase update costs. Available copy protocols [Good83, BeGo84], for instance, assume that every update is immediately performed on all live copies of the replicated object while majority consensus voting (MCV) [Elli77, Giff79] requires a majority of replicas to be involved in every update. In both cases, the number of copies involved grows linearly with the total number of replicas.

There are however situations where neither of these two alternatives is satisfactory as the users of the data object need a higher availability than the one a primary copy protocol would provide but cannot afford the high update costs of voting and available copy protocols. We expect such situations to become more prevalent as the current trend towards decentralized computation continues. A university local area network may soon number more than one hundred data servers and several thousand workstations. We may expect to have at any time a large fraction of these servers and workstations holding copies of the same data.

We propose to provide at the same time high availability and fast updates by extending the primary copy protocol to allow for more than one primary copy. We also propose to identify primary copies by the ownership of a *token.* These tokens are not irrevocably attached to any copy. First, tokens can be transferred from one copy to another to adapt the configuration of the replicated object to changing access patterns. Second, tokens owned by failed primary copies can be reassigned to some live copy.

The remainder of this paper is organized as follows: Section 2 introduces our protocol and discusses its correctness. Section 3 provides upper and lower bounds for the availability of replicated data objects managed by the protocol. Section 4 discusses possible extensions. Finally section 5 has our conclusions.

2. A VOTING PROTOCOL WITH TOKENS

We will consider replicated data objects consisting of *n copies* or *replicas* residing on distinct *sites* of a computer network. Individual sites and the communication facilities linking them are subject to failures. Site failures result in the unavailability of the replica residing on the failed host. This situation will continue until the site has been successfully repaired. We will sometimes refer to the available copies of a replicated object as *live* copies. Failures of the network communication facilities sometimes create situations where some live copies of a replicated object cannot communicate with the other live copies of the object. These situations are known as *network partitions* and may result in inconsistencies if two subset of non-communicating replicas simultaneously accept updates.

We will also assume that the *n* copies of a replicated data object share *m* tokens. A token is essentially a capability to act as a primary copy and assert the state of the replicated object. Copies that do not own a token can only act as passive partners and are therefore similar to the weak representatives introduced by Gifford [Giff79]. In particular, they cannot be included into any quorum and bear no responsibility for the long-term safekeeping of the replicated object. Conversely, the MCVT protocol does not guarantee that the state of these copies reflects the current state of the replicated data object. We will only assume that there is some mechanism for propagating updates to all copies without tokens and that these copies have a reasonable chance to be up to date.

As there will in general be more than one primary copy, we need to specify in our protocol a mechanism guaranteeing that these primary copies will always provide a consistent view of the replicated data object. Although more sophisticated solutions are possible, we decided in favor of *majority consensus voting* with *static* quorums because of its simplicity and robustness. We will henceforth refer to our protocol as *Majority Consensus Voting with Tokens* (MCVT).

MCVT insures the consistency of replicated data objects by honoring read and write requests only when an appropriate quorum of primary copies can be accessed. In its simplest form, MCVT assumes that the current state of the replicated object is the state upon which enough primary copies have agreed to hold a majority of the m tokens. Distinct quorums of tokens for reads and writes can be introduced but they will not be considered here.

As the current state of a replicated object cannot be established without gathering answers from replicas holding a majority of tokens, a replicated object managed by an MCVT protocol remains available so long as such a majority can be gathered. Even number of tokens might cause a problem as draw conditions will occur every time the set of replicas that answered the query holds exactly one half on the m tokens. To break these ties, we will arbitrarily designate one of the m tokens as a *special* token and use it as a tie-breaker.

Protocol Correctness

The correctness of the MCVT protocol depends on the two assumptions that

(1) there will never be more than m tokens among the replicas of a data object, and

(2) there will be never more than one special token.

These two conditions must be enforced by all operations manipulating the tokens.

Transfers of tokens between two replicas do not result into any special problems provided that the replica receiving the token does not record its new token before the replica abandoning it records its loss of a token. Tokens can nevertheless become lost during the transaction if the site holding the replica receiving the token fails while the token is in transit. Such losses do not endanger the consistency of the replicated data object but would affect its availability and reliability. To avoid these occurrences, token transfers will be implemented as *atomic transactions.*

Reassigning tokens owned by failed primary copies is a different issue. Tokens removed from failed primary copies can be reassigned to live copies that do not own a token to transform them into primary copies. The overall effect of the procedure is to allow the regeneration of new primary copies without having to wait for the recovery of the sites holding the failed primary copies. The benefits of this approach are clear even if no copy without token is up to date since bringing a copy up to date will typically require considerably less time than waiting for the recovery of the site holding the failed primary copy. The only difficulty with this procedure is that failed primary copies that loose their tokens cannot be notified of that event.

One solution to this problem would be to require each copy holding a token to keep track of the all other copies that currently hold tokens. Such record would not be different of the *was-available set* used by some available copy protocols [LoPa87, CLP87] or the *partition set* used by optimistic dynamic voting protocols [PaLo88]. We decided instead in favor of a simpler invalidation technique where each token is assigned a *generation number*. These generations number will be initially set at zero for all *m* tokens in the replicated data object. Every time some tokens are removed from one or more failed primary copies, the generation numbers of the tokens owned by all primary copies participating to the transaction are incremented by a constant and all tokens held by copies that did not participate to the transaction become invalid.

This invalidation technique has three important consequences. First, we cannot remove tokens from failed primary copies without first collecting a majority of valid primary copies since doing otherwise could result in the mutual invalidation of two disjoint sets of primary copies. Token regenerations therefore need to be implemented as atomic transactions consisting of an election phase during which votes are collected from valid primary copies and possible new primary copies are identified followed by a commit phase during which the new generation number of valid tokens is broadcast to all participating copies. Second, tokens held by live primary copies that cannot communicate with the primary copies participating to the transaction will also become invalidated. The protocol is therefore free to reassign these tokens to some copies without tokens. Finally, elections will be complicated by the fact that the process tallying the results will have to distinguish between valid votes originating from replicas holding valid tokens and invalid votes coming from other replicas. This determination can be greatly simplified by using the result of the following theorem.

Theorem:

In a replicated data object managed by the MCVT protocol, if there is a majority of tokens share the same generation number, they are necessarily valid.

Proof:

Each regeneration transaction can only reassign the tokens owned by failed or non-communicating copies. Therefore no regeneration transaction will ever result in the existence of more than *m* valid tokens.

Since a regeneration transaction cannot proceed without first collecting a majority of valid primary copies and will necessarily change their generation numbers, it will never invalidate more than a minority of the previously valid tokens. As a result, there will never be a majority of invalid tokens with the same generation number.

The MCVT Protocol

The MCVT protocol requires four procedures, READ, WRITE, EXCHANGE and REGENERATE, respectively implementing the read, write, token exchange and token regeneration operations. Unlike the available copy and dynamic voting protocols, MCVT does not require any specific recovery protocol for failed copies. Any procedure ensuring that obsolete copies are brought up to date within some reasonable time interval will suffice.

The following description of the MCVT protocol assumes that each of the n copy of the replicated data object will never own more than one of the m existing tokens. Each replica will have a version number v_i. Primary copies will also have a generation number g_i representing the generation number of the token it holds. To simplify our description, we will assign dummy negative generation numbers to all copies without tokens.

procedure READ(d : data_object)
begin
  let U be the set of all replicas
  $\langle R, \mathbf{v}, \mathbf{g} \rangle \leftarrow$ START(U, d)
  $S \leftarrow \{r \in R : g_r = \max_{s \in R}\{g_s\}\}$
  $v_{\max} = \max_{t \in R}\{v_t\}$
  if $(|S| > \frac{m}{2}) \vee (|S| = \frac{m}{2} \wedge \text{replica with special token} \in T)$ **then**
    perform the read on any $c : v_c = v_{\max}$
    COMMIT
  else
    ABORT
  fi
end READ

Figure 1: Read Algorithm

The algorithm for performing a read operation is simple. Its major task is to ascertain the current state of the replicated object by computing its current version number. As seen in Figure 1, the algorithm starts by pooling all replicas of the data object. The operation returns R which is the set of reachable replicas and two arrays: **v** and **g** which contain the operation numbers and generation numbers respectively of all replicas that answered the START. It then computes S, the set of all replicas holding a valid token. If the algorithm is able to gather a quorum of such replicas, it can assert that the current version number of the replicated object is the maximum version number $v_{\max}$ of all replicas in S. The read operation can then be performed on any copy in U whose version number is equal to $v_{\max}$.

The algorithm for writing is similar to the algorithm for reading but requires a two-phase commit protocol. As seen on Figure 2, the WRITE procedure first attempts to ascertain the current state of the replicated object and to determine if enough current copies are available. If this attempt is successful, the algorithm commits the write operation, sending the new version number to all the copies that were updated.

```
procedure WRITE(d : data_object)
begin
   let U be the set of all replicas
   ⟨R, v, g⟩←START(U, d)
   S←{r∈R : g_r = max_{s∈R}{g_s}}
   v_max = max_{t∈R}{v_t}
   T←{s∈S : v_r = v_max}
   if (|T| > m/2)∨(|T| = m/2 ∧ replica with special token ∈ T) then
      perform the write
      COMMIT(T, v_max+1)
   else
      ABORT(R)
   fi
end WRITE
```

Figure 2: Write Algorithm

The algorithm for exchanging a token between two replicas is by far the simplest: it uses a two-phase commit protocol to avoid token duplications and aborts if the two replicas do not share the same version number.

```
procedure EXCHANGE(s, t : copy)
begin
   ⟨v, g⟩←START(s, t)
   if v_s = v_t then
      perform the exchange of tokens
      COMMIT(s, t)
   else
      ABORT(s, t)
   fi
end EXCHANGE
```

Figure 3: Exchange Algorithm

As seen on Figure 3, the regeneration algorithm begins as does the write algorithm by attempting to ascertain the current state of the replicated object. If this attempt is successful, it builds the two sets T and V. The set T contains all reachable primary copies whose version number match the current version number v_{max} of the replicated data object. The set V contains

```
procedure REGENERATE(d : data_object)
begin
  let U be the set of all replicas
  ⟨R, v, g⟩ ← START(U, d)
  S ← {r ∈ R : g_r = max_{s∈R}{g_s}}
  v_max = max_{t∈R}{v_t}
  T ← {s ∈ S : v_r = v_max}
  V ← {c ∈ U : v_r = v_max}
  if ((|T| > m/2) ∨ (|T| = m/2 ∧ replica with special token ∈ T)) ∧
      |V − T| > 0 then
    W ← at most m − |T| x ∈ V − T
    if replica with special token ∉ T then
      select new holder c ∈ T ∪ W
    fi
    regenerate
    COMMIT(T ∪ W, g_max+1, c)
  else
    ABORT(U)
  fi
end REGENERATE
```

Figure 4: Regeneration Algorithm

all copies in T plus all reachable copies without tokens whose version numbers also match v_{max}. All copies in V but not in T are therefore good candidates for the tokens held by primary copies that are unreachable or not up to date. The algorithm selects at most $m - |T|$ of these copies. If T does not contain the special token, a new holder is selected. The algorithm commits the regeneration operation, sending the new generation number to all the participating replicas.

3. AVAILABILITY ANALYSIS

Markov models, sometimes supplemented by discrete simulation models, have been the tools of choice for evaluating the reliability and availability of replicated data. Markov models offer the great advantage of providing algebraic expressions for most representative values of the data object availability. Unfortunately they can only model systems whose behavior conforms with a series of hypotheses used by the theory of stochastic processes. While most of these hypotheses are quite reasonable and accurately reflect the behavior of actual systems, some of them, like the assumption that repair times conform to an exponential distribution are much less realistic. Attempts to relax this last assumption have invariably led to intractable models for all but the most basic cases. The analysis we present here does not suffer of these limitations. It only assume that individual site failures and repairs are independent events.

Consider now a replicated system consisting of n identical elements having the same probability A of being operational at any time t. We will refer to the probability A as the *availability* of a single element. Such replicated system is said to be a k-out-of-n system if it continues to operate properly so long as k out of the n entities remain operational [BaHe84].

Assume that the only events affecting the availability of the replicated system are failures and repairs of one of the n elements. Other failure modes that might affect the availability of the replicated system, such as network partitions in the case of a replicated data object, are excluded. As mentioned previously, we also assume that that failure and repair events are mutually independent. The probability that exactly j out of the n elements are available is given by the binomial formula

$$Pr[j \text{ elements available}] = \binom{n}{j} A^j(1-A)^{n-j}$$

In particular we have:

$$Pr[\text{all } n \text{ elements available}] = A^n$$

$$Pr[\text{all } n \text{ elements unavailable}] = (1-A)^n$$

The probability that *at least* k out of the n elements will be available is then given by

$$Pr[\text{at least } k \text{ elements available}] = \sum_{j=k}^{n} \binom{n}{j} A^j(1-A)^{n-j}$$

The availability of a replicated data object consisting of n physical copies managed by a majority consensus voting algorithm with a single quorum for reads and writes and equal weights for all copies is given by

$$A_V(n) = \sum_{j=0}^{\lfloor n/2 \rfloor} \binom{n}{j} A^j(1-A)^{n-j} \quad (n \text{ odd}) \tag{1.a}$$

for n odd, and by

$$A_V(n) = \sum_{j=0}^{n/2-1} \binom{n}{j} A^j(1-A)^{n-j} + \frac{\binom{n}{n/2}}{2} A^{n/2}(1-A)^{n/2} \quad (n \text{ even}) \tag{1.b}$$

for n even since the tie-breaking policy will allow access to the replicated object in one half of the ties. One can show [Pari87] that

$$A_V(2k) = A_V(2k-1).$$

Thus, adding one extra copy to a replicated data object with an *odd* number of copies will not improve the availability of the data object unless the new copy has a higher availability than the existing copies.

Consider now a replicated data object consisting of n identical copies sharing m tokens. Assume that the replicated data object is managed by our MCVT protocol and that no copy owns more than one token. The availability of the replicated data object will depend on the availabilities A of the n replicas and the rate at which tokens owned by failed replicas will be regenerated.

The regeneration of these tokens is a three-step process. First, the existence of such tokens must be detected, which means that the replicated object must be periodically monitored to check that all m tokens are owned by live replicas. This can be done very efficiently for replicated data objects that are frequently accessed by combining the check with the election held at the beginning of the READ and WRITE procedures. Replicated objects that are infrequently accessed or whose access patterns are uneven need to supplement this technique by scheduled samplings of the states of their tokens. Second, up-to-date copies without tokens must be found and out-of-date copies without tokens must be brought up to date. This is a near-trivial task for data objects that are small or rarely updated; it could involve a prohibitive overhead for very large objects that are frequently updated, such as large data bases. However, these objects can be partitioned into fragments of more manageable size. Finally, the distribution of the new tokens must take place. This procedure was described in the previous section. Since it consists of an election followed by a commit phase, it should not take much more time than a normal access to the replicated object.

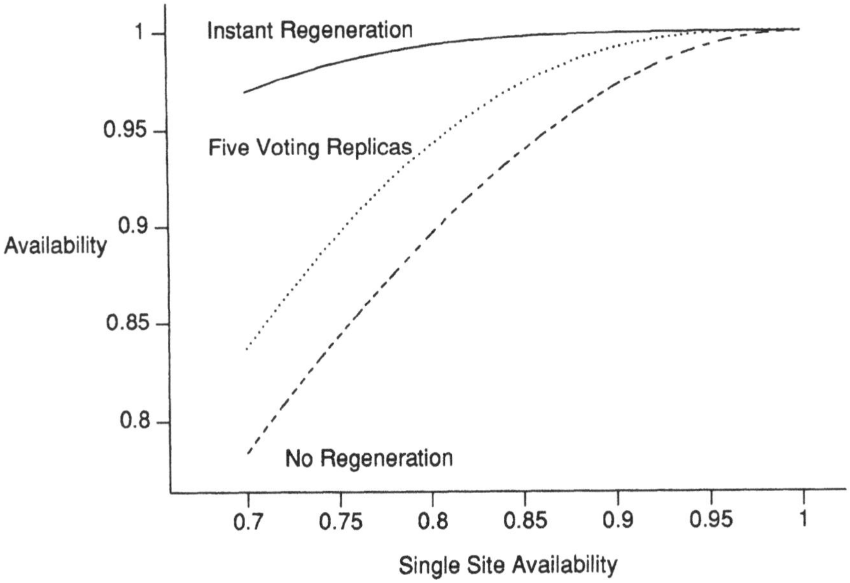

Figure 5: Compared Availabilities for Five Copies and Three Tokens

Should token regenerations never occur, only token exchanges between live copies would remain possible. Since we assumed that failures and repairs are independent events, this procedure would not decrease the availability of the replicated object. It will remain available so long as a majority of its m copies holding tokens remain available. A lower bound for the availability of a replicated file with n copies and m tokens managed by a MCVT protocol is then given by

$$L_{MCVT}(n,m) = \sum_{j=0}^{\lfloor m/2 \rfloor} \binom{m}{j} A^j (1-A)^{m-j} \tag{2.a}$$

for m odd, and by

$$L_{MCVT}(n,m) = \sum_{j=0}^{m/2-1} \binom{m}{j} A^j (1-A)^{m-j} + \frac{\binom{m}{m/2}}{2} A^{m/2} (1-A)^{m/2} \tag{2.b}$$

for m even. Note that this lower bound is equal to the availability $A_V(m)$ of a replicated file with m copies managed by majority consensus voting.

Consider now a replicated object of small size, such as a directory or a tree of indices, that is very frequently accessed. Primary site failures will be quickly detected and their tokens immediately regenerated. The behavior of such an object would be very close to the one of an idealized data object with instantaneous regeneration of failed primary copies. Since live copies without tokens could be immediately replace failing primary copies, the replicated object would remain available so long as enough copies remain available to gather a quorum of tokens, that is, either more than $m/2$ copies or exactly $m/2$ copies including the copy including the special token. The situation would become different after a failure of more than $n - \frac{m}{2}$ replicas. Such a failure would make the replicated file temporarily unavailable and stop the regeneration process as there would not be enough primary copies to gather a quorum. After that failure, we could have more than $m/2$ replicas available but not enough replicas holding valid tokens to assert the state of the file. Such recovery states have been observed in most consistency protocols, including Available Copy [LoPa87, CLP87], the Regeneration Algorithm [PNP86, LoPa88] and all dynamic voting protocols. An *upper* bound for the availability of a replicated file with n copies and m tokens that can be instantly regenerated is then given by

$$U_{MCVT}(n,m) = \sum_{j=0}^{\lfloor m/2 \rfloor} \binom{n}{j} A^j (1-A)^{n-j} \tag{3.a}$$

for m odd, and by

$$U_{MCVT}(n,m) = \sum_{j=0}^{m/2-1} \binom{n}{j} A^j (1-A)^{m-j} + \frac{\binom{n}{m/2}}{2} A^{m/2} (1-A)^{n-m/2} \tag{3.b}$$

for m even.

Our experience with other consistency protocols indicates that this upper-bound provides an excellent approximation of the object availability so long as failures resulting in the temporary unavailability of the file remain exceptional. This is fortunately the case for most reasonable values of the individual site availability and the approximation becomes better as this availability gets closer to one.

The Figure 5 contains lower and upper bounds for the availabilities of replicated objects with five copies and three tokens managed by the MCVT protocol as well as the availabilities of replicated files with five copies managed by majority consensus voting. The values displayed correspond to a range of individual copy availabilities extending from 0.7 (which is unusually low) to 1.0 (which corresponds to a perfectly reliable copy). Lower bounds correspond to the worse case situation where tokens owned by failed primary copies are never regenerated; upper bounds correspond to an optimistic analysis of the best case situation where these tokens are instantly regenerated.

We might reasonably expect most data objects to be accessed much more frequently (daily at least) than site failures occur (from once a week to once a month). Should this not be the case, a process attempting once or twice a day to regenerate tokens would be trivial to implement and inexpensive to run. It is therefore reasonable to expect that the overall availability of replicated files managed by the MCVT protocol would be closer to its upper bound than to its lower one. This could lead us to the conclusion that the MCVT protocol would perform as well as the majority consensus protocol while requiring the update of much fewer copies (two to three instead of three to five in our example).

4. POSSIBLE EXTENSIONS

Token schemes have been widely used to implement concurrency control in many areas as different as replicated data and multiple access channels. These schemes typically include some provision to regenerate lost tokens in some automatic fashion. The key issue of our proposal lies in the usage of multiple tokens to allow more than one primary copy and increase data reliability and availability.

Any concurrency protocol allowing more than one primary copy must include a mechanism guaranteeing that these primary copies will always provide a consistent view of the replicated data object. The MCVT protocol relies on majority consensus voting to achieve this goal. More sophisticated mechanisms are however possible and we will briefly discuss three of them.

4.1. Available Copies with Tokens

Available Copy protocols provide a simple and elegant means for for maintaining the consistency of replicated data when network partitions are known to be impossible [Good83, BeGo84]. These protocols are based on the observation that replicas that have participated in all writes necessarily hold the most recent version of the replicated object. The replicated object remains available so long as at least one of these replicas remains accessible. As a result, available copy protocols provide a much higher data availability than static voting protocols [LoPa87, CLP87]. Moreover, they do not require the minimum of three copies required by voting protocols to improve upon the availability of non-replicated data.

A multiple token protocol based on the available copy approach would require all writes to be performed on all available primary copies of the replicated object. Since all available primary copies would receive each write, they would always remain current: the current state of the replicated object could then be ascertained from *any* available primary copy. Token exchanges would be implemented exactly as in MCVT and token regenerations would remain possible so long as one primary copy remains available.

When a site holding a primary copy recovers following a failure, that primary copy is likely to have missed some updates. The consistency of the replicated data object would not be guaranteed in our new proposal if the recovering copy could act as an available primary copy before having been brought up to date. Any protocol using an available copy mechanism to enforce mutual consistency among its primary copies would therefore need to include a recovery algorithm to be followed at site recovery time. This recovery algorithm should also specify the actions to be taken after a total failure [LoPa87, CLP87].

4.2. Dynamic Voting with Tokens

Another possible method to improve the availability of replicated objects managed by consistency protocols with multiple tokens would be to adjust the necessary quorum of tokens required for an access operation to changes in the state of the network. Unlike available copy protocols, *Dynamic Voting* protocols [DaBu85] operate correctly in the presence of network failures. Although providing much higher data availabilities than static voting protocols, they also require a minimum of three copies to improve upon the availability of non-replicated data.

Dynamic voting protocols differ in the technique used to adjust quorums to changes in the state of the network [DaBu85, BGS86, Jajo87, LoPa88]. They generally operate by disenfranchising all replicas that have become inaccessible because of site failures or network partitions. The protocol checks first if enough replicas remain available to satisfy the current quorum. If this is the case, these replicas constitute a new *majority block* and a new quorum is computed. To enforce mutual exclusion, recovered replicas that do not belong to the current majority block will not be allowed to participate in elections so long as they have not been reintegrated. To keep track of the status of the replicated object, every replica will maintain some state information. This information will include a *version number* identifying the last update recorded by the replica and either a *partition vector* [DaBu85] or both a *partition set* and an *operation number* [PaLo88] identifying the copies belonging to the current majority block. These algorithms perform almost identically so long as the access rate is sufficient to keep the partition sets up-to-date.

4.3. Pure Token Regeneration

Another alternative for maintaining the primary copies of the replicated object in a consistent state would be to use the *Regeneration Algorithm* [PNP86, NoAn87]. The regeneration algorithm would allow reads so long as at least one primary copy would remain available but would require *all* primary copies to be available to to allow a write. Should this not be the case, enough primary copies must be regenerated to bring their number back to its initial value before the write can complete.

Like available copy protocols, the regeneration algorithm does not operate correctly in the presence of network partitions. Unlike them, and like majority consensus voting, it protects the replicated data against irrecoverable failures by never allowing writes on single copies.

5. CONCLUSIONS

We have presented in this paper a new protocol aimed at managing more efficiently highly replicated data. Our protocol, called *Majority Consensus Voting with Tokens* generalizes the *primary copy* approach by allowing for more than one primary copy. Since primary copies are identified by the ownership of a token, the protocol allows for easy transfer of tokens from one copy to another to respond to changes in access patterns. Tokens owned by failed primary copies can also be reassigned to some live copy to enhance data availability.

Upper and lower bounds for the availability of replicated data objects managed by the MCVT protocol were derived under very general probabilistic hypotheses. They indicate that MCVT significantly improves upon the availability and reliability offered by the primary copy protocol without incurring the high overhead of most other extant protocols.

Acknowledgements

We wish to thank S. Toueg for suggesting the possibility of using tokens in a database consistency policy. We are also very grateful to D. D. E. Long and W. A. Burkhard for their comments and encouragements.

This research has been supported by a grant from the NCR Corporation and the University of California MICRO program.

References

[BGS86] D. Barbara, H. Garcia-Molina and A. Spauster, "Policies for Dynamic Vote Reassignment," *Proc. Sixth International Conference on Distributed Computing Systems* (1986), pp. 37-44.

[BaHe84] Barslow, R. E. and K. D. Heidtmann, Computing *k*-out-of-*n* System Reliability. IEEE Trans. on Reliability, R-33, 4 (Oct. 1984), 322-323.

[BeGo84] P. A. Bernstein and N. Goodman, "An Algorithm for Concurrency Control and Recovery in Replicated Distributed Databases," *ACM Trans. on Database Systems,* Vol. 9, No. 4 (Dec. 1984), 596-615.

[CLP87] J. L. Carroll, D. D. E. Long and J.-F. Pâris, "Block-Level Consistency of Replicated Files." *Proc. Seventh International Conference on Distributed Computing Systems* (Sept. 1987), pp. 146-153.

[DaBu85] D. Davcev and W.A. Burkhard, "Consistency and Recovery Control for Replicated Files," *Proc. Tenth ACM Symposium on Operating System Principles,* (1985), pp. 87-96.

[Elli77] C. A. Ellis, "Consistency and Correctness of Duplicate Database Systems," *Operating Systems Review,* 11, 1977.

[Giff79] D. K. Gifford, "Weighted Voting for Replicated Data," *Proc. Seventh ACM Symposium on Operating System Principles,* (1979), pp. 150-161.

[Good83] N. Goodman, D. Skeen, A. Chan, U. Dayal, R. Fox and D. Ries, "A Recovery Algorithm for a Distributed Database System," *Proc. Second ACM Symposium on Principles of Database Systems,* (1983), pp. 8-15.

[Jajo87] S. Jajodia, "Managing Replicated Files in Partitioned Distributed Database Systems," *Proc. Third International Conference on Data Engineering,* (Feb. 1987).

[LoPa87] D.D.E. Long and J.-F. Pâris, "On Improving the Availability of Replicated Files," *Proc. Sixth Symposium on Reliability in Distributed Systems and Database Systems,* (1987), pp. 77-83.

[LoPa88] D. D. E. Long and J.-F. Pâris, "Regeneration Protocols for Replicated Files," submitted for publication.

[NoAn87] J. D. Noe and A. Andreassian, "Effectiveness of Replication in Distributed Computing Networks," *Proc. Seventh International Conference on Distributed Computing Systems,* (1987), pp. 508-513.

[PaLo88] J.-F. Pâris and D. D. E. Long, "Efficient Dynamic Voting Algorithms," *Proc. Fourth International Conference on Data Engineering,* Los Angeles, Calif. (February 1988), pp. 268-275.

[Pari87] J.-F. Pâris, "Operational Analysis of Redundant Systems," *Proc. International Workshop on Modelling Techniques and Performance Evaluation* (March 1987), pp. 41-48.

[PNP86] C. Pu, J. D. Noe and A. Proudfoot, "Regeneration of Replicated Objects: A Technique and its Eden Implementation," *Proc. Second International Conference on Data Engineering,* Los Angeles, Calif. (February 1986), pp. 175-187.

[Ston79] M. Stonebraker, "Concurrency Control and Consistency of Multiple Copies of Data in Distributed INGRES," *IEEE Transactions on Software Engineering,* SE-5, 3 (May 1979), 188-194.

Vol. 296: R. Janßen (Ed.), Trends in Computer Algebra. Proceedings, 1987. V, 197 pages. 1988.

Vol. 297: E.N. Houstis, T.S. Papatheodorou, C.D. Polychronopoulos (Eds.), Supercomputing. Proceedings, 1987. X, 1093 pages. 1988.

Vol. 298: M. Main, A. Melton, M. Mislove, D. Schmidt (Eds.), Mathematical Foundations of Programming Language Semantics. Proceedings, 1987. VIII, 637 pages. 1988.

Vol. 299: M. Dauchet, M. Nivat (Eds.), CAAP '88. Proceedings, 1988. VI, 304 pages. 1988.

Vol. 300: H. Ganzinger (Ed.), ESOP '88. Proceedings, 1988. VI, 381 pages. 1988.

Vol. 301: J. Kittler (Ed.), Pattern Recognition. Proceedings, 1988. VII, 668 pages. 1988.

Vol. 302: D.M. Yellin, Attribute Grammar Inversion and Source-to-source Translation. VIII, 176 pages. 1988.

Vol. 303: J.W. Schmidt, S. Ceri, M. Missikoff (Eds.), Advances in Database Technology – EDBT '88. X, 620 pages. 1988.

Vol. 304: W.L. Price, D. Chaum (Eds.), Advances in Cryptology – EUROCRYPT '87. Proceedings, 1987. VII, 314 pages. 1988.

Vol. 305: J. Biskup, J. Demetrovics, J. Paredaens, B. Thalheim (Eds.), MFDBS 87. Proceedings, 1987. V, 247 pages. 1988.

Vol. 306: M. Boscarol, L. Carlucci Aiello, G. Levi (Eds.), Foundations of Logic and Functional Programming. Proceedings, 1986. V, 218 pages. 1988.

Vol. 307: Th. Beth, M. Clausen (Eds.), Applicable Algebra, Error-Correcting Codes, Combinatorics and Computer Algebra. Proceedings, 1986. VI, 215 pages. 1988.

Vol. 308: S. Kaplan, J.-P. Jouannaud (Eds.), Conditional Term Rewriting Systems. Proceedings, 1987. VI, 278 pages. 1988.

Vol. 309: J. Nehmer (Ed.), Experiences with Distributed Systems. Proceedings, 1987. VI, 292 pages. 1988.

Vol. 310: E. Lusk, R. Overbeek (Eds.), 9th International Conference on Automated Deduction. Proceedings, 1988. X, 775 pages. 1988.

Vol. 311: G. Cohen, P. Godlewski (Eds.), Coding Theory and Applications 1986. Proceedings, 1986. XIV, 196 pages. 1988.

Vol. 312: J. van Leeuwen (Ed.), Distributed Algorithms 1987. Proceedings, 1987. VII, 430 pages. 1988.

Vol. 313: B. Bouchon, L. Saitta, R.R. Yager (Eds.), Uncertainty and Intelligent Systems. IPMU '88. Proceedings, 1988. VIII, 408 pages. 1988.

Vol. 314: H. Göttler, H.J. Schneider (Eds.), Graph-Theoretic Concepts in Computer Science. Proceedings, 1987. VI, 254 pages. 1988.

Vol. 315: K. Furukawa, H. Tanaka, T. Fujisaki (Eds.), Logic Programming '87. Proceedings, 1987. VI, 327 pages. 1988.

Vol. 316: C. Choffrut (Ed.), Automata Networks. Proceedings, 1986. VII, 125 pages. 1988.

Vol. 317: T. Lepistö, A. Salomaa (Eds.), Automata, Languages and Programming. Proceedings, 1988. XI, 741 pages. 1988.

Vol. 318: R. Karlsson, A. Lingas (Eds.), SWAT 88. Proceedings, 1988. VI, 262 pages. 1988.

Vol. 319: J.H. Reif (Ed.), VLSI Algorithms and Architectures – AWOC 88. Proceedings, 1988. X, 476 pages. 1988.

Vol. 320: A. Blaser (Ed)., Natural Language at the Computer. Proceedings, 1988. III, 176 pages. 1988.

Vol. 322: S. Gjessing, K. Nygaard (Eds.), ECOOP '88. European Conference on Object-Oriented Programming. Proceedings, 1988. VI, 410 pages. 1988.

Vol. 323: P. Deransart, M. Jourdan, B. Lorho, Attribute Grammars. IX, 232 pages. 1988.

Vol. 324: M.P. Chytil, L. Janiga, V. Koubek (Eds.), Mathematical Foundations of Computer Science 1988. Proceedings. IX, 562 pages. 1988.

Vol. 325: G. Brassard, Modern Cryptology. VI, 107 pages. 1988.

Vol. 326: M. Gyssens, J. Paredaens, D. Van Gucht (Eds.), ICDT '88. 2nd International Conference on Database Theory. Proceedings, 1988. VI, 409 pages. 1988.